MAN ACROSS THE SEA

Problems of Pre-Columbian Contacts

MAN ACROSS THE SEA; problems of pre-Columbian contacts, ed. by Carroll L. Riley and others. Texas, 1971. 552p il map tab bibl 70-149022. 12.50. ISBN 0-292-70117-9
The 21 papers in this volume were culled from those delivered by recognized and eminent scholars, offering differing points of view and evidence on the pros and cons of pre-Columbian inter-hemispheric contact, at a 1968 symposium. There is an excellent discussion of the past schools and developments of diffusionistic concepts, and fresh attempts are made to delineate the problems involved and to establish a sound scientifically based theoretical framework for future investigation. The book provides no ultimate answers directly bearing on theoretical propositions of independent cultural development versus the effect and impact of trans-oceanic contacts on cultural evolution, but it is an important step in that direction. The bibliography is very complete and should be of great value to any student. The self-critical, nonromantic approach to what is not simply a question of contact, but of the multivariate character of the cultural processes of change and growth toward civilization, makes this book first rate and of prime consideration to all historical and anthropological scholars.

CHOICE   APR. '72
History, Geography & Travel
  Ancient (Incl. Archaeology)

E
103
M26

This book is published with the assistance
of the Dan Danciger Publication Fund

Man across the Sea

Problems of Pre-Columbian Contacts

EDITED BY

CARROLL L. RILEY

J. CHARLES KELLEY

CAMPBELL W. PENNINGTON

ROBERT L. RANDS

UNIVERSITY OF TEXAS PRESS, AUSTIN & LONDON

International Standard Book Number 0–292–70117–9
Library of Congress Catalog Card Number 70–149022
© 1971 by Carroll L. Riley, J. Charles Kelley,
Campbell W. Pennington, and Robert L. Rands
Printed by The University of Texas Printing Division, Austin
Bound by Universal Bookbindery, Inc., San Antonio

PREFACE AND ACKNOWLEDGMENTS

This volume results from a symposium held during the national meetings of the Society for American Archaeology, at Santa Fe, New Mexico, in May, 1968. At this symposium twenty-seven papers and four commentaries were given on various aspects of the broad problem of pre-Columbian contact between the hemispheres and within the New World.

The papers on diffusion within the New World were published in 1969 by the Southern Illinois University Museum (see bibliography entry under Kelley and Riley, this volume), and a few other papers are being published separately. The major portion of the symposium papers, however, are presented here. Section I of the present volume deals with various theoretical and methodological aspects of the diffusion controversy. Section II includes papers on pre-Columbian contact or alleged contact across both the Atlantic and the Pacific oceans. Section III is concerned with the very special problems of plant dispersal around the world and especially with the possibilities of pre-Columbian spread of plant domesticates. The introductory and concluding sections of the book represent an attempt by the editors to interpret the data and to suggest new directions for future work.

We editors have had generous help from a variety of individuals and institutions. Special thanks go to several officials of Southern Illinois University, Carbondale, including Robert W. MacVicar, former chancellor; William Simeone, former dean of the Graduate School; Roger E. Beyler, dean of the College of Liberal Arts and Sciences; Ronald G. Hansen, associate dean for research and projects; and Charles H. Lange and Frank H. Thomas, chairmen of the Anthropology and Geography Departments, respectively. John M. Campbell of the University of New Mexico, program committee chairman, and Stewart L. Peckham of the Museum of New Mexico, local arrangements chairman for the 1968 Society for American

Archaeology meetings, were most cooperative, as were other members of the program and arrangements committees. Phil C. Weigand, State University of New York at Stony Brook, read portions of the manuscript and made valuable critical comments.

A number of individuals at Southern Illinois University helped with the manuscript at various stages of work. These include D. Kathleen Abbass, Toni M. Coleman, Geraldene Kelley, Elizabeth A. Kelly, Theresa A. Page, Susan S. Thomas, and Diane K. Zinkhon.

Last, but certainly not least, we thank the contributors themselves for their cooperation and good humor in the complicated and difficult task of putting together this volume.

CONTENTS

INTRODUCTION

The idea of contact between the Old and New Worlds is almost as old as Columbus himself. For the great navigator, the problem apparently did not exist, since Columbus carried to his grave the idea that he had indeed discovered the east coast of Asia. Other explorers, less myopic or less romantic, realized soon enough that the new expanse of land was indeed a New World and that Columbus' "Indians" were not East Indians—or if so, at some distance removed.

All in all, the Spanish and Portuguese explorers and conquerors were more interested in the here and now than in hypothetical origins. Such speculation as to the origin of American man and American culture was incidental to other and more pressing problems of missionization, conquest, and exploitation. Generally speaking, this was also true of the slightly later English and French explorers.

There were speculations, however. One common early theme that has, indeed, continued to the present would have the American Indian the dusky descendant of the biblical ten tribes of Israel. This nation, with its capital at Samaria in Palestine, was overrun by an Assyrian king, probably Sargon II, sometime around 720 B.C. The ten tribes were, in fact, never lost and continued to occupy their home area; only their political organization had broken down. Still, because of faulty historicity based on uncritical reading of the Old Testament, they have become associated with American Indian origins. Around 1600, Father Gregorio García argued for this lost tribes theory as well as for several others even more improbable. James Adair, in the eighteenth century, believed in the lost tribes, as did Edward King (Viscount Kingsborough) in the nineteenth, and the idea is still current today. As early as the late sixteenth century, however, Joseph de Acosta was calling for more critical evaluation of theories of American Indian origin and suggested the possibility of a land bridge (Acosta, 1940: 77, 87–88). In the seventeenth century, added spice was introduced into the discussion by the scholar Hugo Grotius, who (in 1642) suggested that North American Indians were descended from Norwegians, the Yucatan Maya from Ethiopians, and Peruvians from Chinese. This free-swinging migrationism was immediately attacked by Joannes de Laet, who reintroduced the Acosta arguments. (For a discussion of this dispute see Huddleston, 1967.)

During the nineteenth century there was renewed interest in fanciful theories about Atlantis, the island—or continent—described by Plato that was supposed to have sunk beneath the Atlantic waves only after its peoples had settled and civilized both the Old World and the New. A Pacific equivalent of Atlantis is Mu, and modern adherents of Atlantean and Murian theories usually are so involved in mysticism that it is impossible to deal with their ideas in any reasonable way. On the other hand, the nineteenth century also saw worthwhile consideration of the problem of contacts. A balanced though perhaps overly pessimistic view is that given by Bancroft (1882: 6):

> For my own part I have no theory upon the subject—would have no theory. The problem of the origin of the American aborigines is, in my opinion, enveloped in as much obscurity now as it ever was; and when I consider the close proximity of the north-western and north-eastern extremities of America to Asia and Europe; the unthought of and fortuitous circumstances that may at any time have cast any people upon the American coasts; the mighty convulsions that may have changed the whole face of the earth during the uncounted years that man may have dwelt upon its surface; and lastly, the uncertainty, perhaps I might say improbability, of the descent of mankind from one pair; —when I think of all these things it seems to me that the peopling of America may have been accomplished in so many ways that no more hopeless task could be conceived than the endeavor to discover the one particular manner of it.

A serious study of the question of Old World–New World pre-Columbian contacts has come within the last century and is an offshoot of wider questions of human cultural dynamics. Up until a century ago there was a tendency to look at human cultural growth as a set of particularistic events—or, if man was seen holistically, it was normally in terms of some religious explanation. Beginning in the mid-nineteenth century, however, cultural evolutionism, developing out of an analogy with biological Darwinism, began to gain an increasing hold on ideas about human development. The evolutionists tended to see man as moving from a low (originally an *animal*) state of development through a series of social and technological stages to a culmination in the complexities of civilized life. The varied philosophical streams that collected to form full-blown cultural evolutional theory need not concern us here, but rather the fact that it gave, for the first time, a workable model to explain the parallel growth of complex cultures in distant parts of the world.

By the end of the nineteenth century some explanation of this sort was becoming more and more necessary. As long as there were large areas of the world undiscovered or unexplored, as long as the separate lines of human development in the several parts of the world were largely unknown, then questions of contacts between the hemispheres was not a very crucial one. By 1900, however, the main outlines of human prehistory had been worked out. It had become evident that Old World civilization was largely the result of early growth in favored areas in the Mediterranean Basin, and in south and east Asia. These regions influenced the rest of the Old World in varying degrees, forming what A. L. Kroeber was later to call the Old World oikoumene. The New World had obviously been populated from the Old World at some point in the past, largely, if not wholly, from eastern Asia. Later, within the New World there appeared areas of exuberant culture and finally of native civilization.

Thus, with the broad outlines of human cultural development known, the parallel development in the eastern and western hemispheres emerged as an obvious, crucial test for evolutionary ideas. As more and better controlled archaeological work was done, it became increasingly clear that New World civilization greatly resembled that of the Old World. Could, then, such similarities in broad aspects of technology (metallurgy, writing), economy (irrigation agriculture, organized labor), political organization (priesthoods, monumental structures), plus a multitude of point by point similarities (in art motifs, blowguns, specialized musical instruments, weaving) be due to channelled development of human institutions, or must it be due to some contacts strong enough and persistent enough for one hemisphere to influence the other? This is, in fact, the problem as it exists today, and its importance is hard to overemphasize. (See, for example, Riley, 1967: 17–18).

The naïve assumptions of the more enthusiastic unilinear evolutionists were attacked even by their own members. In 1879 the cultural evolutionist Edward Tylor suggested that the widespread game known as parchesi resembled an Aztec game, patolli, in so many arbitrary points that it could not have been accidental and that therefore the two games must be historically related. Tylor went on to formulate a rule for judging such incidents. According to Tylor, the probability of contact increases in ratio to the number of arbitrary, similar elements in any two trait complexes (Tylor, 1879, 1896).

A direct and concentrated attack on the idea of parallel development of cultural systems was not long in coming. It took two major forms. Borrowing from Friedrich Ratzel, the German and Austrian Kulturkreise group developed an elaborate theory that had cultures everywhere developing as a result of overlapping bundles or complexes of traits carried from some heartland in great waves or circles (Lowie, 1937: 123, 178–179). This theory could be used to account historically for New World–Old World similarities, but, in fact, the Kulturkreise group was more interested in the world-wide mechanics of its hypothetical structures than in hemispheric contact as such.

Not so with a group of English theorists. Beginning in the period around 1880, Miss A. W. Buckland presented a series of papers on various aspects of diffusion or presumed diffusion over vast areas. Although not significant in themselves, her writings foreshadowed the highly organized and sweeping Heliolithic school of Elliot Smith. In the words of Glyn Daniel (1963: 108; see also Lowie, 1937: 90): "According to Miss Buckland—and this is the key doctrine that is implicit in Elliot Smith and his followers—civilization was never, never independently acquired. It *could* not be and it *was* not. If you read Miss Buckland it will give you a foretaste of Elliot Smith, for she was writing about sun and serpent worship, and the spread of agriculture, weaving, pottery, and metals all over the earth."

As one of the incidences of empire, an Australian physician, Grafton Elliot Smith, was sent in 1900 to occupy the Chair of Anatomy at the Cairo Medical School. There he became fascinated with the culture of ancient Egypt and, in the period between 1910 and 1930, shaped a theory that had virtually all high culture spreading from

Egypt to lands beyond, including those of the New World. To Smith and to his adherents, especially the comparative religionist, W. T. Perry, the civilizations of ancient America were clearly derived from Egypt, and the massive superstructure of American high culture was clearly an alien transplant (see especially Smith, 1928; Perry, 1924). This attitude toward man's culture-making abilities—called by Riley (1967: 17) the "Prometheus approach to anthropology"—was to have a considerable vitality. In the 1930's, a later contemporary of Smith, Fitzroy Richard Somerset, fourth Baron Raglan, also postulated a vitalizing Ur-culture, his master-people being the Sumerians rather than the Egyptians. Like Elliot Smith, Lord Raglan essentially denied the possibility of inventions being made more than once. According to Raglan (1945: 17), ". . . every development [of culture] the history of which is known occurred in circumstances which would make its repetition impossible." To Raglan most of civilization was discovered or invented in Mesopotamia by the native priesthoods (Raglan, 1939: 15 et seq.). Again, the theoretical implications for Old World–New World contacts are enormous.

In America, or, at least among Americanists, a considerable skepticism was growing about the possibilities of any significant contact between the hemispheres. Dominated in the first decades of the twentieth century by Franz Boas, American anthropology tended to concentrate on the complex interplay of culture within the New World itself—something also true in cultural geography. One early task was to establish ground rules for examining the nature and kind of contacts and the interpenetration of one culture by another. This was most sharply done by Edward Sapir in his *Time Perspectives* (1916), which laid down strict methodologies for investigating culture flow. The heavy concentration by Boasians and other Americanists on problems of the Western Hemisphere did lead to a certain parochialism. Man was seen as coming across the Bering Strait bringing relatively little in the way of cultural baggage. In the New World man experienced a number of radiations; as part of his adjustment to differing environments, he invented agriculture and eventually built civilizations. Earlier American anthropologists like Lewis H. Morgan would have applauded this demonstration of evolutionism, but the Boasian group were for the most part (at least formally) antievolutionist. They were left with no comprehensive explanation for the similarities of Old and New World cultures, unless accident could be called an explanation. The regionalism reached rather absurd proportions—for example, the southwestern United States, which, for various reasons, was studied rather early and in some depth, was generally considered to be largely autonomous in its development, owing little to the flourishing Mesoamerican civilization in the nearby south. In their more extreme form Americanist studies tended to view New World man as developing in a series of parallel columns from an early stratum. Even the Pleistocene antiquity of man in the New World was doubted by such doughty conservatives as Aleš Hrdlička, thus making for an extraordinary proliferation of New World cultures in a matter of a few thousand years.

For the period between the two world wars and for a few years beyond, the idea of contact between the hemispheres, as far as Americanists were concerned, was kept alive by amateurs like Harold S. Gladwin or by romantics like the Verrills or Thor Heyerdahl. Gladwin, in *Men Out of Asia* (1947), suggested that Alexander's fleet brought civilization to the New World; like the Elliot Smith school, Gladwin stressed the uninventiveness of man in general. Heyerdahl in 1947 sailed from Peru to Easter Island on the raft *Kon-Tiki*. Partly on the basis of this impressive feat he proceeded to build a rambling and ramshackle case for Indian populating of the Pacific in *American Indians in the Pacific* (1952). Even earlier, the Polynesian ethnologist Peter Buck (1959:322–323) had expressed a firm belief that the sweet potato had been brought to Oceania from America by pre-Columbian Polynesian seamen, an idea previously endorsed by Roland B. Dixon (1932). Still and all, the majority of Americanists were unconvinced of any major contact between the hemispheres.[1] As late as 1948, A. L. Kroeber (p. 318) could say that "no specialist in American archaeology at present sees any place where there is room for a significant Old World influence in the unfolding of his story. The various theories 'explaining' the cultures of Mexico and Peru as derived from China, India, Farther India, or Oceania are all views of non-Americanistic scholars or the speculations of amateurs."

This state of affairs was to change drastically within a few years. In September of 1949, the Americanist Gordon Ekholm, in conjunc-

---

[1] Of course, to some anthropologists, including members of the various "functionalist" schools and most social anthropologists, the problem was not a very meaningful one.

tion with the Kulturkreise-influenced German scholar Robert Heine-Geldern, presented a list of traits that the two believed linked Asia historically with pre-Columbian America (Heine-Geldern and Ekholm, 1951). Although various of these presumed contacts were quickly challenged (see, for example, Rands, 1953), the decades of the 1950's and 1960's have seen a renewed interest in the possibilities of pre-Columbian contacts. Not only was contact alleged for the Pacific but also for the Atlantic (see especially the work of Jeffreys, who holds that maize, and perhaps other American plants, were introduced into Africa in pre-Columbian times).

In fact, the statement of Kroeber, quoted above, though perhaps true for anthropologists (at least in terms of the public record), was less true for cultural geographers. Carl Sauer, the doyen of cultural geography in America, seems to have had a long-time idea that inter-hemispheric contact was by no means unknown. Among botanists there has also been a spirited disagreement as to the facts and implications of pre-Columbian diffusion of cultivated plants (for discussion, see Anderson, 1954).

In this symposium we are considering several important lines of evidence pertaining to the problem: archaeological and linguistic evidence, the evidence of present or historically known distributions of traits, and the special problems of plant and animal distributions. Several approaches were followed. These may be reformulated as follows:[2]

1. The validity of actual archaeological data that may relate to pre-Columbian diffusion, or, alternatively, the implications of lack of such data.

2. The implication of trait distributions in the Old World and New World that seem to show relationships. These may take the form of material ethnological objects (blowgun, loom, parchesi and patolli, panpipes) or of large-scale similarities in religious or social organization (totemism, folk tales) or in art ("Circum-Pacific art

---

[2] Parenthetically, we might stress that the formulation of these general points, both here and in the conclusions, represents a kind of minimum concensus among the four editors. We have areas of considerable disagreement, and each of us would occasionally prefer to develop certain theoretical positions much further in one direction or another.

traditions"). The traits compared may of course be archaeological (water lily motif and lotus motif).

3. The incidence of linguistic similarities known from historical sources, especially in the Old World. Examples include the question of early names for maize or for chickens .

4. The significance of plants that are demonstrably or strongly suspected to be pre-Columbian in both hemispheres. Cotton and *Lagenaria* are the strongest candidates, but there are others. Here, the question arises of nonhuman modes of transportation from one hemisphere to the other (flotation, birds as vectors) or parallelisms in development over a long time span. Although not considered in detail by the symposium, the peculiar distribution of disease-producing micro-organisms should be included here.

5. The crucial question of the theoretical and especially the methodological adequacy of past and present models of diffusion and independent invention.

In the context of this symposium, we believe that certain points (admittedly not earth-shaking) can be accepted by all parties.

1. Certain theories of diffusion, especially the seeding of New and Old World from hypothetical continents like Mu and Atlantis, are so far fetched as to not be worth serious discussion. To maintain the argument on a serious level, ideas drawn from basically mystical presuppositions cannot be accepted.

2. Theories that view high cultures in America as the result of historical, datable incidences that are too late in time are not admissible. For example, Mesoamerican and Andean civilization *could not* have been carried by Alexander's sea captains, by Vikings, or by St. Brendan.

In addition to the above, we feel that all participants would agree that one important yet often obscured point needs to be made clear. The fact of contacts or lack of contacts is only a minor part of the problem. Much more important is *the nature* of the contacts. It might not matter a great deal, in terms of the dynamics of culture, if there was a boatload of Polynesians, Japanese fishermen, or Irishmen making a landfall in the New World. The overriding question has always been this: *were there contacts sustained enough or significant enough* to clearly modify the culture of one hemisphere in the direction of the other? In other words, is or is not the New World a cultural "laboratory" in which the channelled development of culture, especially of civilization, can tell us something of the nature of man? If it is, then the implications for a new cultural evolutionism are far-reaching. If it is not, then there are equally tremendous implications of other kinds. This, then, is the question; and, although this symposium will not supply the answer, we hope that it will advance us a little way toward some future time when we will finally have that answer.

MAN ACROSS THE SEA
Problems of Pre-Columbian Contacts

SECTION I

In this section Stephen Jett considers a wide range of theoretical and methodological issues in the diffusion problem. Gordon Ekholm and David Kelley are both concerned with what constitutes "hard" evidence, a subject of primary interest and one taken up by the editors in the conclusions to the volume. Jon Muller also deals with the nature of evidence but, whereas both Ekholm and Kelley think that antidiffusionists demand an unreasonable level of proof, Muller believes that many postulated relationships, especially in design and other art features, result from emphasis on superficial similarities of style. Muller suggests a new approach using underlying structure in comparisons of art styles. Erik Reed discusses not only the papers presently grouped in Section I but also others in the symposium that are concerned with the more general problems of diffusion versus independent invention.

One paper in this section, that of Stephan Borhegyi, is a bit different from the others; it is a stimulating and provocative comparison of Mesoamerican high culture and the Hellenistic oikoumene. At this point we must note, with deep regret, the untimely accidental death of Stephan F. de Borhegyi in September, 1969. His paper is presented here essentially unchanged from the original draft.

1. Diffusion versus Independent Development: The Bases of Controversy

STEPHEN C. JETT

More than thirty years ago, V. Gordon Childe (1937:3) wrote, "Discussions of diffusion are apt to degenerate into combats wherein only dust is diffused or else to ascend into an ether so diffuse that the disputants are left balancing probabilities inherently unsusceptible of statistical treatment." In the period since these words were written, new combatants have joined the lists, but the settling of either the dust or the issues still seems far from imminent, and the growth of sophistication in the application of statistical methods has as yet failed to tip the balance of opinion once and for all.

The present paper deals principally with the most controversial area of discussion relating to diffusion: the interpretation of cultural similarities between the Old World and the New World. Few would contend that significant similarities do not exist; the question is, of course, to what extent these likenesses are the results of completely independent development, and to what extent they are a consequence of interhemispheric contact or migration. Archaeologist Gordon Ekholm (1950: 344) writes, "This is perhaps *the* most important question confronting those working in the field of American archaeology and seeking to make known the true history of the American Indian. It is also a question of outstanding significance to our general understanding of how civilizations come into being, of how simple and primitive cultures develop into more complex ones." This paper does not propose to resolve the controversy; rather, it attempts to define somewhat more clearly the bases of disagreement between "diffusionists" and "independent inventionists." Parties to each of these points of view have accused the adherents to the other of failing to delineate the theoretical underpinnings of their positions (Rowe, 1966: 344; Fraser, 1965: 485).

To the extent that theoretical discussions of the issue in question occur, they tend to be highly partisan. Yet this disunity exists in reference to a single theoretical problem, and simultaneous examination of the assumptions, methods, and predispositions of the proponents of both positions seems desirable (although, obviously, many differences of emphasis are encompassed by the labels "diffusionist" and "independent inventionist," and not every generalization made herein is applicable to every adherent to one position or the other). The present author, though attempting to examine the issues objectively, feels that it is nevertheless appropriate to state at the outset his own leanings, which, though favoring a case-by-case examination of evidence, tend toward diffusionism.

MEANS OF CONTACT: WATERCRAFT

The possibility that some of the similarities between the higher cultures of Asia and the Americas are a result of diffusion via the Bering Strait has occasionally been suggested, but few, if any, believe that massive diffusion of Neolithic or Bronze Age traits occurred via this route. One student of Alaskan archaeology concludes that "northwestern America, and northern Siberia, under present climatic conditions, together form one of the most formidable barriers to human communications one can find anywhere in the world. To refuse Neolithic man the ability to cross the southern Pacific and to accept his ability to cross or penetrate this region is straining at a gnat and swallowing a camel" (Rainey, 1953: 46). These arctic and subarctic environments would not have permitted tribe-to-tribe spread of agriculture or cultivated plants or the many shared culture traits that depend on milder environments, and actual migrants carrying these things would have to have made their way across thousands of miles of occupied land. Nor are many of the other traits shared by the higher cultures of the Old World and the New World found in these subpolar regions—as at least some of them presumably would be if tribe-to-tribe diffusion had taken place. Thus one of the pivotal issues of the interhemispheric diffusion controversy has been the question of the means by which contacts could have taken place. According to Ekholm (1950: 351, 382), "It is largely the difficulties involved in finding an answer to this question that has caused most anthropologists to think of the American Indian civilization as having developed independently." If overland diffusion can be largely ruled out, only travel by water remains as a possible means of contact or migration. If it could be shown absolutely that pre-Columbian watercraft were incapable of ocean crossings, then the issue would be closed. Watercraft, however, are perishable and leave little but ephemeral wakes in the paths of their passing; as a consequence, it has been arguable whether craft capable of transoceanic crossings existed early enough to have permitted the postulated intercontinental contacts. Too, there is disagreement over what kinds of craft are in fact capable of transoceanic crossings under normal circumstances.

Western scholars, particularly Americans (who are imbued from an early age with the doctrine of the discovery of America by Columbus), have tended to assume: first, that the West (including southwest Asia) has always been the leader in technological progress and that, as a corollary, other areas of the world did not have equal or superior sailing craft or navigational knowledge; and, second, that European ships of the fifteenth century, which made transoceanic voyages only with difficulty, must have been superior to those of a thousand or two thousand years earlier. Hence, polygenesists have contended that the watercraft of pre-Columbian times could have crossed the oceans only accidentally and by miraculous good fortune and that, therefore, there could have been no significant influences on ancient America from beyond the seas. "Pity the poor Buddhist missionary," writes Merrill (1950: 29), "who had to make such an impossible voyage across the Pacific in times when boats were crude affairs and distinctly limited in size."

A few Western scholars, however, have been aware that areas of the world other than the West had developed large ocean-going craft and that, in Europe, geographical knowledge and shipping, like most things, suffered a general decline during the Dark Ages. (The "Renaissance" was just that—a rebirth of knowledge and activity, plus, of course, some innovation. When we realize that the spherical form of the earth was taught in Greece by at least 550 B.C., its diameter calculated with an error of only about one-seventh before 200 B.C., and the system of latitudinal and longitudinal coordinates used by 150 B.C. [Tozer, 1964: 167, 172, 343], we gain some idea of the kind of knowledge generally lost to *Europe* until the Renaissance.)

Until fairly recently, diffusionists were little better informed about early watercraft than were the independent inventionists; they have tended to feel that decisions for or against diffusion should depend solely on the evidence of the cultural similarities and that assumptions that the oceans were impassable are completely gratuitous (for example, Meggers, 1964: 511). In fact, opinions like the following are often expressed: ". . . I fail to see why we must wait for evidence of suitable watercraft . . . to evaluate the facts. On the contrary, convincing indications of contact may lead us to infer seafaring abilities at times and places otherwise barren of evidence . . ." (Tolstoy, 1969b; Carter, 1963: 18, expresses a similar view). In fact, some diffusionists have postulated such massive and diverse influences that the amount of voyaging implied has been called by critics "the alleged South Pacific Regatta" (Mangelsdorf and Oliver, 1951: 263).

Since there is such a low probability of ancient watercraft being preserved (with some exceptions, such as occasional submerged wrecks and Viking and Celtic ship burials), their absence in the archeology is not necessarily significant and is not evidence against diffusion. On the other hand, the lack of such specimens does nothing for the diffusionist case either, and it is worth exploring other evidence regarding the possible means of contact, if only because isolationists consider this to be a major factor influencing their stand and accuse diffusionists of ignoring "time, distance, and the difficulties of navigation" (Rowe, 1966: 334).

One may look for other kinds of archaeological evidence of watercraft use: carvings, paintings, or models of ships, parts of watercraft or pieces of associated equipment, and port facilities. Numerous remains of deep-sea fish or mammals might also indicate well-developed ocean-going ability in some areas. A second potential source of information is historical documents—from pre-Columbian times for the Old World, and from European-contact and early post-contact times for the New World. Finally, one may look at the kinds and abilities of craft used by modern "primitives" and, by extension, apply these findings to peoples of pre-1500 times.

Utilizing some of these methods, diffusionists (for example, Heine-Geldern and Ekholm, 1951: 308; Ekholm, 1950: 382; Heine-Geldern, 1956: 94–95; Estrada and Meggers, 1961: 936) have pointed to ancient depictions of large boats in various parts of the Old World and to ancient Asiatic accounts of ships of greater size than those of Columbus and Magellan (Columbus' smallest had an estimated keel length of only 15.46 meters [Martínez-Hidalgo, 1966: 97]). Anti-diffusionists have countered that the ancient documents exaggerate ship size and that, even if the ships of ancient times were in some cases rather large, they were not seaworthy outside of such relatively sheltered waters as those of the Mediterranean or the island-bounded seas off east Asia.

Although some nearly landlocked seas may be more storm-free than some parts of the oceans, we must not fall into the fallacy that mid-ocean sailing is in general more dangerous than longshore sailing. As one sailor puts it, ". . . this is almost the exact opposite of the truth" (Merrien, 1954: 21–22), for the greatest danger at sea is being blown onto a lee shore. Too, although ships used in the ancient Mediterranean were built for Mediterranean conditions, there seems to be little reason to suppose that Mediterranean people were less capable of building seaworthy ships than were the more primitive Vikings, whose craft probably derived in large part from earlier Mediterranean types. There is evidence, which cannot be reviewed here, that voyaging, particularly by Phoenicians, was not uncommon in pre-Christian times in at least the eastern part of the Atlantic. Nevertheless, it is true that the ability of Western ships, particularly larger ones, to make headway against the wind was quite limited. Speaking of ships like Columbus' *Santa María*, Culver (and Grant, 1935: 78) writes, ". . . they went to windward slowly or not at all."

Southern and eastern Asia—particularly the Malaysian region—and Oceania seem from ancient times to have possessed, in addition to large ships, much more highly developed sailing rigs and techniques than existed in the Western world, allowing craft to beat readily to windward (Bowen, 1953b, 1959a, 1959b; Borden, 1967: 219–222; Needham, 1970). A Chinese document of the third century A.D. describes the use of the fore-and-aft-rigged sail in southeast

Asia (Paris, 1952: 271). Geographer Clinton Edwards (1969a), a watercraft expert, writes: "The eastern shores of Asia probably have the greatest variety of watercraft to be found anywhere in the world. This is especially true of southern China, Indochina, and the Bay of Bengal, suggesting the theory that this region was one of the great 'hearths' of original invention and elaboration of many features of watercraft technology." Regarding the distinctive Chinese sail and rig, which dates back to at least A.D. 200 (Doran, this symposium, quoting Needham, 1970: 601), a number of distinguished sailors and yachtsmen pronounce it the world's best for ocean cruising (Borden, 1967: 229, 242, 250), although this conclusion might be debated by other yachtsmen. According to Borden (1967: 56, 64), Micronesian sailing canoes, which are largely derivative from east Asian craft, were, for speed on the sea, by far the best in the world and were able to sail closer to the wind than any other sailing craft: "The best vessels of Micronesia and Polynesia were more weatherly and, despite their matting sails, could outsail the ships of Captain Cook, Bougainville, Kotzebue and other late explorers." There is one record from the Spanish period of a flying proa running the seventeen hundred miles from Guam to Manila in six days. Superior skill in sailing plus the early use of log sailing rafts, which exceed small hulled boats in seaworthiness, are cited by diffusionists (for example, Carter, 1963: 20) to explain the fact that there is a much greater number of Asian-American similarities than Mediterranean-American ones, despite the geographically greater proximity of the Mediterranean to the New World.

Diffusionists and isolationists have often argued about whether or not ships of large size existed in ancient times. It should be pointed out, however, that seaworthiness is not proportionate to size; to the contrary, the larger the size, the greater the stresses set up by wind and wave as they encounter the inertia of the heavy craft and thus the greater the possibility of breaking up. A fairly small craft, if well constructed, is more likely to survive a long sea voyage, especially if it is of flexible construction, as are lashed-log rafts and sewn-plank boats. According to one sailor, ". . . the notion that a small boat cannot go far afield is (granted a perfect knowledge of her sailing qualities) a complete fallacy" (Merrien, 1954: 10–11). Another mariner writes, "Again and again it has been proven that seaworthiness has little to do with size . . . [boats under twenty-five feet] are far the safest for the Pacific" (Borden, 1967: 25, 164).

The earliest suggested transpacific contacts between Asia and America are usually considered to have been effected via dagger-board sailing rafts (for example, Ling, 1956; Estrada and Meggers, 1961: 935). Richard Bowen (1953a: 108; see also Doran, this symposium), an expert on sailing craft, considers the techniques of raft sailing in Asia and in aboriginal America to be too much alike and too complex to have been developed independently, even though the same author considers the lateen-rig sails of the eastern and western parts of the Indian Ocean to have evolved separately (for a discussion of some of the similarities and differences between Old World and New World raft "hulls," see Nelson, 1961; Ling, 1956). Log sailing rafts were once considered unseaworthy for long-distance voyaging, but this contention has now been definitively disproved by Heyerdahl (1950a: 25, 30; 1950b) and others. Edwards (1965: 101), who has carried out the most exhaustive study to date of the aboriginal watercraft of western South America, writes that "the argument that lengthy raft voyages were impossible is no longer acceptable." He further concludes (Edwards, 1969a) that such sailing rafts would have been safer and faster for transpacific crossings than the Spanish ships that plied the Manila galleon route from the latter sixteenth century to the early nineteenth. Chinese documents indicate that seagoing sailing rafts were in common use off China as early as the fifth century B.C. and perhaps more than two millenia earlier (Ling, 1956: 47, 49, 51). According to Chang (1959: 97), "The [ancient] Southeastern [Chinese] Culture is essentially maritime oriented and is historically known as the Pai-Yueh, the navigators," in contrast to the more land-bound north Chinese.

In coastal Peru there are archaeological occurrences of what are usually considered to be paddles and large daggerboards for sailing rafts, although some believe these to be agricultural or ceremonial implements (Heyerdahl, 1959: 335–337). This direct evidence is late (a tentative lower limit is A.D. 1000), but indirect evidence of sea voyaging and trading between Guatemala and Ecuador occurs as early as the Formative period (Coe, 1960: 384–386) and exists for later times for travel between Mesoamerica and Peru (Willey, 1955: 585; see also Edwards, 1969b). The presence of Mesoamerican cultivated plants in the preceramic coastal sites of a Peruvian fishing culture dating from the period about 4000–2500 B.C. is also suggestive (Harris, 1967: 103–104). Unfortunately, Mesoamerican watercraft have not yet received intensive study (but see Thompson, 1950a; Nelson, 1961: 170–175; and McKusick, 1960).

The Polynesians and other Oceanian peoples settled virtually all the inhabitable Pacific islands, a feat that necessitated crossings of up to at least one thousand miles of islandless ocean, often at high angles to the prevailing winds and currents. Whether or not the longer of these voyages were intentional has been debated (for example, Best, 1923; Heyerdahl, 1952; Sharp, 1964; Golson, 1963), but their very occurrence demonstrates that long-distance ocean voyaging in small, primitive craft was possible to some Neolithic peoples. Viking boats, too, though small and open, regularly crossed the storm-lashed North Atlantic, apparently sailing on at least one occasion directly from Norway to Labrador (Weaver, 1965: 7), a voyage duplicated in 1893 in a replica of a seventy-six-foot Viking ship (Villiers, 1962: 63). Carl Sauer (1968) cites evidence of pre-Columbian crossings by Portuguese, English, and Irish mariners (see also Kehoe, this symposium). These cases demonstrate that seaworthy boats existed in pre-Columbian times (C-14 dates in Hawaii, for example, indicate settlement there possibly as early as A.D. 120 ± 120 [Ferdon, 1963: 152]).

It is difficult to obtain a very clear picture of the navigational abilities of ancient peoples. Surviving documents, such as the peripli of the Mediterranean, occasionally offer some help, but relatively few have come down to us, due in part to the studied secrecy of ancient navigators, to whom such esoteric knowledge was an asset in commercial competition. Nevertheless, the sophistication in calendric computations and astronomy in both the Old World and the New World indicates that basic celestial navigation techniques were known. Current investigation is demonstrating the existence of remarkable calendric and astronomical knowledge even in the British Isles, which are usually thought of as culturally peripheral, as long ago as a millenium and a half to two millenia B.C. Referring to the complex celestial orientations within certain British megalithic monuments, astronomer Gerald Hawkins (1965: 190) writes, ". . . the builders may have been aware of some of the fundamental facts which served later as the basis of accurate navigation." It is instructive to note as well the high degree of navigational skill (Gatty, 1958: 34–48, 165–168; Suggs, 1960: 73–85; Lewis, 1964) and extremely extensive geographical knowledge (Lewthwaite, 1966) possessed by the Micronesians and Polynesians, peoples at a much lower general level of technical development than those of the Mediterranean, southern and eastern Asia, and Nuclear America. Ekholm (1964b: 507) suggests that these skills may be derivative from an even more highly developed navigational tradition among Asiatic mainland civilizations. Chinese celestial navigation seems always to have been more advanced than European; Columbus and his contemporaries were certainly not highly skilled in this field (Borden, 1967: 64). In China, calendric and astronomical sciences were, from earliest times, given great attention and received official backing from the sovereign; except, perhaps, for the Babylonians, the Chinese "were the most persistent and accurate observers of celestial phenomena anywhere in the world before the Arabs" (Needham, 1959: 171). The use of the stars for purposes of navigation is specifically mentioned in texts dating to the second century B.C., and the Chinese were the pioneers in the use of magnetic polarity for direction-finding. The use of the lodestone spoon, or "south-pointer," may go back to the fourth century B.C. and is almost certainly earlier than 200 B.C. Magnetized needles were very probably coming into use from the fourth century A.D. on and seem definitely to have been used at sea after about A.D. 850. Magnetic declination values were available probably by the tenth century (Needham, 1962: 271, 281). Geographical knowledge developed early in China, and the spherical-earth theory dates back at least to the first century A.D. there; the system of latitudinal and longitudinal coordinates was known by about A.D. 100 (Needham, 1959: 498, 537). Astronomical science is known to have been at least fairly highly developed in Nuclear America (Teeple, 1931), but the extent to which it was applied to navigation is problematical. In any case, it takes relatively little navigational skill to hit a target of continental size; as Pedro de Quiros put it in 1597, ". . . the most stupid can go in their embarcations . . . to seek a large country—since if they do not hit one part they will hit another" (quoted in Borden, 1967: 44). Edwards (1969a) notes, "The mainland to mainland crossing of the Pacific imposes no navigational difficulties."

It is generally supposed by diffusionists that initial voyages of discovery were accidental (for example, Ferdon, 1963: 502–505), and the frequency in historic times of east Asian fishing boats (to say nothing of net-floats and other flotsam) being brought by storm and current to American shores, even as far south as Acapulco (Brooks, 1875; Sittig, 1896: 531), is cited (for additional discussions of Pacific drift voyaging, see Sharp, 1964; Nelson, 1963; Heine-Geldern, 1952); transatlantic drift voyages have also been recorded (Alcina Franch, 1955: 878). It has been argued that primitive sailors could not have survived transoceanic drift voyages, particularly since provisions would have been inadequate for unexpected voyages of great duration. However, trading and fishing vessels might in some cases have been rather well provisioned; that their carrying capacity was sufficient is indicated by the Kon-Tiki's five-ton cargo. In any case, if adequate water is available, a man can survive for fifty days or longer without food (Critchley, 1943: 42), and, contrary to popular opinion, sea water can be used as a supplementary water source, as can fish juices (Wolf, 1956: 76; Bombard, 1954). At least in some latitudes and at some seasons, rainstorms and the ocean would provide adequate fresh water and food, especially to people familiar with the sea; such was Heyerdahl's (1950a: 28–30) experience in the Kon-Tiki. Alain Bombard (1954), a physician, made a solo crossing from the Canary Islands to Barbados in a fifteen-foot rubber dinghy with sail, voluntarily carrying neither food nor water on the sixty-five-day voyage. There is a nineteenth-century record of nine Japanese surviving an accidental drift of eleven months and landing on Oahu (Sittig, 1896: 530), and Brooks (1875: 53) refers to two accidental voyages from Japan to North American waters, of seventeen and eighteen months' duration respectively, with three of the crew surviving in each case. The usual rate of drift of such junks has been from ten to fifteen miles a day or more, however (Borden, 1967: 228). Thus, much less time would normally be required to cross the North Pacific from Asia to America, since the craft would be propelled by the North Pacific Current, whose attendant winds are prevailingly approximately parallel to the current. These winds would normally add to the rate of travel of a craft even without sail, which, if used, would further increase the speed; Kon-Tiki, though not correctly rigged or sailed, averaged 1.77 miles per hour in the South Equatorial Current (Heyerdahl, 1950a: 30). Estimating the velocity of a sailing craft at only 1 mile per hour, a journey of five-thousand miles (from Japan to Mexico) along a great-circle route in the North Pacific

Current would, if uninterrupted by weather, take 208 days. Of course, storm conditions might greatly increase rate of travel; Heyerdahl (1952: 163) cites the case of a dismasted ship drifting from Japanese waters to Canadian waters in fifty days' time.

It is also conceivable that Old World sailors gradually became familiar with coastlines and islands farther and farther from their homelands and thus eventually gained knowledge of "lands beyond the sea" without ever long leaving sight of land. Scholars are agreed that Malaysians, probably from Borneo, settled Madagascar, probably shortly after the time of Christ (Murdock, 1959: 209–210). If coastal voyaging to Madagascar is assumed, Malaysians or others living in Japan could have reached South America by traveling an equal distance along the island chains and coastlines of Asia and North America. It is also possible to cross the North Atlantic (as did the Vikings) without ever being very far from sight of land.

Heyerdahl (1964; see also Ferdon, 1963; Nelson, 1963) has discussed the most feasible transoceanic routes. In the Pacific, the normally most direct Asia-to-America route is the Japan–North Pacific–California current series originating off the Philippines and continuing parallel to the coasts of Asia and North America as far as Mexico (and on to Costa Rica in winter). A second direct route is the Equatorial Countercurrent; this appears to be somewhat undependable along much of its length but probably not as unreliable as Heyerdahl contends. America-to-Asia routes include the North Equatorial Current (from Mesoamerica to the Philippines) and the Peru–South Equatorial Current sequence (Peru to New Guinea). From Europe and North Africa to America, the most feasible routes include the Iceland-Greenland route and the Canary and North Equatorial currents. A return could be accomplished via the Gulf Stream–North Atlantic Current system; a few pre-Columbian Indians and Eskimos seem to have reached Europe, presumably via the North Atlantic Current (Merrien, 1954: 25; Carter, 1963: 97; MacRitchie, 1912). Other transoceanic routes that seem at the moment less likely to have been important are the West Wind Drift in the South Pacific and the Benguela–South Equatorial Current sequence in the Atlantic from South Africa to Brazil (see *Time*, 1968a; Ferdon, 1963). Each of the currents discussed above is, with the exception of the countercurrent, approximately paralleled by the prevailing winds. It should be kept in mind, however, that sailing craft in the Pacific were quite capable of sailing against normal winds and currents. Too, seasonally and during storms, the prevailing winds and currents may be reversed; almost all Polynesia's littoral plants, which are dispersed in the form of floating seeds, are of Asiatic origin (Guppy, 1906: 64–65), despite opposing prevailing winds and currents.

Antidiffusionists (for example, Rowe, 1966: 336) often contend that a boatload of a few individuals landing on the American coast would almost certainly have been killed or made slaves and would neither have passed on ideas nor have been able to return to their homelands. Such a reception was undoubtedly met at times, but there is no reason to assume that this was always the case; de Vaca's experience was very much to the contrary: "Such [hospitable reception] was indeed almost always the case in the New World and continued to be true until the natives were abused and dispossessed" (Sauer, 1968: 185). A group of seventeen Negroes shipwrecked in Ecuador in the early sixteenth century gained political control over an entire province in short order (Cabello de Balboa, 1945: 133). Some host societies would undoubtedly resist ideas introduced by outsiders, but others might welcome them. For example, a study of pre-European legendary culture heroes in Palau (McKnight, 1968) indicated that the innovator—usually a foreigner—was eulogized, and, in historic times, the Palauans invited individual European sailors to remain as innovators.

Some diffusionists visualize the postulated cultural impact of the Old World on America as being the result of a long series of accidental drifts. Others, however, believe that the number of similarities suggests massive, long-term, intentional voyaging. A group swept accidentally from Asia to North America, if possessed of even the vaguest idea that their direction of drift had been northeastward, might refit and reprovision in America and then sail southwestward; such a course would almost inevitably put them into the returning North Equatorial Current. Assuming that word of a new world was carried back to the old, the question then arises as to what could motivate a return to the newly discovered land. There is a tendency for non-seafaring, machine-dependent, deadline-dominated scholars to overestimate the dangers of transoceanic voyaging, particularly raft voyaging, and to underestimate the willingness of many poor or primitive peoples, especially desperate ones, to take the time and risks that would be involved in transoceanic voyaging. Geographer Carl Sauer

(1959: 120–121) suggests that it may be "our own agoraphobia and thalassophobia as students of New World culture that have so greatly restricted knowledge and consideration of far connections of culture, of mobility of peoples, of communications of ideas beyond the sheltering limits of so-called culture areas."

Yet even in our own times numerous adventurers have made long ocean voyages in small craft, voyages that seem foolhardy or worse to overcivilized man. Perhaps, though, these voyages were not as dangerous as they may appear to have been. Merrien (1954) lists 120 modern intentional *solo and two-man* long ocean voyages (see also Borden, 1967). Among these are a 17-day voyage from the Cape Verde Islands to Martinique by a pair of Estonians in a 29-foot sloop; a 30-day Atlantic crossing in a 24-foot 8-inch sailing craft by a toeless, fingerless sailor; William Verity's 68-day passage from Florida to Ireland in a home-built, 12-foot sloop; a sailless, oar-propelled crossing by two men from New York to the Scilly Islands in 55 days in a dory 17 feet, 8 inches long (see also Ridgeway and Blyth, 1967); a solo, 93-day crossing from Japan to San Francisco in a 19-foot sloop; a 68-day raft drift from California to Hawaii; a solo voyage in a converted Indian dugout canoe (bottom length, 30 feet) from Vancouver directly to the Cook Islands, a journey of some 5,500 miles in 56 days, followed by an ultimate landing in England; a solo, 162-day journey in a 19.5-foot schooner 6,500 miles from San Francisco to Australian waters without a single port of call; the solo, three-year, 46,000-mile, round-the-world voyage of Joshua Slocum in the *Spray* (36 feet, 9 inches); the round-the-world journey of Vito Dumas in a 32-foot ketch, a journey that included a direct 7,200-mile run in the Roaring Forties from the Cape of Good Hope to New Zealand, on to Valparaiso, Chile (5,400 miles in 72 days), and then around the Horn; sixty-six–year-old Francis Chichester's 28,500-mile, one-stop circumnavigation via Cape Horn in a 54-foot ketch; the voyages of Eric de Bisschop—including one with a single companion from Hawaii to Cannes in 264 sailing days in a double canoe, one by bamboo sailing raft some 5,000 miles into the southeastern Pacific from Tahiti (de Bisschop, 1959), and one by raft from Peru 5,500 miles to Rakahanga (Boswell, 1959); the 7,450-mile pontoon raft journey from Peru to Samoa by seventy-year-old William Willis (1965), who eventually sailed 3,000 additional miles to Australia, though suffering an abdominal hernia, a fractured sacrum, and partial paralysis; four other

raft journeys from Peru, with safe landings ranging from the Galápagos to Australia (Heyerdahl, 1966: 704); a journey by three Americans in an old Polynesian outrigger from Oahu to San Francisco
(Heine-Geldern, 1952: 357); a trip down the Amazon and on to
Miami by an eighteen-year-old in a leaky, 19-foot dugout fitted with
sails, including a run of over 850 miles on the Atlantic (Schultz,
1962); a solo, 72-day crossing of the Atlantic in a 17-foot canvas fold-
boat (Lindemann, 1957); an island-hopping expedition by a sixteen-
year-old in a 24-foot sloop from California to South Africa, including
a 2,300-mile run under jury rig due to a dismasting (Graham, 1968);
and a solo voyage in a 6-foot sailboat from Casablanca to Florida in
84 days (*Time.* 1968b). Even transatlantic races for loners have now
been established.

In view of the above, we may consider A. C. Haddon's (1934: 82)
observations regarding motivation for ancient voyages into Polynesia:

A restless disposition has been a fruitful cause of movements. Sometimes
it is a desire to acquire land or wealth, sometimes it is a reaction against
social restraints at home, but it also manifests itself largely as a spirit of
adventure. All these motives occur among many primitive peoples as well
as among civilized nations. In some such way we may account for bearers
of better modes of living and of a higher socio-religious culture adventuring into the Pacific.

Eldon Best (1923: 11–14) also lists some possible motives for intentional voyaging into and within Polynesia, including escape from
war, quarrel, or natural calamity, a desire to find a more fertile homeland, and a search for prestige and adventure. These motives might
apply to transpacific voyaging as well. The population pressures in
Asia and the political expansion of China that are thought to have
caused some of the great migrations of peoples southward in Asia,
into the islands, and as far as Africa and Madagascar may also have
resulted in at least some transoceanic migration to the Americas. Best
(1923: 9) notes that even before initial discovery, the existence of
land beyond the horizon could have been guessed at by the observation of migrating birds and of flotsam arriving with the currents;
North American logs have been observed as far away as the Caroline
Islands (Heyerdahl, 1952: 162).

In regard to postulated intentional voyaging from India, Indochina,
and China to the Americas, Heine-Geldern (1956: 95) suggests that

gold, jade, and feathers may have attracted Asiatic voyagers to the New World. Gold and silver lured sixteenth-century Spaniards to the Americas in ships with less sailing ability than those of pre-Columbian Asia, and in view of the lengths to which men will go for wealth or prestige, it would not be too surprising to discover that Asians came to the Americas for materials they valued highly. Religious motives have also been suggested, particularly the well-known Buddhist predilection for proselytizing (see, for example, Ekholm, 1953: 88; Kirchhoff, 1964).

Extremely long-distance, overland diffusion of objects—and, presumably, of ideas—is well known, even for very early time depths, at least in the Old World (Childe, 1937). Considering the fact that such diffusion required either long chains of group-to-group transfers, or lengthy trading journeys or migrations through alien peoples, or both, and considering the very slow rate of overland travel in early times, prior to extensive road systems and high-speed vehicles, we must realize that if proper watercraft and waterways were available, travel—and therefore diffusion—could often be accomplished much more rapidly and safely by water than by land. As Edwards (1965: v) has put it, ". . . for many inhabitants of the world's islands, seacoasts, and riverbanks, water has not separated places; it has joined them." Cultural isolationists consider that diffusionists overestimate the abilities of pre-Columbian man to traverse the oceans. As Fraser (1965: 468) has pointed out, however, there is a greater potential loss to knowledge in underestimating these capabilities than in overestimating them: whereas an underestimation forecloses any investigation of contacts that may in fact have occurred, an overestimation, though it in no way proves that contact did take place, does encourage the search for evidence of possible contact. In other words, underestimation commits one to a possibly incorrect position relating to contacts and diffusion, whereas overestimation does not. The present author, on the basis of the above discussion of watercraft and navigation, will risk overestimation by concurring with Estrada and Meggers' (1961: 936) conclusion that "it can no longer be realistically argued that either the means or the opportunity to make a transpacific journey from Asia to America was lacking" in ancient times.

A general principle of the theory of overland diffusion is that the greater the time, effort, and hazard involved in traveling between two cultures, the lower the probability of contact and therefore of diffusion, other things being equal. This principle is often erroneously translated into a simple inverse distance/probability-of-diffusion ratio; however, intervening physical and cultural barriers other than distance are often much more important in determining the likelihood of contact. It might be far easier to travel a hundred miles along a flat flood plain than to go half that distance via rugged, waterless mountains. To a boatless culture, a river might represent an impassable barrier, whereas a culture with watercraft might find the same river its most convenient highway. Or the friendliness or ferocity of an intervening tribe might make the difference between intensive overland contact and no contact at all. In the case of oceans, the factor of distance is again only one of many affecting likelihood of diffusion; travel with the winds and currents and in storm-free seasons or areas would make voyages of a given distance far easier than if contrary conditions were encountered (Heyerdahl, 1964). Thus, like the land, the seas have their relative barriers and corridors for the movements of men (but lack, in the open ocean, intervening peoples with which to contend). Again, it should be emphasized that travel by boat, following proper routes, was often safer and swifter than land travel in pre-machine-age times. With this in mind, transoceanic journeying should not be too surprising in view of the well-known examples of tremendously long overland trade routes, such as the Silk Road, and migrations of great length, such as the 10,000-mile journey of the Huns from Mongolia to France and back, the 6,500-mile wanderings over several centuries of the Visigoths in Europe, the campaigns of Alexander the Great and his armies for a dozen years over a route greater than 10,000 miles in length, resulting in the establishment of an empire 3,000 miles long, and the lengthy messianic migrations of Tupian tribes in South America..

Generally speaking, a geographically continuous area of distribution of a complex trait is, if entirely on land, considered to be the result of a single origin and spread of that trait. Diffusion in such a case is conceived of as the group-to-group spread of the trait over time in all directions from the point of origin, with no long-distance traveling required. If two separated areas of distribution of the trait exist, trade contacts across the gap, migration, or independent development are all possible explanations for the similarities. As discussed above, the greater the difficulties involved in traveling between two areas, the lower the probability of contact, and it has sometimes been maintained that "the greater the geographical distance, the stronger have we a right to demand the evidence to be of historical connection, that is, the more rigidly do we apply our criteria" (Sapir, 1916: 39–40). However, reality does not conform to this demand, for an increase in the distance over which contact takes place does not cause a greater degree of similarity to come about; indeed, other things being equal, the greater the effective distance, the less frequent will be the contacts and the fewer the similarities. Other things may not be equal, however. Ease of travel between two cultures is not the only factor that influences likelihood of diffusion. The degree of friendliness, the intensity and the length of contact; the degree of similarity of the values and technologies of the group involved; the degree of conservatism of the cultures, both in revealing and accepting ideas; the practical, prestige, luxury, or religious values of the traits, and the ease of learning them: all affect the probability of diffusion. Since most of these factors may vary a great deal from group to group, diffusion involving separated groups may in some cases be more likely than diffusion among contiguous groups, despite greater physical ease of contact between the latter. Thus we cannot assume when we find a trait in two separated areas that there is necessarily a low probability that the trait spread from one of these areas to the other or from a common outside source to each of these areas. A distant area may for some reason—political, social, economic, environmental— have more attraction than a nearby one, or it may be more receptive to diffusion. Nor is there any means of determining at what rate probability of contact declines with effective distance, even if we do assume other factors to be equal, and it certainly cannot be said that the greater the distance between two areas, the greater the probability of invention occurring in each area.

In addition, the concept of continuity of distribution has a different meaning when applied across large areas of water than it does on land. People do not live permanently in mid-ocean, and we cannot expect culture traits to be found there. Though an ocean may cause an apparent gap in a trait distribution, the distribution *is* in a real sense continuous if it encompasses land areas facing each other across an empty sea, for the trait then occupies all *possible* (that is, land) areas within the boundary of its range. On a small scale, this is demonstrated by the Mediterranean. No one argues that the Roman towns of North Africa were evolved independently of those of Italy or Gaul, yet there is a water gap—and therefore a distributional gap—separating them. In this case, the sea was the main connecting link between these regions. A Soviet anthropologist, speaking of the Pacific, has gone so far as to say, "It would hardly be an exaggeration to call it the interior sea of Ameraustralasia. For that super-continent it played a role—naturally on a different scale—comparable to that of the Mediterranean in the destiny of Afroeurasia" (Arutiunov, 1966: 26).

A second difference between land-bound, group-to-group diffusion and diffusion across water is, as Fraser (1965: 468) put it, the fact that, being by boat, the latter is "linear rather than planar." Therefore the lack in the Pacific Islands of certain traits shared by Asia and America does not, as some antidiffusionists have contended, disprove the ancient intercontinental transfer of these ideas. The transpacific routes considered most probable miss the majority of the Polynesian islands, and, in any event, there is little on the islands of potential attraction for wealth-oriented voyagers; in the later times, the Spanish, during the 250 years they operated in Manila galleons, ignored the Pacific Islands except for Guam, particularly once their routes became well established (Carter, 1963: 14–15).

Ethnobotanical Evidence of Contacts

Because of the impossibility of using the criterion of continuous distribution or of applying an inverse distance/probability-of-diffusion ratio, it would be highly desirable to differentiate between diffusion and polygenesis by the use of criteria that are independent of distance, difficulty of travel, and the like, criteria that apply equally to intracontinental comparisons and to interhemispheric ones—for ". . . clearly the logical consistency of a theory that stops at the water's edge is difficult to defend" (Fraser, 1965: 477). The bulk of the remainder of this paper discusses the possibility of developing such universal criteria.

The existence of means of contact—that is, adequate watercraft—says nothing about whether contact did in fact occur. Diffusionists, in their search for absolute proof of interhemispheric contact, have in recent years turned increasingly to ethnobotanical evidence (for example, Carter, 1950, 1953; Heine-Geldern, 1958; Jett, 1968). Geographer George F. Carter, who has been active in this regard, writes (1963: 8):

Plants do supply absolute evidence. They are not human inventions. Further, a plant accepted in evidence must meet a number of requirements. It must be the identical plant. It must be demonstrated to have been present on both sides of the Pacific. Preferably the plant would have similar usages on both sides of the Pacific. It must be a plant for which the possibility of natural diffusion by sea, by birds, or by winds is negligible. Ideally it would have some nonrational ideas associated with it, such as could be accounted for only by a presumption of human transfer of the plant.[1]

Every cultigen requires a specific wild ancestor (sometimes more than one) as well as a particular history of direct or indirect selection by man and by the environments he creates or alters. Archaeologist John Rowe (1953) questions the assumption that the appropriate wild ancestors must not have existed in an area in the past simply because they are not found in that area today, but plant geographer D. H. Campbell (1926: 26) writes that "the tropical vegetation of the East and West [Hemispheres] is composed for the most part of very different elements. There are very few common species, and to a great extent, the genera and even families differ [the main exceptions among seed plants being littoral species]." Another plant geographer (Polumin, 1960: 166) states that "the chances that two isolated [plant] populations [of the same initial species] will evolve in exactly the same way are incalculably low, while convergence in every respect of previously dissimilar types is even more improbable."

Thus, when identical tropical cultivated species are found in the two hemispheres, we can, with a few exceptions, rule out indepedent selection and evolution. Botanist Elmer Drew Merrill (1954: 236) remarks that, "as a rule, even weeds, much less cultigens, do not extend their ranges from one hemisphere to another without the intervention and aid of man." Many of the relevant cultivated plants are, in fact, tropical, delicate, and essentially or entirely seedless and so could clearly have spread only in the warmer latitudes and through human agency. These and many other cultigens have been so changed under domestication that the wild ancestral species either are not unequivocally identifiable or have become extinct through cross-

---

[1] In *Plants and the Migrations of Pacific Peoples*, ed. Jacques Barrau (Honolulu: Bishop Museum Press, 1963). This and subsequent quotations from Carter's article are used by permission of the publisher.

pollenization with the cultigens and consequent acquisition of traits preventing survival in the wild. As a result, it has in a few cases not been definitively determined whether domestication occurred in the Old World or the New World. Too, until rather recently, most "botanists have studiously avoided study of the domestic plants. . . . Many groups are taxonomically in complete confusion" (Carter, 1953: 62; for a review of recent work on the origins of agriculture and cultivated plants, see Harris, 1967). The above, supplemented in some cases by the archaeological record, indicates a very long period of domestication for these cultigens as well as the impossibility in most cases of even local natural dispersal, much less transoceanic traveling.

There are a few cultivated plants about which there is some argument concerning their ability to spread spontaneously across the oceans; these include the bottle gourd (*Lagenaria siceraria*) and the coconut palm (*Cocos nucifera*), both of which are agreed to have been present in both hemispheres in pre-Columbian times. Carriage by man, however, seems at least as likely as that these plants floated across the oceans, avoided destruction by salt water and pelagic organisms, were tossed ashore on a site suitable for germination, and were taken into cultivation by man. In any case, if any of those cultigens which clearly cannot have spread naturally appear in both hemispheres in pre-Columbian times, contact is proved. This does not demonstrate any diffusion other than of the plants themselves and the specific techniques of their cultivation, but it does show opportunity for additional diffusion.

The best evidence of the pre-Columbian presence of such a plant in both hemispheres would be its occurrence in indubitably pre-Columbian archaeological contexts in both hemispheres. Unfortunately, lack of preservation, lack of clear-cut associations or dating, difficulty of identification, and frequent lack of attention to plant remains on the part of archaeologists have resulted in our having relatively little firm data on this subject.

As far as is known to the present author, the only specimens of American plants that have been found in undoubtedly pre-Columbian sites in the Old World are peanuts in Chekiang Province, China, dated between about 2100–1800 B.C. (Chang, 1968: 157, 445). In the New World, Old World plant remains have been reported only from Peru. Besides the bottle gourd and the coconut, these include: the plantain (*Musa paradisiaca*), which is referred to in archaeological sites by several workers (Towle, 1961: 97; Heyerdahl, 1952: 482); the mangosteen (*Garcinia mangostana*), reported by one nineteenth-century botanist (Towle, 1961: 97); and possibly some others. Ethnobotanist Margaret Towle rejects these identifications as erroneous, not on the basis of the specimens, which are not now available for study, but on the assumption that the species are post-Columbian introductions. The paucity of such "identifications" leaves the question of their usefulness as evidence in doubt; they may be misidentifications, they may come from post-Columbian sites, or they may be genuine pre-Columbian occurrences. Clearly, much additional work is needed.

Hutchinson, Silow, and Stephens (1947), after intensive taxonomic and genetic study, concluded that the New World cultivated cottons and Polynesian wild cottons (*Gossypium* species) were allotetraploids arising from the crossing of some Old World cotton with a New World wild cotton, both of which are diploid. There has been considerable debate regarding how an Old World cotton reached the New World by about 5000 B.C. and perhaps by 5800 B.C., when tetraploid *G. hirsutum* is known to have been at Tehuacán, Mexico (Smith and MacNeish, 1964: 675). Schwerin (1970) and Kennedy (this symposium) suggest transatlantic carriage by man, and Hutchinson (1962: 14–15) has discussed an alternative theory involving an ancient, natural hybridization between wild African and South American cottons. Cotton differs from most of the cultivated plants here under consideration in that it has small, easily transported seeds and can survive in the wild; seeds could conceivably have been transported by birds (see Proctor, 1968), but tests of duration of buoyancy and viability of the seeds of the most likely African cottons have led to the conclusion that the seeds could not have survived a natural transatlantic drift journey (Stephens, 1966).

One particularly promising technique is pollen analysis of datable sediments, mortar, and the like. Pollen is sometimes preserved even under conditions resulting in the decomposition of the rest of the plant. "If pollens of food plants introduced by the early colonists in the Pacific can be recovered and recognized and dated by the radiocarbon method, it will be possible not only to establish the time of arrival of the people and plants, but when, and by what route they came" (Shutler, 1961: 79). As far as I am aware, the only application to date of palynology to the pre-Columbian diffusion problem involves maize (*Zea mays*). Pollen of what is probably wild, ancestral maize appears in Mexican sediments dated at about 80,000 B.C. (Mangelsdorf, MacNeish and Galinat, 1964: 539). In Kashmir, what *may* be pollen of primitive maize has been found in a site dating *possibly* to the thirteenth or fourteenth centuries A.D. (Vishnu and Gupta, 1966: 184).

In the absence of actual plant remains, datable depictions of plants are the next best evidence. Paintings, sculpture, effigy pottery, and the like are found in various parts of the world, depicting, or even being molded on, identifiable plants. An example of the use of depictions is found in the case of the pineapple, a New World plant shown on Inca wooden cups (Towle, 1961: 30). It also appears in a mural at Pompeii (Casella, 1950), its identification having been accepted even by plant taxonomist Elmer Drew Merrill (1954), a very vocal critic of diffusionism.

A third type of evidence is historical documents. Unfortunately, it is not always possible to identify as particular species of plants some of the rather vague descriptions of the early chroniclers; descriptions of yams and sweet potatoes are particularly difficult to sort out, for example. Sometimes only the word for the plant occurs in the documents, and one is not always able to determine whether the writer identified the plant correctly or whether the word was restricted to, or even applied to, the same plant in the past as it is today. How, for example, do we assess the unique occurrence of the present word for sweet potato (*kan-shu*), an American domesticate, in a Chinese document dating to about A.D. 300, when the associated description of the tuberous plant is too vague to make a positive identification (Wallacker, n.d.)?

In the absence of unequivocal descriptions from Columbus' first voyage or from pre-Columbian Old World documents, it can always be argued, if documents are the only evidence, that Europeans were responsible for the plant transfers in question. Despite these difficulties, documentary evidence is sometimes highly suggestive. For example, nearly all scholars agree that the American sweet potato had spread throughout Polynesia in pre-Columbian times (but see Brand, this symposium), and the antidiffusionist botanist Merrill (1954: 274, 307) states that it was also present in Melanesia, Micronesia, and Indonesia. "Even . . . Roland B. Dixon, than whom no more conservative anthropologist ever lived, admitted that someone must have carried the sweet potato westward into the islands several centuries before the time of Columbus" (Coon, 1962: 357). These conclusions are based on documentary evidence from early European contacts and on the great number of local varieties of sweet potato in these regions (but see Purseglove, 1965). "Had cross-Pacific voyages been long and arduous, the sweet potato tubers would either have spoiled or been eaten. Neither was the case, and it is clearly inferable that man made deliberate and relatively easy voyages across the greatest expanses of the Pacific" (Carter, 1963: 9). Another example is the sixteenth-century documentary evidence of the very widespread occurrence of the Asiatic plantain in America (Sauer, 1950: 527); even Merrill (1954: 278) allows that "we may reasonably admit" that the plantain was in the New World before Columbus.

The best-known example of the association of the same *name* with the same plant on both sides of the ocean is that of *kumar, kumara,* and similar words for the sweet potato, or one of its varieties, in Peru and throughout Polynesia; its possible relation to a Sanskrit word for the edible rhizome of the lotus (*kumad*) has also been suggested (Carter, 1953: 64). In another case, the extraction, by similar means, of edible starch from the trunk of a palm and the use of the word *sagu* for the substance in both Malaysia and Brazil (where, however, different palms are used) suggests the possibility of the spread of a technique and a name without the spread of the actual plant (Jett, 1968: 159). Occurrence on both sides of the ocean of similar nonrational mythologies in association with food plants is also suggestive in some cases. Examples include the corn-mother myths of Indonesia and South America (Hatt, 1951) and the origin myth (and name) of the yam in Indonesia and South America (Canals Frau, 1956–57).

There are other sorts of evidence that have been used to support the case for pre-Columbian plant transfers. One is the association of the cultivation of the plant largely with native non-European cultivators, which suggests that the plant was not important to, or spread by, Europeans. The plantain is a case in point (Sauer, 1950: 527). Occasionally, the study of plant parasites or diseases is illuminating. For example, the American sweet potato has been in the Old World long enough for a species of parasitic weevil of Old World origin to become adapted exclusively to it (Merrill, 1954: 317–321).

More than a score of cultivated plants, as well as weeds and some domesticated birds and animals (for example, Carter, this symposium; Heyerdahl, 1966: 700–701), have been suggested as possible transoceanic transfers. This is a field of inquiry in which we can expect to see a good deal more activity in the future, not only by archaeologists, ethnohistorians, and plant geographers, but, of particular importance, by taxonomists and geneticists.

Antidiffusionists have sometimes argued that if significant interhemispheric contacts had taken place, the staple crops of the two hemispheres would be shared. "If someone could only prove that even a few of the *basic crop plants* of American origin, and only a few of the more numerous ones of Eurasian origin, were *universally distributed* in cultivation in both hemispheres in pre-Columbian times, one might be more lenient in judging the matter [of diffusionism]" (Merrill, 1950). As Carter (1963: 10ff.) discusses, however, ". . . there is no law about what plant will diffuse, how far it will go, or where it will have its major development." Indulgents, medicinals, ornamentals (which often bear magic or religious associations), dyes, poisons, and other speciality plants, which may fill an unoccupied cultural niche, may be diffused more readily than staples. A staple may have a low likelihood of acceptance, since an established equivalent against which it would have to compete may exist in the potential recipient area (for example, maize versus rice), or the means of raising the staple may be incompatible with the environment or the type of cultivation practiced in the potential recipient area (for example, a grain crop might be difficult to introduce into an area depending on vegetatively propagated root crops). In any event, some of the food plants suggested as transfers *are* important crops and even staples in some areas. These include the sweet potato, yams, the taro, the plantain, the coconut palm, maize, and *Amaranthus*. As for universal distribution, even today, and much more so in pre-Columbian times, important crops were not universally used even in areas within which much contact and diffusion is known to have taken place. As Carter (1963: 19–20) remarks,

. . . it is often dangerous to assume that modern economic dominants held that same position 2,000 or more years ago. The adoption of a new plant is no simple matter. It requires the adoption of a whole complex of knowledge about the plant's ecological requirements, and often also about the human usages of the plant. The presence of even one transferred plant means that a quite effective and probably relatively durable contact has been made between two peoples. The presence of a number of plants, even as few as ten or twenty, indicates a major cultural contact.

The apparently unequivocal pre-Columbian sharing of at least a few cultivated plants that could have been distributed only by human carriage in warm latitudes necessitates a serious consideration of the possibility that at least some interhemispheric cultural similarities are a result of diffusion. To a certain extent, the question becomes one of economy of explanation. Most scholars would, I am sure, agree that, given the opportunity to observe a technique or practice, man can more easily copy that technique or practice than arrive at it unaided. The theory of independent inventionism requires dual or multiple occurrences of the series of events leading to the development of a trait, whereas diffusionism requires but a single occurrence. Diffusionism, however, does require long, arduous, and, to the isolationist, improbable voyaging, whereas independent inventionism does not. Unless contact is proved, each side can continue to argue that the additional necessary event (repetition of invention versus voyaging) required by the theory of the other side more than offsets the additional event required by one's own theory. Once significant contact is demonstrated, however, as by the plant evidence, the opportunity for diffusion of other items is proved. Under these circumstances, diffusion would seem clearly to be the more parsimonious hypothesis.

Nevertheless, the probability of invention will vary according to such other variables as the nature and level of a culture's technological or other systems and the nature of the physical environment; if the probability of invention is fairly high in a particular instance, the principal of parsimony might not carry a great deal of weight. Therefore, we must look for additional ways of assessing the relative probabilities of diffusion and independent invention actually having taken place.

The Use of Cultural Similarities as Evidence of Diffusion

Since cultural diffusionism is concerned with the spread of culture traits, the traits themselves are its primary evidence. In a few cases, claims have been made for the pre-Columbian New World occurrence of actual objects of Old World manufacture, including a cache of Roman to early Medieval coins from Venezuela, a late Roman torso of Venus from Veracruz state, Mexico (Heine-Geldern, 1967: 22), and "a cache of Chinese brass coins said to be dated 1200 B.C. [sic]" from British Columbia (Larson, 1966: 44). The most convincing case is that of a third century A.D. Roman terra-cotta head in apparently unequivocal association with a twelfth century A.D. tomb in the state of México (Heine-Geldern, 1967). Various ostensibly Norse objects of metal have also been reported, though Helge Ingstad's discovery of a pre-Columbian Norse (?) blacksmith shop in Newfoundland (Weaver, 1965: 9) suggests the possibility of manufacture in the New World. In addition to these objects, various rock inscriptions have been attributed to the Phoenicians (see especially Time, 1968b; Gordon, 1968) and the Norse.

Since few of these objects or inscriptions have been discovered and reported in a fashion that permits confidence in the dating or even in the genuineness of the sites, these finds cannot be accorded much significance. Even if one assumes that all such claims are genuine, their small number prevents them from being particularly impressive evidence of contact. Cultural isolationists feel that this indicates a lack of significant contacts (for example, Rowe, 1966: 336). Diffusionists would undoubtedly feel more comfortable if obvious and abundant imported objects were to be found, but they do not believe that this lack destroys their case. They consider the lack to be the result of incomplete archaeological knowledge, lack of preservation (due, perhaps, to perishable materials having constituted the bulk of the imported goods), and the probably small number of objects imported. The last could be a function of a small number of actual crossings, with colonization rather than exchange being the primary source of contact, and/or of religious rather than commercial motives having been dominant. Jett and Carter (1966: 868) write, "One sometimes has the feeling, too, that even if Old World trade items were found in New World sites, they might not be admitted to be such, due to the assumption of the impossibility of contacts." An imported item, unless it were as obvious as a Roman coin, might not be recognized as being identical to Old World objects; even if formal identity were recognized, it might be attributed to fortuitous convergence. If the object were obviously exotic, it might, if pre-Columbian isolation were assumed, be automatically considered a post-Columbian import and intrusive in the site, in which case it might not even be reported.

Whatever the causes of the apparent lack of imported objects, diffusionists are able to point to discontinuous distributions of clearly related traits without accompanying imported objects. Examples cited by Fraser (1965: 461–462) include significant Hellenistic influence, but no Hellenistic objects, in Han China, and strong Mexican influence in the southeastern United States without the occurrence of Mesoamerican objects. Fraser (1965: 462) makes the point that "the establishment of a relationship between two cultures hinges not on the demonstration of contact [as proved by objects] but of the impact as revealed in the cultural elements themselves. Otherwise the Buddha figures found in Scandinavian graves would be far more significant than in fact they are."

In the comparison of culture traits, the question of their true equivalence inevitably arises. Diffusionists tend to stress formal resemblances, although there is sometimes disagreement as to just how nearly identical objects or ideas or practices must be for the similarities to be deemed significant. It is sometimes held by antidiffusionists that the comparisons of traits outside their cultural contexts, which are often made by diffusionists, is meaningless, since the full nature—and thus degree of true comparability—of these traits can be understood only in terms of their structural ties to each other and to the remainder of the culture (see Muller, this symposium). A corollary is that similar traits found in different cultural contexts, which are often compared, can be considered similar only in a superficial sense and are not valid indicators of diffusion. According to this view, cultures are organically functioning wholes that cannot be considered simply as bundles of individual formal traits. Although it is true that at any one time all the items in a culture are linked in a structural network, nevertheless various traits are of various ages, if viewed evolutionistically, and of various origins, if looked at diffusionistically. As each trait became part of the culture, it had to be integrated within an existing structural network and required a readjustment of that network. Neither form nor structure is immutable. Some of the forms of African tribal art, for example, exerted a powerful influence on certain twentieth-century European styles of sculpture and painting, but the forms were altered and their ceremonial contexts were left completely behind, being replaced by an entirely new set of structural ties. Some traits may be able to diffuse only as parts of complexes, but others may diffuse singly, independent of their contexts (see Barnett, 1942); a single trait, not intrinsically tied to a complex, seems, in fact, more likely to diffuse than an entire complex or part of a complex.

Art historian Douglas Fraser (1965: 473) writes, "Similar roles may be played by radically dissimilar objects (as for instance Pangwe *bieri* and Kota *mbulu-ngulu*), just as identical forms may function in strikingly different ways within a single Camaroons village," suggesting that form and context may in many cases not be interdependent and that similar forms may be comparable despite different contexts. Fraser (1965: 469) further points out that, in any event, broad, interacting complexes of traits can frequently be compared. Following techniques also used by Heine-Geldern (1937, 1966), Fraser (1962) compares art styles in various parts of the world in terms not only of their visual content but also of their iconography, ceremonial contexts, and, frequently, their associations with other, functionally unrelated aspects of culture. Complexes of technique, form, and function are also compared by Heine-Geldern (1954) and Tolstoy (1963, 1966, 1969). In a few cases—for example, tribal Malaysia and tropical America (Jett, 1968)—it is possible to compare very large percentages of the total cultures. As will appear below, however, the usefulness of such comparisons varies inversely with the strength of the structural ties between the components.

Perhaps the most frequently offered alternative to diffusionist interpretations is the concept of the limitation of possibilities: that ways of doing things are limited or channeled by biological, psychological, sociocultural, and physical environmental possibilities (or demands) and by limitations or efficiencies intrinsic in the materials used or in the functions of the objects or practices, and that a trait may therefore have a fairly high probability of arising more than once. Charles Erasmus (1950: 386), referring to G. P. Murdock (1945: 139), writes:

He points out that in some cases the "limitations on potential responses are slight" and in others they are greater. Languages, folktales, and ceremonials permit great variety of detail, but every society can affiliate its children with groups of relatives through only three possible rules of descent: patrilineal, matrilineal, or bilateral. Similarly there are limitations to the number of possible ways of disposing of corpses. In such cases it is to be expected that different and even historically unconnected peoples will frequently chance upon the identical solution to the same problem.

Elaborating on this concept, Robert Rands and Carroll Riley (1958) suggest that convergent or parallel development may often arise from similar "complex nuclei" (simpler, basic forms of the complex) by "pattern elaboration," whose directions are to a variable degree controlled by those characteristics of the complex already in existence or by external factors. As a postulated example, they cite the blowgun complex of Southeast Asia and the Americas, in which, according to their view, the functions of the complex suggested or channeled the lines of its elaboration; this they term "complex demand" (for discussion of the blowgun from a diffusionist viewpoint, see Jett, 1968, 1971). A second example discussed is the captive complex within the New World, in which universal human biological and psychological characteristics are suggested as limiting or channeling factors. Rands and Riley do not contend that the concept of convergence or parallelism via pattern elaboration precludes the possibility of diffusion, but they present pattern elaboration as an alternative explanation. Diffusionists probably generally agree with the basic hypothesis of the limitation of possibilities, but they differ with independent inventionists on just how narrow these limitations actually are. Some diffusionists also feel that such concepts as complex demand have a slightly teleological flavor; they agree that there is in some cases a limited number of choices for elaboration, but they feel that this explains neither the existence of the original complex nucleus nor why that particular complex has been elaborated in some areas and not in others.

For traits that are limited or favored by, or dependent on, a particular cultural situation, the requirement, discussed earlier, that both trait and cultural context be similar before diffusion can be considered loses all meaning. In fact, other things being equal, traits that are found in similar contexts constitute the *poorest* evidence of diffusion, since they may well have arisen due to their similar contexts. A corollary is that if similar contexts tend to yield similar traits, different contexts should tend to yield different traits, and if similar traits are found in two very *different* contexts, the traits must be anomalous in one of the contexts and must be, in that area, the result of diffusion. Noting a large number of motifs shared by two cultures otherwise extremely different in structure, level, content, and physical environment, Fraser (1965: 474–475) writes, "To reconcile the Northwest Coast–Meso-American resemblances with the completely hermetic doctrine of New World invention, it is virtually necessary to admit that convergence may result from the operation of dissimilar factors as well as from similar—a conclusion that is logically inconsistent with itself."

In cases like that of the Northwest Coast–Mesoamerican resemblances, there are only four conceivable explanations for the likenesses: (1) universal or very widespread factors caused them—but this cannot be the case, for many of the similarities are found only in certain parts of the world and not in others; (2) *different* and distinctive local causes—environments and cultural contents, for instance—had similar effects; this seems a very unlikely explanation for a large number of common motifs, and is, in fact, no explanation at all in the sense of being a generalization with predictive value; (3) "pure accident" caused the likenesses; the probability of this is by definition low when a large number of separate resemblances are involved; (4) diffusion, probably from a common outside source (but see MacLeod, 1929), occurred; this may also appear unlikely, but only because of assumptions of lack of means for contact, not because of statistical improbability or impossibility as in the case of hypotheses one, two, and three.

When we deal with traits not strongly favored in, or tied to, a particular context, their co-occurrence with other, unrelated traits in separated areas improves the case for diffusion, as will be discussed below; but due to their lack of interdependence, this is not truly a question of structural context. Thus, although traits may diffuse with their favoring contexts or may be more readily accepted where a similar cultural structure already exists, nevertheless, as *evidence* of diffusion, *similar* traits in *dissimilar* contexts seems superior to *similar* traits in *similar* contexts.

If diffusion did in fact take place in the Northwest Coast–Mesoamerican example, then the traits must either (1) have been especially favored by the context of the donor area (and at the same time have been acceptable to the recipient cultures) or (2) not have been particularly favored by any context and so not have had a very high probability of arising even once, to say nothing of more than once. Traits of the latter type are what we may call "arbitrary" and are identified by their not being observably required or favored by their materials or function, by psychology or biology, or by a particular physical or cultural environment. There are, in other words, a large number of alternatives to such traits; the most probable alternative may, in many cases, be nonoccurrence. Although diffusionists and independent inventionists tend to disagree in their identification of just which traits can be considered arbitrary, there is probably general agreement that the more arbitrary a trait is, the better evidence its duplication is for diffusion.

The most obvious of arbitrary traits are linguistic, for, although language has practical functions, there are nearly infinite numbers of possible sound combinations that can perform these functions. The choice of any particular combination can thus be considered essentially arbitrary (onomatopoetic words and the like excepted). It is generally supposed, then, that although chance duplication of a particular set of sounds and associated meanings may occasionally occur, any large overlap between the vocabularies of two languages must be due to a historical relationship. David Kelley (1964: 17) writes:

Methods for the comparative study of languages have steadily become more rigorous, and the results have emphasized the general isolation of the New World from the Old World. No competent linguist has suggested that any language or language family of the New World is genetically related to any of those of the old World in the period since the rise of civilization, and few have suggested relationships at any time depth, although there have been many attempts by amateurs to show that Aztec is Indo-European, Quechua is Sumerian, or the Algonquian languages really Norse. It seems unlikely that future work will do much to change the evaluation of such attempts as worthless.

However, the position with respect to borrowed words is far different.

Linguist Morris Swadesh (1964: 538) writes:

Though it turns out that neither Australian nor any other language of the Old World that might have come across the Pacific has lived on in the Americas, this does not prove that there were no transpacific contacts. A number of archaeological traits, several common agricultural plants, and certain features of calendars represent parallels that could hardly have come about either by pure chance or by migration across Bering Strait. If there has been diffusion of any sort, there is every reason to suppose that some loan words must also exist. A number of concrete similarities can be mentioned.

Swadesh (1964: 538–539) discusses methods of distinguishing between loan words (such as *kumara* for the sweet potato) and those shared due to an ancient common origin (as the similarities between certain American languages and Australian ones): "We can . . . infer borrowing between unrelated languages by certain types of evidence, such as similar form and meaning; absence of similar forms in related languages on one side of the comparison, presumed to be the receiver; phonetics at odds with what is usual in the borrowing language." To this list of criteria he adds geographical restriction of the term in the recipient area as compared with widespread distribution in the area whence came the donors. Of course, the greater the length of the words, the less the chance of duplication, and the larger the number of such words, the lower the probability of any one of them being independent. Some of these criteria may not be met even if borrowing did take place, but the more of them that do pertain to a word, the higher the probability of borrowing.

Little scholarly work has been done in regard to the question of words lent between Old World and New World languages, although some suggestions have been made concerning possible Polynesian–Northwest Coast and Polynesian-Andean correspondences (see Heyerdahl, 1952: 155–156, 762–763, for a summary), and Kelley (1964: 18–19) points to scores of vocabulary and grammatical identities between Uto-Aztecan and Polynesian-Rotuman, suggesting Mexican influences bridging almost the entire Pacific. It is possible that additional work of this kind will provide important clues regarding transoceanic contacts. The widespread use around the Pacific of similar terms for certain types of watercraft seems particularly significant and should be the object of further investigation. Terms for rafts include: *p'ai* or *b'ai* in China, *paepae* or *pahi* in Polynesia; *paltsam* in southern China, *palson* in Korea, and *balsa* in Ecuador (Ling, 1956: 45; Lou, n.d.); and *ikada* in Japan, *cankatam* in southern India (Tamil language, from the Sanskrit *samghata*), and *jangada* in Brazil. Terms for dugout canoes include: *banga* in Taiwan, *banca* in the Philippines, *pongayi* in southern India (Tulu language), *pongo* in Oaxaca, Mexico, *bongo* in Panama, and *panga* on the Colombian coast (Ling, 1956: 47; Thompson, 1950a: 73; Jett, n.d.). Terms for rudders include *duaran* in southern China and *guare* in Peru (Lou, in press).

Kelley (1960) and Kirchhoff (1964) detail a large number of exact correspondences between Hindu and Mexican calendars and their religious and mythical associations, suggesting diffusions from India or Southeast Asia to Mexico. The nature of these correspondences, all seemingly highly arbitrary, is such—a combination of gods and their attributes, associated animals and concepts, and order of occurrence in sequence—that they constitute what may be considered among the most compelling cases suggesting diffusion.

Other examples of studies of similarities in magic and iconography include Obayashi (1959) on divination from entrails in Southeast Asia and Peru, and Ekholm (1953) and Naudon (1962) on Hindu-Buddhist and Late Classic Maya iconography. Heine-Geldern and Ekholm (1951: 303–307) list Southeast Asian–Mesoamerican similarities in ritual (for example, the volador), mythology (as the concepts of hell and its punishments), political systems and rank recognition (including such symbols of rank as thrones, litters, parasols, and fans mounted on poles), among others (see also Heine-Geldern, 1968).

Similar mythologies have sometimes been compared by diffusionists (for example, Hatt, 1949, 1951). One objection (Luomala, 1940) to this type of evidence is that similarities may be due to universal psychological factors. This would seem to be more true of some mythic elements than of others, but certainly such factors must be taken into consideration when making comparisons.

"Another important area in which there are . . . indications of value is that of games. Various types of arrow-throwing or shooting games show remarkably similar terminology, from Egypt through Polynesia and much of the New World, and some board games show similar terms in widely separated areas" (Kelley, 1964: 17). The most frequently cited example of correspondences in games is the near duplication of the complex Indian and Southeast Asian game parchesi in the Aztec game patolli. Although Erasmus (1950) believes this duplication could be explained by the principal of the limitation of possibilities, diffusionists consider the probability of its independent development to be very low (for example, Heine-Geldern and Ekholm, 1951: 299; Carter, 1963: 8). Kroeber (1948: 550–552) has said of this game that, although the odds against its duplication are high, its standing alone as a complex shared trait argues against its having spread from Asia to Mexico. However, as Heine-Geldern and Ekholm (1951), Tolstoy (1963, 1966), Kirchhoff (1964), and others have demonstrated, it can hardly any longer be considered as standing alone.

Art styles and motifs have been very frequently used as evidence of transoceanic diffusion (Heine-Geldern, 1959a, 1959b, 1968; Fraser, 1962, 1967; Meggers, Evans, and Estrada, 1965), in their roles both as iconography and as noniconographic forms. The analysis of styles and the taxonomy of motifs are specialized tasks and, by their very nature, somewhat imprecise. Too, because of being due in part to creative motivations, styles may change fairly rapidly. Nevertheless, despite the difficulties and dangers of working with this sort of data, it may contribute to the body of evidence regarding diffusion; music and the dance, which present somewhat similar problems and possibilities, have been little studied from this point of view. Anti-diffusionists contend that there is a limited number of likely motifs and combinations of motifs, that many of these can be explained in terms of function or of observation of nature (see Fraser, 1965: 470–474), and that duplication would not be surprising. Diffusionists are more impressed by the observable diversity in styles and believe that when similarities are found they are suggestive of diffusion.

Somewhat less useful than the more arbitrary of the traits discussed above are complex technologies. Isolationists often consider such shared techniques to be simply reflections of similar levels of cultural evolution, arguing that similar levels share similar problems and possibilities and thus favor the emergence of similar technologies. Diffusionists feel that this contention begs the question of why certain cultures evolved to high levels and others did not. Independent inventionists frequently contend that environmental factors strongly influence both cultural level and specific culture content, but certain diffusionists (for example, Carter, 1964) have argued that, empirically, there is little correlation between environment and cultural level or content. It has also been pointed out that America's earliest "high" culture, the Olmec, apparently arose in what most would consider one of the worst possible environments for spontaneous cultural evolution: ". . . certainly by the ninth century B.C., ceremonial centers were constructed in a most unlikely area, the hot, humid swamps in the states of Vera Cruz and Tabasco, facing the Gulf of Mexico. Here appeared an art style with no known antecedents. . . . The oldest evidence of mathematics and written dates are here" (Lothrop, 1964:

16). Bernal (1955: 349) adds "that the first appearance of high culture and all its development during the classic period occurred in a rather unfavorable habitat." Meggers (1954), among others, has suggested that this type of environment limits *in situ* cultural evolution and that high culture can occur in such areas only by introduction. This, taken in conjunction with similarities to certain Old World cultures, has suggested interhemispheric diffusion, both direct and stimulus, to some scholars. Diffusionists tend to feel that complex technical processes "stem from a unique concatenation of historical circumstances; and the chances of these circumstances being duplicated they regard as relatively slim" (Fraser, 1965: 456–457). ". . . for an event of this nature to have really occurred [that is, the duplication of many Old World inventions in Mesoamerica], such an accumulation of particular . . . geographical, cultural, spiritual, technological, and other circumstances—the same in both cases—had to be united that it makes this supposed parallelism very doubtful" (Alcina Franch, 1955: 875; my translation).

Heine-Geldern (1954) compares the metallurgies of Southeast Asia and South America and finds that the metallurgical processes, including the lost-wax method of casting, are nearly identical, as are many of the types and styles of the objects produced. Archaeologist Paul Tolstoy has made a remarkably thorough and rigorous study of bark-cloth and primitive paper-manufacturing industries. Tolstoy (1966: 72, 77–79) recognizes 121 distinct traits within this complex as a whole and categorizes each of those shared by Southeast Asia and Mesoamerica (92 traits) as to whether or not the choice to adopt that trait or an alternative is forced upon the manufacturer at any point in the development of the industry and whether or not the choice made is contingent upon past decisions. Thus traits can, to a certain degree, be rated in reference to the limitation of possibilities. Forty-four of the 92 shared traits are "not required by any of the other steps in procedure of which they are part or by the goal itself of making bark cloth. . . . Even when essential, many of these traits are still but one of several known alternatives. . . . [Thirty-seven of the traits] are redundant, i.e., they co-occur with their alternatives, thus casting doubt on their competitive advantage or determination by function" (Tolstoy, 1969b). It is certainly significant as well that the traits that rate highly as evidence for diffusion on the basis of their being optional or redundant also rate highly when tested against criteria of distribution and world frequency (Tolstoy, 1966, 1969; these criteria are discussed below).

Spatial and Temporal Distribution of Traits

Diffusionists have frequently been accused of "trait-chasing"—the out-of-context comparison of Old World and New World traits, often from various time levels and from different parts of the two hemispheres. The question of cultural context has already been discussed; however, it is true that since contacts occur within spatial and temporal zones of limited extent, the items diffusing at each contact should exhibit the following characteristics:

1. Spatial overlap or clustering in the donor area and in the recipient area
2. Co-occurrence at the same point in time in both areas
3. Earliest appearance in the recipient area at least slightly later than first appearance in the donor area.

If archaeology or history demonstrates that these criteria are in fact met by a set of traits, the case for diffusion is greatly strengthened, but the collecting of similarities scattered in space and time contributes much less toward demonstrating diffusion. It is conceivable that a series of contacts occurred, each at a different point in time and space and each contributing but a single trait; but unless the traits are rather complex, it seems equally conceivable that scattered cases of independent invention occurred. Still, it may be that the apparent spatial and temporal incongruities of these traits are the result of the imperfection of our archaeological and ethnographic data:

it is possible that certain of the introduced ideas or traits might have taken root more readily in some centers rather distant from where the primary contact occurred . . . a number of mechanical and other techniques, including the compass, paper, printing blocks, and the crossbow . . . found their way to the West [from China]. . . . We know of these historically, but, if there were no historical accounts, it would be very unlikely that we would ever be able to work out a history of this diffusion by archaeological reconstruction . . . [or] to localize any one center or complex in the Western world that would help to prove the Chinese origin of these various traits

(Ekholm, 1964b: 503; for an archaeological example within the New World, see Meggers, 1964: 521).[2]

It might also be added that if diffusion between two areas were continuous over a long period of time, geographical, but not temporal, clustering would be expected (see, for example, Jett, 1968).

Despite these possibilities of diffusion without apparent clustering, the greater the degree to which traits do cluster in space and time in separated parts of the world, the lower is the probability of their having arisen independently in the two areas, for "the probability of the simultaneous or successive occurrence of two or more independent events is equal to the product of their separate probabilities" (Downie and Heath, 1959: 104). Thus, if the probability of trait x being twice independently developed were one in two (fifty-fifty), and if the probability of unrelated trait y being twice independently developed were also one in two, then the probability of x and y *both* being independently developed at the same or successive times at each locality would be one in four. The co-occurrence of a third, equally probable invention would reduce the combined probability to one in eight, and so on. Of course, it is impossible to calculate the degree of independence of various traits or to ascertain the probability of their being invented in a particular cultural context, but we may certainly say that the greater the degree of clustering of shared traits in space and time, the lower the probability of their having been developed independently. The probability would be further lowered geometrically to the extent that the traits (if truly mutually independent) occurred *together* in more than two separated places at appropriate time levels. Thus, the criterion of arbitrariness should be used in conjunction with that of clustering.

As Fraser (1965: 465–466) argues, it is irrelevant that some or all of the traits in a postulated donor cluster occur at earlier dates in various other areas, a point used by Kubler (1962: 12) in an attempt to refute Ekholm's (1953) evidence of clustering in Hinduized South-

---

[2] In *Prehistoric Man in the New World,* ed. Jesse D. Jennings and Edward Norbeck (Chicago: University of Chicago Press, 1963), © 1963 by William Marsh Rice University. All rights reserved. This and subsequent quotations from Ekholm's article are used by permission of the publisher.

east Asia and certain parts of the Maya area. "The point is not that earlier instances are known, but that the traits studied by Ekholm cluster at more or less the same time in two widely separated areas, the one being the result of a long sequence of invention and diffusion, the other appearing suddenly and without observable precedent" (Fraser, 1965: 466; a point to be discussed below).

The case for diffusion is improved by rarity of the shared traits—that is, their restriction to two or a few areas of limited size (or, rather, to two or a few *cultures*) at appropriate time levels. As Kroeber (1948: 550) puts it, "Anything innate ought to be breaking out normally, instead of at certain times and places only;" thus, the very rarity and geographical restriction of the traits indicate that they are not highly favored by nature, psychology, function, or the like and do not, therefore, have a high probability of independent invention. Tolstoy (1966), for example, favors the idea of diffusion of the Celebes-type bark-cloth industry to Mesoamerica, in part because the distinctive traits involved are confined to restricted geographical areas in the postulated donor and recipient regions. He further notes (1969b) that the Celebes and Mesoamerican industries have more in common than do the admittedly related industries of Java and Celebes.

The very *wide* distribution of a trait in the world may be the result of very early or very rapid diffusion, or it may be that the simplicity and "naturalness" of the trait allowed its frequent independent invention; such a distribution says little in itself regarding diffusion or polygenesis. On the other hand, the identification of a trait at several widely scattered times and places with no possibility of temporal or distributional overlap would demonstrate that independent development can occur, at least in regard to those particular traits and, by extension, to traits of similar complexity. Independent inventionists frequently declare that "it seems to me illogical to hold that if human beings can make an invention once they cannot make it twice. There are so many examples . . . of duplicate inventions which can be definitely shown to have been made in entire independence" (Kidder, 1953: 47). Of course, this is one of the basic points of contention between isolationists and diffusionists; the similarities that to the latter suggest diffusion are to the former examples that prove the possibility of independent invention. Thus Alfonso Caso (1964: 67) asserts that "there is no possibility of . . . [Mesoamerican agriculture, writing, or calendar systems] having arrived from across the oceans" and asks why simpler traits could not be reproduced independently if these complex systems were; whereas Kelley (1960) and Kirchhoff (1964) consider the calendar one of the best pieces of evidence for diffusion and question the assumption of the complete independence of agriculture and writing. Very little real effort has been made by polygenesists to test their theories by demonstrating independent duplication of a significant number of complex traits. One exception is Caso's (1964: 55) attempt to amass a number of such cases. "They are not intended as a demonstration of *lack* of connections between the Old and New Worlds, but only as a demonstration of the weaknesses in a method which seeks to use similarities in the forms of objects as proofs." Caso (1964: 55, 57) believes that his examples demonstrate that "resemblances of form have very little value as evidence even when they are obvious. They do not constitute proofs even when the resemblance extends beyond form to concept (the idea inspiring the object) and function (the end served by the object)." Although few of Caso's examples satisfy diffusionists as having been demonstrated to have had no interconnecting links, a few of his examples seem unquestionably independent, although they are not particularly complex traits. Other examples could be added—the dome in Roman architecture (coursed stone) and in the Eskimo igloo (spirally laid snow blocks) and the tonsure among Medieval European monks and certain Amazonian Indians—but few unequivocal examples of this sort have been forwarded. Even in invention-oriented Western industrial civilization, remarkably few independent inventions have been cited by independent inventionists (but see Ogburn, 1938: 90–102). Of those listed by Kroeber (1948: 341–342), Tertius Chandler (1960) finds that upon close scrutiny only one or two can be called truly independent, and these occurred within a common cultural matrix specifically oriented toward the search for more efficient methods (see also Barnett, 1953: 44–45). Diffusionists conclude that man is not very inventive and that diffusion is a more probable explanation of similarities than duplicate invention.

It has been suggested above that, since temporal overlap must exist between traits in separated areas if diffusion took place between those areas, evidence for diffusion would, ideally, include proof of such overlap, and evidence against diffusion would include the demonstration of an insuperable time gap between occurrences. This requirement, though eminently valid, is often difficult to meet in practice because of imperfections in preservation, in dating, and in thoroughness of archaeological investigation and publication. For example, there are striking similarities between Late Chou decorative styles of China of 700–200 B.C. and those of the Tajín culture of Veracruz, Mexico, of A.D. 500–1000 (Heine-Geldern, 1959a). The time gap would suggest independence, but, as Ekholm (1964b: 493–500) writes:

. . . there are various possible explanations [of the gap that are consistent with a diffusionist interpretation of the similarities]. Contacts could have occurred closer to the time of the full development of the style in Asia, and it could have been maintained in [perishable] wood-carving for hundreds of years before it appeared in stone in Veracruz. Or, as we know to be partly true, elements of Late Chou style continued into later dynastic periods and may have diffused at that time. Furthermore, the effective contacts could have been with a peripheral style in China that retained the full Late Chou pattern much longer than was the case in central China, where our known Chinese sequence obtains. Many complex problems arise, of course, in the attempt to equate ethnographically known traits that leave little or no archaeological traces. . . . Certain ideas about divine kingship might also have been introduced, [for example,] but these would be mainly lost to us [archaeologically] except as they might be apparent in associated elements, such as [depictions of] the use of the umbrella or the litter as insignia of rank.

Heine-Geldern (1960: 279) also points out that the increasing time depth that is being demonstrated for American cultures is tending to reduce many apparent chronological gaps between Asia and America.

Presence or Absence of Developmental Series

Sharing of a trait by two separate cultures may be a result either of direct or stimulus diffusion or of parallel or convergent evolution. It is assumed that the evolution of a complex trait occurs through gradual change and elaboration over time or by a recombination of existing traits rather than arising suddenly and without precursors in a kind of cultural spontaneous generation. Direct diffusion, on the other hand, involves either the importation of an actual item or its manufacturer or the learning and implementation of the trait by members of the recipient culture through contact and imitation. When direct diffusion occurs, the trait involved may first appear in the recipient culture in developed form; its development occurred elsewhere, and so it may not have been preceded in the recipient culture by earlier, less evolved forms.

Stimulus diffusion consists of the imitation of a material culture trait without knowledge of the processes that produced that trait; thus, the separate devising of a process of manufacture is required of the recipient culture. The newly devised process may be the same as, or different from, that used by the donor culture. If it is different, it may convey the impression of convergence, even though in fact it was stimulated by outside influence. In such a case, however, we would not expect to find evidence of developmental stages in the recipient area. (It is possible that one or more abortive attempts at duplicating the object or process prior to eventual success might be difficult to distinguish from developmental stages; too, stimulus diffusion might result in the creation of a simpler form of the trait by the recipient culture or the copying of certain forms without a full understanding or implementation of their original functions.)

Parallel, independent evolution of a complex trait in two separate cultures involves two independent, but similar, series of developmental stages, beginning at similar starting points and arriving by similar steps at similar or identical end points. Convergent evolution consists of two or more cultures developing similar or identical traits by gradual change from different starting points, with developmental stages that become increasingly alike until similar or identical end products are achieved. Sudden appearance of a trait in history or archaeology has, therefore, been used as an indicator of diffusion; conversely, a temporal continuum with simple forms at the early end, followed by increasingly more complex forms, has been considered evidence of evolution. This principle is valid for testing diffusionist or evolutionist hypotheses but is not always, or even usually, conclusive by itself. For example, sequential diffusion of each of the developmental stages could occur. In questioning Heine-Geldern and Ekholm's (1951: 299–302) contention that the lotus motif and its use in art and ritual was diffused from Asia to Mesoamerica, Rands (1953) shows that the motif has considerable antiquity in America and appears to have become more highly elaborated over time. Rands (1953: 121) concludes in favor of local evolution, but he admits, without accepting, an alternative hypothesis: "To explain the elaborated water lily as of Asiative derivation, it would appear necessary to postulate a complex series of waves of fundamental influence which accounted for new traits at various time levels. This seems, in fact, to be the position taken by Heine-Geldern and Ekholm." Jett (1968) has also postulated that a series of introductions of traits into South America over a long period of time occurred in such a way as to simulate the evolution of a total culture. Another possibility is the occurrence, in two separate areas, of evolution to a similar level, followed by innovation in one of the areas and diffusion from that area to the other. As Tolstoy (1969b) points out, similar developmental levels in each of two cultures not only increases the likelihood of similar inventions but, given contact, also increases the probability of diffusion between the two areas.

On the other hand, the *lack* of discoverable developmental stages is not necessarily decisive evidence of diffusion, for isolationists can invoke the same concepts of incomplete investigation and perishable earlier forms that diffusionists use to account for time gaps between occurrences in postulated donor and recipient areas. (Morley, 1946: 46, takes this position in reference to the lack of known direct antecedents of Maya culture in the Maya region.) An illustrative case is that of Mesoamerican writing. Even in its earliest known forms, it is a highly evolved system; no earlier, simpler forms of writing out of which it might have grown are known anywhere. In this case, then, the absence of a *known* developmental sequence proves nothing about diffusion, for previous to its use on stone monuments this writing and its precursors must have been used on wood or bark-cloth paper or leaves, no example of which is known to have survived from this early period. This writing system may have evolved in Mesoamerica, it may have evolved in the Old World and have diffused to the New World, subsequently dying out in the Old World, or it may have come about through stimulus diffusion from the Old World. The system and its known history provides no solution to the problem of origins.

One can imagine several possible sorts of occurrences resulting in culture change: the independent occurrence of similar complex nuclei, with their independent elaboration yielding at least some similar traits; the independent occurrence of similar complex nuclei, the elaborations of one diffusing to the area of the other (whose similar nature favors acceptance); diffusion of a complex nucleus and subsequent independent elaboration yielding similar as well as dissimilar traits; diffusion of both the complex nucleus and later material and nonmaterial elaborations, the latter in both directions and over long periods of time, with separate similar and dissimilar undiffused elaborations occurring simultaneously and continuously in each area, and other traits from other sources adding to or hybridizing with all these elaborations. The last of these hypothetical situations, which may be closer to reality in many cases than any simplistic diffusionist or independent-inventionist scheme, would be, to say the least, challenging to interpret on the basis of presence or absence of developmental stages.

Although the criterion of presence or absence of developmental stages has definite shortcomings that must be understood, it may nevertheless be a very useful tool for assessing the possibility of diffusion versus evolution. It would be most conclusive in cases revealing convergent developmental stages or in cases involving lack of antecedents for types of objects whose precursors could have been fashioned only of nonperishable materials. Certainly the search for such antecedents is, in any case, incumbent upon anyone concerned with cultural origins and processes, whether he be of diffiusionist or isolationist inclination.

Absence of Traits

An argument frequently used in support of the isolationist viewpoint is that, if significant contact had occurred, important Old World culture traits missing from the Americas would have been adopted in the New World. Art historian George Kubler (1961: 32–34) writes: "The diffusionists have never given any explanation of the absence of large-wheeled vehicles and of Old World beasts of burden in America. Would these powerfully useful instruments not have survived the displacement more readily than Hindu and Buddhist symbols?" Other significant absences have been discussed. Kroeber (1948: 776), though not arguing this point specifically, also lists proverbs, divination from viscera, ironworking, stringed instruments (other than the monotone bow), and oaths and ordeals as not present in the Americas. The true arch, draft animals, the plow, milking, the potter's wheel, and coined money have also been mentioned, and other traits, such as glassmaking and the crossbow, could be added.

Actually, not all the above traits *are* missing in the Americas; divination from entrails was practiced in Peru (Obayashi, 1959), where the dome—the arch rotated—was also constructed in chulpa tombs; draft animals (dogs), oaths, and ordeals were used by some groups of American Indians (Hoebel, 1949: 373); and what may be unmarked coined money is known from Colombia (Irwin, 1963: 262). In any case, absences are not considered decisive by diffusionists.

In a consideration of these absences it is most important to remember that the process of diffusion is primarily a process of one culture's making selections from such portions of another culture as are made available to it by contact. . . . the items selected must [further] be absorbed into, and adapted to, the purposes of the receiving culture. What is selected . . . is dependent on a multitude of factors that combine in innumerable ways, so general rules of how it can be expected to work [for example, Kubler, 1961] in any given situation are almost impossible to make. It is certain, however, that the selection . . . will be especially restricted if the donor and receiving cultures are distant from each other and if the contacts are intermittent (Ekholm, 1964b: 501).

Heine-Geldern (1960: 278–279) writes:

. . . the absence of coined money in America has been mentioned as one of these alleged proofs [of isolation. Yet] coinage was not adopted by most of the ancient hinduized countries of southeastern Asia despite the close connections they had with India where coinage was used since the time of the Mouryan kings. The absence of the true arch in America is often stressed by Americanists. They obviously believe that the arch was known in eastern Asia since hoary antiquity. Actually, it became known in China only at the time of the Han dynasty [205 B.C. to A.D. 220]. . . . Again . . . it was never adopted by the peoples of Champa [in Annam], Cambodia, Java, etc. who were in close contact with the Chinese. . . . [In] the case of the wheel and the plow . . . Americanists who cite their absence in America . . . have so far failed to tell us how they could have been used in America without the necessary draft animals.

Fraser (1965: 460–461) argues:

If we judge West African culture by the absence of wheeled vehicles, the plow, the true arch, draft animals and milking, then the well-documented Islamic penetration of the western Sudan cannot have taken place. For these traits are all well known in Moslem North Africa. . . . the ancient Greeks also rejected [the true arch] though it was known earlier in Sumer, Babylon, and Egypt. The absence of horses and other beasts of burden in the New World may be attributed to the same difficulties of transport across open sea that prevented Norsemen who colonized Newfoundland from successfully introducing such animals in this hemisphere. . . . We [also] know that the Norsemen worked bog iron in the New World, but they never passed the technique on to the Indians. . . . Moreover, such New World traits as the corbel arch, pyramid, and ball court, present in Meso-America, were not invariably adopted in adjacent areas to which diffusion is known to have occurred.

One might add to these observations that milking was absent in east and southeast Asia (Simoons, 1970) and that, even if it had been possible to import Old World draft animals, if trading or missionary activity, rather than colonization, had been the form of contact, it is unlikely that such importation would have taken place. It has also been pointed out by diffusionists (for example, Heine-Geldern, 1964: 53; Birrell, 1964: 35) that ironworking and the like are highly specialized occupations and that specialists in such activities might well have been absent on craft engaged in even intentional transoceanic travel; too, the technical level of the receiving culture may not in some cases have been adequate to permit the transferal of certain complex technologies. "A further problem is caused by the fact that the individuals responsible for introducing an innovation to another culture are often dissidents in their own culture. If a group leaves an area because they dislike certain aspects of their own culture, they can hardly be expected to introduce these traits into another culture" (Kelley, this symposium).

Diffusionists have noted that if the New World had been as inventive as the isolationist position implies, then one might expect to find either the missing Old World traits or, alternatively, important New World inventions that were absent or late in the Old World, just as some Old World inventions are lacking or late in the New. Fraser (1965: 475) writes:

Apart from platinum working, there are remarkably few; these include the stirrup-spouted vessel, whistling jars, stepped-fret pattern, porcupine quill work, hammocks [infant hammocks are also used in Indonesia], certain specialized weaving processes, and a variety of natural and agricultural products [like the rubber complex, depending on the native flora]. Interestingly enough, the majority of these traits appear to derive not from New World high-culture centers, as we might expect, but from the more primitive American societies. This goes in the face of [isolationist Erland]

Nordenskiöld's [1931: 24] own observation that "the higher the development of a civilization, the greater the probability that new inventions will be made independently."

In addition to trait absences in the New World, antidiffusionists have pointed to the lack of Old World records of ancient voyages to the New World. Those diffusionists who believe accidental voyaging to have been paramount in introducing Old World ideas note that such unintentional, one-way journeys would have left no record of their landfalls at their points of origin. Those who favor the idea of significant intentional voyaging attribute the paucity of records of the Americas to the studied secrecy of commercial voyagers (Irwin, 1963), the destruction of ancient records (as at the libraries of Alexandria, Carthage, Islamic Iberia [Jeffreys, 1953], and Southeast Asia [Heine-Geldern, 1964: 52]), and the probable one-way nature of missionary voyages. The vagueness of those accounts of voyages which do survive (Heine-Geldern, 1964: 52) inhibits their interpretation, but diffusionists have also pointed out that some Old World records and traditions do exist that are at least suggestive of possible ancient transoceanic voyaging (for example, Irwin, 1963; Larson, 1966; Li, 1961; Doran, this symposium) and that such New World legends as that of Quetzalcoatl may reflect visits from outside the Americas (for example, Irwin, 1963; for a dissenting view, see Hedrick, this symposium), as well as American voyages into the far Pacific (Heyerdahl, 1966b: 96–99).

PHYSICAL ANTHROPOLOGICAL EVIDENCE

It is generally believed that the pre-Columbian peopling of the Americas was, for the most part, accomplished by paleolithic man via the Bering Strait region. Most transoceanic-diffusion theories postulate contact diffusion rather than major migration as the source of cultural similarities. Physical anthropologist Carleton Coon (1962: 352) has asserted that, if transoceanic voyagers visited America, "they left no visible imprint on the racial composition of the [American Indians]"; Coon concludes that contacts, if any, were transient and could have had no great cultural impact. On the other hand, rather vague and loose suggestions of correlations between interhemispheric cultural similarities and racial ones have been made occasionally by diffusionists (for example, Gladwin, 1947), and Heyerdahl (1952: 224–345) discusses archaeological evidence of Caucasoids in South America, but, to my knowledge, the only study that attempts to compare in detail the racial characteristics of specific Old and New World groups is Jett (1968). It compares data for certain Indonesians and certain tropical-forest tribes of South America and concludes that these two groups are physically more like each other than they are like any other groups in the world, including their near neighbors. Based upon these and other findings, a hypothesis of migration from Malaysia to tropical America is forwarded.

There are, of course, problems involved with the use of physical anthropological data, including nonavailability for many areas. Another problem is the possibility of overland migration via Alaska. If, however, the traits are missing in the intervening areas, as in the example cited, such migration would seem unlikely; had it been early, pockets of population of that type might be expected to have survived in intervening marginal areas, and had it been late, ten thousand miles of miscegenation would have greatly altered the physical type of the migrants. Another difficulty is possible parallel or convergent evolution or phenotypic response resulting from similar physical-environmental, nutritional, or cultural pressures. The case for such influences is weakened in the example cited by the existence of traits that are nonadaptive or that have negative adaptive value in the environment involved.

It has become increasingly clear that the use of blood groups in racial comparisons must be carried out with caution, since evidence now indicates that diseases are important in selecting for certain blood factors, although the mechanisms and impact of such selection are still not clear (Otten, 1967). There is reason to believe that the American disease syphilis selects against blood types A, B, and AB. "In highly syphilitic populations it might lead to the fixation of the O gene, and a frequency of 100 percent of group O" (Coon, 1965: 283). "Blood group gene frequencies as we know them now may be purely temporary, no accurate indications of past conditions. . . . Thus, it is not necessary to assume that ancestral Amerindians [who are now almost exclusively O and A] were derived from a B-free population. . . . They may have lost it in transit. But it is equally likely that B had adaptive value in Asia but none in America" (Garn, 1957: 220, 222). Nevertheless, blood group data can in some cases be useful, taken in conjunction with other data, as indicating relationships between populations (see Matson *et al.*, 1967, for a discussion and an example). The recently discovered Diego factor has received some attention, since it appears to be confined to widely scattered American Indian groups and to certain Mongoloid south and east Asian peoples (Comas, 1965). It, too, has been said to be an inhibitor of syphilis (Coon, 1965; 283). Geographically restricted blood factors like this one may serve as evidence even of contact not involving massive migration, although it is always conceivable when dealing with a single factor that the mutation(s) producing it occurred more than once in the world. The whole pattern of blood groups should be used in comparisons relating to large-scale migration, and data of this kind should be supplemented by other kinds of evidence.

Certain other characteristics may also prove useful as research progresses. Among these are the chemistry of body secretions (saliva, tears, colostrum and milk, earwax, sebum, urine, nasal secretions, perspiration, and sexual secretions), chemical tasting ability, dental configuration, and dermatoglyphics. Many—perhaps all—of these traits will certainly prove to be adaptive, responsive to environment or nutrition, or interdependent, and must therefore be used with caution (see Otten, 1967).

Not strictly physical anthropological evidence, but mentioned here for convenience, are studies of human parasites. For example, Soper (1927; see also Darling, 1920; Heyerdahl, 1966b: 700–701) notes that two hookworm species that could not survive slow migration through the Arctic are found in China and Japan and among certain American Indians; one of these species is not present in Polynesia. The conclusion is that man carried them across the North Pacific.

CONCLUSIONS

The evidence of means for contact and diffusion (watercraft and navigation techniques) and the evidence, particularly botanical, that contact did, in fact, take place, providing opportunity for diffusion, is of such a nature as to leave no doubt that the question of transoceanic diffusion is a real one. Means, opportunity, and plausible motives do not, however, prove that significant transfers of ideas took place; it is for that reason that an attempt has been made to discuss systematically criteria for determining whether or not such transfers did occur. There has been, and will, no doubt, continue to be, much disagreement concerning such criteria and how much weight to assign to them. Evaluating the degree of diffusion can never be an exact science, and it seems inevitable that a wide range of opinion will always exist on this subject. It is to be hoped, however, that the uncritical acceptance of diffusionist or antidiffusionist assumptions and the careless and all too often acrimonious rejection of the opposing point of view that have characterized much of the diffusion controversy in the past can be avoided in the future. Criteria such as those discussed herein must be developed, refined, and applied, and it is incumbent upon all concerned with the history of culture to test their data in the light of such criteria. The diffusion question is a serious one, with far-reaching implications for the understanding of the nature of culture, and it deserves as close and as objective attention as we can give it.

2. Diffusion and Archaeological Evidence

GORDON F. EKHOLM

The interest that some of us have expressed in recent years in the question of transpacific contacts has met with mixed success. Although we have seen a gradual increase in willingness to accept the idea—as evidenced by this symposium—still there remains a large hard core of resisters who continue unshaken.

There are, of course, many problems concerning the kinds of evidence that have been presented in the area of transpacific contacts, but the principal difficulty appears to be a kind of theoretical roadblock that stops short our thinking about questions of diffusion or culture contact. This is true in anthropological thought generally, but the obstruction seems to be particularly solid and resistant among American archaeologists.

The purpose here is to make a foray or two against this theoretical roadblock. I have questions of transpacific contacts in mind, but I will be referring to somewhat more manageable situations and will be directing my attention to our view of culture-historical processes generally. My ultimate aim is to establish a proper and adequate theoretical understanding of the importance of diffusion, or of culture contacts, which it seems to me we sadly lack. At this time I will offer only scattered suggestions, not a finished statement of my theoretical position on the subject. For examples I will be referring mainly to Mesoamerica, the area I am best acquainted with.

I will begin by describing in very brief form my own personal, speculative view of ancient Mesoamerican society, which is somewhat different from the usual conception. I see this society as one composed of seven or eight regions, each with its own special character or style, but all sharing in and forming what we have come to call a unit of civilization or early civilization. This general sharing of the over-all culture and, in part, its origin, was made possible by a process of continual interaction—by constant travel back and forth between the areas of the several subcultures.

This view is engendered in part by my thinking of what it means for these people to have reached a stage of social complexity we can call civilization. Their societies were probably class-structured and were undoubtedly composed, too, of many persons or groups with specialized occupations. There were many individuals who spent all or most of their time as religious functionaries, architects, sculptors, politicians, entertainers, traders, or were engaged in a number of other things. These specialists, if we can judge from similar and better known societies, were highly interested in the activities of their counterparts in other regions. We must imagine, for instance, that a priest-philosopher in Teotihuacán would on occasion make a pilgrimage to Copan to confer with a famous guru of whom he had often heard. It would not be different from the travels of the Chinese pilgrims who traveled to faraway India to visit the holy places of Buddhism.

In the same way, we must imagine many kinds of persons traveling about Mesoamerica for a variety of purposes. Certainly there were embassies sent from one town or one capital to another—and espionage in times of stress. Most likely there were traveling magicians or curers and troupes of players, dancers, or acrobats who made regular tours of the capitals or the provinces, depending on their skills. Also, there were probably professional ball players who made the rounds of various towns or cities—perhaps organized like our major and minor baseball leagues. Finally, of course, there were the ever-present traders or businessmen who traveled widely from region to region and who, like the others, continually carried news and knowledge of all kinds back and forth.

According to this speculative view of Mesoamerican society, one would suspect that the leaders or certain classes of people in each major center would know in rather complete detail what was happening in other centers. They would know more, of course, of what was happening in the places nearest to them, but it should be emphasized that they would know from *direct* reports what was happening in distant areas as well. There is some evidence of this kind of widespread trade and travel on the eve of the Spanish conquest. The Aztec had observers in Veracruz watching the landing of Cortez. There was also a regular and active trade route from central Mexico to the Yucatan peninsula, and it is known that a group of Aztec traders were in Panama when the Spanish arrived. It is absurd to think that the same kind of activity was not going on in Classic times, if not long before that.

To speculate further and to generalize on the basis of this view of Mesoamerican society, I would suggest that it is this kind of interaction—continual goings and comings between a number of somewhat distant centers—that would be particularly favorable and perhaps essential to cultural growth or to the emergence of the civilized life we see to have existed in Mesoamerica. Other things being equal, isolation brings stagnation; extensive and continuing contacts with other peoples bring change and development. Cultures or civilizations do not evolve without large doses of culture contact or diffusion. It is an essential ingredient in any theoretical conception of the culture historical process.

This kind of speculation may be considered by some to be unscientific and a waste of time, but I would insist on its being just the opposite. It is essential, because the degree, or extent, of culture contacts between regions, such as that described for Mesoamerica, does not come through archaeologically; it can never be seen or fully understood by looking solely at hard archaeological evidence. Judging the extent of culture contact by archaeological evidence alone is difficult or impossible for several reasons.

We might consider first to what extent the finding of trade objects is indicative of the amount of trade from one region to another in Mesoamerica. As I have pointed out elsewhere, a look at the Aztec tribute rolls is most illuminating in this regard. These are lists of vast amounts of materials and objects that the Aztec demanded periodically from the various portions of their empire. The control and carrying of these materials to Tenochtitlán must have occasioned very close cultural interaction. We have found little archaeological evidence of this tribute, however, although careful and extensive excavation of many central Aztec sites would undoubtedly provide more. Nevertheless, the record will always be tremendously incomplete, for most of the tribute was in the form of foodstuffs, textiles, feathers, paper, and other completely perishable materials. Small amounts of stone and metal objects are included in the lists, and these would be, of course, potential archaeological records. Interestingly, however, the only pottery included are jars containing honey and small amounts of a special yellow pottery that was demanded from the west. It may be, of course, that the process of trade in earlier periods and in other regions would involve different kinds of materials than did this tribute system, but the chances are that the assortments would nowhere be different to any significant degree.

The extent to which pottery may have been traded or transported from place to place in ancient Mesoamerica is of very special interest because so much of our reconstruction of the history of the area is based on this enduring material. The tribute records have been cited, and one can argue further on other grounds as well that its transport was probably minimal. Every major center had its own pottery factories, and it is, after all, a heavy product to carry. The wide distribution of Plumbate ware must have been due to some very special demand for it.

There are still other reasons why through purely pragmatic archaeology we cannot hope to get a true picture of the extent of culture contacts in ancient times. One is that much of the culture of any society is nonmaterial. Many culture-contact situations might well be channeled in such a way that much nonmaterial culture is exchanged but that little or no material culture objects are traded.

Another factor in our dossier on the limitations of archaeology is the always incomplete nature of our knowledge. The history of archaeological research seems to be that with any increase of our archaeological knowledge of two neighboring cultures, we find increasing evidence of their relatedness. This will continue to go on, for we must all agree that we still have much to do in Mesoamerica as in most areas of the world.

It is my view, however, that we can never fully document by concrete archaeological evidence the degree to which the cultures of neighboring peoples were dependent on each other.

My speculative view of the nature of Mesoamerican society must therefore stand without definite proof in the form of hard archaeological evidence. We can search for such evidence, and, of course, we must do so, but we must also maintain something like this speculative view, refining it where possible, but basing it mainly on our whole conception of the nature of human society and of the culture-historical process. Every archaeologist should have his own version of such a speculative view and, ideally, should make it explicit from time to time, so that potsherds do not tend to take the place of people in our thinking.

It is clear that this speculative or theoretical view of the culture-historical process tends to put considerable emphasis on the importance of diffusion or culture contact. I have used Mesoamerica as a unit of civilization and have been speaking of culture-contact processes within it, but I do not separate it completely from the rest of the world.

There must have been periodical contact of various kinds between Mesoamerica and the southwestern and southeastern United States, and the more advanced cultures in these regions must have been dependent in considerable degree on those contacts. Certainly not everything in these areas was dependent on diffusion from Mesoamerica, but the areas would not have developed in the way that they did if Mesoamerica had not been down there in the south.

Another interesting opportunity for the consideration of archaeological evidence and diffusion is that of relationships between Mesoamerica and the Antilles. It has long been assumed that there was little direct communication between the two, this based mainly on stylistic differences and the nearly complete lack of trade objects in either place. We find, however, that in Puerto Rico there were specially constructed ball courts and a ball game very similar to that played in Mesoamerica. Furthermore, the participants played with stone belts or had stone belts that were replicas of ball-playing belts made of other materials. These are remarkable similarities in a profoundly elaborate complex of things that speak of intercommunication. It calls for a total reassessment of our usual conception of relationships between the two areas.

In considering the interrelations of cultures one must also look from Mesoamerica to the south. In this speculative view of how human beings are interested in other peoples and places and of how they tended to travel over much larger distances than we are inclined to believe they did, it is quite probable that there was periodic travel of various kinds between Mesoamerica and the Andes. There is more than speculation for this. There is some fairly hard evidence of such contacts and other indications of cross currents of influence between the two areas, and those who ignore the importance of this inter-influence will eventually discover that they have backed the wrong horse.

Finally, and as a summary, we might come back to the question of transpacific contacts. I admit that there is no hard evidence of such contacts, unless some of the botanical studies now in progress will serve as absolute evidence that they did occur. No trade objects have been found, and the probability is that they never will be found, even though contacts may in actuality have been numerous and of great significance to the American scene.

In my speculative view very important contacts did occur. I base this view on my conception of how culture contact is the most important factor in cultural evolution. I base it, too, on the timing or chronological fit of happenings in the major culture centers of eastern Asia and the Americas and on the number of fairly convincing parallels that have so far been suggested, but which I cannot discuss here.

I make no excuses for the fact that my speculative view is way ahead of the archaeological evidence. The point I have been attempting to make is that this is as it should be—that because of the nature of archaeological evidence we must always be far ahead of it when it comes to the consideration of culture contacts.

3. Diffusion: Evidence and Process

DAVID H. KELLEY

A major problem of any attempt to show long-range transmission of objects or ideas from one culture to another lies in the fact that the best proof of such transmission is normally to be found in those cultural elements which are of least importance in the receiving culture.

A Roman figurine head was found at Calixtlahuaca. Assuming the circumstances of the find are correctly reported, it proves that a Roman figurine head could, somehow, have reached Mexico and that the date of the level in which it was found is later than the date when such figurines were manufactured in the Roman empire. These conclusions have almost no value either for the study of culture history or for the study of cultural processes. We do not know whether the figurine was brought by one lost Roman or whether it had passed through a hundred intermediary hands. It might stimulate some scholar to examine possible Roman influences in Mexico but could have little other value.

At the opposite extreme, one of the most distinctive and important characteristics of Mesoamerican civilization is the use of a wide range of writing systems. If the idea of writing was introduced from Eurasia or Africa, this is an important datum both for culture history and for our understanding of the cultural factors involved in the development of writing systems. Conversely, if it could be shown that there was no reasonable possibility that the idea of writing was of foreign origin, it would be helpful to our understanding of cultural processes. However, the idea of writing was of such utility in Mesoamerican culture that different groups adopted widely different forms of writing. Only a few elements in any of these systems suggest the possibility of Eurasian origin. No serious scholar has, to my knowledge, made any explicit proposal that Mesoamerican writing systems derive from any specified Old World writing system. If Mesoamerican writing represents an example of stimulus diffusion, it is quite possible that we will never get adequate proof of the fact. The very success of writing in Mesoamerican culture created the conditions for the transformation of the initial system into several very different ones. This is true in varying degrees of all items that become of central cultural importance in the receiving culture.

There are other factors that make it difficult to establish whether particular changes are due to diffused innovations or not. The first, as Tolstoy has pointed out, is that a culture must reach a certain level of complexity before the people have the capacity to adopt certain innovations from other cultures. In effect, this means that most innovations can be adopted only when the receiving culture is at a level of technological or social complexity that would make the innovation seem a plausible possibility, even without outside stimulus.

Another difficulty is caused by the fact that the stimulus of an innovation often seems to prompt further innovations. Diffusion and independent invention are usually presented as polar opposites in the interpretation of evidence, but as processes they seem to be complementary. Many of the factors leading to the acceptance of innovations are probably the same whether these innovations are external to the culture or internal.

A further problem is caused by the fact that the individuals responsible for introducing an innovation to another culture are often dissidents in their own culture. If a group leaves an area because they dislike certain aspects of their own culture, they can hardly be expected to introduce these traits into another culture. The traits are transformed and deformed by the transmitting agents as well as by the receiving culture. In an evidential sense, the most valuable items are those which are least transformed, which are generally relatively superficial items. The criterion of functional equivalence between compared systems or artifacts as a test for historical relationships seems almost completely invalid. In general, functional similarities between cultures may be presumed to have arisen through equivalent functional needs. Basic functional similarities must be present if two systems are to fulfill the same needs. Superficial similarities in subsidiary aspects of the system or trait are then more valuable as evidence, despite their lesser importance in the culture. Thus specialized cutting tools must, of necessity, share certain characteristics of the cutting edge and weight, but when an ax shares with those of another culture the addition of a bird head with no discernible functional reason, the evidence of relationship is much more convincing.

In other cases, unexplained cultural resistances may prevent the acceptance of apparently useful or interesting ideas, or the technical incapacity of the receiving culture or the transmitting agents may block transmission of some segment of the parent system. The very considerable emphasis of Hindu culture on eroticism represents the type of cultural phenomenon that may cause strong reactions in some segments of the culture. Much of Aztec religion looks like a modified Hinduism in which one important change was the deliberate abandonment of religious eroticism. The reasons for cultural blockage here seem fairly clear. It is much less clear why neither the true arch nor the wheel were to be found in Egypt for more than a thousand years after Mesopotamian influences transformed Egypt from a Neolithic farming stage to a semiurban, literate society, although they already had a long history in Mesopotamia. In the light of such evidence, it is surprising to find scholars of the capacity of Kroeber arguing that the absence of the true arch and the wheel in the New World proved that there had been no contacts between New World and Old World.

The differential effects of different kinds of contacts in terms of the evidence that might be left behind have been most inadequately considered in the existing literature. Studies of the processes involved have usually been labeled acculturation and their relevance to prehistoric problems has seldom been considered. Among pertinent factors are the size of the introducing population, the size of the receiving cultural unit, the occupation or occupations of the members of both the transmitting and receiving groups, the social status of both, the nature of the innovation, the physical means of transport, the degree of knowledge or skill required for the innovation, and the nature of the motivation. In many cases it is clear that the nature of the factors known or postulated is such that the kind of evidence demanded by critics would be extremely unlikely.

Although the effects of some of these traits are difficult to appraise, we have some useful data on others. Evidence of the arrival of a single man is unlikely to be found under normal circumstances, but an entire trading post or military colony may be recognized with ease. Foot transportation may leave little later evidence, whereas wheeled vehicles demand roads and ships need harbor facilities, which may be located. An intrusion involving a marked change in settlement pattern leaves relatively obvious evidence, such as the orientation of the Toltec buildings at Chichén Itzá; however, such evidence in itself may not be adequate to prove an intrusion. In conjunction with other evidence, it may furnish a marked aid to determining the extent and nature of an intrusion.

A close appraisal of the effects of different classes of occupation is not warranted here, but the nature of the changes brought about by sailors are apt to be quite different from those brought about by wandering bands of hunters. Merchants and missionaries differ equally in their effects and in the probability of proving that they have affected a culture. The merchant, dealing in trade objects, often supplies distinctive items that can be recognized in different cultures. The missionary, on the other hand, supplies ideas, which may have a much more tremendous influence and yet, at the same time, may be greatly transformed. The perfectly sound observation of some primitive philosopher that matter might exist in four states—solid, liquid, gaseous, and fiery—was early transmuted into the strange doctrine of the "four elements"—earth, air, fire, and water—and was associated with cosmological schemes that were spread across Eurasia and that are found in recognizable form in the *Bodleian codex* and elsewhere in Mesoamerica. Yet recognition of the underlying physical base of the scheme tends to cut down on its value as evidence of contact. If contact of a sort that might have transmitted these ideas is accepted on other grounds, it is certainly entirely reasonable to regard these ideas as part of the material transmitted. The changes in Mesoamerica seem no greater than those found in many parts of Eurasia.

During time periods when only specialists, usually in the service of rulers, and a few of the rulers themselves were literate, an inscription commemorating a contact between two cultures normally is found only when the upper classes are involved in the contacts. "Ptolemy was here" is the best type of evidence, if found in a good context. Unfortunately, this type of evidence seems particularly likely to be forged and has not been an important part of modern discussions on contacts between New World and Old World. The only inscription that has entered at all importantly into the discussion is the Kensington stone, which seems to be a forgery. The alleged coat of arms of the Sinclairs, earls of Orkney, in Massachusetts may ultimately be of some importance, but the details are so eroded that a certain skepticism seems warranted. When found, such evidence may have some interesting historical value, but only careful comparative studies can determine its cultural importance. The general similarity of the Iroquois long house and the Scandinavian buildings of the tenth and eleventh centuries can hardly be denied, but it is not clear whether this extends to the kind of petty details that would lend conviction to a hypothesis of historical relationship, and no Iroquois long house has been found with a runic inscription inside.

For these reasons, many of the most important cultural changes occur without presenting clear-cut evidence of the derivation of the change. There seem to be several major classes of phenomena for which adequate proof of contacts can be shown, and it seems worthwhile to summarize these here.

1. The "hard" evidence of trade objects or inscriptions.

2. Those relatively trivial phenomena which are so little integrated into the receiving culture that their foreign origin is still obvious.

3. Biologically distinctive entities, such as the domesticated dog or the sweet potato. Clear-cut representations in art of such objects may be as valuable as their remains, or even more valuable as indicating more of the role they played in the culture, but problems of interpretation may enter if the representation is doubtful, and a painting may sometimes be forged.

4. Those technical processes which can be shown to have a long and complex history behind them in one area and which appear in another area without local antecedents and with close similarities to a single temporally and geographically restricted variant of the donor culture. The first attempt of this sort with

which I am familiar was Elliot Smith's study of mummification. By far the best evidence of this sort is Tolstoy's data on the introduction of barkbeating into Mesoamerica from the Celebes. The most widely accepted study of this sort seems to be the attempt of Estrada, Evans, and Meggers to show the derivation of Valdivia pottery from Jomon. The quality of the evidence is substantially lower than that of Tolstoy's study but has the psychological advantage of belonging to a class of comparisons from which archaeologists frequently draw comparable, though less far-reaching, conclusions.

5. Certain classes of systematically arranged data having common components that seem to vary randomly, where common patterns provide clear-cut evidence of relationship of the system. Such systems are susceptible to statistical analyses of various sorts, which may provide proof at a very high level of probability. Linguistic comparisons are of this sort. My own studies of the Mesoamerican calendar system and its Oceanian and Eurasian relatives are comparable in nature. Some studies of mythology may fall in this category, but the evidence is often difficult to appraise because of the psychologically important nature of the content. Stylistic comparisons in art are of this sort, although the statistical validation is tenuous.

6. Sometimes a group of innovations may appear together even when they have no obvious functional interrelationships, and it may be found that all have prototypes in a single culture elsewhere. This is a very good indication of cultural derivation, even when none of the individual items are adequate to prove that contact occurred.

New data and new techniques of analysis will eventually show that a great many contacts have occurred between far separated cultures, and more sophisticated analyses of the processes of cultural change will eventually allow clear-cut positive or negative conclusions about many cases that now remain in doubt.

4. Style and Culture Contact

JON MULLER

Invention, migration, and diffusion are not opposing theories of culture change, but merely mechanisms. As such, the importance of the issue of invention versus diffusion has often been grossly exaggerated. Attempts to deal with this problem must do so within the realm of more general culture theory. Such studies as those of Renfrew (1969) and Jacobs (1969) have shown how hypotheses regarding the role of trade, for example, may be generated by a broader theoretical outlook. Nonetheless, it remains very difficult to verify or reject hypotheses concerned with diffusion, invention, or other similar mechanisms even where these are appropriate. In some instances, spectrographic or other physical methods may serve to demonstrate contacts between two areas; but far more often similarity or dissimilarity of art styles may be the only available evidence. Anthropologists, however, and other students of these matters have usually used the concept of style with all of the finesse of a steamshovel. The purpose of this paper is to indicate briefly some ramifications of the concept of style and to see how these may be used to deal with questions of culture change in general and of culture contacts in particular.

To be sure, there are reasons why anthropologists, and archaeologists especially, have chosen to emphasize diffusion or invention at the expense of other mechanisms of culture change. Some of these reasons simply have to do with the weight of nineteenth- and early twentieth-century traditions, and at least one individual committed to a form of "evolutionary" theory seemed to feel that one had either to be a diffusionist or a racist!

Even if one ignores this extravagance, it is clear that such methods as cross-dating have often predisposed archaeologists toward diffusionist explanations. Yet it remains difficult to understand how anthropologists, faced with the incredibly complex picture of change in contemporary societies, came to be committed to consideration of only certain mechanisms. Despite a relative scarcity of studies of culture change where variables can be controlled, such works as Barnett's *Innovation* (1953), Hodgen's *Change and History* (1952), or even certain archaeological studies like those of Lewis R. Binford, depending on one's outlook, serve to indicate the multivariate character of culture change.

At the very least, it may be suggested that it is necessary to examine particular situations to determine which processes are involved. The procedures traditionally used by many to discover "contact," however, can be shown to be inappropriate and inadequate. For example, diffusion and independent invention have often been postulated on the basis of "complexity" and "simplicity." But can "complexity" actually be judged without attention to the particular styles involved and without attention to the cultural and ecological context?

A recent article by Douglas Fraser (1966a) serves to illustrate how difficult this decision may be in abstract terms. Fraser has attempted to trace the diffusion of a formal pattern that he calls "the heraldic woman." This design consists of a female figure viewed from the front with the knees apart exposing the external genitalia. In certain data that Fraser presents, this woman is flanked by two other figures of some kind. Fraser considers this formal pattern too complex to have been the result of the "common interests of mankind the world over" (Fraser, 1966a: 36). Though it is not my intention to go into a long critique of Fraser's thesis, it is interesting to note that the position Fraser describes is one that occurs very widely in childbirth. Furthermore, in Oceania, where this design seems to have its most continuous distribution, very similar positions are among the most common for coitus (Ford and Beach, 1951: 24). There is little reason to agree with Fraser's view that the bilateral symmetry in the heraldic woman and the flanking figures is a product of only highly stratified societies

(Fraser, 1966a: 79) and therefore must have diffused from "higher" centers. In short, there is no real reason to suppose that a common position for childbirth, a common position for coitus, and the principle of bilateral symmetry need to have diffused as a unit involving this "heraldic woman" design. The cultural context suggests that such patterns may truly be somewhat closer to the "common interests of mankind the world over" than Fraser indicates. Further examples of this kind may be found in Rands and Riley's paper on diffusion and discontinuous distribution (1958).

But the archaeologist does not often have anything approaching complete data on the total culture, so that it is understandable, though not commendable, that archaeologists have tended to concentrate on purely formal (in the sense of "pertaining to forms or shapes") similarities and differences. There are, however, many different kinds of analysis of forms, a factor that tends to obscure the basically nonstructural or "formal" nature of most classificatory systems. There is little enough reason to object to typologies of the traditional archaeological sort as specialized tools, but these are usually tools for archaeological research of a historical rather than an anthropological nature. The archaeologists of the 1920's and 1930's who developed these methods to their present status were aware of the historical orientation of taxonomic approaches (for example, Gorodzov, 1933), but as anthropological theories have developed and turned away from the predominantly historical emphasis of those times, the "tried and true" methods have been retained despite their general inappropriateness for newer problems. Indeed, the method has developed into a kind of implicit culture theory in its own right —a culture theory that has little support once it is made explicit. As an implicit theory, people have not chosen to question it. In the first place, the assumption that typologies and classification are the major means of organization of human cultures is open to serious question. Second, the typologies used are all too often based on quite arbitrary distinctions. Classification, after all, should be a preliminary step in analysis, not the end product.

For these reasons, purely typological comparisons are inadequate tools for the investigation of culture contact. Most types, such as pottery types, are too gross and too arbitrary to be of much use in the detection of the very subtle phenomena that may indicate trade, for example. All too often, vast trade networks have been postulated on the mere occurrence of a particular "type" of artifact, without any real attempt to discover whether this apparent identity of type simply reflects the inadequacy of the taxonomic procedures employed. Such typological categories as "megalith" or "bell beaker" come readily to mind. At present the goal seems to be to assign the object a name and pigeonhole at any cost. In fact, there seems to be some recognition of these difficulties, since many scholars involved with contact situations have avoided the use of formalized types and have concentrated on such smaller units as motifs. Nonetheless, the approach has remained basically taxonomic. Units or classes of forms are described and compared without any reference to nonformal characteristics.

It should come as no surprise that both classificatory and individual comparisons based on form alone are open to question. Art historians have been working with these problems for some time, and some of them have come to the conclusion that a study of a style must treat structure as well as forms (Schapiro, 1953). Structure, of course, is somewhat of a fad at present, and the term is sometimes used very loosely, even to indicate what most art historians would speak of as forms. If the outward shapes and visible characteristics are meant by *form*, then *structure* can be taken to refer to the organizational principles involved.

There are other problems with analysis of forms besides a linkage with taxonomic and often "Platonic" models of culture, and there are other reasons why purely formal analysis is less than adequate in dealing with hypotheses of culture contact. Although this problem cannot be treated in detail here, a few examples may help to illustrate this point. In some cases, similar visual forms may be present that appear "too complex" to have arisen independently. Yet detailed structural analysis may be able to show that the two forms are only superficially similar and that the underlying chains of derivations are quite different. Also, structural similarities that do exist may prove to be only of a very general nature, despite the similarity of forms; in some cases, generalized structural similarity may create a kind of illusion of formal resemblance. A good example is a certain similarity between materials from the southeastern United States and from northeastern Mexico. What appear at first glance to be very similar designs seem much less similar when it is realized that the major resemblance lies in the simple crowding of the design. In short, analysis of forms deals with only a portion of the complete style. Even where the formal similarity is real rather than apparent, it is still possible that the similarity is merely the chance overlap between two entirely separate and unrelated styles. One is tempted to ask whether the resemblances that do exist between the prehistoric pottery of Japan and Ecuador may not be of this character (Meggers, Evans, and Estrada, 1965).

One failing in Meggers, Evans, and Estrada's treatment of cultural context is that their stylistic comparisons are not sufficiently controlled. Material from a very broad range in time and space from Japan is compared with material from a very broad range in time from Ecuador (Lathrop, 1967; Pearson, 1968; Muller, 1968). Little attention is paid to the question of whether cultural and ecological similarities between Japan and Ecuador at that time may not have led to a potential for similar inventions. Of course, it is also possible that such similarities might have made it easier for innovations to have been accepted if diffusion did occur (Tolstoy, 1969a: 556). The stylistic basis for the judgment of close similarity is of more interest here, however.

These stylistic comparisons are done within the boundaries of traditional ceramic types, at least on the American side of the Pacific. Designs on particular sherds are treated as representative of a pottery type at Valdivia, but no indication is given of the precise provenience of the illustrated sherds. Thus it seems possible that these sherds could be from either the earliest or the latest levels in which the type was recovered. It is apparently assumed that types were stable units for a long period. Indeed, as Lathrap has pointed out (1967), some materials are compared that do not occur at all in Valdivia A (for example, zoned punctation of Valdivia Incised in Meggars, Evans, and Estrada, 1965, plate 168*i–m*, see pp. 65, 207; and some whole types like Valdivia Broadline Incised, plate 190*d–f*). It is also worth noting that no comparisons of "the most popular decorated pottery during Period A" (Meggers, Evans, and Estrada, 1965: 67), Valdivia Modeled, are made with Japanese ceramics. Further, Japanese ceramics are quite diverse, and it is not proper to treat material from this large area as a stylistic unit (Kidder, 1957; Pearson, 1968; Muller, 1968).

It is just as important to determine whether the detailed resemblances cited by Meggers, Evans, and Estrada do hold up. The

Figure 4.1. Jomon sherd (Meggers, Evans, and Estrada, 1965).

Figure 4.2. Valdivia sherd (Meggers, Evans, and Estrada, 1965).

comparisons are based almost completely on similarity of form and similarity of line. Even a partial examination of structure throws doubt upon these formal resemblances. Although only a single example can be given here, similar criticisms may be made of all too many of the comparisons of Valdivia and Japanese sherds. In Meggers, Evans, and Estrada's first plate of comparisons (plate 160), Japanese sherds decorated with parallel straight and zig-zagging lines are compared to Valdivia sherds. The similarity of the designs (especially plate 160g and l, which are reproduced here as figures 4.1 and 4.2) lies in the use of parallel lines which have a sharp change of angle on the lines. On the Japanese sherd (fig. 4.1) the decoration seems to be close to and parallel to the rim of the vessel. As far as can be told, the Valdivia sherd (fig. 4.2) is a step design from the base of a bowl (such as Meggers, Evans, and Estrada, 1965: plate 42e). Quite aside from the matter of placement on the pot, there is a real difference between a design in which parallel lines are abruptly changed into parallel zig-zags and one in which the straight lines are connected with a step pattern, especially when the latter is only a part of a larger design unit. In short, stylistic resemblances will not be meaningfully assessed in these cases until whole designs and their arrangements are analyzed.

There are, of course, some anthropologists who have been concerned with structure. Lévi-Strauss's structural studies of myth are the most famous, although his use of structure is not always in complete agreement with the narrow definition given here. Perhaps the most notable recent structural study in archaeology is Roark's paper on Nasca pottery (1965). In a different sense, Anna Shepard's section on design analysis in *Ceramics for the Archaeologist* (1963: 259–305) is also structural. The absence of such analyses in many archaeological reports is regrettable. Of course, it must be recognized that structural analysis is not a panacea for the ills of anthropological archaeology and should be used only where appropriate for the matters being investigated. In other areas of anthropology, there are many kinds of structural analysis, ranging from the developed structuralism of most of linguistics to the incipient structuralism in the art studies of Franz Boas. However, many recent discussions of culture contact have been based upon archaeological and artistic materials, and it is on this problem that attention will be focused here.

There are already many kinds of structural interests in the study of so-called material culture. These range from the structural school of Guido Kaschnitz von Weinberg and Friederich Matz in Germany to the efforts of Watt (1966, 1967) and myself (Muller, 1967) to develop "generative grammars" for art styles. The notational system for this latter approach may vary widely without affecting the basic character of these "iconic" statements. For example, Watt's notation is computer oriented, whereas mine is not. Both Watt and I, however, are stimulated by the theoretical position developed in linguistics by Noam Chomsky and others. The major contribution of Chomsky and his colleagues, from this point of view, however, is not so much the concept of transformational grammar as it is the basic question of theory—given two alternate explanations for the same data, for what reasons is one rejected. One such basis is simply the "power" of the explanation, that is, to what extent a particular theory accounts for the material. A second basis is that of relative simplicity, or what the mathematician calls "elegance." To make these judgments, it is necessary to adopt a metatheory that is essentially a philosophy of enquiry or scientific method. These kinds of criteria allow the conclusion that classifications of forms alone have neither the power to deal with variation meaningfully nor the elegance that can be achieved through the use of structural analysis.

How then, may structural analysis help in the specific problem of culture contact and in the larger problem of culture change? First of all, change cannot be understood if *only* environmental, historical, or similar "external" factors are considered. It is also necessary to understand *what* is changing. Culture is a part of an ecosystem, but it is also more than that. To understand the relationships of all these systems, it is necessary to understand the internal operation of the systems as well as the relationships of subsystems.

A practical argument in favor of using a structural approach to culture contact problems is that this kind of close study of style may help in formulating hypotheses on the nature of a particular contact between two societies. In eastern Tennessee and western North Carolina, for example, there are three styles of engraved shell work that all share a single theme, a rattlesnake design. These three styles, which I have named Lick Creek (fig. 4.3), Citico (fig. 4.4), and Saltville (see fig. 4.5) after sites in the area, show certain similarities of form to one another; indeed, the Lick Creek and Saltville styles have many similar design motifs. Yet if these three styles are examined more closely, the Lick Creek and Saltville styles have relatively little in common in the use of design, whereas the Lick Creek and Citico styles tend to use elements in the same way despite differences in form. Furthermore, the forms of the Saltville style sometimes suggest that these have been derived from a visual misunderstanding of the Lick Creek forms. The differences between the Lick Creek and Saltville styles, taken altogether, suggest the hypothesis that contacts between the two societies in which these objects were made may have been indirect. On the other hand, the kind of structural closeness of the Lick Creek and Citico styles suggests direct relationships— for example, that the former developed into the latter. This postulated change in the Lick Creek style seems to coincide with the dispersal of the stylistic tradition into a much wider area, so it may be that there is an expansion of one society, a cultural consolidation, or the growth of a sphere of interaction, or all of these. In turn, it may be possible to show ecological concomitants of these changes. It should be remembered, however, that an analysis of cultural systems in structural terms is ultimately justified on the basis of general theory and not merely upon the ability to generate hypotheses to be tested by other means.

The ability to specify structures makes it possible to see how one

Figure 4.3. Lick Creek shell gorget.
Diameter approx. 3″.
(Peabody Museum, Harvard).

Figure 4.4. Citico shell gorget. Diameter approx. 5.5″.
(Maiden Collection).

Figure 4.5. Saltville shell gorget
Diameter approx. 5″.
(Maiden Collection).

kind of cultural system may develop into another and actually to specify the nature of this change. It is futile to attempt to determine whether a particular hypothesis regarding changes in a system may be accepted if the system itself has not been carefully studied. In dealing with structures in art styles, for example, it may be possible to specify the nature of changes through time, the impact of trade and other kinds of culture contact, and whether contacts are at all likely.

One documented case of diffusion may help to clarify the need for this "internal" understanding. It is known that the Norman invaders came into England and imposed new social, economic, and, incidentally, linguistic systems. In each of these spheres the dominance of the new leaders was by no means complete, and, as any anthropologist might have expected, the systems were modified to a greater or lesser degree in the process of change. As Anglo-Saxon became modern English, many of the forms and even many of the structures of Norman French were accepted and assimilated into the language. It is true that these events are the result of diffusion, and it is undoubtedly possible to discover social and economic concomitants of these changes in the language. For all this, the changes and the nature of the various factors involved simply could not be understood in any really complete sense until the structures and forms of the languages had been carefully studied. In dealing with this question of understanding in social anthropology, Lévi-Strauss (1960:52) has come to somewhat similar conclusions:

Therefore when presented with a structural model which departs from empirical reality he feels cheated in some devious way. To him, social structure is like a kind of jig-saw puzzle, and everything is achieved when one has discovered how the pieces fit together. But, if the pieces have been arbitrarily cut, there is no structure at all. On the other hand, if, as is sometimes done, the pieces were automatically cut in different shapes by a mechanical saw, the movements of which are regularly modified by a camshaft, the structure of the puzzle exists, not at the empirical level (since there are many ways of recognizing the pieces which fit together): its key lies in the mathematical formula expressing the shape of the cams and their speed of rotation; something very remote from the puzzle as it appears to the player, although it "explains" the puzzle in the one and only intelligible way.

In order to explain a change in a cultural system it is not enough merely to point to a possible cause, whether that be a transatlantic voyage or a decline in the number of rabbits. It is also necessary to show how this cause works its effect. Thus, although structural analyses of style may seem at first glance to be primarily synchronic, the fact is that it is not possible fully to treat a change in a style without understanding the style as it operated. To choose a trivial example, it may be observed that a certain line on a design field is widened through time and eventually replaced by cross-hatching. This may be remarked upon as a curiosity of some value in dating the object, but very little has been said about the change. Yet a structural analysis may be able to show that the change is neither sudden nor really new—that a rule that has held in the style for a much longer period of time had simply been extended to a new context, and in this sense the change is perhaps simply a regularization of the system of rules. Viewed in this light, the change is far easier to understand than in terms of some massive series of events that mysteriously produce such a small effect.

Still another argument for dealing with structure—which really implies the concept of style in art and material culture—is that styles seem to be very useful in dealing with what Chang (1967: 38ff.) has called a "settlement," the "meaningful unit in archaeology." However, I do not agree with Chang that "model building" in archaeology need be "essentially a typological operation" (1967:90). On the contrary, I suggest that archaeologists can and should attempt to build models fully as powerful as those used in the rest of anthropology. If Chang is right in seeing the "settlement" as a relatively "stationary state" (1967: 38), a concept that many archaeologists are willing to accept as a working hypothesis, then it is especially important to describe this more or less stable system in some more culturally meaningful way.

The concept of structure has been emphasized precisely because it is so often ignored, but form is also important. Formal typological treatments do perform some kinds of tasks with relatively little investment of research time. A certain "trade ware" may sometimes be recognized without understanding the style involved, and this recognition may be of significance in testing some hypothesis that has little to do with the style of the pot as such. Here the danger is that the "trade ware" may be no such thing and that ignorance of the local style may lead the researcher into a complete misunderstanding of the situation. Lest there be any question, however, it must be understood that the careful analysis of styles is not simply a more complex way of creating types anymore than the study of German syntax is simply a good way of learning to distinguish German from French.

Form is important, aside from these typological usages, because, after all, structure involves the manipulation of forms. Accordingly, the basic taxonomy of forms in stylistic analysis is a crucial problem, but one that does not need to be detailed here.

Given a hypothesis of contact between societies, there are a number of general ways of testing the concept. First, it seems reasonable that forms may "diffuse" more easily than the principles governing the use of these forms in a particular style. Since formal components of styles are often very simple when considered in isolation from structure, similarity of form may be accidental, so caution is required. If the forms are truly similar, the nature of the resemblance must be sought out. For example, do the formal units of one style show irregularities in use which might indicate naïveté in interpreting another style (as in Gaulish coinage)? Are the formal units that are similar treated in the same fashion as elements previously used in the style?

Comparison will necessarily involve the use of structural criteria, and there are also comparisons that may be pursued independently of the precise formal similarities. Despite many formal differences between certain woodcarving styles of the Northwest Coast of North America and the weaving styles of the same area, it is possible to show in some of these styles that the principles of organization, the rules of structure, are very similar (Holm, 1965: 10–11). Although this example is within a single culture, the same kind of relationship might hold between different cultures in very intensive contact situations.

If it seems likely that structures may not be learned as easily as forms, it follows that lack of structural similarity does not rule out the possibility of contact. It surely must tell a great deal about the nature of interaction, however. Very close structural and formal correspondence between two very simple styles, of course, may also result from limitation of possibilities.

The study of styles is important because of what can be learned about the operation of culture. In addition, stylistic analysis can provide a more complete and theoretically justified approach to problems that have already been defined. By careful examination of the nature and kinds of similarity it will prove possible to make archaeological inferences concerning change and contact more meaningful in anthropological terms. Structural analysis is not an alternative goal for anthropological research but rather a necessary concomitant of any attempt to understand the operation of cultural systems.

5. Pre-Columbian Contacts—The Dryland Approach: The Impact and Influence of Teotihuacán Culture on the Pre-Columbian Civilizations of Mesoamerica

STEPHAN F. BORHEGYI

In assessing the extent and duration of the cultural contacts certain pre-Columbian Mesoamerican civilizations were able to exert upon other cultures in the New World, one can easily point out that such lasting and effective impacts emanated primarily from three nuclear sources, during three different time periods.

1. During Preclassic times, the nuclear source of cultural influence radiated from the Olmec heartland on the Gulf Coast of Veracruz in Mexico.

2. Throughout Early and Middle Classic times, the influence of Teotihuacán, located on the central plateau of Mexico, was felt as a principle power in almost every corner of Mesoamerica.

3. During Postclassic times, the impact of the Toltecs of Tula, and later, that of their heirs, the Aztecs of Tenochtitlán, penetrated and affected the same areas.

If one transposed these Mesoamerican overlapping routes of influences on a map of the Old World, one would find a closely parallel, if not analogous, situation of cultural contacts, expansions, and lines of diffusion around the shores of the eastern Mediterranean. Here, too, during the late Neolithic and the Copper Age, the sphere of influence of Cycladic and Minoan civilizations was in turn succeeded by the Mycenean and the Archaic Greek, only to be followed later on by the Classic Greek- and Macedonian-inspired Hellenistic world. The heir of Greek culture, the Roman Empire, brought a three-century-long and much misinterpreted Pax Romana to the same area, part of which in turn was gradually transformed into the thoroughly orientalized empire of Christian Byzantium.

The topic of this paper, then, is an exercise in theory to study the structure, model, causes, extent, and success of Teotihuacán over-lordship and dominance over other Mesoamerican civilizations during the Classic period. For the sake of such an exercise, we will compare from time to time the basic motivating forces behind the ascendancy of Teotihuacán with the analogous sway that Hellenism exerted on the eastern Mediterranean world.[1] It is an accepted fact that Alexander's Macedonian military conquest of the greater part of the then known world, or oikoumene, for the next three hundred years brought to the Asiatic lands occupied and colonized by the Greeks a radically new philosophy and a world view commonly known as Hellenism, a new way of life hitherto unprecedented in the Old World. Unlike their Minoan and Mycenaean predecessors, the great swarm of widely scattered Greek and Macedonian migrants (slave and free) who followed in the footsteps of Alexander and settled around the eastern shores of the Mediterranean, the Levant, Egypt, and Asia Minor, not only represented mercantile and commercial outposts of individual and independent Greek city-states (polis); they also brought Hellenic ways of life massively to the attention of Oriental peoples and succeeded in amalgamating peoples of different cultural, linguistic, and religious origins. The Greek style of life rapidly became fashionable among the native Oriental upper classes who were eager to learn the Greek ways and adopt Greek styles. By the

[1] For studies on Hellenism and its impact on Asia Minor, see Badian, 1958; Muller, 1958; Tarn, 1961; Burn, 1962; McNeill, 1965; and MacKendrick, 1966; on the Italian Renaissance and humanism, see Ferguson, 1939; for the use of historic analogues in archaeology, see Asher, 1961; Binford, 1967; and Schuyler, 1968.

second century B.C. Hellenism was an already recognizable syncretizing cultural force, a new world outlook and philosophy that could rise above the particularism of the polis and could successfully transcend the boundaries of cities, national states, and national cults by flexibly adjusting itself to local needs. Basing itself on Iranian and Persian prototypes, Hellenism (and its Stoic and Cynic philosophy) was able to envisage for the first time in the history of the Old World a resplendent hope (which has never quite left men since) of a boundaryless ideal state and to formulate a concept of a universal brotherhood and equality of man, a "unity of concord" or "unity of hearts" achieved not by human laws, but by love (*homonoia*). As a result of all this, a truly cosmopolitan city dweller, a "Hellenistic" individual who could choose his own way of life and feel at home anywhere in the then known civilized world, came into being. Hence Hellenism, as a cultural force, prepared the grounds for Christianity and foreshadowed the Italian Renaissance by some fifteen hundred years.[2]

When one studies Teotihuacán and the far-reaching cultural influences of this great Mesoamerican *tollán*, or metropolis, it becomes tempting to compare it with the impacts of Hellenism on the various

[2] Since this paper is primarily a theoretical exercise demonstrating the use of analogues and historical models in archaeological interpretation, Hellenism as compared to Teotihuacán will be treated throughout not only as a political but as a syncretizing spiritual force, a force that could transcend cultural boundaries and was primarily operative from the time of Alexander's conquest and political unification of much of the Orient until the gradual take-over and occupation of the Hellenistic lands by the Roman Empire. It should be understood that the impact of the political and economic influences of the numerous Hellenistic monarchies, the Antagonids (in Macedonia), the Seleucids (in Syria), the Attalids (in Pergamum), and the Ptolemies (in Egypt), that succeeded the united and utopistic realm of Alexander varied from time to time and from country to country. These Diadoch kingdoms, each composed of different native, ethnic, and linguistic groups, were far from being uniform, were ridden with internal disorders, and frequently competed with or opposed each other. Nevertheless, the highly adaptive and appealing supracultural, artistic, intellectual, "Eurasian" spirit of Hellenism, regardless of the temporary political boundaries of the Diadoch states, remained more or less uniform throughout the entire eastern Mediterranean world and continued to remain so, with minor modifications, even through the Roman occupation of the same area. Only the growing influence of Christianity was able to obliterate and ultimately absorb the last remaining vestiges of "profanity" and Hellenism.

Oriental civilizations that once ruled Anatolia, Syria, Persia, India, Egypt, and North Africa. The secret of the initial success and ready adaptation of Hellenism in the Orient can probably be best ascribed to the fact that the Greek immigrants built on earlier Minoan, Mycenaean, and Archaic Greek migrations and colonies, in much the same way as Teotihuacán culture of the Classic period followed in the footsteps of earlier Olmec expansions into the Valley of Mexico, Oaxaca, the Mexican isthmus and the Gulf Coast, the Pacific coast of Guatemala, El Salvador, and the Maya countries.

However, in order to assess and understand how Teotihuacán was able to master much of Mesoamerica, it will be necessary to examine the various cultural changes this contact has caused to other cultures of Mesoamerica. This influence, even if distant, can perhaps be best observed in the Maya area in general and in the highland Maya area in particular. For this reason, the specific and abrupt changes or the new cultural traits that were perhaps the results of the spiritual and political influence of Teotihuacán over the Maya cultures of highland Guatemala and Chiapas (during the Early and Middle Classic period from A.D. 250 to 650) are listed in detail as an appendix and are contrasted there with the Late Classic period (from A.D. 650 to 950), when the decline and fall of Teotihuacán caused the gradual reemergence of the popular Preclassic highland Maya folk-cults. (For Teotihuacán's influence over the lowland Maya of the tropical rain forest, see W. R. Coe, 1964; Borhegyi, 1964a; Greene and Moholy-Nagy, 1966.)

The stage, then, is set in Mesoamerica; the date is about A.D. 250; and the act is about to begin in the greatest of all cities of the New World, Tollán-Teotihuacán. The origins of Teotihuacán are lost in myths. The city was already dead when the Aztecs arrived to found their empire at Lake Texcoco. But they were awed by the magnificence of the place and knew that they were walking on sacred grounds. The city's grandiose "sun" and "moon" pyramids, probably created during the later part of the Preclassic (Teotihuacán I or Tzacualli phase), are mute testimonies to the existence of an already stratified society with marked specialization and function. It is evident that a well-organized priestly hierarchy, which undoubtedly constituted the top of the social ladder, must have directed and supervised the city's master plan and its massive civic building activities. Already by Late Preclassic times the influence of Teotihuacán's priestly bureaucracy was apparently felt as far east as the Gulf Coast and probably as far south as Oaxaca. At any rate, it is quite clear that by A.D. 250 Teotihuacán was a settlement of great size, housing about fifty-thousand people, and that it provided a developmental base for the rapid growth that followed. Covering more than eight square miles with its carefully laid out grid pattern streets, with well-planned market places, civic structures, ceremonial precincts, long processional avenues and canals with sewers and rain gutters, residential and slum (?) districts, hostels and warehouses for traveling merchants and foreign emissaries (?), and its uniform "city blocks," the huge metropolis must indeed have been an awesome sight (cf. Millon, 1960, 1964; Bernal, 1963).

The continued expansion of the urban population, which probably soon included an impoverished and hungry city proletariat, necessitated a new form of coordination of the labor and food supply, a new way of storing surplus food, and resulted in an innovative, full-scale, highly productive irrigation system that brought life to the rich but previously unused alluvial plains south of the expanding metropolis. In turn, the introduction of irrigation agriculture created a possibility of increased population density (see Armillas, Palerm, and Wolf, 1956). Indeed, the growing economic network of Teotihuacán must step by step have incorporated and systematically exploited such neighboring valleys and lakes as Texcoco and included or intensified such new cooperative and exploitative activities as saltmaking, fishing, collecting lake plants and insects, hunting waterfowl, and collecting forest resources. With superb organizational mechanism, the Teotihuacán governmental machinery gradually began to expand its power over the entire Mexican tableland, at the same time pulling in and attracting large masses of people from faraway distances and coercing and coordinating them into an effective centrifugal megapolitan system (see Linné, 1942). If the original bearers of the Teotihuacán culture (I and II) were Nahua-Totonacs (see Jiménez Moreno, 1966: 43), they certainly succeeded by Classic times in attracting Chocho, Popoloca, Mazatec, and perhaps even Mixtec peoples and continued to coexist with them for centuries to come. Such a polyglot linguistic situation coupled with an ever-expanding and multiple economic base was most conducive to the development of far-reaching and lucrative trading activities and to the progressive evolution of an independent and wealthy merchant class. This con-

dition in turn favored a dramatic increase of such specialist classes
(or castes?) as various types of teachers, scribes, artisans, craftsmen,
healers, carpenters, painters, architects, stonecutters, masons, lapi-
darists, featherworkers, potters, weavers, spinners, acrobats, ball-
players, athletes (?), actors, and the like, and a standing army or
strong military class to protect and garrison the newly mastered and
incorporated tributary lands. By Middle Classic times, the economic
and religious influence of Teotihuacán was felt over most parts of
Mexico and penetrated even into the neighboring lands of the Mayas.
And so the city of Teotihuacán found itself in the role of a supracommunity center of authority. For all practical purposes, a new era, a
Pan-Teotihuacán world was in the making.

However, unlike Hellenism, the New World order of Teotihuacán
was not the dream of one single man (for Alexander's utopian concept of a "World State" and the "unity of mankind," see Badian,
1958). Lacking an Alexander and a professional and superbly trained
Macedonian infantry and cavalry, the expansionistic and political
aims of Teotihuacán were perhaps only implemented by trained military units like the Eagle and Jaguar Knights and were in reality
guided by a well-organized priestly bureaucracy ever watchful for
new economic riches and tribute possibilities. However, a simultaneous and perhaps originally peaceful propagation of a "Teotihuacán
faith" combined with a missionizing zeal may well have been the initial vision of one single person, that of a "pacifist New World Alexander," the culture hero Quetzalcoatl, the legendary high priest of the
God Tlaloc-Quetzalcoatl-Ehecatl. But apart from this one difference,
the spread, impact, and success of the Hellenistic spirit in the Old
World and that of Teotihuacán in the New World follow practically
the same paths of history.[3] The *koine* (a simplified version of the
Greek language) was paralleled in the Teotihuacán way of life by the

---

[3] The influence of Teotihuacán over the lowland Maya inhabitants of the
tropical rain forest may well have followed a somewhat different path from
that of their highland cousins. The uninterrupted cultural continuum of such apparently popular Preclassic Maya cults as the stela and altar cults, the ritual
calendar and its related glyphic system, all of which ceased to be in use among
the highland Mayas by Classic times (probably as a result of Teotihuacán
disapproval or taboo), appears to have continued in their popularity until the
end of the Classic period in the Maya lowlands. This may indicate that the
Early Classic highland Maya theocracy was probably less cohesive and as a
result of this perhaps more adaptive. The highland Maya would have therefore

use of Nahua speech as a *lingua franca*, which no doubt soon became prestigious and fashionable, especially among the native, priestly, upper classes and wealthier merchant classes of the various Classic period Mesoamerican cultures. The incorporative potentials of these cultures, whether Maya, Zapotec, or Huaxtec, were apparently ripe and of a sufficiently cosmopolitan outlook to seek out such foreign mastery, since their own theocratically oriented bureaucracy, affected by previous Olmec contacts, prepared them to accept with ease such supplementary adaptations from outside cultures. As with Hellenism, the initial foreign contacts of Teotihuacán were probably continuously reinforced with a search after such new and marketable export-import and luxury commodities as chicozapote wood, jaguar hide, and quetzal and macaw feathers, and were eventually cemented by the gradual monopolization of perhaps such key products as cacao, amber, salt, hallucinogenic mushrooms (?), peyote (?), *ololiuhqui* (?), rubber, copal-incense, cotton, amate fiber, jade, liquid mercury, cinnabar, ochres, iron pyrite, rare marine shells, and perhaps others. "Hellenism" in the Old World became synonymous with trade and commercialism, art forms, sports, games, philosophy, astrology, eclecticism in religion, and a utopian belief in a good life. One can perhaps safely assume that the word *Teotihuacán* meant something similar to most of the people of Classic period Mesoamerica.

1. *Trade* in Mesoamerica during the Teotihuacán interlude was extensive both on land and water. Simplified by the unification of large areas and by a new common (?) currency system based on cacao beans (?), market and trading centers were springing up in many parts of Mesoamerica, but primarily in the midst of many of the former, Olmec-influenced Mesoamerican *necropoli*, or burial precincts. As a result of the abundantly available craft and food surpluses, groups of itinerant merchants were forming themselves into fraternities or guilds, especially around trading posts and ports

---

incorporated more willingly and perhaps without much pressure, any "exported" Teotihuacán religious beliefs. On the other hand, the more complex and more cohesive and geographically more isolated lowland Maya theocracy remained selective and resisted and rejected a total acceptance of Teotihuacán overlordship. It may also be that the lowland Mayas had already by late Preclassic times developed and "invented" independently a form of celestial (and terrestrial?) paradise or heaven and, having such a concept and coercive power, were in no need to emulate literally a Teotihuacán-designed Tlalocán.

manned or dominated by Teotihuacán. Motivation to gain wealth by means of trading was becoming a safe and increasingly enterprising secular occupation, especially since the trade routes, trading posts, hostels, warehouses, and rest stations were undoubtedly policed and supervised by Teotihuacán-controlled military garrisons, led perhaps by the fearsome Eagle and Jaguar Knights. Like Hermes in the Old World, the black god Ek-Chu-Ah (one of the many manifestations of Tlaloc?) became the protector of wary travelers and of the increasingly cosmopolitan and rapidly growing rich *pochteca* merchant class, whose members began to reside in comfortable suburbanite quarters associated with the market and trading centers. The gradual formation of an independent and wealthy *pochteca* league must have contributed greatly to the secure economic base of the Teotihuacán world, allowing an ever greater channeling of energy to the arts and to the service of the gods and the dead. Nor should the manipulative, political, and proselytizing power of such organized guilds be underestimated. They may also have constituted the invaluable fifth column so essential to the successful expansion of all kinds of colonizing empires and nations. Furthermore, this new commercial base under increasingly secularized control favored the accumulation of wealth by individuals other than priests and bureaucrats and provided an outlet for social mobility and population expansion, a broader market for new and imported exotic luxury goods, many of which (like copal incense) were rapidly becoming necessities, and a further incentive for *pochteca* enterprise (see Acosta Saignes, 1945).

2. In *the arts*, Teotihuacán, like Hellenism, influenced both the secular and the sacred fields. The cities, old or new, vied with one another in the splendor of their works. Every city of any consequence influenced by Teotihuacán had its temples, statuary, ball courts, markets, and communal plazas. The massive and monumental architectural style of Teotihuacán, featuring the combination of inclined and vertical planes, the use of *talud* (slope) and *tablero* (panel), along with the market and plaza form of settlement pattern, was imitated with considerable success all over Mesoamerica. The strongly theatrical, sculptural, and pictorial representation of the gods of Teotihuacán, like those of Greece, merged easily in form as well as in function with their Zapotec, Huaxtec, Chontal, Totonac, and Maya counterparts. Like the "Cloud Gatherer" Zeus-Amon, Tlaloc-Chac, the hurler of thunderbolts (fire serpents) and rain, ruled supreme.

The mural and fresco art as well as the pottery styles, forms, and wares of Teotihuacán, like the painted *amphoras* and *kylixes* of the Greek commonwealth, were richly covered with many-colored allegoric and thematic motifs as well as with narrative or descriptive illustrations of standardized mythological events, legends, and rituals and with the portrayals of the favored gods of Teotihuacán. These soon became coveted and prestigous export items. They were rapidly imitated everywhere in Mesoamerica and were in many instances manufactured in local styles and clay.

3. In *sports*, with wealth and sufficient leisure time assured by the readily available surplus food supply, communal and spectator games accompanied by betting became increasingly popular. Various types of intercity and interarea competitive rubber ball games (*tlachtli*) flourished and, like the Pan-Hellenic Olympic and Isthmian games of the Greek commonwealth, were perhaps officially encouraged and sponsored by Teotihuacán. Ball courts were numerous, and almost every city, trade and market center in Mesoamerica boasted at least one or two sizeable I-shaped formal courts (*tlachco*). The rather amazing uniformity of these courts and of the numerous ball-game paraphernalia used by the players (stone and wooden yokes, stone *hachas*, *palmas*, ballgame handstones, bats, clubs, helmets, face masks, knee and wrist pads, leather aprons) over a large portion of Mesoamerica argues for a common origin of these games and attests to the widely accepted popularity of these friendly, competitive hip-and-hand-ball games, irrespective of linguistic and culture area boundaries. Whether or not these Teotihuacán-inspired competitive games originally included a not so friendly trophy head cult, with its human sacrifices and decapitation, is not altogether clear, but perhaps this aspect of the game was only a local elaboration that developed at and was diffused from the Gulf Coast of Mexico during late Early or Middle Classic times.[4]

4. Of all the influences, however, the *religious ideology, world*

---

[4] For the description of the pre-Columbian ball games and on the various and occasionally regional uses and restrictions of the ball-game paraphernalia, and on the "trophy head" cult as related to the games, see Borhegyi, 1960a, 1961c, 1963b, 1965a: 22–23, nn. 23, 28, 1965c, 1968a, 1968c. It should be noted that the stone *palmas* popularly used in connection with the rubber ball game in Mexico (especially on the Gulf Coast) during Classic times seem for some reason to be curiously absent in both the highland and lowland Maya areas.

view, and philosophy of Teotihuacán left the greatest impact on the Classic cultures of Mesoamerica. Like the Greek gods of Hellenistic export, the Teotihuacán gods were venerated and lived side by side with the gods of native lands. Like the members of the Greek pantheon, the gods of Teotihuacán, too, gradually assumed supremacy while taking the form and iconography of their Maya and Zapotec counterparts (cf. Borhegyi, 1965a: 28–30, 1966a). To satisfy the spiritual needs of their heterogenous and polyglot public, the priests and artisans of Teotihuacán, like their Hellenistic counterparts, must soon have felt the need to develop a new visual, narrative, and forceful muralistic "language" to express their encyclopedically systematized collections of legends and myths (see Kubler, 1967a, 1967b). Since there was no stela cult or glyphic system, so important in other areas of Mesoamerica, this well-ordered, visual, "Teotihuacán-Esperanto" language, as depicted on the various realistic fresco murals at Teotihuacán and also on the ritual pottery vessels (especially on the fresco-painted, cylindrical tripod vases and on the *adorno*-covered censers), may have been essential as a new form of billboard-like mass communication system. It would have guided and visually instructed the recently initiated novices and converts and appealed to the large flocks of multilingual, but largely illiterate, uneducated, and somewhat superstitious pilgrims who thronged to the various market centers, to whom an esoteric or parochial "glyphic" and "calendric" language would have been totally incomprehensible.[5] As in the Old World, these pilgrim centers were theatrically situated on the shores of sacred lakes, wells, and waterholes or near sacred

[5] It is interesting to realize that bilingual or even trilingual (cf. the Rosetta Stone) public and civic inscriptions make their first appearance in the Old World during Hellenistic times. It is probably also relevant to note here that Christianity in general, and sixteenth-century Spain in particular made a systematic and conscious use of the sumptuous and dynamic Baroque and Churriguresque art forms as a visual communication, a message frozen in clay or wood, to facilitate and expedite the conversion of the Indian masses in sixteenth-century Central and South America. Also, it may not be entirely accidental that the greatest and most sacred pilgrim shrine of Mexico, the miraculous shrine of the Virgin of Guadalupe, was erected in the outskirts of Mexico City so near to the ancient pilgrim center of Teotihuacán. Thus the pre-Columbian goddess Tonantzin was transmuted into a Christian Virgin of Guadalupe, much in the same way as Demeter (Persephone), the Mediterranean goddess of the underworld, became a Black Virgin Mary.

mountains and volcanoes, where the water gods and "Earthshaker" jaguars were believed to dwell. In many ways the great metropolis of Teotihuacán must have closely resembled the Alexandria of Hellenistic fame: a city planned both for comfort and beauty, where the erudite priests, sages, philosophers, and scientists congregated and lived on state support while engaged in writing, editing, compiling, stabilizing, and copying a systematized encyclopedic corpus of the accumulated scientific, astronomical, calendrical, mythological, ritual, and epigraphic knowledge.[6] But unlike Alexandria, Teotihuacán was also a "City of the Gods," the place where the earthly representatives of the gods—a chosen and most probably self-perpetuating sacerdotal nobility—lived. Here, too, dwelled the gods themselves. Here resided Quetzalcoatl and his high priest, who went by the same name and title. Here lived brothers and relatives of the divine Quetzalcoatl—Xolotl, Xochiquetzal, Xipe Totec, Xiuhtecuhtli, and Tezcatlipoca (the setting sun)—whose priests ultimately challenged the rule and supremacy of Quetzalcoatl and his acolytes. However, Teotihuacán was not just the dwelling place, the Mount Olympus of the gods, but, as Dr. Caso (1942) so well put it, it was also the locale and entrance to a terrestrial paradise, the Tlalocán, where Tlaloc, the rain god, held court with his jade-skirted wife, Chalchihuitlicue, goddess of the living water. Here, under the protective eyes of Tlaloc and Chalchihuitlicue, the living and the dead found themselves in a state of bliss and eternal happiness, as depicted on the frescoes at Teotihuacán. Here in the Blue House of Tlaloc, where the clouds gather, they amused themselves by singing and dancing or by playing ball, chasing butterflies, picking flowers, swimming in swift rivers, eating fruits and drinking cacao (?), or just dozing under the shade of giant *ceiba* trees.

Fray Bernardino de Sahagún quoted his aged informant as saying that the place was called Teotihuacán, burial place of kings, where those who died became gods and to speak of a person as a god meant that he had died. Indeed, to die or to live on as a deified mortal (either in the form of a reborn soul, or as a precious butterfly, or

---

[6] For the history and development of the city of Alexandria, the intellectual capital of the Hellenistic Age, symbolized by one of the Wonders of the Ancient World, the four-hundred-foot Pharos or lighthouse in its harbor, see Forster, 1961. The Museum in Alexandria and the Library at Pergamum were state institutions where a salaried staff carried out literary and scientific work.

quetzal-papalotl) and to become a part of this terrestrial and heavenly paradise not only had vast incorporative and export potentials; it
was perhaps the greatest universal attraction, the most important
integrating force or secret weapon that could best explain the rapid
success of the spiritual and political expansion of Teotihuacán. For
the city of Teotihuacán was not merely an administrative and spiritual center, a pontifical seat like Rome, but it was the physical entrance, the *porta de cielo*, the gate of the heaven through which the
living and the dead, the converts, the believers, the initiated, the mis-
treated, and the penitents could enter the Tlalocán, where they could
find compensation for their earthly sufferings and were promised a
joyful, happy, and perennial existence. In the concept of the Tlalocán,
Teotihuacán offered something tangible, something desirable, a rich
and readily available compensation that no previous Mesoamerican
culture was able to offer. Appropriate initiation rituals perhaps included bloodletting or self-torture, or baptismal rites by the use of
holy water, or purification rites with copal incense (the "blood" of
the copal tree) and the ceremonial consumption of such mind-
changing hallucinogens as the *ololiuhqui*, the sacred mushroom (*teo-
nanacatl*, "the flesh of god"), or *peyote*. Through these individual-
ized initiation rites, Teotihuacán tendered salvation and a joyful life
to the sufferers, the sick and maltreated, to the living and to the
deceased, to peoples and perhaps even classes of all types, to Huax-
tecs, Zapotecs, and Mayas, to everyone who believed and lived in
accordance with the new universe created by Teotihuacán. Through
the autosacrifice and self-immolation of the Orpheus-like redeemer
god, Quetzalcoatl-Nanhuatzin-Xolotl (the living and deified Que-
tzalcoatls), the peoples of Classic Mesoamerica were now able to
hope for a compensation in the present, and for a happy continuation
of life after death.[7]

[7] The Tlalocán, or earthly paradise, of Teotihuacán of the Classic period as
described in the sixteenth century by Sahagún was to become by the time of the
Aztecs or perhaps even by early Postclassic times, the second of the nine resting
places of the deceased, on the arduous road to the *Mictlán,* the ninth and final
resting place of the Aztec dead, which was equivalent to total immersion or
disappearance. According to Sahagún, the Tlalocán of the Aztecs (even only as
a temporary resting place) must still have been a wondrous site since "never
was there a lack of green corn, squash, sprigs of amaranth, green chiles, to-
matoes, string beans in pods, and flowers," and because also "there dwelled
some gods called Tlaloques" (Sahagún, 1946: I, 317–318).

This belief ultimately was formed into a powerful "monopoly" through which Teotihuacán could rule and maintain its adaptive power for five hundred years. In exchange for gaining a joyful terrestrial and eternal life in the Tlalocán, the subject people, especially their priestly and upper classes, were willing and perhaps even eager to abandon or supplement some of their own religious beliefs and surrender and submit themselves and their lands to the political and spiritual hegemony and economic exploitation of Teotihuacán.[8] Thus the tributary power of Teotihuacán could transcend classes, cities, national cultures, and national cults and in the concept of the Tlalocán could offer in return a universal brotherhood for all mankind in Mesoamerica (and perhaps even to some of the peoples in North and South America?), along with a terrestrial paradise in which perhaps every man (living or dead) was considered equal. In this New World concept of Teotihuacán, there appears to be no longer any importance placed on separately existing cities with strong local and parochial allegiances, but rather an emphasis on one supracommunity, a great city, under one divine law, with citizenship open for all classes and walks of life, initiates and believers who were entitled to a share in the utopian belief of the Rain God's happy terrestrial realm. In the then known inhabited world, in the oikoumene of Teotihuacán, a member of another linguistic group would probably no longer be regarded *ipso facto* an enemy, but a "soul" brother, a cosmopolitan member and a shareholder of the Teotihua-

[8] The successful, rapid spread of Teotihuacán religious ideas does not necessarily imply that other Mesoamerican cultures (like the Mayas or Zapotecs) had not already developed by Preclassic or Protoclassic times some equally if not more complex forms of religion. On the contrary, it would indicate that other Mesoamerican cultures did develop and practice analogous but perhaps less adaptive religions and were therefore always ready to accept and incorporate new, attractive religious or philosophical concepts, such as the ones offered by Teothihuacán to supplement their basically similar cults. For the possible association of regular-sized and miniature effigy mushroomstones with the cult of the nine gods of the underworld among the highland Mayas in Preclassic times, see Borhegyi, 1961a: 501–503.

In many ways the adaptability and rapid acceptance of the Classic period Teotihuacán-designed "earthly paradise" and afterworld, the Tlalocán, closely parallels the immense popularity of the Hellenistic mystery cults and redeeming religions with their concepts of trial on earth followed by a happy afterlife in heaven, and salvation through initiation and knowledge of God, concepts that continued to play an important role in Christianity and in gnosticism.

cán commonwealth in which Nahuas, Totonacs, Zapotecs, and Mayas all could participate. Such melting-pot conditions were especially conducive to the development and formation of merchant classes, no longer dependent on priestly authority, but composed of peoples of various ethnic and linguistic groups whose common interests and goals transcended ethnic and village boundaries and whose secular and cosmopolitan orientation in turn gradually led to a progressive loss of theocratic control. Thus, certainly by the end of the Early Classic period, Mesoamerican man had a unique chance and opportunity. He could cease to remain, if he so chose, a member of an isolated, self-contained autonomous village or urban community and could become a citizen of the Teotihuacán oikoumene. There he had the potential to become a veritably "reborn" individual, a "renaissance" man of the then known cosmos, a cosmopolitan in the true sense, whose allegiance and loyalty belonged to the one great earthly and heavenly city of gods and men, a city that had no visible and no artificial boundaries.

Aside from the lacustrine resources and the rich, green-colored obsidian sources located at Pachuca, the barren lands of Teotihuacán in Preclassic times could offer nothing of world-wide attraction or notice.[9] But as with Hellenism, Classic Teotihuacán, through the concepts of individual salvation and the Tlalocán, was able to tender a spiritual and real reward, a magic, coercive, and popular holding power that remained unparalleled in the New World until the arrival of the Spanish conquistadores and Christianity. I therefore believe that the terrestrial and heavenly paradise, the Tlalocán and its widely acceptable mystery cult religion, was the best and perhaps, next to obsidian, the only "marketable" and diffusible commodity Teotihuacán ever possessed. It was the magic key that opened the door to the hearts of all classes and individuals among practically all Classic cultures of Mesoamerica.[10] But to perpetuate and continually rein-

---

[9] On the obsidian industry of Teotihuacán and Pachuca, see Linné, 1934: 143–153; Spence, 1967. For the occurence of green obsidian, imported from Mexico, in the lowland Maya area during late Early Classic times, see W. Coe, 1962: 500.

[10] It may be important to note here that the Hellenistic-inspired and immensely popular oracular shrines and chthonic mystery rites and Orphic or Hermetic cults also involved a confession, atonement of sins, and gradual initiation trials (as perhaps did the Tlalocán with its nine or thirteen obstacles). In a

force the belief in an earthly and heavenly Tlalocán open to all peoples, it was necessary to develop new art forms, suitable architectural styles, and a new method of non-glyphic but realistic mass communication. To maintain such a boundaryless commonwealth or coalition, there was also a need for a large, bureaucratic governmental machinery and a sound economic base; and so the Teotihuacán cacao, salt, amber, and liquid mercury monopoly, under the divine protection of Ek-Chu-Ah, came into existence. The tribute system, a Teotihuacán-controlled market and pilgrimage pattern, the competitive and theatrically rendered ball games that spellbound masses of polyglot spectators, and the lake ceremonies, dramatically staged to entice and entertain the flocks of pilgrims, formed a formidable and much sought after Teotihuacán "export cluster," one that long held under its spell and power the then known world of Mesoamerica.

However, not even magic spells or utopistic coercive powers can last forever. As the Hellenistic Orient lost its independence to Rome, Teotihuacán, too, fell to one of its more barbarous protectors, the Otomí. With the fall of the eternal city, the earthly and heavenly paradise, too, was lost. If this theory is correct, it would help to explain the chain reaction that occurred after the fall of Teotihuacán, causing the abandonment, throughout Mesoamerica, of many of the sacred cities influenced by Teotihuacán and ultimately bringing about the gradual disintegration of theocracy and the Classic world. The Teotihuacán outposts, like the Greek colonies and Hellenistic cities of Asia, Africa, and Europe, became gradually absorbed by the native cultures, and the long-subdued and nearly forgotten local folk customs, village cults, and fertility gods reemerged. But, like the utopian ideas of Hellenism that lived on in books and thoughts and, when time was ripe, kindled the flames of the Renaissance, the impact of Teotihuacán lingered on, even after the destruction of the city of the gods. That many Teotihuacanos survived and that a diaspora followed we know, and for a while the exiles in Azcapotzalco, Cholula, Tajín, and Xochicalco carried the torch and the teachings of Teotihuacán (see Borhegyi, 1965a: 35, nn. 44, 49). Then, in the eleventh century, the Toltecs of Tula reestablished themselves as the inheri-

---

somewhat similar fashion to the public cult of Tlaloc at Teotihuacán, the mystery cult and worship of Serapis, the patron god of Alexandria was also a deliberate syncretizing invention during the time of the first Ptolemy.

tors of Teotihuacán under the leadership of a new culture hero, Ce-Acatl-Topiltzin, a new divine Quetzalcoatl, much as Rome ruled the captive Hellenistic lands under the divine Augustus (and his heirs), who continued to emulate Hellenism and the deeds of the deified Alexander. During the militaristic and nationalistic rule of the Toltecs and their followers, the Aztecs of Tenochtitlán, the Teotihuacán ideology and pantheon was again revived, but, as one might expect, in considerably altered form. The terrestrial paradise, the commonwealth of the Tlalocán of Teotihuacán was replaced by a "nationalistic" heaven, the Mictlán of the Aztecs, reserved, like the Valhalla of the Germans and Scandinavians, primarily for the Aztec warriors who died on the battlefield or on the sacrificial altars. And Tlaloc, while still important, had lost out to the Aztec warrior god Huitzilopochtli. In the final act, the Spanish sword and the Christian cross, like the Arab scimitar under the banner of the Prophet, brought to an end the remaining vestiges of Teotihuacán. But even today, thirteen centuries after its violent destruction, Teotihuacán is an awesome and unforgettably theatrical sight, a monumental dead city that spread over more than five square miles, with gigantic pyramids towering over two hundred feet high, and with countless temples, fresco-painted palaces, avenues, ceremonial plazas, and residential quarters. Like the literary and art products of Hellenism, the mural frescoes and architecture of ancient Teotihuacán continue to remain a source of inspiration to the artists and architects of today, while the concepts of its terrestrial and heavenly paradise, the Tlalocán, merged invisibly with the christo-pagan folk beliefs of heaven and hell.

In summary, this brief exercise in the use of analogy in archaeological interpretation relative to the structure of contact situations of Hellenistic times in the Old World and the Classic period in pre-Columbian Mesoamerica suggests some general implications about the mechanism of *culture change* that might be worthy for future research and exploration, which can be summarized as follows:

1. The use of analogy in the comparative and structural studies of otherwise unrelated and distant societies indicating similar acculturative and social and historical evolutionary processes appears to have theoretical validity (see Asher, 1961; Binford, 1967; Schuyler, 1968).

2. If we accept the axiom that similar environments are likely to produce similar cultural adaptations, even among distant cultures, it

appears that similar sociohistorical conditions or stimuli could also elicit analogous responses to a given environment and result in similar or parallel cultural evolutionary processes (cf. Hellenism and Teotihuacán). In other words, certain cultural changes will "automatically" set into motion analogous cultural responses, even among distant and perhaps otherwise unrelated cultures (cf. M. Coe, 1957).

3. Societies living far apart but within similar *ecosystems*—that is, within a similar cultural, biological, and physical environment—will be likely to have parallel cultural evolution with comparable incorporative and expansionistic (diffusive) potentials.

4. The functional prerequisites for urbanism do not necessarily lie in an ecological zone, rich in farming, mining, or other potentials, but can also be sought for even in a desolate or barren region, provided that the locality has sufficiently recognizable and widely acceptable *sanctity* to attract pilgrims and trade. Places like Mecca, Delphi, Athens, Rome, Teotihuacán, or even Lourdes appear to be good candidates for such studies.[11]

5. An expansionistic or colonizing society of a sacerdotal or hierarchic character that has entered the road toward secularization (and will, consequently, gradually lose its former coercive power) will most likely pass through an Indian summer in which some utopian precepts will be generated to arrest or delay the inevitable decline, especially when some of its elite or enlightened members realize that further progress is unlikely. These utopian precepts will usually stress the unity and brotherhood of mankind, a state that can perhaps best be achieved through a kind of religious mysticism involving individual and equalitarian salvation and eternal life. The Persian Empire under the Achaemenids, the Hellenistic period, and Mesoamerica during the Teotihuacán-influenced Classic period, may well be considered representative models for such usually brief but brilliant utopian periods.

6. The success of an expansionistic, theocratic society does not always necessitate a solid economic base, since its best export commodity may be a widely acceptable and intangible esoteric theological concept or reward rather than locally grown or produced surplus

---

[11] On the sacred architecture of the ancient Greeks and its relevance to the landscape and to such hallowed topographical features as mountains, rivers, springs, wells, and clearings, see Scully, 1962.

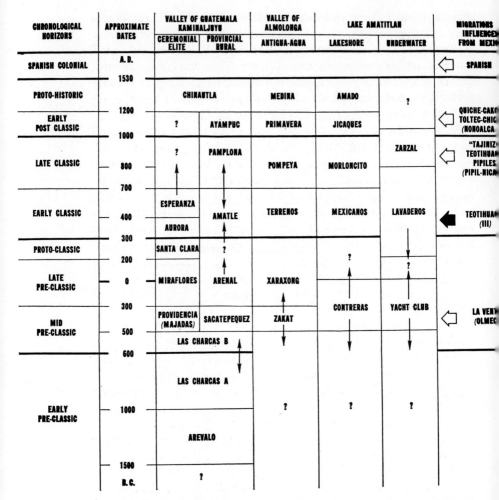

| CHRONOLOGICAL HORIZONS | APPROXIMATE DATES | VALLEY OF GUATEMALA KAMINALJUYU | | VALLEY OF ALMOLONGA | LAKE AMATITLAN | | | MIGRATIONS INFLUENCES FROM MEXICO |
		CEREMONIAL ELITE	PROVINCIAL RURAL	ANTIGUA-AGUA	LAKESHORE	UNDERWATER		
SPANISH COLONIAL	A. D.							SPANISH
	1530							
PROTO-HISTORIC		CHINAUTLA		MEDINA	AMADO	?		
	1200							QUICHE-CAKC
EARLY POST CLASSIC		?	AYAMPUC	PRIMAVERA	JICAQUES			TOLTEC-CHIC (NONOALCA
	1000							
		?	PAMPLONA			ZARZAL		"TAJINIZ TEOTIHUAC
LATE CLASSIC	800			POMPEYA	MORLONCITO			PIPILES (PIPIL-NICA
	700							
EARLY CLASSIC	400	ESPERANZA	AMATLE	TERRENOS	MEXICANOS	LAVADEROS		TEOTIHUAC (III)
		AURORA						
	300							
PROTO-CLASSIC	200	SANTA CLARA	?		?	?		
LATE PRE-CLASSIC	0	MIRAFLORES	ARENAL	XARAXONG				
	300				CONTRERAS	YACHT CLUB		LA VEN (OLMEC
MID PRE-CLASSIC		PROVIDENCIA (MAJADAS)	SACATEPEQUEZ	ZAKAT				
	500							
		LAS CHARCAS B						
	600							
		LAS CHARCAS A						
EARLY PRE-CLASSIC	1000			?	?	?		
		AREVALO						
	1500							
	B. C.	?						

Figure 5.1. Chronological table showing various Mexican and, in particular, Teotihuacán-inspired ceramic influences in the Central Highlands of Guatemala at Kaminaljuyu (Valley of Guatemala), Antigua (Valley of Almolongal), and at Lake Amatitlán.

goods. However, such theological or political concepts, in order to be successful and adaptable to different peoples and classes, must have at least certain universally acceptable elements and doctrines that

can transcend cultural, political, ethnic, or class boundaries. Therefore it is apparent that the Teotihuacán religion, like the popular
Hellenistic mystery religions, like Mithraism, Christianity (and
Gnosticism), Islam, or Buddhism, must have possessed, at least
initially, such universally acceptable and eclectic concepts. Otherwise
their rapid diffusion, adaptability, and power of attraction could
never have been so irresistible and so eminently successful.

7. The inherent failure and the ultimate doom and fall of an expansionistic, theocratic society lies in its tendency to develop a nationalistic, frequently corrupt, and intolerant bureaucratic governmental machinery, usually under the hereditary rule of a divine mon-
arch or priest king. Such a totalitarian ruler, in his ambivalent dual-
istic role as King and God of Many Lands, cannot any longer super-
impose the religious concepts over the various alien cultures under
his rule. In other words, *nationalism breeds counternationalism,*
and even universally acceptable religious ideas cannot be diffused
or exported with lasting success and by divine authority alone into
alien or subject countries unless the separate roles of church and
state are clearly marked and well defined. The decline and fall of
Teotihuacán may well be ascribed therefore to the growing secularization, nationalism, and bureaucratic intolerance of its Nahua priest
rulers, a rule that by its nature became increasingly corrupt, slack,
restrictive, tyrannical, and exploitative. As such, it generated only
repugnance, antagonism, and counternationalism instead of its former
prestige and pride and therefore proved to be no longer acceptable
or adaptive either to allies or to alien subject cultures. Such a state of
a culture almost inevitably invites counterrevolutions from its subject
cultures (with various degrees of intensity and violence) and sets into
motion a trend toward the forcible or peaceful secularization and na-
tionalization of all institutions formerly controlled by the absolute authority of the old established priestly bureaucracy and ruling class of
more or less cosmopolitan outlook.

8. The decline and fall of civilization need not necessarily be inevitably precipitated or caused by ecological or economic failures,
but can also be explained by esoteric, nonmaterialistic cultural or
historical events. The decline of Hellenism, the fall of the Roman
Empire, the doom of the Arabic and Ottoman expansions, and the
end of the Teotihuacán may well serve as future models to more detailed studies of such internal cultural changes and events.

APPENDIX

The following archeological checklist attempts to enumerate various types of cultural traits that are assumed to represent abrupt and marked modifications in the essentially self-contained and parochial highland Maya culture patterns of the beginning of the Classic period.[12] The author's conjecture is that in one way or another these changes are indicative of Teotihuacán influences. Also listed are certain popular Preclassic traits like the stela, mushroom, and figurine cults, all of which are believed to have been temporarily discontinued during Middle Classic times, perhaps as a result of Teotihuacán pressure tactics or prohibition. The fact that many of these Preclassic traits gradually reemerge after the fall of Teotihuacán, in somewhat changed forms, to be sure, seems to indicate that at least the core elements of these popular folk or peasant cults of Preclassic origin survived and must have continued to be practiced by some of the Maya village farming communities, which tenaciously clung to their ancient ways beneath a veneer of Teotihuacán culture. They perhaps professed little interest in the Teotihuacán, urban way of life or for those things for which this stood.[13] By Late Classic times, however, when the mastery of Teotihuacán began to fade away, the folk cults that these objects represented made a strong comeback and, once revived, continued their existence throughout the Postclassic, with some of their vestiges surviving as part of the present-day practices of folk-catholicism in highland Guatemala and

[12] For a checklist comparing the similarities and differences between the highland Guatemalan and tropical rainforest lowland Mayas, see Borhegyi, 1964. The reader is also referred to the author's more detailed publications on highland Maya archaeology and settlement patterns presented as syntheses in the *Handbook of Middle American Indians*, II, pt. 1 (see Borhegyi, 1965a, 1965b). For publications describing and illustrating the ceramics, figurines, and lapidary arts of Teothihuacán and their New World distribution, see Linné, 1934; Seler, 1961; and Séjourné, 1966. For the influences of Teotihuacán on Mexican highland cultures, see Linné, 1942. On the impact of Teotihuacán on Zapotec cultures in Oaxaca, see Linné, 1938.

[13] For a more detailed study of the reemergence of the Preclassic Maya folk and peasant cults after the collapse of Teotihuacán in A.D. 650, see Borhegyi, 1956a, 1965a.

Chiapas. As in many other parts of the world, the anonymous peasant masses were apparently little affected by the change in their religious or political masters.

Early and Middle Classic Period (A.D. 250 to 650) Aurora-Esperanza and Amatle phases; Tlamimilolpa (Teo. IIA–III) and Xolalpan (Teo. IIIA) phases.

Late Classic Period (A.D. 650 to 950) Amatle-Pamplona phases; Metepec (Teo. IV) phase

A. *Settlement Pattern & Architecture*
  1. Intensified, extended, and controlled terrace and valley irrigation agriculture (see Borhegyi, 1965a: 19, nn. 19, 20).

A. *Settlement Pattern & Architecture*
  1. Same, extending even on to the hilltops.

  2. Discontinuation of subterranean, bottle-shaped food storage pits in favor of (state-controlled?) elevated wooden silos or *trojes* above ground (see Teotihuacán frescoes depicting the use of such *trojes;* see also Borhegyi, 1965a: 20, n. 5).

  2. *Trojes* and use of large ceramic storage jars exist even today (cf. Borhegyi, 1965a: 32–33, n. 42).

  3. Plaza-oriented, nucleated open-valley settlements with temple mounds surrounding enclosed courts, replace the former *necropoli* layout (cf. Borhegyi, 1956b, 1965b).

  3. Preference for dispersed, but compact, smaller family or clan open-valley or hillslope settlements.

  4. Temple (or burial) mounds decrease in size; urban residential zones appear around the outskirts of ceremonial centers.

  4. Gradual shift away from the large open-valley settlements toward hillslopes and ultimately to hilltops.

  5. Use of Teotihuacán *talud* (slope) and *tablero* (panel) features on the façade of temple mounds (see Kidder, Jennings, & Shook, 1946: 17, figs. 10–11, 107–109; Borhegyi, 1965a: 21, n. 22).

  5. Use of *talud* and *tablero* discontinued; altar mounds, round structures, and colonnades first appear.

6. Discontinuation of adobe structures, beginning of stone (or carved tufa) masonry.

6. Increased use of stone masonry.

7. Appearance of I-shaped, open-ended ball courts with paved playing floors and sloping inner walls and benches (see Borhegyi, 1965a: 21–22, nn. 23, 24).

7. Sunken and *palangana*-type ball courts.

8. Several settlements assume urban size and dimensions, to accomodate population expansion and/or concentrations.

8. Decrease in size of settlements as settlements become more dispersed.

9. Drainage and sewer systems become regular part of urban planning.

9. Continues.

10. Subterranean beehive and circular-shaped community and family sweathouses with concentric benches first appear.[14]

10. Continues.

B. *Burial Customs*
1. Seated (mummy bundle) burials replace the former extended and flexed burials (cf.

B. *Burial Customs*
1. Continues, but extended and flexed burials make a comeback.

[14] The Classic period appearance of subterranean, community and family sweathouses may be of special importance. If indeed the roles of incense burning, and holy water and baptism as ritual purifying agents were essential parts of the soul's acceptance into the Christian and Islamic paradise, and into the Tlalocán of Teotihuacán (see also n. 7), the ritual use of sweathouses both in the Old and New World could have served a similar "soul-cleansing" or purgative purpose for the living and especially for sinners. Perspiring or "sweating-out" sins or sin-caused illnesses is an integral part of the various cathartic religious ceremonies throughout the world. It is very likely that the Teotihuacán-inspired use of community and family sweathouses in Mesoamerica served (and still does) for similar magico-religious cleansing or curative rites. The circular shape of the Classic period subterranean sweathouses in Mesoamerica suggests a close relationship with Quetzalcoatl as Ehecatl, the wind god, whose temples in Late Classic and Post Classic times were frequently constructed in circular form. For a distribution of such round temple structures in the highland Maya area, see Borhegyi, 1965a: 32, n. 41; 44, n. 52.

Borhegyi, 1965a: 22, nn. 26, 27).

2. Dogs included as sacrificial retainers with burials (see Borhegyi, 1965a: 23, n. 29; Kidder, Jennings, & Shook, 1946: 155, fig. 138b). This Teotihuacán-inspired custom perhaps relates to the cult of the dog-headed Xolotl (an alter-ego of Quetzalcoatl), the Hermes-like guide to the underworld.

2. Gradually discontinued.

3. Tombs with horizontal passageways first appear.

3. Continues, but urn burials also appear by end of the period (cf. Borhegyi, 1965a: 32–33, n. 42).

C. *Lapidary Work*
1. Preclassic stela and altar cult and the use of carved protoglyphs diminishes, except on the Pacific coastal slopes.

C. *Lapidary Work*
1. Stela cult with stone altars and carved glyphs reappears on the Pacific coastal slope due to Mexican "Pipil" influence.

2. Monumental lapidary craft on the decline, except on the Pacific coastal slopes.

2. Continues.

3. Popular use of Preclassic effigy mushroomstones and "toad bowls" (miniature and full size), colossal heads, potbellied stone statues, and their associated cults are temporarily discontinued (cf. Borhegyi, 1961a, 1963a, 1965c: For the ritual consumption of hallucinogenic mushrooms and their association with the above cults, see Borhegyi, 1965a: 17–18, n. 16).

3. Carved effigy and plain mushroomstones, "toad bowls," colossal heads of Preclassic reappear, but in somewhat changed forms and with a marked preference for tripod mushroomstones (cf. Borhegyi, 1965a: 36–37, nn. 45, 46, 47).

4. Preclassic use of vertically tenoned stone sculptures is replaced by horizontally tenoned ones (cf. Borhegyi, 1965c).

4. Use of horizontally tenoned stone heads increases.

5. Mexican Gulf Coast–style, carved-stone ball-game paraphernalia, such as yokes (usually plain), *hachas, manoplas,* and spherical stone balls, first appear (cf. Borhegyi, 1963b, 1965c, 1968a, 1968c).

5. Use of Mexican Gulf Coast–style, carved-stone ball-game paraphernalia increases with growing tendency of chthonic symbolism (human and monkey skulls, vultures, reptiles, dissected and decapitated human bodies) (see Borhegyi, 1965a: 36, n. 46).

D. *Ceramics*
1. First appearance of Teotihuacán-type cylindrical tripod vessels with apron covers, slab feet, and Teotihuacán-style carved or painted designs (cf. Kidder, Jennings, & Shook, 1946: 159–170; Borhegyi, 1968b: 228–230).

D. *Ceramics*
1. Gradually replaced by hard-fired, tall cylindrical vases, bowls, and jars.

2. Teotihuacán-style plain or carved polychrome stucco (or in-fresco) decorated vessels (see Rands and Smith, 1965: 127–130).

2. Replaced by red-on-buff or red-and-black-on-orange or buff geometric, anthropomorphic or zoomorphic designs (see Borhegyi, 1965a: 34–35).

3. Thin Orange and Tiquisate A ware effigy and plain vessels (dogs, seated and lying human beings).

3. Replaced by Fine Orange Z and Y wares and by San Juan Plumbate and Tiquisate B wares (see Borhegyi, 1965a: 34–35).

4. Incised, painted, or stucco-decorated two-part human or animal effigy vessels.

4. Gradually diminish.

5. Teotihuacán-type *floreros, candeleros,* and cream pitcher vases (Kidder, Jennings, & Shook, 1946: 202–203, 216).

5. Discontinued.

6. Teotihuacán-type Tlaloc vases with tri-mountain symbolism (cf. Borhegyi, 1950a).

6. Discontinued.

7. Teotihuacán-style rimhead vessels replace Preclassic Maya-

7. The popular Preclassic Maya-style rimhead vessels reemerge

style rimheads (cf. Borhegyi, 1950b; 1951a, 1951b).

in somewhat changed forms (cf. Linné, 1934: 114–115).

8. *Sartenes* roasting dishes (for cacao?) or "frying pans" (for beans?) become popular (cf. Linné, 1934: 184–186).

8. Continues through present day.

9. Popular Preclassic three-pronged censer and its associated cult is temporarily discontinued (cf. Borhegyi, 1951a, 1951b).

9. Popular Preclassic three-pronged censers reemerge in somewhat changed forms and continue to exist to present day.

10. Ladle censers make their first appearance.

10. Continue in changed form, with two or three legs added and decoration in Mixteca-Puebla style (cf. Borhegyi, 1965a: 55).

11. Teotihuacán-style, elaborate, "built-up," two-part censers with funnel-shaped censer covers, resting on tubular or hourglass-shaped receptacles, both lavishly decorated with small applied moldmade *adornos* featuring shell, water, and rain symbolism (cf. Borhegyi, 1960a, 1966b).

11. Use of Teotihuacán-style censers gradually diminishes, replaced by less elaborate, spiked effigy censers and by censers representing seated persons holding containers in their laps (cf. Borhegyi, 1965a: 34–35, nn. 44, 49).

12. Preclassic figurine cult is temporarily discontinued (cf. Borhegyi, 1956a, 1965a: 24–25, n. 32).

12. Preclassic figurine cult reemerges, but most of the figurines are by now moldmade. However, Tiquisate ware figurines continue to resemble Teotihuacán (IIIA and IV) figurine shapes and forms (cf. Borhegyi, 1965a: 34).

13. Popular use of Preclassic effigy whistles is temporarily discontinued (cf. Borhegyi, 1956a, 1965a: 24–25, n. 31).

13. Popular Preclassic effigy whistles reappear but in mold-made forms and continue to exist to present day.

14. Use of flat and roller stamps

14. Flat and roller stamps re-

is temporarily discontinued (cf. Borhegyi, 1950c, 1965a: 25, n. 33, 1965d).

15. Spindle whorls first appear (Kidder, Jennings, & Shook, 1946: 215–216; Linné, 1934: 126–128).

E. *Miscellaneous Objects*
1. Stone barkbeaters (used perhaps to make bark paper, *amatle*, for painted divinatory "books") first appear (cf. Borhegyi, 1965a: 27, n. 36).

2. "Doughnut" stones appear (see Borhegyi, 1965a: 26, n. 35).

3. Jade, shell, and bone crafts are intensified.

4. Increased use of such marine shells as oliva, spondylus, strombus (cf. Borhegyi, 1966b, 1968b).

5. Shark teeth and stingray spines as burial offerings indicate extensive trade with littoral cultures (cf. Borhegyi, 1961b, 1965a: 23, n. 30).

6. Pyrite-encrusted mirrors (see Borhegyi, 1965a: 27, nn. 37, 48; Woodbury, 1965: 172–175).

7. Use of liquid mercury.

8. Use of pottery drums, flutes, and flageolets.

F. *Religion*
1. Various forms of representations, on pottery vessels and

---

appear in somewhat changed shape (cf. Linné, 1934: 125–126), with marked preference for flat, stemmed forms.

15. Continues through present day.

E. *Miscellaneous Objects*
1. Continues.

2. Continues.

3. Continues, with metallurgy (gold and copper ornaments) added by the end of the period.

4. Diminishes.

5. Gradually diminishes.

6. Gradually diminishes.

7. Disappears.

8. Continues (cf. Borhegyi, 1965a: 35).

F. *Religion*
1. Gradually disappear, although representations of such

censers, of such popular Teotihuacán gods as Tlaloc, Quetzalcoatl, Ehecatl, Xolotl, Tezcatlipoca, Xipe, Dios Gordo
(cf. Kidder, Jennings, & Shook,
1946; Borhegyi, 1965a: 28–
30).

Teotihuacán-derived gods as
Tlaloc, Quetzalcoatl, and Xipe
continue in changed forms. Div-
ing god and Jaguar god gain in
importance.

2. Various forms of Teothihuacán religious symbolism depicted on pottery vessels and censers
such as the "reptile's eye motif,"
treble scrolls, tabbed speech
scrolls, dripping rain water,
waves, tri-mountain (volcano?)
symbol, goggle-eyed owls, various forms of shell and marine
life, vines, flowers, and cacao
pods and cacao leaves (cf.
Linné, 1941; von Winning,
1947, 1948, 1949, 1961; Borhegyi, 1966b).

2. Gradually disappear.

3. Child, animal, and other sacrifices to sacred lakes and waterholes, especially at the time of
the corn-planting season (cf.
Borhegyi, 1958a, 1958b, 1959,
1966b).

3. Continues in various changed
forms and survives through
present day, as an important
"Christian" ritual to assure the
fertility of the crops.

6. Commentary: Section I

ERIK K. REED

In my comments I shall discuss not only papers in my section, but others that seem germane to a consideration of theoretical and methodological problems.[1] Interestingly, most of the participants seem favorably inclined toward the possibility that transoceanic voyages offer partial explanations of some features of culture history in pre-Columbian America. Of course, they may not be a statistically valid random sample or truly representative cross-section of Americanists today. But at least those who hold such notions can freely speak out now. Thirty-three years ago, when the Society for American Archaeology was being organized, surely no such heresies could safely have been uttered publicly. In fact, the brief paper by W. C. McKern, in the third volume of *American Antiquity*, which proposed the Asiatic origin of Woodland pottery of North America, was bold and radical for 1937.

As a former employee of Mr. Harold Gladwin and as a fellow-traveler (literally, that is) of Thor Heyerdahl, I am glad to encounter

---

[1] Stephan F. Borhegyi's paper was originally assigned to another section. For technical reasons I regrettably did not receive the revised manuscript soon enough to include it in these comments. I would say from hearing the original presentation that the paper is exciting and worthwhile, but in subject matter it deals with somewhat different aspects of the contact problem than those I discuss here.

increasing open-mindedness and imagination and particularly grati-
fied at recognition that oceans may have been highways, not always
barriers, ever since the development of navigation in sea-going vessels
a few thousand years ago.

The first paper in Section II makes this point clear in some detail.
It is a fine, thorough, yet imaginative treatment, establishing firmly
the probability—not mere possibility—of transpacific voyages, primarily eastbound, over a long period. The speculation Doran gently
brings forward in connection with the voyage of a Chinese fleet into
the Pacific in 219 B.C. is daring but not palpably unreasonable. Surprisingly, there is little mention in the whole symposium of the far
earlier material in Ecuador, also discovered by the late Emilio
Estrada, indicating contact from ancient Japan; I shall return to the
Valdivia complex shortly.

Ekholm speaks of the isolationism that long afflicted and crippled
American archaeology. Probably this is a better, more general term
than Doran's (and Carl Sauer's) thalassophobia. It has been more
than that, a localism—or, at most, regionalism—that in the past often
tended to see independent, local development in each culture province or in even more sharply restricted areas, with separate invention
of various traits in different regions postulated.

In contrast with that approach, the trend in recent years has increasingly been toward emphasis on interrelationships and on diffusion of both specific elements and general influences. Thus, in considering Middle American civilization, Ekholm sees an oikoumene
comprising several distinct but fundamentally connected regions,
with continuous interaction, active widespread trading, and considerable traveling. Contact by sea between Middle America and western
South America has received attention lately and will come up again
later in this symposium. In the southwestern United States, the basic
importance of Middle American influence has been emphasized in
recent years, for the Pueblo area as well as for the obviously Mexican-
derived Hohokam culture of southern Arizona.

Ekholm brings out the limitations and pitfalls of archaelogical evidence. This need not discourage us too much; the situation is not
hopeless, as long as perceptive interpretations like Ekholm's are
offered. Now, he also speaks of the lack of "hard" evidence of transpacific voyages and contacts. The ceramics of the Valdivia complex,
on the south coast of Ecuador at about 3200 B.C., probably the oldest

known pottery in the New World, resemble the contemporary Middle Jomon ware of Neolithic Japan so closely that a direct transfer by a voyage around the North Pacific from southern Japan to Ecuador has been postulated.

In discussion from the floor during the session, Jon Muller pointed out numerous discrepancies in the Valdivia-Jomon comparisons and asserted that the case was not adequately supported by the evidence (as he has published; see Muller, 1968). Presumably he is correct on specific details cited, but the over-all resemblance is too striking for me to believe it could be sheer coincidence. Incidentally, also, the small series of crania from a Valdivia context are not of the characteristic early physical type of the Americas, not at all "Otamid" or "Australoid"—undeformed brachycephals with little development of brow ridges, they seem to resemble, surprisingly enough, not the Ainu, but medieval Japanese or, possibly, Indonesians.

In the first paper, Stephen Jett offers a lengthy compilation bringing together a variety of pertinent material, with a number of penetrating observations. He manifests a grasp of the essentials of ocean voyaging and the antiquity of seaworthy vessels, and of how to look at trait distributions when the sea is involved. A topic of interest Jett mentions that could stand elaboration is the matter of Spanish voyages across the Pacific: (1) beginning with Magellan in 1521, several westward crossings were made from America to the East Indies, but not until Urdañeta's discovery of the Japan Current route and the prevailing westerlies at 35° N in 1565 were the Spaniards able to sail back eastward successfully to America; (2) from 1568 on, to about 1810, the annual Manila galleon regularly sailed from Acapulco straight west, touching at the southern tip of Guam and continuing right on to the Philippines, then returning by the Japan Current around the North Pacific to the coast of California—traveling well south of the Hawaiian Islands outbound and far north of them on the return, not knowing of them until Captain Cook's discovery.

Jett summarizes the ethnobotanical situation, bringing out the tenuousness of much of the evidence, and the few, and generally dubious, alleged finds of Old World artifacts in supposedly pre-Columbian contexts. Various points of view on diffusion of cultural features are discussed. Similar words for certain types of watercraft in some Asiatic languages and in parts of South America are mentioned. Comparisons that have been made between Asiatic and

American mythologies, calendars, magic, and religions are cited. Theoretical views and principles on diffusion and independent invention receive further attention, particularly in connection with such items or processes of material culture as barkcloth and metallurgy.

Finally the possibilities—and the difficulties—of physical anthropology are taken up. Here Jett mentions a new and important study of his own, in which he found certain Indonesian groups and certain tropical forest tribes of South America to be so closely alike physically that he postulates an Indonesian migration to South America. In reading the final version of the paper, 1 could not recall having heard this in Jett's original presentation at the meeting, which reminded me of a bit from the latter that I do not now find in the former—a neatly put comparison to criminal investigation, which must consider means, opportunity, and motive and which often must proceed on the basis of interpretation of evidence rather than conclusive proof. We are not so badly off, really, in comparison to the historian working from documentary sources. His material is either hearsay, which is not admissible in court, or eyewitness report, which any lawyer or police officer can tell you is highly untrustworthy. In archaeology we are working with circumstantial evidence, the best kind.

The paper by David Kelley presents clearly and concisely important basic theoretical considerations, bearing particularly on the difficulties in recognizing stimulus diffusion and pointing out the unreasonableness of insisting on exact and complete parallels in cases of probable diffusion. He rightly emphasizes acceptance of innovations, and their modification, and general aspects of acculturation, rather than the radical dichotomy so often indicated between diffusion and evolution.

More surprising and heretical than renewed consideration of transpacific voyaging are the comparatively few serious and sensible presentations in behalf of transatlantic contacts before the fifteenth century A.D. (aside from the well-known Viking settlements in Greenland and less clearly understood landings in Vinland, on or close to the mainland of northeastern North America, between 1000 and 1350). At this juncture the thought strikes me that it would not be illogical, whether or not the evidence really supports this, to envision a party of advanced folk from over the sea, or a single black-skinned Quetzalcoatl-figure, arriving without seeds but initiating agriculture in the New World by domesticating plants recognizably close to some they or he had previously known—to wit, *Canavalia* beans and white-flowered gourds, and perhaps cotton—the distinctively American plants being brought into cultivation only later. (For a discussion of diffusion—especially plant diffusion—see Schwerin, 1970.)

The paper by M. D. W. Jeffreys (Section III) revives a claim previously brought forward some twenty years ago, which I had thought had been disposed of, or at least widely disregarded. But it is desirable to re-examine such proposals, in the light of recent developments, changing attitudes, and increasing quantities of pertinent evidence available. On this one, however, I feel the case still is undemonstrated. This paper is based largely on documents and traditions. The Portuguese and Chinese references cited are post-1500, with only one exception, and it is merely opinion, not evidence, to state that maize could not have spread as rapidly as post-Columbian introduction to the Old World would necessitate. Other contributions from the New World spread with almost comparable rapidity. For example, turkeys were introduced to Europe by the Spaniards a few years after their conquest of Mexico in 1519–1521, and, though little known until about 1530, were being raised in large flocks in parts of western Europe by 1560–1570; a turkey, surely drawn from a living model, is depicted in a miniature painting from Mogul India under the Emperor Jahangir (1605–1625).

Admittedly, the apparent references to maize as a well-established crop in China and southern Asia come so fast and thick after 1500 as to make almost incredible the accepted idea of post-Columbian spread. The possibility of misinterpretation then must be considered. Reliance on what should be the proper meaning of one or another Portuguese word for some cultivated plant used by a sixteenth-century historian or administrator strikes me as unsafe, though a good case is made for Pigafetta's "miglio" in the Philippines in 1521. The one citation from an earlier period I find unconvincing; there should be, if any at all, numerous references instead of one dubious one. The various Turkish and Italian words for maize impress me even less as evidence for events of four hundred to five hundred years ago. Again, consider "turkey fowl." Maize was, I understand, being raised in Portugal by 1515.

However, if the two identifications of plant remains from archaeological contexts of the thirteenth or fourteenth century and early fifteenth century in India are correct, then Jeffreys is right despite the weakness of his linguistic, historical, and traditional evidence, and at least some of this material is valid as given.

Finally, the paper by Jon Muller treats of important theoretical approaches, basic to this or any similar discussion. It does not apply these principles to the specific problems of this symposium, and so I have no comments on it beyond remarking that Muller's cautions and guidelines should be kept in mind in all such investigations.

To conclude, perhaps the following still is pertinent after the passage of a hundred years: "Certainly there is nothing unreasonable or improbable in the supposition that the countries on the Western Mediterranean . . . communicated with America in very remote antiquity; nor is it improbable that there was communication across the Pacific. The objections raised against it come chiefly from the gratuitous assumption that such enterprise was impossible in ancient times, and from the influence of thought and imagination preoccupied, perhaps unconsciously, by an invincible determination to deny it" (Baldwin, 1869).

SECTION II

This section on transoceanic contacts begins with a paper by Edwin Doran discussing possible means of transport across the Pacific and ends with papers by Robert A. Kennedy and Alice B. Kehoe doing the same for the Atlantic. Daniel R. Beirne traces certain material cultural items, axes and adzes, that appear in both the Old and the New Worlds. George F. Carter is concerned with the possible pre-Columbian entry of the chicken into the New World, and John L. Sorenson discusses the significance of a number of cultural features shared by the two hemispheres.

Two papers relate to presumed specific examples of diffusion. Herbert C. Taylor examines the Viking data on Vinland and suggests certain lines for further work. Basil C. Hedrick reexamines the Quetzalcoatl story and concludes that this legend, at least, cannot be used to demonstrate interhemispheric contact.

The summary by Clinton R. Edwards not only deals with many problems raised by the various authors in this section but also adds additional critical evaluation on methods of transport.

7. The Sailing Raft as a Great Tradition

EDWIN DORAN, JR.

The papers presented at the contacts symposium touch only a portion of the great variety of data that must be considered in evaluating the possibilities and probabilities for transpacific diffusion before Columbus. Sailing rafts are only a small aspect of the problem but have some value as evidence. Others have considered at length the idea that the rafts of Ecuador and of coastal Asia probably are connected genetically (for example, Hornell, 1931; Ling, 1956; Estrada and Meggers, 1961; and Edwards, 1965); this paper adds little in the way of new evidence on rafts as such.

It is hoped, however, that two limited objectives can be reached. By examining models of boat antiquity and distribution that are well documented and then arguing by analogy, perhaps the plausibility of considering rafts on opposite sides of the Pacific as one connected distribution can be enhanced. Further exposition of the seaworthiness and good sailing characteristics of rafts may assuage the thalassophobia that has been one of the most critical deterrents to rational evaluation of common traits on opposite sides of the Pacific. Most anthropologists have not been sailors, a fact that may have contributed to their hesitation in admitting to contacts across the oceans.

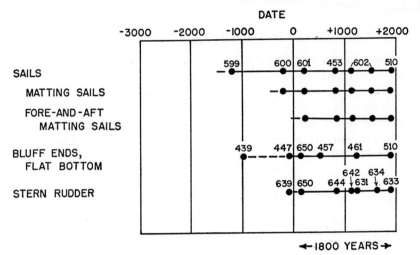

Figure 7.1. Historical development of Chinese craft. (Numbers refer to pages in Needham, 1971.)

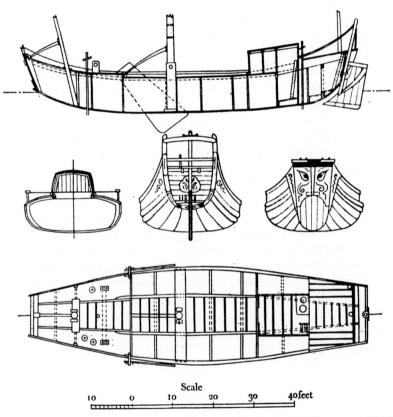

Figure 7.2. Typical Chinese junk. (Drawing by G. R. G. Worcester, 1966: 29. Courtesy of Mr. Worcester and the Science Museum, London.)

Let us begin with Chinese craft, which offer perhaps the simplest and most clearly documented model (fig. 7.1). Although the Chinese character *fan,* meaning sail, dates from earlier than 1000 B.C. and matting sails are described in earlier Han times, it is not until after A.D. 200 that a definitive text permits us to assert without question that fore-and-aft matting sails were in use in China (Needham, 1971: 599–601). The typical shape of Chinese craft, relatively flat-bottomed and with bluff bow and stern (fig. 7.2), is foreshadowed by the shape of the Shang dynasty radical for boat (Needham, 1971: 439). Again, however, a millennium must pass before conclusive evidence is at hand, in this case two models, one wooden and a later one of pottery, that were excavated from Han tombs of about 100 B.C. and A.D. 100 respectively (Needham, 1971: 477, 650). The shape of the vessels, with transom bulkhead and gallery extending aft, and a trapeziform, balanced stern rudder on the latter, constitute proof of the full development of the typical Chinese model by this date. Characteristic Chinese craft have been in use at least two thousand years and during that period spread over the area shown in figure 7.3,[1] perhaps two thousand miles in widest extent.

For millennia European craft could be identified by a complex of traits: single mast, square sail, quarter rudders, inserted frames, and a basic skeleton of keel, stempost, and sternpost (fig. 7.4). The single mast with square sail is depicted on Egyptian pottery of about 3000 B.C. and continued as the classical means of propulsion until about A.D. 1400, when multiple masts became common. The quarter rudder, a steering device attached to the after quarter of the ship and often doubled, one on each quarter, has as long a history. It was replaced by the stern rudder about A.D. 1400 also (fig. 7.5).

Less certainty is possible about the construction techniques and interior structure of ships. Paintings and drawings are of little assistance; we must depend on descriptions, models, and, latterly, marine archaeology for information. In contrast with modern practice, ships through most of European history were built plank by plank, the edges carefully tenoned and dowelled together and the frames or ribs then shaped and inserted to provide the necessary

[1] All the maps in this article are based on Map 101M of the Goode Base Maps Series, Department of Geography, the University of Chicago. Coypright by the University of Chicago and used by permission of the publisher.

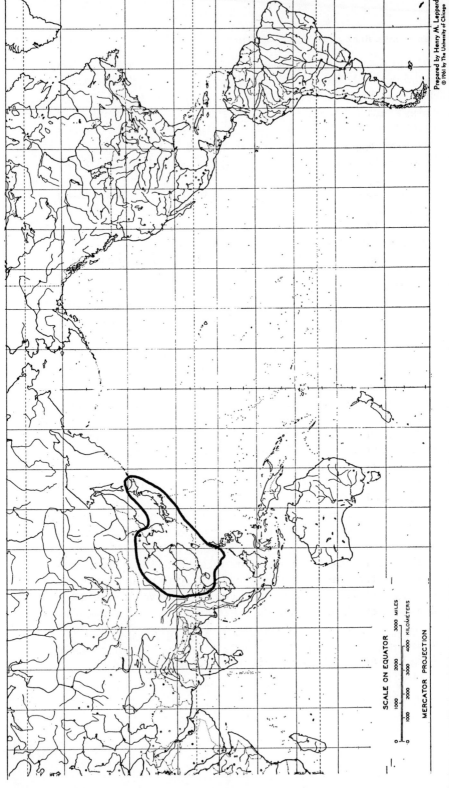

Prepared by Henry M. Leppard
© 1961 by The University of Chicago

SCALE ON EQUATOR

MERCATOR PROJECTION

Figure 7.2. Distribution of Chinese craft, A.D. 100–1900. (Doran 1967: 42, 46; Needham 1971: Paris, 1955: map 2; Suder, 1930: 71.)

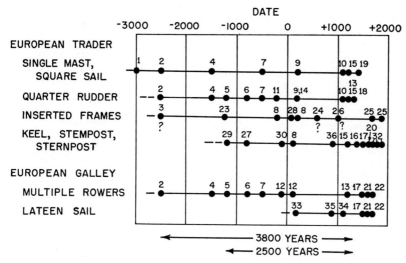

Figure 7.4. Historical development of European craft. (Numbers refer to sources listed in Appendix A.)

strength. There is some difference of opinion on the degree to which the Egyptians framed their vessels (see Casson, 1964: 23; cf. Marx, 1947: 169), but use of frames by Minoan times appears to be generally accepted. Tenoned planks taken from a Mediterranean wreck of about 1200 B.C. provide a reasonably firm minimal beginning date for this technique, which in places has endured to the present (Bass, 1963a: 243; Hasslöf, 1963: 243). Keel, stempost, and sternpost are also generally accepted as having been in use since about 1200 B.C. The history of European galleys is much the same. The only complexity enters with the partial substitution of lateen sails for square sails about A.D. 200.

The documented continuous history of this distinctive ship type thus extends certainly over a period of 2,500 years, and its recognizable antecedents existed for an additional 1,300 years. The antiquity of the skeletal framework is the only uncertainty, and archaeology may provide more data on this in the future. The distribution of European craft, a maximum that includes all points of use at any time during nearly four millennia, is shown in figure 7.6.

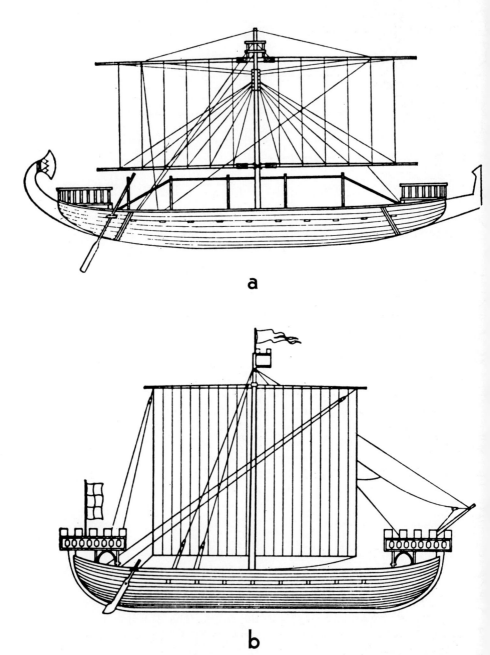

Figure 7.5. Typical European craft. *a.* 1500 B.C. (Canby, 1963: 14). *b*, A.D. 1284 (Canby, 1963: 30). (From Courtland Canby, 1963, *A History of Ships and Seafaring*. Courtesy of Hawthorne Books, Inc.)

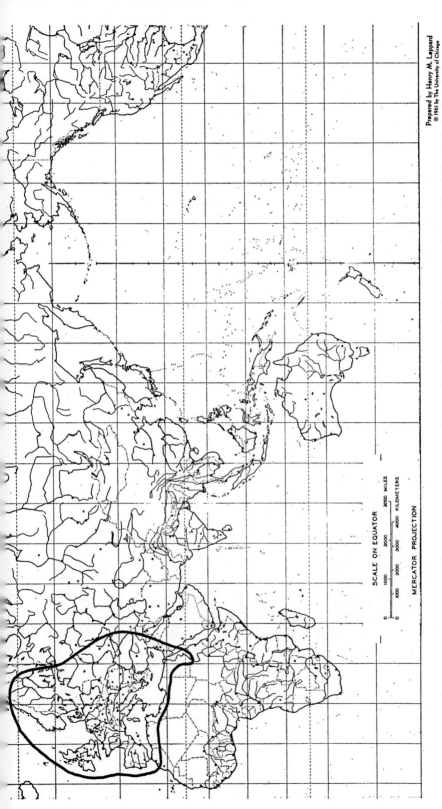

Figure 7.6. Distribution of European craft, 1200 B.C. to A.D. 1300. (Anderson, 1963; Casson, 1964; Hornell, 1964; Suder, 1930.)

SCALE ON EQUATOR

MILES

KILOMETERS

MERCATOR PROJECTION

Prepared by Henry M. Leppard
© 1961 by The University of Chicago

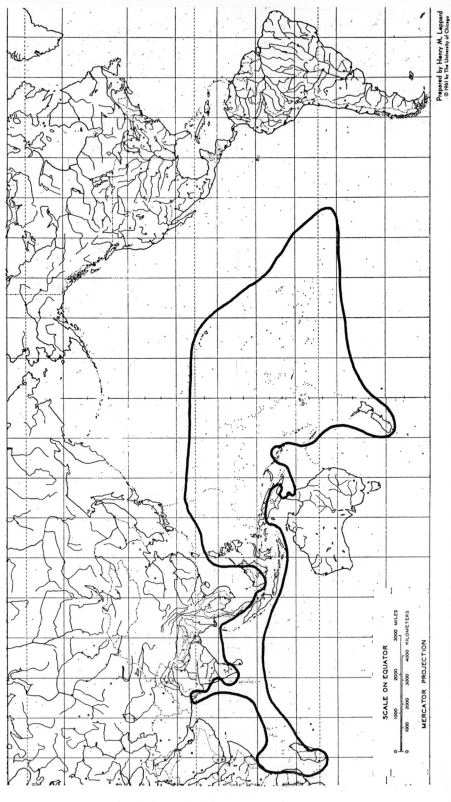

Prepared by Henry M. Leppard
© 1961 by The University of Chicago

SCALE ON EQUATOR

1000   2000   3000 MILES

1000 2000 3000 4000 KILOMETERS

MERCATOR PROJECTION

Figure 7.7. Present distribution of outriggers. (Greenhill, 1956: 57; Hornell, 1946: end map: Suder, 1930: 79.)

The two complexes sketched are the best examples we have of the manner in which boat types arise and diffuse. The data result from centuries of maritime detective work, made relatively easy by the clues available in cultures that have been literate for thousands of years. Even now, despite the accumulated detail, there is much that remains unknown. Only in the last decade have we suddenly realized that ships in the West have been built for only a few centuries according to techniques we once thought age-old. Shell construction—sewing or pinning planks together into boat form before inserting the framework—has been the dominant mode of construction for most of history.

Despite obvious imperfections, a useful model emerges from this discussion. A boat type is a coherent, recognizable entity, a cultural pattern, a significant portion of a great tradition. Once developed, a type spreads gradually over a wide, contiguous area. Boat types are conservative features in which major changes are quite infrequent; they seem to endure for millennia in essentially unchanged form.

Let us begin to use this model by deducing what we can from a map of the distribution of outrigger devices (fig. 7.7). Since we are dealing here with peoples who are largely illiterate, the evidence is very scanty, but there are some C-14 dates and other data. The only early time fix is the well-known outrigger ships of Borobudur, about A.D. 800, an advanced type that must be quite a late part of the story (Hornell, 1923: 218). Although the eastern and western extremities of this distribution may have been reached less than two thousand years ago, it should be a safe assumption, based on the distributions already examined, that outriggers constitute a single cultural tradition that begins several thousand years ago, probably in Southeast Asia.

There is an additional hypothesis, largely speculative. Underlying both the European and Chinese boat traditions, there seems to be an extremely ancient sewn-plank tradition (fig. 7.8) that extends all the way across the Old World and has some tantalizingly possible extensions in Chile and California (Casson, 1963: 258; Wright, 1964: 91). This hypothesis will be accepted or discarded only after a great deal of future work in archaeology.

As we did with outriggers, let us now look at what we know about rafts and see what results when the model is applied. The world distribution of rafts is presented in figure 7.9. Somewhat arbitrarily, the

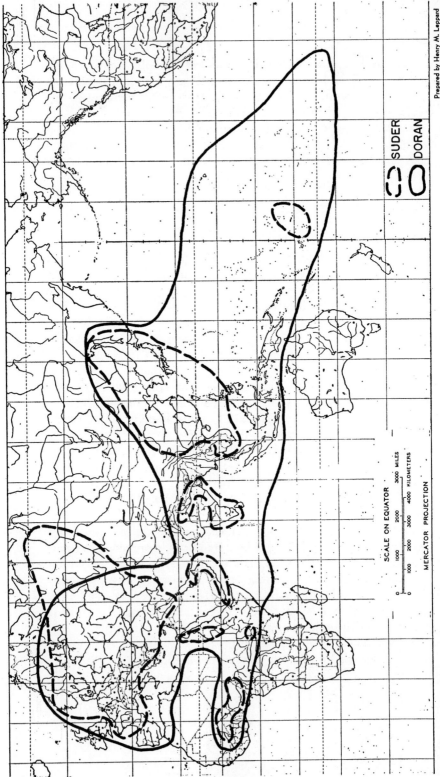

SUDER

DORAN

SCALE ON EQUATOR

1000   2000   3000 MILES

1000   2000   3000   4000 KILOMETERS

MERCATOR PROJECTION

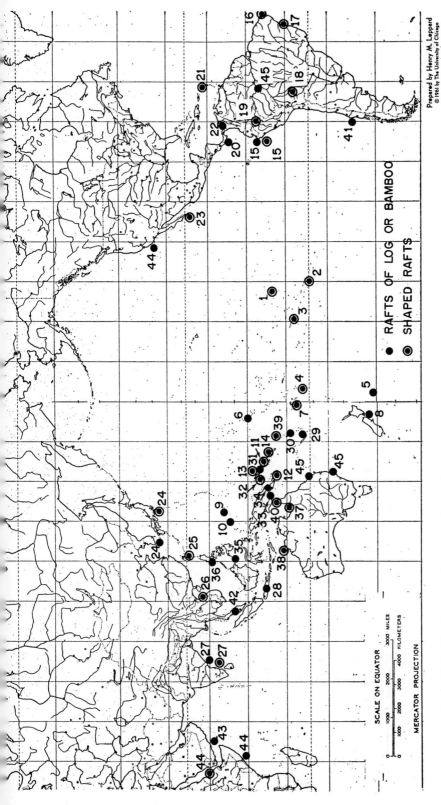

Figure 7.9. Distribution of rafts used on salt water, present and past. (Numbers refer to sources in Appendix B.)

RAFTS OF LOG OR BAMBOO

SHAPED RAFTS

SCALE ON EQUATOR

1000   2000   3000 MILES

1000 2000 3000 4000 KILOMETERS

MERCATOR PROJECTION

Prepared by Henry M. Leppard
© 1961 by The University of Chicago

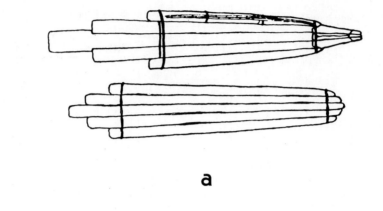

a

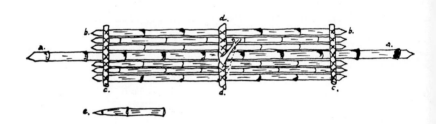

b

Figure 7.10. Shaped rafts from *a*, India (after Hornell, 1923: 172), and *b*, New Ireland (after Bell, 1949: 211).

ambatch rafts of Africa and various reed rafts (Mesopotamia, Peru, Lower California) are excluded, as are the many riverine log and bamboo rafts of interior Asia. In equally arbitrary fashion several Amazonian fresh-water rafts are included. Essentially all rafts used on salt water are located. It should be noted that rafts are not just a bunch of logs or bamboos tied together in random fashion (fig. 7.10). There is a very wide distribution of carefully shaped rafts, either varied in length of logs or tapered by arranging all butt ends of log or bamboo in the same direction.

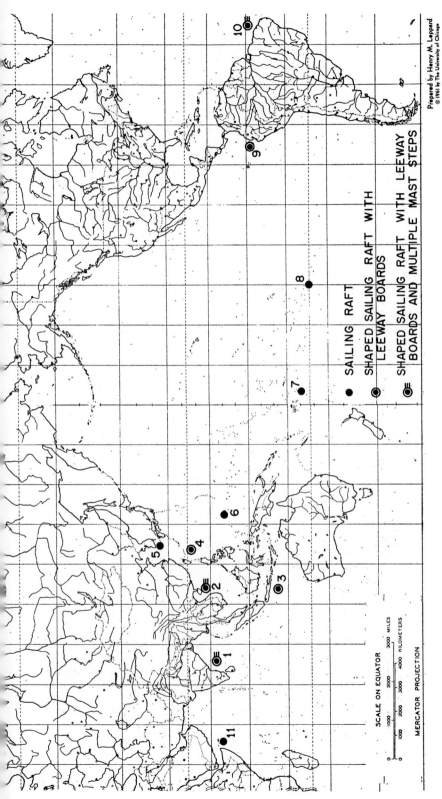

SAILING RAFT

SHAPED SAILING RAFT WITH
LEEWAY BOARDS

SHAPED SAILING RAFT WITH LEEWAY
BOARDS AND MULTIPLE MAST STEPS

SCALE ON EQUATOR

1000   2000   3000 MILES

1000 2000   3000   4000 KILOMETERS

MERCATOR PROJECTION

Prepared by Henry M. Leppard
© 1961 by The University of Chicago

Figure 7.11. Distribution of sailing rafts, present and past. (Numbers refer to sources in Appendix C.)

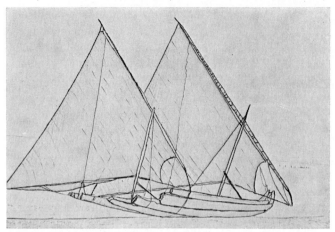

Figure 7.12. Raft of the Coromandel coast, India. (After Hornell, 1946: pl. 11.)

Figure 7.13. Raft of Borobudur in Java. (Krom, 1920–1922: pl. 22.)

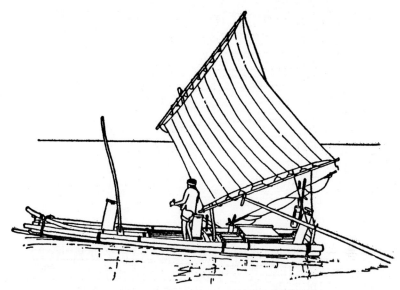

Figure 7.14. Raft of Annam. (Ling, 1956: pl. 9)

The distribution of sailing rafts is indicated in figure 7.11. Leeway boards, which are thrust down to prevent sideward movement and thus permit the raft to make headway in a windward direction, are found in at least six locations—Coromandel, Java, Annam, Formosa, Ecuador, and Brazil. These are emphasized because it is the combination of the raft's flotation and sails and leeway boards that produces a craft capable of proceeding in any direction for almost unlimited periods of time.

A quick look at these rafts will permit some comparisons. Figure 7.12 illustrates Coromandel rafts, which inhibit leeway by means of two leeboards and a steering paddle (Hornell, 1946: 66). On the stupa of Borobudur in Java, a panel illustrates what seems to be a raft with sailors fore and aft manipulating daggerboards as they assist in the rescue of a man threatened by a sea monster (fig. 7.13). Figures 7.14 and 7.15 may be taken together because of their proximity (Annam and Formosa), their use of bamboo as construction material, and their multiple daggerboards (Paris, 1955: 59 ff.; Ling, 1956). Figure 7.16, an old drawing taken from Spilbergen, is probably the best approximation of the aboriginal form of Ecuadorian rafts

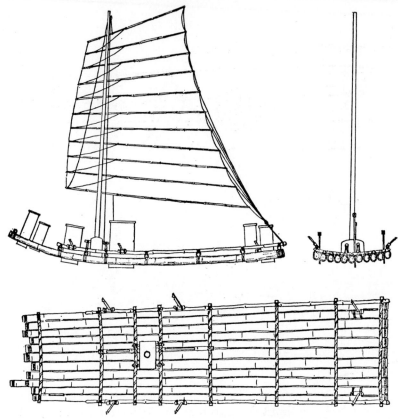

Figure 7.15. Raft of Formosa. (Ling, 1956: pl. 2.)

Figure 7.16. Raft of Ecuador. (Spilbergen, 1619. Reproduced in Heyerdahl, 1952: pl. 67.)

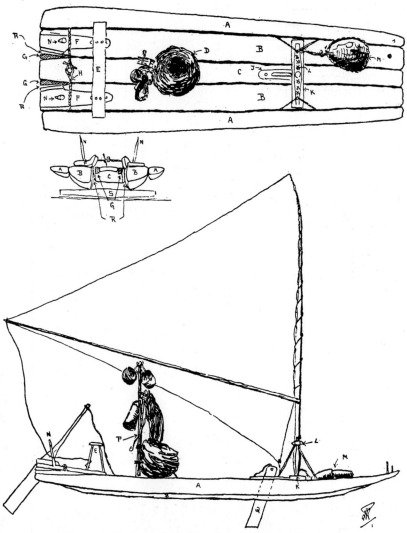

Figure 7.17. Raft of Brazil. (Lane-Poole, 1940: 334.)

(Heyerdahl, 1952: pl. 67; Edwards, 1965: 61 ff.). Multiple dagger-boards can be noted by careful inspection. Figure 7.17 illustrates a Brazilian raft, the jangada, with its single daggerboard (Lane-Poole, 1940; another good discussion of the jangada is found in Hornell, 1946: 82 ff.).[2]

---

[2] Let me digress to note by belief that the jangada , the sailing raft of Brazil,

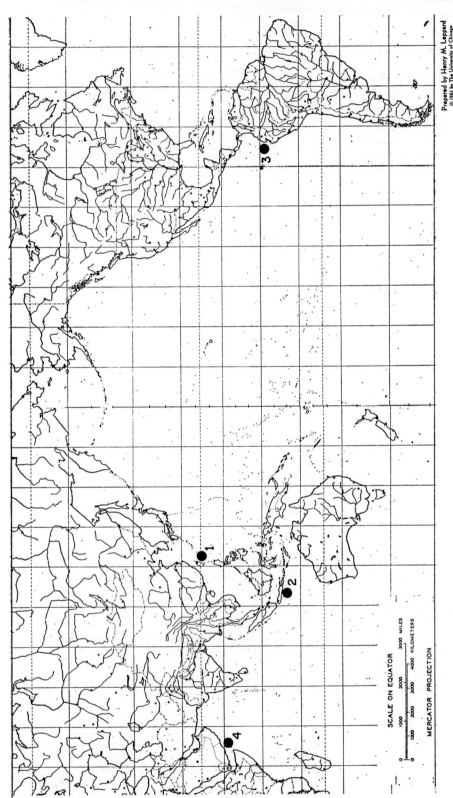

Figure 7.18. Known pre-Columbian sailing rafts. (*1*, Ling, 1956: 47; *2*, Krom, 1920–1922: pl. 22; *3*, Edwards, 1960: 384; 1965: 107; *4*,

Prepared by Henry M. Leppard
© 1961 by The University of Chicago

SCALE ON EQUATOR

MERCATOR PROJECTION

Finally, in figure 7.18, we have the world distribution of sailing rafts that are unquestionably pre-Columbian in time. Fortunately the extremes of raft distribution are documented. Although unproven in detail, there is a very strong indication that the entire raft complex is also pre-Columbian.

Two maps already cited are now superimposed for comparison (fig. 7.19). If the model of boat traditions derived from the Chinese and European examples carries conviction, then the outrigger distribution can be considered a genetically related distribution of great antiquity. And if that is the case, then it should require little further stretch of the imagination to conclude the same for the raft tradition. From the areas occupied by each, it would seem that both the outrigger and the raft are much older than either the Chinese or European traditions, and these we know to have minimal ages of two to four thousand years.

The second objective mentioned earlier—that is, to emphasize the seaworthiness and excellent sailing characteristics of rafts—may now be considered. The *Kon-Tiki* voyage by Heyerdahl from Peru to the Tuamotus is well-known proof of the possibility of drifting across this particular course (Heyerdahl, 1952). Less known, but more spectacular, are the two drift voyages made by de Bisschop between 1956 and 1958 (Danielsson, 1960). From Tahiti he and companions drifted and sailed more or less poleward to 35° south latitude, then east almost to the Juan Fernández Islands, a distance of over five thousand miles in over six months' time. From southern Chile via Callao in Peru, they drifted north and west on another raft until they were wrecked on Manihiki some six months and seven thousand miles later. A similar distance across the northern Pacific would take one from Japan to California, a voyage that may have been made many times. Of sixty cases of inadvertent drifts of Japanese junks into the Pacific, at least a half dozen reached the coast of America between Sitka and the Columbia River and another half dozen were wrecked on the Mexican coast or encountered just offshore (Brooks, 1875: 53–59; Nelson, 1962). Survivors of such drift voyages were not un-

---

is post-Columbian in origin. The name itself is Tamil, derived from Sanskrit, and has been associated with the Portuguese since at least 1600 (*OED*, 1933: V, 550). In addition, multiple steps are provided for the mast, a trait found also only in India and Annam, where the most complex of all sailing rafts are located.

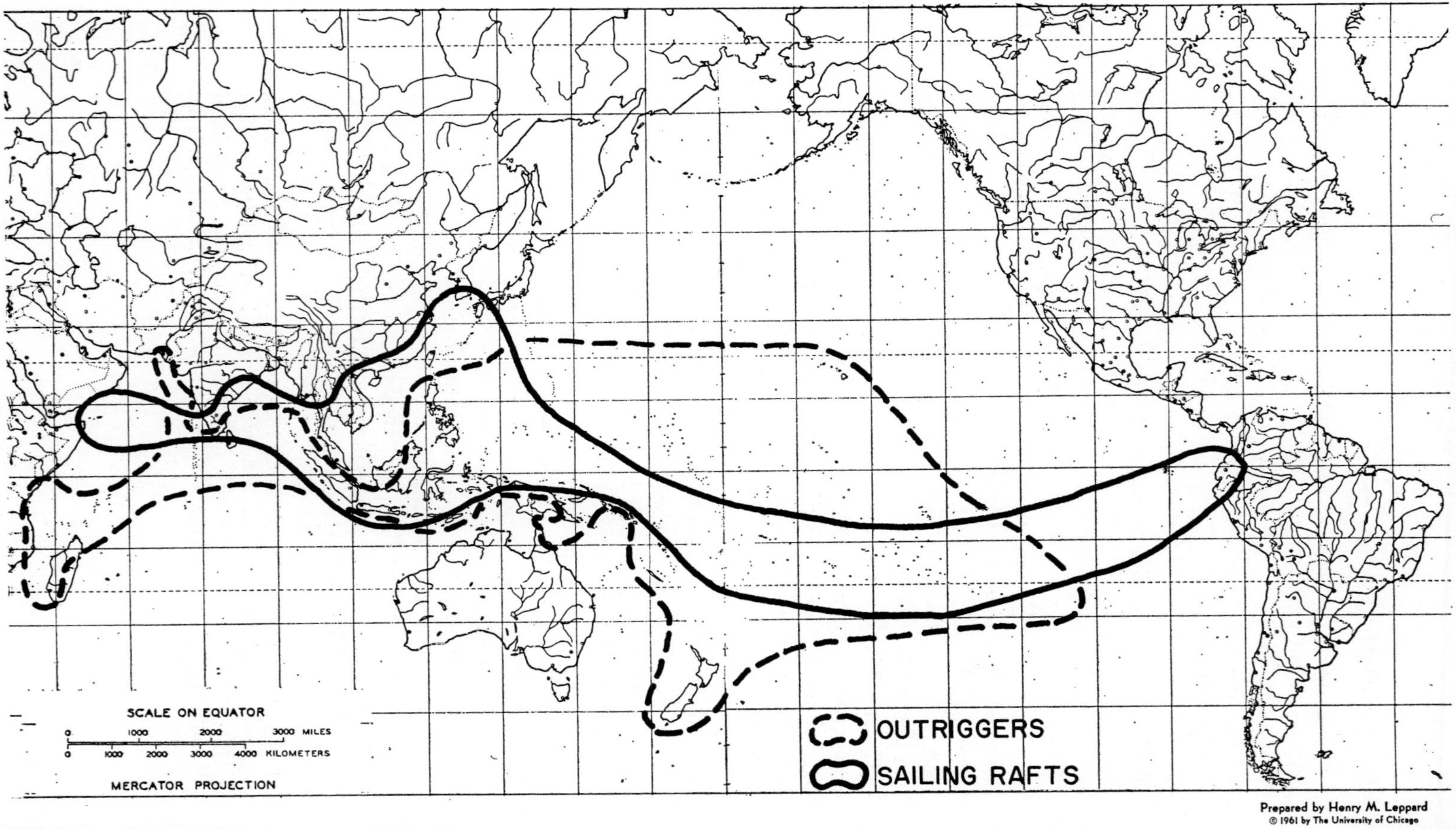

Prepared by Henry M. Leppard
© 1961 by The University of Chicago

OUTRIGGERS

SAILING RAFTS

SCALE ON EQUATOR

1000   2000   3000 MILES

1000   2000   3000   4000 KILOMETERS

MERCATOR PROJECTION

Fig. 7.10. *Comparison of outrigger and sailing-raft distributions*

common, and Japanese slaves were held by Salmon Indians of the northwest coast of America when they first were visited by whites (Brooks, 1875: 54). Drift voyages between Asia and America not only are clearly possible but actually have occurred repeatedly in historic time. In view of the ability of rafts to sail close-hauled against the wind in remakably effective fashion, a phenomenon noted repeatedly and with great surprise by early Western mariners who encountered rafts off the coast of Ecuador and Peru (Edwards, 1965: 73–77), an even greater feasibility for early transpacific raft voyages can be inferred. There appears to be no question that rafts could have crossed the Pacific, repeatedly and in appreciable numbers.

The likelihood that such voyages did indeed occur was increased by Estrada and Meggers' (1961) discovery of a cluster of probable Asiatic traits in an Ecuadorian site, dated at about 200 B.C. Although these traits (house types, net sinkers, coolie yoke) occur widely in Southeast and East Asia, each of them also is known specifically to have occurred in early Han dynasty China. This leads to my last point, which I advance simply as pleasant speculation.

In a period during which there was much concern to locate new medicinal drugs, one Hsü Fu received permission and an "enormous" subsidy from the emperor of China to search for drugs in the Eastern Ocean (Needham, 1971: 552, 3). A fleet (which may well have been rafts) and some three thousand young men and women of good character were assembled, and in 219 B.C. Hsü Fu and his company sailed east into the ocean, never to return.[3]

The nearly exact juxtaposition in time of early Han traits in Ecuador with a historically documented voyage of no return by early Han people into the Pacific is intriguing. I am well aware, however, that this will be insufficient to the logical positivist until he finds C-14–dated ideographs in Ecuador that state, "Hsü Fu was here."

In summary, our model of boat types, based on the Chinese and European traditions, is one of great conservatism, very slow rates of change, and rather slow rates of diffusion. If applied to outriggers, which are widely accepted as a single, diffusion tradition, the model

---

[3] Although it is more commonly accepted that Hsü Fu sailed to Japan (Hsieh, 1967: 88–89), "nevertheless it may be almost equally likely that the story of Hsü Fu's disappearance conceals one voyage at least to the American continent" (Needham, 1971: 533).

suggests a very ancient and long-continued spreading of the out-rigger idea. By analogy we arrive at the same result when we examine rafts. The ocean gap that has been such a barrier to acceptance of the derivation of American traits from the Old World is a lesser obstacle when the seaworthiness of rafts, their sailing ability, and the fortitude of man are demonstrated as adequate for transpacific crossings. By analogy with the better-known models, and considering their striking similarities, the sailing rafts of the Old World and the New World may be considered as one widely distributed tradition of great antiquity.

APPENDIX A

European Types: Sources for Figure 7.4

1 Casson, 1964: 19
2 Casson, 1964: 20
3 Casson, 1964: 23
4 Casson, 1964: 24
5 Casson, 1964: 29
6 Casson, 1964: 30
7 Casson, 1964: 44
8 Casson, 1964: 47
9 Casson, 1964: 48
10 Casson, 1964: 62
11 Casson, 1964: 38
12 Casson, 1964: 40
13 Casson, 1964: 41
14 Casson, 1964: 55
15 Casson, 1964: 64, 65
16 Casson, 1964: 68
17 Casson, 1964: 69, 71
18 Casson, 1964: 76

19 Casson, 1964: 77
20 Casson, 1964: 107
21 Casson, 1964: 121
22 Casson, 1964: 122
23 Bass, 1963a: 243
24 Bass, 1963b: 156
25 Hasslöf, 1963: 172
26 Hasslöf, 1966: 137, pl. 8
27 Lethbridge, 1956: 564
28 Marsden, 1965: 61
29 Marx, 1947: 169
30 Throckmorton, 1964: 206
31 Needham, 1971: 635–636
32 Chapelle, 1935: 21, 102, 294
33 Casson, 1956: 5; 1966: 199–200
34 Casson, 1964: 73
35 Anderson, 1963: 102, 103
36 Casson, 1964: 58, 60

APPENDIX B

Rafts: Sources for Figure 7.9

1 Hornell, 1936: 48
2 Hornell, 1936: 93
3 Hornell, 1936: 143
4 Hornell, 1936: 274
5 Hornell, 1936: 219
6 Hornell, 1936: 355
7 Hornell, 1936: 330
8 Hornell, 1936: 217
9 Hornell, 1936: 412

10 Hornell, 1936: 435
11 Haddon, 1937: 114
12 Haddon, 1937: 241
13 Nelson, 1961: 184
14 Brindley, 1926: 444
15 Edwards, 1960: 383
16 Lane-Poole, 1940: 334
17 Nelson, 1961: 169
18 Nelson, 1961: 168

19 Nelson, 1961: 168

20 Nelson, 1961: 170

21 Nelson, 1961: 170

22 Nelson, 1961: 171

23 Nelson, 1961: 172

24 Nishimura, 1925: 26, 62

25 Ling, 1956: 27

26 Paris, 1955: map 1

27 Hornell, 1946: 61, 65

28 Krom, 1920–1922: pl. 22

29 Haddon, 1937: 13

30 Haddon, 1937: 24

31 Haddon, 1937: 120

32 Haddon, 1937: 135

33 Haddon, 1937: 217

34 Haddon, 1937: 288

35 Hornell, 1946: 70

36 Hornell, 1946: 70

37 Hornell, 1946: 71

38 Hornell, 1946: 71

39 Hornell, 1946: 75

40 Hornell, 1946: 76

41 Hornell, 1946: 80

42 Mitman, 1923: 262

43 Bowen, 1956: 289

44 Suder, 1930: 85

45 Suder, 1930: 88, 89

APPENDIX C

Sailing Rafts: Sources for Figure 7.11

1 Hornell, 1946: 61

2 Paris, 1955: map 1

3 Krom, 1920–1922: pl. 22

4 Ling, 1956: 27

5 Nishimura, 1925: 62

6 Hornell, 1936: 412

7 Hornell, 1936: 274

8 Hornell, 1936: 93

9 Edwards, 1960: 384; 1965: 107

10 Edwards, 1960: 386

11 Bowen, 1956: 289

8. Cultural Patterning as Revealed by a Study of Pre-Columbian Ax and Adz Hafting in the Old and New Worlds

DANIEL RANDALL BEIRNE

How did man develop culturally in South and Central America? Were the pre-Columbian cultures of this continent the result of independent evolution untouched by, and unknown to, the cultures of the Old World? Or was there contact between the Old World and the New World long before Columbus thought of a voyage to India? The intriguing theories supporting either diffusion or independent invention have their respective protagonists, and a constant parade of evidence in support of one or the other has given the subject a lively aspect. To the parade of evidence is now added another regiment of facts from the study of early ax-hafting methods to provide new insights into this controversial subject.

The evidence poses several problems. Either man has repeatedly reinvented methods of ax hafting of a most specialized type, or man has spread the ideas of the variations in ax hafting very widely over the world. If the former is the case, then the coastal area of northwestern South America was the center of an ax culture of limited dispersion throughout South and Central America. It was a culture that was advanced technologically in the skills of axmaking far beyond other cultures in the Western Hemisphere. If the latter prevails, then the civilized area of coastal northwestern South America may have been a junction point of cultural streams that crossed both the Atlantic and the Pacific from the Old World.

The data presented here suggest some evidence of diffusion from the Old World to the Pacific coastal regions of northwest South America. This evidence, studies of ax-hafting techniques, suggests that there were more influences from the Far East than from Europe, Africa, and the Near East. Hence all the techniques used in the Western Hemisphere will be analyzed to show that several specific types of these intimate transpacific diffusion from the Far East.

GENERAL CHARACTERISTICS OF THE PERCUSSION CUTTING TOOLS

Ax, Adz, and Celt

A detailed analysis of the early percussion cutting tools, the ax and the adz, cannot be made, nor can the tools be compared in various regions of the world, until certain common, fundamental terms of typology and nomenclature have been explained. Various scholars have created their own terms. Others, erroneously or carelessly, have given improper terms to many common types of percussive cutting tools. Clear and precise definitions for the percussive cutting tools, ax, adz, and celt, are essential to further discussion of typology and nomenclature. The terms used here as the basis of comparison have been compiled after extensive research in the field in an attempt to meet the need for precise terminology.

The ax, for which the entire family of this tool and weapon is named, is a thick, shock-resistant implement of stone and metal whose blade edge is equally faced and parallel to the handle (figs. 8.1, *a* and *b*). The characteristics of the ax were determined by its earliest function of felling trees by chipping and then splitting and shaping the logs. Strength as well as resistance to shock were essential elements in its construction.

The adz is a thin tool of stone or metal, designed to withstand excessive shock. The edge of the blade (fig. 8.1, *d*) is tapered on only one side and the plane of the blade is perpendicular to the plane of the haft (fig. 8.1, *c*), resulting in a restriction of the penetrating power of each stroke of the arm. The ax can achieve a deeper penetration with each stroke because it is easier for the arm holding the ax to vary the angle of penetration from one side to the other and cut out larger

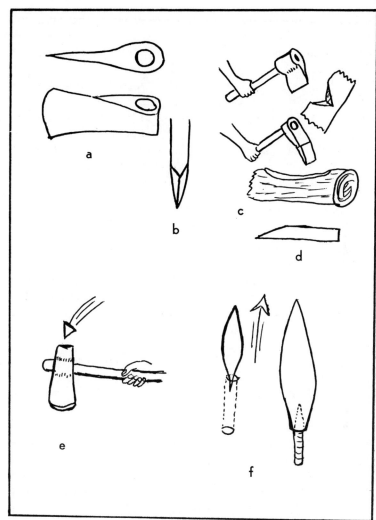

Figure 8.1. Percussion cutting tools. *a*, Ax. *b*, Profile of an ax. *c*, Cutting techniques, ax and adz. *d*, Profile of an adz. *e*, Direction of force (perpendicular) of ax. *f*, Direction of force (parallel) of spear.

chips. The adz, on the other hand, is a more effective woodcutting tool for cutting wide, thin slips, as in hollowing out a log (fig. 8.1, *c*).

The term *celt* lacks precision. It is a general term applied to un-specialized, simple forms of percussion tools of indeterminate func-

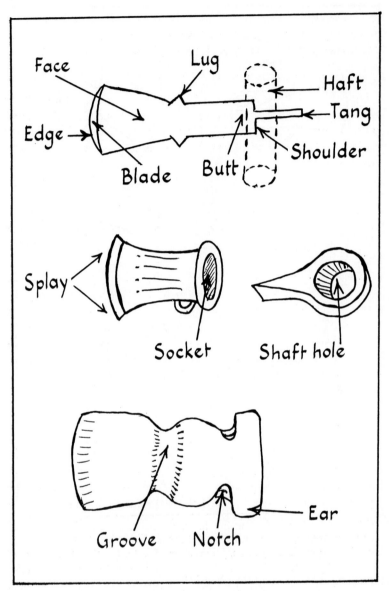

Figure 8.2. Nomenclature.

tion. Most primitive or prehistoric, ungrooved, stone axes and adzes are called celts. To distinguish between ax and adz at early stages in tool development is sometimes quite difficult.

Nomenclature: Parts of Axes and Adzes

Figure 8.2 includes most of the terms used in any comparison of axes and adzes. Some of these terms are controversial, both because names differ regionally and because writers are careless in their usage. In all cases every effort is made here to use the term that is most common in the world.

Topology

The study of axes and adzes is complicated by the difficulty in finding an efficient method of distinguishing one type from another. There are many systems of classification in use. The most common systems base comparisons of types on function, form, composition, and hafting. Form is largely dependent on composition and hafting. Certainly a thinner blade can be made with tempered steel than with stone, and the steel blade normally cuts deeper and dulls its edge less than the stone. The method of attaching the axhead to the haft influences not only the way the blow is struck but also how the butt and body of the implement are shaped. In a study of axes and adzes a consideration of hafting is clearly the primary means of distinguishing between various types of axes and adzes.

Hafting

Hafting has always been a key part of any study of axes and adzes. Early man faced a difficult problem when he found that for a percussion implement of this type the handle had to be mounted at a right angle to the force of the blow (fig. 8.1, e). Because the blows are repetitive as well, he found that the assemblage was put under extreme and continuing shock and strain. Consider how simple he found the attachment of a projectile point by comparison (fig. 8.1, f). Here the direction of impact is parallel to the shaft and thus much more easily contained. In most cases only one or two impacts had to be sustained, because the implement—for example, an arrow or spear —had done its work or else had been lost or shattered.

If there is a best way to haft a cutting implement, it is the shaft-hole method, which has now swept over most of the civilized world.

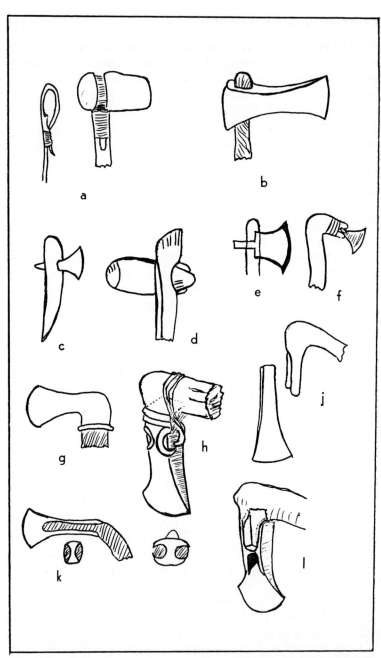

Figure 8.3. Methods of hafting. *a*, Grooved axhead with bent-stick haft.
b, Shaft-hole method. Shaft, normally wood, passes completely through
the head. Used for ax or adz. *c*, Slotted-handle method of tang hafting
with the tang wedged into the wooden haft. *d*, *e*, Another version of
slotted-handle hafting. *f*, *j*, Bent-handle and split-stick techniques of
tang hafting. The tang of the head is wedged between a split-stick haft.
g, *h*, Socket hafting. The haft is wedged into the butt. In some cases the

Yet in the past, this method had a quite limited and, for most of the world, a very late occurrence. Instead, many other ways of solving the problem of hafting the ax and the adz were worked out. Some of these are so complex and clumsy and individual that their independent invention is virtually assured. Others appear widely enough throughout the world to challenge any theory of independent invention. Distribution data will be presented later to support these judgments.

Hafting powerfully influences the shape of the ax. For instance, wrapping a stick around a stone is greatly facilitated by cutting a groove into which the stick can fit. This shaping of the head greatly reduces its slipping under the shock of repeated blows. Thereby a particular type of ax comes into being. The technique of hafting thus creates a typical form and a recognizable ax type. Figures 8.3 and 8.4 show the major methods of hafting throughout the world. Once the forms of hafting are understood, the types of axes and adzes, which are created largely by differing approaches to the hafting problem, can be considered.

Composition

Unfortunately it is not possible at this time to treat the subject of composition in axes as fully as we can hafting. There is limited variation in composition; nearly all axes are made of either stone or metal. Both these materials, however, are susceptible to detailed study, although such studies have seldom been done. For instance, stone is available in a great number of forms, but only certain ones— granite, quartz, basalt, jade, diorite, flint, and obsidian—have the necessary resistance to shock, combined with hardness (Martin, Quimby, and Collier, 1947: 8). Since the availability of such stone varies regionally, it would be most revealing to know what was available in any area and what choices were made. If men over a wide area chose one type of stone, when within that area there were other equally desirable types of stone for the purpose, then cultural factors probably influenced the choice. But in order to make such judgments, there must be many more detailed studies than are now available.

The same is true of metals. The study of the composition of the metals of ancient weapons could be extremely revealing and, in time,

---

ıaft enters a socket at the base of the butt and in others at the end of he butt. Some sockets are round and others are square. Some are reinorced with bindings from a ring on the head to the haft. *k, l,* Flange ınd wing methods of socket hafting. Flanges and wings on the head of netal axes and adzes hold the shaft end securely. In the Palstave (*1*), ı ridge was added to the wing to stop vertical slippage.

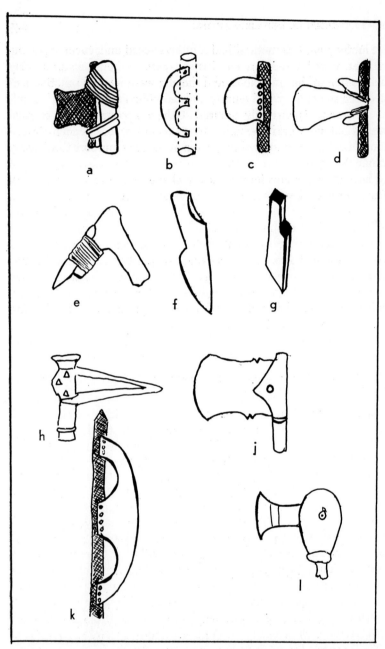

Figure 8.4. Methods of hafting. *a, d,* Butt hafting. *a,* **T**-shaped or lugged with the top of the **T** lashed to the haft. *b,* Simple tang hafting with tangs of the butt resting on or partially inside the haft. *c,* Perforated butt with holes in the tang to assist in securing axhead to the haft. Both these methods (*b* & *c*) could be considered tang hafting. *d,* Eared hafting. Ears are cut in the axhead to secure the bindings. Head is usually made of stone. *e,* Elbow (bent-handle) hafting. The head is

undoubtedly will be. Not only must the composition and the smelting and treatment (annealing, tempering) methods be studied, but the composition of the ore bodies from which these metals were obtained must be known as well. Detailed studies of this sort are just beginning to appear. Regrettably, in this study composition will get only passing notation and attention must be centered on hafting. Fortunately hafting is most revealing and of great importance in determining the shape or form of the implement. Further, methods of hafting have great longevity and usually characterize large, contiguous areas, which suggests the results of diffusion.

Function

That function had a major influence on hafting is an understatement. It also had a major influence on composition and form. Heavy work demanded a secure haft as well as sturdy blade material. The shape and size of the head as well as the angle of the blade were predetermined by the work requirements. Nonetheless, caution must be taken with generalizations, since such forms as ceremonial axes often violate these basic rules of function. Since a detailed discussion of the world-wide function of axes and adzes is impossible here, function will be discussed only in those specific cases where pre-Columbian diffusion has been suggested.

WORLD DISTRIBUTION PATTERNS

World distribution patterns of the six hafting techniques discussed reveal that all appeared in the Western Hemisphere during pre-Columbian times. These forms are not limited to the Western Hemisphere alone; all are found to some extent in various regions of the Old World. Until a detailed analysis of each is available, however, it is not safe to say that these patterns are evidence of diffusion.

The patterns of the bent-stick and split-stick hafting techniques for grooved axes (fig. 8.5) reveal heavy distribution in most of the Western Hemisphere, particularly concentrated in the United States and the Caribbean. Africa displays dense concentration along the west coast as well as in much of the area south of the Sahara. These distribution patterns alone suggest that diffusion across the Atlantic between the West African coast and the Antilles is a strong possibility. The patterns for shaft-hole hafting (fig. 8.6) show a very dense

---

shed to the end of a bent haft. More commonly used for adzes than xes. *f, g,* Various shaped adz heads with grooves to help secure the ead to the bent haft and prevent any slipping. *h,* Rivet hafting. Pins r rivets are used to secure very heavy axheads. Sometimes associated vith tanged and socketed axes when used to reinforce those methods of afting (*j, k, l*).

concentration in the Mediterranean, northern Europe, and the Middle East. Isolated concentrations appear in eastern Asia and northwest South America. The generally accepted route of movement begins in northwest Europe during the Middle Stone Age and spreads across Eurasia as far as Indonesia after the Bronze Age (Werth, 1954: 95). The distinct absence of the shaft-hole method in North America, the Caribbean, Africa, and the Pacific rules out any attempt to establish links between the Old World and the New World, even by tracing directions of possible movements.

Maces, which are shaft-hole hafted, reveal quite different distribution patterns than the axes (fig. 8.7). Both the Atlantic and the Pacific oceans figure in some of these patterns. The concentrations of the cigar-shaped club link northwest Europe, the place of origin of the technique, with the Atlantic and Central America. The Pacific Ocean patterns of the star and ring maces, which link Japan and northwest South America, however, give greater credibility to a suggestion of transpacific diffusion of shaft-hole hafting.

Tang-hafting patterns (figs. 8.8 and 8.9) show concentrations over most of the world, with the greatest New World densities in Central America, the Caribbean, eastern United States, and northwest South America. Forms that are classified as shouldered and perforated have been found in enormous numbers in the Cañari country of the Andes (Bushnell, 1951: 117). In the Old World the spread of simple tang hafting is extensive, with heavy concentrations throughout Europe, the Middle East, and eastern and southern Asia. This technique is so basic and the distributions so widespread throughout the world that distinguishing independent invention from diffusion is almost impossible. Only in such specific forms as the perforated or the shouldered can any close analysis really be made. Even with these the distribution patterns reveal nothing to encourage any argument for diffusion.

The socket method (fig. 8.10) has very limited distributions in the Western Hemisphere, although they are quite extensive in the Old World. The strongest possibility for diffusion rests with a transpacific link. The densities of full socket hafting are marked throughout China and Southeast Asia and extend out into the Pacific. Directly across the Pacific lies Peru, where the technique of full socket hafting is quite common along the coast (Bushnell, 1951: 116). Such distribu-

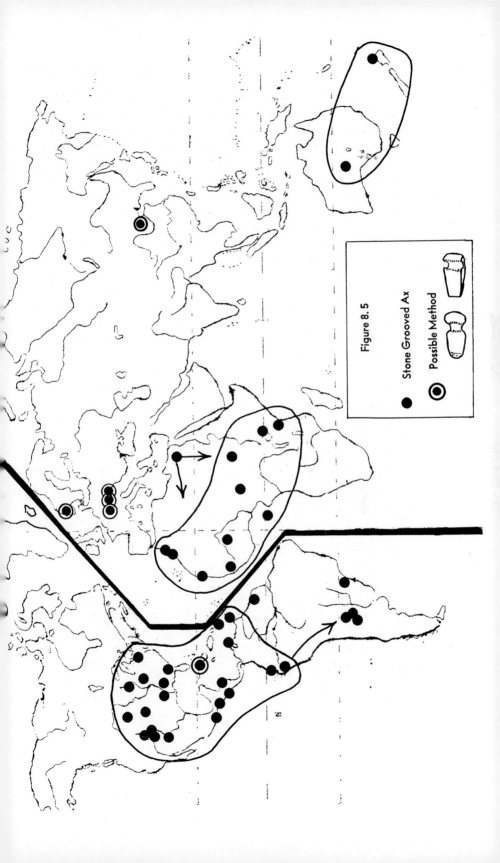

Figure 8. 5

● Stone Grooved Ax

◉ Possible Method

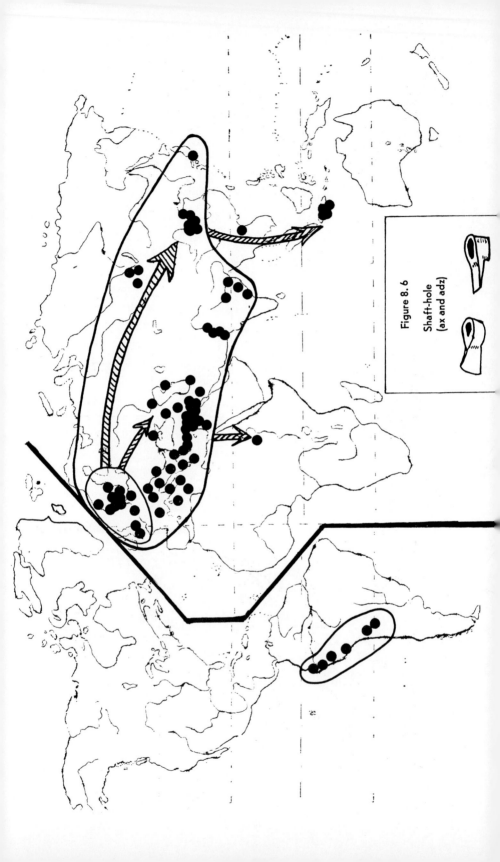

Figure 8.6

Shaft-hole
(ax and adz)

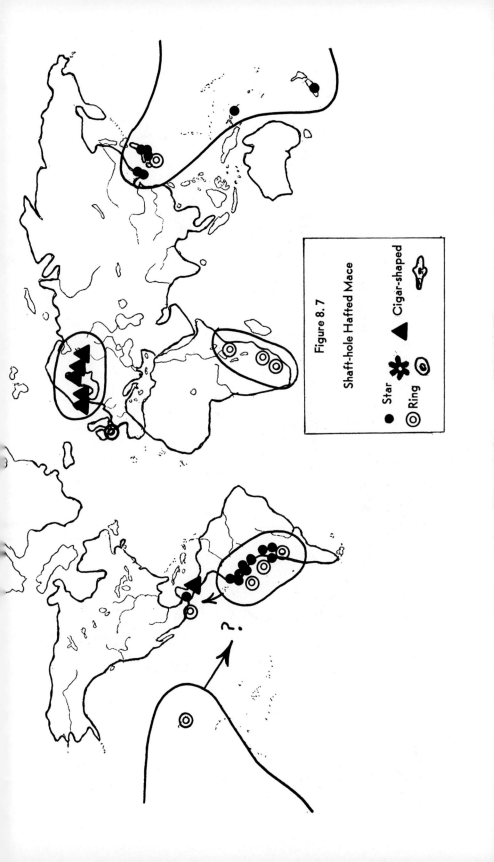

Figure 8. 7

Shaft-hole Hafted Mace

● Star

▲ Cigar-shaped

◎ Ring

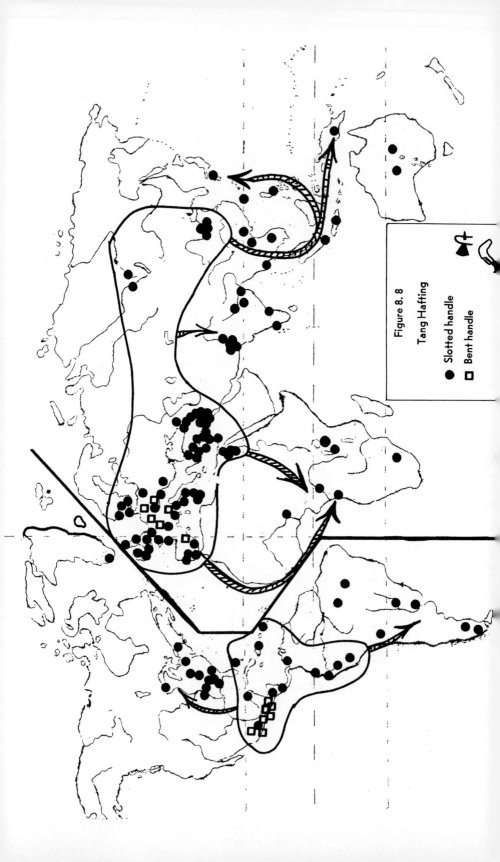

Figure 8. 8

Tang Hafting

● Slotted handle
□ Bent handle

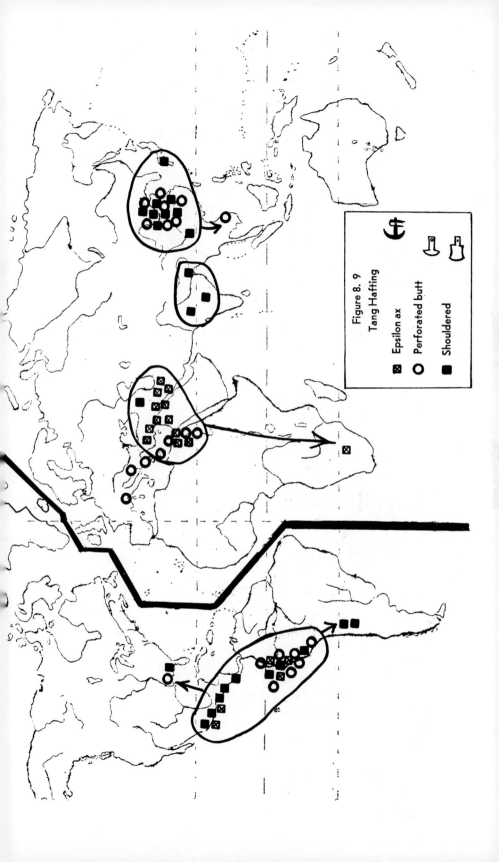

Figure 8. 9
Tang Hafting

Epsilon ax
Perforated butt
Shouldered

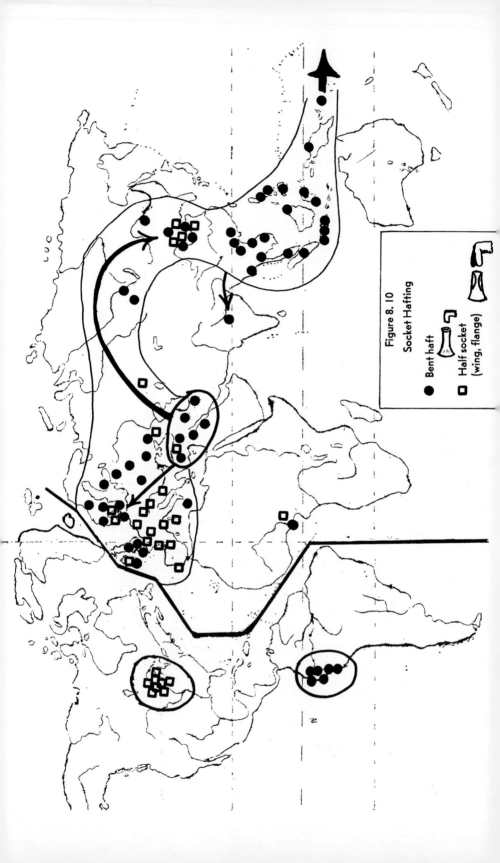

Figure 8. 10
Socket Hafting

● Bent haft
▢ Half socket
  (wing, flange)

tion invites further investigation of this method of hafting, which might reveal more evidence of diffusion.

Elbow hafting (fig. 8.11) shows a pattern of extreme density of stone forms in Asia and the Pacific and of metal forms in the regions bordering the Mediterranean. Both forms exist in the area of northwest South America, but any case for diffusion would have to be built on some of the stone forms that exist throughout the Pacific Ocean area. The grooved adz appears to follow a definite course from Japan across the North Pacific to Alaska and then extends down the northwest coast of America as far as California. The appearance of similar forms in northwest Argentina and on Easter Island raises the question of route of diffusion if diffusion did take place. Did it follow the Central Pacific route from the Asian mainland to Easter Island, or did it follow the Heyerdahl hypothesis (Heyerdahl, 1952) and leave from South America? In either case a good argument for diffusion can be maintained.

The metal adz forms, on the other hand, show no Pacific or Atlantic link. The people of Polynesia never reached the metal stage. Proponents of independent invention in South America can use this fact to support their position.

The butt-hafting patterns (fig. 8.12) are the most interesting of all because they are densely concentrated in only two areas of the world—northwest South America and Egypt. Why is this hafting method not found in other parts of the world? Why are the distributions so dense in these two regions, with almost no spread to other geographically close cultural regions? No evidence of transatlantic links between these two regions is available. The argument for the concentrations along the Guiana coast as evidence of transatlantic links falters with the revelation that these concentrations have eighteenth-century dates and were brought about by a people who moved into this region from the west (Jennings and Norbeck, 1964: 434). Here again the independent inventionist finds support.

Study of these eight hafting distribution patterns and the seventeen specific types of axes and adzes associated with them reveals only three types that strongly suggest diffusion between the Old World and the New World. These three are (1) the bent-stick haft for the grooved ax, (2) the shaft-hole mace, and (3) the elbow-hafted grooved adz. Two others, the perforated tang of the slotted-handle

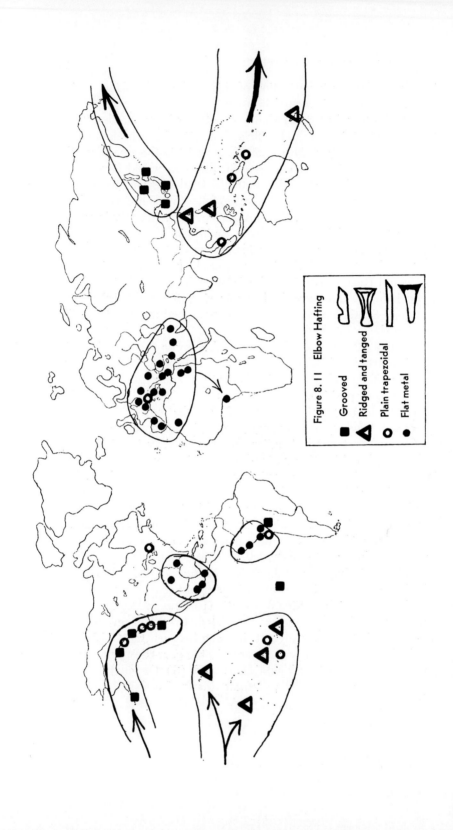

Figure 8.11 Elbow Hafting

■ Grooved
◁ Ridged and tanged
○ Plain trapezoidal
● Flat metal

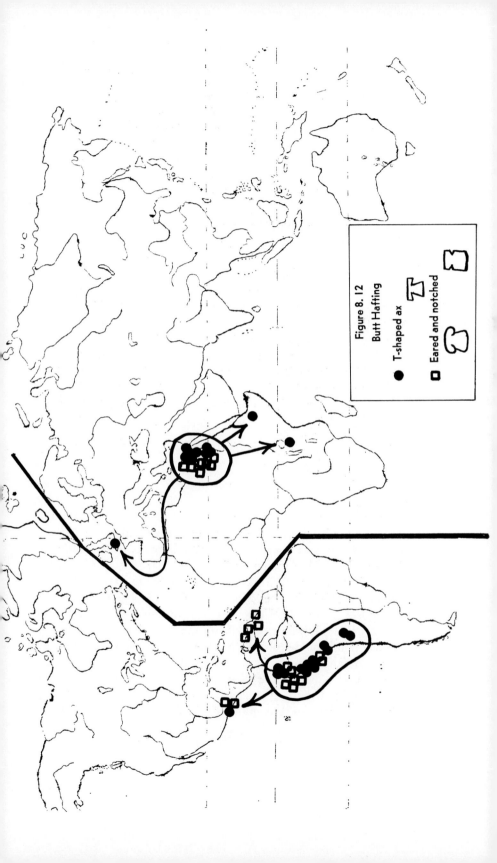

Figure 8.12
Butt Hafting

● T-shaped ax

□ Eared and notched

haft and the verticle-hafted full socket, offer possible indications. The argument for diffusion grows weaker, however, when the patterns of the remainder of these axes and adzes are studied. It must be remembered that this opinion so far is based solely upon distribution patterns. Further study of the shape and function of each type is necessary before more definite conclusions can be reached.

ANALYSIS OF SHAPE, FORM, AND FUNCTION

In order to discuss the hafting techniques in detail for further evidence of pre-Columbian contacts, it is necessary to establish a systematic approach. The method of approach employed here is to base the sequence on the findings from the distribution patterns. The first group studied will be those whose patterns suggest diffusion and whose form and shape look very much alike. It should be borne in mind that distribution patterns are not necessarily conclusive proof of either diffusion or independent invention, since the areas of greatest density are often areas where most of the excavating has taken place. For this reason the author feels that the similarities in form and shape of axes should be analyzed in spite of the limited support of arguments for diffusion as revealed by the distribution patterns of hafting methods.

Axes Similar in Shape and Form; Distribution Patterns
Suggest Diffusion

Shaft-hole Mace. Introduction of shaft-hole hafting into South America might be attributed to transpacific diffusion of some forms of the mace. The shaft-hole, star maces of Ecuador, Peru, and Bolivia (figs. 8.13, *a, b, d, f, h, j*) and those of Japan and Korea (figs. 8.13, *c, e, g, i*) possess common shapes and forms. The Asiatic forms have dates of Late Jomon period, about 1000 B.C. (Heine-Geldern, 1954: 360; Kidder, 1959: 55), whereas the South American dates are of the considerably later Mochica and Cara phases, A.D. 500–1500 (Meggers, 1966: 146; Univ. of Penn. Museum). The Asiatic forms are of stone only whereas the South American forms are of stone and bronze. This would probably indicate a late development of the metal form from the stone.

Arguments against diffusion spring from the simplicity of form, particularly of the ring mace, and the limited distributions of both ring and star maces throughout the Pacific. The functions of war and

Figure 8.13. Star-shaped mace heads. *a, b,* Stone, Ecuador, Cara phase, A.D. 500–1500 (after Meggers, 1966). *c,* Stone, Japan, Jomon period (after Kidder, 1959). *d,* Stone, Bolivia, Tiahuanaco (Univ. of Penn. Museum). *e, i,* Stone, Korea, 1000 B.C. (after Heine-Geldern, 1954). *f, h,* Stone, Ecuador (after Rivet and Verneau, 1912). *g,* Stone, Japan, Later Jomon, Negano Prefecture (after Groot, 1951). *j,* Bronze, Peru, Moche (Univ. of Penn. Museum).

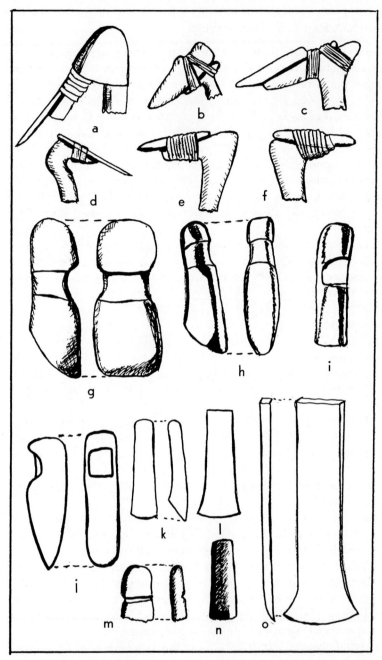

Figure 8.14. Elbow hafting. *a*, Copper blade, wood haft, Inca, Peru (Baessler, 1906). *b*, Stone, Haida, N.W. Coast of N. America (Hodge, 1905). *c*, Stone, Hawaii (Smithsonian). *d*, Copper blade, Egypt, 3400–3200 B.C. (Emery, 1961). *e*, Stone, Alaska (Martin, Quimby, and Collier, 1947). *f*, Stone, Portugal, Neolithic (Oakley, 1957). *g*, Stone grooved adz, N.W. Argentina (Willey, 1946). *h*. Stone, scarfed-butt variety (grooved), Easter Island (Duff, 1959). *i*, Stone grooved axe, St. Lawrence Is., Bering Sea (Geist and Rainey, 1936). *j*, Stone, N.W.

ceremony, common to most cultures, might encourage men in different areas to develop a common style of weapon whose common shapes would be the result of logical, progressive development.

The argument for diffusion would be supported if these maces were found in areas of Ecuador with other artifacts that have been linked with Japan (Meggers, 1966: 146; Estrada and Meggers, 1961). The limited dispersion of this style into the other areas of the Western Hemisphere discourages arguments for independent invention. The conclusion reached is that transpacific diffusion of shaft-hole hafting into Ecuador from Japan is suggested by the similarity in the shapes, forms, and distribution patterns of the star-shaped and ring maces.

Elbow-Hafted Grooved Adz. The stone adz was common to much of the Western Hemisphere, but the methods of hafting are doubtful in some regions. The Moche and Inca cultures of the Andean region of South America used copper adzes and employed the elbow method of hafting them (Baessler, 1906: table 2; Univ. of Penn. Museum). The function here appears to be that of a carpenter's woodworking tool as well as a scraping tool. Some may have been used in agriculture and for working the earth. Except for this region, however, and among the Haida of the northwest coast of North America, the elbow-hafted adz was not extensively used in the Western Hemisphere.

That concentrations of this hafting method in the Western Hemisphere are limited to the areas along the Pacific Ocean suggests links with other Pacific cultures and, possibly, transpacific diffusion from Asia. The stone grooved adzes (fig. 8.14, *g–i*) of northwest Argentina, Easter Island, St. Lawrence Island, Alaska, and the northwest Pacific coast of North America all look much alike, having a similar form of groove for hafting. Whether these are related beyond this is pure speculation, since actual dates of these are not available. General knowledge, from comparisons with other cultural traits, would indicate their dates to be fairly recent. What is important is that the Easter Island variety (fig. 8.14, *h*), according to Duff, is one of a family of adzes whose origin was the Late Neolithic scarfed-butt adz of Formosa (Duff, 1959: figs. 1, 6). Heyerdahl supports this concept to some degree by associating hafting techniques of Peru and Ecuador with Polynesia (1952: 108). Since the Argentine adz (fig. 8.14, *g*)

Pacific Coast (Martin, Quimby, and Collier, 1947). *k*, Stone adz, plain trapezoidal, Tuamoto, Polynesia (Duff, 1959). *l*, Copper adz, Egypt, XXVI Dynasty (Petrie, 1917). *m*, Stone scarfed-butt, Formosa, Late Neolithic (Duff, 1959). *n*, Stone, Oregon (Martin, Quimby, and Collier, 1947). *o*, Copper adz, Moche and Inca, Peru (Univ. of Penn. Museum).

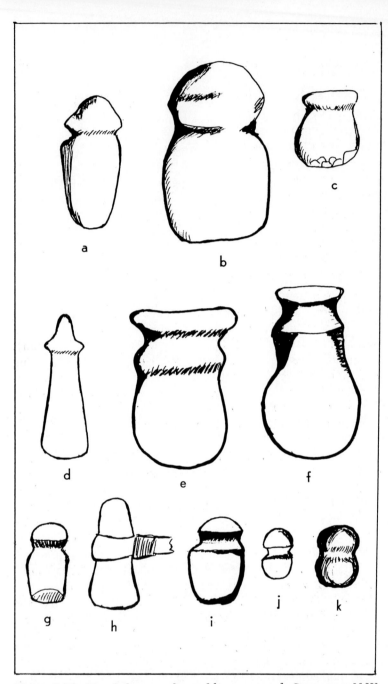

Figure 8.15. Grooved axes, celts, and hammers. *a, b*, Stone axes, N.W. coastal Africa (after Forde-Johnston, 1959). *c*, Stone ax, Fernando Po, West African coast (after Werth, 1954). *d*, Petaloid celt, Haiti. *e, f*, Stone grooved axes, St. Vincent, Antilles (after Fewkes, 1914b). *g*, Stone full-grooved ax, S.W. United States (after Hodge, 1905). *h*, Stone ax, Mexico, 1500–100 B.C. (after Bushnell, 1956). *i*, Stone ax, Cara phase, Ecuador (after Meggers, 1966). *j, k*, Stone hammers. *j*, Europe, pre-1500 B.C., (after Childe, 1944). *k*, S.E. Brazil (La Plata R.) (after Hrdlička, 1912).

most resembles that of Easter Island, a link between these two locations can at least be suggested.

Arguments for parallel development stem from comparisons with other Pacific cultural traits that, in spite of having the same probable origin, appeared in regions extremely distant from each other. Examples of this would be the similarities in buildings, carvings, and customs, as well as elbow adz hafting (fig. 8.14, *b, c, e*), between some of the peoples of the Pacific and coastal Alaska. Both cultures may have originated in the vicinity of Japan many years ago and spread in two directions. What we see in the adz form is the result of logical parallel development.

In spite of this argument the appearance of the Easter Island and northwest Argentina adzes suggests two possible links with Asia. One link begins at a very early date in the vicinity of Japan and moves by way of Alaska into North America (Duff, 1959: 121). The other begins in the Late Neolithic in Formosa and spreads very slowly across the Pacific, possibly reaching coastal South America just prior to the Spanish.

Grooved (Bent- and Split-stick) Hafting. The grooved method of hafting is one of the early forms. In Europe it was associated with Mesolithic stone hammers that were used to drive wedges into logs. Later, according to Childe, about 1500 B.C., this function merged into the shaft-hole-hafted ax that was strong enough to split the logs from the dense forests of northern Europe (Childe, 1944: 25).

In North America and Africa, however, this grooved hafting method was associated with stone axes only; here the distributions cover both fostered and arid regions. Since the shaft-hole ax is not found in these two regions, it could not have followed the North European pattern of functional development. It might appear then that this grooved ax was designed for less arduous tasks than tree splitting.

Since the distribution patterns of West Africa and the Caribbean might suggest transatlantic diffusion, a closer study of the various grooved axes of these regions is necessary (fig. 8.15). A careful study of these does reveal that the ones most alike in shape and form are found in West Africa and Ecuador, not West Africa and the Caribbean, as implied by the distribution patterns (fig. 8.15, *b, i*). Explaining this contradiction is not easy. The simplicity of the ax form, together with the functional requirement of the groove for tighter se-

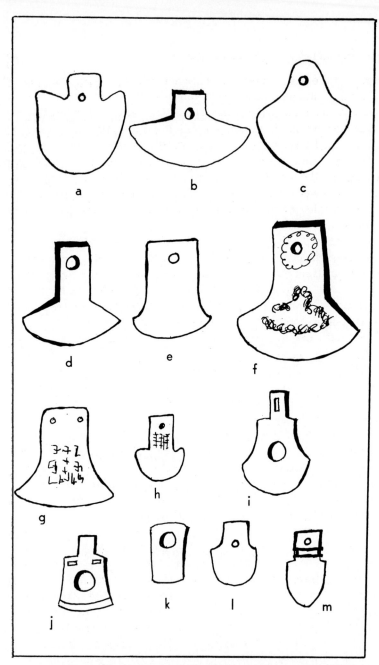

Figure 8.16. Perforated tang, wide-blade cutting axes. *a*, Stone, *c*, Copper axes from Ecuador (after Rivet and Verneau, 1912). *b*, Copper cutting tool, Milagro phase, Ecuador (after Meggers, 1966). *d, f*, Copper, Peru and Ecuador; *d*, Inca (Univ. of Penn. Museum; Smithsonian); *f*, 400 B.C. (after Heine-Geldern, 1954). *g, h*, Copper and gold (after Rivet and Verneau, 1912). *i, j*, Bronze, China, pre-Anyang (after Loehr, 1956). *k*, Copper ax, Milagro phase, Ecuador (after Meggers, 1966). *l*, Stone, Ga., USA (Smithsonian). *m*, Stone, Ecuador (Univ. of Penn. Museum). *e*, Bronze, Tonkin, Vietnam, Dongson (might be socketed; after Janse, 1958).

curing of the haft, makes it an extremely common type, very difficult to distinguish from others of its kind. Unlike many of the other ax forms, it does not have many distinct features that stand out and make recognition of different cultures a simple matter. In addition, it is associated with simple cultures whose movements were probably limited to land, which may explain the great number of locations throughout the world. If it can be proved that these simple, grooved-ax cultures were capable of building boats that could cross over two thousand miles of the open South Atlantic, then perhaps the diffu-sionists have a case.

Perforated Tang (Slotted-Handle) Hafting. Tang hafting is com-mon throughout the world and is probably a logical, progressive de-velopment from the simple, stone wedge. Mesolithic Europeans ap-pear to have been the first people to fit the top (butt) of a wedge into a handle (Childe, 1944: 7). The butt was wedged tightly into the handle, thus creating a chopping tool strong enough to perform simple tasks like hollowing out canoes and cutting paddles. This so-called slotted-handle stone ax was too light and brittle for extensive tree-felling and probably too crude for performing any detailed woodwork. According to Childe, the need for a stronger precision tool led to the development of the socket-hafted ax in Europe about 1200 B.C. (1944: 7).

The perforated forms (fig. 8.16) are limited to relatively few regions in the world. Some regions, such as Shang China, specialized in the large circular perforation on the face of the ax (fig. 8.16, *i, j*). Small circular perforations are common in Ecuador (fig. 8.16, *a–d, f–h*) and in Vietnam. (fig. 8.16, *e*) Whether this is a result of parallel development or diffusion is a matter of opinion.

The dates of the Asian forms are considerably earlier than those of Ecuador. Most Chinese forms are Shang dynasty, twelfth or eleventh century B.C. (Watson, 1966: 77). Lohr (1956: 19) gives dates for some forms (fig. 8.16, *i, j*) as pre-Anyang, which would have been even earlier. Heine-Geldern (1954: 395) gives a date of 400 B.C. for a copper, butt-perforated ax in Ecuador (fig. 8.16, *f*). An ax much like it is found in Peru (fig. 8.16, *d*) and is associated with the Incas, a much later culture (Smithsonian). Other forms in Ecuador (fig. 8.16 , *k*) are called Milagro phase (Meggers, 1966: 139). On the other hand, stone perforated axes were found by Meggers with the

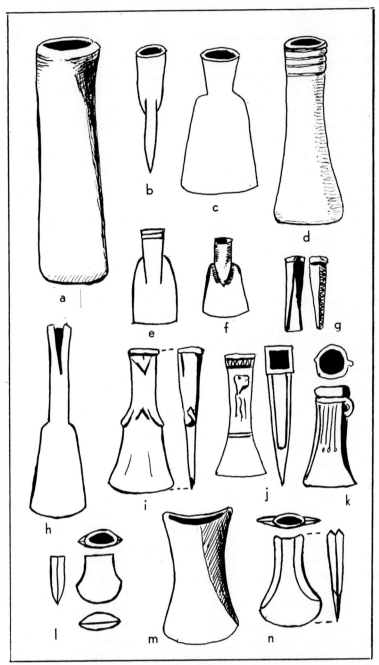

Figure 8.17. Socketed axes and spades. *a, b,* Copper ax, Moche, Peru (Univ. of Penn. Museum). *c,* Metal hoe, Celebes (Cheng, 1960). *d,* Bronze ax, Indochina (Heine-Geldern, 1945). *e,* Bronze spade, Shang China (Cheng, 1960). *f,* Bronze spade, Celebes (Heine-Geldern, 1945). *g,* Bronze socketed tools, England, Late Bronze Age (Childe, 1940). *h,* Copper spade, Peru (Meade, 1924). *i,* Bronze ax, Sicily, 1000–850 B.C. (Brea, 1957). *j,* Bronze ax, Yunnan prov., China, 1st

ring and star-shaped maces and were called Cara phase, A.D. 500–1500 (1966: 146). South of China, in Tonkin (North Vietnam), perforated axes are linked to the Dongson culture (Janse, 1958: 54). From these few examples it appears that the Asiatic dates do reach forward and the South American ones backward, enough to make diffusion appear possible.

What then is the significance of these correlations? Were the late copper axes of Ecuador copies of earlier stone ones? Are the stone ones linked to the Shang or Dongson cultures of Asia? Is it coincidence that the star-shaped mace, so much like the Jomon mace of Japan, was found with the perforated stone ax? Why are these forms limited primarily to the coastal regions of Ecuador and Peru? This all seems to suggest some possible link between eastern Asia and Ecuador between 400 B.C. and A.D. 500.

Full Socket (Vertical Haft). Full socket hafting is quite common in the Old World, where it appears in a number of distinct styles (fig. 8.17). It spread from northwest Europe to Indonesia, where it functioned as a tool, a weapon, and a ceremonial symbol. In the New World, socket hafting was used for both tools and weapons (fig. 8.17). It was not a common method of hafting here and has been found only in the region of Peru and Ecuador.

The similarities between hafting methods of Southeast Asia and Indonesia (figs. 8.17, *c, d, f*) with those of Peru (figs. 8.17, *a, h*) are strong. The shape and form, especially of the shouldered spades, bear a strong resemblance to each other. The dates of the Asiatic ones are estimated at about the fourth century B.C. (Heine-Geldern, 1945: 146), whereas those of Peru belong to the Mochica culture, almost eight hundred years later. In Peru the axes functioned as tools; in Indonesia they were used not only as tools but also as ceremonial symbols. (Van Heekeren, 1958: 9) The sockets of Peru are round like those of Indonesia and south Asia, not square like those of China (fig. 8.17). This square form is unique and is found only in China; the rest of the world employed the round or oval style.

What conclusions can be reached from this close study of the socket? First, the sockets of Indonesia and Vietnam (Indochina) look very much like the Mochica ones of Peru. Second, the only full sockets in the Western Hemisphere found so far are those in coastal Peru. Third, the dates given for the south Asian and Peruvian sockets

---

ent. B.C. (Watson, 1962). *k*, Bronze ax, England, Late Bronze Age Childe, 1940). *l*, Stone or shell ax, Choiseul, Solomon Is. (Fritot, 938). *m*, Bronze celt, Philippines, Late Neolithic (Beyer, 1948). *n*, Bronze ax, Indonesia (Van Heekeren, 1958).

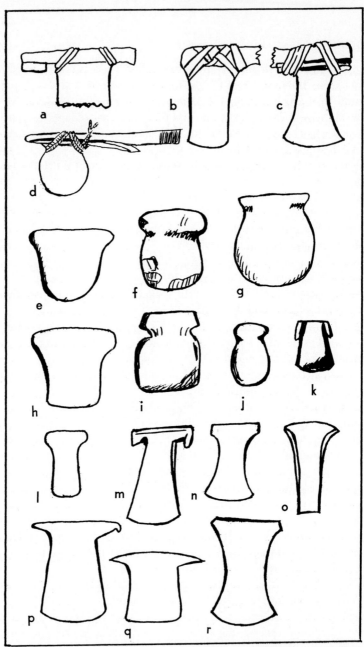

Figure 8.18. Butt hafting: eared and T-shaped axes. *a*, Butt-hafted ax, Egypt, XII Dynasty (Petrie, 1917). *b*, Butt-hafted ax, Egypt, XVIII Dynasty (Petrie, 1917). *c*, Butt-hafted, metal T-shaped ax, Peru (Rivet and Verneau, 1912). *d*, Butt-hafted, stone eared ax, Bolivia (Nordenskiöld, 1924). *e*, Stone eared ax, Egypt, VI Dynasty (Petrie, 1917). *f*, Stone eared ax, Old Egypt (Berlin Museum; Werth, 1954). *g*, Copper or bronze ax, 2400–2200 B.C., Egypt (Petrie, 1917). *h*, Stone ax, Valdivia phase, 1500 B.C., Ecuador (Meggers, 1966). *i*, Stone eared ax, Río Naupes, Ecuador (Berlin

make diffusion a possibility. Fourth, the distribution patterns (fig. 8.10) show the socket technique extending quite a distance into the islands of the South Pacific. Last, the square Chinese form seems to eliminate any link between east Asia and the Western Hemisphere. All these facts suggest the possibility of diffusion from Indonesia or Indochina across the Pacific to Peru sometime before A.D. 200–600, the dates of the Mochica culture, according to Alfred Kidder (1964: 465).

Axes Similar in Shape, Form, and Hafting Method; Distribution Patterns Suggest Independent Invention

A number of axes of similar hafting method that look very much alike in shape and form reveal distribution patterns that suggest independent invention rather than diffusion. Any conclusions drawn from the distributions alone should not be final, however, without at least a brief résumé of some of the rather curious similarities.

Butt-Hafted (T-Shaped and Eared) Axes. Butt hafting (fig. 8.18) is unique because it is found only in Egypt and parts of northern South America, centering in Peru. Both regions had the eared forms in stone at very early dates. The Egyptian ones are of the Sixth Dynasty (2200 B.C.), whereas those of Peru are early Tutiscainyo (500 B.C.) (Petrie, 1917: pl. 8; Lathrap and Roys, 1963: 37. With the advent of metallurgy in both regions the T-shaped ax appeared with more defined lugs on the butt. Various perforated forms were even developed to help secure the butt to the haft (fig. 8.19). A narrow version of the T-shaped ax was designed to penetrate armor and was used by both Egyptians and Incas for this purpose (Yadin, 1963: 60; Rowe, 1946: 276). In spite of all these similarities, however, parallel development must be assumed until further evidence to the contrary is found. As part of an over-all Egyptian complex in Peru, this evidence might help the diffusionist cause, but the evidence standing alone is not sufficient proof.

Tang (Bent-Handle) Hafting. The bent-handle haft for the tang ax was common in pre-Bronze Age Europe but was rare in the Western Hemisphere and has been found so far only in the Toltec ruins

Museum; Werth, 1954). *j*, Stone eared ax, Ecuador (Rivet & Verneau, 1912). *k*, Stone eared ax, Cara phase, A.D. 500–1500. Ecuador Meggers, 1966). *l*. Stone, East Africa (Cole, 1963), Ecuador and Bolivia (Rivet and Verneau, 1912). *m*, Copper T-shaped ax, Peru Baessler, 1906). *n*, Copper T-shaped ax, Moche, Peru (Univ. of Penn. Museum). *o*, Copper T-shaped ax, Diaguita, Argentina (Miranda, 1946), also found in Costa Rica (Stone, 1958). *p, q*, Iron T-shaped ax, Egypt, 500 B.C. (Petrie, 1917). *r*, Bronze T-shaped ax, Gaza, Egypt, 2nd mill. B.C. (Metropolitan Museum)

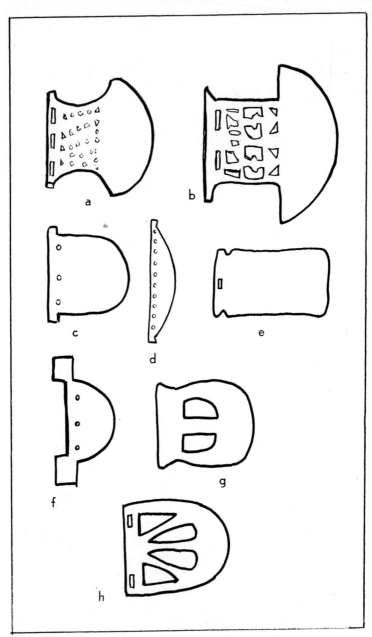

Figure 8.19. Forms of T-shaped, wide-edged, short-bladed cutting axes. *a*, Copper perforated ax, Ecuador (after Rivet and Verneau, 1912). *b*, Similar copper ax from Ecuador (courtesy of the Smithsonian). *c, d*, Copper or bronze perforated axes, Egypt, ca. 2400 B.C. (after Yadin, 1963: I). *e*, Form of copper, perforated, notched ax, near Lima, Peru (after Baessler, 1906). *f*, Egyptian perforated ax, with lugs that were square in shape and fitted into recesses in the haft (after Petrie, 1917). *g, h*, Forms of perforated axes from Egypt, copper or bronze, ca. 2100–1570 B.C. (after Petrie, 1917).

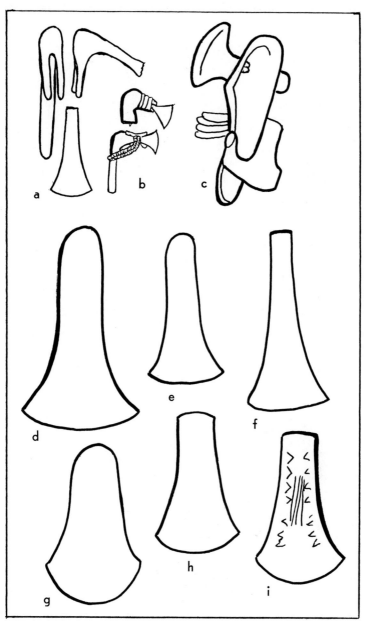

Figure 8.20. Some methods of simple tang hafting (*a–c*). Examples of tang-hafted axes: long-blade, penetrating type (*d–i*). *a*, Bent-handle, split-stick hafting with bronze blade, Europe (Childe, 1944). *b*, Simple bent-handle method, Aztec, Mexico (Saville, 1925; from codices). *c*, Copper tanged ax, Maya, Mexico, Early Classic period (Wauchope, 1964). *d*, Stone ax, St. Vincent, Antilles, 500 B.C.; also found Caribbean side of Costa Rica (Fewkes, 1914b; Fritot, 1938; Stone, 1958). *e*, Bronze ax, Wessex culture, England, 16th cent. B.C. (Piggott, 1965). *f*, Bronze ax, Portugal (Petrie, 1917). *g*, Stone ax, St. Vincent, Antilles (Fewkes, 1914b). *h*, Bronze ax, England, Bronze Age (Petrie, 1917). *i*, Bronze Ax, Ireland (British Museum).

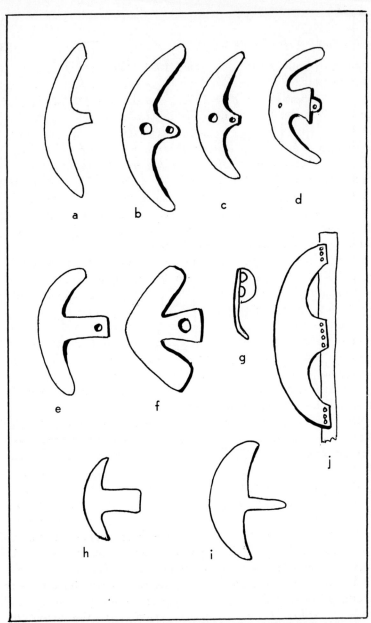

Figure 8.21. Forms of epsilon axes. *a, b,* Bronze or copper axes from Palestine, ca. 2400 B.C., and Mesopotamia, ca. 2100–1570 B.C. Note perforations on *b* (after Yadin, 1963: I). *c, d,* Perforated epsilon axes from Soli, S. Turkey, ca. 2600–1700 B.C. (after Schaeffer, 1948). *e, f,* Stone, perforated epsilon axes from Ecuador (after Rivet and Verneau, 1912). *g, j,* Epsilon axes from Carthage and Egypt (after Petrie, 1917). *h,* Copper ax money, Mexico, ca. A.D. 1000 (after Coe, 1962). *i,* Stone tanged ax, Tope Sialk, Iran, ca. 1200 B.C. (after Schaeffer, 1948); copper cutting tools, smaller but identical in shape, are found in Milagro phase Ecuador (after Meggers, 1966).

in Mexico (Childe, 1944: 26; Seler, 1904: 349). The technique is rather simple, and this explains its wide spread in early Europe (fig. 8.20, *a*). If it was so simple to design, why did it not spread beyond Mexico? Perhaps it was superseded by the slotted-tang method (fig. 8.20, *c*). In either case much more evidence is necessary to suggest diffusion, and independent invention seems more plausible.

Tang (Slotted-handle) Hafting: Epsilon Ax. The epsilon ax stands out because of its distinct shape and form (fig. 8.21). The very narrow face for the extremely wide cutting edge lightens the weight of the ax considerably. The wide blade suggests an implement for cutting fields of grain. Unless extremely sharp, the blade would have been of limited use except as a ceremonial symbol.

The similarity in shape and form between those of the ancient Near East and those of Ecuador is remarkable. The large axes of Ecuador, however, are of stone and appear to be close copies of some metal forms known only in Egypt and the Near East. What purpose they were designed for is unknown, but stone forms certainly could not cut grain. Perhaps they functioned as some form of war club. Nevertheless, in spite of the implication of parallel development in these two regions, an explanation needs to be found for the occurrence of these stone forms in coastal Ecuador as well as the very limited distribution in the Western Hemisphere.

Tang (Slotted-handle) Hafting: Long-bladed Penetrating Ax. The long-bladed, penetrating ax is the most common ax found throughout the world. It became man's basic cutting tool in both stone and metal. What is interesting to those seeking transatlantic contacts is the striking similarity between the polished stone axes of the Antilles and the Bronze Age metal axes of England (fig. 8.20, *d, e*). Even Fewkes noted this similarity quite a number of years ago: "In considering the shapes—we are reminded of the forms of bronze axes so common in the Old World. They have the same symmetrical form and the sharp edge, showing that they are implements used in cutting" (1922: 99). Perhaps they are copies of metal forms, but why have none of the original metal forms been found? The simplicity in design and wide distribution of the symmetrical metal form throughout the Western Hemisphere suggests that these polished stone axes of the Antilles were copies.

A study of dates for metallurgy in South America might challenge this theory. Fritot (1938: 101) gives a date of 500 B.C. to the stone forms. Yet Easby (1966: 73–74) claims that metallurgy was, prior

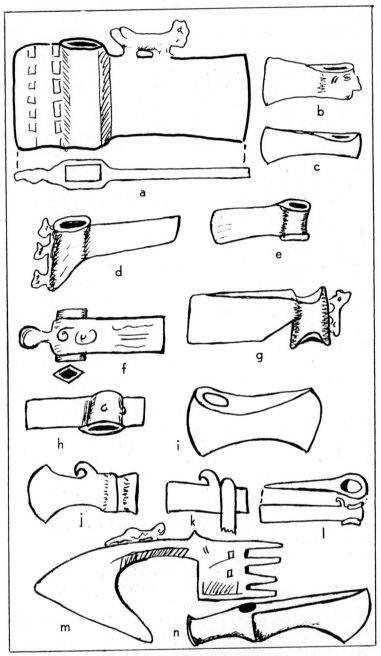

Figure 8.22. Shaft-hole axes. *a*, Copper ax with animal figure, Trujillo, Peru (Baessler, 1906). *b*, Copper ax shaped into figure of a head, Sissig, Ecuador (Rivet and Verneau, 1912). *c*, Bronze ax, Sicily, 1000–*e*, Copper, Mesopotamia, 2600 B.C. (Childe, 1926). *f*, Bronze ax, Shang China, 1300 B.C. (Freer Gallery, Smithsonian). *g*, Bronze ax, Luristan, Iran, 8th–7th cent. B.C. (Smithsonian). *h*, Bronze ax, Minusinsk, Siberia (Loehr, 1956). *i*, Copper ax, N.W. India, 2000 B.C. (Piggott, 1950). 850 B.C. (Brea, 1957). *d*, Metal ax, Syria, 4000–2100 B.C. (Yadin, 1963).

to that time, limited to the Old Copper culture of Wisconsin in North America (400 B.C.) and to parts of Peru (500 B.C.). "In Peru, however, the metal was not copper but gold. This was a stage of development that was not attained in North America until Hopewell times" (Easby, 1966: 74). So far no gold axes of this style have been found. What is the mystery? Perhaps they are the result of independent invention, but until some metal forms are found in that region the mystery will continue.

Shaft-holed Ax. The shaft-holed ax, centered in Europe and Western Asia, is found only in the northern Andes of the Western Hemisphere (fig. 8.22). Why is it limited to this region only, and why are only metal forms found? Nordenskiöld (1930: 43) answers this by saying that the shaft-hole method employed here was derived from the T-shaped ax (butt-hafted) and its rawhide fastening; "on other axes this binding was at a later stage imitated in metal and a handle-holed (shaft-holed) axe resulted."

Similarities in shape and form between those of the Near East and those of the northern Andes suggest cultural links (fig. 8.22). Both regions made use of animal and human motifs as decoration. Those of Syria and northwestern Argentina even used the same form of hook on the upper edge (fig. 8.22, *j, k, l*). Perhaps this was merely a functional innovation, but why the same size hook, bending in the same direction and extending from a point on the upper edge directly in front of the haft hole? Perhaps this was the only way it could hang and be properly balanced.

The major evidence available seems to favor independent invention in the Andes over diffusion from the Old World. The dates for those axes from the Near East average about three thousand years earlier than the South American ones (Schaeffer, 1948: figs. 44, 45, 265). Dates are not known for the Andean forms, but they would appear to belong to the Inca period. Since the number of shaft-hole axes found is limited and all are of metal, more evidence is needed before any conclusions can be reached. Nordenskiöld's theory is certainly possible, and there is still the possibility that the shaft-hole ax was introduced from an outside origin. In any case, more axes with accurate dates must be found before any conclusion can be reached.

Elbow Hafted Flat Adz (Metal and Stone). Mention of the flat adz

---

, k, Copper axes with hooks, N.W. Argentina (Nordenskiöld, 1930).
*, Bronze ax with hook, Ugarit, Syria 1900–1750 B.C. (Schaeffer, 1948).
n, Bronze battle-ax with cast figure, Luristan, Iran (Ghirshman, 1961).
, Jadeite battle-ax, South Russia, second mill. B.C. (Pigott, 1965), and Turkey, 2500 B.C. (Yadin, 1963); this style is common for the period of stone battle-axes and is found over most of northern and central Europe.

is made briefly to reveal that the copper form was quite common in the New World, as well as in the Old World. To distinguish one type from another, or even to determine its method of hafting by observation alone, is quite difficult. For reasons of limited information in general, as well as limited distinguishing characteristics, no evidence of diffusion has been produced, and therefore independent invention must be assumed.

SUMMARY

This study has discussed many characteristics of the two primary percussive cutting tools, the ax and the adz, and has shown that the key to their classification is hafting. By mapping these hafting techniques on a world-wide scale, it was shown that all of the six basic hafting methods were found in both the Old World and the New World. The question next asked was, "Which of these resulted from diffusion?" To answer this, the distribution patterns of seventeen specific characteristics of the hafting methods were analyzed. The result showed that the patterns of five—(1) the shaft-hole, star-shaped mace, (2) the elbow-hafted, grooved adz, (3) the bent- or split-stick, grooved ax, (4) the slotted-handle hafted, perforated tang ax, and (5) the vertical-hafted, full-socket ax—suggested transoceanic diffusion from the Old World.

Detailed analysis of the shape, form, and function of each of these five revealed that the grooved ax, because of its simplicity in form and its very early origin, was probably the result of independent invention in the Western Hemisphere. The weighing of the evidence also shed some doubt on diffusion of the perforated tang ax because of its absence among the islands of Polynesia.

The strongest cases for transoceanic diffusion rest with the elbow-hafted, grooved adz, the shaft-holed star mace, and the vertical-hafted, full-socket ax. Of these, the grooved adz appears to have the strongest case because examples, similar in hafting, shape, and form, have been found in both northwest Argentina and Easter Island. Peter Buck (1938: 322–323) discounts Easter Island as the route to South America from Asia because of the lack of timber there for building suitable canoes. He supports diffusion but believes that the link was from the Marquesas to the north Peruvian coast instead. At this stage the author will not contest Buck's theory until more research is done in the northern Chile–northwestern Argentina region. The conclusion reached about the grooved adz is that diffusion to South America in slow, progressive steps across the South Pacific from China appears possible and that, if the carriers of this adz did leave from Easter Island and were carried directly across, they would have landed on the north coast of Chile, not too distant from where the Argentine adz was found.

In the case of the shaft-holed star mace, the link suggested is between Japan and Ecuador sometime before A.D. 500. This relationship coincides with other possible patterns of diffusion previously introduced by Meggers (1966) and may be part of a complex.

The full-socket method of hafting is very rare in the Western Hemisphere and is limited to the Mochica of coastal Peru. In Indonesia and parts of Melanesia, on the other hand, the concentrations are so dense that some spread into the islands of the Pacific seems likely. Buck (1944: 136) mentions a form of socketed adz "known from Hawaii to New Zealand." Although the type of socket mentioned here is somewhat different from that used in this study, nevertheless the principle is much the same and reinforces the case for transpacific diffusion to Peru. Other comparisons should now be made between the cultures of the Mochica and those of early Southeast Asians to determine any other cultural links that might help to substantiate this concept of the diffusion of the full socket.

Although the patterns of the socket, the elbow, and the shaft-hole hafting methods encourage arguments for transpacific diffusion, those of the plain tang, epsilon, perforated, and butt-hafted, T-shaped axes leave many questions about their independent invention unanswered. Further discoveries will most certainly amplify, clarify, and extend these findings to more specific dates and locations.

How diffusion came about and what routes were used are at the moment mere speculation. What has been established here is that there is enough similarity in shape, in form, in distribution, and in dating of the three forms of hafting—the shaft-hole star mace, the elbow-hafted, grooved adz and the full-socket ax of coastal northwest South America and eastern and southeastern Asia to give the proponents of the theory of "pure coincidence" cause to pause and consider.

9. Pre-Columbian Chickens in America

GEORGE F. CARTER

Plant evidence suggesting pre-Columbian contacts with America has played a considerable role in gaining serious consideration of transoceanic contact with America (Cook, 1901; Sauer, 1952; Hutchinson, Silow and Stephens, 1947; Carter, 1963), but there has been little recent discussion of the zoological evidence. There is the interesting case of a human parasitic worm that man could not have carried through the arctic and that points to an origin on the China or Japan coast (reviewed by Heyerdahl, 1952: 508). There are Mexican hairless dogs for eating that have Chinese counterparts. There is the curious question of the turkey, the data for which closely parallel that for maize in suggesting an introduction into Europe in the fifteenth century via the Near East (Bökönyi and Janossy, 1958). Although Schorger (1966) cites expert opinion that questions the identification of the pre-Columbian turkey bone, I will publish elsewhere data tending to support Bökönyi and Janossy. And there is the case that will be discussed here—that of the chicken.

The question concerning early voyages has progressed. We less frequently hear the dogmatic assertion that they never occurred. Some contact is now generally admitted, and the questions now asked are how early, by whom, how often, how intense, and, the ultimate question, what role did these contacts play in the development of

Amerind civilization? I have pointed out that plant transfers indicate contacts beyond casual touch-and-go situations (Carter, 1963) and that the successful transfer of domestic plants suggests a relatively swift voyage. Should we now find that not only plants but even domestic animals were transferred, we would have further evidence suggestive of extensive contacts by relatively swift voyages rather than drift voyages.

I propose here to build historical models for testing the data already presented, and to introduce some new data. The end product will be probabilistic, and my findings perhaps can be most fairly stated to have shifted the odds a little.

The chicken should not be viewed in a vacuum nor as necessarily a single occurrence. The chicken, turkey, maize, sweet potato, blowguns, and musical instruments may be parts of cultural complexes of differing times and places of origin but all seemingly pointing to meaningful transoceanic contacts, and the full significance of the data can be grasped only when all these cases are considered as a whole or as parts of a series of complexes. Something of the magnitude of the items in question can be gained by consulting Sorenson (this volume), Rowe (1966), Nordenskiöld (1929), and Ferguson (1958). Ferguson alone presents a list of 298 items shared by the Old World and the New World. Despite great unevenness in selection of traits and occasional errors and distortions, there are approximately 500 cultural traits at issue. This is the context of the chicken-in-America problem.

THE CASE OF THE CHICKEN

Whether or not chickens were in America before 1492 has been discussed periodically. Acosta in 1590 concluded for pre-Columbian chickens. Nordenskiöld (1922) concluded for early post-Columbian diffusion and introduction in eastern Brazil, Latcham (1922) and Sauer (1952) for pre-Columbian introduction, and Gilmore (1950) for a post-Columbian introduction, but with reservations. There is general agreement on most of the facts but wide disagreement concerning the interpretation these facts allow.

There is also a tendency to treat the chicken either as a cultural fact, ignoring the biological data, or vice versa. In most cases the chicken is discussed within America with little or no checking of data outside America. All these generalizations are only partial truths.

Sauer, for instance, called attention to the biology of the chicken in America and noted the implications. Nordenskiöld, on the other hand, considered the chicken as a linguistic abstraction and assumed its post-Columbian introduction to be an established fact. There are, of course, reasons for such partial treatment of any question. Time and competence and interests are all limited, and the result is that we are always working with less than complete knowledge bearing on even so limited an item as the chicken. This study too is incomplete; no claim is made other than that it advances the evidence a step or two.

The accepted facts, already amply presented, seem to be these. The chicken was present over most of South America within forty years of the first European contacts (Nordenskiöld, 1922) and seemingly well established in southeast Brazil as early as 1519. The name for the chicken in the Inca Empire precedes the Spanish by at least two generations, though no one can prove that it then meant chicken. Names for chickens in South America are usually not Spanish or Portuguese. Chickens in the hands of Indian groups in remote areas of America are Asiatic in type, not European.

The principal questions are: (1) Is the chicken pre-Columbian in America? (2) Or is this a case of nearly instantaneous diffusion over vast distances? (3) If the chicken is a European introduction, why does it have names unrelated to European origin and why is it biologically unlike European chickens? (4) What other lines of evidence might we seek that would tend to decide the case? Obviously, the key piece of evidence would be a chicken bone from a pre-Columbian archaeological level. Although such a find has been claimed[1] in Chile and the bone identified by experts at the Smithsonian as *Gallus gallus*, adequate proof of pre-Columbian time was not supplied. We can, however, develop some other lines of evidence.

One crucial point is the rate of diffusion of the chicken in America. Is it expectable, or not? Another is the names for the chicken. If they are not European, do they reveal any other relationships? Another is the races of chickens. Are they European? If not, where do they

[1] Dillman S. Bullock found chicken bones in graves on Mocha Island, Chile, that must date before 1687. Chickens are documented on the island by 1600, but there is no dating on the critical grave finds (Bullock, 1956, personal communication).

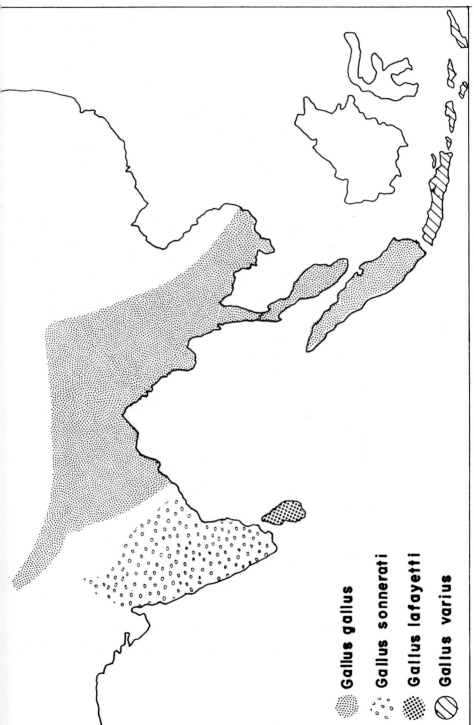

Figure 9.1. Distribution of four species of jungle fowl.

Gallus gallus

Gallus sonnerati

Gallus lafayetti

Gallus varius

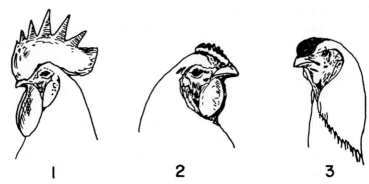

Figure 9.2. Races of chickens as seen in heads and combs. The combs shown are *1*, single; *2*, pea; and *3*, strawberry. The races are Mediterranean, Sinitic, and Malay. The breeds are Minorea, Brahma, and Malay. The Mediterranean birds are flyers and perchers, the Sinitic and Malay birds ground dwellers and almost nonflyers. Temperament, color of eggs, and other characteristics vary along these same lines. Sufficient study probably would allow quite sharp division of the original racial lines. In some cases, details of skeletal structure should allow racial identification from the bones. Malay bones, for example, are much heavier and thicker than Mediterranean bones.

occur? And, most importantly, how early can they be documented in aboriginal America?

In order both to obtain basic data and to develop a basis for judging such things as rates of spread, this study will begin in the Old World. The underlying assumption is that there is at least a modicum of regularity in cultural processes and that what we learn in one area has some application in others.

Origin of the Chicken

The European Model

There is considerable uncertainty concerning some details of the origin of the chicken. *Gallus* has four species in India and Southeast Asia (fig. 9.1). *Gallus gallus* ranges from northwest India through Cambodia and into Sumatra. It lays buff-colored eggs. *Gallus lafayetti* is limited to Ceylon and lays spotted eggs. *Gallus sonnerati* occupies peninsular India and lays spotted or plain (white?) eggs.

Gallus varius is found from Java through Flores. All are interfertile, and domestic chickens may be hybrids containing mixtures of two or more of these species (Hutt, 1949). Note that all the wild chickens lay tinted eggs, with the possible exception of *sonnerati*, which may lay white eggs, if that is the meaning of "plain."

The different areas of the Old World have (or had) differing chickens. The Mediterranean class of chickens is characterized as follows: small body, nervous temperament, large, single comb, white-shelled eggs, early feathering, early sexual maturity (Warren, 1949: 402). East Asian chickens lay tinted (usually brown) eggs and are often pea-combed. Chickens of the Chinese mainland are very heavy bodied, have feathered tarsi, and may also have feathered wattles. They seem to be a breed adapted to cold. India and Indonesia are centers of a great variety of chickens—true bantams, melanotic strains, and silkies. Japan is unlike China but more like India in its chickens.

Some features, such as combs, offer good evidence of origins. Asian breeds may have pea, single, double, or rose combs. European fowls may have single, rose, leaf, V-shaped, or no comb. Pea comb is Asian and is dominant over single comb. Had this gene been introduced into Europe, it would have tended to displace the European single comb. Feathered shanks are Asian: China, India, and Vietnam. Feather-footed chickens probably were reaching eastern Europe via inner Asian routes prior to the arrival in western Europe of the sea-borne Asiatic chickens. Russian chickens have numerous Asiatic traits. Brown (1929) draws the line between Mediterranean races and Asiatic races along the lower Danube. Magyar chickens are related to Italian chickens, but beyond that one enters the Asiatic chicken realm. Shank color also varies systematically. Most European breeds have white shanks, a trait absent in Asia. Asiatic birds have dark shank colors, and this is associated with the odd characteristic known as rumplessness—absence of the final segments of the spinal column. Ear lobes tend to be white in Europe, red in Asia. Black ear lobes mark the Asiatic silkies and Sumatras and accompany other extreme melanotic traits—black skin, flesh, and bones. The silkies are of special interest; their imperfect feathering can only be maintained by rigid selection, since it is a recessive trait. They have ritual importance in Asia. The rumpless chicken is also genetically strange. Rumplessness is dominant over normal vertebrae and is very hard to breed out of a line of chickens. The trait is thought to be Chinese in origin, reaching Persia about the seventeenth century.

These markers allow us to state, with some caution, that fowl with certain characters have specific origins, and that it is possible to distinguish with some certainty between European and Asiatic fowl. If the American Indians had rumpless, silky, feather-wattled, feather-shanked, red-ear-lobed, pea-combed, melanotic, or brown- or tinted-egg-laying chickens, then they had Asiatic and not European chickens. Unless some other explanation were supplied, the implication would also be that these were pre-Columbian Asiatic introductions.

Most of the Indian, Indonesian, and Chinese fowl were unknown in Europe until the nineteenth century, when the so-called hen-craze led to wholesale importations of exotic fowl. McGrew (1926) says that large fowl (Sinitic race) were unknown in Europe until 1816. Aldrovandi (1604), writing at the end of the sixteenth century, describes chickens known to Europeans at that time, as well as chickens reported from the Orient and those known to the classical world. It is most difficult material to use, but it seems to indicate the existence of more chicken varieties in classical times than later. There apparently were real losses, for the Guinea hen (*Meleagris*), which was important in Roman times, disappeared from Italy for nearly a thousand years after the collapse of the Roman Empire. In the sixteenth century, the Europeans were receiving reports of wooly, hairy (silkies), very large races of chickens (or turkeys[?], for they were compared in size and flavor to peacocks), tailless, and aberrant (to them) color types in Asia. Heavy-bodied and feather-footed (Sinitic) chickens are mentioned in Germany, but it is difficult to tell when and from where they were introduced. An Asiatic source perhaps via the Ukraine seems probable, as Brown (1929) has suggested on his maps of the spread of the chicken. In the main, the European race prevailed, and the other races were described as oddities. Even today one can, to a considerable extent, use races of chicken much as we have used races of maize to determine origins and movements of people.

Spread of the Chicken in the Old World

We are concerned with evaluating data, the kind of evidence we should expect for recency or antiquity, for the spread of a domestic fowl. One of the key questions concerns probable rates of diffusion.

I propose to begin by reviewing the data for the spread of the chicken in the Old World. This should give us some insight into the processes involved in the spread of this domestic animal over a large area and through varied cultures and languages.

Diffusion

Domestic chickens are documented for the Indus Valley, and a probable date somewhere between 3000 and 2000 B.C. seems indicated. Since this may not be the point of domestication, the actual date may be considerably earlier. Beebe (1931) favors Burma and eastward. If one assumes "normal" diffusion rates, one thousand years or more might be assumed for domestication prior to the Indus appearance.

It would be useful to have exact dates for domestication and each step in diffusion, but this is seldom obtainable, and we must use approximations. Chickens are not mentioned in the Rig-Veda, but are mentioned in other Vedic literature. It seems likely, therefore, that the Aryan invaders did not know the chicken prior to their entry into India. Chickens are mentioned in Sumeria in the second millennium B.C. The Sumero-Babylonian word for the cock was *tar-lugal,* the King's bird.[2] This seems to indicate that the chicken then had somewhat the position that the peacock had in later times—an ornament for the royal grounds and perhaps an occasional banquet item. The probable dates would then seem to be domestication about 3000 B.C. and diffusion to the West reaching Sumeria around 1500 B.C. Chinese tradition is that they first obtained chickens around 1400 B.C. from the West (Robinson, 1913). The Chinese name for the bird, *ki* or *kai,* can be traced to the Chou dynasty, 1122 to 249 B.C. (Beebe, 1931). The early use of fowl in China was for sacrifices.

It has often been noted that although the Egyptians were greatly interested in birds and kept many kinds—ducks, geese, even pelicans —for food and for eggs, and portrayed them frequently, the chicken never appeared in any of the classical material. It was considered

---

[2] This was taken over into Hebrew in Talmudic sources. In biblical times the word was *zarzir,* and Hebrew seals carry drawings of the chicken at that time (N. H. Tur-sinai, President of the Academy of the Hebrew Language, Jerusalem, 1964, personal communication).

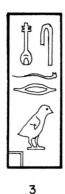

Figure 9.3. Representations of the chicken in classic Egyptian art. *1*, From the tomb of Rekhmara. *2*, From the tomb of Tutankhamen. *3*, The "chick" as portrayed in Egyptian hieroglyphics. The differences between *1* and *2* may be only formal versus informal art style. However, *1* strongly suggests the Malay race and *2* is clearly a cock of the Mediterranean race type. Compare figure 9.2.

that the chicken was introduced into Egypt only in Roman or Ptolemaic times (Meinetzhagen, 1930). Although a figure suspiciously like a chick is common in the hieroglyphs (fig. 9.3), it has not been considered identifiable, especially in the absence of any evidence for adult chickens. It is an interesting example of the danger of negative evidence, for two apparent chicken references have now appeared along with two pictures of cocks. In Ikhnaton's (1379–1362 B.C.)

Hymn to the Sun, the chick is referred to in stanza seven (Hawkes, 1962). Translations are always suspect. In the annals of Thutmose III, however, there is a list of tribute from an Asiatic land: "Lo! four birds of this land, which bring forth every day." Domestic chickens, but not wild chickens, lay eggs frequently. Still, one could argue endlessly about the identity of this bird if there were not an accompanying scene in the tomb of Rekhmara, at Thebes, showing tribute brought to Thutmose. It shows several races of men and many animals. Among them is one cock with an erect, single, three-lobed comb and bilobed wattles (fig. 9.2,1). The time is about 1501–1447 B.C. (date from Lowe, 1934). There is also a sketch of a chicken on an ostracon from the talus of Tutankhamen's tomb, dating to about 1400 B.C. (Lowe, 1929) (fig. 9.2). Both these chickens are single combed, and the one from Tutankhamen's tomb is typical of the wild jungle cock of northwest India, the probable ancestor of the European chickens. After this time there is no record of chickens in Egypt again until about 50 B.C. Zeuner (1956) concluded that the chicken had been introduced as a royal bird but was lost thereafter and was then later introduced into common usage about 50 B.C., a date that would fit fairly well with the chicken's appearance in Palestine about 200 B.C. (Beebe, 1931), following its popularization in Greece after Persian contacts.

From a base date of about 3000 B.C. in India, we find a fifteen-hundred-year lag in the introduction of the chicken to the Mesopotamian and Nile areas. Since he lacked evidence of chickens in intervening land area, Zeuner (1956) suggested that these introductions were by sea routes. Since the Mesopotamians were then engaged in active sea trade with the Indus cities, this is not improbable, but we know so little of the chicken in Persia at that time that it is not a very strong argument. Wood-Gush (1959) cites Dhella to the effect that the cock is prominant in Zoroastrian literature as early as 2000 B.C. Although Zoroaster's dating is uncertain, this seems early, but Beebe's suggestion of a time before 600 B.C. seems late. Since chickens reached Greece in the eighth century, a date in Persia well before 1000 B.C. seems indicated. Perhaps 1500 B.C. is a fair compromise. Egypt may also have had direct sea contacts (Hornell, 1923), since the Egyptians refer the chicken's origin to an Asiatic country and portray it among tribute brought back seemingly by sea. Whether the chicken then disappears for fifteen hundred years or whether the record fails us is more difficult to determine, but the Egyptian record is so rich that a loss seems indicated.

During the first millenium B.C. the chicken spread rapidly westward into Europe. The Greeks called it the Medean bird (rare) or the Persian bird. Representations in Greek art are rare in the eighth century but common in the sixth, by which time the bird was important in religion and in cockfighting. Early in the third century there were special eating breeds that were nonflyers and nonfighters. Although there was no taboo against eating chickens, their primary function was egg-laying. The time intervals are highly significant; centuries were required for these changes.

The Greeks spread the chicken to Sicily by 500 B.C. By 161 B.C. the chicken was conspicuous in Roman menus, and the Romans were fattening and castrating chickens and had laws governing various fowl. When the Romans moved north, they found that the Celts had chickens (first century B.C.) and that the British had them (43 B.C.) but did not eat them. In Cornwall the tradition is that the Phoenicians brought them, which suggests a sea route. The Scots have a similar legend for the origin of their ancient breeds of chicken. Cornishmen also have a rare white-legged breed of gamecocks that they call Persian birds (Johnson and Brown, 1913). Linguistic data on introductions (see below) suggest a Danubian route to northern Europe and a Mediterranean route to southern Europe, with a convergence in northwest Europe (see below). Beebe (1931) considered that the chicken first reached northwest Europe and was carried back into Italy by the Romans after their conquest of Gaul, but he probably was overly influenced in this by the Latin word for chicken, *gallus*. As will be shown below there is a better origin for *gallus* than Gaul.

The spread of the chicken from the Near East to England, the equivalent of spanning North America, or South America at its widest, required about fifteen hundred years from its first introduction in the Near East and Egypt or about eight-hundred years from its establishment in Greece. Not all areas were penetrated at the same speed. From probable Persian contacts, the chicken spread to Palestine about 200 B.C. and is a familiar figure by New Testament time, as is shown in the story of Peter's three denials before the cock's crow. The chicken is established in common usage in Egypt only about 50 B.C., after an earlier 1500 B.C. introduction, which, as

TABLE 9.1
Chicken: Diffusion in the Old World

				Time (Years)	Distance*	Rate (Miles per year)
India	3000 B.C.	China	1400 B.C.	1,600	2,500 L	1.5
India	3000 B.C.	Sumeria	1500 B.C.	1,500	1,500 S	1.0
India	3000 B.C.	Egypt	1500 B.C.	1,500	3,000 S	2.0
India	3000 B.C.	Persia	2000 B.C.	1,000	1,000 L	1.0
Greece	800 B.C.	Sicily	500 B.C.	300	500 S	1.6
Greece	800 B.C.	England	50 B.C.	750	1,500 L	2.0

* L: land route.
  S: sea route.
Distances are air line approximations. The margin of error is probably so high that these rates should be viewed as indicating something between 0.5 and 4 as outside limits and something between 1 and 2 as the best estimate.

we have seen, was perhaps only as a curiosity. The rate of spread to England seems, then, to be best thought of as a rapid one.

Rate of Spread

With the crude data at our disposal it is possible to make some estimates of rates of diffusion. These are shown in table 9.1. In the period about 1500 B.C., the chicken reached China "from the West." This is roughly 2,500 miles in two thousand years, or about one mile per year. I hasten to add that the real travel time may have been quite different, for we do not know if a pilgrim took some chickens and carried them home in one year or if the spread was slow and steady. India to Sumeria (by sea) is fifteen hundred years. Assuming a 3000 B.C. time of domestication and a 1500 B.C. appearance in Sumeria, we again have a travel time of one mile per year. Egypt, nearly twice as far away, yields a two-mile-per-year figure for the first introduction, but if the time of establishment of the chicken about 50 B.C. is used, the rate goes back to about one mile per year. Again, it seems likely that the beginning of extensive sea trade is the key to the appearance of the chicken in these places at these times, and not slow seepage overland. As the Egyptian data show, however, the matter is complex and the "rare bird" phenomenon is different from adoption by the people.

The later data are more suitable for judging overland diffusion rates. The chicken spread from India to Persia at some early date and became extremely important in Zoroastrianism. A time about 1000 or 1500 B.C. for chickens in Persia is suggested. The distance is about one thousand miles and a travel time of about one mile per year would be indicated. Chickens arrived in Greece from Persia in the eighth century, a distance of about two thousand miles in twelve hundred years, or about 1.66 miles per year. Greece to Sicily, five hundred miles in three hundred years, seems slow, especially when sea routes linked Greece to Greek colonies in Sicily. It should caution us against assumptions of instantaneous diffusion, for here the same people (Greeks) were linked by rapid sea transport; yet, so far as the data show, it was three hundred years before the chicken was carried to these nearby colonies. Greece (Turkish coast) to England via the Danubian countries, a probable route, yields a travel rate of two miles per year. This may be our best figure for a land route, since we have better control of the dates at both ends and know the actual route.

Despite the crudity of the data, the range is clearly between one and two miles per year, and our best figure is two miles per year for spreading over a fifteen-hundred-mile area by land through tribal people. A rate of spread over a comparable distance through tribal groups might well be at one-fourth, or four times this rate of one to two miles per year, but a rate ten or twenty times as fast would seem suspect. It is reassuring to find that this is exactly the order of magnitude of diffusion time that Doran finds for the spread of boat traditions (this symposium) and that Edmonson (1961) found for a number of traits spread on a Neolithic cultural level.

Just why the spread of so useful an item as a domestic bird should be so slow is intriguing and deserves more extensive analyses than can be done here. It should be noted that there are many cases of failures of diffusions of domestic animals. The turkey, although wild and hunted in eastern America north of Mexico, was not accepted as a domestic bird, in spite of the considerable Mexican cultural influence in that area. Neither did the turkey spread into South America, with a possible exception in a small part of the Ecuadorian-Colombian region. Neither did reindeer husbandry spread from Siberia to America, or llama-keeping from the Andes to Mexico, despite evidence of sea-trade contacts that served to spread other ideas (see

Meighan in Kelley and Riley, 1969). The record does not suggest that men quickly seize novel ideas.

The early spread of the chicken was as a sporting bird (cockfighting) and as a cult animal (for divination and sacrifice). In both cases a whole complex of ideas, attitudes, and skills had to be passed along with the bird. Cockfighting could not spread into areas where other men did not have fighting cocks. Divination with domestic fowl implies a whole complex of ideas: keeping fowl with all the required knowledge on care, feeding, and propagation; and another set of magico-religious ideas and practices that must sometimes have conflicted with preceding notions. Case studies of spreads of comparable items would probably show that the role of individuals in accepting or rejecting such novelties would give us a pattern of intermittent spurts and delays. Notice, for instance, the relatively rapid Graeco-Roman acceptance of the bird compared with the slowness of its establishment in the Palestinian area. In the Palestinian area the bird was first a sacrificial animal; "there was at first considerable opposition to the ordinary economic breeding of fowls, by those who considered the birds as special objects of religious significance" (Beebe, 1931: 241). And as already indicated, there may have been considerable delays in Egypt between the appearance of the chicken as a novelty in 1500 B.C. and its acceptance in the culture as an economic item about 50 B.C. The record, poor as it is, is more suggestive of slow acceptance by individuals and cultures than of rapid diffusion and acceptance. Acceptance rather than contact seems to be the key to the slowness of spread.

Linguistic Data on Routes

When the names for the chicken from India to the Atlantic are mapped, certain relationships stand out clearly. From the Sanskrit *kukuta* (cock), to Persian *khurus* (cock), to Old Slavic *kukuta* (cock), Latin *cucurio* (cock), German *kucklein* (chicken), and Dutch *kieken* (chicken), to English *chicken* is a rather simple and direct trail (fig. 9.4). One should note that linking *kukuta* to *chicken* would not be simple if the intermediate steps had been lost. The *Oxford English Dictionary* (1961) gives the derivation of chicken as from Old Teutonic (early centuries A.D.): *kiukino*, a diminutive of *kiuk*, an ablaut form of *kuk*, whence cock. The closeness of *kuk* to such Indian forms as *kukut* is obvious. *OED* also notes that *cock* in

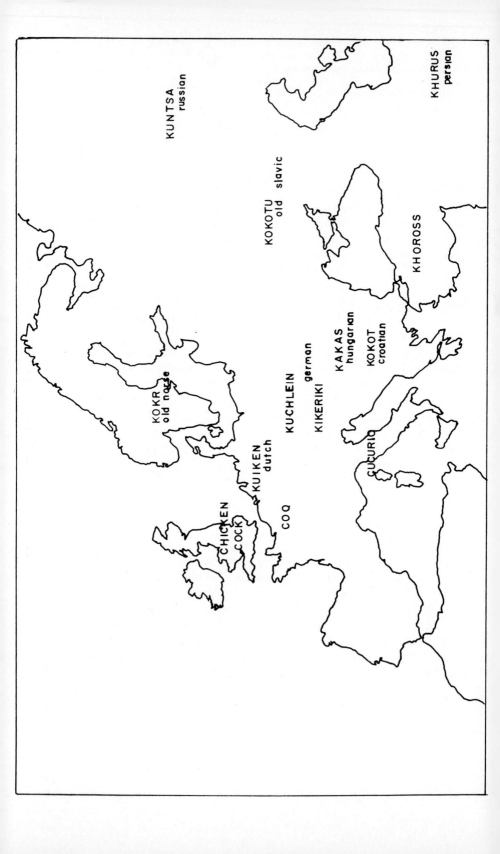

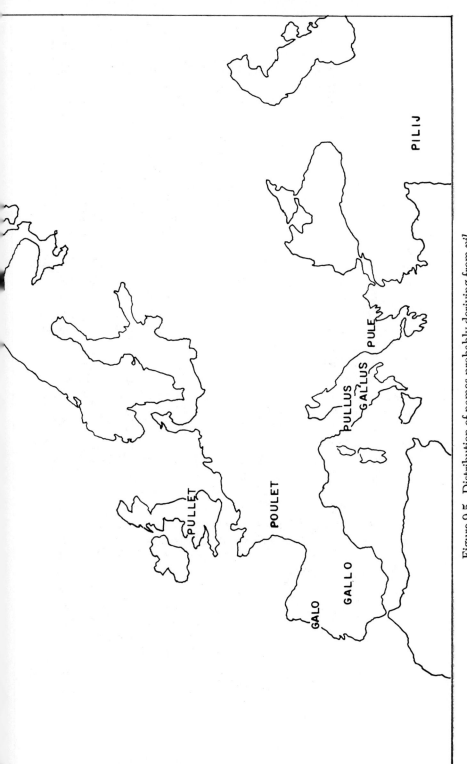

Figure 9.5. Distribution of names probably deriving from *pil.*

Old Teutonic is usually spelled *kok*, indicating a foreign origin. This suggests that the chicken was a relatively recent arrival at that time. Given the well-preserved intermediate steps, the trail stemming from India about 3000 B.C. or earlier is quite clear even today. Obviously, this sequence is selective and avoids the Latin *gallus* from which apparently springs *gallo* and *pollo*. *Gallus* seems to derive from Hindu *pil*, from which stem *pilij*, *pule*, *pullus*, and *gallus* (fig. 9.5). The Romans also used *cucurio*, and this seems likely to have been derived from the *kuk* series, suggesting plural times and routes of diffusion. Since these series are continuous and historically linked, an explanation based on repetitive invention of onomatopoeic names seems out of the question.

Southward in East Africa, one finds *kuku*, *kuki*, and *koko* with modifiers (Senga, *n kuku*; Wisa, *n koko*; Kaffir, *kuku*). These seem clearly to point to Indian origins, and probably few would quarrel with such an interpretation of the evidence by appealing to onomatopoeic naming, independent invention, psychic unity, or the like. *Kui* (Bornu, West Africa) also probably belongs in this series. The linguistic evidence is supported by zoological data. African chicken eggs are dark brown, indicating that their chickens do not belong to the Mediterranean race. Africa also has melanotic strains with black flesh; these also are found in India, but not in Europe.

Richness of names often is a clue to both importance and antiquity of an item in a culture. The diversity of names in Asia suggests antiquity. Within India, there are not only differing names—*kukut*, *murgh*, and *pil*, all forming bases for names—but also specific names for special fowl. Thus, black-fleshed fowl are *chogho khara*. A breed of small fowl (bantams) is *kharcha* and its varieties are *teni*, *kulang*, *kokni*. A variety of this small race with black bones and skin is called *karaknath* or *karnatak*. Such wealth of varieties and names for them suggests both importance and antiquity for the chicken in India.

Elsewhere in Asia there is considerable linguistic diversity. Much of Indonesia has *ayam* as a root for chicken. Southeast Asia, including South China and the Philippines, have *kai*, *ke*, and *kei* forms, and, as was noted earlier, the Chinese have these names as early as the Chou dynasty. The Japanese have separate sets of names for fowl, cock, hen, and chick (*totori*, *ondori*, *on*, *hina*, *hiyokko*), and the early poultry specialists noted that Japanese chickens were quite different from Chinese chickens. Nevertheless, certain things are apparent.

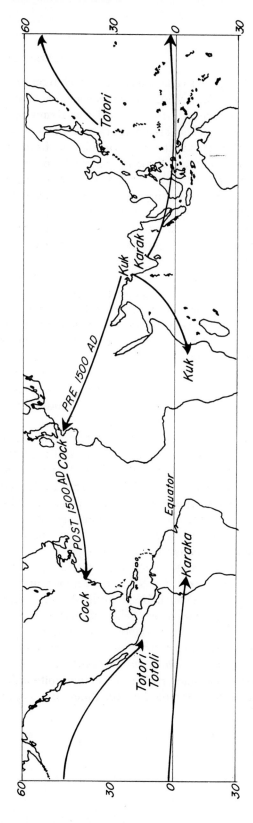

Figure 9.6. Transoceanic name similarities. The case of *kuk* to cock in Great Britain and thence across the Atlantic to the United States is a model of distant travel of the bird and its name. The *kuk* name also crossed the Indian Ocean to Africa virtually unchanged. The *karak* root as a chicken name seems to belong in this same category for the name, the race of chicken, and the uses are Asiatic. *Totori* in Japan seems to be repeated among the Tarahumar and the Aztec, and again the Indian attitudes and the races of chickens present are Asiatic rather than 16th-century European.

Names can be followed over long distances and large time expanses, including across oceans. They are almost universally explainable on the basis of diffusion of the bird as well as the name for the bird. Onomatopoeia, so often invoked, seems rarely applicable.

In passing, it is important to note that in Guam, where the Spanish influence was overwhelming, the name of the chicken is *gallo* and *pollo*. In the Philippines, where the Spanish were a tiny minority, pre-Spanish, apparently Chinese, names, *ke, kaki*, were retained. When Asiatic chickens were introduced in the nineteenth century into Europe, an area where chickens had long been established, they did not carry their Asiatic names with them, although the various breeds were often named according to their origin—bantams and cochins for instance.

The rule seems to be that where the chicken was well established among a population that remained numerically dominant, the native name was retained, just as in America *maize* was retained in the area where Indians survived, whereas *corn* was substituted in the British lands where the Indians were extinguished.

The Chicken in Polynesia

The Pacific is of particular interest as a diffusion model, and there is a modest amount of data available due to Ball's study, *Jungle Fowls from Pacific Islands*. The Polynesian attitude was distinctly Asiatic. The chicken was primarily for cockfighting; flesh and eggs were of little importance. White chickens were used in Hawaii for necromancy—again the Asiatic pattern of the importance of white chickens for ritual. Quiros also reported white fowl on the Santa Cruz islands in the New Hebrides. That the Maori had known chickens is suggested by their calling the large ground-dwelling birds there by the general Polynesian name for chicken, *moa*.

Melanotic strains were widespread. Combs are all single and often large. In Fiji and the Marquesas the birds were larger, and on the Marquesas they had feathered tarsi. Large birds with feathered feet strongly suggest the presence of genes of the Sinitic race of chickens. Variation is greater in the Society Islands and Marquesas than in Fiji or the New Hebrides. The Marquesans depart from standard Polynesian in calling the chicken *kuku* instead of *moa*. *Kuku* is clearly related to the Sanskrit name, and the presence in the Marquesas of an inscription in letters belonging to the fourteenth-century kingdom of

Majapahit and ultimately of Hindu origin (Handy, 1943) seems to tie this together. Ball cites Handy on the frequent use of cock feathers in the Marquesas in headdresses and gives the names as *hei kua, hei mekameka,* and *hei pe afe a. Hei* is Chinese for chicken and the large size and feathered tarsi are specific Chinese chicken traits. We have here, then, linguistic and zoological evidence suggesting plural introductions of fowl to the Marquesas with both India and China as sources. Such complexity of origins probably underlies the greater variation in chickens in the Polynesian islands than in the Melanesian islands.

The most ancient game among the Tahitians was cockfighting, and they believed that the chicken had been on the islands as long as the people. They actually have conflicting legends: that the chickens were always there, and that the first colonists brought them. The Polynesians had special gods for cockfighting, and even the natives that did not have chickens had names for them. The Marquesans had a legend that a man named Haii had brought chickens twenty generations before 1812. *Hei* is the Chinese word for chicken, and, as was noted earlier, the Marquesans not only have traces of Sinitic chicken races but also attach the Chinese name to the feather ornaments that they make from chicken feathers. Some of the Hawaiian feather cloaks are said to be made with chicken feathers.

Easter Island, the closest of the Polynesian group to America, is of special interest, even though this was not necessarily the springboard for voyages to and from America. Metraux (1940) has supplied considerable information on the chicken in his study of the island. Chickens were found abundant at the time of contact. They are described as a small, long-legged fowl. They were of great social and economic value and were one of the five gifts that one gave to honored persons. There were henhouses, and chickens were important as food as well as used for feathers. Perhaps significantly, there is no mention of cockfighting on Easter Island. The legend of the arrival of Hotu-Matua includes a long list of the things that he brought and the chicken is included in this list. The chicken is involved in numerous ceremonies and sacrifices, and white chickens, especially cocks, were prominent. A white cock was used by sorcerers to cause the death of another person. The most cherished feathers were those of white cocks, which were kept in gourd containers and taken out when headdresses were to be made. The white chicken was also used to conjure with—for example, the case of the driftwood tree, which could be made to obey a boy through the power of a white chicken. If chickens were carried to America by Asiatics, these are the kinds of cultural patterns to be expected.

Ball considered the jungle fowl on the Polynesian islands to be feral birds and the domestic breeds to be post-1840. He is almost surely wrong. His own evidence suggests plural introductions before 1540 of fowl that were close to the wild jungle fowl, and also of domestic strains of white fowl and of some seemingly large Chinese mainland chickens, at least in the Marquesas. The early accounts (Quiros, Leza, Cook, Bougainville) all state that the islanders had fowl like European chickens, even at times saying "exactly like ours" and specifying races of white chickens.

The data suggest early introductions of chickens similar in appearance to wild jungle fowl. These have often gone wild. Later (see Metraux, 1940, on Easter Island) such developed breeds as white fowl and large feather-footed fowl were spread to some of the islands; the linguistic and zoologic data suggest Hindu and Chinese sources. A considerable time span may be indicated. For America, it seems relevant that the wild jungle fowl types are not in question but that the later developed breeds are. Seemingly fully domesticated chickens do not become feral, and it was only the fully domestic types that reached America. Such breeds in Polynesia are hinted at by the feathered tarsi and virtually proved by the presence of white chickens even as far east as Easter Island.

Polynesia is of particular interest as a model, for the distances traveled are immense; but there is no resistance to the idea of Asiatic origins for cultural traits even in that distant outpost, Easter Island. The scattered notes above suggest that the Asiatic chicken was carried into the Pacific through a series of introductions. Asiatic attitudes, customs, and even names at times accompanied the bird. The complex of biological, linguistic, and cultural data consitutes the evidence of the Asiatic origin for this immense spread. Similar data elsewhere should have similar meaning.

Summary of Old World Model

The chicken spread relatively slowly at first, requiring fifteen hundred years or more to reach the eastern Mediterranean effectively. Thereafter, about eight hundred years or more were required for the spread to England. Over this time span, the linguistic relationships are quite clear, and onomatopoeia, chance convergence, and similar explanations seem inapplicable. In East Asia linguistic relationships are not so clear. Indonesians, Polynesians, Chinese, and Japanese have very divergent names for their chickens. Presumably, the time span in Asia is much greater and divergence has obscured any original relationships. Occasional relationships to mainland names appear in Polynesia (Hawaii, Marquesas, and Mangareva). Africa presents a case contrary to Asia. The relationships are close and point to India, and, presumably, the time span since introduction is less great. The biological strains are markedly different in Asia and Europe. Asiatic attitudes toward chickens in ritual remained much closer to the probable original pattern than was true of sixteenth-century Europe. All these items afford possibly useful clues for Americanists studying chickens in America.

DATA FOR AMERICA

Concerning the chicken in America, there is basic agreement on the facts between those who consider it post-Columbian and those who consider it pre-Columbian. Gilmore (1950: 394), who holds a relatively neutral position, summarizes the data as follows:

> The first authentic landing of Europeans on the coast of Brazil was near Bahia on April 22, 1500, by Cabral who brought chickens.[3] Pinzon and Lepe had landed a few months earlier somewhere north of the Amazon River. Unless one accepts the rumored earlier landings by the Portuguese (said to have been as early as 1448), 31 years is the maximum time for this remarkable diffusion of the chicken (to Peru) but Nordenskiöld clearly showed that extensive trade routes were well established and that the chicken was treated as a special pet. However, if this explanation is unacceptable, the origin of a true chicken in pre-conquest Peru must be sought in Polynesian transoceanic voyages.

That it had to be Polynesian is an assumption in keeping with the thought of that day.

Gilmore uses thirty-one years as the diffusion time, for he accepts both Nordenskiöld's 1500 date for the Portuguese introduction on the coast of Brazil and his philological argument for the Inca's knowing

---

[3] Sauer (1952: 58) has commented, "No document mentions anything of the sort [leaving chickens], though the journals of Cabral's voyage are quite detailed."

the chicken prior to the arrival of the Spanish in 1532. Nordenskiöld pointed to the Quechua name for the last Inca, Atahualpa, as evidence that the chicken preceded the Spanish to Peru. He also noted that the last Inca's uncle had been named *hualpa* (Huallpa Túpac Inca Yupanqui). Either these men were named after the chicken, or the chicken was named after them. Garcilaso de la Vega says that the chicken was named in memory of Atahualpa so that each time the cock crowed, he would be remembered. This leaves unexplained the naming of Atahualpa's uncle. Naming of Inca after birds was usual, as Nordenskiöld points out, so that the probability that the chicken name preceded the Spanish by a generation or so seems slightly favored. Whether it was then applied to the chicken or not must be decided on some other basis. We now turn to our European models as aids in evaluating the data.

The evidence indicates that chickens were very widespread in South America within twenty to forty years of first contact. These spot records indicate that the chicken was established from the Atlantic to the Pacific and from northwest Brazil to Argentina in less than forty years. In terms of established dates as opposed to assumed introductions, the earliest record is 1519, on the coast of southern Brazil, and if this date is used as a base, this enormous diffusion occurred in less than fifteen years. The first Spaniards into the interior of Brazil (upper Amazon, 1560; Río Ucayale, 1544) found chickens already established. And, of course, Atahualpa in 1533 had been so named at least a few years before the arrival of the Spanish, and his uncle some years before that. We are faced with a spread of the chicken over an area larger than the United States within fifteen to thirty years. The diffusion time to some of these points (see table 9.2) seems quite rapid: for example, from southern Brazil to Ucayale River, two thousand miles away, took twenty-five years—eighty miles per year. To have reached Peru before the Spanish, rates of one hundred miles per year would have been required for the Cabral assumption, or two hundred miles per year for the 1519 date. This rate of diffusion of the chicken from eastern Brazil to Peru is totally out of step with the parallels from Eurasia.

Nordenskiöld emphasized the existence of developed trade routes in South America, but even older and equally efficient ones existed in the Indo-European area. Romans and Greeks had trade relations with India from 200 B.C. to A.D. 400. Hindus and, later, Arabs used the monsoon to sail freely in the Indian Ocean. The spread of objects and ideas (silk, cotton, rudders, papermaking) still required millennia. One could argue that the Spanish changed these rates. But this does not seem to apply to the chicken in South America. The sixteenth-century Spanish explorers of the interior were hungry men seeking food, not dispensing chickens, and Egyptians and Jews caution us that not all people quickly adopt a strange plant or animal. (Also see Carter, 1963, for a discussion of the phenomenon.) The great tribal migrations set off by the European colonization will not help explain this apparently rapid rate of diffusion, for the chicken was widespread prior to the migrations. One must move the chicken by virtually unchanged Indian routes and connections to account for the time of reported observations of chickens among the Indians. So rapid a spread in the New World as has been generally accepted is an assumption that the model of chicken diffusion in the Old World and other studies of rates of acceptance and diffusion seem to make questionable.

TABLE 9.2

Spread of Chicken in South America
Nordenskiöld's assumption: Chicken introduced in northeast Brazil at 1500

			Distance (Miles)	Travel Time (Years)	Rate (Miles per year)
Cabral	1532	Peru	3,000	30	100
Cabot	1526	Southern Brazil	1,500	25	60
Orellana	1541	Amazon	2,000	40	50
Federman	1531	Orinoco	2,500	30	80
Correa y Acuña	1543	Paraguay River	1,600	40	40
Rojas	1542	Northern Argentina	2,500	40	60

Names as Evidence

In an exhaustive study of words among the Indians in South America, Nordenskiöld examined the evidence for domestic fowl, horse, cow, banana, iron, firearms, scissors, and European knives. The work is biased by his unquestioning acceptance that all these were post-Columbian in time of introduction. As students in this area know, both the banana and the chicken are questionable.

If we examine Nordenskiöld's conclusions, we find the following. Of the alleged post-Spanish names, the chicken name was most wide-spread and Nordenskiöld attributed this to more time for spread (1922: 143). He noted that the Guaraní from Paraguay to Guiana shared similar words for banana, fire arms, needles, steel knives, and scissors but that their names for domestic fowl were quite different in different localities. He thought this could be explained by invoking plural routes and earlier spread, and he noted that his evidence showed that the Guaraní had chickens before their great north-to-south migrations occurred. For the eastern and western Carib, his evidence pointed to similar conclusions. They share a common name for chickens but have different words for metal needles and knives and firearms; this indicates that they had the chicken (and also the banana) before their migrations separated them. Finally, he noted that the *takara-karaka* name for the chicken was more widely spread than any other post-Columbian cultural element and that this must be due to the fact that chickens were spread more rapidly, more widely, and earlier than the other European cultural elements. Nor-denskiöld's data flatly state that the chicken surely precedes European cows, horses, iron, scissors, guns, fishhooks, knives, and needles. How much earlier in time the chicken was, his data do not tell us.

The variety of names for the chicken and the scarcity of European names are suggestive of antiquity and of non-European origins. Acosta, in 1590, pointed this out clearly: ". . . I must say that I was astonished at the fowls which without doubt were kept there even before the coming of the Spaniards, this being clearly proved by the fact that the natives have names of their own for them, calling a hen *gualpa* and an egg *ronto*" (from Castello, 1924: 116). One is left wondering if Acosta was astonished that they had chickens, or at the kinds of chickens, or both. Capa says: "In the first accounts of the conquest, we frequently hear of hens and the name leads us to be-lieve that they were like our own; this however, is not so and only the birds of Paraguay and Tucumán were somewhat similar to ours" (Capa, 1915: V, 427). Capa had access to original sources, but he neither cites nor quotes them on this topic. His comment would seem to verify chickens for Paraguay and Tucumán at contact time. These areas border the Inca Empire, where the *hualpa* names suggest pre-Columbian age for the chicken. The diffusion may have been from west to east in pre-Columbian times! Acosta, who was much closer to

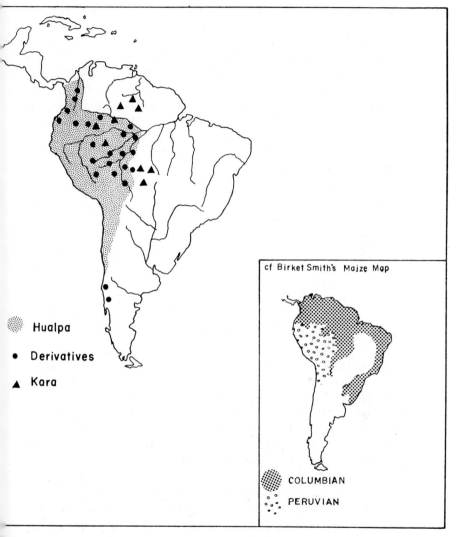

Hualpa

Derivatives

Kara

cf Birket Smith's Maize Map

COLUMBIAN

PERUVIAN

Figure 9.7. Distribution of maize names and chicken names in South America. Nordenskiöld's map has been simplified here to show the distribution of *hualpa* and its derivatives and the *kara* names. The association of the *hualpa* names with the Andean civilizations seems clear. The general distribution for these names is suggestive of an introduction at some point on the Pacific coast somewhere in Ecuador or northern Peru. Birket-Smith's map of the names for maize, virtually a duplicate of this map, documents diffusion from the Ecuadoran region dating back to about 1500 B.C.

the data than Capa and also used linguistic evidence, was much surer of pre-Columbian chickens, especially in Peru.

Nordenskiöld mapped his data for South America (fig. 9.7). The Inca Empire and adjacent regions are marked by the use of *hualpa* and its derivatives as a name for chicken. This includes Chibchan, Quechuan, Aymaran, and Araucanian linguistic groups. In addition, this type of name appears sporadically in the headwaters of the Amazon in Pano, Tupi, and Arawak territory and far north into Ecuador, and in Chile almost to the island of Chiloe in the south. The north-south distance is about three thousand miles. Both the distance and the variation in names is comparable to the spread from Persia to northwest Europe. As we have seen, however, not less than fifteen hundred years was involved in that case. A comparable distance in America would be an introduction at New York, spreading north to Ottawa and south to Miami and then west in a long tongue through the south to Los Angeles. This kind of spread was assumed by Nordenskiöld to have occurred in about thirty years; in hard data (1519–1533) less than fifteen years seems available. I am unaware of any comparably rapid spread over so vast an area resulting from European contact. On the contrary, diffusion of traits with very considerable antiquity in South America has produced a pattern almost exactly like that of the chicken.

Birket-Smith (1943: 32–33) reduced the names for maize in South America to two great groups: Peruvian and Colombian. The Peruvian group included the old Inca Empire and extended into the lowlands to the east—Jívaro, Zaparo, Panoans, Moseteñe, and the neighboring Arawakan tribes. This is strikingly parallel to the distribution of the *hualpa* names for the chicken. The Colombian maize names had an even wider distribution—to the northwest: northern Peru (Chimu) to Honduras (Lenca), Guatemala (Xinca), and southern Mexico (Chiapanec, Mazatec); to the east: Tupian, Cariban, Tucanoan, and most of the Arawakan. Here, as with the name for chickens, the Arawak divide. This would be consistent with their originally lacking both maize and chickens and, after their spread into South America, their obtaining them from adjacent people. Maize is now considered to have been carried from Mexico to South America around 1500 B.C., and the linguistic linkages to southern Mexico thereby gain considerable interest. If maize, spreading after 1500 B.C., has a distribution comparable to that for the chicken, as it does, then there is more reason to think of the diffusion of the chicken as pre-Columbian than as post-Columbian. It is pressing the data rather hard, but if the rate of spread of ideas is taken as about one mile per year, as the Old World model suggests, and if the spread of the chicken from a Pacific coastal point of introduction is assumed, then the distance traveled in South America is about three thousand miles. The indicated time of introduction would be 1500 B.C., about the same time as the intro- duction of maize. The similarities in distribution and changes in forms of the words are sufficiently parallel to be reinforcing.

Capa (1915) gives some relevant data for rapid spread, however. He cites an introduction of chickens in the Caribbean, followed by a very rapid build up of large flocks, and their spread subsequently to many parts of America. "Those (chickens) called 'from Castille' were with the famous explorers in the island of Gallo and they increased so that there was an abundance of eggs in all the viceroyalty which was no small assistance to the traveler and merchant, because of the scarcity of other foods in the Indian towns. The Spanish worked hard to multiply so useful a bird, imposing tributes of chickens and eggs" (my rough translation).

The situation in the Caribbean is not clear. Why designate some chickens as "from Castille" if not to differentiate them from other chickens that were not "from Castille"? One could argue that it was chickens versus turkeys, but supposedly there were no turkeys in the Caribbean. On the other hand, there were both European and Asiatic races of chickens in the Caribbean relatively early. Wafer (1903: 121) in describing his experiences as a buccaneer from 1680 to 1700 clearly describes both a European race and a Sinitic race type. The Sinitic fowl were small, feather legged, bush tailed, and avoided the larger European birds. Probably the European birds would be prolific egg layers, since they were bred for this trait. The Sinitic birds prob- ably would not be. The Spanish would expectably promote the dis- persion and keeping of the European types, and the early records show that the Indians were required to pay taxes in eggs.

There is a persistent discrimination between *gallina de Castille* and *gallina de Mexico* (or other areas in the New World) that invites careful scrutiny. All poultry experts agree on the presence of Asiatic races, and they almost equally uniformly blandly assume post-1500 introductions. No proof is ever offered. It may be important to recall that although chickens were surely absent in some parts of America, they may have been present in others. Chickens may have been absent in Mexico and the Caribbean but present in Peru and adjacent (but not all) South America.

Additional evidence for a pre-Columbian chicken comes from the Arawak who live in the Orinoco drainage area and scattered through the headwaters of the Amazon. The northern Venezuelan Arawak had no chickens at contact, lack an Indian name for them, but call the chicken *gallina*, clearly revealing a Spanish source.

Among the central and western Guiana Arawak the name for the chicken is *takara, karaka,* and related forms, and seemingly their source was non-Spanish. *Takara* and *karaka* strikingly recall the Hindu names for small melanotic strains of chickens, for *karaknath*[4] is close to *karaka* and *khara,* since they all share *kara* as an apparent root. A Hindu name in America may be unexpected, but intermittently since the late nineteenth century it has been pointed out that *kumar* is an ancient word in India with wide associated meanings, whereas in America it has a very narrow meaning (sweet potato) and a limited area (northern Andean). I have argued elsewhere (Carter, 1950) that this could be explained as a Hindu word applied in one local area in America to an American plant and have learned since that many others had preceded me in discovering this. The parallel would be the English naming *Zea mays* "corn," thus utilizing an old English word that had wide, nonspecific meaning (any small, hard object, hence, a grain, a pepper corn, and so forth). The Hawaiian name for chicken also seems significant here. *Moa kakala* is virtually identical to Arawakan *takara,* which in turn approximates Hindu *khara.* The shifts are closely parallel to the *kumar, kumara, kumala, umala, uwala* series for the sweet potato, and some of the key locations (coast of South America, Hawaii, India) are the same. And again, context is important; religion, calendar, plants, animals, and linguistic evidence all suggest a Hindu element in America.

We are here confronted with near identity of names and things and a similar geographic distribution. The things are biological entities not subject to independent invention and not capable of transoceanic transfers by natural means. The chances against one occur-

---

[4] Beebe (1931) attributes "*karnatak* to a non-fighting breed in which the skin, bones, tongue, eyes, and blood are all black." He cites an Urdu source on cock-fighting.

rence of this type must be reckoned as very high. For two of them (chicken and sweet potato), the odds are immense, and the list can be expanded (see below). Note, for instance, that the Guaymi word for chicken is *kui*. This is distinctly different from the name for the Spanish introduced guinea fowl which they call by the Spanish name, *perdis*. If they took Spanish names for Spanish introductions, why was the chicken not called *gallina? Kui,* on the other hand, is close to Hindustani *kukri,* from which such African forms as *kuki* probably derive. The *kukus, kuki,* or *kui* series seem genetically related and point to an Old World origin in India. One would hesitate to use names separated by such vast distances if these were not the connecting links of East Africa, India, and the Pacific. The Guaymi are neighbors of the Cuna, who possessed writing, and among whom Metraux, attempting to debunk Hevesy, found a dozen signs duplicated in both Easter Island and the Indus Valley.

The *kara* name in India refers specifically to melanotic strains; just such chickens were reported on the coast of Ecuador in the early nineteenth century (Punnett, 1933) and are amongst the fowl of Brazil described by Finsterbusch (1929: 462 ff.) as clearly Asiatic. In India, melanotic traits and silky (wooly) feathers are genetically linked. Possibly a genetic complex of silky melanotic fowl is ancient in this area. If so, we have the curious situation of a name, signs, and a biological entity, all pointing to India and all in one area. A caution must be entered here.

Capa says that a line of chickens with black flesh was brought from the province of Guinea. They were considered unappetizing and were not liked in Peru (1915: 444). He does not cite his sources, and such an introduction would leave the name unexplained. It is, of course, possible that melanotic strains were pre-Columbian and that the Spanish introduced more of them, in this case seemingly from Africa, but the name linkage, though weakened by lack of knowledge of races of chickens in the hands of the Indians in the *takara-karaka* area, strongly suggests non-Spanish and non-African origins. Students of fighting cocks freely acknowledge that the South American cocks were oriental (cf. Finsterbusch, 1929).

Among the curiosa of this collection of names is the discovery that among the Tarahumar the name for chickens is *totori,* which duplicates the Japanese name. Naked-necked chickens (Malay race) are numerous in the Tarahumar area today (Pennington, personal communication). Both archival and archaeological research seems desirable to see what this means. We often too quickly get into either/or arguments. There is no reason that a separate introduction of chickens might not have been made on the northwest coast of Mexico. Nor must one assume that this would automatically have spread to Mexico City. It could have spread in any direction, to the Pueblos, for instance. Or it might have remained localized. It is an intriguing situation that deserves investigation.

The point of Spanish versus non-Spanish names deserves stressing. In northern Venezuela we have an explicit account of the absence of chickens at contact time and of these people obtaining chickens from Europeans. In this area today the Indian names are derivatives of *gallo* and *gallina*. Since this is Arawak territory, it suggests something other than a northern or Caribbean source for the Arawak chickens south of Venezuela. There the name is similar to a Hindu name, the attitude toward chickens is Asiatic (non-eating), and Nordenskiöld found that the chicken name preceded all the known European-introduced names. The parallel is, again, close to the Eurasian model. The spread of the chicken into new areas tends to carry the name used by the introducer. Once the chicken is established, it tends to retain its name unless the impact of the incoming people is overwhelming (consider Guam versus the Philippines). From the Venezuelan case, it seems clear that the chicken did not have a universal spread in South America. This cannot be used as evidence of recency of introduction, for domestic turkey keeping did not have a universal spread in North America and seemingly failed to spread in pre-Columbian time into the Caribbean or even into the Southeast, despite Mexican influences and the presence of wild turkeys. Neither did turkey keeping spread into South America, despite the contacts with Mexico.

Rivet (1957) discussed some data on names in Asia, Polynesia, and America, and his comments are so pertinent as to deserve summarizing here. He pointed to the sweet potato names, noting that the *kumar-kumara* linkage to Polynesia extended on into New Guinea (*kumala*) and even into certain Mon-Khmer and Indian dialects. He cited:

Sweet potato	*kumadjang* in Java
Yam (cultivated)	*kemarung* in Saka of Pahang
Yam (wild)	*kemahang* in Malay and Semang of Kedak

Yam	*kambar* in Madagascar
Yam	*kamalu* in Bengali (cf. *kumala*)
Yam	*kumara* in Telugu
Plectanthera tuberosa	*kumali, gumeli* in Sunda
Solanum nigrum	*kamal* in Cachemise

These all share *kuma, kema, kamba, kama.* He contrasted the wide-spread use of this word in the Old World, where it was apparently applied to several root crops, with its narrow application in America, which he assigned to a narrow group of northern Quechuan (in Ecuador) and to the nearby Cuna (*kwalu*). Of equal interest, he cited Frederici's discussion of another word for root crops in Oceania (yam, taro, sweet potato) and similar relationships that are general in Oceania, localized in America. This is *kapa,* from which in Oceania one gets *ape, ep, up, ebe, ebi, ubi;* the intervocalic can become *b, v, w, f,* or *h* or be eliminated. *Apitchu* in Quechuan would very easily derive from this series. As with the chicken, it is possible that we are looking at two or more word introductions. As Rivet noted, these words do not stand alone. There is the *maho-mahagua* series for the *Hibiscus tiliaceous.* Further, *toki,* meaning adz and applied to an adz used as a symbol of a chief, is also common to Polynesia and to the Arawak in America. It may be widespread on the South American coast, for *toki* is also the Araucanian word for ax (adz). As Beirne (this symposium) shows, Polynesian adz types are definitely present in this same area. Again, the word is variable in Polynesia—*t'oi, koi, toki,* derived from *taka* 'to strike'—but of isolated and limited form in America. It is surprising that E. D. Merrill paid so little attention to these papers, originally published in the 1920's, when he was flailing away at the proponents of plant diffusion, often using barrages of linguistics.

The gist of the data from names is that, except in areas where the chicken was absent at contact times and the introduction is known to have been by Spaniards, the names used are non-Spanish. Names vary considerably, suggesting plural introductions, or much time, or both. Three names, one in South America, one in Central America, and one in Mexico, seem directly related to Asiatic names for the chicken. This is far from being an isolated case; two Oceanian-American linkages for names for sweet potatoes have long been in the literature, and there are other plant and artifact name linkages.

Zoological Data

The data so far suggest that the chicken might have been pre-Columbian in America and possibly of Asiatic origin and that at least one strain might be expected to be related to an Asiatic Indian type. It has frequently been pointed out that there are non-European chickens in the hands of remote Indian groups (Sauer, 1952; Castello, 1924; Latcham, 1922). Castello, starting with an interest in the unusual fowl of Chile that has puffs of feathers on the sides of its head, gave papers at two successive international poultry congresses on this matter. The second paper had the advantage of information elicited from all over the poultry world by the first paper. He stated that there were then five types of chickens in Chile, though now badly mixed: the common European fowl; curly or frizzle-feathered fowl (the type Columbus mentioned [?]); ear-tufted fowl that rarely lay blue eggs; a fowl that normally lays blue eggs; and blue-egg-laying fowl with a hairlike covering, recognizably the silky character usually associated with such melanotic features as black skin. One can add that peacomb is also commonly present among these fowl, and, according to Hutt (1949:386), peacomb and blue eggs are genetically closely linked. Taillessness is also a common feature in Chile and is found in China, Japan, and also in Persia, according to Aldrovandi (1604). Castello's sources informed him that up to 95 percent of the Araucanian chickens were tailless at the time of the Pacific War. From his informants, he also got a distribution of blue-egg-laying chickens—Chile to Ecuador and even into Mexico. Presumably much of the genetic complex had a similar distribution, and this is supported by Punnett's (1933) citation of black-fleshed chickens on the coast of Ecuador in the 1820's. Black-fleshed chickens are best known from India, although, as noted, they are also present in Africa. The Ecuadoran coast is adjacent to the Arawak of the Orinoco-Amazon area, and these people had a seemingly Hindu name for their chicken that would be appropriate for a silky-feathered, melanotic chicken.

Finsterbusch (1929: 86) specifies for Brazil: "The best breeds there are straight Oriental, Malays, Indian type, naked neck Madagascars (Tamatavas) and a silky variety with top knot which proves to be a descendant from the original Black Game-fowl." Finsterbusch simply assumes these to be Portuguese imports, but there seems to be considerable reason to consider them pre-1500 imports. Scholars opposed to Castello's theory that the chicken was pre-1500 in America hypothesized recent genetic changes to account for the blue egg (which is otherwise unknown in the poultry world) and introductions from Asia at contact times of the obviously Asiatic races to the coast of Brazil, and instantaneous diffusion.[5]

It seems significant that the location of our best zoological record is among the Araucanians. In this area of minimal Spanish influence, among an Indian people who remained fiercely free into the nineteenth century with their culture fairly intact until well toward the end of the nineteenth century, we find fowls with the unique character of blue eggs. They also possess Asiatic characters: ear puffs, tail-lessness, melanotic, silky (or hairlike) feathers and peacombs. None of these are traits known early to Europeans. The poultry world was startled by the blue egg, and the ear puff is so unusual that Castello persuaded the First International Poultry Congress to adopt a specific name for this chicken: *Gallus inauris*. Actually, Chinese chickens have comparable, although not identical, feather puffs (McGrew, 1926). One can find European books that discuss breeds of chickens where, as late as 1890, there is speculation as to the origin of the recently arrived silkies and a concensus that they had come from Japan. They are then most unlikely European exports. On the other hand, we have seen that they were widespread in Southeast Asia and the Pacific. One would have to look far indeed to find a situation better suited to preserving a precontact record of chickens (if they were precontact) than the Araucanian situation. If the Araucanian evidence validly indicates pre-Columbian, non-European chickens, then their name for the chicken, *atalpa*, an obvious derivative of the Quechua *atahualpa*, would also support the argument that the vast spread of this name suggests a pre-1500, not a post-1500, date. The Araucanian chickens surely have a complex of Asiatic genre, and it is possible, but not proved, that this is pre-Columbian in origin.

Uses, Attitudes, Cockfighting

Throughout the books on chickens runs the theme of nonutilitarian

[5] See Finsterbusch (1931), who, admitting typical Oriental fowl to be common in Chile, invoked Dutch pirates bringing them from Bali, even though he had no evidence for such an importation. Castello countered with the citation from Acosta already quoted to show that the linguistic data supported the zoological data in suggesting pre-Columbian importations.

use in the earliest periods of domestication. Cockfighting is so important, both in the probable homeland of the chicken and among the routes of earliest spread, that numerous authors have suggested this as the original reason for domestication. An equally important theme is that of a cult or sacrificial animal. In Zoroastrianism the dog and the chicken are the important sacred animals. As we have noted, the chicken was originally a sacrificial animal for the Jews, and this use was so entrenched that it inhibited the breeding of the birds for flesh and for eggs. Caesar's note that the British had fowl but did not eat them is part of the evidence that the original spread was not associated with the use of flesh or eggs. The same pattern extends into Polynesia. Cockfighting is very important. Chickens are important for their feathers for headdresses and other featherwork and of only minor significance as a food source. The African pattern of uses of the chicken was similar. Cockfighting was widespread, and I assume that, along with races of fowl from India and a Sanskrit name for the chicken, the Africans took over some of the ritualistic uses of the bird. The few notes on cockfighting in the Old World indicate that this sport has regional and, at times, national characteristics. Asiatic and European spurs are distinctive, and the Spanish preferred no spurs. In Spanish America the situation can be summarized as follows. Where the native population disappeared early and the Spanish were numerically dominant, the custom is Spanish—no spurs, as in Cuba and Puerto Rico, for example. This was also true along the Rio Grande, where there probably was no preceding pattern of cockfighting. In Brazil, the custom is to use blunt natural spurs, as is also the Japanese and Polynesian custom. I do not know the Portuguese custom, as my sources (Johnson and Brown, 1913; Pridgen, 1938) omitted that area. All the rest of Spanish America fights its cocks with Asiatic slashers. This is not only an Asiatic pattern of cockfighting; at times it is found associated with Asiatic fowl and Asiatic names.

One could well argue that once the Manila galleon began its run and Asiatic slashing spurs were introduced, their deadly effectiveness would quickly displace the Spanish custom of naked heels. However, it must be noted that the Spanish retained "bare heels" in Europe in competition with deadly stabbing spurs, introduced "bare heels" to America, and long continued to fight cocks that way in the few areas in Spanish America where the Indian population was swept away or for which there is no probability of pre-Spanish chickens, as in the Rio Grande area. The total picture of cockfighting is more suggestive of a pre-Spanish pattern of Asiatic practices. Authors flatly contradict one another on the pre- or post-Spanish presence of cockfighting in America and seem unaware of the wider implications of their data elsewhere. Thus Pridgden (1938) is mystified by the appearance of Malay-type cocks in Madagascar. No ethnologist knowing of Madagascar's Malayo-Polynesian speech and outrigger canoes would find Malay fighting cocks there very mysterious, though he would be interested in evidence of diffusion of fighting cocks. C. O. Sauer (personal communication) says that he knows of no early references to cockfighting in America. Absence of record does not mean absence of trait. In England cockfighting is not mentioned for a thousand years after Roman times, but it was surely flourishing throughout that period..

Asiatic spurs were bound onto the cock's leg by extremely complicated bindings. Bronze spurs were used, and Romans used silver at times. One wonders if study of Asiatic spurs by American archaeologists might lead to identification of cock spurs in pre-Columbian America, or if somewhere in the contact literature there may not be some mention of cockfighting.

One of the striking features of the chicken situation is the usage in tropical forested South America. The Indians seldom ate chickens or their eggs.[6] Their primary purpose seems to have been to supply feathers for decoration. White chickens seem to have been especially prized for this, and it may prove significant that the black-skinned silkies have white feathers, for *kara* names would be appropriate for them in India. This is clearly a non-European pattern, more in keeping with Asiatic practices, where the chicken's primary function was often for ritual or for cockfighting and where avoidance of eating eggs is a well-known trait. This is also a strong argument against sixteenth-century European introduction, for the accompanying pattern of use should then have been strongly for flesh and eggs with cockfighting secondary and religious significance lacking.

---

[6] Further work shows that this is true also of parts of North America and that there, too, it is associated with Asiatic races of chickens with Asiatic names.

Plural Introductions?

We seem rather quickly to assume that we are dealing with single contacts and one transfer of a trait. In the chicken case, we have hints that we may have had plural introductions. Note, for instance, the Japanese name among the Tarahumar and the Hindu names among the Arawak and the Guaymi. Note also that there seem to be two or three Asiatic varieties—naked-necked, rumpless, melanotic, frizzled, silky, peacombed, feather-puffed—in various combinations. Although these could have come in one mixed lot, we have a curious hint from Easter Island that varieties of chickens arrived there sequentially, for Metraux (1940: 90) records, "Finally, white fowl—hitherto unknown—began to multiply." Chickens clearly arrived at this outpost in the Pacific in a sequence, and the varietal differences record this sequence. Although the Spanish surely introduced chickens, they may only have been adding complexity to an already varied set of Asiatic fowl. The plurality of names and plurality of races of fowl in South America is more suggestive of multiple introductions and antiquity than single introductions and recency; and, as we have seen, the chicken does not stand alone. In the field of ethnobotany there are plants shared by Oceania and America with comparable, similar names. As Sorenson (this symposium) shows, the list of parallels in general cultural anthropology is enormous.

Conclusion

The accumulated case now stands: (1) diffusion rates suggested for America are several orders of magnitude too fast when compared with a comparable situation elsewhere; (2) names for the chicken in America parallel the name relationships in the Old World and suggest antiquity beyond A.D. 1500, and Nordenskiöld actually demonstrated the precedence of chicken names to known European introductions; (3) the biological data indicate a Southeast Asian rather than a European source; (4) names for chickens in two areas in America adjacent to a region of survival of melanotic strains suggest a Hindu origin; (5) among the chickens in the hands of remote tribes are non–Indo-European races that survive today in Japan and India; (6) one of the genetic traits (blue eggs) is known only in America (although mutations occur at random rates, this may be better evidence for a pre-1500 than a post-1500 introduction and the genetic linkage is to an Asiatic trait, peacomb); (7) the spurs used on cocks in parts of the Indian-dominated areas of Latin America where there is linguistic and biological evidence suggestive of Asiatic influences are Asiatic in type; and (8) the usage of chickens in America is more in keeping with early Asiatic practices than with sixteenth-century European practices.

The contrary position would be: (1) the Spanish surely brought chickens to America; (2) these included African melanotic strains, according to Capa; (3) they also brought Asiatic animals (pigs and dogs) and it is not inconceivable that they also brought Asiatic chickens;[7] (4) the Spanish could have spread chickens far up the South American rivers, where they could penetrate easily with shallow draft boats; and (5) both the Spanish and the Portuguese were sailing to India and the East Indies and could have brought back Asiatic fowl to South America, especially via the Atlantic.

It seems to me that the case for the Spanish and Portuguese introduction is weaker than the case for a pre-Columbian Asiatic source, but it is easy to underestimate the Spanish. Who, for instance, would have suspected that one of the first settlers in Peru introduced camels (Capa, 1915: 443)? However, one can also ask why the Spanish would introduce Asiatic fowl to South America but not to Europe, and why the names, attitudes, and uses of fowl in South America among the Indians should follow Asiatic rather than European patterns. The matter of context must be dealt with also. We do have Asiatic arts in America, and even Asiatic names for Amerind cultural items are not rare: patolli, *toki*, *kumar*, balsa, *mahagua*, and *karaka* all have Asiatic equivalent names for the identical objects. And, finally, if chickens were indeed carried to America by pre-Columbian mariners, it would be a very significant fact, for it would indicate that some voyages were made with such speed that they allowed the carriage of animals who had to be fed and watered and would surely not have survived a long drift voyage. In total, the picture is one more readily interpreted as due to pre-Columbian introductions of Asiatic

[7] One need only read of the starvation on the Asia-to-America galleon trips to realize that this was not a favorable route for introducing Asiatic (Philippine, probably Sinitic type) chickens to America.

fowl into America than by post-Columbian introductions. Admittedly, this falls short of absolute proof.

SOURCES FOR FURTHER EVIDENCE

No study exhausts a subject, and surely the question of pre-Columbian chickens is not settled. There are some obvious and some unusual avenues for further information. Clearly, we need bird bone identification, for, if chickens were present, their bones must be in the archaeology. Southern Ecuador, Peru, and northern Chile, because of good preservation and because varied data suggest the possibility of chickens there before 1500, are logical places to begin. Shell, even pieces of fingernail size, are identifiable by X-ray diffraction, according to Dr. Robert Howes, Texas A&M University. Forms as closely related as the turkey and chicken are readily separable, although races of chicken cannot be so identified. White, brown, and blue coloring of egg shells is, as we have seen, of some diagnostic value in identifying chicken races. Feathers have some value and the feathers of the silkies should be identifiable. Since this is one of the breeds possibly in America in pre-Columbian time, this clue may be helpful, and an examination of very early featherwork for silky-type feathers might be revealing. Chickens have blood groups comparable to the human pattern, and a world-wide collection of data would almost surely yield important insights.

Finally, the literary material needs reexamination, with attention to the details of the fowl described. If chickens were already present when the Spanish arrived, the picture would be a confused one. They would see a strange bird, the turkey, and would describe it as a sort of peacock. How then would they describe a not so strange chicken? The differences would not be as great as between peacock and turkey, and only if they commented on egg color, lack of tail, abnormal feathering, strange crowing, or the like, would the distinction be evident. In the main, one would expect the Spanish to describe the turkey as something new and strange but to say of chickens: "They have chickens like ours." Equally frequently they would not think chickens worth commenting on. As Nordenskiöld found, the Spanish seldom mentioned dogs, even though we know they were present. From Capa's comment that the letters of the contact period frequently mention chickens, we can assume that there is more in the archives than has been examined with the possibility of pre-Columbian chickens in mind.

How far we may be from the full picture of the history of the chicken in America can be indicated by a few notes from North America. Lewer (n.d.: 502) states that in 1693 in Virginia "most cocks and hens were without tails" and English stock tended to lose their rumps. Furthermore, in 1872 most West Indies fowl were rumpless. This absence of the terminal skeletal segment is an Asiatic trait, not a European one. In 1700 the Indians in the Lower Mississippi Valley were keeping chickens and using them for ceremonial purposes. No Spanish, French, or British introduction could account for this ceremonial use. One thinks of escaped Africans, but it is just possible that one should think of pre-Columbian chickens in southeastern archaeology. If a chicken bone were found in Virginia, it would probably be considered evidence of post-Columbian age. Such an assumption may be unwarranted.

The obvious place to begin is with identification of bird bones. It would be most informative if we knew that the Jomon-like pottery on the coast of Peru was accompanied by chicken bones. This seems unlikely, for our records do not suggest chickens in China until 1400 B.C. On the other hand, Japanese chickens seem to be derived, not from China, but from some other, probably seaborne, source; we have no idea of the date of introduction. It would be less improbable for chicken bones to appear about 300 B.C., the time suggested for the later wave of influences on the coast of Ecuador. Such a time of arrival would be appropriate to one other interpretation of the data before us. It would allow a more reasonable period of time, consistent with that time suggested by the Old World model, for the diffusion of the chicken over much of the length and breadth of South America, together with development of divergent names. Clearly, the archaeological record is going to be the ultimate test. Perhaps the material is already on hand among the many bags of carefully salvaged but unidentified bird bones from the controlled excavations of recent decades. The results of identification will be awaited with interest.

Finally, one last caution. This is not a definitive study of the chicken, not even of the data available. The genetics and distribution of comb types, for instance, could be the basis for an equally lengthy paper. The linguistic section could become another. The greatest stumbling block, however, is lack of detailed descriptions of chickens from all parts of the world. We are in the same position in relation to chickens as the domestic plant studies were before Vavilov began his systematic world-wide collections and before Carter, Anderson, and Mangelsdorf developed the concept of races of maize. We desperately need ethnological reporting of details of chickens in the hands of native people as well as a wealth of information on names, uses, attitudes, customs, and mythology related to chickens. When this material is obtained, someone should write a book on the subject.

10. The Significance of an Apparent Relationship between the Ancient Near East and Mesoamerica

JOHN L. SORENSON

The aims of this paper are (1) to draw attention to the theoretical and methodological significance of the question of transoceanic diffusion to nuclear America from the Near East, (2) to present a body of evidence relevant to the problem, and (3) to point out some requirements for further research in the area.

The present status and future needs of these studies cannot be adequately understood without examining the historical background of research on the topic, for the expectations of scholars working in the field constitute an important variable.

It seems a fair assessment that most of the arguments from the first third of this century that claimed transoceanic sources for native American cultures by utilizing archaeological and related data were thoroughly naïve. Under the influence of Franz Boas the small corps of American anthropologists relentlessly attacked such naïveté to the point where only a handful of professional Americanists continued even to believe that a legitimate issue existed.

In the last two decades or so the culture history of the New World has been of concern to two professional wings in American anthropology. One wing has been concerned with the development of one or another variety of evolutionary theory—whether of the persuasion of Steward or of White or of some variant of these. To these students of the New World peoples, the culture-historical data have been useful in illustrating and clarifying evolutionary theory. The second group has been occupied with clarifying local and regional cultural sequences. Neither has given serious, consistent consideration to the possibility of significant communication of culture from the Old World to the New World. To be sure, there have been increasingly frequent discussions of some of the elements of the problems, as witnessed by this symposium, but at no time in the modern era of anthropology has a serious attempt been made to relate the historical issue to theoretical currents in anthropology, other than incidentally to evolution.

Two examples from the literature show how representatives of these two sectors of American anthropology treat the transoceanic contact issue. Adams (1966) acutely compares sociocultural aspects of life in early Mesopotamia with conditions in late prehistoric central Mexico. At the level of abstraction and with the approach he employs, he apparently considers it irrelevant to be concerned with possible historical sources for the behavioral patterns that constitute the grist for his mill. To answer the kind of question facing him, he simply notes that such patterns as kingship "appear"; the real problem, for Adams, concerns the degree to which similar adaptive patterns seem to have been employed in the two distinct settings.

Phillips' (1966) treatment is poles apart. He treats the evidence for diffusion as readily divisible into a set of discrete features or traits. This conceptual scheme, a product of midwestern archaeological research of the thirties and forties out of the cultural anthropology of the twenties and thirties, seems unable to avoid simplification almost to the point of caricature. (For example, Phillips suggests that the clay figurines of Mesoamerican settings cannot be related to those of the Old World, where they are supposed to connote fertility, because the American examples are "unsexy.") Yet one must admit that this simplistic view of culture as a set of discrete traits—which is fairly common among archaeologists concerned primarily with clarifying local or regional sequences—has also been the style of the diffusionists until now.

In studies of Old World culture history a different situation prevails. There the concept of evolution has not dominated the study of events since post-Neolithic times, nor have archaeologists been left alone with their sequences. Instead historians, philologists, linguists, art historians, and other specialists have, along with the area-specialized archaeologists, constructed an over-all picture of inter-related culture growth that has rarely been phrased even in anthro-pological, let alone evolutionary, terms. Kroeber was the American anthropologist par excellence who dealt with these Old World ma-terials. His attempt to conceptualize that complex segment of culture history gave rise to the concept of the oikoumene (or "ecumene," as Hewes spelled it in elaborating on Kroeber's work—see Kroeber, 1952; Hewes, 1961). A partial equivalent of the Old World oikou-mene, built around the concept of Nuclear America, has been used in the New World. "Yet," Kroeber stated, "the story of major civiliza-tional growth in America, as we are beginning to adumbrate its totality in outline, gives no indication of integrating with the cor-responding story in Eurasia. The two are not, so far as we can yet see, parts of a single plot" (1952: 392).

Dissatisfaction with both the substance and form of the evidence for Old and New World connections as diffusionists have presented it heretofore has prompted me, over the last fifteen years, to accumu-late my own corpus of evidence. The appendix to this paper summar-izes much of it. My present professional position and interests ensure that so long as this corpus of data remains only in my files, it will not be criticized, clarified, or supplemented as it ought to be. In view of the significance of the issue involved, I am obliged to offer the ma-terial for use by scholars who may be in a position to consider it more fully.

Purists may object that the documentation is inadequate. Indeed few of the topics have been pursued in depth, yet the citations seem sufficient to provide access to the literature for future workers who wish to deal with any point in more detail. Popular and polemic literature is cited where it appears to control reliable factual evidence not readily available in more authoritative sources. Where no docu-mentation is given, it is either because the point seems so well known as not to require a citation or because sources cited just earlier are clearly applicable. A few cited works I have not personally seen.

Three problems require discussion in order to clarify the nature of the material presented: (1) Why emphasis on the Near East? (2) What about time relations? (3) What criterion of significance is em-ployed?

Many diffusionist hypotheses suffer from a lack of nucleation of the evidence used—the cultural features considered are not grouped in time and space in a manner persuasive of their origin in a single area. Yet it seems that there might be some area within the Old World civilization where most or all of the diffused features were simultaneously present. Inasmuch as civilization developed earliest in the Near East and since that area remained a communications heartland for millennia, it is plausible that complexes might be found there that eventually reached the New World. Thus that nuclear area might be a more logical source of diffusion to America than locations along the ecumenical periphery, such as Southeast Asia. The bulk of evidence presented in the appendix confirms this supposition, even though the matter of a transmission mechanism and route remains unresolved (and wholly untreated in this paper).

It should be emphasized that my concern here with the Near East (by which I mean the entire area from Iran to Egypt and Anatolia to the Persian Gulf, although most of the evidence refers particularly to the Levant) as a possible source for cultural elements transmitted to America in no way rules out the possibility that the features cited could and did move from some other Old World area where they also occurred. Also, the distinct possibility exists that some of the parallels may be due to convergence.

Time relations of the paired features have not been tabulated systematically; however, most or all occur earlier in the Near East than in Mesoamerica. The chronological period for the former is in most cases from the Middle Bronze Age (ca. 2000 B.C.) through the Iron Age (middle of the first millennium B.C.). For Mesoamerica much of the evidence is necessarily drawn from the conquest period, although it is becoming increasingly evident that many of the essentials of Mesoamerican civilization have a time depth of upwards of three millennia (see Nicholson, 1967).

The criterion for deciding whether parallels are due to diffusion has been that used by Kroeber and Hewes in studying the Old World oikoumene. On the basis of the whole range of culture known for the world a judgment is made, admittedly intuitive, that a feature is, or is not, so specific and so abstract or complicated that it is not reasonable for it to have been developed independently in a second, distant location. I have tried to avoid comparisons less specific than Kroeber's and Hewes's work employed.

The most convincing type of cultural parallel would be, ideally, something discrete, concrete, and visible, like two patently Egyptian statuettes that purportedly "come from three meters in depth at the eastern beaches of Acajutla," El Salvador (and are now in the Museo Nacional "David J. Guzman," San Salvador). If one could locate and accept without question a number of such evidences, at least the barebones historical problem of intercontinental contacts might be simplified. (Yet even if the statuettes—or a Roman figurine—could be proved ancient and authentic, we would probably be unable to connect them in any meaningful way with the process of Meso-american culture growth.) But of course items like these have so often proved elusive, unreliable, faked or with such other disabilities as evidence that they must be ignored for practical purposes. Rather, we must make do with comparative evidence, which is less discrete and more ambiguous and which, therefore, some critics will doubt.

My selection, phrasing, and display look to concepts rather than to traits as such. Partly for that reason and partly because the criterion of specificity fails there so often, technology is given short shrift. Social features too are largely omitted from consideration, since they seem not unlikely to arise by convergence in separate areas. Most of the items included are in the area of cultural values, where the most arbitrary and abstract concepts lie. Unfortunately the necessary tabular format hinders adequately representing the multiple interconnections and pyramiding of concepts that in fact exist. Indentation and parenthetical cross-references are used to suggest some of these complexities.

What then does this evidence show? First of all, some twenty-five features considered significant by students of the Old World oikoumene are also found in Mesoamerica. This suggests at least a generic connection between the two areas, although not a strong one.

The total number of parallel features displayed below is less important than their general position in the two civilizational traditions. The usual view of transoceanic influence on Nuclear America has been, in recent years, that although some interesting minor cultural elements might have come across the ocean by some means, none of these seriously influenced the indigenous tradition. Meggers (1963a), despite believing that such movements were very important, implies that the evidence available to support such a view is limited—that diffusion led more to "embroidery" than to core contributions. This paper, however, shows that some rather basic ideas seem to have been shared in the two areas. Even should some of my evidence have to be put aside when examined more closely, it appears to require that the "embroidery" position be seriously modified. Of course it is obvious that the *style* of Mesoamerica is highly distinctive (as Kirchoff, 1933, and Nicholson, 1967, point out), but so was the stylistic expression of Egypt, the Aegean, and India, as each utilized the general ecumenical inventory.

Unless further research disqualifies a great deal of the evidence presented here, one must conclude that a substantial number of cultural features of much more than peripheral significance in Mesoamerican civilization either originated or were at least present even earlier in the heart of the Old World oikoumene. The exact medium of communication, the times, the route, and the specific content transmitted are unclear, just as details about Mesopotamian-Egyptian communication in the Protoliterate (see Frankfort, 1954) remain hazy, yet the fact of relationship is forced upon us by the circumstantial evidence. We share with Kroeber (1952: 391) "a dilemma, even when the total context of a situation leaves little moral doubt of there having been a connection of some sort. Was the connection due to a conscious and specific imitation of something foreign, though perhaps also with deliberate adaptation to a different environment? Or was it an ideational germ which was transported and which slumbered, perhaps for centuries, until its environment awoke it. . . . The temporary verdict may often have to be: 'Nothing provable.' But the problem remains to vex and intrigue us."

Is there any chance that Nuclear America, or at least Mesoamerica, should actually be included within the Old World oikoumene? No, it seems to me—at least on the basis of the present evidence and definition of the oikoumene. Of about two hundred cultural features listed by Hewes (omitting those ruled out as possibilities by faunal and floral absences), one in eight is found in Mesoamerica and another one-tenth might prove to be there also. Perhaps this indicates that Mesoamerica is in approximately the same relation to the Old World oikoumene as

the primitives in the area or adjoining it, [who] derive their cultures mainly from the civilization characteristic of the Oikoumene as a whole, through reductive selection. They preserve old elements largely discarded elsewhere, and they do without elements which their retardation makes them unable or unwilling to accept. Basically, however, these retarded or primitive cultures in or adjacent to the Oikoumene are fully intelligible only in terms of 'Oecumenical' civilization. They usually add to what they share some lesser measure of their own proper peculiarities and originations, and they have often developed a distinctive style of their own. But in the main these backward cultures depend and derive from the greater ones whose nexus we have been considering.[1]

What does the issue of intercontinental cultural connections signify for anthropological thought? Meggers (1963a: 142) considered it "one of the most significant theoretical problems in anthropology." Scholarship appears to have demonstrated that civilization—that most complex manifestation of man's cultural behavior—wherever it manifests itself in the Old World, is part of one great ecumenical web. If it now turns out that New World civilization is seriously related to (that is, dependent upon) that of the Old World, then there can be no ultimately satisfying scientific answer to the question of how men became civilized, for there will be but a single case of the phenomenon. One cannot generalize from a single case. To be sure, some of the factors, environmental or otherwise, involved in producing variations on the process can be clarified (as Adams, 1966, attempts to do), but key questions would inevitably remain unanswerable.

This theoretical point has important methodological implications. Kroeber (1952: 391) anticipated one such difficulty: "Nineteenth-century anthropologists could still fall back on a sort of spontaneous generation to explain cultural likenesses remote in space or time. Today we hesitate to invoke autogenesis; we shrink from it almost as fervently as do biologists. . . . Specific universals in human culture have shrunk to be vanishingly few. *There is thus as much evidence needed for an assumption of independent origins as of a connection: the burden of proof is equal*" (my italics). Given the soundness of the last statement, perhaps we should expect that in some professional meeting to come we may hear a symposium presenting actual evidence and arguments for the independent origin of American civilization, as a logical follow-up to the present symposium. It is surely fair

[1] Alfred L. Kroeber, *The Nature of Culture* (Chicago: University of Chicago Press, 1952), p. 393. Copyright 1952 by The University of Chicago. All rights reserved. Copyright 1952 under the International Copyright Union. This and other quotes from Kroeber's book are used by permission of the publisher.

to state that most archaeologists do not follow Kroeber's dictum, but assume rather than demonstrate that external cultural influences were insignificant to their area.

A related point has been made by Naroll (1961) in discussing cross-cultural survey methodology. He showed how one must, and may, guard against bias in sampling, which could derive from historical (that is, diffusionary) linkages. Few scholars using the cross-cultural survey method yet seem to appreciate the point. Nor do those treating the problem of multilinear evolution generally recognize the care with which they ought to proceed in making assumptions about the (in)significance of diffusion in the cases they treat.

In summary, an evolutionary or social anthropology that fails to control for historical diffusion seems to rest on grounds potentially as weak as that unrestrained diffusionism which lacks appreciation for the adaptive power of man. On the basis of the evidence presented, it is plausible, and perhaps necessary, to interpret the rise of civilization in Mesoamerica as significantly dependent upon communication from the heartland of Eurasia through intermediate steps that are unclear. If this conclusion is correct, it has important implications for all anthropological research upon the nature of civilized societies. It seems incumbent upon concerned scholars to pay early, serious attention to the quality and meaning of the evidence used here and to pursue the leads it opens up.

APPENDIX

Table of Shared Cultural Features

	Documentation	
Cultural Features	Mesoamerica	Near East

Temple and Its Platform

An artificial representation or natural elevation of cosmic significance	Wicke, 1965; Holland, 1964	Frankfort, *et al.*, 1949: 30–31, 59–60; Hastings, 1951: VI, 678; Wales, 1953: 8–10
Ascent signifies rising to heavens	Holland, 1964: 303; Vaillant, 1950: 157–158	Wales, 1953: 8–11
Temple atop		Parrot, 1949: 211; Wales, 1953: 8
Interior partitioned, "holy of holies" idea, which is contact point with heavenly powers	Wicke, 1965: 412; Holland, 1964: 303–305	Wales, 1953: 8
Omphalos concept, "navel of the world"	Thompson, 1950b: 71; Alexander, 1916: 286–287	Wales, 1953: 8; Nibley, 1951: 229; Wensinck, 1916; Burrows, 1941: 43–53
Waters confined beneath temple[2] (cf. Overflowing Vase motif and Tree of Life scene, below)	Prescott, 1877: II, 20	Hastings, 1951: II, 705 & IV, 128–129; Ezek. 47
Cosmic axis, connection of heavens, earth, underworld at the point	Holland, 1964	Wales, 1953: 8–13; Burrows, 1941: 44–45
Occasional burial beneath this point (cf. Burial, below)	Wicke, 1965: 410–412	Hastings, 1951: I, 609; Edwards, 1961
Ascent via stairway up the center on one side		

NOTE: Throughout the table an asterisk (*) is used on the left of an item to signify that Kroeber (1952) or Hewes (1961) included that feature in his list of ecumenical sharings.

[2] At the great pyramid at Cholula, when Cortés was attacking, native priests in their extremity (in accord with a "tradition") expected water to flood out of the structure when they made an opening in its side. The temples at Byblos and Jerusalem were believed to be over the watery abyss, confining the contents from bursting forth. (On this motif in Ezek. 31, Farmer, 1956: 18.)

| | Documentation | |
Cultural Features	Mesoamerica	Near East
Levels, terraced form	Holland, 1964	Hastings, 1951: VI, 678; Langdon, 1931: 159
Symbolizing sky and/or cosmos	Holland, 1964	Langdon, 1931: 159
Usual number—3, 4, 7 levels	Thompson, 1950b: 99	Hastings, 1951: VI, 678
Planting on terraces	Kirchoff, 1944	Starr, 1937: 374–375
Orientation of sacred sites to cardinal or solar directions	Dow, 1967	Finegan, 1964: 37
Particularly, temples faced east to catch rising sun	Dow, 1967	Finegan, 1964: 37; Hollis, 1933
"South" means "on the right hand"	Thompson, 1960: 249	(Hebrew)
World quarters	Nuttall, 1901	Nuttall, 1901
Colors symbolize the quarters		
Patolli-parchisi game[3]		Culin, 1898: 854 ff; Piggott, 1950: 190–191
Swastika	Nuttall, 1901	
Pattée cross	Covarrubias, 1946: 134	Perrot, 1884: I, 286–294
Cross within a cross	Ferguson, 1958: 102–103	Frankfort, 1939: pl. 30
Astronomy, Calendar, Writing		
Highly developed astronomy		
Articulated lunar, solar, stellar calendar counts		
360-day calendar plus 5 extra	(Mexico)	(Egypt)
Cycle of 7 days	Thompson, 1954: 144	
Day measured sunset to sunset	Dow, 1967	Finegan, 1964; Gen. 1:5
*Observatories		
*Eclipse records		
*Nonpermutating eras and year counts		
Day-name list ordered like alphabet order, and lunar houses; similar names and associations in sequence[4]	Kelley, 1960	

[3] Indian parchesi was known as far west as Syria. A similar dice game was shared between Sumer and the Indus Valley as early as the Early Bronze Age (Piggott, 1950).

[4] Kelley shows Maya day name *manik*, represented by a hand glyph, prob-

| Cultural Features | Documentation | |
	Mesoamerica	Near East
Day names with associations like Eurasian constellations[5]	Kelley, 1960	
Place value notation	Kroeber, 1948: 468–472	Neugebauer, 1951: 18, 20, 26, 140–146
*Zero concept	Kroeber, 1948: 468–472	Neugebauer, 1951: 18, 20
*Zero sign		Kroeber, 1948: 468–472
Hieroglyph system (ca. 750 signs; use of ideographs, rebus, affixes)	Thompson, 1965: 652; 1950b	(Egypt)
*Paper		
*Papermaking Lime sizing of writing surface	Thompson, 1954: 169	Funk & Wagnalls, 1936: 716
Burial Tomb in elevated structure with or without temple atop	Wicke, 1965; Linné, 1942	Edwards, 1961: 199–204 (Egypt); Hastings, 1951: I, 690–691 (Mesopotamia)
Burial chamber with hidden entry	(Palenque)	Edwards, 1961
*"Royal tombs" (conspicuous display)	Adams, 1966: 145	Kroeber, 1952: 389–390
Dedicatory sacrifice, subfoundation burial of children	Vaillant, 1950: 76	Bailey, 1943: fig. 53; Hastings, 1951: XI, 32 & VI, 114
Urn burial of children	Meggers & Evans, 1963: table 2, appendix 1	Macalister, 1912; Free, 1956: 47

ably pronounced *ka*, corresponding in sequence to Hebrew letter *k*, probably representing the hand, pronounced *kaph*. (Cf. Hebrew *kaph* 'hand,' with Yucatec *kab* 'hand,' or Mam *kop* 'hand.') Following letter of the alphabet is Hebrew *lamed*; cf. next Yucatec Maya day name *lamat* (or Greek *lambda*; cf. Tzental-Zotzil *lambat*). Next is day-name *mulu*(c), which is ruled by shark and has the Aztec equivalent "water." Greek *mu* (from Assyrian *mu*, "water?"), or Hebrew *mem,* is next in alphabet sequence. I suggest the possibility that the Hebrew second month, *Ziv*, may relate to the third of the Yucatec Maya list, *Zip*.

[5] Kelley also shows that half the names and animals of Aztec days recur in Eurasia in correct sequence as the same or related animals in the constellation list.

| Cultural Features | Documentation | |
	Mesoamerica	Near East
Deep-shaft tombs	Covarrubias, 1957: 89	Franken & Franken–Battershill, 1963: 70–71
Bench, niche arrangement along walls of tombs	(Monte Alban, Kaminaljuyu)	Franken & Franken–Battershill, 1963: 70–71, 160
Family re-use of tombs	Sellars, 1945	Franken & Franken–Battershill, 1963: 159
Retainer sacrifice	MacLeod, 1923: 424; Tozzer, 1941: 129–130	
Stone sarcophagus	Stirling, 1943: 59	Irwin, 1963: 159
Rope motif surrounding	Stirling, 1943: 59	Irwin, 1963: 159
Ancestor heads preserved	Morley, 1956: 206	
Fires made at burial site upon death of notable (cf. second item below?)	Bancroft, 1883: II, 799; Kidder, Jennings, & Shook, 1946: 93	Pedersen, 1945: 484; Jer. 34:5; 2 Chron. 16:14
Incense and Incense Furniture		
Strong emphasis on, accompanying most rituals	Kidder, Jennings, & Shook, 1946: 260; Tozzer, 1941: 163–164 ff.	Hastings, 1951: VII, 202–205
As route for ascent of soul	Bancroft, 1883: II, 799	Pedersen, 1945: 484; Hastings, 1951: VII, 202–203
For purification	Tozzer, 1941: 163–164	Hastings, 1951: VII, 204
For offering to gods, sweet, attractive	Kidder, Jennings, & Shook, 1946: 93	Hastings, 1951: VII, 204
Symbolizing prayer	Bancroft, 1883: III, 7	Hastings, 1951: VIII, 204; Psalms 14:2
To hide holy object in temple by incense smoke	Satterthwaite, 1946	Pedersen, 1945: 266
Required to be used with "holy," special fire	Tozzer, 1941: 153, 155, 158	
Incense a gum procured from trees after ritual preparation of gatherers	Tozzer, 1941: 143	Pedersen, 1945: 357; Hastings, 1951: VII, 201
Considered the "blood" of tree producing it	Tozzer, 1941: 142 (rubber)	Pedersen, 1945: 357 (frankincense)

	Documentation	
Cultural Features	Mesoamerica	Near East
Fertility, rain association	Sahagún, 1946: 482–483 Brinton, 1885: 14	Hastings, 1951: VII, 202–203
Serpent association[6]	Hastings, 1951: VII, 203	Schaeffer, 1936: fig. 3; Hastings, 1951: VII, 201
Tall, cylindrical ceramic burners	Borhegyi, 1950c, 1951a, 1951b	Cook: 1930: 29–31; May, 1935: 13; Albright, 1942–1943: I, 30–31, & III, 28–30; McCown, 1947: I, 236 ff.
Horizontal rows of inverted-triangle "windows"	Borhegyi, 1950c, 1951a, 1951b	Ibid.
White surfaced	Borhegyi, 1951b: 112	McCown, 1947: I, 236
Horns on rim	Borhegyi, 1951b: 112	McCown, 1950: 211; May, 1935: 13
Four horns	Ferguson, 1958: 87; García Payón, 1966: 49	Albright, 1949: pl. 19
Burners of limestone	Borhegyi, 1951b: 110	May, 1935: 12
Feline associations[7]	Borhegyi, 1951b: 110	Kelso and Thorley, 1945: 91; Starr, 1937: I, 437–441; Albright, 1938: 1–2; Burrows, 1941: 209
Feline-human hybrid motif with fertility associations	Borhegyi, 1951a	Burrows, 1941: 209; May, 1931–1932: 73–98; Albright, 1938: 1–2
Standing Stones (Stele) as Cult Objects	Shook, 1952; Williamson, 1879	Wales, 1953, 14; Macalister, 1912: I, 105–107, & II, 381
A series placed in a row (astronomical function?)	Shook, 1952; Williamson, 1879: 418–421	Hastings, 1951: VI, 681; Thompson, 1967: 122
Event and time commemoration	Proskouriakoff, 1960	Levy, 1953: 183; Thompson, 1967: 126
Memorial, mortuary	Proskouriakoff, 1960	James, 1966: 36

[6] According to Hastings, incense was said to be favored by Quetzalcoatl, represented as the feathered serpent, as a form of bloodless sacrifice, while frankincense was gathered from trees in Arabia that were supposedly guarded by winged serpents.

[7] Reclining jaguar appears atop the rim of a Guatemalan example (Borhegyi, 1951b). Three reclining lions appear on top of one from Nuzu (Starr, 1937).

| Cultural Features | Documentation | |
	Mesoamerica	Near East
Figurines[8]		
Human female, ceramic, apparently connected to fertility cult concept	Vaillant, 1950: 50–51	Pritchard, 1943
Pregnant woman Woman holding own breasts	Covarrubias, 1957: pl. 3	May, 1935: pl. 31
Occurrence in burials	(Mexico)	Elderkin, 1930; Pritchard, 1943
Movable limb figurines	Borhegyi, 1954b	Riefstahl, 1943; Elderkin, 1930
Animal figurines, apparent cult rather than toy significance		Thompson, 1967: 123
Wheeled animal figurines	Ekholm, 1946; Irwin, 1963; 131–135	May, 1935: 23–24. Speiser, 1935: I, 68 ff.; Starr, 1937: I, 425
Ceramic models of cult scenes	(West Mexico)	Bossert, 1951: pls. 96–99, 39
*Sacrifice Complex Animals slain		
Offerings burned	Lothrop, 1926: I, 71–73	
On altar in ceremonial area		
Communion sense in consumption of part of the sacrifice	Tozzer, 1941: 120; Hastings, 1951: XI, 6	Lev. 3
Accompanied by censing		
Incense mixed with cereal, as one type of offering	Tozzer, 1941: 104, 142	Lev. 2:1–3
Parched grain or meal as offering	Tozzer, 1941: 144	Hastings, 1951: XI, 34
Blood offered as sacrifice	(Mexico)	Hastings, 1951: XI, 32; Exod. 30:223
Blood scattered over area and participants	Lothrop, 1926: I, 71–73; Squier, 1860: 71	Lev. 1:11; Lev. 3:8; Squier, 1860: 71
*Fermented and non-fermented drink offerings	Tozzer, 1941: 110, 145, 165	Hastings, 1951: XI, 32

[8] Constructional features shared, which may or may not be significant, include both hand- and moldmade, both hollow and solid, two-part construction, elaborate headdresses, use of white slip.

| Cultural Features | Documentation | |
	Mesoamerica	Near East
Libation vessels of similar shape	Museum of Primitive Art, 1965: 22	Museum of Primitive Art, 1965: 22
Human sacrifice when prominent person was near death	Hastings, 1951: VI, 842	Hastings, 1951: VI, 842
Child sacrifice	Vaillant, 1950: 200	Isa. 57:5; Jer. 19:5; Irwin, 1963: 164–165
Child of leader offered at time of national danger	Tozzer, 1941: 184, 223; Bancroft, 1883: II, 796	Hastings, 1951: VI, 842
Scapegoat concept	Tozzer, 1941: 226	Lev. 16
Foundation burials (see above)		
Accomplished by throwing down from an elevation	Tozzer, 1941: 116, 184	Irwin, 1963: 164
Sacrificial cutting of self to cause bleeding	Tozzer, 1941: 113; Loeb, 1923	1 Kings 18:28; Loeb, 1923
Circumcision	Loeb, 1923	Loeb, 1923
Sacrificial connotation	Loeb, 1923	Loeb, 1923
ᵤustration[9]		
Representation of crossed streams over a subject figure	Seler, 1906: II, codex, 31 Gardiner, 1950	
"Life" signification of stream[10]		
Being poured from vessels		

[9] Upon being shown the Seler-Gardiner comparison, the doyen of American orientalists has said, in private correspondence, that in his opinion, had the Mexican scene come from, say, Mesopotamia, where transmission distance (to or from Egypt) is no issue, there could be no question that historical connection existed between the two.

[10] Water on the one hand and *ankh* symbols on the other both specifically denote "life." The Borgia figures are Mictlantecuhtli and Mictlancihuatl, lord and lady of the region of death (Vaillant, 1941: 172). Egyptian scenes of this type show Horus and either Thoth or Seth. Horus stands for the east and Thoth for the west, the region of death. Seth is of the north and also was associated with illness and evil (yet he could also connote the reverse; see Thompson, 1967: 120–122). The Mexican divinities are associated with the north, or sometimes the south, quarter. Ixtlilton, the center figure in the Borgia scene, was a god of healing; Thoth was emblematic of healing in Egyptian medicine (Hastings, 1951: IV, 751). Nepthys, wife of Seth, was sometimes queen of the night and of the dead, like Mictlancihuatl.

	Documentation	
Cultural Features	Mesoamerica	Near East

By a divinity on either side
  Healing connotation[11]

Directional identification of
divinities[12]

Characteristics of spouse[13]

Dark, death connotation[14]

Purificatory Aspersion Rite	Tozzer, 1941: 105	Hastings, 1951: II, 831
Using an aspergillum	Tozzer, 1941: 105	Hastings, 1951: II, 831
Renewal, rebirth concept	Tozzer, 1941: 105; Sahagún, 1946: bk. 6, chaps. 32, 37	Hastings, 1951: II, 831
Divination		
Astrology (elaborated)	Hastings, 1951: IV, 780–782	Hastings, 1951: IV, 780–782
Astrological almanac	Thompson, 1954: 138	
Mirror gazing (captoptromancy)	Besterman, 1965 73–77; Museum of Primitive Art, 1965	Hastings, 1951: IV, 807
Illness		
Breach of taboo, cause of illness	Handy, 1936: 127; Tozzer, 1941: 106	Handy, 1936: 127
Confession to cure illness	Tozzer, 1941: 106	Handy, 1936: 127
Snake Symbolism		
Signifying wisdom, knowledge	Ixtlilxóchitl, 1952: I, 21	Burrows, 1941: 106–107
Signifying healing	Ixtlilxóchitl, 1952: I, 21	Hastings, 1951: XI
Signifying fertility		Thompson, 1967, 123–124; Burrows, 1941: 106–107
Associated with water holes	Smith, 1919	Hastings, 1951: XI, 403
"Flying," feathered	(Quetzalcoatl)	Hastings, 1951: XI, 406; Num. 21:4–9; 2 Kings 18:4

[11] See note 10.
[12] See note 10.
[13] See note 10.
[14] See note 10.

Cultural Features	Documentation	
	Mesoamerica	Near East
Motif, undulating serpent (or intertwined serpents)	Vaillant, 1935: 53; Paddock, 1955, Fig. 8a	Perrot, 1884: I, 286–294
Seven-headed serpent motif	García Payón, 1948–1949; Ferguson, 1958	Frankfort, 1955: fig. 13
Rain, fertility association	Ferguson, 1958; Caso, 1959: 45	Budge, 1926: 132
Dragon, water-monster	Thompson, 1950b: 75, 110	Hastings, 1951: IV, 128–129, 154
Feline Symbolism		
Power, dominance, rulership	Holland, 1964: 303	Thompson, 1967: 117–119
Fertility, rain, abundance	Covarrubias, 1946	Thompson, 1967: 117–119; Hastings, 1951: 147–149
Symbolizing night aspect of sun which enters underworld at night; feline is lord of underworld	Thompson, 1960: 134	Thompson, 1967: 118
Radial whorl design on joint in feline representations[15]	Gann, 1926: 198–199	Kantor, 1947: 118
Hybrid Human-Feline (cf. above on incense burners)		
Mountain/Rain/Cloud Divinity[16]		
Mountain dwelling	Seler, 1902–1903: 106 ff.	James, 1966: 105, 14–16
Rain (regularity), life controlling	Seler, 1902–1903: 106 ff.	James, 1966: 105, 14–16
Full-bearded[17]	Irwin, 1963: 171–175	Irwin, 1963: 171–175
Represented carrying bolt of lightning	Irwin, 1963: 171–175	Irwin, 1963: 171–175
Overflowing Vase Motif[18]	Ferguson, 1958: 78–85; Covarrubias, 1957: pl. 50	Van Buren, 1933; Nibley, 1951: 235–236

[15] H. O. Thompson considers the whorl in Asia to indicate deity.

[16] Tlaloc in Mexico, Baal/Hadad in Palestine and Syria.

[17] Irwin's illustrations are rather striking on this and the following feature.

[18] Stela 25 at Izapa shows a remarkable linkage: a highly conventionalized tree ("of life"?) has atop it a bird(?). The tree grows out of a vase while an

Cultural Features	Documentation Mesoamerica	Near East
Lotus or Water Lily Symbolism (as emergent life, primeval and ultimate abundance)	Thompson, 1960: 72–73; Rands, 1953	Thompson, 1967: 122; James, 1966: 132
Guilloche (Double S) Sign	Groth-Kimball & Feuchtwanger, 1954: fig. 32	D'Alviella, 1894: 184
Rain, water association	Groth-Kimball & Feuchtwanger, 1954: fig. 32	Ackerman, 1950
"Tree of Life" Scene Representations include: tree in center, two (or four) figures facing—one (or two) each side, serpent/monster element beneath, and bird/(winged) motif above	Briggs, 1950	Briggs, 1950
"Tree of God" Cedar[19]	Tozzer, 1941: 197	Hastings, 1951: II, 705; James, 1966: 33
Named after deity[20]	Tozzer, 1941: 197	James, 1966: 33
Sacred tree bears blue/green stone[21]	Henning, 1911	James, 1966: 13; Kramer, 1952: ll. 620–626; Kunz, 1938: 232–238

aquatic monster beneath and at one side is connected in a manner to suggest overflowing water. See James, 1966: 13, on the Mesopotamian concept of tree nourished by the sweet waters beneath. Cf. vase overflowing at hierocentric point (Nibley, 1951: 235).

[19] Cedar of Yucatan was called *kuche*, "tree of God"; it was the preferred wood for idol-making. In Babylonia the sacred cedar had the name of Ea written in its core (Hastings, 1951: XII, 456); at Susa the cuneiform sign for cedar tree was part of the name of the dominant deity (Hastings, 1951: II, 705).

[20] See note 19.

[21] Jade is referred to figuratively as the "heart" of the maize plant (which appears as the "tree" of life); a codex apparently represents jade leaves; jade, "the exudation of leaves," was fed to the infant ancestors of some Middle American peoples. In Mesopotamia the sacred *kiskana* tree was shown with leaves that appear to be lapis lazuli; the Epic of Gilgamesh mentions the tree of life bearing lapis lazuli fruit.

	Documentation	
Cultural Features	Mesoamerica	Near East
Tree representing a people	Henning, 1911	Henning, 1911; Ezek. 17; Gen. 49:22; Isa. 61:3
World tree spreading protectively over all[22]	Thompson, 1950b: 71; Tozzer, 1961: 131–132	James, 1966: 13, 143
Rooted at contact point with upper and underworlds (cf. above on cosmic axis)	Thompson, 1950b: 71	James, 1966: 13, 143
Route for movement up, down	Thompson, 1950b: 71; Cf. Holland, 1964: 303	James, 1966: 13, 143
Various Motifs and Aesthetic Features		
Double-headed eagle	Barlow, 1954: 57	Ward, 1910: 420
Winged sun disc (globe) or sun as body of bird[23]	Barlow, 1954: 59; Kroeber, 1948: 474–514	D'Alviella, 1894: 207; Hinke, 1907: IV, 89
Pennated tail, dependent from a circular feature	Barlow, 1954: 59; Kroeber, 1948: 474–514	D'Alviella, 1894: 212
Horseshoe-shaped, curled-end device	Ferguson, 1958: 118–125	Ferguson, 1958: 118–125
Representing hair curls of a female deity[24]	Covarrubias, 1957: fig. 87; Thompson, 1958: 300–306	Hinke, 1907: IV, 19; Frankfort, 1944: 198–200
With childbirth associations, "Mother," "Lady"[25]	Covarrubias, 1957: fig. 87; Thompson, 1958: 300–306	Hinke, 1907: IV, 19; Frankfort, 1944: 198–200
With vegetational fertility meaning	Covarrubias, 1957: fig. 87; Thompson, 1958: 300–306	Hinke, 1907: IV, 19; Frankfort, 1944: 198–200

[22] See Count (1952: 56), where this and other folkloric motifs, not all mentioned in this paper, are considered as to significance for interhemispheric movement.

[23] The Mexican version shows the disc as the body of a partially stylized bird with outstretched wings and pennated tail below. The Assyrian example is more stylized, lacking the bird's head and feet, although wings and tail are very similar to the Mexican one.

[24] This is Ishtar/Hathor in Mesopotamia/Egypt. Cf. fertility figurine complex above.

[25] See note 24.

| Cultural Features | Documentation | |
	Mesoamerica	Near East
Associated with Venus as Morning Star	Covarrubias, 1957: fig. 87; Thompson, 1958: 300–306	Hinke, 1907: IV, 19; Frankfort, 1944: 198–200
Star of David, intertwined triangles	Smithsonian, 1883: 57	
Motif, ring (plate?) transfixed from below by a stick with pentad showing on ring face	Caso, 1947: figs. 1, 4, 21, 62	Ackerman, 1950; Ferguson, 1958: 115–116
Motif, ritual bucket (bag?) held by figure in hieratic scene	Drucker, Heizer, & Squier, 1955: 198	Frankfort, 1955: pl. 83
Motif, floating figure (*"Seraph?")	(La Venta Stela 3)	Irwin, 1963: 169
Frontality in representations of human figure (head in profile; eye, torso, and shoulders full front)	Ferguson, 1958: 112	Ferguson, 1958: 112
Mosaics[26]	Kidder, Jennings, & Shook, 1946: 115–117; Vaillant, 1935: 245	Woolley, 1934
Panpipe		
Trumpets (several types)	Thompson, 1954: 185	
Cylinder stamps[27]	Borhegyi, 1950c	Woolley, 1937: 76; Frankfort, 1939
Flat stamps	Borhegyi, 1950c	
Antiphonal poetic style[28]	Thompson, 1950b: 61–62	Ginsberg, 1945: 55–56

[26] Turquoise (blue) is the material for the earliest known Mexican example. Lapis lazuli (blue) was the favorite stone for mosaics in Sumer.

[27] "The cylinder seal is a peculiar type not likely to be invented independently in two different countries. . . . Paper-using people would never invent the cylinder seal" (Woolley, 1937). Frankfort (1939: 311) suggests a link in art styles between the Near East and Mexico.

[28] "There are close parallels in Maya transcriptions of the colonial period, and, I am convinced, in the hieroglyphic texts themselves to the verses of the Psalms, and the poetry of Job" (Thompson, 1950: 61–62). Ginsberg (1945) shows that the same style was Ugaritic.

| Cultural Features | Documentation | |
	Mesoamerica	Near East
arious cosmological and other eatures		
*Paradise concept	Tozzer, 1941: 131–132	James, 1966: 74
*Underworld, "hell" concept	Borhegyi, 1961; Tozzer, 1941: 132	Smith, 1966: 11; Sellars, 1945
Dualism (strongly manifest)	Thompson, 1950b: 83	Briggs, 1955; Count, 1952
Earth, air, fire, water as basic elements[29]	Nuttall, 1901: 143–146	Nuttall, 1901: 143–146
Deluge motif	Moura Pessoa, 1950: 7–48	
Produced by rain A few persons saved in a vessel Bird sent forth to check drying		
Pyramid tower built for safety against deluge	Bancroft, 1883: V, 200	Gen. 11
Destroyed by being blown down by wind[30]	Ixtlilxóchitl, 1952: I, 21	Parrot, 1949: 33–36
ingship complex	Honoré, 1964: 21–24; Adams, 1966: 132–150	Hastings, 1951: X, 632–638; Frankfort, 1948
King concept	Honoré, 1964: 21–24; Adams, 1966: 132–150	
Divine mandate	Honoré, 1964: 21–24; Adams, 1966: 132–150	
Throne	Honoré, 1964: 21–24; Adams, 1966: 132–150	
Canopy	Brinton, 1885: 20	Varron, 1942
*Umbrella, parasol, sign of dignity, rank	Heine-Geldern & Ekholm, 1951: 306	Varron, 1942
Sceptre		
Crown or diadem		

[29] Nuttall reports the concept(s) present in Greece and perhaps in India as early as the seventh century B.C. The intervening area likely shared them, too.
[30] Note that this destruction concept is not biblical, hence unlikely to have been transmitted by post-conquest Spanish.

| Cultural Features | Documentation | |
	Mesoamerica	Near East
Gold necklace, sign of office		
Heraldic devices		
*Litter	Tozzer, 1941: 165; Miles, 1966: 258	Oppenheim, 1944: 63
Deference of bowing, downcast eyes		
Technology		
*Textiles		
Purple dye	Nuttall, 1909; Born, 1937	Jackson, 1916; Born, 1937; Wright, 1943: 3
Prepared from coastal mollusk		
By "milking," then replacing it		
Elite and hieratic connotation		
Scarlet dye (cochineal/ kermes)	Born, 1938; McBryde, 1945	Born, 1938
Prepared from plant louse		
*Resist dyeing		
*Loom		
*Cotton		
Clothing		
Turban	(On figurines)	
"Nightcap"	Stirling, 1940: 317	Albright, 1949: 211–212
Pointed-toe shoes	Stirling, 1940: 327	Chiera, 1938: 205; Irwin, 1963: 146–157
Long robes	Irwin, 1963: 145–157	Irwin, 1963: 146–157
Sash, mantle, sandals, loincloth		
Weapons, armor		
Kettle-shaped helmet	Irwin, 1963: 145–157	Irwin, 1963: 146–157
Sling	Vaillant, 1950: 210	
Thickened textile armor	Follett, 1932; Vaillant, 1950: 210	Smith, 1905: 158; Miller & Miller, 1944: 187
Metallurgy		
*Lost-wax casting	Meggers & Evans, 1963: app., table 2	
Smelting, alloying, forging, hammering, gilding, etc.	Linné, 1938: 74	

	Documentation	
Cultural Features	Mesoamerica	Near East
Building Colonnade, aqueduct, canal, cement-lined reservoir, high- way Corbelled arch *True arch[31] Walled city *Fired brick Ceramics highly developed[32]	Satterthwaite, 1944: 217	
ocial organization *Merchant class or caste *Organized trade, "caravans" *Corvée labor	Museum of Primitive Art, 1965: 123 Museum of Primitive Art, 1965: 123	
iological modifications Cranial deformation Trepanation	Tozzer, 1941: 88 Romero, 1951: 318	Irwin, 1963: 105; Lev. 19:27 Wright, 1938: 28–29

[31] "It has been usual to suppose that the principle of the true arch was unknown to the American Indian, though here and there in some particular structure it has been argued that the principle, though not obvious, was really present. If the reader will turn to Figures 22 and 23 and Plates 3b and 4a of this report, I believe he will have no doubt that the Maya at La Muñeca roofed a long room with the true arch, and that they knew exactly what they were doing" (Satterthwaite, 1944: 217).

[32] Shared features include unsupported spout, multiple, bridged spouts, pattern burnishing, applique strip with thumb-press decoration on it, negative painting, rocker stamping, tripod support, four-handled crater, flat-based bowl, composite-silhouette bowl, neckless storage jar, multiple brush decoration, ribbed and twisted-strand handles, handle in form of effigy hand grasping rim, loop legs, vertical "market-bag" handles. Marked uncertainty on my part as to which, if any, of these are significant leads me to note them here rather than in the main tabulation.

11. Vinland and the Way Thither

HERBERT C. TAYLOR, JR.

> When once the Northmen had
> found their way to Cape Farewell,
> it would have been marvelous if
> such active sailors could long have
> avoided stumbling upon the con-
> tinent of North America.
>
> (Fiske, 1902: I, 177)

In 1965 Messrs. Skelton, Marston, and Painter published *The Vinland Map and The Tartar Relation*. It is intended as no denigration of this learned work to observe that the report on the Vinland Map created far more excitement in scholarly and cryptoscholarly circles than it deserved.

A sort of miasma surrounds the study of Norse contacts with the New World, an atmosphere quite different in kind from that involved in any other aspect of pre-Columbian New World archaeology and history. Periodically a publication or an archaeological interpretation will be adduced as evidence that the Norse occupied a given piece of North American real estate. The work is first hailed as an important discovery and then denounced upon more careful scrutiny. To mention only a few such instances over the past century and a quarter, there was the publication of the voyages of the Zeni, the Kensington Stone, the Newport Tower, and now the Vinland Map. In each case very substantial interest was created, in each case the discovery came under scholarly and scientific fire, and in each case the debate tended to obscure the solid body of historical and archaeological evidence that strongly indicates the Norse knew and utilized portions of the northeast American littoral at least sporadically from the end of the tenth to the middle of the fourteenth century, and perhaps later. In this paper it is proposed to present an encapsulation of historical and archaeological evidences for Norse Greenlandic acquaintance with North America during these centuries, followed by some comments on the controversy over the Vinland Map.

The Vinland Map is, of course, so termed because it locates an island to the west of Greenland, the island of Vinland, discovered in company by Bjarni and Leif. *Inter alia*, the map raises the name of an explorer long buried in Eric the Red's Saga, that of Bjarni Herjulfson.

Every schoolchild dutifully learns that Columbus discovered America in 1492. The schoolchild, grown older and more literate, learns that Columbus came late. Leif Ericson discovered America "fourteen or fifteen summers after Christianity was made law in Iceland," that is to say, about A.D. 1000 or 1001. Leif Ericson was not, however, the first European to make landfall off North America. As a matter of sober fact, at least according to the saga, the American mainland was first seen by white men because a Viking sailor had an overpowering desire to drink the yuletide ale with his father. Thereby, of course, hangs a tale, and in order to tell the tale, we must go back in time to the great age of Viking exploration.

Iceland was settled by the Northmen in the eighth century. By the tenth century the Icelandic skald (singer or teller of tales) was famous throughout the Christian world. Icelanders were present at the courts of England, Scotland, Norway, Sweden, and Denmark. The Icelandic tongue was understood throughout Scandinavia and in parts of England, Iceland, and France, and down the length of the Dnieper across to the banks of the great bend of the Volga. Scandinavians, including Icelanders, made up the famed Varangian guard of the Byzantine emperors (Craigie, 1913: 1–12). In the following century the rulers of both Norway and Denmark took the Cross and fought in the Holy Land. That many Icelanders were in their armies is attested by the frequency with which the cognomen Jorsalfar (Jerusalem-farer) occurs in the Icelandic genealogies.

Lying on the western edge of the known world, however, the Icelanders not only voyaged east and south to the Old World—they also began to push back the shadows that lay over the western seas. Greenland was evidently known to the Icelanders from about A.D.

900, when Gunnbjorn's ship (out of Norway for Iceland) was blown off its course and made landfall off either Greenland's east coast or some skerries to the east of Greenland.[1]

In the year 981 a red-headed Icelander named Eric (who just happened to be one of the finest navigators known to history) got himself into trouble. Trouble ran in the family. Eric's father had been exiled from Norway, due to a touch of homicide, and had settled in Iceland. (Iceland seems to have served as the same sort of malefactor's haven in the early Middle Ages, as did Texas to nineteenth-century Americans.) In Iceland, Eric continued the family tradition by killing two of the more redoubtable local gentry—Eyiulf the Foul and Duelling-Hrafn. Local opinion seems to have been that Eric may have done a public service but that he was much too handy with a broadsword. He was banished by the Thing-moot to northern Iceland. Here he killed two sons of one of the more solid citizens "and certain other men besides" (*Flateyjarbok*, in Gray, 1930: 29). This was too much. Eric was given the lesser outlawry of three years. Instead of spending the time in Norway or other parts of Scandinavia, he chose to seek for the land which Gunnbjorn had reported, off to the westward, nearly a century before. In one of the great feats of exploration, Eric found Greenland and voyaged along its southwestern coast for three years, A.D. 981–984. The following year he led an expedition of twenty-five Icelandic ships to colonize the new area. Fourteen of the vessels actually reached Greenland. The land was divided between the leaders of the expedition, each being awarded a fjord with grazing land. The colonists pushed up the fjords and built their farms some distance inland. The first comers all settled in the so-called East Colony. In the century following, other immigrants augmented the population of the East Settlement and founded the West Settlement farther up the coast (northwestward).

Medieval Greenland was almost two weeks' sail from Norway in good weather (Bardarson, 1906: 163–164), and if the ship were blown off course it might be, and frequently was, a matter of months. Moreover, the sagas and historical records inform us that many of the ships that sailed for the colonies were lost. The Norse settlements, lying under the edge of the great icecap, represented an outpost of

---

[1] *Landnamabok*, bk. II, chap. 7, par. 1, and bk. II, chap. 12, par. 3, in Vigfusson and Powell, 1905: I. Secondary accounts are Stefansson, 1944: 65–67; Norlund, 1936: 16–17.

Christendom and the end of the known world to the medieval European scholars. To the north of these settlements lay arctic desolation and the whirlpool that marked the edge of the world, according to Adam of Bremen (in Fiske, 1902: I, 210).

Nonetheless, it must not be thought that the Norse colonists were always hopelessly isolated. The men who settled the land were Icelanders and, therefore, seamen. Not only did they maintain contact with Europe, but they also gave the motherland its first glimpses of a new world. Within a year of the settling of Greenland, the coasts of North America had been sighted.

It was the custom of Bjarni, Herjulf's son, to spend alternate yules with his father in Iceland. Bjarni, though young, was a man of substance—a trader and ship captain. In the summer or early autumn of 986 he returned to Iceland from a year's trading in Norway to find his father gone. Herjulf had been one of the leaders of the expedition that had accompanied Eric to Greenland in the preceding year. "Bjarni was much surprised when he heard this news, and would not discharge his cargo. His shipmates inquired of him what he intended to do, and he replied that it was his purpose to keep his custom, and make his home for the winter with his father; 'and I will take the ship to Greenland, if you will bear me company.' "[2]

Thus imbued with filial and bibitory zeal, Bjarni set sail from Iceland with only rough directions for locating Greenland. Evidently passing well to the south of Cape Farewell, he sailed on until he came to a rocky coast; steering south, he encountered a second, forested coast; sailing still further south, he came to a gentler coastline with meadows, which was to be Vinland the Good. Without landing, Bjarni turned back and made landfall at Cape Farewell and found a safe harbor at Herjolfsnes, where, the saga tells us, he found his father and drank the yuletide ale.

This voyage of Bjarni was, according to Eric the Red's Saga, the basis for Leif Ericson's voyage to seek new lands in the west. Whether Bjarni made such a voyage is highly conjectural. But Fiske is certainly right when he remarks that such active sailors as the Greenland Norse could not long have avoided stumbling upon the continent of North America. In any case, it seems clear that three lands to the west of

[2] Eric the Red's Saga, *Flateyarbok*, ca. 1387, col. 222b, line 44, to col. 223b, line 40, tells Bjarni's tale. Translation appears in Gray, 1930: 38–40, and in Harvard Classics, *American Historical Documents*, 1000–1904, pp. 5–8.

Greenland were located by Leif, Eric the Red's son, around the year 1000 (Eric the Red's Saga, in Vigfusson and Powell, 1905: II, 598–608). These lands were named Helluland (Stoneland), Markland (Forestland), and Vinland (Wineland, Vineland, or Grassland, depending upon which translation one accepts). Although some scholars have professed to be able to state which side of what bay Leif landed on, the writer confesses that after a fairly detailed study of the literature, he is unable to come to any definite conclusion concerning the location of these three areas. Probably the best discussion of their location is contained in Hansen's *Outlines of the Geography and History of Greenland for the Use of Anthropologists* (1915: map facing 12).

After Leif's expedition there seemed to be several voyages to the eastern coast of North America by the Greenlandic Norse. According to Eric the Red's Saga, Thorfinn Karlsefni attempted to found a colony in Vinland during the first decade of the eleventh century (Vigfusson and Powell, 1905: 11, 610–625). The expedition is said to have included 160 men, several women, and some cattle. At first the Norse maintained peaceful relations with the Scraelings whom they found in the new land and did a brisk trade in cloth in exchange for furs. However, fighting broke out and the Norse were forced to abandon the colony. A son, Snorri, was born to Thorfinn and his wife, Gudrid, during the first year in Vinland (A.D. 1007?), and he is said to have been three years old when the party returned to Greenland.

Evidently Greenlandic Norse ships visited North America sporadically for centuries thereafter. At least some of the timber used in the construction of later Norse settlements in Greenland has been identified as American larch and we learn that in 1347 a ship returning to Greenland from Markland was blown over to Iceland (Nicol, 1840: 264; Nørlund, 1936: 88–89).

This contact with the New World was well enough known to cause Vinland to be accepted as an actual geographic locality lying west of Greenland. The first mention of Vinland in any known document is that of Adam of Bremen in 1073; he tells us that out on the ocean beyond Greenland lies another island called "Vinland" where, according to trustworthy reports of the Danes, corn grows without cultivation.[3]

---

[3] "Praeterea unam adhuc insulam recitavit a multis in eo repertam oceano,

In *Landnamabok* Vinland is more than once tacitly assumed to be a known geographical locus. Thus we are told that Ari Marsson made a voyage to a place near Vinland (*Landnamabok*, bk. II, chap. 19, par. 2, in Vigfusson and Powell, 1905) and in one of the detailed genealogies of *Landnamabok* we learn that "their son was Thord Horse-Head, father of Karlsefni, who found Vinland the Good, Snorri's father" (*Landnamabok*, bk. II, chap. 11, par. 2, in Vigfusson and Powell, 1905). There are also historical mentions of the location of lands beyond Greenland, including Vinland, in "The King's Mirror" of the thirteenth century and in the *Icelandic Geography* of either the twelfth or the fourteeth century.

Thus there can seem to be no doubt that the Greenlandic Norse knew of the existence of the lands to the west and visited on occasions from the eleventh to the fourteenth centuries. Although the records speak of timber brought to Greenland from the New World and this may be buttressed by archaeological data, there was little other economic exploitation of the western lands and the Scraelings made colonization impossible.

Until recently, no undisputed archaeological record of Norse settlement on the North American continent had ever been found. Dighton Rock, the Newport Tower, and the Kensington Stone have been successively disproved as evidence of Norse occupancy—at best, the verdict of "not proved" must be, for the nonce, accepted.

Shortly before the publication of *The Vinland Map*, Helge Ingstad (1964) published an article in *National Geographic* entitled "Vinland Ruins Prove Vikings Found the New World (see also Borden, 1963: 580; 1964: 539; 1965: 294–295). Excavations at L'Anse aux Meadows in Newfoundland have uncovered houses, a smithy, and a soapstone spindle wheel of a type commonly found in Norse ruins in Europe and Greenland. Radiocarbon dates indicate the site was occupied about A.D. 1000. In the opinion of a number of authorities, notably including Junius Bird, the site is indisputably Norse. In the opinion of the excavator, Helge Ingstad, the site probably is the "Vinland" of the sagas. Which Vinland of the sagas, or whether the several may be regarded as one, only additional excavation can make clear. In any

---

quae dicitur Vinland, eo quod ibi vites sponte nascantur, vinum bonum gerentes; nam et fruges ibi non seminatas abundare, non fabulosa opinione, sed certa comperimus relatione Danorum" (quoted in Fiske, 1902: I, 210).

event, for the first time we evidently have unquestioned archaeological data to support historical evidence that the Norse on occasion utilized the northeastern American littoral.[4]

It is, after all, not surprising that we have thus far had small success in locating the settlements of the Greenlandic Norse on the North American continent. There was a time when the Greenlandic settlements themselves were thought by many scholars to be mythical, and it was the work of nineteenth and more particularly early twentieth-century Scandinavian archaeologists that proved the authenticity of saga and historical accounts of the settlement of Norse Greenland. However, Norse Greenland was, on the basis of the historical record, occupied for over four hundred years, and the archaeological record would indicate somewhat longer occupancy (A.D. 986–1500). At maximum the population of Norse Greenland probably reached three thousand. On the other hand, the historical records of landings and attempted settlement in Markland and Vinland indicate very brief occupany by only a few individuals. Thus each new historical or archaeological discovery that promises to shed light upon the whereabouts and character of Norse Greenlandic occupancy of the New World is received with ravenous attention.

This brings us to the Vinland Map. The map and a manuscript known as "The Tartar Relation" were acquired from a European collector by Laurence Witten, a bookseller. At about the same time the Yale Library obtained a manuscript portion of Vincent of Beauvais' *Speculum Historiale*. It was discovered that this manuscript—in handwriting, watermarks, and, above all, worm holes—exactly fitted the Vinland Map and "The Tartar Relation," indicating that they had been at one time bound together. Careful analysis presented at length in *The Vinland Map and The Tartar Relation* led the several authors to the conclusion that all these documents had been prepared in the Upper Rhineland during the middle of the fifteenth century, quite possibly during the Council of Basel, which flourished from 1431 to 1449. What fired the imagination of the scholarly world was one por-

---

[4] The data and the weight of authority supporting the finds at L'Anse aux Meadows as Norse in character appear overwhelming. The current writer does sympathize with such critics as Christopher Collier (1967: 31–41), who observed that "perhaps the most striking thing about this article is the uncharacteristically misleading tone of the illustrations and picture captions provided by the *Geographic* editors."

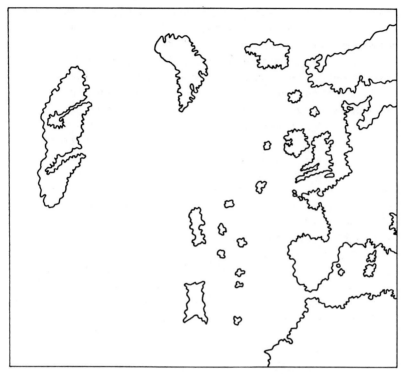

Figure 11.1. Detail from Vinland Map.

tion of the so-called Vinland Map, whence the map derives its name.
This section shows in recognizable form the western coast of Europe,
and, in the North Atlantic, three islands identifiable as Iceland, Greenland, and Vinland. Detail from this map is shown in figure 11.1. Generally the earlier reviews of this work tended to accept the analysis
presented by Skelton, Marston, and Painter but were careful to point
out that in fact this added little to our knowledge of Norse contacts
with the North American mainland. Relying upon sailing directions
and without cartographic tradition, the Norse in their heyday of exploration did not produce maps.

The location of Vinland on the Vinland Map "does not help us in
the least to locate Vinland—whether it was Baffin Land, Labrador,
Newfoundland, Nova Scotia, or further south is still uncertain" (Morison, 1965: 92). Furthermore, as early as 1912 A. A. Björnbo had re-

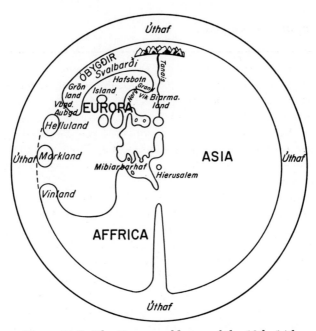

Figure 11.2. The Norse world map of the 12th–14th centuries reconstructed. After A. A. Björnbo, *Cartographia Groenlandica* (from *Vinland Map*).

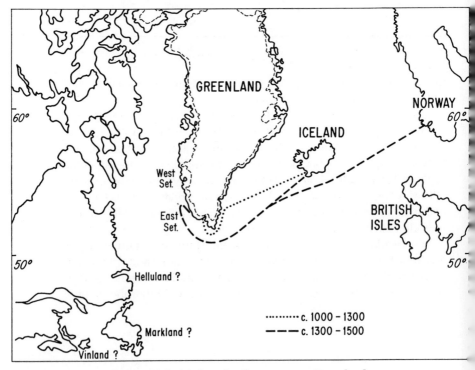

Figure 11.3. Medieval sailing routes to Greenland.

constructed in cartographic form the world view of the twelfth- to fourteenth-century Norse. Aside from showing Greenland as an extension of Asia and Vinland as a horned extension of Africa, thus providing the necessary symmetry and leaving Jerusalem as the center of the world, this reconstruction tells us at least as much as does the Vinland Map. Björnbo's reconstruction is presented as figure 11.2. For purposes of comparison, see figure 11.3, a map on a modified mercator projection, showing the North Atlantic and medieval sailing routes to Greenland.

In February and March, 1966, G. R. Crone (1966a: 75–78; 1966b: 75–80), the map curator of the Royal Geographical Society, first raised serious question concerning the dating and hence in some sense the authenticity of the Vinland Map. Mr. Crone agrees with Mr. Skelton that the Vinland Map is without the slightest doubt based on Andrea Bianco's world map of 1436 (which is, and, so far as we know, always has been in the Marciana Library in Venice) or that both were based on a common model. However, Mr. Crone goes further. He points out that a fold in the Bianco map has been copied into the Vinland Map. Thus, in his view, the man who produced the Vinland Map was a copyist, not a cartographer. He further concludes that, granted the estimated date of 1430 for the Bianco map, we must allow at least fifty years for the telltale fold to have developed and that, this being so, the Vinland Map dates to later than 1486 and probably is post-Columbian. If it is post-Columbian, like the Zeni Map before it, one is left free to assume that retrospective attempts were made to indicate knowledge of the New World before the voyages of Columbus.

Crone further points out that the most notable section found in the Vinland Map not found in the Bianco map is in the addition of the New World lands, and "another point as to date may be deduced from the apparent use of the ellipse in the general design. No other contemporary cartographer used it for this purpose. Though the ellipse was known in the early fifteenth century, its formula had not been determined. This evidence, such as it is, points to a later, rather than an earlier date" (Crone, 1966b: 80). Crone then proceeds to point out that his questioning the cartographic authenticity of the Vinland Map raises the difficulty of reconciliation with the paleographical evidence, which, as previously indicated, would seem to date the work to the middle of the fifteenth century. One possible explanation is that the map was both prepared at a later date and bound with the other portions of the manuscript at a later date, most likely in the early sixteenth century.

At this juncture, it would seem that the Vinland Map is apt to go the way of the Kensington Stone and the Zeni Map as hard evidence of Norse occupation of the New World.

Probably archaeologists ought to cease attempting to find their pre-Columbian salvation in cartographic or manuscript sources primarily and should turn instead to the Greenlandic archaeological record. It has been asserted by Scandinavian archaeologists, and supported by historical referents, that some of the timber used in the construction of late Norse Greenlandic forms was North American in origin. It should be possible both to check this assertion and to form some idea of the provenience of the wood. Further, it might still be possible to obtain C-14 dates on this North American timber. Is it not also possible that the checking of already excavated Greenlandic sites by New World archaeologists or the excavation of additional Norse Greenland sites might yield other artifacts that would give evidence of location and duration of Norse use of the northeastern American littoral?

APPENDIX
Brief Chronology of Historical Events in Norse Greenland

Date	Event	Remarks
A.D. 981–984	Eric the Red explores Greenland	
986	Immigration fleet of fourteen ships arrives	Possibly 985
987	Bjarni Herjulfson sights Helluland, Markland, and Vinland	Possibly 985
1000	Christian missionaries appear	Christianity speedily adopted
1000–1001	Leif, Eric's son, explores Markland, Helluland, and Vinland	Date uncertain
1004	Leif's brother, Thorwald, attempts colonization of Vinland (?)	Doubtful
1005	Thorwald slain by Scraelings; Vinland abandoned (?)	Doubtful
Before 1010	Thorfinn Karlsefni attempts colonization of Vinland but is later repulsed by Scraelings	Probably authentic
1023	Greenlanders subject to Norwegian Crown but later become independent again (?)	Doubtful
1121	Bishop Erik goes to Greenland and thence to Vinland	Doubtful
1124	Bishop Arnald arrives in Greenland	
1156	Johann Knut, bishop	
ca. 1188	Johann II, bishop, d. 1209	
ca. 1200	First contact with Greenland Eskimo	Date uncertain
ca. 1212	Helgo, bishop, d. 1230	
ca. 1234	Nicolas, bishop	
ca. 1247	Olaf, bishop, d. 1280	
1261	Greenland subjected to Norwegian Crown	
ca. 1288	Theodore, bishop, returns to Norway in 1299, d. 1314	

Date	Event	Remarks
1314	Arne, bishop, d. 1325	
—	Johann III (Skalle), bishop	
1347	Last known visit of Greenlandic ship to Markland and (accidentally) to Iceland	
1370	Approximate date of publication of Ivar Bardarson's account	
1376	Alf, bishop, d. 1378	
ca. 1389	Henry, bishop	Last known to reside in Greenland
1390–1400	Alleged voyages of the Zeni	Probably not authentic
1410	Last certain historical contact with the outside world	
1492	Alexander VI's papal letter on Greenland	Reports no news from Greenland for 80 years
1540	Jon Greenlander's voyage	Doubtful
1577	Martin Frobisher "discovers" southwest Greenland	

12. Quetzalcoatl: European or Indigene?

B. C. HEDRICK

It must be clarified from the outset that this paper deals ultimately with the man, or men, Quetzalcoatl, if, indeed, it is possible to separate the man from the god and myth.

In 1957, as a novice ethnohistorian first embarking on the trail of the elusive personage known as Quetzalcoatl, I wrote: "A complete study of Quetzalcoatl would require many years of work, and the concurrence of several investigators would be necessary due to the great abundance and complexity of the material which is found dispersed throughout widely scattered sources. . ." (Hedrick, 1957: v). Eleven years later, I am still on that trail, and, either because of or in spite of the passage of time, the ultimate solution to the riddle of Quetzalcoatl seems little nearer.

This paper is an attempt simply more specifically to delineate and identify the man, or men, known as Quetzalcoatl and to demonstrate that this man, despite past and present claims to the contrary, was born, bred, and buried within the geographic regions encompassed by contemporary Mexico. My thesis is simply stated: there is no evidence that Quetzalcoatl, man or men, had any origin not indigenous to the New World—more specifically, within the confines of Mexico as presently delineated.

It is my contention that Quetzalcoatl, at least the Quezalcoatl who was worshiped by the "Toltecs" and later the Aztecs, was an evolutionary being; that is, that he was, in fact, a true, blood-and-bones man, that he was later deified (probably prior to his death), and that from the humanitarian acts of the man and from the functions of the god, a many-faceted myth sprang up, which surrounded and enveloped both the man and god.

Before progressing further with this account, it is probably well to outline a bit of the history of the Toltec culture. The word *tolteca* not only signifies an inhabitant of Tollán (Tula), the traditional cultural centre of the Toltecs, but also means "artist," "artisan," or "capable worker," as opposed to the word *chichimeca,* another loosely defined but widely used term for barbarous groups of Mexico, the word signifying "barbarous." Thus, the word *tolteca* was not (or should not have been) given to a determined tribe or group of people, but to men in general who were distinguished by their higher knowledge, by their capabilities in business, and for their refined customs, as opposed to the uncultured and ignorant peoples.

According to legend, the Toltecs originally came from a city called Huehuetlapallan, which means, approximately, "the old red land" (earth). It has been suggested by various individuals that this location may well be between the Gila and Colorado rivers in present-day Arizona. Caso (1945b) places the movement of the Toltecs from Huehuetlapallan at about six centuries before Christ. Tradition has it that in the year 544 B.C. the Toltecs left this place, going southward. After a protracted pilgrimage fraught with hardships that lasted approximately 104 years, they arrived at Tollán, or Tula, situated in the modern-day state of Hidalgo, Mexico, where they established their capital (Sáenz, 1962: 3).

The chroniclers of pre-Hispanic Mexico tell us of a culture hero, governor, and high priest of Tula. This man's name was Quetzalcoatl. The indigenous mind and imagination wove about this personage all types of legends, so that it is virtually impossible to ascertain where the narration of fact ends and where the mystique of religion, combined with the passage of time, begins. Historical sources preserve the following. In paragraph fifty-four of the *Historia tolteca* in the *Anales de Cuauhtitlán* (II), "One reed [843 A.D.]; . . . it is told, that in this (year) Quetzalcoatl was born, whom they called 'Topiltzin' (Our Prince), the priest, one reed, plumed serpent (or precious twin)" (my translation).

The purported father of Quetzalcoatl, Iztac Mixcoatl (who also is deified and who has other names ascribed to him), appears as the chief of a group of invaders, possibly less civilized than the people they conquer, who do conquer the northern part of the Valley of Mexico, establishing themselves in Colhuacán. In their later warring excursions, they come into contact with other Nahuan groups—that is, those who settled some time prior in the southern part of the Valley and who had incorporated into their culture the most advanced elements of their neighbors. Iztac Mixcoatl united with a woman, possibly of Huitznahua origin, named Chimalma (Chimalman). From this union came Ce Acatl Topiltzin Quetzalcoatl. Quezalcoatl, whose mother died during childbirth, was educated by his grand-parents (*Histoire du Mechique*, quoted in Sáenz, 1962: 3), even-tually became head of the group, tribe, or clan formerly led by his father, and headed to the north.

Following the chronology of the *Anales de Cuauhtitlán* (par. 60), we find that in the year *dos conejo* (two rabbit—A.D. 870) Quetzal-coatl arrived at Tollantizinco. There he remained four years, then moved on to Cuextlan (la Huasteca) (par. 61). Then, in the year *cinco casa* (five house—A.D. 873) (par. 68), the Toltecs allegedly sent for him, electing him as head man of Tollán, and thus he became the priest-king of Tula. There can be no doubt that this priest-king, Que-tzalcoatl, was an indigene. The path from his birth to his "enthrone-ment" is too clear to allow for any extrahemispheric origin for the hero of Tula.

Further documentation of the indigenous origins of Quetzalcoatl is given in *La relación genealogía* (III, 263–281), although the year of his establishment in Tula is different. The *Relación* gives his ap-pearance there as *dos acatl* (A.D. 883). The time discrepancy between these two sources, though admittedly somewhat wide, does not de-tract in any way from the native aspect of Quetzalcoatl's origin.

Quetzalcoatl obviously not only acquired governmental and politi-cal functions in Tula. He was also considered as a priest par excel-lence. He had been a highly pious individual, possibly the originator of autosacrifice and of penitence, a man who had led an austere life. He was, therefore, the predicator of a new religion that combatted excesses and human sacrifices practiced by other religious tendencies of the day. Thus we find the mythicized fight between Quetzalcoatl and Tezcatlipoca (as narrated by Orozco y Berra, 1880: I, 64) rep-

resenting the conflict that the man, Quetzalcoatl, engendered between his humanitarian, socioreligious aims and those of the opposing trends.

If I may digress for a bit, it should be pointed out that there were,
in fact, various indigenes who bore the name of Quetzalcoatl. As an
example, we may cite the custom, at least among the Aztecs, of referring to the priests who represented given deities by the name of
the respective deity. We find men (all indigenes, of course) under
the name of Quetzalcoatl not only in Tula but also in Tenochtitlán,
Texcoco, Cholula, Cempoala, and in other areas where there were
priests dedicated to his culture. Sahagún (1938: I, 218–219) describes how and for whom the election of the priestly ranks were
made and the names that were given and customs that these min-
isters followed. He also tells how they elected the high pontificate,
who was the king or *señor* of all the principals of the religious body,
and how to this *señor* they gave the name Quetzalcoatl. He continues, pointing out that still other priests received the name or
title Quetzalcoatl. Vaillant (1951: 182) notes this arrangement also:

In Tenochtitlan . . . two high priests directed cult activities in honour of the
War God, Huitzilopochtli, and the Rain God, Tlaloc, the chief divinities
worshipped in this city. They were called *Quetzalcoatl-Totec-tlamacazqui*
and *Quetzalcoatl-Tlaloc-tlamacazqui*. The name Quetzalcoatl was given
them perhaps as an honorific title in memory of the God of Civilization and
Learning . . . archetype of the priestly ideal. The second names refer to the
gods of the respective cults, and the third word means priest.

The whole point of this digression is to acknowledge the existence
of various individuals called Quetzalcoatl, to highlight the fact that
it is recognized that many men went under this name at one time or
another, to underscore the deductive fact that they were all native
to the region in which they existed, and to demonstrate that there is
no evidence whatsoever for believing that they had extrahemispheric
origins.

Returning to the Quetzalcoatl of Tula fame, we find it possible
that this man was, in fact, the same individual who later appeared in
Cholula, and it is even conceivable that it was he whom the Mayas
called Kukulkan. In both instances I refer to the probability that, in
addition to the cult worship of the god Quetzalcoatl, there was, in

fact, at least one man by the name of Quetzalcoatl in these geographic areas. That the man of Tula, Cholula, and Yucatan could have been one and the same may be demonstrated as follows. For one reason or another, the reign of Quetzalcoatl came to an end in Tula. Legend gives us various choices, among which are the seduction of a young maiden, the invention and imbibing of *pulque* to the point of inebriation, thus disgracing himself with his subjects, and the loss of a battle with Tezcatlipoca (see above). Whatever the cause for the abandonment of Tula by Quetzalcoatl, it seems evident that a hegira by a man, not just a mythicized flight, took place. There is an extremely interesting, if stylized and legendary, account of Quetzalcoatl's flight in Sahagún (1932: 187). Closer to fact is the rendition in Torquemada's work, *Monarquía indiana* (1943: I), wherein it is recounted that the last "chief" of Tollán led to the downfall of this important center. The chief's name is Topiltzin, an apellative of Quetzalcoatl. Cholula became the inheritor of the culture of Tollán. Upon the destruction or decline of Tollán, many of the inhabitants were supposed to have gone to Cholula, where they inculcated their culture into that of the natives of the area. Orozco y Berra, in his monumental work *Historia antigua y de la conquista de México,* along with Sahagún, gives an intriguing story of the trip made by Quetzalcoatl from Tollán to Chollolan (Cholula). Having once reached Cholula, where he purportedly was very well received, he remained there for some twenty years, teaching his mysteries to the people. These people became the primary priests of the Aztec religion, and their city with its great temple pyramid grew to be the Mecca of the Aztec empire. Cholula was, of course, famed for the work of its artists in the precious metals, excavations in the area having corroborated that this fame was justly deserved (Spence, 1912: 27).

After his long stay in Cholula, Quetzalcoatl arrived at the seashore and is supposed to have sailed on a raft (described variously as made of balsa, writhing serpents, and reeds) out into the sunrise, promising one day to return to his people. It should be called to mind that, on leaving Tollán, Quetzalcoatl was departing for the area known as Tlillan Tlapallan, generally conceded to be the Yucatan region of Mexico.

Whether or not Quetzalcoatl traveled to Yucatan and was transformed in name to Kukulkan, which in Maya signifies "plumed serpent" (as does one of the meanings of the word Quetzalcoatl), I am not prepared staunchly to say with any amount of surety. However, it is not out of possibility that such an occurrence did take place. That there was a man (not just a god) called Kulkulkan in Yucatan is highly probable. It has also been told, as will be shown, that this man was "Mexican" (that is, not indigenous to Yucatan). Referring to the figure carved in stone at the entrance to the temple on the pyramid of Kukulkan, T. A. Willard (1941: 174) has this to say:

. . . this majestic figure of the great leader is not that of a native of the beardless race of Mayas, but a tall stately figure with a very long beard and the features of a white man, which a well-known archaeologist has likened to that of our "Uncle Sam." And in a way, the simile is not as absurd as it may sound. After all, Kukulcan too was representative of his government.

We are informed by Bishop Landa and others, that a great leader known as Kukulcan—the name meaning "The Plumed Serpent"—appeared in Yucatan in the forepart of the eleventh century, where he became a powerful political figure. He ruled in Chichen-Itzá until he became a very old man, and then left in the same manner as he came, by way of Champotón.

Documentos inéditos contain among other things, the history of Tecauto and Tepecán written by Juan de Magana, who states: ". . . it is said that the first inhabitants of Chichen-Itzá were not idolators until Kukulcan, Mexican captain, entered these parts and taught idolatry and the necessity of it."

The attention of the reader is called to the statement in the penultimate paragraph, "Kukulcan . . . appeared in Yucatan in the forepart of the eleventh century." I should like to point out the fact that Kukulkan and Quetzalcoatl could, then, be one and the same man. For, if, as Sáenz (1962: 5) points out, the date of the abandonment of Tula was A.D. 999 (based on the conclusion of Jiménez Moreno that the date of the exodus of Quetzalcoatl from Tula should be advanced one or two cycles of fifty-two years), and if we presume that Quetzalcoatl did spend twenty years in Cholula, then his arrival in Yucatan (allowing approximately one year for travel, to be generous) would fall roughly at A.D. 1020. Two other possible arrival dates I have concluded on the basis of approximately two years' travel time (from Tula, eventually to Cholula, and from Cholula eventually to Yucatan), basing them on the different dates as given in the appendix of this paper, are A.D. 969 and A.D. 999, either of these dates being sufficiently near to "the forepart of the eleventh century" to be seriously considered in the search for the synonomy of Quetzalcoatl and Kukulkan. The very latest date at which I arrived for Quetzalcoatl's (Kukulkan's) arrival in Yucatan was A.D. 1072.

Further substantiation of the theory that Quetzalcoatl and Kukulkan were one and the same man is that, although I cannot find any specific primary source that witnesses the fact that Quetzalcoatl had with him any great number of people on his departure from Cholula, it is known that many of the people from Tula did follow their fallen leader to Cholula. Then, if the hypothesis that Quetzalcoatl and Kukulkan could have been the same individual can be accepted, we find that Molina Solís (in Willard, 1941: 160), the recognized historian of Yucatan, writes, "It is stated authoritatively that with Kukulcan were many people and they all came from outside of the country." Further, according to Molina Solís (in Willard, 1941: 174, 179), "civil war came between Kukulcan's *Toltecs* [my italics] and the Itzá-Mayas, and the reason for which is unknown. . . . Further proof of the Toltec invasion and conquest of the Itzáes in Chichen-Itzá is found on the embossed metal disks brought up from the sacred Well by Edward H. Thompson."

The famous historian Justo Sierra (1948: I, 15) also lends credence to our theory, when he states that "the Mayan culture, that of Mayapán, begins its intimate contact with the Nahao culture, that had now infiltrated in the Quiché groups. A prophet and legislator, or better said, perhaps, a priestly family founds the new cult of Gugumatz on the shore of the Usumacinta, and penetrating into Yucatán through Campotón [sic] establishes in Mayapán the altars of Kukulcan; these terms Gugumatz and Kukulkan are the exact transcriptions of the Nahoa Quetzalcoatl."

Although still another date is interjected, Coe (1966: 138–139) writes that "another version of the tale, the one known only too well by Moctezuma II, tells us that he did not perform an act of self-immolation, but rather set off . . . on a journey to the east, from which he was supposed to return one day. It is evidence of the historical core within this legend that Maya accounts speak of the arrival from the west, in the year A.D. 987, of a Mexican conqueror named in their tongue Kukulcán ('Feathered Serpent'), who with his companions subjugated their country. There is also ample evidence in the arch-aeology of Yucatán for a sea-borne Toltec invasion, successfully initi-ating in the late tenth century a Mexican Period."

I do not, of course, claim dogmatically upon this evidence that the two principals are unequivocally one and the same, but I do put forth the theory for further, critical evaluation and study. Of course, if the above hypothesis contains any basic truth, then Kukulkan also was obviously of native origin, with no extraterritorial roots. It is acknowl-edged that, as in the case of Quetzalcoatl on the "mainland," there probably were at least two men bearing the name of Kukulkan, but again there is no evidence whatsoever—whether or not Kukulkan was indeed Quetzalcoatl—that the man was from any other land but Mexico.

Some of the claims to the extrahemispheric origins of Quetzalcoatl border on the ridiculous when seen in cold, analytical, and retrospec-tive light, but undoubtedly they served the purposes or were (or are), indeed, seriously believed by some of the proponents of transoceanic contact, either corporal or spiritual. Most of these claims, of course, grew out of religious zeal or intent. For example, when the Catholic friars came to New Spain, they used the fact that Quetzalcoatl was supposed to have civilized the Toltecs and left for the east to return again at a later date "as evidence that St. Thomas the Apostle had visited the Mexican nation and converted its inhabitants, who later slid back into pagan ways" (Vaillant, 1951: 182). The oddest element of this claim, aside from the obvious proselyting intent, is that the Quetzalcoatl of the Mexican Valley documents was never blond (or fair), as stated by the friars, but virtually always pictured as black-bearded and, in illustrations, at least, had his face painted black. This fact did not, however, hinder the Spanish priests from trying to justify many of their over-zealous evangelistic acts in the name of bringing new salvation to the back-slid natives who had been visited and con-verted by St. Thomas.

There are also those people who see in Quetzalcoatl an Irish priest. The most serious attempt to establish this claim came in an article by D. Daly (1891), in which he endeavored to show, on the basis of the fair, blond man reported by the Spanish priests, and on certain out-of-context quotations from early Mexican manuscripts, combined with a time lapse in the whereabouts and activities of the future Irish saint, that Quetzalcoatl was, in fact, St. Brendan. Additional attempts have been made to associate Quetzalcoatl with religious personages, an extreme example being Hanson (1949), *Jesus Christ among the Ancient Americans* and *In the Land of the Feathered Serpent.*

From time to time, others have assayed the theories that Quetzalcoatl was an errant Norseman, or perhaps even an Atlantean who somehow came to Mexico to spread sweetness and light throughout the land. I find no credibility in any of these opinions and set them down as romantic thinking with no documentary, or even legendary, basis.

I strongly feel that one of the most picturesque of pre-Columbian Mexico's figures is Quetzalcoatl, although I concede that his renown is due less to the undoubted importance of his acts and subsequent religious cults than to his association with the arrival and the beliefs of the white man. As has been mentioned previously, Quetzalcoatl had been a wise and good ruler in Tula—lawgiver, teacher of the arts, and founder of a "purified" religion. Driven from his rule for one reason or the other, he departed for Tlillan Tlapallan, the land of plenty, promising to return and reinstitute his kindly creed on some future anniversary of the day of his departure. As some manuscripts have, indeed, described him, he was bearded, light-skinned (except when ceremoniously painted), clad in a long over-garment, and, as with other demigods, identified with things celestial; crosses were associated with him (both the man and the god). When Cortés landed, the Mexicans were expecting the return of Quetzalcoatl, and the very Indian sentries who first beheld the Spaniards' ships are purported to have been posted to watch for the coming of the now-god, Quetzalcoatl. The white men (their image perhaps augmented by their shining mail, the robed priests, the crosses) were inevitably assumed to be the expected deity, and among the gifts sent to them by Moctezuma II were the turquoise masks, feather mantle, and other apparel appropriate to Quetzalcoatl. It has long been felt that the belief in Quetzalcoatl's return materially aided the Spaniards in the early stages of their advance, and it is small wonder that the myth that was helpful to their ambitions should have appealed to their imaginations. The missionary priests, gaining some idea of native traditions and finding among them ideas, emblems, and rites analogous to those of Christianity (the cross, baptism, confession), saw in the figure of the robed and bearded reformer of religion a Christian teacher, and they were not hesitant to identify him with St. Thomas, the Apostle. It is virtually a *non sequitur* to state it, but once again we are reminded that indigenous religious artifacts, both physical and spiritual, quite naturally give rise in the minds of the innocently naïve to the belief that there must, perforce, have been *some* European or other transoceanic culture contact. We know today that these artifacts—the cross and baptism, for instance—were common among the Amerind, ranging virtually from British Columbia to the tip of South America. There is absolutely no extrahemispheric presence identifiable, at least insofar as the topic of this paper is concerned.

As Carroll L. Riley (1969: 212) has said:

It is clear that no significant amount of the native American civilization came from the Old World. Proponents of schemes that have American Indians dependent on the Old World for their complex societies simply ignore the implications of time, space, and common sense. It is possible that a few items, pottery types, certain art motifs, one or two food plants, were so transported, but there is, as yet, no definite proof even for any one of these. It is then reasonable to believe that, in the Old World and the New, very similar civilizations grew up independently. This . . . is no more than an indication of the basic unity of the human species and of the mechanistic and channeled nature of the steps that lead to civilization.

The subject is a completely fascinating one. Alexander (1920: 67) states:

. . . whether we view the Quetzalcoatl myth in relation to its association with European ideas or with respect to its aboriginal analogues in the two Americas, it presents a variety of interest scarcely equalled by any other tale of the New World.

Vaillant (1951: 175) says:

I, personally, believe that the introduction of superior culture elements and the creation of local arts as well might not only lead to the invention of a God of Civilization, but also endow individual innovators with the name of that god. [The concept of the god Quetzalcoatl] resulted . . . from the experience of many peoples over a long period of time in explaining and honouring the introduction of those benefits which ensure their corporal and spiritual well-being.

I have no quarrel with Vaillant in the foregoing, succinct statement concerning Quetzalcoatl.

In conclusion, I should like to restate that the man known as Quetzalcoatl was, in my opinion, an evolutionary being; that is, he was originally a flesh-and-blood "Mexican," he was deified, and from the deeds of the man and from the functions of the deity a many-faceted and complex system of mythology sprang up, which surrounded, enveloped, and obfuscated both the man and the god. But, man that he was, Quetzalcoatl was indigenous to the New World, beyond any reasonable doubt.

APPENDIX

Chronology of Toltec History*

Event	Dates from manuscripts	Ruin of Tula		
		1116	1156	1168
Birth of Quetzalcoatl	1 Acatl—843	895	935	947
His establishment in Tula according to the *Anales de Cuauhtitlán*	5 Calli —873	925	965	977
His establishment according to the *Relación de la genealogía*	2 Acatl—883	935	975	987
Abandonment of Tula by Quetzalcoatl	1 Acatl—895	947	987	999

After Sáenz, *Quetzalcoatl en México y Centro América.*

* Jiménez Moreno, after a careful study of various genealogies, proposed in the Round Table, dedicated to "Tula y los Toltecas," which was held in Mexico City in 1947, that a correction of dates be made, advancing them one or two cycles of fifty-two years. Great confusion of dates in regard to Tula exists, for the *Anales de Cuauhtitlán* place the beginning of the reign of Mixcoamazatzin (Mixcoatl-Totepeuh or Iztac Mixcoatl) in A.D. 752. But the "Leyenda de los Soles" puts the birth of his child, Topiltzin, at thirty-nine years of his life or reign; thus it appears to be A.D. 804, which is the initial date of Toltec history. And the latter date, according to the three hypotheses of the proposed correction, would correspond to A.D. 856 or 908. The penultimate column above owes its authorship to César Sáenz.

13. A Transatlantic Stimulus Hypothesis for Mesoamerica and the Caribbean, circa 3500 to 2000 B.C.

ROBERT A. KENNEDY

In America as in other regions of the world, increased knowledge of the subject, with the appreciation that the range of enquiry cannot be confined by modern regional boundaries, has allowed diffusion—without the "ism"—to take its rightful place in the theory and process of elucidation of prehistory. But diffusion by land is still easier to accept than that by sea. The reason is, quite simply and bluntly, that precious few prehistorians are small-boat

NOTE: The publication by the *Southwestern Journal of Anthropology* in the spring of 1962 of Dr. Alice Kehoe's paper, "A Hypothesis on the Origin of Northeastern American Pottery," prompted me in that year to draft the basis of this paper. Shortly afterward I was fortunate in being able to discuss this draft in detail with Professor Gordon Willey while he was at Cambridge University. From him I got much valuable advice concerning the then recent work by American scholars and the kind suggestion to rewrite my paper, basing it upon the pottery evidence alone. This was not possible, for I had to return to Oxford and my African thesis, the studies for which had originally led me to the evidence of interest here. In fact, until now and even now, pressure of work and ill health have prevented me from returning wholeheartedly to the increasingly important and absorbing subject of transoceanic contacts.

sailors, let alone experienced in the navigational conditions and seas familiar to men during that truly great period of voyaging four to five thousand years ago. In all humility I must, for the sake of brevity and as one who is thus experienced, claim that the "navigational problem" of transatlantic contacts can be dismissed. The consideration of such possible contacts has been hampered by this lack of essential experience and resulting understanding. Research has largely been of the kind to be expected of landsmen; and consequently dugout canoes—with certain exceptions, essentially craft of sheltered waters —or rafts, have been somewhat rashly invoked in this context and are persistently plotted on the distribution maps or even launched into the unpredictable currents of archaeological thought. Unfortunately they continue drifting therein far beyond their actual survival potential. It is surprising that the American Indian bullboats have not been cited as more suitable examples of *inland* craft and comparable to the Welsch coracle. And it is still more surprising that the closely related curragh, the *sea-going* craft that still survives on the west coast of Ireland, is generally ignored. Though planked craft were already in use by about 3000 B.C. in the Mediterranean, it is most likely that it was in craft like the curragh that transatlantic voyages were made during the period under consideration.

In studying the problem alluded to above we must remember the limitations of archaeology—and ethnography. We must bear in mind not only the special qualities but also the perishable nature of such craft. Not least must we ponder on the psychology of immigration after a long, terrifying, and probably accidental ocean crossing. It is here, incidentally, that I see an important avenue for study. The possibility of theorizing usefully and with the aid of data from known models is surely not remote. To my mind the facts and theory of migration and resultant immigration and colonization, or survival and acculturation, in prehistoric times have not received enough attention.

The results of radiocarbon dating have recently given us a clearer picture of cultural sequences in the Old and New Worlds and have suggested that there are at least two separate, original pottery traditions in the New World. Of these, the East Woodland pottery has been thought to be part of the Asiatic tradition, whereas the Middle American pottery appears to have an earlier and separate tradition. Recent work has also suggested that a transpacific source may be in some way responsible for pottery development in Middle and South America. Furthermore, the Asiatic origins of Woodland pottery have been questioned, and it has been ably suggested that a more likely source is northwestern Europe, by means of seaborne contact utilizing the Irminger Current and the islands of Faroe, Iceland, and Greenland as stages (Kehoe, 1962). In view of these suggestions, it is my aim to point out the existence of a strong case for a transatlantic stimulus by means of the southern route and to suggest that this is the probable source of many traits in Middle American cultures, particularly in their pottery.

If we accept that pottery is one of the most diagnostic classes of artifact, the distinct occurrence of a high number of technical and decorative traits (which are undeniably at home in the Eur-African/ Atlantic Late Neolithic context) in the areas of Middle America, in the Caribbean and southeastern North America, and, moreover, at approximately the right time, must seem to us significant.

The earliest pottery in the New World seemed to occur in southern Middle America or Mesoamerica and southeastern North America. And any valid list of Old World traits noticeable in the earliest pottery must, it seems, include the following minimal choice of headings: (1) coil-building; (2) fibre-tempering; (3) "impressed" decoration by the use of rockering, Cardium shell, cord, punctation, and scoring; (4) certain distinct motifs executed by one of these methods (for example, scoring)—such as concentric arcing or hatched triangles—or by zone-burnishing; (5) Mediterranean Chassey A. style decoration; (6) carinated vessels and polypodal forms; and (7) mammiform feet.

I am not clear as to the distribution of coil-building. It is, anyway, one of the traits in the fabric that often go undetected. But I should expect its occurrence along with the other traits, since it was common in Atlantic Europe and Northwest Africa.[1]

Fibre-tempering, which has been reported to be typical of the "earliest pottery north of Mexico" (Bullen, 1961), is also typical of Saharan ware from Tibesti (Kennedy and Vita-Finzi, 1965) to the Maghreb and the Río de Oro. It also appears to have gone unnoticed

---

[1] The origin of this technique was long thought to be North Africa and, ultimately, Egypt, though its distribution is not confined to the African shores of the Mediterranean and it may be at least as early as the Neolithic culture stage itself.

in some Neolithic wares from the Mediterannean, for I have detected its occurrence in pottery from Malta. "Impressed" decoration belongs to an ancient tradition with significant maritime associations, which certainly had not died out along the Moroccan coast in Atlantic Late Neolithic–Chalcolithic times. Rockering and the use of a cardium or similar shell were decorative treatments that seem to have been used by at least about 1500 B.C. in the earliest pottery from Mexico (Coe, 1962) and also in Guatemala (Willey and Phillips, 1958), where cord marking and zone-burnishing are also recorded for the Ocòs culture. The latter technique is notably typical of the European Western Neolithic period and also, perhaps significantly, of southern Spain (see below). Rockering has also been reported from Ecuador about 2000 B.C. (Willey and Phillips, 1958). For what it is worth by judging from the comparison of illustrations alone, the so-called check-stamped wares of the American Southeast appear identical to the dentate "impressed" ware of Spanish Morocco, while this treatment is common to Saharan ware as a whole. Furthermore, these Southeastern wares, the earliest of which are about 2000 B.C., are also fibre-tempered (Willey, 1962, personal communication).

The execution of certain motifs that are equally at home in Atlantic Late Neolithic Europe and the Hispano-African Mediterranean zone from at least 3000 B.C.—for instance, scored concentric arcing and triangular hatching (though in Atlantic Europe the latter seems to become more popular in Beaker times)—appears to occur very early in the New World. The latter motif apparently occurs in the "orange incised" wares of the Southeast (Griffin, 1952), in "pre-Guangala" pottery of Ecuador (Bushnell, 1957) and also in the "Machililla incised" ware of the Machililla culture (Meggers and Evans, 1962), which in 1962 seemed to me similar to the "pre-Guangala" pottery. Taken together, the last three culture groups of pottery evince distinct Chassey A. style decoration. Not merely one motif, but several typical motifs on several separate vessels, and this in each culture group. Moreover, in both the "pre-Guangala" and the Machililla cultures this decoration is executed on carinated vessels, in a horizontal zone complete with defining lines and—be it emphasized—by *incising upon the hard clay before firing* (Bushnell, 1957). This is identically the technique evinced by the Western Neolithic Chassey A. wares in Europe (Childe, 1957).

The common decorative motifs occurring on these European wares are a hatching-defined broad zigzag, triangular hatching, alternate cross-hatching, cross-parallel hatched squares, punctuation (only present in the combination alluded to above on "pre-Guangala" wares, so far as I could ascertain), and diamond or lozenge shapes. Perhaps it is also significant that this last motif occurs in the Machililla culture, along with parallel zigzags, on "Machililla red-banded" (painted) wares, an apparent inconsistency that need not be important or surprising in what is anyway likely to be a post-stimulus-source culture in the New World. For both "pattern" (zone)-burnished and *painted* wares are associated with the so-called trading colonies complex about 2600 B.C. in southern Spain (Blance, 1961) and later with Beakers, there and also in Spanish Morocco (Evans, 1958).

The significant quality of these transatlantic coincidences of decoration and technique is enhanced by the shapes of the vessels upon which they have been executed. Carination has already been mentioned, and in the "Machililla incised" wares this feature is embellished by nicking (Meggers and Evans, 1962), a treatment characteristic of the earlier Western Neolithic wares. In El Salvador tetrapodal carinated pottery is also said to occur early on (Lothrop, 1927), though probably not quite early enough for this hypothesis (Willey, 1962, personal communication). It would interest me to know if this example is comparable to the similar but more recent finds reported from Ecuador (Bushnell, 1957).

Polypodal vessels have a most ancient ancestry in the Neolithic period of the Old World (Mellaart, 1962). They also occur sporadically and widely in the later contexts of the Western Neolithic and have a resurgence in Beaker times, which as we now know have been extended back into the third millennium B.C. by radiocarbon dating. Reddish colored wares might also indicate a transatlantic influence in Beaker times, as Kehoe (1962) has suggested for the American Northeast. One might extend this to apply to the well-developed early pottery already described from the Southeast, Middle, and Central America. But when this color is due to the use of a slip we may look further back, to the middle of the third millennium, for a source in southern Spain or Northwest Africa.

The presence of mammiform legs among the early polypodal "orange" wares in El Salvador "at approximately 1500 B.C." (Haberland, 1969) is particularly striking, while Lothrop showed one with a "skirt" that recalls skirted bowls with Chassey A. type decoration from Malta (Evans, 1958). Mammiform legs also occur on some late Predynastic Egyptian pottery (Petrie, 1920); and this is not so far-fetched a comparison as it may seem. There are strong elements of a Predynastic character in the European Late Neolithic and, more significantly, in prehistoric Berber culture and, of course, the Saharan Neolithic. Some of these elements certainly found their way to the Canary Islands with the Late Neolithic colonization. Another apparently significant, though unexplained, fact that must not be overlooked is that almost the whole repertoire of the so-called Chassey A. style decoration is also distinctive of the Nubian C. Group pottery (of the last quarter of the third millennium B.C.). This significance is apparent because similar ware has turned up across the Sahara westward and has been recorded from several sites in Northwest Africa as well, opposite the Canary Isles (Almagro-Basch, 1946; Kennedy, 1965).

At this point, if not before, it may be as well to state that I am perfectly aware of the wide-ranging and therefore potentially dangerous approach of this paper. But if we recall the period under review, from about 3000 to 1500 B.C. on the western side of the Atlantic and about 3500 to 2000 or perhaps 1800 B.C. on the eastern side (that is, allowing an arbitrary time lag for the establishment of the stimulus cultures), the similarity of traits—by no means confined to pottery—cannot be dismissed in entirety as mere coincidence. Also, the wide-ranging approach is essential if we are to begin to understand more fully the great period of prehistory under review here, for it was itself essentially a wide-ranging period. In my opinion we are dealing with Pan-Atlantic cultures, even if the stimulus *did* move in only one direction, though some colleagues think the opposite (west-east) movement took place (on botanical grounds, for instance).

In my original draft three main classes of artifactual evidence were considered. These were arrowheads, stone axes, and the pottery. These represent by no means all the purely archaeological evidence, let alone the more dubious welter of intangible traits or customs that could, but might better not, be invoked. The climate of opinion and the breadth of vision among archaeologists have changed enormously. One need not compile a monumental thesis, followed by an unorthodox (but none the less valuable experimental) voyage. The case can be argued archaeologically first, as it should be. The study of the intangibles can, must, and will come later, when a substantial archaeological foundation has been established for it. And I have to admit to the serious consideration of an experimental voyage in a curragh. However, for the time being we can all regard with interest and also admiration the voyage of the papyrus vessel, *Ra*, while pursuing the primary archaeological research.

A major problem in the consideration of a southern stimulus route has up to now been disguised as it were by the use of such terms as "Saharan Neolithic," "Beaker times," or "Late Neolithic–Chalcolithic times." This now needs some explanation. The problem is dominated by the question of the origin of the Beaker culture. This has received much scholarly attention, but, partly because of a mainly European or mainly African approach in archaeological research and partly because of the dearth of reliable evidence, this vital Old World problem remains unsolved. However, the presence of a strong African, even Saharan, strain in the Spanish Neolithic has long been appreciated (Childe, 1957). The distribution of a large number of Beaker sites in otherwise advanced Neolithic contexts in Northwest Africa (Camps, 1961) suggests a connection with exploitive, industrial activity (see Kennedy, 1965). This was apparently directed with the necessary specialist skills at exploiting natural mineral resources valuable at that time (copper, salt, stone). It also suggests a continuity of industrial or craft knowledge from Egypt through northern Africa on the one hand and throughout the Mediterranean area and particularly in Spain on the other. It is also necessary at this juncture to emphasize that the prehistory of the Iberian peninsula is still by no means satisfactorily resolved. Evidence vital to this hypothesis has usually been glossed over by those working on the Iberian material. All that can and should be said here, however, is that whoever and whatever the Beakers represent, certain things are reasonably clear. The so-called Beaker culture is marked by an exceptional *mobility*, both by land and by sea. But the routes followed must have been established for at least a millenium. And the Beaker and Late Neolithic Eur-African cultures are only the end products of the complex acculturative processes that concern us here.

The amazing continuity of the "Libyan" (Berber) culture right across the Sahara westward from the Nile—retaining at least until the second millennium B.C. what was in part essentially a Predynastic

Egyptian character minus the settled, urban life—is demonstrated by the fibre-tempered pottery, the arrowheads (also extending into Atlantic Europe), and the Saharan rock art illustrating the use of the throwing stick, the wearing of plumes in the hair, and fringed leather clothing. This evidence, with that of certain ritual practices like trepanning (which also developed obsessive proportions in Late Neolithic and Beaker times in Western Europe), dog veneration, and mummification, (both incidentally attested for the Canary Isles by Hooton, 1925; Espinosa, 1907), suggests that the ancient Libyans may have been involved by means of the contacts and opportunities inherent in the nomadic way of life, in the development of the C. Group in the East and of the Hispano-African Beaker complex in the West. But these are, I repeat, end products. And we have to face the cold fact that we still do not know what was really happening, during the two millennia or so before, among the Neolithic cultures present in the embarkation zone for our hypothetical stimulus or series of stimuli. I hope, however, that I have managed to convey some idea of the cultural complexity in the Atlantic Eur-African zone, from which comparatively remote traits could *all* become available to the bearers of transatlantic stimulus.

Although by the end of the third millennium B.C., from Brittany to Northwest Africa and the Canary Isles, a similar combination of influences was playing its part in a broad culture period that was or had been essentially Atlantic Late Neolithic, the archaeological record in the Canary Isles and the adjacent African mainland alone fails to show all the traits that we could claim as of Old World origin and that are found in the New World. But we must accept as hardly likely that all these traits would have been carried by one boatload of accidental migrants, especially during one of the greatest periods for group mobility or voyaging in man's history. We must surmise that many boats would be forced off course during some two and a half millennia. We can only wonder, at this stage, how many safely crossed and how many were lost. One could speculate on the cultural affiliations and dates of the several likely and successful groups of stimulus bearers, but there is not time for this. If we assume our hypothesis is to be a valid one, it is, however, worth speculating upon where ultimately successful landings took place. And it is to these areas that further study should be applied.

It is superficially disconcerting that of the earliest cultures in the

New World known to me that possess "advanced" traits, none are what I could seriously regard as true stimulus-source cultures. But their distribution must be significant. This suggests two main land-fall zones, in the Southeast, and along the Mesoamerican and Carib-bean coasts. A third zone, the Antilles, should also be mentioned, but this elucidation awaits further study; probably the islands merely became what might be described as a "fossil" stimulus-source culture zone. An obviously disconcerting factor is the occurrence of many apparently significant sites along the wrong coastline. This, how-ever, may reflect the more congenial conditions for life along the Pacific coast and littoral, not only for prehistoric man but also for archaeologists. The original landings must have taken place on the eastern coasts and the survivors must have penetrated westward. Clearly the Gulf and Caribbean littorals must be explored thoroughly and particular attention paid to the ancient shorelines. Recent work in South America is, I understand, producing important results in this direction.

To sum up this distinctly preliminary presentation of my hypothesis for Old World stimulus via the South Atlantic route, transatlantic immigrants are more than possible. We know they had the craft—and they were *not* dugouts. There were probably many landings over a long period, giving rise to several stimulus-source cultures. The ultimate influence of these was probably largely dependent upon fortune, fortitude, and geography.

14. Small Boats upon the North Atlantic

ALICE B. KEHOE

Was there contact between Europe and northeastern North America before Cabot brought America's North Atlantic coast into the orbit of the European powers?

The query divides into three: Was transatlantic voyaging possible before the late fifteenth century A.D.? Is there historical documentation for transatlantic voyaging before A.D. 1492? Is there evidence for undocumented voyaging before 1492? The first question can be unequivocally answered in the affirmative. One and perhaps two or three cases can be adduced for North Atlantic crossings in answer to the second question. For the third question, there are substantial, but not conclusive, clues suggesting limited contacts between northern Europe and America in the late Archaic and Early Woodland periods of the American northeast.

That the Atlantic could have been traversed before the development of the fifteenth-century caravels is amply proven by hundreds of authenticated crossings in small boats of every description. At least two rafts, two dugout canoes, two dories propelled only by oars, several dories fitted with sails, conventional sailboats as small as five feet eleven inches in length, and unconventional boats including kayaks, folding boats, and an amphibian jeep have successfully floated across the ocean.[1]

The most instructive voyage, for students of transatlantic diffusion, was that of Dr. Alain Bombard in 1952. To prove his doctoral thesis, that shipwrecked persons can remain alive on the products of the sea alone, Dr. Bombard rode an inflatable rubber liferaft from Casablanca to Barbados via the Canaries. The raft, *L'Hérétique*, was fifteen feet long, six feet wide, and equipped with a rigid keel, two leeboards, and a dinghy sail of limited usefulness, as her mast was set so far forward she could not sail into the wind. Bombard resolved to manage without any stored food or water, claiming (1954: 12) that a man can maintain himself indefinitely on the sea if he is provided with a cloth net for small sea fauna, fishing line and hook for tunny, a small spear or harpoon for sea perch, and a large harpoon for larger fish. Bombard did survive his sixty-five consecutive days at sea in reasonable health.

A German medical doctor, Hannes Lindemann, tested Bombard's thesis with two Atlantic crossings, first in an African dugout and later in an Aerius folding boat. Lindemann (1958) would amend his predecessor's survival kit only by adding a simple fruit press, to squeeze liquid out of fish when this might be the only drinking liquid available. Although both Bombard and Lindemann floated along the warm mid-Atlantic trade winds belt, generally supposed to be richer in marine life than the more northern latitudes, the comments of North Atlantic small-boat sailors such as Manry (1966) and Ridgeway and

[1] Merrien (1954) includes an appendix listing noteworthy small-boat ocean crossings. Others are recorded by Mr. Jean C. Taupin, secretary of the Slocum Society, East Setauket, New York, an organization devoted to singlehanded ocean voyages. Currently, the smallest vessel known to have been successfully sailed across the Atlantic is the *April Fool*, in which Hugo Vihlen traveled alone from Casablanca to just off the Florida coast (*Newsweek*, July 1, 1968, p. 57; *Time*, June 28, 1968, p. 31). Also pertinent to the thesis of this paper is the Eskimo kayak preserved in the Aberdeen, Scotland, Museum since it beached upon the Scottish shore in the late seventeenth century. The kayak seems to prove that Eskimos, probably from Greenland, were able to paddle their light skin boats across the North Atlantic, and that they are to be identified with the "Finn-men" of Scottish legend (Whitaker, 1954), who "have the power to take any shape of marine animal, as also that of human beings. . . . In the seal-form they came ashore every ninth night to dance on the sands" (Andersson, 1967: 2). (Joan Baez sings the ballad of a Finn-man, a "Silkie"—more correctly, *selchie*—of Sule [seal] Skerry, on one of her early records.)

Blyth (1967) suggest the colder waters could also sustain human life.

The history of watercraft further supports the possibility of early transatlantic contacts originating from Europe. American craft, however, cannot be satisfactorily discussed. At the beginning of the historic period, sewn-bark canoes seem to have been the predominant, perhaps the only (Rogers, 1965: 457–458) boats used by the Indians of northeastern America. Primarily riverine transport designed for easy portage, the bark canoes were used for salt-water journeying by the coastal tribes. Prehistoric boats have not, to my knowledge, been discovered in northeastern America, and the circumstantial evidence of site locations and food debris implies that watercraft were not intensively employed in the northeast until the second millennium B.C. (MacLeod, 1967, and Michels, 1967).

Europe, in contrast, has yielded a dugout canoe at Pesse, Holland, dated about 6000 B.C. (Piggott, 1965: 66, n. 26). Evidence for even earlier boats comes from the Early Maglemosian site of Star Carr, Yorkshire, where a boat paddle was excavated from what had been a lakeside camp, dated about 7500 B.C. (Clark, 1954: 12). According to pollen analysis, Star Carr in the mid-eighth millennium was surrounded by birch forests, but not by any trees suitable for dugouts. Clark therefore inferred (1954: 23) that the occupants of Star Carr must have used sewn-skin boats for their fishing and fowling. The first historic documents on Atlantic Europe—for example, the Roman descriptions of the Celts—mention sewn-skin boats as typical of the region, so it is reasonable to assume they were indigenous and possibly ancient. As Lethbridge remarks (1952: 120–123), it is hardly likely that the Neolithic stock-keepers who settled Britain around 3000 B.C. ferried their cattle across the Channel in dugouts; large sewn boats, such as the Aran Islanders still use for transporting cattle, would have been more suitable.

Basically, European boats either were constructed of a sewn, flexible covering stretched over a light wooden frame or were built of wooden planks braced in shape by a frame. The sewn type would logically be older, since its construction would not have demanded the tools and woodworking skill necessary to split and bend planks. Sewn boats persist into the present in Europe as survivals on the impoverished margins of the plank boats' sphere of diffusion. The curraghs to be seen off Ireland's west coast are the best known of the survivals. It should be noted that modern curraghs' distribution, size, uses, and functions are all markedly reduced from those described by classical authors for the curraghs of the premedieval periods.

Curraghs and the closely similar riverine coracles were exhaustively studied by James Hornell (1936, 1937, 1938). In the present century these boats were made of canvas coated with a mixture of pitch and tar; previously they were made of hides coated with grease or oil. Hornell reported a coracle maker at Bewdley around 1895 who used damaged cowhides discarded from a tannery, sewing up the cuts in the hides and making them waterproof, the informants recalled, with neat's-foot oil (Hornell, 1936b: 273). The Irish saint Brendan is said to have sailed upon the sea in a curragh covered with cowhide tanned with oak bark, tarred at the joints, and carrying butter "to dress hides for covering the boat" if it should need repair (Hornell, 1937: 79). Roman geographers described seagoing curraghs as the principal ocean transport of Britain and Ireland, and they continued to be preferred by Irish sailors during the Dark Ages (Lewis, 1958: 106–107). Used as regular merchant vessels across the Irish Sea, some are said to have been large enough to mount a sail and to hold up to twenty men.

Curraghs differ from most ocean ships of today in that the sewn boats are designed to ride over the waves, whereas our usual ships cut through the waves, relying for stability upon heavy keels and cargoes (or ballast). The curragh is actually more seaworthy than the heavy-keeled ship because, although a curragh may capsize, she is essentially unsinkable (Merrien, 1954: 11; Ellam and Mudie, 1953: 14–15; Le Toumelin, 1955: 290–291; Manry, 1966: 231). She gains seaworthiness also because of her shortness (above citations; Lethbridge, 1952: 179): "under the thrust of the waves . . . and the lash of the winds . . . the small vessel is . . . theoretically safer than the big one" (Merrien, 1954: 11). Le Toumelin (1955: 290) explains, "The safety of a ship depends more on her proportions than on her dimensions. . . . In planning a sea-going vessel, the main preoccupation should be threefold: beam, freeboard, and absence of overhang. . . . The stability of the hull of a sailing vessel is a fundamental factor. That implies beam. To obtain stability merely by weight is to be deprecated, if only because of the fearful rolling this causes." Curraghs admirably fit Le Toumelin's formula.

Not only curraghs, but also plank boats, can demonstrate deep roots in Europe. Presumably evolved through the building up of the sides of dugout canoes, comparatively large, probably plank-built boats are shown in northwestern European Bronze Age rock engravings and on a Danish sword dated to the middle of the second millennium B.C. (Piggott, 1965: 144). An impressive example of Early Iron Age British boatbuilding is the sewn-plank boat from Yorkshire, about 750 B.C. (Piggott, 1965: 187). This type of boat, of which two specimens are known, was approximately 15.35 meters long by 2.60 meters wide (Clark, 1952: 290). Caesar and Strabo describe the Breton merchant vessel of the era of the Gallic Wars as the *ponto*, a broad-bottomed, high-ended, carvel-built oaken ship with leather sails (Clark, 1952: 292; Lewis, 1958: 46).

Ships of Mediterranean design may have been seen on the Atlantic during Phoenician voyaging or even a thousand years earlier, when the Bronze Age Wessex culture of England was trading with the Aegean. The Romans employed Mediterranean ships in their trade with Gaul, though not all such ships could handle the heavy Atlantic swells. By A.D. 700, the Swedes were sailing large clinker-built vessels that seem to represent the first of the Norse *knerrir* (singular, *knorr*), the merchant ship as contrasted with the long warship (Lewis, 1958: 171). *Knerrir* dating from about A.D. 1000, found in Denmark, are about sixty-five feet long, with broader beam, deeper keel, and higher freeboard than the Viking raiding ships; the *knerrir* depended upon heavy woolen sails, not oars, for propulsion (Jones, 1964: 21–22, n. 1). Farther south, Carolingian merchant vessels were either the Roman-derived, carvel-built coasting *scaphae* and ocean-going *barcae*, or the clinker-built *kogges* employed by the Frisians, the principal traders between the former Roman provinces and the northern lands (Lewis, 1958: 241). Frisians sailed as far as Greenland from their home port on the Weser, A.D. 1035–1045 (Lewis, 1958: 431–432).

It is not known when the skill of sailing into as well as before the wind was perfected. Lethbridge (1952: 164) argues that the Romans may have had this skill, although the Norse did not learn it until the ninth century A.D. Lewis (1958: 316) mentions that the Norse may have learned it from the Irish, with whom they were mingling in Ireland, Britain, and Iceland.

To summarize, curraghs—excellent craft for the Atlantic—were probably available in Atlantic Europe from the eighth millennium

B.C. Plank boats were probably present from the late Bronze Age, about 1500 B.C. Boats capable of crossing the Atlantic were thus to be found in Europe from the Mesolithic period on. Bombard's and Lindemann's experiments show that sailors in even the smallest boats could have survived a crossing. Incidentally, prehistoric voyages would probably have been shorter than these doctors' trips, because modern small-boat sailors deliberately go north or south of the optimum routes in order to avoid the danger of collisions in the regular shipping lanes.

Most small-boat Atlantic crossings attempt to utilize the trade winds for a westward traverse, traveling from Iberia or northwest Africa via Madeira, the Canaries, and the Azores to the West Indies. Eastward traverses use the Gulf Stream drift and its accompanying westerlies from off the United States direct to Iberia or Britain, or to Britain via Nova Scotia. A second westward route, most pertinent to this paper, takes the Irminger Current, moving west across the far northern Atlantic, often accompanied by northerly winds. The Irminger route has the advantage of passing near the possible provisioning stops of Iceland and Greenland. A much less probable route would be the present Le Havre–New York shipping lane. The geographer Taylor (1964: 106) has noted that "what must be studied is not wind averages but meteorological situations . . . at intervals of perhaps half a century or more. A powerful east wind persisted for weeks on end, blowing right across the ocean in a belt centering on about latitude 50° N. . . . A ship approaching the Channel entry could be swept away as far as Cape Race." A curragh or dory-type wooden boat provisioned for a Channel crossing and coasting journey could in this situation reach Newfoundland (1,750 miles from western Ireland) without severe physical strain upon its crew. Such freak meteorological occurrences can be invoked to postulate only unique transatlantic contacts, of course; sustained or intermittent contacts between prehistoric northern Europe and northeastern America would have necessitated use of the Irminger Current.

If boats have been available for millennia in Europe, and currents and winds are propitious for westward crossings, transatlantic contacts originating from Europe would seem probable. America's exclusion from the universe of the European literati more likely stems from the influence of Rome upon the scholars of Western Europe than from any absence of contacts. "The Romans," admitted Mortimer Wheeler (1954: 31), "were timid sailors." They applied their sophisticated engineering skills to the development of land roads, towns, and forts, neglecting sea routes (Lewis, 1958: 4–6). Unlike the Phoenicians and Greeks who had preceded them, the Romans did not rely upon a merchant marine to maintain intercourse between the mother power and her colonies. Roman shipping lagged behind other aspects of Roman civilization in both technological progress and sociopolitical importance.

Medieval scholars, consciously pursuing the Roman tradition, similarly neglected marine matters. Shipping along Atlantic Europe was in any case hindered during the Dark Ages by piracy, during the Middle Ages by the focus of European interests on the Arab expansion in the eastern Mediterranean, and in the fourteenth century by the plagues that decimated the Atlantic countries. The fifteenth century finally saw a rebounding population and the European conquests of the Arab borderlands fostering a growing merchant class. Some of these merchants entertained the theory that a westward ocean route around the earth might prove to be the cheapest way to import Eastern luxury goods (Williamson, 1962: 6–8). Spurred by this hope, Columbus, Cabot, and others forced the European seafaring nations to compete in western exploration, and transatlantic voyages entered the history books.

Slighted by the conventional histories, the Norse must be credited with the first historically documented discovery of America. The record of exploration in the North Atlantic may be begun three centuries before Christ, when Pytheas of Massilia described a distant northern land, Thule, probably Norway (Jones, 1964: 4). Pytheas' manuscript has long been lost, so any contextual clues it may have contained on the true extent of pre-Roman Atlantic exploration are beyond recall. Roman geographers' lack of interest in the farther reaches of the western ocean obscures their references to Pytheas.

In the eighth century A.D., Bede mentioned Thule in his *De ratione temporum*, but as Jones (1964: 8) cautions, Bede's account may be no more than a recension of the then surviving fragments from Pytheas. By A.D. 825, new data on Atlantic exploration appeared in the work of Dicuil, an Irish monk. Writing *De mensura orbis terrae*, Dicuil stated that thirty years earlier, in 795, he had spoken with *clerici* "who lived in that island" known as Thule (Jones, 1964: 8), now definitely to be interpreted as Iceland. Dicuil does not indicate when the Irish first discovered Iceland.

"The Irish proved themselves the most intrepid mariners of the Atlantic prior to the age of the Vikings" (Lewis, 1958: 168). From the sixth until well into the eighth century, Ireland shipped imports and also her own products to Britain and Gaul, Scotland, the islands beyond it, and Norway (Lewis, 1958: 158–159). Parallel to the Irish commercial venturings were the pilgrimages of the Irish monks to desert places suitable for hermitages. As long as Celtic sailors dominated the waters around Scotland, the Orkneys and Hebrides provided such refuges, but by 795 the colonizing expansion of the Norse southward threatened the loneliness of the monks, so some sailed as far as Iceland to continue their retreats (Lewis, 1958: 237–238). There seems no sound evidence that the Irish penetrated farther than Iceland. Their principal shipping routes went north and east, and the *clerici* who pushed on to Iceland sought to be on the margins of civilization, not to break beyond.

The ninth century saw the tremendous expansion of the Norse—to Russia, to France, England, and Ireland, and to Iceland. Irish knowledge of that island may have stimulated the Norse entries to it. When the Vikings raided and colonized Ireland, they must have become familiar with her seafarers' exploits. Lewis (1958: 269–270) implies that the Norse should be considered the inheritors, as well as the successors, of Irish maritime adventuring.

Norse utilization of the most distant western colonies—Greenland, Vinland, and Markland—is imperfectly known in comparison even to the records for early Norse occupancy of Iceland. The sagas telling of the westernmost settlements are family histories, not national chronicles. With the recent archaeological corroboration of the sagas' descriptions of American exploration (Ingstad, 1964), however, these become the best historical documentation of pre-Columbian contact between Europeans and American natives. The problem of recognizing contact in the absence of literary documentation is highlighted by the sagas' account of Norse trade with the Vinland natives. The *Groenlendinga Saga* tells of exchanges between the party of Thorfinn Karlsefni and groups of indigenes who had obviously come to trade. Expressly forbidding his people to give the savages Norse weapons, Thorfinn found the natives would accept buckets of cow's milk as payment for their bundles of furs (Jones, 1964: 157–158). *Eiriks Saga Rautha,* written down later than the *Groenlendinga Saga,* varies the account only by relating that red cloth, not milk, was exchanged for the furs (Jones, 1964: 182). The intention of the Norse to trade only perishable (even ephemeral, in the case of milk) goods to the Americans clearly precludes any archaeological records of these contacts. It is striking, too, how closely parallel are the Norse trade items, milk and red cloth, to the historic northeastern Indians' desired trade goods, liquor and red cloth.

There is no documentation for Norse trade or utilization of America after Eric the Red's kindred lost interest in the land, except for the Icelandic Annals' mention of a Greenland boat storm-driven from Markland to Iceland in 1347 (Jones, 1964: 96). Nevertheless, Markland (probably Labrador) would have been the most sensible source of the timber required by the Norse culture in Greenland. In addition, Markland could have supplied other commodities valuable to the Greenlanders. Iceland was regularly exporting to Norway walrus hides (preferred for ships' rigging), falcons, and polar bears caught in Greenland and Baffinland (Lewis, 1958: 340). Norwegians in turn exported these products, plus furs, south and east throughout Europe. If Greenlanders obtained furs from the Markland natives, the furs would have been favorable to Greenland's balance of payments in the trade she maintained with Iceland and Norway. Some furs of Canadian origin could have been included in the lots exported by Norway without necessarily being documented in surviving records. Considering the Greenlanders' need for timber, the most reasonable assumption is that there *was* intermittent contact between the Norse and the Labrador Indians from the eleventh to perhaps the fifteenth century.

Less solid than the Norse sagas are hints that some Englishmen may have known of land across the western ocean before Columbus' first voyage. Bacon stated in 1622 "that there had beene before that time [1492] a discouerie of some *Lands,* which they tooke to be *Islands,* and were indeed the *Continent* of *America,* towards the *Northwest.* And it may be that some Relation of this nature comming afterwards to the knowledge of COLUMBUS was by him suppressed, (desirous rather to make his Enterprise the *Child* of his *Science* or *Fortune,* then the *Follower* of a former *Discouerie*) did give him better assurance" (quoted by Quinn, 1961: 284). As early as A.D.

1325, an island called "Brasil" was drawn on charts of the Atlantic (Quinn, 1961: 278). In the second quarter of the fifteenth century, two islands, "Antillia" and "Salvaga," of which the east coasts strongly resemble the coasts of Newfoundland and Labrador, appear on maritime charts of the Atlantic. E. G. R. Taylor (1964: 105) argues that the presence of these "islands" on the charts demonstrates pre-Columbian European knowledge of northeastern America's coast (but not interior), for "it has always seemed out of the question that a cartographical establishment, employing skilled craftsmen and carrying on the business of supplying seamen's charts, would insert imaginary islands on these maps."

Merchants of the port of Bristol, England, engaged in the distribution of dried cod had sufficient confidence in the charts, or other sources of information, to send out several ships later in the fifteenth century "to serch & fynde a certain Isle called the Isle of Brasille" (quoted by Quinn, 1961: 278). That Bristol men discovered "Brasil" and that "Brasil" was probably Newfoundland, is claimed by a well-connected English gentleman (Ruddock, 1966), John Day, in a letter written during the winter of 1497–1498 to a high Spanish official, thought to be Columbus. Day mentioned that such cod as were caught and dried in Iceland were numerous off "Brasil," but he was maddeningly vague about the year of the discovery of "Brasil," saying only that this occurred *"en otros tiempos"* before Cabot's first voyage.[2]

Day's letter, buried in Spanish archives until 1956, illustrates the elusive and inconclusive nature of the documents referring to North Atlantic voyages prior to the sixteenth century. Until the last decade of the fifteenth century, literate Europeans thought the North Atlantic useful principally as a source of cod. Traffic in cod invited the attention of neither poets nor princes; if it did, those who earned their living from the business took pains to protect from common knowledge the locations of their best fishing grounds, in order to exclude competitors. Unambiguous historical evidence for pre-Columbian contacts across the North Atlantic cannot be expected.

Where historical documentation is lacking, archaeological data would be particularly desirable. Resting a case for transatlantic contacts solely on the presence or absence of definitely diffused objects might be ideal, but would be unrealistic. Not all contacts need have

[2] The John Day letter and its significance are fully discussed by Williamson (1962).

involved imperishable, diagnostically distinctive artifacts.[3] Even if they did, the sites of contact, presumably on the North American shore, are not likely to be discovered.

About 5000 B.C., the sea level off eastern North America was some ten meters lower than it is at present. A wide stretch of coastal plain now under water was then available for habitation. Geologists differ on whether the sea level has been rising slowly and steadily for the last seven thousand years, or whether the sea rose comparatively rapidly between 5000 B.C. and 3000 or 1000 B.C., subsequently either remaining stable or oscillating around its present level (Curray, 1965: 725). Whichever geological school may be correct, the conclusion for archaeologists is that sites of initial transatlantic contact dating from the pre-Christian era should be assumed to lie inaccessibly buried under the Atlantic, except north of the St. Lawrence where isostatic rebound has raised some beaches. Sites that anciently lay a little distance inland may now be so close to the water's edge that proper excavation and evaluation is impossible (see Powell, 1965), or they may be covered by bogs, dune sands (Schafer and Hartshorn, 1965: 125), or landfill. So long as the continental shelf remains unexplored (Emery and Edwards, 1966: 736; Salwen, 1967), and the bogs, dunes, and urban substrata untested, no reasonable scientist can demand direct archaeological evidence of transatlantic contact sites.

Appearing in periods early enough in northeastern America that their coastal sites should be submerged today, two clusters of traits solicit examination as possible American adaptations from European stimuli. The traits seem to lack American antecedents, but parallel traits occurred directly across the North Atlantic in cultures that demonstrably were sea-oriented, fishing and trading from ocean harbors or open beaches.

The first cluster of traits suggesting transatlantic contact is in the Laurentian aspect of the northeastern American Late Archaic. Beginning about 4500 B.C. (Cotter, 1966: 901) and continuing into the second millennium B.C., the Laurentian occupied Canada south and east of the Pre-Cambrian shield, northern New England, and north-

---

[3] This paper is considering only archaeological material. Lopatin's (1960) discussion of the restricted (northwestern Europe—northern America) distribution of the sweatlodge complex is an ethnographic contribution of great relevancy, suggesting considerable antiquity for the presumed transatlantic diffusion of this trait.

ern New York. Trade extending westward along the Great Lakes links the Laurentian with the contemporary Old Copper of Michigan and Wisconsin (Ritchie, 1965: 79–83). Diagnostic traits for the Laurentian include gouges, adzes, plummets, ground slate points and knives (among them the semilunar form), barbed bone points, chipped stone projectile points (broad side-notched and, later, slightly hollow-based triangular forms), and bannerstones (Ritchie, 1965: 79–80).

All these traits except the two associated with the atlatl (the side-notched point and the bannerstone) occur in northwestern Europe contemporary with the Laurentian (Childe, 1957: chaps. 10, 11). Similarities in artifacts are matched by similarities in cultural patterns; on both sides of the North Atlantic there were mobile hunter-fishers who used ground stone woodworking tools and animal-tooth knives (boars' tusks in Europe, beaver incisors in America). In many regions of the Baltic and Scandinavia, the people chose to camp on beaches affording access to the open sea, a circumstance implying the use of boats for ocean fishing; this pattern is noted as early as about 7000 B.C. in Scandinavia (Hagen, 1967: 34).

Although immigrant Neolithic farmers moved into Atlantic Europe about 3000 B.C. (Piggott, 1965: 57–64), especially in the north they failed to displace entirely or to acculturate the indigenous hunter-fisher groups (Piggott, 1965: 64). Instead, there is evidence that the hunter-fishers increased their traditional subsistence activities in order to produce surpluses to trade to the grain-growers. Cod fishing in particular seems to have increased substantially after the advent of farming into Scandinavia (Clark, 1952: 85), either through the development of a symbiotic relationship between the aborigines and the immigrants or through the creation of what Lethbridge (1950: 131–132) terms the "crofting culture," farming supplemented by regular sea fishing as an adaptation to the ecology of coastal northwestern Europe. It is when this relationship or pattern becomes solidly attested, about 2000 B.C., that the use of ground slate for tools first appears (Hagen, 1967: 79). Clark (1952: 88) points out the efficiency of ground slate fish-gutting knives.

The possibility emerges that the impetus given to cod fishing by the demands of Neolithic immigrants to Scandinavia may have resulted in Norwegian fishermen being caught by the Irminger Current and northeasterly winds, eventually to land near the mouth of the St. Lawrence. Conceivably the fishermen found the Grand Banks and used the Canadian shore for cod-drying stations, as was done in the sixteenth century A.D. Some fishermen might have settled in Canada to be rid of the Neolithic homesteaders back in Norway (cf. the Norse settlements in Iceland, spurred by Harald Fairhair's revolutionary unification of Norway and its consequent sociopolitical upheavals [Jones, 1964: 19]). A hypothesis of two-way diffusion across the North Atlantic in the third millennium B.C. could explain the innovations of woodworking tools and fishing gear in the Laurentian Archaic and the innovation of ground slate knives and points in Scandinavia and the Baltic countries. This diffusion could include the strikingly similar bird-headed combs, one found by Ritchie on Frontenac Island, New York, dated about 2000 B.C. (Ritchie, 1965: 116, 107), and others from Varanger Fjord, Norway, dated some centuries later (Hagen, 1967: 74, figs. 24, 26; cf. discussion of combs in Ford, 1969: 77).

The foregoing hypothesis is, in this writer's opinion, tenable but incapable of a more detailed and convincing demonstration until current efforts to distinguish, date, and define the various phases of the Laurentian Archaic can be brought to published fruition. The second cluster of traits to be discussed contrasts with the first in centering on a class of artifacts, pottery, that exhibits very specific European/American parallels at precisely the same time period on each continent. These parallels are made more significant by the great potential variability inherent in ceramics. The case for a northwestern European origin for northeastern American pottery is one that cannot be ignored.

The orthodox stand has been that Early Woodland pottery migrated from Asia to eastern North America via Bering Straits. Somehow the pottery hid all traces of its passing between the Yukon and the Pre-Cambrian shield. This gap notwithstanding, archaeologists will envision hunters trudging with unbroken pots across the Straits and two thousand miles of Arctic coast or boreal muskeg (Wright, 1967: 130–133). A far more comfortable hypothesis is that the pots skimmed over the Atlantic in fishermen's curraghs. To reiterate what I remarked several years ago (Kehoe, 1962), as long as the Asiatic derivation of Woodland ceramics in northeastern America remains unproved, an alternative derivation of these ceramics from the nearer, European edge of Eurasia ought to be studied.

The earliest pottery known in northeastern America is the Vinette 1 ware discovered by Ritchie in New York. Dated about 1000 B.C. (Ritchie, 1965: 193), the ware marks, by definition, the Early Woodland period in the region. Vinette 1 pots were coil-made, grit-tempered, tall conical jars, cord-roughened on both exterior and interior (Ritchie, 1965: 192–193).

Wright (1967: 131) tries to argue that Vinette 1 is a manifestation of a ceramic tradition originating, through independent invention, in Georgia and Florida about 2000 B.C. Inconsistently, compared with his theories on later Woodland pottery, Wright invokes the negative evidence of the lack of Early Woodland sherds in western and northern Canada as his principal reason for assigning Vinette 1 a southern derivation. Vinette 1 is, however, entirely distinct from the earliest southeastern wares (Ford, 1966: 783–787; 1969: 91) and the earliest Middle Atlantic states pottery (Ritchie, 1965: 150–151). The southeastern pottery consists of flat-bottomed, open, hand-modeled bowls or pans, paste tempered with crushed steatite or fiber, surfaces at first plain, then (after about 1600 B.C.) decorated by pointed tools. Technologically, it seems highly improbable that the southeastern complex could have given rise to Vinette 1 (table 14.1).

In the Baltic area of Europe, on the other hand, the typical pottery of the second millennium B.C. was the Comb-ware—coil-made, grit-tempered, conical jars with all-over decoration made on the exterior by toothed tools (see Childe, 1957, and Kehoe, 1962, for primary references on European pottery). Late in the second millennium, textile impressions replaced "comb" (dragged-stamp and dentate) and "pit" (punctate) as the preferred exterior surface treatment on the pottery of the nonagricultural groups of northwestern Europe. Comb ware dominated the eastern Baltic from about 3000 B.C. to about 1600 B.C. (Kivikoski, 1967: 31–32), while in Norway, textile-impressed pottery is dated about 1000 B.C. (Hagen, 1967: 74). Textile-impressed pottery (*cord-roughened* is an American archaeologists' portmanteau term that may include textile impressions [Quimby, 1961]) thus appears on both sides of the North Atlantic just at about 1000 B.C. On the east side, it is a development in the tradition of coiled, grit-tempered, conical jars, the manufacture of which began

TABLE 14.1

Comparison of Vinette 1 and Early Southeastern Pottery

Trait	Vinette 1	Georgia	Florida	Middle Atlantic States
Temper	grit	fiber	fiber	steatite
Shape	straight-sided jars	simple or carinate bowls	simple bowl or pan	simple bowls (copied from steatite bowl)
Base	conoidal	flat	flat	flat
Surface	cord or fabric over entire surface, inside and out	plain until 1600 B.C., then decorated	plain until 1600 B.C., then decorated	plain
Decoration	none (by Ritchie's definition); Vinette 2 has toothed-comb variations	drag-and-jab, punctate, incising, cross-hatch	incised scrolls	none
Appendages	none	none	none	lugs
Manufacture	coil	modeled	modeled	modeled or patch

two millennia earlier in the region. On the west side, it is the first ceramic, with no antecedents anywhere in the continent.

Pitted-ware (related to Comb ware) sites of second millennium B.C. Sweden are so situated that it seems evident they were occupied by a seafaring people (Stenberger, 1962: 71). Scandinavia, the Baltic, and Britain were then linked in an extensive trade network that extended southeast to the eastern Mediterranean. About 1200 B.C. the Mediterranean empires experienced a series of attacks and piracies that led the civilized nations into the Dark Ages (Piggott, 1965: pp. 155–160) and caused repercussions the lengths of the old trade routes. Some of the northwestern European hunter-fishers may have been stimulated by the shattering of the southern empires to seek refuge in the west, where they may have carried their conical pots bearing the recent fashion of textile impression. It would not be amiss here to record that some European authorities infer from distributions that the Comb-ware makers spoke Finno-Ugric languages and included Mongoloid racial admixture (Kivikoski, 1967: 46–47).

Vinette 2 pottery is a decorated ware that Ritchie (1965: 205) believes appeared during the final years of Vinette 1 manufacture, to become subsequently the dominant ware of northeastern America. According to D. F. Dincauze (personal communication, 1969), the ware is well represented in Maine and New Brunswick. Wright (1967: 109) would separate the diagnostic features of Vinette 2 into two sets of modes, rocker-stamping from the Hopewell ceramic tradition and pseudo–scallop-shell from his Laurel tradition. Either or both traditions could have contributed dentate stamp and incising. Tenaciously insisting that the Laurel tradition came from Asia via Bering Straits, although there is a lack of closely similar pottery in Siberia so far as is known and a complete absence of Laurel pottery west of central Canada (Wright, 1967: 132–133), Wright (1967: 126) postulates a southeastward-moving Laurel meeting a northeastward Hopewell diffusion into the St. Lawrence region.

A more parsimonious explanation for Vinette 2 pottery seeks its origin in the Impressed wares of western Europe. Exhibiting all the decorative techniques seen in Vinette 2, the ancient Impressed or Cardial ware (Kehoe, 1962: 24) occurred along the Mediterranean coast from Italy west and into Portugal during the fifth millennium B.C. (Piggott, 1965: 57–58). The third millennium B.C. saw a preference for plain-surfaced pottery in Atlantic Europe, except in Scandinavia, where impressed decoration could be found on the Funnel-necked ("TRB") Beakers of the First Neolithic immigrants. Then, about 2000 B.C., there was a resurgence of all-over impressed decoration, rapidly diffused through Europe by the Bell-Beaker people, who may have been the descendants of the Impressed ware culture in Iberia (Piggott, 1965: 98).

The Bell-Beaker carriers used the sea as their avenue of expansion and communication from Portugal to France (Ushant) and Britain (Piggott, 1965: 101). Their ceramic influence continued in Britain through the second millennium B.C., fused with native traditions to varying degrees (Clark, 1966: 183–184). Vinette 2 techniques were thus available in Europe throughout the millennium before they appeared in North America, and in Europe they were associated with peoples not afraid of Atlantic voyaging.

Vinette 2 may have been transmitted to the northeastern American coast after Vinette 1 pottery had become established, or its features may have been part of the initial introduction of pottery, the decorative techniques moving inland more slowly than the simpler cord roughening. It should be pointed out that Ritchie (1965: 205) has somewhat arbitrarily excluded Vinette 2 features from his Early Woodland Vinette 1 trait list: "We have no satisfactory type or closed site for what I am currently designating the Early Point Peninsula culture" for which Vinette 2 is the index fossil.

Less clear-cut by their very nature but worth considering in the context of possible European contributions to Early Woodland cultures are the similarities in burial customs on the two sides of the North Atlantic about 1000 B.C. Both continents showed marked concern for the higher-status deceased, who were often cremated and placed in graves situated on high knolls or ridges (Ritchie, 1965: 173–177; 1955: 7; Stenberger, 1962: 77–82). The New York area funereal ritual included orientation of the graves toward the east.

A few centuries later the Celts of Atlantic Europe were giving their leaders "elaborate burial, often in timber mortuary houses and under barrows" (Piggott, 1965: 196). These sixth-century B.C. tombs could serve as the prototype in form, if not precisely in content (they contained wagons and draft animals), for the Middle Woodland burial mounds then arising in eastern North America. The origin of classic Hopewell is surely a complex problem, but the possibility of transatlantic influence on it should not be neglected. Not only burial traits, but also such important Hopewell ceramic modes as footed vessels, zoned-stamped or incised decoration, and rocker-stamping have European parallels (Kennedy, this volume). Even panpipes occurred in Europe (Piggott, 1965: 35) preceding their eastern North American appearance.

This paper has suggested contacts that could have been made between the prehistoric peoples of Europe and of northeastern America. Particular attention has been given to the Scandinavian fishing groups who seem to have possessed the boats and the seafaring temerity later documented for the Celtic peoples of Britain, Brittany, and Ireland. These fishermen seeking cod could have repeatedly visited North America, most likely the Canadian Maritimes. The similarity of their basic material culture to that of the Laurentian Archaic and the Early Woodland in northeastern America would render it very difficult to distinguish the debris of their cod-drying stations (if such existed and are still above water) from the camps of American natives. Only the priority of Laurentian-like woodworking tools and fishing gear and Woodland pottery and burial traits on the eastern side of the Atlantic implies a possible origin for these artifacts there. Conversely, the earlier use of ground slate knives in America implies a transoceanic origin for the slate implements appearing in Europe. Given the presence of seagoing curraghs, marine diffusion is to this writer the most satisfactory explanation of the similarities between northwestern European cultures and those of northeastern America in the third and at the end of the second millennium B.C.

15. Commentary: Section II

CLINTON R. EDWARDS

Upon reading these papers it occurred to me that in discussing pre-Columbian contacts between the Old World and the New World, we have reached a point that allows more precision in our terminology for the time and regions involved. I shall not presume to introduce a new set of terms, but a discussion of our present usage might put some of our objectives into clearer perspective.

The most obvious point is that *pre-Columbian* is too inclusive a term to use in the context of the papers, since none of them deals with the original and early entries of man into the Americas. There seems to be tacit agreement that by *pre-Columbian contacts* we mean those contacts that may or may not have occurred during times much later than man's early migrations via (presumably) the Bering Strait region to North America. We are thus talking about post-Pleistocene, pre-Columbian contacts, not about those far pre-Colombian contacts that did indeed result in the introduction of many culture traits to the Americas. We do not know precisely what kinds of traits were possessed by the initial and early immigrants, but we can reasonably assume that such things as varied weapons kits, utensils, use of fire, intimate knowledge of wild flora and fauna and their uses, probably clothing, possibly some kinds of watercraft, and many other traits were introduced.

A major assumption of many students of American prehistory is that these introductions stopped at an early date, not to be resumed effectively until Columbus, leaving a gap of more than a few millennia in which no contacts or introductions occurred. This assumption should be converted to a question: when did these contacts stop (if in fact they did), and why? To my knowledge the only answers essayed have involved some kind of late Pleistocene change in the physical geography of the Bering Strait region that cut off the entryway.

With one exception the authors of the papers in this section are obviously open to the possibility that the contacts and introductions of culture traits did not stop, but continued by different routes—oceanic routes that required some degree of nautical skill.

Let me digress for a moment to deal with the exception. B. C. Hedrick's concern is not with pre-Columbian contacts, but with demonstrating that if such did occur, the person who became deified as Quetzalcoatl had nothing to do with them. Hedrick means to quash once and for all the many attempts to invoke an Old World "bearded white god" with entourage as bearer of civilization and origin of the Quetzalcoatl tradition. I do not believe that most serious, knowledgeable students of American prehistory will feel the need for Quetzalcoatl's establishment as an indigene, but now at least they have a well-argued and relatively short and succinct essay to which they can refer those avid questioners whose imaginations have been fired by the more romantic versions of Quetzalcoatl's origin.

Our terminological problem is rendered more difficult by the accumulating data on pre-Columbian voyages by Norsemen. To remind us that there were indeed post-Pleistocene, pre-Columbian crossings of one fairly large segment of the world ocean, Herbert C. Taylor, Jr., provides a brief review of what is known about Norse contacts with northeastern North America. The burden of his useful summary is neither to question nor to prove Norse contacts, but to urge the seeking of unequivocal archaeological evidence in Greenland to support the already widely accepted evidence of the sagas.

The time period that concerns most of the rest of the contributors comprises the millennia between what for convenience I shall call the "Bering Strait era" of contacts and about A.D. 1000. Sometime during this period certain human groups in the Americas acquired, by unknown processes and to varying degrees, practically all the accoutrements of civilization known to the contemporary Old World. A basic question that concerns us all, and that is stated explicitly by George F. Carter and John L. Sorenson, is how the New World civilizations got started and developed to the high degree observed by such as Cortés and Pizarro. Carter does not dwell on this, since he has expressed himself quite straightforwardly in previous publications. Sorenson devotes a lengthy passage to the concept of a world oikoumene in which the Old World and the New World are far from discrete entities in terms of cultural change and the processes of that change.

This leads to the even more basic question, one of the most fundamental in the study of man: how do human cultures change? The first section of this volume deals more specifically with theory that bears on this question within the context of extra-American contacts. But implicit in all papers under review here except Hedrick's and Taylor's is the notion that at least some specific traits of American cultures were the result, not of independent American conception and development, but of introduction by people who had developed those traits previously in the Old World, and that these introductions played some role in American cultural change. The authors deal with such disparate elements as pottery, sailing rafts, methods of hafting axes and adzes, domesticated chickens, and, in Sorenson's case, with an impressively long list of traits he thinks worthy of detailed investigation as possible indicators of transoceanic cultural contact.

Among the papers there is welcome departure from a formerly widespread and tacit assumption that all elements under consideration in the context of transoceanic contacts originated in the Old World and were conveyed to the New World. This assumption has led more than one opponent of transoceanic contact theories to ask, in effect, "Why must all these putatively similar traits be of Old World origin—in lieu of proper dating, could not many have originated in the New World, and have been carried to the Old World?" They did not really believe in the possibility of this alternative but hoped that the seeming ridiculousness of the notion might squelch the enthusiasms they so heartily deplored.

Here again our terminology has led us into difficulty. *Old World* and *New World* have been too strongly suggestive, and perhaps are no longer appropriate regional terms for our context. We now know that human occupation and use of the land in much of the Americas is as old or older than in much of Eurasia and certainly much older than in the farther Pacific islands. Agriculture in southern Mexico is much older than in many parts of Europe or Africa. The Norsemen in coming to Vinland encountered a land that may well have been occupied by man longer than most of Scandinavia. The abundant evidence of drastic ecological, pedological, and general environmental change through human agency in the pre-Columbian Americas destroys the notion of a pristine New World awaiting the European touch. *Old* and *New* are only truly appropriate in terms of priority of original human occupation. These designations have influenced our thinking overmuch when we have tried to discover the human relationships between the world's two major land masses in the last few millennia. The equations "Old equals origin" and "New equals introduction" have indeed invited the criticism of the antidiffusionists.

It is true that practically all the authors emphasize Old World to New World dispersals of the traits in question (Kehoe's ground slate knife is an exception), but there are attempts to assign at least tentative dates that indicate hypotheses of Old World temporal priority.

As I see it, the pre-Columbian contacts problem as discussed in the symposium reduces to the determination of whether or not extra-American stimuli for cultural change, including those changes leading to civilization, continued during a relatively short time period in human history. It was, of course, a crucial period in which that most significant of cultural changes occurred—the accretion of all those traits and social attitudes that in the aggregate constitute civilization.

If these papers are representative of our present progress in piecing out what happened during this period, we seem still to be at the stage of discussing discrete elements that may or may not prove to be significant indicators of magnitude of transoceanic contact. Sorenson writes on this point, suggesting that we now need to make further efforts to relate the data to a general theoretical framework. This has been attempted by the contributors to the first section of the symposium, and the results seem very promising. We seem finally to be pulling away from the ancient and overworked diffusionist-isolationist dichotomy as the only argumentative framework for discussion. In the Section II papers, however, most authors felt it still necessary to challenge the isolationists to propose alternative hypotheses to that of transoceanic conveyance of their several traits and aggregates.

To paraphrase another of Sorenson's points, trait plus trait plus trait does not make a culture; nor does trait plus trait plus trait make a civilization. Civilization is in large measure a complex network of social attitudes, only partly definable by material culture. We still find it very difficult to decide on the basis of archaeological material whether or not a civilized state was reached by various peoples. Until we can decide on criteria for this human condition that can be judged from archaeological remains, we shall have to continue for some time to consider only the pieces, the individual traits, that are but parts of the whole.

Criticism of the "where-there's-smoke-there's-fire" approach is, I think, justified. That is, claims that a few "significant" kinds of artifacts are sufficiently alike on opposite shores of an ocean to force the conclusion that they are indicators of a massive transoceanic transferral of culture seem still premature. But the list of traits is growing impressively long, and, as demonstrated in these papers, the degree of sophistication in judging the comparisons is generally higher than formerly. We may soon reach the point at which we shall have to decide just how many traits we can acknowledge as having been introduced by transoceanic dispersal and still insist on very predominantly autochthonous development or change in aboriginal American cultures. The danger is that, even though we shall have proved circumstantially (assuming that all the comparisons are acceptable) that hundreds or even thousands of traits were introduced from overseas, through this approach alone we still shall not have shown how the spark of societal change leading to civilization (however we finally define it) was ignited. Nor shall we really have identified the processes of cultural change. It is, however, precisely from this kind of investigation (and it need not be confined to transoceanic problems) that we are most likely to find answers if we can devise more pertinent theoretical frameworks within which to discuss the role of introduced traits in the origins and nature of cultural change.

We have had at hand for some time a theoretical framework that may be more fruitful in the transoceanic context than those frameworks by which Sorenson characterizes many Americanists' past

endeavors. We have abundant evidence from archaeology and ethnology that human groups in long-standing isolation from others
change very slowly, at least technologically, and that groups in
frequent contact with others are characterized by most rapid change,
especially in the frontier zones of interchange of ideas. This is not
the place to elaborate the theory or to discuss its general application
to the question of how cultures change. But we do have the problem
of explaining how and why, after tens of thousands of years of very
slow technological change and lack of any attributes of civilization
anywhere in the world, both the world's great land masses should
rather suddenly and in many similar ways experience almost con-
temporaneously the phenomenon of change from the precivilized to
the civilized state. As outlined by Sorenson when he discusses Kroeber's wrestling with this problem, students of Old World prehistory
and history seem fairly well in accord that the major generator of
change is the dispersal and interchange of ideas within a single,
uncompartmented oikoumene. On the other hand, many scholars in
the United States assume that the forces and processes engendering
change stem predominantly from the individual group itself, not from
outsiders. The result of this latter theoretical persuasion was the
compartmentalization of cultures as discrete entities in the Americas,
with emphasis on such problems as local developmental sequences
and the definition of "culture regions." Thus, in gross simplification,
there was in pre-Columbian times a single African-Eurasian oikoumene, extending eastward into the Pacific, and an American land
mass with a large number of separate oikoumenes. We are all aware
that this characterization of Americanist thought in the United States
is no longer entirely true; far-reaching relationships among New
World cultures have been demonstrated, and there are more to come.
Perhaps in the not too distant future American ecumenists will predominate; this seems to be the present trend. What does this bode
for the question of the role of transoceanic dispersals as a mechanism
for cultural change? How broadly will we ultimately stretch our
ecumenical web?

One test of the efficacy of introductions in shaping cultures might
be to attempt a reconstruction of what some of our aboriginal American cultures might be like if we excluded from their inventories all
those elements that we can demonstrate to have originated outside
their regions (but still in the Americas). I suspect that with such

subtraction we might well bring many to the point of bare survival, or even perhaps to extinction. But we are too busy for such exercises—much better to explore conscientiously and in detail the external ramifications of the traits we find among particular peoples and to try to evaluate the role of such introductions as we may detect in cultural change.

So far I have been concerned mainly with broader theoretical issues suggested by the papers. In the balance of my commentary I shall deal more closely with the ideas and data presented by the Section II authors, excluding Sorenson, Hedrick, and Taylor, whose contributions have been discussed above.

Judgments about the degrees of similarity among the pottery types, decorative styles, other kinds of artifacts, and cultures to which Alice B. Kehoe and Robert A. Kennedy refer must be left to their fellow workers, who can evoke readily in their minds' eyes the entities identified by the labels. In these writers' own judgments the similarities among the various elements are sufficient to warrant discussion of possible means and routes of transoceanic dispersals, in these cases across the Atlantic.

I concur in their opinion that from the standpoint of available nautical capabilities ancient crossings of the Atlantic were entirely possible. As I have written previously in the context of Pacific crossings, there are no navigational difficulties—the target could not be missed. Kehoe presents a very useful summary of what is presently known about ancient European watercraft and of the many modern crossings by small craft. The latter do not of course prove that ancient crossings did in fact occur, but they do indicate very strongly that we cannot, as a theoretical point, dismiss such voyaging as impossible.

The characterization by Kennedy and, more gently, by Doran of most prehistorians as landlubbers in thought as well as fact is perhaps now a bit hard. True, most prehistorians have not had small-craft experience, especially oceanic. But, just as they rely upon the researches and opinions of experts in other special fields of knowledge, so they rely with equal courtesy upon those of us who have been blue-water sailors and have made maritime prehistory our special interest. Our antidote for thalassophobia is not to require seagoing apprenticeships of all prehistorians, but to continue the collection and well-reasoned discussion of data on watercraft, seafaring, and man's prehistoric relationship to the sea, relating them as best we can to the theoretical and substantive issues at hand.

Kehoe and Kennedy favor the curragh or some similar vessel as the most probable candidate for ancient Atlantic crossings. This is reasonable for the time and the part of the Atlantic discussed by Kehoe in her hypothesis of contact between northern Europe and northeastern North America during the American Late Archaic and Early Woodland periods. It seems to me somewhat less reasonable for the time period and part of the Atlantic with which Kennedy is concerned. As he notes, planked craft were available; so, too, were dugout vessels and reed-bundle floats. Although craft similar to curraghs or coracles were probably not unknown in Mediterranean or nearby lands (for example, the *quffa* of Mesopotamia and hide-covered craft of Asian rivers), I know of no evidence for use of this genre at sea except in the north circumpolar distribution where it predominated as curragh, kayak, or umiak.

For Kehoe's case it is plausible and desirable to investigate possible relationships between curraghs and conceivably related northeastern American vessels like the bark-covered, framed canoe. If such could be established, not only the other artifacts but also the means of transport would support the theory of contacts.

For Kennedy's case there are no known curragh counterparts in the American tropics, and planked, framed vessels of any known European design were entirely absent from aboriginal American waters. The known distribution of the reed-bundle float in the Americas was distinctly Pacific-side and largely peripheral to Kennedy's hypothetical contact areas. This leaves the dugout vessel, which, despite Kennedy's low esteem of its seagoing capabilities, is in many parts of the world, anciently and now, far from being "essentially [a] craft of sheltered waters." The Caribbean example suffices: it is from just this region, within his contact area, that we have the earliest and best European contact descriptions of seagoing dugout vessels capable of carrying numerous crewmen and large cargoes.

All this is not to insist that record of similar or identical vessels should be found at both ends of a transatlantic route. I have argued elsewhere that sea-oriented American aborigines had craft well suited to their purposes long before any possible introduction of types built to the Mediterranean (or east Asian) plank-frame tradition (Edwards, 1969a). If European or Asian planked and framed vessels did indeed cross the Atlantic or Pacific in the millennia before the Norse voyages, it is not necessary to require that they should have been adopted at voyage's end and preserved until ethnographic records began.

In my opinion, the notion that curraghs bore Eur-African goods to Mesoamerica yields no leads to further inquiry on the American side; on the other hand, the dugout story is intriguing and awaits elaboration.

Kennedy's brief mention of Thor Heyerdahl's voyage in *Ra* permits the airing of a view or two, with the reservation that I know of it only from newspaper accounts. My published data and interpretations of the dispersals of reed-bundle floats preclude my entertaining seriously the notion that such craft were introduced to the Americas at the late date of the putative Egyptian voyages.

Perhaps Heyerdahl's greatest contribution has been to show by example that long voyages in "primitive" craft were not impossible. This may have been necessary for some Americanists; it was not for those who know the sea. Despite the fact that *Kon-Tiki* was not a particularly faithful reproduction of the aboriginal sailing raft of western South America, a point essential to the discussion of the times was well made by the voyage: balsa wood would indeed float long enough to convey men over great oceanic distances. I tend to accept in principle Heyerdahl's rationalization that the failure of *Ra* to reach its destination was due more to inadequate knowledge of how to design and build a seagoing papyrus float than to inadequacies in the material itself. Under more usual meteorological conditions he might well have completed the voyage. After all, the reproduction of ancient and all but forgotten technologies is tricky business, and we can be sure that the ancient mariners were better at their particular skills than we could ever hope to be. How many of us could reproduce an ancient hunter's kit of weapons with, say, an atlatl as principal means of killing game and survive any length of time on the results of the hunt? On these grounds, we should not dismiss out of hand the possibility of Atlantic crossings by bundle floats. Such questions as whether the ancient Egyptians ever used them along Atlantic shores and the matter of sails must be left for another time.

My final comments on the Atlantic question concern the continued preoccupation in some of these papers with prevailing winds and currents. In two recent publications (Edwards, 1969a, 1969b) I have discussed the possible misconceptions that derive from uninformed use of oceanographic, meteorological, and climatological data. At the moment I have no new thoughts to offer, but since the matter of ocean and weather conditions is obviously pertinent to this volume, some repetition may be excused. In the following paragraph I have combined my previous comments, paraphrasing slightly. Although they were written in transpacific and Pacific-side inter-American contexts, I believe they are appropriate for the Atlantic as well.

Wind and current directions and strengths are by no means as persistent as pilot charts and climatic atlases suggest—they are presented only as averages. Various authors have proposed as possible routes those oceanic pathways (for example, the Irminger and North Equatorial currents, West Wind Drift, tradewinds, and westerlies in the Atlantic) favored by winds and currents as depicted in these publications. Faith in the persistence of direction and strength has engendered much debate, and often the winds and currents flow in the same direction as the favored theory. But this faith is not shared by oceanographers and meteorologists, and many a sailing man has had occasion to be skeptical. They know that the average conditions portrayed on pilot charts and in atlases often do not represent the actual conditions as they are experienced on an individual voyage. Recent investigations of ocean and coastal currents reveal that they are anything but ever-flowing and unidirectional. Thus we are misled by the concept that "prevailing winds" and "rivers in the ocean" were the main determinants of possible ancient sailing routes.

I do not think we have any hope of reconstructing with any precision the sea and atmospheric conditions of an individual voyage or of a potential route at any given time. I suggest that we concede the point that individual parts of oceans were neither consistent barriers nor aids to voyaging. The significant point for us here is that the Atlantic could have been crossed, given the ancient nautical technology for which we have some evidence. The specific routes are of only secondary interest and not crucial to the discussion of transoceanic dispersals of culture traits.

On present evidence the sailing raft was not part of the Atlantic scene, so we shift now to the Pacific and Edwin Doran's paper. Since most of his data on rafts are those which I have also used in previous publications (Edwards, 1960, 1965, 1969a), and since his interpretations are very similar to mine with respect to the possibility of Pacific crossings in sailing rafts, I shall comment only on a few points that seem to need further elaboration before they can be incorporated into a body of good evidence.

Those who have discarded the "age and area" construct as a viable theoretical base will probably not accept parts of Doran's argument about extent of dispersals and analogies among the distributions of the various watercraft types. However, if space had allowed elaboration of the descriptions and technical features of the Coromandel, Vietnamese, Taiwanese, and aboriginal Ecuadorian rafts, I believe the imaginative effort to base the hypothesis of transpacific crossings on other than just the similarities among the Ecuadorian and Asian rafts would have offset age-area prejudices.

In my opinion, the Borobudur and Gulf of Aden examples are not sufficiently well described, nor is there adequate corroboration by other occurrences in these regions for them to be included more than very tentatively in discussion of the vessel type in question. One may see daggerboards and a raft hull on the former, but one may just as easily see the men, obviously under some duress, as are others aboard, clinging to the high prow and sternpost of a more conventional vessel like others portrayed in Borobudur reliefs. In the original of the Egyptian example the lower structure is shown merely as a featureless platform with rounded sides, much obscured by damage to the painting and with no suggestion of daggerboards.

I have argued for the ancient provenience of Vietnamese sailing rafts with daggerboards (Edwards, 1969a); they may deserve a place on Doran's map of known pre-Columbian sailing rafts. If sailing rafts were absent from Taiwan before the ancestors of fishermen who use them there today brought them from the Chinese mainland some three hundred years ago (according to Ling, 1956: 26), the map symbol should be shifted appropriately. Their pre-Columbian provenience on the mainland stems from Chinese historical accounts, but technical details are lacking.

On the point of daggerboard sailing rafts' seagoing capabilities, I am glad to see that a fellow sailor with good practical as well as intellectual experience in things nautical shares my views. Let me reiterate with him that from the practical seaman's point of view Pacific crossings in such craft were entirely feasible.

Carter's and Beirne's papers are, to me, the most educative in this set, in that they present their data in great detail, allowing those whose acquaintance with domesticated chickens and primitive wood-working tools is less than intimate to judge their cases without reference to numerous other publications.

Although some of the first and early European-American contact data on the rapid dispersal of the chicken seem arguable (they were argued in the symposium meeting), some of the linguistic and biological evidence is impressive, so that one almost expects that archaeological chicken bones will be found in time for the next symposium. Besides his not inconsiderable work on the botanical evidence, Carter is credited with engaging a number of botanists in overseas contact problems. We wish him equal success with the zoologists.

Beirne's paper is long on data and short on theory; he sticks closely to his specialty and provides us with a valuable set of data, described and discussed in minute detail. It is the kind of work that serves so well when the search is on for elements of cultural complexes that may figure in the story of human dispersals.

It is fortunate that discussion of the role of introductions in cultural change is now focused strongly in the context of transoceanic dispersals. The attention of many specialists well qualified to pass judgment on the degree of similarity among particular kinds of artifacts or traits has been attracted, I suspect, originally by the more adventurous claims of nonspecialists. As Kennedy, Kehoe, Carter, and Doran emphasize, another factor has been the former general disbelief in the possibility that before the European Age of Discovery or before the Norse voyages there were people in the world who had the nautical skills required for transoceanic voyaging.

Another benefit is that the discussion is creating new young specialists as well as inducing our veteran jousters in these lists to branch into additional fields of special knowledge. How impressive it is to see one of our most enthusiastic pioneers amassing a remarkable set of data and educating himself and us on the domesticated chicken! Would pottery types, axes and adzes, or any of the other traits mentioned in these papers have received so much detailed attention in a more prosaic context? Perhaps most rewarding has been the increasing attention of the botanists and plant geographers. For the most part their role in this symposium has been to set us straight on former misconceptions, but new leads were also opened; if their suggestions for further study, especially those in Baker's excellent commentary, are followed by the specialists, we can expect to learn much more about the relationships between plants, man, and culture change.

NOTE: In August, 1970, after this paper was written, Thor Heyerdahl completed a successful voyage in a papyrus float.

SECTION III

Some students of culture history concerned with the question of Old World and New World contacts in pre-Columbian times have long wondered if such contacts are indicated in the world of plants, especially those important to man. During recent years most attention has been focused upon the genera considered in this botanical section. Jonathan Sauer believes that the wide distribution of the coconut probably does not demonstrate cultural contact, except in the case of the Caribbean-Atlantic region, where the tree is known to have been introduced within historical times and where it does not grow in a wild state. Thomas W. Whitaker states that, although the bottle gourd is known to be endemic to subtropical and tropical portions of Africa, we have no clear picture as to how it appeared in the Americas, whether by the influence of man or by drift from Polynesia or Africa. Cultural contact with respect to diffusion of the bottle gourd is demonstrated for the New World. In discussing the sweet potato, both Douglas Yen and Donald D. Brand agree that according to present knowledge the genus is native to the Americas. These authors are not in agreement on the question of how and when the sweet potato reached the island world of the Pacific; Yen tends to support a pre-Columbian introduction into that area by man, whereas Brand inclines to an early post-Columbian dispersal from the Americas. Hugh C. Cutler and Leonard W. Blake, commenting on the travels of corn and squash, suggest that there is no good evidence for diffusion of maize from the New World in pre-Columbian times, particularly in view of what we know about the Spanish trade routes in immediate post-Columbian times. M. D. W. Jeffreys, on the other hand, pleads for a pre-Columbian diffusion of maize from the New World to the Old World, basing his evidence largely on linguistics. Stanley G. Stephens in discussing cotton concludes that the present wide distribution of the four cultivated forms of this genus results from post-Columbian contact; he does not, however, exclude the possibility of earlier transoceanic contacts. Lawrence Kaplan's paper is concerned with the diffusion of certain species of the genus *Phaseolus* within the New World, there being no evidence of transoceanic movement of the American—or for that matter, of the Old World—species of *Phaseolus* in pre-Columbian times.

Herbert G. Baker's spritely commentary not only includes a critique of what the above writers offer but also points out in cogent fashion some of the paths we must follow to obtain more precise knowledge of the development and use of some of our important cultigens.

16. A Reevaluation of the Coconut as an Indicator of Human Dispersal

JONATHAN D. SAUER

Cocos nucifera is commonly regarded as a strictly cultigen species, domesticated in antiquity in some unknown region from wild palms that are presumably extinct (Fosberg, 1962; Corner, 1966). In this view, any coconut groves that appear wild are assumed to be feral relics of human planting. The tremendous prehistoric range of the species, spanning the Indian and Pacific oceans from East Africa to Panama, is thus seen as dramatic testimony of long-range plant dispersal by ancient voyagers. An alternative, which will be favored here, is to accept the possibility that spontaneous coconut populations may be truly wild and capable of wide natural dispersal. The mere presence of the species would then fail to qualify as prima facie evidence of cultural contacts. These conflicting interpretations have both had venerable champions, but rather than review the long history of this argument in the literature, the aim here will be a brief summary of evidence now at hand.

It should be stipulated at the outset that the entire distribution of the coconut in the Atlantic-Caribbean region is an artifact. The

NOTE: This essay is an offshoot of field work on tropical coastal vegetation sponsored by the Coastal Studies Institute, Louisiana State University, with financial support from the Geography Branch, Office of Naval Research.

Figure 16.1. Coconut plantation extending for miles on Barrier Beach off Nariva Swamp, east coast of Trinidad (August, 1958). The monotonous palm stand has replaced a complex native vegetation of sea-grape thickets and other coastal pioneers and has barred sea turtles from a formerly major nesting ground.

Figure 16.2. Village with planted coconuts and pandanus near Black Point, east coast of Saint Vincent (July, 1967). Like the coconut, the pandanus is native to Indo-Pacific islands and was introduced to the West Indies in the colonial period. Remnants of the natural sea-grape thicket persist between the houses and the beach.

species was brought from the Indian Ocean region to West Africa and Brazil by the Portuguese, and its diffusion through the Caribbean during the colonial period is a coherent and well-documented story (Patiño, 1963). There are no traces of early aboriginal cultivation or of natural groves in this region, and the present distribution pattern is transparently dependent on commercial planting (figs. 16.1, 16.2). In extensive studies of Caribbean and Gulf of Mexico coastal vegetation, I have encountered only scattered volunteer coconuts that show little promise of forming self-reproducing stands. It is small wonder that O. F. Cook (1901, 1910) and others whose knowledge of the species stems from this region have emphasized man's role in its dissemination.

In the Indo-Pacific region, the story is far longer. Fossils closely resembling or identical to modern coconuts are known from the Tertiary of India and New Zealand (for bibliography, see Sauer, 1967). On Pagan Island in the Marianas, a fossil palm seedling, said to be reliably identifiable as a coconut, was found in Quaternary tuff overlaid by lavas from a volcano older than the existing calderas; subsequently, during a period when sea level was higher than now, seacliffs were cut back into these lavas and reefs were deposited on the wave-cut platform (Fosberg and Corwin, 1958). This was suggested as evidence of a postglacial high sea stand, on the assumption that the coconut was introduced by man, who probably reached the Marianas no more than four thousand years ago. However, worldwide geological data do not show any such sea stand after the last interglacial (Shepard, 1964; Russell, 1967), and the fossil may actually document prehuman presence of the species in the Pacific Islands.

There are various reasons for believing the species to be a native member of the cosmopolitan Indo-Pacific strand flora. It shares with members of this flora from other families convergent adaptations that are exceptional in its own family and explicable by long evolution in seashore habitats (Copeland, 1906; Chiovenda, 1921–1923; Burkill, 1935). The nuts are adapted for dispersal by ocean currents over distances of at least a few thousand miles; experiments have shown they remain buoyant and viable after several months in sea water (Docters van Leeuwen, 1936; Edmonson, 1941; Borssum Waalkes, 1960). The period of four months that usually elapses between falling of the ripe nut and germination may be correlated with the period of viability when drifting in the sea (Corner, 1966). A germinating

Figure 16.3. Sprouted coconuts intended for planting being loaded onto copra schooner from pirogue, Silhouette Island, Seychelles (May, 1963). The coconut monoculture that now blankets this Indian Ocean archipelago was established in the nineteenth century by planting nuts from local wild palms.

Figure 16.4. Drift coconuts germinating on beach, West Island, Cocos-Keeling (April, 1963). Establishment of volunteer coconuts is commonplace on beaches of tropical Indian Ocean islands. Cocos-Keeling atoll had a fringe of wild coconut palms when it was colonized in the nineteenth century.

coconut is a self-potted plant, the roots growing entirely inside the fibrous husk until after the leafy shoot has emerged and become well developed (fig. 16.3). Stranded nuts can thus be shifted up the beach by waves long after they have begun to sprout (fig. 16.4). The natural habitat of the palms is an extremely narrow zone near the limit of wave reach, where the crowns overhang the outpost thicket of shrubs and beach creepers (figs. 16.5, 16.6). Like other coastal pioneers, the coconut is a heliophile, barred by shade and competition from spreading into stable inland habitats. Coconut palms thrive under constant wind and are exceptionally resistant even to hurricanes (figs. 16.7, 16.8). Their root systems give incredibly firm anchorage in loose sand and are not readily excavated by storm waves (fig. 16.9). The roots tolerate occasional flooding with sea water and effectively tap the fresh water lenses in sand aerated by rising and falling tides.

The role of coconuts in unmodified seashore vegetation is best documented in the Indian Ocean, which has a constellation of islands that were probably undiscovered and certainly uninhabited before European exploration and colonization. In case after case, explorers reported beaches of these archipelagos fringed with coconut palms, which they had no doubt were wild and derived from seaborne nuts (Sauer, 1967). In the Pacific, it is scarcely possible to be sure that any island was unvisited by prehistoric voyagers, but some apparently virgin islands certainly had thriving coconut groves. For example, on Palmerston Atoll, where Captain Cook "saw no traces of inhabitants or any human being having been there before," his men spent some days catching birds so tame they could be taken in the hand and gathering hundreds of coconuts (Beaglehole, 1967). One of the most remote of all Pacific atolls, Palmyra, was uninhabited and rarely visited from its discovery in 1802 until well into the twentieth century but had thousands of coconut palms before any were known to have been planted (Rock, 1916; Dawson, 1959). Spontaneous coconuts whose wild status is debatable are commonplace on inhabited Pacific islands.

On the Pacific coast of Central America and offshore islands, coconuts were discovered growing along the beaches by Spanish explorers in the early sixteenth century (Patiño, 1963). They were noted specifically at Punta Burica on the present Panama–Costa Rica border, at Natá and Chimán on opposite sides of the Gulf of Panama, on islands in that gulf, at a bay near Cabo Corrientes in Colombia, and

Figure 16.5. Coconut palms in natural beach vegetation, Anse Kerlan, Praslin Island, Seychelles (May, 1963). The fabulous coco-de-mer, or double coconut, a palm not closely related to the true coconut, is native to the interior of this island, which was first explored in 1768. The coconuts and other coastal trees in this picture are the same species encountered by the first colonists.

Figure 16.6. Native beach vegetation, West Island, Cocos-Keeling (April, 1963). Although separated by about 3,000 miles of the Indian Ocean, this atoll has a beach flora virtually identical to that of the Seychelles (fig. 16.5), including the Scaevola in the left foreground and two dozen other sea-dispersed species.

Figure 16.7. Hurricane-battered coconut plantation, Point Piments, northwest coast of Mauritius (June, 1960). Three months before, the island suffered a direct hit from the most violent tropical cyclone in the recorded history of the southwestern Indian Ocean (Sauer, 1962). Storm waves reached through the plantation and excavated roots of the outermost palms, as in the left foreground. Winds up to 150 m.p.h. killed the casuarinas on the point at right and removed most of the coconut fronds.

Figure 16.8. Same view as in fig. 16.7, three years after the hurricane (April, 1963). Recolonization by beach morning-glory and pioneer grasses and sedges, which had barely begun in previous picture, is well advanced. The coconuts that had not been decapitated are recovering.

Figure 16.9. Coconut plantation on north coast of Isla del Carmen, Campeche (July, 1962). The palms in the foreground are still alive in spite of erosion exposing much of their root systems.

on Cocos Island. The nuts were immediately recognized as the same as ones seen in Spain that had been brought from India, and the Portuguese name, *cocos*, was applied. No local name was reported nor was there any mention of aboriginal utilization, in spite of much attention being given to native crops in some of the same chronicles.

Peter Martyr heard in Spain that trees that bear the same fruit as in the land of Calicut were cultivated on islands in the Gulf of Panama, but he was also told that at Natá the coconuts germinate and grow spontaneously on the seashore and that it was believed they had been borne there by ocean currents from unknown regions. Likewise, Oviedo noted that the coconut palms on the coast of Cocos Island appeared to be adventive, like those of Burica. In 1685 a French freebooter saw the Burica coconuts fringing the coast so evenly that they appeared to have been planted with care, even though they were only "a simple work of nature without any aid of artifice" (Patiño, 1963: 70). A recent description (Allen, 1956: 178–179) of the region just west of Punta Burica agrees: "Coconut palms are the dominant element along sandy beaches in the entire Golfo Dulce region, forming small picturesque groves or, particularly from the delta of the Río Coto to Banco Point, stretching out in a thin line for miles in front of the darker, broad-leaved vegetation. The trees have every appearance of being wild and are universally believed to be so by the local inhabitants, since they regenerate spontaneously without the aid of man, far from any present habitation."

Coconut groves still grow on beaches of uninhabited Cocos Island off Costa Rica; the species does not extend into interior forests of the island, statements to the contrary being due to presence of an unrelated palm that superficially resembles the coconut (Cook, 1940).

Early records of harvesting coconuts in Central America all refer to Spanish, not Indian, activities (Patiño, 1963). The first known case of planting occurred in 1539, when nuts from the coast of Panama were shipped to western Mexico, probably Colima, where a thriving coconut wine industry soon developed with techniques imported from the Philippines (Bruman, 1947).

Pre-Columbian planting and use of the species are established only for the western and central Pacific islands, Malaysia, and parts of the Indian Ocean. The recorded history is longest in India, beginning with some of the most archaic post-Vedic sources. Medieval Arab literature has much to say about coconut products, which were major exports of the Maldives, Laccadives, and some East African islands. There are traditions of coconut planting in the Maldive region as early as the ninth century, and there is little doubt that many other Indo-Pacific peoples have been planting these palms for a long time over a very wide area (for bibliography, see Sauer, 1967).

During the last hundred years, with the rise of international commerce in coconut oil and copra, coconuts have been planted so assiduously that the species looks like an artificial introduction even where it is native. In some Indian Ocean islands now blanketed with a monoculture of coconuts, it is a matter of historic record that the plantations were made with seed from native seashore palms (Sauer, 1967). Although necessarily speculative, it seems likely that prehistoric planting of local wild varieties occurred repeatedly, particularly on atolls. The aboriginal colonization of Pacific atolls would have been impossible without the coconut (Mascal and Barrau, 1956). Since years must pass between planting and the first harvest, postulating that the species was introduced in cultivation implies expeditions in advance of settlement or a long, hungry, thirsty wait. It is interesting that in the Gilbert Islands the natives had a tradition that breadfruit and taro had been introduced by their ancestors but that the coconut was already there (Wilkes, 1845). Such traditions are, of course, not reliable, but they might be worth canvassing for possible ecological or geographical patterning. In Hawaii, for example, which is unfavorably situated to receive drift seeds from other islands and lacked most of the cosmopolitan Indo-Pacific strand flora, native traditions speak of the coconut as introduced by Polynesian navigators (Degener, 1930).

Sorting out natural and artificial dispersals might be greatly aided if subspecific entities could be distinguished within *Cocos nucifera*. The diversity of the species in the Indo-Pacific region is famous but has not been systematically studied. Most of the so-called varieties mentioned in the literature are local names based on single characteristics that may segregate within the same progeny. Comparative morphological-geographical surveys of the kind recently initiated by Whitehead (1966) may eventually permit recognition of coherent varieties, wild and cultivated.

At present it is not at all clear how much of the evolution of the species is attributable to human selection. The species' biology makes it peculiarly intractable breeding material. Except for dwarf forms, which are probably strictly cultigens, the coconut is predominantly outbreeding, pollination being largely by the wind, so that genetic fixation would be difficult even if generations were short. The individual palms commonly live for over a century and, even though old trees decline in yield, primitive cultivators may be reluctant to replace them because of the long wait for a young tree to begin bearing (Luomala, 1953). Moreover, in folk economies the coconut is a multiple-purpose plant, so that the goals of selection are highly diffuse. In Guam, Safford (1905: 242) noted that "many of the natives pay no attention to selection, but plant sprouting nuts indiscriminately." Even in commercial plantations, attempts at selection have been rather desultory and ineffective; scientific coconut breeding programs have been initiated at various agricultural experiment stations, but progress has been slow (Charles, 1961; Liyanage, 1961).

Thus *Cocos nucifera* is best regarded as a semidomesticated species, a complex of local populations with all degrees of dependence on man, from nil to complete. Any blanket explanation of its gross prehistoric distribution by either natural or human agency is therefore inappropriate, and the story will have to be disentangled piecemeal. At our present level of understanding, the transpacific distribution of the species is not reliable evidence of human dispersal.

17. Endemism and Pre-Columbian Migration of the Bottle Gourd, *Lagenaria siceraria* (Mol.) Standl.

THOMAS W. WHITAKER

The ubiquitous bottle or white-flowered gourd, *Lagenaria siceraria* (Mol.) Standl., surely one of man's first cultivated plants, should have a great deal to contribute to our understanding of the migration of peoples and the diffusion of cultures. Up to the present time, however, archaeological and distributional studies of *Lagenaria* have not fulfilled this promise. Actually, such studies have raised more questions than they have answered. In only a few instances, where controversies have arisen over the course of migration and cultural diffusion, have the data from *Lagenaria* been particularly instructive. This state of affairs probably exists because we are not clever enough to exploit the data at hand, or the data are not sufficiently critical to make a convincing argument.

Archaeological remains of *Lagenaria siceraria* are perhaps more numerous and more widespread in the Americas than those of any other plant species. Fragments of the rind occur most frequently, but seeds, peduncles, and even intact fruits are not uncommon. Aside from identifying the species, and with the possible exception of the seeds[1] (fig. 17.1), plant remains of *L. siceraria* have furnished little

---

[1] Seeds are a promising source of comparative data for archaeological pur-

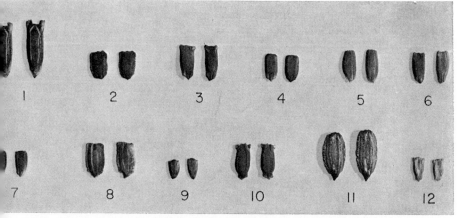

Figure 17.1. Seeds of *Lagenaria siceraria*, showing variation in morphology of collections from different geographical areas. *1*, Ghana. *2*, Bola Redonda, Chiama Valley, Peru. *3*, Semilla de Bule, Tuxpan, Jalisco, Mexico. *4*, Los Amatos, Chiapas (Sauer Collection). *5*, Ovamboland, S.W. Africa (Rodin Collection). *6*. Zacatecas (Sauer Collection). *7*, Chiapas (Sauer Collection). *8*, New Zealand, large round. *9*, Teotitlan del Camino, Oaxaca. *10*, Zucca Melon. *11*, Nigeria. *12*, Long-handled dipper.

information of a comparative nature that would be helpful in deciphering the migration of this species. Even when present together, rind fragments, seeds, and peduncles of *Lagenaria* do not provide as much botanical information as a single corncob.

In this report, after reviewing the evidence for endemism, I propose to bring together the scattered archaeological references to *Lagenaria siceraria*, with the purpose of improving our understanding of the migration of pre-Columbian peoples in the Americas.

ENDEMISM

As a reference point for the study of plant migration, particularly of a cultigen, the location where the species is endemic must be firmly established. For a trash-heap plant, and such a persistent fellow-traveler as *Lagenaria siceraria*, it is vitally important to know

---

poses. This possibility is presently being investigated by Professor C. B. Heiser, Jr., Indiana University (see Heiser, 1969).

Figure 17.2. Fruit of *Lagenaria sphaerica* (Sond.) Naud.

Figure 17.3. Fruit of *Lagenaria siceraria* (Mol.) Standl. cv. "Small Kettle." This type of cultivar was much used for making containers of various kinds in preceramic cultures.

its origin. Up until about 1962, there was really no convincing evidence to indicate where *L. siceraria* was indigenous; it could have come from tropical America, tropical Africa, or tropical Asia. Some recent studies by Meeuse (1962) and Jeffrey (1967) have clearly demonstrated that *L. siceraria* is endemic to tropical Africa. In fact, both Meeuse and Jeffrey report that plants of this species have been collected at locations in Africa where it is difficult to think of them as being other than wild plants. Thus plants collected in other areas, notably the American and Asian tropics and subtropics and Polynesia, are almost certainly cultigens or trash-pile weeds. Furthermore, *Lagenaria* is not a monotypic genus as treated by J. D. Hooker (1867) and other early workers. Jeffrey (1961) has shown there are at least three other species closely allied to *L. siceraria*, all indigenous to tropical Africa.[2]

One species of the genus, *L. sphaerica* (Sond.) Naud., crosses readily with *L. siceraria*, as Charles B. Heiser, Jr., and I have shown independently. Our work, however, was anticipated by St. Pierre (1866), who reported this cross more than a century before we commenced our experiments. The F_1 hybrid plants from the cross, *L. siceraria* × *L. sphaerica* (figs. 17.2 and 17.3), are tremendously vigorous and have beautiful staminate flowers, but the pistillate flowers abort in the early stages of development. Thus the plants are self-sterile. Furthermore, pollen of the staminate flowers is so poor it cannot be used in backcrosses to either parent.

We must conclude that the probable occurrence of indigenous wild plants and the presence of closely related species clearly suggest that *L. siceraria* is endemic to tropical Africa. A further argument favoring this idea is the wide spectrum of variation found in fruits and seeds in collections of *Lagenaria siceraria* from tropical Africa.

CONTACT WITH THE WESTERN HEMISPHERE

If we assume that *Lagenaria siceraria* is endemic to tropical Africa, the next questions demanding answers are readily identified: (1) Was *L. siceraria* transported to the New World by man, or did it come to the Americas by other means? (2) When and where did *Lagenaria* arrive in the Western Hemisphere? We only have vague, but perhaps

[2] There is a single collection of *L. breviflora* (Benth.) G. Roberty, from Brazil, but it is probably adventive.

suggestive answers to these questions. For example, the question of how *L. siceraria* came to the New World is, at least in part, susceptible to experimental approach. Carter and I (1954, 1961) have shown that it is entirely possible for gourds of *L. siceraria* to float from the coast of Africa to the Brazilian bulge and retain viable seed with the ocean currents as these currents are today. This does not mean, however, that *L. siceraria* was introduced into the New World without the assistance of man. In fact, it seems unlikely that *L. siceraria* was established in the Americas by fruits that floated to these shores from Africa, mainly for the reason that it is not known to be a strand plant. Jonathan Sauer (personal communication), who has made extensive studies of the peripheral plants of the Caribbean, tells me he has never encountered *L. siceraria* on or near the strand. It could be argued that this is not a valid objection, because people are always picking up things on beaches; but the initiation of bottle gourd cultivation from this source implies a sophisticated agriculture of reasonably high level, which probably did not exist at the time the first bottle gourds were reported from the Americas. The problem, however, is not simple. One can speculate that man picked up a stray fruit on the beach and transported it to his dwelling, where it was broken or smashed by natural means, and that the remains were thrown on the community trash pile. In such an environment the seeds would probably germinate and later produce a crop.

The question of when and where the bottle gourd arrived in this hemisphere is equally frustrating. Archaeological recoveries from the Ocampo caves in the state of Tamaulipas, Mexico, indicate that the gourd was in the Western Hemisphere prior to 7000 B.C. (Whitaker, Cutler, and MacNeish, 1957). Rinds identified as *Lagenaria* were recovered in strata with a radiocarbon date within the range 7000–5500 B.C.

The earliest cultivated bottle gourds from South America are those identified from Huaca Prieta on the northern coast of Peru by Whitaker and Bird (1949). They are radiocarbon dated at about 3000 B.C. Also, Engel (1963) has identified bottle gourds in plant remains from Asia, Unit I, a preceramic settlement on the central coast of Peru. These materials of Engel are dated at 1942 B.C. ± 100. An unusual aspect of the gourd collections at Huaca Prieta and Asia, Unit I, is their presence in levels known to be preceramic and pre-maize.

Lanning (1963) has explored a number of preagricultural sites on the central coast of Peru. These sites antedate the introduction of cotton and other cultivated plants. Bottle gourds were found in the refuse deposits from some of these sites. There are no radiocarbon dates for these preagricultural sites, but Lanning suggests dates on the order of ten thousand years or more. The end of the pre-agricultural stage in this area took place about 2500–2000 B.C. with the establishment of permanent villages. In two of the principal pre-ceramic villages, Yacht Club and Tank, excavated by Lanning, cotton was present and used for a variety of purposes. Also, there was an abundance of gourd remains, suggesting these two crop species were cultivated, not merely gathered.

It is evident from these observations that *Lagenaria siceraria* was in South America at an early date, definitely as early as 3000 B.C., perhaps much earlier. It is also clear that *L. siceraria,* along with cotton, was cultivated in relative abundance in preceramic, pre-maize sites on the coast of Peru. It is unfortunate that we have no critical information about the comparative morphology of the intact fruits, the rinds, or the seeds of these gourds that might give us a clue to their origin, but transpacific transport from Asia through Polynesia cannot be ruled out.

Dissemination of the Bottle Gourd in North America

Mesoamerica. If we return to the idea that *Lagenaria siceraria* is indigenous to tropical Africa, the path or paths by which it reached Mesoamerica are erased, perhaps permanently. We can state, however, with some confidence that *Lagenaria* was in Mesoamerica at an early date, probably as early as 7000–5500 B.C. at the Ocampo caves and somewhat later in the Tehuacán Valley (4900–3500 B.C.).

It is no accident that reports of the earliest cultivated bottle gourds are from sites in northern Mesoamerica as defined by Armillas (1964). The sites concerned are the Ocampo caves of the Sierra de Tamaulipas in northeastern Mexico, and the rock shelters of the Tehuacán Valley in the southeastern corner of the central plateau of Mexico. These sites are in the areas where plant materials are most likely to be preserved. The mild, warm, dry climate minimizes bacterial and fungal activity, leading inevitably to the preservation of much trash-heap material. Furthermore, the soils and the availability of water for irrigation are suitable for the development of a primitive agriculture. It is entirely plausible, as others have suggested, that these favorably located areas served as dispersal centers for cultivated plants.

The Southwest. The first record of bottle gourds from the American Southwest is from the Cordova and Tularosa caves in New Mexico (Martin, *et al.*, 1952). The date is firmly established as 300 B.C., and *Lagenaria siceraria* was grown continuously at these sites up to A.D. 1200. *L. siceraria* appears to have entered the area from the south at about the same time as such crops as *Cucurbita pepo L.* (summer squash), maize, and beans. By the time of contact, *L. siceraria* was widely dispersed over the Southwest. Bottle-gourd fragments have been recovered from numerous sites in Arizona, New Mexico, southern Colorado, and northwestern Mexico (Cutler and Whitaker, 1961) with dates ranging from A.D. 150 to A.D. 1346.

The Eastern Woodlands. Yarnell (1964) has shown that plant cultivation was practiced in the Eastern Woodlands as early as 1000 B.C. In the Mammoth Cave and Rock Shelter areas of Kentucky there are radiocarbon dates of 1125 B.C. for Salts Cave (Bennington and Watson, 1962)[3] and 690 B.C. and 640 B.C. for Newt Kash Hollow. Among the earliest cultigens at these sites were bottle gourd, squash (*C. pepo*), sunflower, marsh elder, and perhaps chenopod, according to Yarnell. Thus the pattern of crop production is not unlike that found along the coast of Peru, where bottle gourds and squash (*C. moschata* Duchesne ex Poir.) preceded maize and beans. The best clue we have to the migration of *L. siceraria* into the Eastern Woodlands is the suggestion of Griffin (1964) that a simple, early agriculture from the south infiltrated the eastern United States between 2000 and 1000 B.C. This early, primitive agriculture was centered around the cultivation of gourd, squash, and locally domesticated food plants.

The Plains. There is much evidence that agriculture was relatively late in the Plains area. The earliest bottle gourds and squash (*C. pepo*) were first reported from the Sterns Creek level of the Walker-Gilmore site in Nebraska, excavated by Strong (1935). The dates are A.D. 500–1300. Material of both gourds and squash was present

[3] Dr. Richard A. Yarnell, Emory University, Atlanta, Georgia, informs me that the earliest firm date for gourd in the Eastern Woodlands is 620 ± 140 B.C. from Salts Cave. This date is from human feces containing gourd fragments. The 1125 B.C date is from sooty material scraped from the cave wall.

in abundance, suggesting that these items were cultivated and important in the economy of the people. Considering the late date, it is surprising that corn and beans were not present. Strong, however, is specific on this point: "It seems remarkable that neither corn nor beans were found" (1935: 194).

SUMMARY

1. *Lagenaria siceraria*, the white-flowered or bottle gourd, is shown to be indigenous to tropical Africa.

2. The gourd could have been introduced into the Americas by drift from Africa or Polynesia, but introduction by human transportation remains a distinct possibility.

3. The earliest firm date for *L. siceraria* in South America is about 3000 B.C. at Huaca Prieta on the northern coast of Peru. Lanning, however, has estimated that gourd remains from a site on the central coast of Peru may be older than 3000 B.C. The gourds described by Lanning were probably gathered, not cultivated.

4. On the northern border of Mesoamerica, *L. siceraria* is reported from strata radiocarbon dated at 7000–5500 B.C. This is the earliest date for this species in the Americas.

5. The suggestion that bottle gourds and squash (*Cucurbita pepo*) moved from northern Mesoamerica into the American Southwest and the Eastern Woodlands is well supported by present information. By 300 B.C. these crops were being grown in New Mexico (Tularosa and Cordova caves); bottle gourds and squash were cultivated in the Eastern woodlands much earlier (1125 B.C.). Migration of bottle gourds into the Plains area was comparatively late (500–1300 A.D.).

6. In the early preceramic strata excavated in both North and South America, the white-flowered gourd and squash (either *Cucurbita pepo* or *C. moschata*) preceded maize and beans. The significance of this observation is yet to be determined.

18. Construction of the Hypothesis for Distribution of the Sweet Potato

DOUGLAS E. YEN

The construction of a hypothesis to account for the widespread distribution of a cultivated plant species requires evidence for four obvious parts: the center of domestication of the species, the direction of its movements, the time of transfer, and the identity of the agency for transfer. Despite the general consensus that the sweet potato is an American plant, the botanical evidence has never been clear. Thus the speculation that has accompanied botanical discussion on the issue from Candolle (1886) to the post–*Kon-Tiki* controversy (see Merrill, 1954), has pervaded the ethnological issue on the relationship of the plant to the prehistory of man in the Pacific. From the earliest surmises concerning the provenances of the peoples that inhabit the widespread islands, the cultivated plants have been associated with the migration of man. With the recent establishment of the center of domestication in the New Guinea area of such Pan-Pacific plants as sugar cane (*Saccharum officinarum* L.) by Warner (1962), and the *fehi* banana (*Musa troglodytarum* L.) by Simmonds (1962), as well as other cultigens of narrower distribution by Barrau (1963), the association with the generally accepted direction of migration is well founded. For the roster of plants cultivated by the Polynesians at the time of European discovery were mainly the Indo-

Malayan taro (*Colocasia esculenta* [L.] Schott.), the yam (*Dioscorea* sp.), the Eumusa series of bananas, the breadfruit tree (*Artocarpus altilis* [Parkins.] Fosb.), and the New Guinean plants. In the broad scheme of west-to-east migration in the Pacific, the long period of sojourn in the Melanesian area that produced linguistic differentiation (Grace, 1964) finds further support, in the evidence from the New Guinea highlands (Bulmer, 1964), for a great time depth for human occupation. In this period plant domestication was probably achieved, and the agricultural systems based on the combination of the indigenous domesticates and the Indo-Malaysian plants of earlier introduction were formed, to expand, with adaptive modifications, first to the peripheral areas of Melanesia and then into the heart of Polynesia.

The sweet potato has an adventive place in such systems, as typified in the interpretation of Buck (1938) that the plant was the main indication of contact of Oceania with South America. The degree of contact implied was thus below the level of migration, although Heyerdahl (1952) was to use the plant's distribution as one of the evidences for peopling of Polynesia by Amerindians.

In the account that follows, a reconstruction of the sweet potato hypothesis has been made. The most recent botanical evidence that serves as a basis is summarized. Following the prescription of such construction procedures, one may see that the plant data contribute to the first topics—center of domestication and direction of transfer— but in themselves affect the aspects of time and identity minimally. The interdependence with human studies in their historical perspectives is brought out in what I have called the agricultural relationships. The focus of the study, of which this is a condensation, is on the Pacific, but I have concluded with some comment on the sweet potato in its intra-American distribution.

THE HYPOTHESIS

1. The sweet potato reached Polynesia from America in prehistoric times. It may have been a part of the crop-plant array of the eastern Melanesian islands by the time of European discovery.

2. In the western Pacific, the plant was unknown in pre-Columbian times. Its distribution in Asia is accounted for by its introduction by the Spanish trading galleons plying between Acapulco, Guam, and Manila in the sixteenth century. In western Melanesia, the plant is

one of the residual results of the complicated trading chain established by the Portuguese in the fifteenth and sixteenth centuries, which encompassed Brazil, Portugal, coastal Africa and India, and the East Indies.

There is no element of surprise here, since the hypothesis is the composite of a number of claims that have appeared in the literature on the subject and was presented in almost identical form by Barrau (1957), who was seeking the most logical explanation of sweet potato distribution on a Pacific-wide basis. Before we proceed to examine the construction of the hypothesis, however, the isolation of some salient implications may be useful.

1. The plant originated in America.

2. The species was distributed widely in Mesoamerica and South America in pre-Columbian times.

3. The species is the same throughout its distribution.

4. After the introductions of prehistoric and historic times, the roles of indigenous peoples must be imputed, especially in the intra-Polynesian distribution and its possible westward extension and in the Melanesian distribution from the East Indies.

THE BOTANICAL EVIDENCE

The taxonomic unity of *Ipomoea batatas* has been demonstrated by the investigations of material collected from Asia, the Pacific Islands, and America. The cytological survey disclosed uniformity of features of chromosome numbers (2n = 90) and agreed with Jones (1965), who worked with North American materials, on the presence of secondary associations of chromosomes in meiosis in plants from Peru, Ecuador, the Cook Islands, New Guinea, New Caledonia, the Philippines, and Thailand (Wheeler and Yen, unpublished data). Breeding experiments between varieties from the different areas are incomplete, but certainly no breeding barriers may be suggested on a geographic basis. The expansion of the preliminary study (Yen, 1963) of sixteen morphological characters to over forty, in a greater number of varieties represented in a greater area, still did not produce any discrete characters on which species or subspecies separation might be proposed. It is apparent from the same data that separation of geographic races due to differential selection has not occurred (Yen, 1968). The contrasts are patent with cotton, with its differentiation of the Old and New World forms at the specific level (Hutchinson, 1959), and maize in America, with its regional development due to different introgressant species (Mangelsdorf and Reeves, 1959).

THE CENTER OF ORIGIN

Despite the counterclaims for alternate hypothetical origins, the American center has by far the strongest evidence. The distribution of the species of the family Convolvulaceae taxonomically closest to *I. batatas* (Ooststroom, 1953) has been the basis for this claim. House (1908) was satisfied that the species was derived by cultivation of the wild American species *I. tiliacea,* but subsequent cytological considerations have made this unlikely. Nishiyama (1959) reported a Mexican find of an *Ipomoea* form K123, which he and his coworkers were subsequently to identify as *I. trifida* (H.B.K.) G. Don. This, Nishiyama suggested, could have been the progenitor of the sweet potato. Subsequent analyses of this material suggested to many of us that it was representative of the *batatas* species, being of the same chromosome number (2n = 90), exhibiting homologous variation of many morphological characters, and having the same reproductive modes. Jones (1967) has published this viewpoint. We had independently reached such a conclusion on the following bases:

1. The lack of resemblance between the herbarium specimens of *I. trifida* at the U.S. National Herbarium and Nishiyama's material.

2. The collection of clonal material from sweet potato fields in Colombia that resembled K123. On subsequent analysis this could have been *I. batatas* on all counts, including chromosome number, with the exception of the ability to set edible roots. The cultivators had objected to my collection of these samples on the score that they were unproductive weeds.

3. My collection of Ipomoean weeds from sweet potato cultivations in the *montaña* area of the eastern Andean region. These proved to be thirty- and sixty-chromosome forms, some of which bore absolute resemblance to the herbarium specimens cited above.

That K123 and some of the weed specimens resembling the sweet potato from South America are the "wild" forms of the cultigen, often claimed to be lacking, is an obvious suggestion. They are not, however, necessarily the progenitor forms, but may be the result of parallel development as hybrids—perhaps from the same parentage. Despite the incompleteness of the theory of descent of the species, the case for American domestication is rather firmly made on the basis of incidence of feral forms demonstrably related to *I. batatas*.

With the elimination of cytological and taxonomic differences in sweet potato varietal populations as factors in geographic distribution, the focus here has been on the morphological and physiological variations that exist within the species. As in the preliminary study (Yen, 1963), the American population again displayed wider ranges of variation than Polynesian, Melanesian, and Asian populations, even though some forty different characters were taken as indices, compared with the initial sixteen, and even though the numbers of representatives of the latter three areas were significantly increased, whereas the American additions were limited to only a few from the West Indies and Mexico. There were only two transgressions from the American variation ranges: one variety from Thailand has a glabrous condition of the internal flower structure, which in all other varieties shows degrees of hairiness, and one from the Marquesas Islands recorded the lowest specific gravity figure for the edible root of any variety investigated. These instances were attributed to the action of mutation or random genetic effects (Yen, 1968). Earlier, the occurrence of a form with extremely divided leaves had been found only in New Guinea. The view that this was a third transgression from the American variation range, however, has had to be revised following my 1967 visit to Haiti, where a variety common to rural areas exhibited the same condition. That a similar form was reported in breeding material from Uganda by MacDonald (1967) is suggestive of the West Indies–Africa–New Guinea line of Portuguese introduction.

THE DIRECTION OF PLANT MOVEMENT

The indications of direction of plant movement from variation data are founded on two simple models of geographic distribution. With allowance for such influencing factors as the possibilities of evolutionary change after distribution, the reproductive system of the plant, the propagation practices under cultivation, and the selection pressures to which the plant is subjected (Yen, 1968), these schemes can be regarded as valid. If the Pacific distribution was the product of a single and diffusive introduction, then the range of variability

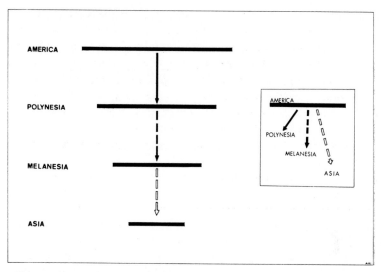

Figure 18.1. A model of reducing variability that should result from the successive transfers of sweet potato clones. The solid horizontal lines represent plant variation ranges; the vertical lines are the putative transfers. No such patterns were suggested by the present botanical study, but three separate lines of introduction from America to Oceania and Asia, as represented in the inset figure, were indicated. (Prepared with the help of Aki Sinoto.)

of most of the plant characters would conform with the diagram presented as figure 18.1. No such consistent pattern of variability was achieved in the sweet potato material. Instead, the seemingly random geographic patterns of the characters investigated indicated conformation with the model of separate introductions from a common provenance, where the variability from character to character has no order other than inclusion within the American range. The material is actually more striking in its uniformity than in its variation on a geographic population basis, so that differences at the extremities of the ranges have taken on more significance than is the norm in population study. This has been taken to be the function of the heterogeneous nature of the genotype and the lack of interest by native cultivators in the selection of nonfunctional characters.

The possibility of the spread of the Polynesian sweet potato into Melanesia is based on two observations: the rare occurrence of va-

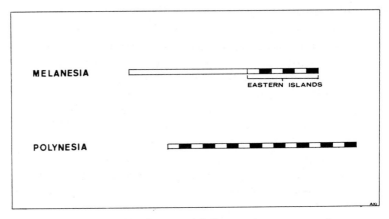

Figure 18.2. A possible inter-areal diffusion of sweet potato between Melanesia and Polynesia as indicated by plant variation in some characters. The barred portion of the Melanesian variation range (upper line) is representative of varieties of the Eastern Islands, suggesting that they may be derived from Polynesian stock (lower line), rather than from the founding population of Melanesia. (Prepared with the help of Aki Sinoto.)

rieties common to the two cultural areas, and the incidence of the type of variation pattern in the confluent area in some of the botanical characters studied (figure 18.2).

When one turns to comparison of the Polynesian populations, it is almost impossible to describe adequately the sequence of introduction in the area. In the Marquesas, the Societies, and the Cook groups, the varieties tend to replicate, with less range of variation than the American, the type of random-patterned variation that applies to the varietal populations of Asia, Melanesia, and Polynesia. The explanations for this may lie in the plant's lack of agricultural importance in the area, which has been conducive to losses of different phenotypes in the different locations. The indications of the Easter Island population, however, appear contrary to the claim of Heyerdahl (1963) that the island was the gateway to Polynesia for American cultigens, since the variation there seems to be derived from within the range of the Marquesas and Society Islands materials rather than in the opposite direction.

HISTORY

A reexamination of historical sources has not revealed new information, though it has perhaps strengthened the view that the sweet potato may have reached eastern Melanesia in prehistoric times. Thus we may briefly summarize the evidence for antiquity, in terms of the records of the early discoverers, as follows:

1. The plant's presence in America is so well documented—for example in the account of Columbus' first voyage to the West Indies (Jane, 1960), in the chronicles of the Spanish pioneers of western South America summarized by Yacovleff and Herrara (1934), in early texts from Mayan Mesoamerica (Bronson, 1966) and from Brazil (Marcgrav, 1648)—that nothing more need be said of the earliness of the American distribution.

2. The antiquity of the plant in China has been denied on documentary evidence by one of its proponents, Bretschneider (in Candolle, 1886). Further, such evidence for Hunan has been produced by Ho (1955), who offered the overland route from the south as an additional route for adventive American plants into China. Burkill (1935) was unable to find evidence of pre-European cultivation of the plant in India or Southeast Asia .

3. The assessment by Dixon (1932) of the Pacific distribution, which gave the Polynesian plant prehistoric status, is unarguable. This was based on the incidence of the plant in the records of the first explorers at the apex of the Polynesian triangle—Hawaii, Easter Island, and New Zealand. Its early record in Tahiti would seem to attest to its antiquity there also, but the later records from the remainder of tropical Polynesia may indicate European introduction of a secondary agricultural status in the indigenous economy.

Although Barrau (1957) has expressed the opinion that most of the traditional Polynesian varieties have been replaced in recent times by imported varieties, this does not appear to be borne out in the fieldwork associated with this project. Certainly, the activities of the missionaries may have transported varieties with them, but this amounted to a shuffling process within a single area. The possibility of introductions into Polynesia, however, is a real one in the case of the nineteenth-century whalers who plied the whole Pacific, including Peru. This activity, hinted at by Melville's (1847) reference to Tombez potatoes in the Society Islands, may well have been responsible for a somewhat greater variation in modern Polynesian sweet potatoes than was evident in the pre-European times.

ARCHAEOLOGY

Direct evidence of the plant in archeological contexts is restricted to areas of the Peruvian coast. Tuber remains identifiable as sweet potato have been ordered in time by Towle (1961), with the earliest placed in the Formative epoch (750 B.C.–A.D. 1) of the south coast. The phytomorphic pottery representations in the Mochica style (Tello, 1924) would allow for the expansion of the plant's cultivation between the period immediately prior to the Christian era and approximately A.D. 500. The most recent finds, however set its possible cultivation at much earlier levels. The report of Lanning (1965) of sweet potato remains from one central coastal site at the 2500 B.C. level takes the plant back to near the beginning of the Preceramic VI period (Lanning, 1967). Although this is earlier than the periods at which systematic agriculture is promulgated for Peru, an earlier find has been reported. Engel (1967–1968, personal communication), has found tuber remains in the Chilca area south of Lima, deposited between carbon levels at 8000 B.C. and 10,000 B.C. There is little doubt that some of these are sweet potato.

The significance of such finds is manifold, and, in the scope of our problem, they transcend intimation of antiquity of the plant in the areas and constitute evidence for origin of the plant. In fact, if our evidence for jungle or *montaña* origin (cf. Kidder's 1964 attribution of coastal cultivars to tropical forest derivation) was firmer, the early date of the coastal finds forces a view of earlier horticultural activity in *montaña* subsistence or, minimally, the exploitation of an economic feral form of *I. batatas* there, and the action of domestication and horticultural experimentation on the western side of the Andes.

Apart from remains reported by Skjölsvold (1961) from Easter Island, associated with a date of A.D. 1526, the findings of pits in New Zealand comprises the only other evidence for the sweet potato in the Pacific. Although indirect, assigning the function of such groundworks to the storage of the sweet potato is justified on the grounds of historical and contemporary reports of the practice. Golson (1959) first queried the validity of earlier suppositions, based on traditional materials, that Maori agriculture was introduced in the fourteenth century A.D., since his excavated pits were associated with this date. The lack of any indication of such storage in the rest of Polynesia suggested a New Zealand invention, which must have pre-dated or approximately coincided with the evidence of the structural finds. The resultant agricultural sequence (Yen, 1961), which incorporated this invention on the deteriorating climatic background in the temperate zone, has been used in the reconstruction of the local cultural sequence (Green, 1963; Golson, 1965).

With the securely dated sequence for New Zealand culture going back only to the eleventh century A.D. (Green, 1967), although the earliest date published is A.D. 800 (Groube, 1967), and with reported agricultural association, there is a comparatively narrow time span for agricultural crop introduction and adaptation. Over the broadest basal dates for the association of plant with man in South America and New Zealand, the direction of plant transfer is implicit. Eastern Polynesia, as the immediate source of New Zealand culture, provides the only identification of the intermediate stopping point.

LINGUISTICS

The vernacular names for the sweet potato in the Pacific have provided clues indicating the provenances of the plant in the various areas of distribution since the time of European discovery. An overview of them all shows a close correspondence to the hypothesis that has been outlined. The commonest gloss in Chinese belies its basic importance in modern peasant economies (for example, Yang's 1945 account of subsistence in a Shantung village), for it is the equivalent of "foreign tuber." The Japanese and Okinawan equivalents also connote importation, with the beginning of an agricultural chain in China, indicated as the source of the plant in some Japanese and Okinawan names.

Conklin (1963) has produced the most comprehensive analysis for vernacular names in the western Pacific and has consolidated the evidence for the *batata* word forms as Portuguese transmissions, and the *camote* as Spanish.

The word and its association least questioned have been *kumara* and its cognate forms in Polynesia, and the Quechua *kumar*. Swadesh (1964), examining the word form, states that it is not typical of

338 DOUGLAS E. YEN

Quechua or Aymará; he seems to infer a borrowing from Polynesian. That a Polynesian linguist, Biggs (1968, personal communication), has expressed some reservations in attributing the Polynesian forms to direct borrowing casts further doubt on what has been a cardinal point in the sweet potato problem. A more motivated construction has suggested itself, involving the compositing of *kuu* and *mara* ("watery" and "soft"). The uses of *mara-tawhiti* in an old Maori chant and *pakamara* in a Moriori (Chatham Island) context, both referring to the sweet potato, may be considered as some support for the contention. Biggs does not insist on the significance of his observations, but they do bring into focus the danger of presuming contacts among human groups because of one lexical item in common.

Although the linguistic materials support the tripartite theory accounting for the Pacific sweet potato, the identity of the prehistoric contact between Peru and Polynesia hardly emerges from the closer examination of the lexical items and their apparent cognation. Further, the problem of suggested contact is confused by the lack of record for the *kumar* word on the Peruvian coast in contemporary times, in the earlier dictionaries, or in the vestiges of defunct languages.

The Agricultural Relationships

The recent increase of archaeological evidence from eastern and western Polynesia has strengthened the theory that the immediate origins of the immigrants who were to become known as Polynesians were in eastern Melanesia. Green's review (1967) of the sequence of settlement, based on interpretations of the C-14 dates, on the artifactual comparisons, and on the language relationships, makes the following further points.

1. The first settlement of eastern Polynesia was not much earlier than the beginning of the Christian era.

2. The expansions to the peripheral areas of Polynesia are dated subsequently. The Easter Island contact is debatable—A.D. 400 dates at one site and ninth-century dates with more secure artifactual associations. Migrations to Hawaii and New Zealand are viewed as having occurred by the ninth and eleventh centuries respectively.

The eastern Melanesian agriculture, then, as a part of the original cultural transfer, expanded into eastern Polynesia, with some of the associated technologies that were developed in the intervening period. The preparation of the root of *Piper methysticum* L. for kava drinking and the semianaerobic fermentation of breadfruit in pits for storage of food are two examples of techniques that may have developed in the eastern Melanesian–western Polynesian island region, since they are not Southeast Asian or general Melanesian practices. The introduction of the cultigen array, followed by adaptive processes in the new environments, resulted in the dominance, at least on the volcanic islands, of the taro and breadfruit, an agricultural pattern not too different from that of the West. The shared primary status of the yam species there, however, appears to have been reduced.

It is against this agricultural background that the introduction of the sweet potato is most likely to have been effected—an already developed subsistence of agriculture and the exploitation of marine resources. The claims that poor adaptation to the environment account for the plant's secondary role in tropical Polynesia (for example, Brown, 1935: 238) would seem to be negated by current observations of the yielding ability of the plant in the Marquesas and of its commercial exploitation, in modern times and in the period of supply of the whaling ships (see Melville, 1848: 261). Rather than being an environmental effect, the explanation may be viewed as a conservative cultural one, resulting from the transfer of a traditional agricultural system into new but broadly similar environments, where adventive plants would find difficulty in attaining dominance.

The agricultural accompaniments of the later Polynesian expansions, however, were probably the full issue of the cultigen array. If there were more than isolated contacts, then the later ones were achieved before the established systems of tropical Polynesia, without sweet potato, were achieved or adapted. This applies especially to Hawaii, where all the plants were reported but where taro and sweet potato are the traditional dominants, and Easter Island, where historical reports indicate dominance of the sweet potato and where all but breadfruit and coconut are mentioned. Temperate New Zealand is the one example in Polynesian crop distribution where even the human technological adaptation processes would not overcome the effects of the inclement weather on the tropical cultigens. Some forms of taro are the only possibilities among the starch staples, apart from the sweet potato, whose adaptation there constitutes one of the major achievements of Polynesian agriculture. This would appear to invert the claim against environment as the major factor in sweet potato adaptation, but a further, corollary statement could be made: If the sweet potato had come into eastern Polynesia *simultaneously* with the eastern Melanesian plants, its agronomic advantages of yield, earliness of production after planting, ease and fecundity of vegetative propagation, and adaptability to soil variations would have exerted a greater agricultural influence. The even temporal start with the other crops in the pioneering of the peripheral environments —especially Hawaii and, to a lesser degree, Easter Island—enabled the recognition and exploitation of these qualities.

On such reasoning, it is possible to arrive at some limits of time within which the introduction of the sweet potato from America was made. If some two centuries are allowed for the adaptation of the western Polynesian agricultural pattern in the eastern tropics, the addition occurred between the second and third centuries A.D. or, if the early Easter Island settlements are unacceptable, between the second and eighth centuries.

The vexing question of the identity of the human contact with America finds no solution in the agricultural approach. The theory of Polynesian contact, based on the choice of transfers for the vegetative sweet potato rather than the more easily transported Peruvian grain plants (Yen, 1963), is little modified by the counteropinion of Heyerdahl (1966a) that a plant like maize does not grow in the Marquesas, for it does. If, however, the landfalls of Peruvians in Polynesia were of cultural consequence, as acceptance of the evidence (Heyerdahl, 1952) would imply, one might reasonably expect the perpetuation of the grain plant. This may be contrasted with the extinction of maize in the Marquesas after its planting by Mendana in the solitary contact before the eighteenth century. With the neutralization of the lexical similarity as evidence of contact, it is necessary to move beyond the issues directly connected to the plant. The strongest indication of American contact is in the study of the blood group genetics of Polynesians by Simmons (1966); the results have prompted the conclusion that the modern Polynesian has resulted from a gene pool whose contributions were derived from Indonesia, western Polynesia, and South America. This may indeed be the thread of correlative evidence that confers the greater security of identification of American carriers of the sweet potato into the Pacific in its prehistoric distribution.

THE AMERICAN SWEET POTATO

The unitary nature of the sweet potato species in its distribution has been indicated. Specific or subspecific differentiation on a geographic basis that would indicate independent domestications have not been found, either in the populations that have been adjudged as derivative from different areas of America, according to the tripartite hypothesis of Pacific distribution, or from comparisons of the American variation. Evidence for diffusion, nevertheless and hesitatingly introduced, is provided by the lexical items, this time in a distribution without the geographic barrier of the dimension of the Pacific Ocean.

The vernacular names—*camote*, from Nahuatl; *kumar*, from Quechua; *batata*, of doubtful origin but thought to be Caribbean or from Darien (Burkill, 1954)—may help to convey exclusiveness between areas. However, indications of the antiquity of the plant among the ancient Maya (Bronson, 1966) adds the base-form *'iis* to the list. The relationship of this with the Arawakan Goajiro form of *haisi* remains unknown, but Taylor (1957) has related the latter to a series of cognates that include the Taino *hage* (the *age/aji* of Columbus, in June, 1960), the Lokono *haliti*, Yavitero *kaliti*, Carutana and Arequena *kariri*, all meaning the sweet potato. Other words found in the eastern Peruvian jungles that appear to be cognative—*haritshi* for the Culina, *curiiti* for the Nomatsiguenga, *coricha* for the Campa—may indicate Arawakan connection. The Pano languages like Shipibo, Cashibo, and Cahinawa all have forms very similar to *cari*, while the Venezuelan Yaruro use *oa' 'ri*, according to Leeds (1961). The Tupí-Guaraní *jetica* recorded for Brazil by Marcgrav (1648) has a distribution reaching the upper Amazon, with the Cocama *itica*.

Although directions of transfer cannot be postulated from this, at least some diffusion of plant and word is implied. The Arawakan distribution, covering a considerable area of the southern continent, offers some indication of an agricultural expansion from the mainland to the Antilles—a possible complement of the reconstruction from prehistory by Rouse (1964) of the Neo-Indian cultural expansion in the early Christian era. Such evidence for sub-Andean origin of the plant is tenuous, and the true location may yet prove to be Amazonian. Whatever the case, the plant's very early appearance on the coast of Peru allows a considerable time depth for intracontinental diffusion.

NOTE: The collection of sweet potato varieties, on which my studies have been based, was made with the financial assistance of the Rockefeller Foundation, New York, from 1957 to 1967. The laboratory and experimental field facilities for the study were provided by the Department of Scientific and Industrial Research, New Zealand, at the Vegetable Station, Otara.

In the preparation of this paper, I am especially indebted to Dr. Frederic Engel of the Instituto de Antropología y Agricultura Precolombina in Lima, Peru, who allowed me to quote some of his recent and unpublished findings; to Dr. Bruce Biggs of the University of Hawaii, whose evaluative discussions have produced a more cautious approach to the lexical situation that I have considered; and to my colleague Dr. Roger C. Green, who has offered critical and very useful comments. However, I cannot burden these friends with any responsibility for the statements I have made herein.

19. The Sweet Potato: An Exercise in Methodology

DONALD D. BRAND

Probably the sweet potato has been cited and discussed during the past fifty years by proponents and opponents of pre-Columbian contacts between the Americas and the rest of the world more than any other cultivated plant. It now seems timely to survey the results of the principal lines of research. Furthermore, a number of unfounded statements and assumptions have been converted into "facts" through much repetition, and these putative facts require examination.

Modern methodology for the determination of the origins of cultivated plants began with Alphonse de Candolle (1886: 8–28), who insisted on the combination of botanical, archaeologic, historical, and philologic data. Although techniques and materials within each of these fields have improved considerably since Candolle, the only new field that has been added is the mythologic—which considers data from myths, legends, and ceremonies.

BOTANICAL

The sweet potato, *Ipomoea Batatas* (L.) Poiret in Lamarck 1804, has been adequately described and classified taxonomically since the first half of the nineteenth century. It belongs to the morning glory or Convolvulaceae family, which contains some fifty genera and nearly two thousand species, mainly tropical and subtropical in habitat. According to Candolle (1886: 12–13), we should look for the region with the greatest number or concentration of species of a genus. The genus *Ipomoea* has more than five hundred species, most of which are native to the New World, with the greatest concentration apparently in Mexico (House, 1908; Matuda, 1964–66; Ooststroom, 1954; Wilson, 1960). Within the genus *Ipomoea* is the section or sub-genus *Batatas*, all of whose species are found in the New World, and only four of these species are found elsewhere (Bois, 1927; Candolle, 1886; House, 1908; Ooststroom, 1954).

Candolle also urged the determination of the closest wild relatives. This was not possible until the genetic studies of the last forty years, carried out by Tioutine (1935), King and Bamford (1937), Miller, Kehr, and Ting (Miller, 1939; Ting and Kehr, 1953; Ting, Kehr, and Miller, 1957), and notably in recent years in Japan, China, New Zealand, the United States, Uganda, Trinidad, and elsewhere by Poole (1952, 1955), Nishiyama (1963; Nishiyama and Teramura, 1962), Yen (1960, 1963), MacDonald (1963), and Martin (1965). It was determined that the basic chromosome number for the genus was fifteen, and that the sweet potato was a hexaploid with ninety chromosomes ($2n = 90$). *Ipomoea tiliacea* (Willd.) Choisy, now known to be conspecific with *Ipomoea fastigiata* Sweet (Matuda, 1964; Nishiyama and Teramura, 1962), has been considered by Asa Gray (Gray and Trumbull, 1883) and Homer House (1908: 255) to be the ancestral form of the sweet potato. Ting, Kehr, and Miller concluded in 1957 that such could not have been the case because *Ipomoea tiliacea* is a tetraploid. Then Nishiyama and Teramura (1962; Nishiyama, 1963), on the basis of study of wild forms collected in the United States and Mexico in 1954–1955, concluded that *Ipomoea trifida* (H.B.K.) G. Don and *Ipomoea Batatas* were the only hexaploids in the genus and that probably the sweet potato was derived by cultivation from *Ipomoea trifida*. Heiser (1965: 939), although accepting the close relationship of these two, surmises that *Ipomoea trifida* may be no more than an escaped form of the sweet potato. Furthermore, Heiser suggests that tetraploid *Ipomoea tiliacea* might have hybridized with various diploid species in different areas, and, if chromosome doubling occurred in the hybrids, several different types might result that would be sufficiently similar to be grouped within the confines of a single species.

Another type of analysis also was used to strengthen the case for the close relationship of the two species. In 1926 Stout suggested that self-incompatibility might be present in the sweet potato (Martin, 1965: 407). Many species of *Ipomoea* are self-fertile, such as *Ipomoea tiliacea*, but *Ipomoea Batatas* and *Ipomoea trifida* are predominantly self-sterile or self-incompatible (Nishiyama and Teramura, 1962; Martin, 1965). A common incompatibility group of the sweet potato and *Ipomoea trifida* indicates close relationship. Nishiyama concludes that incompatibility seems to be one of the most useful characters for study of phylogenetic relationships between the wild forms and the cultivated sweet potato and that analysis of incompatibility groups could aid in understanding the dispersion process from the original habitat. Martin (1965) concludes that probably the sweet potato is an amphiploid of a self-incompatible species and a self-fertile species.

It would seem, therefore, that *Ipomoea trifida* is the best candidate so far for either the ancestral wild form or the nearest relative of the sweet potato (see Yen, this symposium, for a more recent treatment of this matter). The range of *Ipomoea trifida* (H.B.K.) G. Don, which is conspecific with *Ipomoea trichocarpa* Elliot (Wilson, 1960), is from Sinaloa, Chihuahua, and Texas at the north (Matuda, 1964: 142; House, 1908) through Mexico, Central America, the West Indies, and into Colombia and Venezuela. The southern limit of the range is unknown, but this species is not reported in the floras of Peru by Weberbauer (1945) and Macbride (1959). It is of historical interest that the type locality of *Ipomoea trifida* is in Venezuela, where it was collected by Humboldt.

The sweet potato is commonly considered not to occur wild (Bois, 1927). However, Peter Martyr (1944: Dec. II, bk. 9, chap. 1) mentions that delicious sweet potatoes were collected wild by the Indians of the Urabá region of northwestern Colombia. Burkill (1954: 233) solves this problem by suggesting that the Indians probably left some sweet potatoes unharvested in the ground until needed for "seed," and the Spaniards reported this as collecting from the wild. Besides the possibility of overlooked roots left in abandoned fields giving the appearance of wild plants, some seedlings might occur from seeds defecated by birds, as reported by Bulmer (1965) for New Guinea. In any case, all known examples of possible wild sweet potatoes have been few in number and restricted to regions of known cultivation of the plant.

As yet we know relatively little about the nature and distribution of horticultural varieties of the sweet potato. Analysis of the literature from the first 150 years after Columbus' discovery indicates that sometimes a distinction was made according to flavor or taste, but most commonly the varieties were identified primarily according to root color. To the best of my knowledge, the country people (both Indians and mestizos) from Peru to Mexico still differentiate varieties by exterior skin color first and then by interior flesh color of the root. Going by skin and flesh color may be sound practice in any given area with well-established varieties, as witnessed by Oviedo (1950: 234) in the West Indies, where the purplish *ajes* were good but the tan or brownish *batatas* were better. However, the Inca Garcilaso de la Vega (1943: 179) commented of Peruvian sweet potatoes that they were of four or five colors but that in flavor they differed very little one from another; and in Mexico about 1570 Dr. Hernández (1959–1960: II, 173) listed five varieties based on combinations of skin and flesh color and referred to all as having an agreeable flavor like chestnuts.

Actually we know very little about the relationship of flavor or sweetness to any of the morphologic, cytologic, and other characteristics that have been studied to date. Classifications have been made of commercial varieties raised in the United States and the West Indies by Price (1896), Groth (1911), and Thompson and Beattie (1922), but none of these classifications shows any relationship of sugar content to the classificatory criteria used. This is to be expected, since the nature of leaf and vine and the color of the roots vary with climate and soil (Thompson and Beattie, 1922: 3–4). Soil affects the shape, size, and starch contents of the roots (Price, 1896: 14–15), and climate, season, and soil strongly affect the texture and sugar content (Price, 1896: 50; Groth, 1911: 37–41). It cannot be stressed too strongly that cooler climates, whether from latitude or elevation, will increase starch at the expense of sugar, and the reverse takes place in warmer climates. It was probably because of such deterioration produced by planting in the relatively cool climate and high latitude of New Zealand that Captain Wilkes (1845: II, 389) in

1840 considered the sweet potato found at the Bay of Islands as being a small watery root much inferior in quality to those grown in the other Polynesian islands.

Despite what has been said, it remains true that within a homogeneous environment certain recognized horticultural varieties will consistently produce roots that are referred to as dry, mealy, or starchy as opposed to others that are called moist, mushy, or sugary. It should be pointed out that when raw all varieties are hard or firm; that after cooking the moist fleshed become soft, whereas the dry fleshed remain relatively firm; and that the so-called dry-fleshed varieties have a higher percentage of water than do the moist fleshed (USDA, FB2020, 1950). Storage, incidentally, results in a loss of water and an increase of sugar content (Price, 1896: 5–8; Groth, 1911: 41–45). In general, it is popularly assumed that the yellow- or rose-fleshed sweet potatoes have more sugar than do the white-fleshed roots (Bois, 1927). Most of the experimentation, by both governmental and private plant breeders, has been to increase yield, and it is interesting to note that the best yielding strains or varieties tend to be of the so-called starchy, rather than the sugary, type (MacDonald, 1963).

Except for purposes of experimentation and breeding, the sweet potato is almost universally grown vegetatively–that is, from the tuberous root itself (like the *Solanum* potato) or from slips from the roots or from vine cuttings. The early accounts from the Americas unanimously agree that the Indians used only these parts in propagating the sweet potato. Because of this, it is often claimed that wherever a number of varieties are cultivated a considerable antiquity or period of cultivation is involved. However, as Price (1896: 23, 51, 67–69, 98–100), MacDonald (1963: 222), and others have remarked, the sweet potato is subject to sudden mutations or appearance of sports and, in fact, has a marked tendency to mutate. Furthermore, Yen (1960: 369–371; 1963: 112–114) has pointed out that natural seed production and accidental germination of seeds in sweet potato plots would accelerate the process of forming new varieties.

Although the consensus among botanists from Clusius (L'Ecluse, 1576) to the present generation has been that the sweet potato was a native of tropical America, no representative sampling of cultivated varieties from this region was made until that by Vavilov and his associates in 1923–1933. Without giving any details on the nature and distribution of varieties found, Vavilov (1931) listed the sweet potato as originating in South America. Probably because of the South American collections made in 1932–1933, Vavilov stated in 1935 that the South Mexican–Central American–Antillean region was "probably . . . the home of the sweet potato," although he gave no reasons for his change of opinion (Vavilov, 1951: 40).

Now it is appropriate to acknowledge our indebtedness to Douglas Yen, who, along with Nishiyama, has done more to clarify the origins of the sweet potato than anyone else. On the basis of varieties from Asia, Oceania, and northwestern South America, Yen (1963: 110) concluded that the maximum range of variation in the sixteen characteristics studied was provided by the South American material. Unfortunately, no comparable sampling from Middle America has been reported upon as yet, since Nishiyama concentrated mainly on wild forms. Both Yen and Nishiyama agree, however, that the sweet potato probably originated in tropical America in the region from Mexico into South America, although Yen inclines toward a South American origin. Sauer (1950: 509) also favors a South American origin, on the philosophic grounds that the sweet potato belongs in a cultural complex that operated by vegetal means of reproduction, whereas Mesoamerica relied on seed reproduction. Nevertheless, it must be pointed out that as yet we do not know whether northwestern South America or Mesoamerica has the greater varietal diversity in the local cultivated sweet potatoes. Perhaps I should mention, for whatever it is worth, that I have noted just as much flowering and seed-setting of sweet potatoes in southern Mexico as in coastal Peru.

The botanical evidence for the age or relative antiquity of the sweet potato as a cultivated plant is unclear and leads to contradictory conclusions when not supported by other kinds of evidence. A possible line of inquiry would be pollen analysis along with C-14 dating.[1] The

[1] There have been rumors of sweet potato pollen recovered in Melanesia in an archaeologic context dated earlier than 1500. Dr. Richard Schutler, Jr., in a letter of August 12, 1968, wrote me saying, "What sweet potato pollen we have (*Ipomoea*) was identified by Dr. James Schoenwetter (now at Arizona State University, Tempe) from the surface of Rockshelter 12, Trench 7, Futuna Island, southern New Hebrides. So, as of now, we can't say anything about its antiquity on the island." Some recent publications on the sweet potato in New Guinea are Bulmer, 1965; Watson, 1965; Walker, 1966; Watson, 1967; and also Barrau, 1958: 47–48.

sweet potato has distinctive pollen (Selling, 1947: 267, pl. 35), and it flowers much more commonly and abundantly than most people residing in temperate areas realize. But although sweet potato pollen grains can be distinguished from those of other cultivated plants, I do not know to what extent the pollens of the different species of the subgenus *Batatas* are distinguishable from each other or from other species of *Ipomoea*.

In addition to palynology, two quasi-botanical lines of research that might help in clarifying the history of the sweet potato are the diseases and the pests of the cultivated plant. Unfortunately, the work in these fields has been too spotted, too local, and too lacking in historical awareness to be of much help so far. However, it is of interest that the chief pest on Trinidad (*Megastes grandalis* Guenée) has not yet reached the Antilles (Kennard, 1944: 75).[2]

In summary, the results of botanical investigations indicate that the sweet potato is a single species, of American origin, and probably derived from *Ipomoea trifida*. Furthermore, the evidence points toward tropical continental America—most likely northwestern South America—as the region where the sweet potato was first cultivated. Here I should like to point out that Merrill was a tired old man, who acknowledged his waning intellectual faculties, and he should be forgiven his very tentative suggestion that Africa might be the home of the sweet potato (Merrill, 1954: 371–372).

ARCHAEOLOGICAL

The archaeological evidence is of three types: (1) remains of the sweet potato roots, (2) representation in an archaeological context, and, possibly, (3) evidence connected with tillage techniques. Since most of the areas of actual or possible prehistoric cultivation of the sweet potato are humid all or part of the year, the preservation of dessicated remains can scarcely be expected except in dry areas with irrigation. So far as I know, dessicated roots of the sweet potato have been found only in coastal Peru in sites from Cahuachi in the Nazca Valley to the Ancón area north of Lima (Towle, 1961: 78–79). The

---

[2] See Pierce (1940: 230), whose incomplete data and misleading conclusions concerning the implications of the distribution of *Cylidinae* weevils apparently somewhat influenced Merrill (1954: 321–323). To keep abreast of developments, one should check each issue of *Field Crop Abstracts* (Commonwealth Bureau of Pastures and Field Crops, vol. 16, 1963–), beginning with vol. 16: 223.

first published illustration and description is that of the one sweet potato root found in the Necropolis de Ancón remains in the 1880's by Reiss and Stübel (1880–1887: III, pl. 107, fig. 18; Harms, 1922: 184). Other illustrations will be found in Safford (1925), Towle (1961: pl. 1, fig. 5), and Heyerdahl (1952: pl. 63, fig. 3). Tello, excavating on the peninsula of Paracas in the 1920's, found small, fusiform sweet potatoes among the food offerings associated with the mummy packs in the cemeteries on the slopes of the Cerro Colorado (Tello, 1929: 123, 164). Altogether, the finds indicated that the sweet potato was being cultivated during the Formative (perhaps as early as 1000 B.C.) and was well established by Classic times. More recently, during excavations carried out in 1961–1963, Lanning has uncovered sweet potatoes at Punta Grande in the Ancón area, as part of an agricultural village complex with an initial C-14 date of about 2500 B.C. (Lanning, 1965: 74). Such a date does not make the sweet potato one of the older cultivated plants, but it does give the root a more respectable antiquity.

Archaeological remains of the sweet potato in any form have not been found to date outside of Peru, not even in the old agricultural sites of the Mexican states of Puebla and Oaxaca. Here I must refer to one possible exception. Skjölsvold and Smith (Heyerdahl and Ferdon, 1961: I, 297, 303, 394) reported in 1961 that remains of sweet potato were found at site E-2 on Easter Island, in a context with a radiocarbon date of A.D. 1526, plus or minus a hundred years. If the dating has been accurate, this would mean presence of sweet potato about 1420 or earlier, or as late as 1620. One wonders, however, as to the state and nature of the so-called remains of sweet potatoes, and whether any botanist identified these remains. In this connection it is appropriate to recall some remarks made by Cutler (W. Taylor, 1957: 39) in 1957: "A botanist frequently cannot identify scraps from archaeological excavations. . . . For example, of nine root and tuber crops under such names as *ubas, jannes, and pataddes,* and the Span- be found in the herbarium of the institution with the second best South American collection in the world." It must be kept in mind that Roggeveen and Bouman as of 1722 apparently mention three root crops under such names as *ubas, jannes,* and *pataddes,* and the Spanish expedition of 1770 also reported three root crops (Mulert, 1911: 120, 125, 189; Corney, 1908: 13, 21, 101, 123, 135).

Modeling in terra cotta and depiction by painting on cotton cloth are the only forms of archaeological representation known for the sweet potato, and they are known only from Pachacamac to Lambayeque in central and northern coastal Peru. Nearly all the modeled forms are stirrup jars and other vessels of the Classic Mochica, as illustrated by Disselhoff (1967: 49) and others (Herrera, 1942: pl. 2, figs. 2, 4; Tello, 1938: pl. 90; Vargas, 1962: fig. 8; and Verrill, 1937: pl. 4, figs. 1, 2). Disselhoff (1967: 18, 30) reproduces in colors two fragments of cotton cloth from Pachacamac in the Berlin Museum für Völkerkunde. The first is a polychrome painting of a landscape with sweet potato blossoms and roots; the second is also a polychrome painting, which shows leaves, roots, and blossoms.

A possible archaeological expression of a tillage practice associated with the sweet potato is found in the New Zealand sand and gravel pits whence the Maori obtained materials to spread on their cultivated fields and plots. Because of the extension and size of these diggings, some writers, like Best (1925: 60–68) and George Carter (1950: 163), consider them to be proof of an ancient cultivation of the sweet potato. But yams and taro were also extensively cultivated at the time of Cook, and sand and gravel were used in the preparation of fields and plots for these plants.

The main conclusions from archaeological research are that the sweet potato was cultivated in the Americas two thousand or more years B.C., that is was an important food crop in coastal Peru, and that possibly it was on Easter Island by 1620, 1520, or earlier.

HISTORICAL

Considering the claims that have been made for the pre-Columbian occurrence of the sweet potato in Europe, Africa, and Asia, it is most interesting that there is no description of the plant and root in the literature that would be accepted by a botanist until that of Oviedo in 1526 (1950: 234). Before we can sketch the occurrence and spread of the sweet potato, however, we must anticipate the linguistic discussion to identify the words used for the sweet potato in early accounts.

The first mention of the sweet potato is by Columbus, in Cuba, who applied a West African generic term for yams (*Dioscorea*) *niame* in his journal entry for November 4, 1492. A notation by Las Casas on the abstract of the journal identifies these *niames* as *ajes* or *batatas*. Later on, in Hispaniola, by which time the natives captured earlier were able to serve as interpreters, Columbus himself uses the native Taino term *aje* and likens the flavor to that of chestnuts (Navarrete, 1945–1946: I, December 16 and 21). The proper pronunciation of *aje* or *age* is given in 1494 by Dr. Chanca as *hage*, and he further identifies this root as the sweet potato by citing the Carib word *nabi*, which is still used in some areas in South America (Navarrete, 1945–1946: I, 347). Later writers indifferently wrote about *ajes* and *batatas*, and *ajes* or *batatas*; and Oviedo (1950: 234; 1959: 234), Gómara (1877: 201), and other writers make it clear that they considered these two plants as essentially the same except that the roots of the *batata* were sweeter and tastier.[3] By the end of the sixteenth century the term *aje* practically disappears from the literature, probably because the Spaniards preferred the sweeter varieties and consequently encouraged the raising of this type. Incidentally, the first mention of the sweet potato (under the name *age*) in printed literature is not in the often-cited 1511 edition of Peter Martyr's *First Decade*, but in chapter six of the little-known *Libretto de Tutta la Navigatione de Re de Spagna*, published in Venice in 1504, which contains early letters by Peter Martyr (Travigiano, 1504).

Unfortunately, due to the great influence of Humboldt (1811: III, 127–133) and of Asa Gray (Gray and Trumbull, 1883: 241–255), *aje* or *age* frequently has been equated with a *Dioscorea*. As a consequence there has arisen the so-called Aje Problem or Enigma concerning which numerous authors have written (Zayas y Alfonso, 1914; Henríquez Ureña, 1938; Cárcer y Disdier, 1953; Friederici, 1947; Williams, 1953; Burkill, 1954).

The next word to appear is *batata* and its variant *patata* (the Spaniards always have had difficulty with initial *b*, *p*, and *v*). Sixteenth-century writers actually acquainted with the Caribbean region are in nearly unanimous agreement that *batata* is also a word of the Hispaniola Tainos. It first appears in printed literature in 1516, however, in Peter Martyr's description of the crops of northwestern Co-

---

[3] Benzoni, who was in the Americas in 1541–1556, considered the *haie* better flavored than the *battata* (Benzoni, 1857: 86). Martín Enciso wrote of *batatas*, *aje* along the northern coast of South America (Enciso, 1519: fol. 51v). Sweet potatoes as *batatas* are mentioned for the Santiago de Cuba area by 1538 (Gentleman of Elvas, 1905: I, 13–14). Fr. Vicente Valverde, first bishop of Cuzco, was in 1539 the first Spaniard in Peru to write of sweet potatoes, using the terms *ages*, *batatas* (Valverde, 1865: III, 98).

lombia and Panama (1944: dec. II, bk. 9, chap. 1). Peter Martyr goes on to mention seeing and tasting these delicious roots, known to the natives as *batatas*. From the context it seems probable that what he ate were sweet potatoes brought in 1513 by Colmenares—almost undoubtedly from Hispaniola, since the roots probably would not have been edible after the time necessary to go from Urabá to Santo Domingo and thence to Spain. Here we should note that Gómara (who was not present) mentions that Columbus brought back sweet potatoes in 1493, which were tasted in Barcelona by Isabella and Ferdinand (Gómara, 1877: 167); and Oviedo at some time between 1515 and 1534 brought back from Santo Domingo *batatas* that were still edible and well considered when he reached Avila (Oviedo, 1959: 235).[4]

The Taino Arawak name for the sweeter type of sweet potato, *batata*, early in the sixteenth century became the generic term for all kinds of sweet potatoes in most of the European languages. As a consequence we find Italians, Spaniards, Portuguese, and Germans in the first half of the sixteenth century referring to sweet potatoes in Brazil (for example) by recognizable variants of this word: Pigafetta in 1519 (*batate*), Schmidel in the 1530's (*podade*), the Núñez Cabeza de Vaca expedition in 1541 (*batata*).[5] The Spanish conquerors carried the word onto the mainland from Mexico to Peru, and for some years the native names in these areas do not show up in most of the reports from the field and not at all in the general histories by Oviedo, Las Casas, and Gómara, who use either *aje* or *batata*. Unfortunately, through a series of accidents and events that have been discussed frequently (Cárcer y Disdier, 1953, 1955; Friederici, 1947; Hawkes, 1947; Henríquez Ureña, 1938; Laufer, 1938; Safford, 1925), confusion began to arise at the very end of the sixteenth century between the common names for the sweet potato and the *Solanum* potato in various languages. Some of the results are shown in table 19.1.

---

[4] The Venetian ambassador Navagiero (1879: 274, 389) ate sweet potatoes in Seville in 1526. The physician Nicolás Monardes (1925: II, 36), who was born in Seville and who practiced there from about 1529 until his death in 1588, wrote of sweet potatoes being so common in southern Spain in his time that ten or twelve caravels laden with sweet potatoes sailed every year from Vález-Málaga to Seville.

[5] See Pigafetta, 1906: XXXIII, 40–41; Schmidel, 1938: 60; *Comentarios de Alvar Núñez Cabeza de Vaca*, 1877: XXII, 553; *Hans Staden's Wahrhaftige Historia*, 1964: 195.

TABLE 19.1

Selected Names for the *Ipomoea* and *Solanum* Potatoes

	Names for the Sweet Potato 16th–18th Centuries	Current	Names for the Solanum Potato Current
Castilian	batata, patata	batata patata dulce	patata
Portuguese	batata	batata doce	batata batata ingleza
Italian	batate	batate patata dolce	patata
French	batate, patate	batate, patate patate douce	pomme de terre patate
English	potato	sweet potato	potato
German	podade, etc.	Batate Suesskartoffel	Kartoffel
Dutch	patade, etc.	bataat	aardappel

Beginning in 1534 with the men who came from Guatemala and Mexico with Pedro de Alvarado, and accelerated in 1551 with the arrival of the former Mexican viceroy Mendoza and his followers, the hispanized Nahuatl word *camote* rapidly replaced all other names for the sweet potato among the Spaniards and mestizos and many of the Indians within the Peruvian viceroyalty from Ecuador to Chile. The transition is apparent in two writers who were in Peru in the 1540's: Cieza de León (1553: chap. 46) writes of *ajes o batatas*, but Zarate (1944: 37–38) mentions *ajis y camotes*. The dominance of *camote* is outstanding in the various Peruvian reports from 1582 to 1586 in the *Relaciones geográficas* (1881–1897).[6]

The net result of these events and changes is that during the sixteenth century the Americas became divided into two sweet potato areas. From the Antilles to southern Brazil the sweet potato is *batata* for most Europeans; from Mexico to Chile the sweet potato is *camote*. The importance of these facts is that the sweet potato moved east-

[6] For other early Peruvian illustrations see Acosta, 1940: 112; Cabello Balboa, 1951: 233; Cobo, 1890–1895: I, 355–356; Ortiz de Zúñiga, 1920: I, 32; Poma de Ayala, 1944: 69; and the citations (some erroneous) in Yacovleff and Herrera, 1934–1935: 273–274.

ward from the Atlantic shores of the Americas with the name *batata*, whereas the sweet potato carried westward by Spaniards went by the name *camote*, whether from Mexico or Peru. However, a most unfortunate exception must be made to the clean-cut dichotomy established. Most of the European explorers and entrepreneurs of the sixteenth and seventeenth centuries knew neither botany nor farming, and consequently they very commonly would use the name of some previously known or reported rootcrop (like *niame*, *batata*, or *camote*) for the rootcrops in newly discovered lands. Unless there is other supporting information, a name alone is not adequate evidence. One can be almost certain, however, that a sweet potato is meant if its shape is described as that of a turnip or carrot *and* the flavor is likened to that of chestnuts or as being sweet or sweetish.

The distribution of the cultivated sweet potato in the Americas at the contact period (roughly the fifty years from 1492 to 1542) was practically restricted to the regions between the two tropics. The sweet potato was not cultivated in what is now the United States, not even in Florida, as Sturtevant has ably demonstrated (1960: 11–12). A survey by Beals (1932: 101–102) draws the northern limits in Mexico with the Huastecs of Veracruz and Tamaulipas and uncertainly into Jalisco and Nayarit of western Mexico.[7] I have studied most of the extant material on western Mexico, and I find no definite evidence for the sweet potato in Nayarit as of 1524–1530 nor in most, if any, of Jalisco (Tello, 1891: 86).[8] Actually, the unequivocal evidence indicates that the sweet potato did not reach the northern limits of Mesoamerica and that it was found only from the lowlands of Veracruz and Michoacán southeastward through Central America into South America. In South America the sweet potato was reported widely from Colombia, Venezuela, and the Guianas southward into

[7] The citation by Beals in his table 12 (p. 162) actually is to a report of about 1608 for the Villa and Provincia de Pánuco (Martínez, 1868: IX, 133, 141, 150).

[8] Antonio Tello, a Spanish priest who came to New Spain in 1619 and wrote in 1650–1653, mentions "camotes (que son las batatas de Castilla)" for Tonalá as of the 1530 Guzmán expedition, but the extant original Guzmán accounts do not mention sweet potatoes. However, Ponce (San Juan, 1872: LVIII, 18) mentions sweet potatoes at Jocotepec on Lake Chapala in the 1580's, and there are numerous other mentions from the second half of the sixteenth century for places in Jalisco, Nayarit, and Sinaloa.

Peru, Bolivia, Paraguay, and Brazil. Latcham (1936: 181–184) is the authority for the widely quoted statement that the sweet potato reached the province of Quillota on the Río Aconcagua north of Valparaiso in Chile, but he gives no evidence for this conclusion. The southern limits of agriculture among the Gês-Tapuya, Tupí-Guaraní, and other groups of southern Brazil, adjacent Uruguay, and northeastern Argentina, seem to be the southern limits of the sweet potato, according to the scattered observations collected by Hoehne (1937) and reports by Spaniards like those of the Núñez Cabeza de Vaca expedition of 1541–1542.

Here one might comment on the claim that the Maori of New Zealand had developed the most poleward-growing varieties of the sweet potato. We do not know how long before 1769 the sweet potato had been cultivated in these latitudes of the high thirties and low forties, but long before 1769 the sweet potato was being cultivated in comparable or higher latitudes of what is now eastern United States.

Conklin (1963: 129–136) and Ho (1955: 193–194) have fairly well eliminated pre-Columbian sweet potatoes from Africa and eastern Asia. The claims for the circum-Mediterranean lands are too weak to merit discussion. The oceanic islands of the Pacific, however, still pose questions as to time, mechanism, and direction of introduction of the sweet potato. Most of the theories and literature will be found in Dixon (1932), Hornell (1946), Heyerdahl (1952), and Yen (1963). The current consensus is that the sweet potato originated in the Americas and was taken thence into the Pacific in pre-Columbian times.[9] Here we are concerned merely with the historical evidence for the sweet potato in the Pacific Islands at the time of initial contacts by Europeans. Most of the literature stresses the Dutch, British, and French voyages of the eighteenth century, especially for the outer Polynesian islands from New Zealand via Easter Island to Hawaii. Dixon (1932) has listed the sweet potato as being found on Easter Island by 1722, Society Islands by 1768, New Zealand by 1769, Tonga by 1777, Hawaii by 1778, and the Marquesas by about 1790–1804. I do not challenge any of these except Easter Island, since with that exception sweet potatoes are described fairly circumstantially.

[9] For a representative sampling see Baker, 1965: 51–55; Cooley, 1951: 378–386; Haudricourt and Hedin, 1943: 157–163; Macnab, 1967: 219–221; Martínez del Rio, 1952: 328, 336–341; Sauer, 1952: 46–47, 60.

It must be kept in mind, however, that the Spaniards and Portuguese were the first Europeans in the Pacific (Sharp, 1960; Friis, 1967). The Spaniards discovered Polynesia, Micronesia, and eastern Melanesia, and the Portuguese discovered western Melanesia. Furthermore, the first ethnographic data for a Polynesian people were obtained by the Mendaña-Quirós visit in 1595 to the Marquesas. Some years ago, in another connection, I made a careful study of nearly all the extant published materials on Spanish exploration in the Pacific, in the original Spanish and Portuguese. Contrary to the assumptions of Friederici (1929, 1936) and his followers (Sapper, 1966; Nordenskiöld, 1931), I could find no mention of the planting of sweet potatoes by Mendaña or Quirós in the Solomons in 1568, in the Marquesas and Santa Cruz in 1595, or in the New Hebrides in 1606— although such items as maize, cotton, melons, squash, broad beans, kidney beans, lentils, and chickpeas were planted (see Zaragoza, 1876–1862; Markham, 1904; Stevens, 1930; Kelly, 1966; and Friis, 1967: bib. nn. 68, 70, 72 to chap. 7). Nor is there a record anywhere else that the Spaniards planted sweet potatoes in Polynesia. But it is possible that the sixteenth-century Spaniards did see sweet potatoes in Micronesia, Melanesia, and the Philippine Islands when they mention *batatas, patatas,* and *camotes* repeatedly.

The men of the Legazpi expedition, for example, mentioned *patatas* and *niames* in 1565 for what must have been one of the Marshalls (*Col. Doc. Ultramar,* 1886: II, 228). In this and most of the other cases, however, we probably should assume that these words were used descriptively for rootstuffs and not specifically for *Ipomoea Batatas.* Nevertheless, if we rule out the Legazpi record of *patatas* sweet potatoes in the Marshalls, then in all fairness we must rule out the Roggeween record of *pataddes* sweet potatoes on Easter Island, since both accounts lack a description of the root or the vine.

The strongest historical evidence for the sweet potato in Oceania during the sixteenth century comes from the southern Marianas. Pigafetta (1906: XXXIII, 98) laconically refers to the presence on Guam in 1521 of *batate,* which is the same word Pigafetta used in Brazil for the sweet potato. We assume that Pigafetta, either in southern Spain or through members of the Magellanic expedition who had been in the Antilles, was familiar with the sweet potato under the name *batata.* Andrés de Urdaneta, as a member of the Loaisa expedition, was present on Guam in 1526 when Gonzalo de Vigo (a deserter from the *Trinidad* in 1522) was picked up. Urdaneta refers to Gonzalo de Vigo (*Col. Doc. Indias*, 1866: 17) as being very useful because he knew the local language. In another account, published by Navarrete (1945–1946, V, 51–53), this information is repeated, and *batatas* are mentioned among the local foodstuffs. Urdaneta was again on Guam in 1565 with the Legazpi expedition. *Batatas* (also *patatas*) and *ñames* are mentioned in several of the accounts of Guam (*Col. Doc. Ultramar*, 1886–1887: II, 236, 245, 250, 392; *ibid*, III, 438). The pilot major Estevan Rodríguez mentions that Urdaneta repeated some of the words he remembered to the natives who recalled Gonzalo de Vigo, and then Rodríguez gives a brief list of Chamorro words and their Spanish equivalents (apparently derived from Urdaneta, who presumably remembered them from the days of his association with Gonzalo de Vigo). In the list of fifty-six words and the numbers from one to ten (*Col. Doc. Ultramar*, 1886: II, 392–393) is given the Chamorro word *azuiban*, meaning *batata*. Although the Spanish equivalent *batata* could have been used in the general sense of root, this does not seem reasonable, since Urdaneta had lived for some eight years in the Moluccas (1526–1535) as well as in New Spain later, and he surely would have differentiated among yam, taro, and sweet potato. Years later such writers as Safford (1905: 297–298) and the philologist Preissig (1918: 156) wrote that the sweet potato had no vernacular name on Guam, but was known as *camote*. Preissig, incidentally, goes on to give Chamorro names for aroids (*suni, piga, papao, baba*) and for yams (*dago, nica, gado*). All this might indicate a pre-Magellanic introduction of the sweet potato into the Marianas, where it became known as *azuiban*, but with frequent Mexican contacts after 1565, the term *camote* took over for the root that the people from New Spain certainly would ask for rather than yams or taros.

A review of the historical evidence would indicate the following. The sweet potato was definitely cultivated at the contact period in the Americas from Michoacán and Veracruz and Cuba in the north to central coastal Peru, the Corrientes region of Argentina, and Santa Catarina of Brazil in the south. It had been introduced into southern Spain and Portugal before 1500 and possibly as early as 1493. No definite historical record of the sweet potato in the Pacific Islands exists before the 1760's and 1770's, although the sweet potato possibly is indicated for Micronesia in the sixteenth century and for

Easter Island in 1722. Here it should be noted that in 1595 the Men-daña-Quirós expedition did not mention sweet potatoes for the Marquesas. This may have been an oversight, or the sweet potato may not have reached the Marquesas as yet, or it may indicate that the sweet potato was not yet anywhere in Polynesia.

Here I wish to outline my theory of the introduction of the sweet potato into Oceania, which may not be better than any other theory but certainly is no poorer in terms of the actual facts known. I assume that the sweet potato was cultivated in Portugal before 1500; that it was taken from Portugal to western India by the Portuguese between 1498 and 1505; and that the sweet potato was then carried by Persian, Arab, Hindu, or other traders from the Malabar coast to Indonesia, where it became established discontinuously from Sumatra to the Moluccas. Moluccan and Papuan traders carried the sweet potato along the north coast of New Guinea in the first two decades of the sixteenth century; and accidental and sporadic voyages from the Moluccas, Celebes, Philippine Islands, or New Guinea placed the sweet potato in the Marianas before 1520. From northern New Guinea the sweet potato moved gradually eastward into eastern Melanesia, whence it reached some one of the Polynesian groups, perhaps the Society Islands. Here the sweet potato obtained the name *kumala, umara,* or the like, and was thence dispersed to the outer Polynesian islands by sporadic one-way voyages. Back in Indonesia there were other sixteenth-century introductions of the sweet potato by Portuguese and Spaniards that tended to overlie and black out the earlier non-European introductions to such an extent that in only a few areas, such as that of some of the mountain people of Luzon (Safford, 1925: n. 23), did there remain the tradition that the sweet potato was pre-European.

LINGUISTIC

The linguistic or philologic evidence will be discussed only in terms of the diversity within tropical America and the possible relationships between South America and Polynesia. As has been pointed out from Candolle to Nordenskiöld, linguistic diversity or variety probably indicates relative antiquity. Unfortunately, with the exception of the South American studies by Nordenskiöld (1930: 168–171), there are no extensive lists of the words for sweet potato in American Indian languages (see also D. Taylor, 1957: 704–705). I

have compiled a brief but broadly distributed list to show some of
the differences from Mexico to Brazil, and within as well as between
linguistic families.

uarhás (Tarasco; Tarascan)
buz-cua (Otomi; Otomian)
camotli (Nahuatl; Utoaztecan)
ñu-yaa (Ixcatec; Popolocan)
muen (Zoque; Zoquean)
iz (Maya; Mayance)
batata and *hage* (Taino; Arawakan)
cari, curiti (Central Arawakan)
napi, nabi (Calinya and Galibí;
   Cariban)
chacu, chaco (Cumanagoto;
   Cariban)

unt (Paez; Chibchan)
comal (Cañari; Cañari)
cumar (Chinchasuyo Quechua)
apichu, apisu (Quechua;
   Quechuan)
tuctuca (Aymará; Aymaran)
chapru (Sek; Yuncan ?)
open, opoen, opene (Mochica;
   Yuncan)
bem (Huallaga Colon; Cholón)
inchi (Jívaro; Jívaro)
yeté (Guaraní; Tupí-Guaraní)
yetica (Tupinamba; Tupí-Guaraní)

Actually, such a list as the above must be used with the greatest
caution, since the date of the earliest available vocabulary varies
greatly from one language to another. Furthermore, the Otomi and
Ixcatec and perhaps other words for sweet potato seem to be com-
pound or double-barrelled words, and these usually are not what
they seem—as witness our own sweet potato and jerusalem arti-
choke. About the only valid conclusion we can reach is that the
sweet potato was a cultigen long enough ago in the Americas to result
in quite different words from one family to another, and even within
some families. Here we should remember, however, that some of the
linguistic families established by philologists are rather questionable
in whole or in part.

Seemann and Markham (Cieza de León, 1864: 234) opened a
Pandora's box in the 1860's when they pointed out that there was a
similarity between the *cumar* of the Quito dialect of Quechua and the
kumara of some of the Polynesian islands. This similarity, which probably has no more genetic significance than does the similarity of Nahuatl *teotl* to Greek *theos* or Quechua *marca* to German *mark*, has
led many writers to extravagant statements that have no basis in fact.
I will quote three statements that are representative of scores of
others. Dixon (1934: 173) wrote that *kumara* was a word of the "supposedly older Chinchasuyo dialect spoken along the coast for a hundred miles or more north and south of Lima." Hornell (1946: 42)

wrote that *kumar* or *kumal* was the name for the sweet potato "in the Quichuan language of the Lima region of coastal Peru." Sharp (1964: 126) wrote of "cumar, the Quichua Indian word for sweet potato." None of these statements is at all correct. There was not a Quechua language of coastal Peru; the word *cumar* is not a Quechua word; and the word *cumar* never was used for sweet potato anywhere along the coast of South America.

The consensus of archaeologists, historians, and philologists today is that the coasts of Ecuador, Peru, and Chile were occupied by non-Quechuan and non-Aymaran peoples until less than a hundred years before the Spanish conquest (Rowe, 1946: II, 204–208; Rivet and Créqui-Montfort, 1951: vii–xxxv). Quechua-speaking peoples and the so-called Inca Empire were restricted to a small region in the interior near Cuzco until the beginning of the fifteenth century. The coastlands of Peru and Ecuador were not conquered until after 1455, and the very important Chimu country of the north coast was not conquered until about 1470. The conquered coastal Indians who wished to participate in the benefits and offices of the Inca Empire had to learn Quechua, but the Quechua language was not the language of the people, and it died in the coastal area almost immediately after the Spanish conquest of the 1530's. What obtained from perhaps 1000 B.C. or earlier until the Quechua-Inca conquests (according to the archaeologic evidence) was a number of local cultures and peoples whose descendants are represented in the three or four families of languages recognized in the Ecuadorean-Peruvian coastlands from Manta to Nazca. The languages along the coast were Sek, Yungan, and Chinchan, with such names for sweet potato as *chapru* and *open* (Carrera, 1939; Larco Hoyle, 1938–1939; Rivet, 1949; Villareal, 1921; Zevallos Quiñones, 1946).

The Quechua word for sweet potato is *apichu*. Despite the statement by Henríquez Ureña (1938: 31), the Inca Garcilaso de la Vega did not use and probably never had heard the word *cumara*. This Spanish-Quechua mestizo was born in Cuzco in 1539 and went to Spain in 1560. In his only remark about sweet potatoes (Garcilaso de la Vega, 1943: 179) he states that the Indians of Peru called them *apichu*. In the literature of colonial Peru one will read about *batatas* and *ajes* in the earlier years, then about *camotes* and *apichu*, but never about *cumar* or *cumara*, except in dictionaries. In the dictionaries, from the anonymous first dictionary of 1586 (*Arte, y Vocabu-*

lario en la Lengua General, 1586) on through that by Torres Rubio-
Figueredo in 1700 (1754), *camote, batata,* and *apichu* are the main
headings, and *cumar* is mentioned only as occurring in the Chinchasuyo dialect of Quechua. Unfortunately, the best-known Quechua
dictionary, that of González Holguín in 1608, copied widely from
earlier dictionaries but neglected to point out that *cumar* was used
only in the Chinchasuyo dialect. His laconic statements (González
Holguín, 1952: 31, 429, 444) were: "Apichu, o cumar. Camote o batata"; and "Batata camote. Apichu"; and "Camote. Apichu." Please
note that *cumar* was never defined as a special kind of sweet potato,
but merely as the word used in the Chinchasuyo dialect. A further
bit of evidence that *cumar* is not a Quechua word is that this word
does not occur in the regions to the west, south, and east of Cuzco
into which the Quechua was carried—only *apichu.*

Despite the mention of *cumar* as a word for sweet potato in the
Chinchasuyo dialect of Quechua, this means neither that it was a
Quechua word nor that it was used on the coast. The Chinchasuyo
dialect was spoken by the Quechuized Indians conquered in the
Andean highlands to the northwest from Cuzco, chiefly from Junín to
Cajamarca. We do not know what the original languages of these
conquered peoples were; possibly Arawakan, Panoan, Chibchan, or
other. There were strong influences between the Chinchasuyo and the
Ecuadoran highlands conquered later. By the end of the sixteenth century it is apparent that *cumar* and *cumal* were common
words for the sweet potato among the Quechuized Indians of the
Ecuadoran highlands from Cuenca to Quito (Cordero, 1955; Cordero
Palacios, 1924; Friederici, 1947: 225; Guzmán, 1920; Seemann, 1852–
1857: 319). The word apparently was originally a Cañari word, as
recorded for the Cuenca area in 1582 in the form *comal* by the priest
of the doctrina of Cañaribamba (*Relaciones geográficas de Indias,*
1881–1897: III, 186). The appearance of a form of this word in the
Urubamba valley near Cuzco, as first recorded by Cook in 1916, is
explained by the massive exchange of *mitamaes* between the Cuzco
area and the Cuenca area (Cieza de León, 1943: 262; *Relaciones
geográficas de Indias,* 1881–1897: III, 171). According to Cieza de
León, more than fifteen thousand Cañari men with their wives were
sent by Túpac Inca to the Cuzco area. Since *mitamaes* normally were
settled in areas with climates similar to those with which they were
familiar, it would seem reasonable that the Cañari were settled in

the warmer valleys like that of the Urubamba rather than at the cold levels of Cuzco itself. Probably Christian missionary activity from the Ecuadoran and Chinchasuyo highlands explains the findings of such words as *cumari* and *cumal* by Veigl and by Poeppig (Friederici, 1947: 225) in the Maynas and adjacent areas of northern Peru.

It is very interesting that Peruvian botanists and anthropologists were unaware of *cumar* or *cjcumara* until after Cook's report of 1916. I believe that we can logically conclude that neither *cumar* nor any word like it was a Quechua word for sweet potato. Furthermore, the Indians of Peru and Ecuador, with the possible exception of some in the Chinchasuyo and the lower Urubamba, so far as I know make no distinction between a "starchy" and a "sugary" sweet potato.[10] What is absolutely definite, is that nowhere on the Ecuadoran or Peruvian coast was there a people cultivating any kind of sweet potato under a name even remotely resembling *cumar* or *cumara*. Consequently, Polynesians could not have obtained the sweet potato with such a name on the coasts of South America, nor was there a coastal people to take the sweet potato with such a name into Polynesia.[11]

MYTHOLOGICAL

Under mythological lines of evidence I will only mention briefly the role of tradition and genealogies and that of ceremonies. Traditions and genealogies tend to feed upon themselves and to grow expansively under the tender care of ethnologists and antiquarians. The sweet potato is involved in tradition, myths, and genealogies chiefly, if not entirely, in Oceania. This indeed speaks for the important role of the sweet potato in parts of that region. But perhaps this is more an expression of cultural poverty than of great antiquity. It is possible that the sweet potato has been substituted among the Maori for a folk-memory of rice once possessed by their ancestors

---

[10] Herrera (1941: 345–346) gives a detailed terminology which apparently has only a very limited distribution. See also Pérez Arbelaez, 1956: 305–308, for Colombia, and Pittier, 1926: 127, for Venezuela.

[11] Discussions of words for sweet potato in South America and Oceania will be found in Cook and Cook, 1916: 339–347; Dixon, 1932; Imbelloni, 1940: 202–204, 1956: 389–390; Rivet, 1928: 583–609. Although Paul Rivet rectified a number of Imbelloni's false or doubtful citations (in Imbelloni's first edition of *Esfinge indiana*, 1926), Imbelloni continued to use them in his later publications and these citations have been uncritically copied by other writers.

(Best, 1925: 49). If it were not for the breakdown of Maori culture it would be interesting to speculate as to what the role of the white or *Solanum* potato would have been in view of its rise to superiority as the favored tuber in some fifty years.

Traditions must be handled with the greatest of care, and much, if not most, of what has been collected after the initial years of contact with Europeans is greatly contaminated. There are scores of examples to warn us, such as Kroeber's recording about 1911 that the Mohave considered wheat and melons to be indigenous (Kroeber, 1925: 735), or the Maori traditions, mentioned by Best (1925: 147, 152), that they had the turnip and the *Solanum* potato before the coming of Europeans. Yen (1960: 372) and others in New Zealand and Hawaii have reduced the supposedly large number of pre-European varieties drastically through historical, linguistic, and botanical studies.[12]

The analysis of genealogies 120 years ago and now yield rather striking differences. Currently there seems to be an agreement among most students of the New Zealand situation that the sweet potato reached those islands in the fourteenth century at the latest. However, Pickering and Hale, who were on North Island in 1840, concluded from a genealogy collected at Bay of Islands that the sweet potato was brought to New Zealand by Pani and his sister in A.D. 1740 (Pickering, 1879: 1017; Wilkes, 1845: II, 377–414). Perhaps the most disruptive event in the lives of students of the Maori has been the thesis of "accidental" one-way voyages propounded by Sharp (1964: 62–92; Golson, 1963), the logic of which gives the lie to many of the traditions concerning the bringing of the sweet potato to New Zealand. A comparable thing has happened to the traditional chronology and genealogy of the Incas in Peru as a result of careful analysis of both written accounts from the colonial period and the results of archaeologic research (Rowe, 1946: II, 192–209).

Despite what has been said above, the important place of sweet potatoes in ceremonialism from New Zealand to Hawaii is quite impressive. It certainly speaks for the importance of this root in the economy of a number of the islands, whether the sweet potato dated from 1700, or 1600, or 1500, or earlier.

---

[12] For some other discussion of sweet potato varieties in Polynesia see Best, 1925: 55–56; Chung, 1923: 15; Tapsell, 1947: 325–332.

Conclusion

My own reaction to the survey that I have made is to conclude that the matter of diffusion (time and method) is still far from settled. Although I hold for a relatively late introduction of the sweet potato into Polynesia, and from the west, I would not be greatly surprised if it were a few centuries earlier and from South America—but *not* with the name *cumara*. This name must be explained in some other fashion, just as someone should explain how the Mexican word *coa* for a digging stick shows up in Polynesia as *ko* (Barrau, 1961: 14; Best, 1925: 32–42), also for a digging stick. Also the suggestions by Yen (1960: 373) and Bulmer (1965) as to the role of birds should be given more attention.

20. Travels of Corn and Squash

HUGH C. CUTLER AND LEONARD W. BLAKE

The plants man uses reflect his activities and environment at the time he collected the plants. Cultivated plants are especially informative. They are chosen, planted, and carried by man on his travels. They are changed by mutation, environmental selection, hybridization with wild and weedy plants and various cultivated selections, by seed selection, growing methods, and other factors. Most cultivated plants depend upon man, and man frequently has become so dependent upon them that his activities may be governed by the life cycles of his crops.

A cultivated plant and the technique associated with growing it spread from a definite center. Beyond this center, each area tends to harbor a series of local refinements. Frequently it is possible to distinguish the forms of a major cultivated plant grown in one village from those of another village only a few miles distant. If enough material is available for study, each major crop plant grown by a group of people may be distinguished from the kinds of the same species grown by another group, even a closely related one, that is separated to a slight degree by distance, culture patterns, or time.

From our studies on plants used by living peoples and from the large collections of archaeological materials sent to us in recent years, we have become convinced that the assemblage of plants used in one place at one time differs from that found at any other place or time. The entire aggregation of useful plants, wild and cultivated, edible and used for such things as cordage, textiles, medicine, and decoration, forms a unique pattern, one that is recognizable when the elements can be precisely identified. The degree of similarity of one assemblage to another from a different site or time period will reflect cultural connections and environmental conditions.

Archaeological plant collections can be studied effectively only by specialists. They must know enough about minor variations, environmental effects, and accidents of preservation to be able to interpret as well as identify specimens. Their results should be intelligible and useful. Relatively few botanists take the time to become such specialists, largely because they do not understand that archaeological sites may provide usable records of the past history of plants and that these materials can often be dated or placed in order by archaeologists. The need for more specialists is even greater now than it was in 1956, when a conference, "The Identification of Non-artifactual Archaeological Materials," held in Chicago (Taylor, 1957) pointed out the problems involved in utilizing all the resources of a site.

Corn and squash are two of the best plants for the study of relationships of plants and humans. The volume of corncobs alone exceeds the mass of all other cultivated plants found in archaeological sites. Most casual descriptions of corn are based on the color and character of kernels, but the cob bears structures better suited for the investigation of relationships and the definition of natural groups. Cobs were usually brought to the house or storage site and are extremely durable. Consequently, we have many excellent specimens and do not have to depend upon scarce and scanty materials like the Old World clay impressions and carbonized fragments of wheat and barley used so effectively by Hans Helbaek (1963). The fruit stems and rinds of squash and gourds are not as useful as corncobs, but usually enough were left at a site to make identifications possible (Cutler and Whitaker, 1961).

The nearest relatives of corn are the purely New World grasses in the genera *Manisuris* and *Tripsacum* and the many *Tripsacum*-corn intermediates called teosinte. These have been included in a separate genus, *Euchlaena*, but should be considered as a variable hybrid involving maize and *Tripsacum*. Wilkes (1967) provides a thorough survey of present knowledge of teosinte and its relationships.

The species of *Tripsacum* may be arranged in three groups:

1. Slender, *Manisuris*-like species, such as *T. floridanum* and *T. lanceolatum*, with restricted distribution and usually thirty six chromosomes.
2. More vigorous species that may have hybrid or polyploid vigor sometimes appear to have been involved in hybridization with maize, teosinte, or maize-contaminated species of *Tripsacum,* and may have thirty-six or seventy-two chromosomes—for example, *T. dactyloides*, *T. laxum*, and *T. australe*.
3. Vigorous tropical species like *T. pilosum*, which apparently bear considerable amounts of maize germplasm and usually have seventy two chromosomes.

The center of diversity of *Tripsacum* and of teosinte lies in Mexico. There, too, are located most of the archaeological sites in which *Tripsacum* or teosinte have been found.

The oldest known corn has been found in Mexico. Most ancient are some pollen grains identified among fossil pollen isolated from a drill core taken at a depth of more than seventy meters below present-day Mexico City (Barghoorn, Wolfe, and Clisby, 1954). The identifications were questioned (Kurtz, Liverman, and Tucker, 1960), but later studies by Barghoorn and his associates confirm that at least some of the fossil pollen grains were those of corn (Mangelsdorf, Macneish, and Galinat, 1964: 539). The pollen is believed to have been deposited during the last interglacial period, estimated to have occurred about eighty thousand years ago.

The oldest corn plant remains were found by MacNeish about 125 miles east-southeast of Mexico City, in the Tehuacán Valley. The earliest are from levels dated about 4800–3500 B.C. and are believed to be wild corn. The cobs are small, usually eight-rowed, the kernels partially covered by the glumes as in weak forms of pod corn, but the structure is essentially that of modern corn. The Tehuacán corn is likely to have been wild, self-propagating, and not dependent upon man for its care, and thus may be considered to be wild corn.

There remain two questions: From which grass did the wild-growing corn evolve? Did man play any part in the creation of the Tehuacán corn? It is possible that man gathered related grasses from different habitats, brought them to his homesite, and enabled them to hybridize on his dump, where they grew together from seeds cast out with refuse. The scarcity of corn in the El Riego phase (6500–4000 B.C.) of Tehuacán and its absence in levels where wild plant materials and some possible ancient cultivated plants like gourds, squash, and some beans are found suggest that, if present, it was not abundant or was not used.

Tripsacum, teosinte, and many other grasses were gathered by Indians for food. Gathering and transporting edible seeds from varied habitats back to the living site is a practice far older than man. The seeds may be brought home in stomach contents, accidentally attached to body or clothing, in bedding, or a purposefully gathered food. Man probably recognized that plants grew from seeds long before he attempted gardening. Scattered clues as to how man began to propagate plants suggest that agriculture began on a small scale and for a long period was an incidental source of food.

Maize appears late in South America. The oldest cobs, dated between 1400 and 1200 B.C. (Collier, 1961: 107) resemble the earliest northern corn specimens of pre-Columbian times, from the Hopewell period of Ohio, Mill Creek of Iowa, and the lower levels of Bat, Ventana, and Tularosa caves in the American southwest. This corn, related to Chapalote, Reventador, and Nal-Tel of Mexico (Wellhausen *et al.*, 1952) and the Southwest, differs from the Tehuacán wild maize but resembles corn from later periods of Tehuacán and from many other sites in Mexico (Mangelsdorf, MacNeish, and Galinat, 1967). Such corn was relatively common in Mexico and the Southwest until about A.D. 1100 and, only slightly changed, is still grown as popcorn in many places from Argentina to the Great Plains. Relative uniformity of the widespread early kinds of Chapalote group corn implies a limited source and limited time for the first distribution of maize. In both Mexico and Peru there was a long period of gardening with beans, gourds, and squash. Before this, we suspect that beans, gourds, and squash may have been gathered from wild-growing weedy plant associates of man (Cutler and Whitaker, 1961). In Peru maize appears after ceramics. In Mexico and the Southwest corn was considerably earlier.

The basic pattern of the maize ear and tassel and of the tassels of *Tripsacum* and teosinte is a pair of rows of paired spikelets. The next step, probably caused by genes for fasciation, is to an eight-rowed (four rows of paired grains) ear, then to sixteen-rowed and to thirty-two-rowed ears. This sequence is apparent in South America (Cutler, 1946), where several small-cobbed races of corn have eight rows, the common and commercial kinds have fourteen or sixteen rows, and sweet corn has from twenty to as many as thirty-two rows of grains. The eight-rowed types have twelve to twenty-four tassel branches, the sixteen-rowed maize has around thirty-six tassel branches, and the pure sweet corn has an average of about eighty tassels.

The earliest corn from Tehuacán and the ones considered wild by Mangelsdorf, MacNeish, and Galinat (1967) usually have eight rows of very small grains. When eight-rowed ears appear in most other sites, they usually have large grains and large cobs, are considerably advanced in their features, and are considerably later. Usually there is a gradual decrease in the number of rows of grains; this has been interpreted (Cutler, 1960) as evidence that hybrids of the older, many-rowed corn with later, eight-rowed kinds had more vigor and adaptability than the eight-rowed parent (considered to be similar to the race called Harinoso de Ocho, or eight-rowed Flour corn). It is more likely that larger-grained forms evolved and were selected and that in the process there was a selection for fewer rows of grains. These newer kinds spread as they evolved, so that we have a sequence culminating in eight-rowed, large-grained, large-cobbed corn rather than a series with corn like one of the parents.

Plant uses change slowly. Present distribution is a key to past use patterns. Sweet corn distribution among recent Indians appears to offer evidence of gradual flow of a cultivated plant from a center. Extremes of sweet corn are found in highland valleys of Peru and Bolivia. The ears are small, many rowed, shaped like rounded, miniature pineapples with deformed tips, and have relatively long and slender red or golden grains. Glumes are weak, the cob white. Plants are paler green and bear many more tassel branches than the common corn of the region. As one moves northward, sweet corn still differs, in nearly all the ways it did in the Andes, from the common corn of the region in which it is found. The change is gradual and consistent. In the pueblos of the Southwest, the grains are still mainly red or golden, the cobs white, soft, and with more rows than most Pueblo corn, except for the dents we will mention later. On the Plains, where most corn has quite hard cobs and usually eight or ten rows of grains, golden and red sweet corn has softer cobs and more rows (Will and Hyde, 1917). The sweet character is governed by a single recessive gene, but the many other characters and modifiers associated with it accompany sweet corn on its northward migration, gradually becoming less pronounced as the distance from Peru increases.

Dent corn is complex. Unlike the common sweet character in corn, which is governed by a single recessive gene, dent corn is governed by many genes and is poorly understood. Like sweet corn it may be associated with many characters and have modifiers. There is some evidence that the dent character came from *Tripsacum*. Mexico is the center for dent corn, but there is a secondary center in the valleys of the Andes, apparently derived from Mexico but possibly affected by introgression of maize and the native *Tripsacum* of the eastern Andean slopes.

In Utah, just west of the Colorado and Green rivers, and in a few valleys like the Yampa in Colorado, a pyramidal-eared dent corn, typical of western Mexico, has been found associated with Fremont culture sites, dated from about A.D. 1000 to 1150. Fremont dents traveled northward from the Mexican center of dent corn through the region about Zion Canyon and continued as far northward as the region of Yampa Canyon. They did not spread out, apparently had little or no influence outside the area affected by Fremont culture, and disappeared from the region with that culture.

There is no evidence of dent corn in what is now the United States until long after Europeans arrived. Apparently the first Spaniards out of Mexico brought little corn to the Southwest and depended upon the native varieties. Not until their return after the Pueblo Rebellion of 1680 did they bring the typical large-cobbed, many-rowed, long-eared, dent corn of western Mexico, which is the dominant recent corn of the Rio Grande pueblos. This is shown in an excellent series of pre-Rebellion and post-Rebellion specimens excavated by Herbert Dick at Picuris. There are no dents among the many corn specimens Alden Hayes recovered from Gran Quivira, which was abandoned just before the Pueblo Rebellion. Some of the corn from the mission of San Juan Capistrano in San Antonio, Texas, about 1762, is dent, whereas earlier sites in Texas had nondented corn. Our recent southern dents are almost identical to some of the dent corn races of Mexico. This fact and the absence of any pre-Columbian or even pre-Pueblo Rebellion specimens of dent corn from any area of the United States (except the isolated one occupied for a short time by Fremont people) indicate that southern dents were introduced by Europeans. It was from mixtures of these with the eight-rowed eastern and northern flints that our corn-belt corn was selected.

Before we discuss the spread of corn from the New World to the Old World, we must briefly review the origins of the squashes and pumpkins. All the twenty-six wild and cultivated species of *Cucurbita* are found in the New World, nearly all of them in Mexico and adjacent countries. All species, cultivated and wild, will cross with at least some of the other species, although some crosses can be made only with difficulty and after many attempts, and some crosses produce only sterile fruits (Whitaker and Davis, 1962).

Cucurbita pepo is the most northern of the cultivated annual species. Examples are the Halloween pumpkin, summer squashes, acorn, white-bush scallop, and zucchini (Cutler and Whitaker, 1961; Whitaker and Davis, 1962). *C. pepo* is the most common squash from the high valleys of Guatemala and Mexico to Canada; it is the most ancient squash in the United States and the only one grown in pre-Columbian times in areas north and east of the Southwest. It is associated with cool climates. Seeds found in the Ocampo caves of Tamaulipas are the oldest known for any of the cultivated species. Their seeds, however, may be from an early wild-growing, man-associated weed plant.

Cucurbita moschata is more tropical, found from Arizona to Peru and Brazil in prehistoric times, usually in the warmer regions. Examples are Kentucky field pumpkin and butternut squash. There are many variants in lowland tropical areas from Mexico to South America.

Cucurbita mixta is an unusual squash with a restricted distribution. The best known cultivar in the United States is green-striped cushaw, a cultivar found in many sites in the Southwest dated after A.D. 1000, and grown in the southern states. Two seeds from the El Riego phase of Tehuacán, about 6500–4800 B.C., may belong to this species, and there are good specimens from later phases.

Cucurbita maxima was restricted to South America in pre-Columbian times, and we have no very ancient archaeological specimens. It prefers cool climates. Modern examples are Hubbard, banana, and turban squashes, and mammoth chili pumpkin. *C. maxima* and the weedy *C. andreana* of Argentina with which it will hybridize are far removed geographically from most other cultivated and wild *Cucurbitas*. It has been suggested that both were carried by man to South America from Mexico. There is some similarity of *maxima* and *mixta*. Both have corky stems and series of forms with white-bodied and with brown-bodied seeds. It is difficult to distinguish the brown-bodied seeds of the Taos cultivar of *C. mixta* from some of the brown-bodied seeds of *C. maxima* and the hybrids of *C. maxima* × *C. andreana* found in eastern Bolivia.

No *C. maxima* or *C. mixta* has been collected between Peru and Mexico from archaeological sites and the few specimens grown there in recent times are post-Columbian introductions. The area is occupied by *C. moschata*. (A perennial squash, *C. ficifolia*, is also grown and is being studied.)

It is possible that very early weedy or wild species of *Cucurbita* were carried to South America and that *C. maxima* and *C. andreana* descended from these. Lanning (1965) and Engel (1963) have both reported on early preceramic settlements on the Peruvian coast. We recently studied fragments of gourd (*Lagenaria*) and unidentified *Cucurbita* species, perhaps wild, from one of Lanning's locations. This has recently been described from wild-growing material from Ecuador as a new species, *Cucurbita ecuadoriensis* (Cutler and Whitaker, 1969). This *Cucurbita* resembles the smallest ones, identified as *C. moschata*, from Huaca Prieta preceramic levels dated 3000–1000 B.C. (Whitaker and Bird, 1949). Bottle gourd is found in the same preceramic levels of Huaca Prieta. Recently we identified a fragment of gourd from a site near Talara, Peru, recovered by James B. Richardson and estimated to date about 5500–4500 B.C.

This suggests that early wild species of *Cucurbita* may have grown in the same places as wild-growing or weedy *Lagenaria*. Perhaps several *Cucurbita* species once grew as far south as the Andes, but the wild plants growing in the intervening area became extinct. Another possibility is that mature and almost mature fruits were carried to the coast of Peru or Ecuador before 5000 B.C. and grew and evolved to become the weedy plants gathered on the Peruvian coasts. These, then, may have been ancestors of *C. maxima* and *C. andreana*. This is speculation. Bottle gourds can float in sea water for nearly a year, lie exposed to great temperature and humidity changes for six years, and still contain viable seeds (Whitaker and Carter, 1961). Occasionally, we have found small, round, and ovoid fruits of the ornamental gourd *Cucurbita pepo* var. *ovifera* in beach drift along the Missouri, Mississippi, and Illinois rivers, bearing viable seed. Seeds of the wild southwestern species, *C. foetidissima, C. digitata,* and *C. palmata,* taken from fruits that have been stored for several years at room temperature, have germinated.

A few authors have claimed that cultivated plants offer certain proof of transoceanic human contacts. So far we have been unable to find any positive and undeniable evidence. That cotton and bottle gourd will float and that both have centers in Africa opens the possibility that the American forms were carried by the prevailing winds and currents running northwestward from Africa. But if *Lagenaria* was wild and did drift from Africa, why do we not find it still growing wild in some places?

A secondary center for *Cucurbita pepo* and the great importance of *pepo* from the Balkans to Turkey and adjacent southwestern Asia suggested to Vavilov that this might be a center for the species. The kinds of corn and *pepo* grown there are the same ones found associated on the Gulf Coast and the Caribbean. In the same areas of the Old World sunflowers are frequently grown. When one considers the trade routes of the early Spanish, this similarity in crops of the two areas is not surprising. Witthoft (1966) has mentioned the persistent trade in gun flints between the Balkans and Spain, and the lists of seamen on the early ships include Italians and Greeks, who are likely to have carried these plants home.

In southeast Asia, the group of cultivated plants is different. There the plants are distinctly South American, in particular from the west coast, south of central Peru. So far we have found no indisputable evidence for pre-Columbian introduction. The major cultivated squash found in India and other regions of Southeast Asia is *Cucurbita maxima*. The corn is typically South American, and there are records of peanut, of the South American amaranth, *Bixa,* of several species of *Inga,* of *Capsicum* sp. peppers, and of papaya and sweet potato (Drury, 1858). Many of the common beans (*Phaseolus vulgaris*) we have seen from India are varieties typical of coastal Chile and Peru.

The diversity of forms of *Cucurbita moschata* in China and the origin of the many New World food plants grown there have been studied, and nearly all authorities agree that these can be traced back only to post-Columbian introductions. The fact that closely related wild species and ancient archaeological remains of corn and squash are only found in the New World seems proof that their origins must be American.

The similarity of the assemblage of New World crops grown in southwest Asia to those of the Gulf and Caribbean region and the similarity of New World crops of Southeast Asia to those of Peru and Chile indicate that these regions had extensive contacts. There are records of such contacts in early post-Columbian times.

21. Pre-Columbian Maize in Asia

M. D. W. JEFFREYS

Introduction

Zea mays is an American plant, but there is considerable
evidence that maize was cultivated in Asia even before Columbus
discovered America. Because maize is incapable of self-propagation,
its presence, wherever it is found, implies an introduction by man.
The issues of who initially brought maize to Asia and by what routes
are, however, beyond the scope of this paper (see Jeffreys, 1963).[1]

The antiquity of maize in the East Indian Archipelago had, 150
years ago, impressed Crawfurd, the British resident at the court of
the Sultan of Java in 1808. As a result of his investigations in the Indian Archipelago, Crawfurd was convinced that maize had been cultivated there before the discovery of the Americas and concluded
that maize was indigenous to these islands. Crawfurd (1820: I, 365)
wrote:

After rice, maize or Turkey corn (Zea Maiz) is the most important production of agriculture among the great tribes of the Archipelago. The word,
Jegung, which I imagine to be purely native, is the term by which this plant

[1] I must stress the fact that maize is an American plant because Stamp (1968)
in a recent abstract stated not only that I have shown maize to be "an Old
World crop" but also that Professor Hui-Lin Li has demonstrated how it could
have reached America. Neither of us has ever written anything like this. Each
accepts the New World origin of maize.

is known from one extremity of the Archipelago to another. There can, therefore, be little doubt, as in the case of rice, that one tribe instructed all the rest in its cultivation. As far as a matter of this nature is capable of demonstrating it may also be conjectured, that maize was cultivated in the Indian islands before the discovery of America, and that the plant is an indigenous product.

Rev. Leibbrandt (1882) also claimed that maize was indigenous to Amboyna, one of the Molucca islands. While agreeing with Crawfurd that "one tribe instructed all the rest . . . [and] that maize was cultivated in the Indian islands before the discovery of America," I cannot accept the claim that maize was indigenous to the Old World.

MAIZE INTRODUCED BY THE ARABS

What was the tribe that introduced maize under the name of *jegung* to the Indian Archipelago? Arab trade by sea and land shows that Arabs were the distributors. Hence a preliminary study of such trade is essential. Hirth and Rockhill (1911: 14) wrote: "By the beginning of the seventh century the foreign colony at Canton, mostly composed of Persians and Arabs, must have been a numerous one, for Islam seems to have been brought there between 618 and 628. . . . By the middle of the eighth century the Mohammedans at Canton— which they called Khanfu—had become so numerous that in 758 they were able . . . to sack and burn the city." Kenyon (1931: 262) wrote: "At the time of the revolution in Canton in 876, there were said to be 120,000 Mohammedans, Jews and Christians and Parsees in the city, many of whom were killed. The Persian trade, no longer supported by a strong empire at home, did not survive this blow, and their place in the Chinese trade was taken by the Arabs."

When Europeans entered these waters they found Arabs established in every port from Arabia to Canton. According to Hazard (1954: 41). "By 1290 they had acquired a permanent toe hold at Parlak on the tip of Sumatra and from there they spread along the coasts and into the other islands, settling in the ports, marrying native girls, adopting the local language and culture, allying themselves with the aristocracy, purchasing slaves, and finally converting the coastal rulers and people. . . . The Southern Philippines adopted Islam shortly before the arrival of the Spanish." Magellan, according to Robertson's (1906: I, 135) translation of Pigafetta's account, met Arabs at the court of the King of Cebu.

It is now necessary to review the ancient Asiatic caravan trade, which later became an Arab monopoly. Before Christ, the land route, according to Mackiner (1929: XXII, 369), "through the heart of Asia had penetrated to northern China, and silk from that source was finding its way to the Mediterranean through Tyre. . . . The fact that at this time [the twelfth and thirteenth centuries] a single race, the Arabs, dominated the caravan tracks of the near East and also the seaways of the Indian Ocean undoubtedly favoured the development of the trade with the Middle and Far East." Bretschneider (1888: I, 267, 269) wrote:

There can . . . be no doubt that at the time of the T'ang [dynasty, A.D. 618–907] many Mohammedans were settled in China. In early times, when the Chinese began to extend their power over the countries west of China proper, they denominated them by the general term *Si yü*, or *western countries*. It seems this name came first into use when Chang K'ien had returned from western Asia [136 B.C.]. In the history of the former Han . . . where the countries of the *Si yü* are first described, it is stated that the *Si yü* begins at the Chinese fortresses of *Yü men kuan* and *Yang kuan*. Both were situated in the western part of the present *Kansu*, west of *Kia yü kuan*, one of the principal gates of the Great Wall. . . . The name of *Si yü* is still applied in a general sense to the same regions of Central and Western Asia inhabited by Mohammedan people. . . . In the T'ang history, where they are first mentioned, they go under the name of *Ta shi* (Arabs). *Hui-hui* is now the common Chinese name for all professors of Islamism. . . . The Mongol emperors patronized the colonization of China by foreigners; and with respect to the Mohammedans, it seems that since Hulagu, the brother of Mangu Khan, ruled over western Asia, emigration from Persia to China had considerably increased.

Hazard (1954: 42) remarked that "Kublai Khan (1260–1294) appointed many Persian officials, who encouraged Moslem immigration, especially in Yünnan, and a steady influx continued until the Ming revolt of 1368/9. Thereafter gradual infiltration, some conversion, rapid reproduction—the Chinese imperial census estimated six persons per Moslem family, to five for other Chinese—and purchase of Chinese children in times of famine increased the Moslem population so that they may now be estimated at five per cent of China's proper 400,000,000." Concerning these western foreigners, Ping-ti Ho (1955: 195) wrote: "Ever since the beginning of the Ming period (1368–1644) these western tribesmen, who had a great demand for

Chinese fabrics and especially for tea, had been trading their horses for Chinese products at various government trading posts along that thousand mile frontier."[2] This merchandise passed to Europe through the hands of the Arabs along the Great Silk Road. This road was equally available for the reverse transportation of maize.

Botanists and the Antiquity of Maize in Asia

The type of maize found along these trade routes is important. Stonor and Anderson (1949: 383) described the maize found among the Naga and other tribes of Assam: "Types of maize fairly similar to those grown around the Caribbean basin are widely distributed in the Orient and were apparently introduced by the Spanish." The evidence that will follow does not support the conclusion that the Spaniards introduced this type of maize. These authors observed that these types of maize "seem to be the prevailing type in the Philippines and in Guam and they or mixtures of them make up the bulk of the maize grown in Asia, particularly at lower elevations and along the coasts." These two botanists pointed out (Stonor and Anderson, 1949: 387) that before 1928 Russian plant research into types of Asiatic maize "demonstrates that varieties similar to those described from the Naga country are widespread in central Asia from Persia and Turkestan to Tibet and Siberia." It is apparent that Caribbean types of maize are found along the Arabian Sea and land trade routes.

Some Characteristics of Asian Maize

The Russian botanist, N. N. Kuleshov, who published in 1928 the results of his investigations, was also impressed with the antiquity of maize in Asia. As translated by Kidd and Reynolds (1954: 271–299), Kuleshov reported waxy maize as peculiar to eastern Asia, with a wide distribution from 5° to 45° north latitude. He noted that "dwarf plants are peculiar to vast areas of central Asia; while the sheltering of the panicles by the upper leaves and the concealment of the silking ears in the leaf sheaths are encountered in eastern and central Asia, Transcaucasia, etc."[3] He continued: "we arrived at the

[2] This and subsequent quotations from Ping-ti Ho, "American Food Plants in China," are reproduced by permission of the American Anthropological Association from the *American Anthropologist*, 57 (1955): 194, 195.

[3] This and subsequent quotations from Kidd and Reynolds' translation are used by permission of the *Annals of the Missouri Botanical Garden*.

conclusion that in the maizes of Asia we have observed an array of characters and peculiarities which are unknown in America, or which are extremely rare in America." Kuleshov reviewed the work of Vavilov and concluded that "the striking facts . . . inevitably lead to the idea that Asian maize, if it be not viewed as native, at any rate is very ancient. These characteristics which are seen in Asiatic maize attest to this explanation. . . . Waxy endosperm, which was discovered in Asiatic maize, was also discovered in the most ancient crop of Asia— sorgo. Dwarfness, which is characteristic of Asiatic maize, is also a characteristic of sorgo, flax, and other ancient crops. But these characters are found in large areas, and for them to be manifest in maize, time, of course, is required." Kuleshov, alluding to another worker in this field, remarked, "If we agree with Collins, we must assume that waxy endosperm arose in the maize in Asia by means of mutation and has its place of origin in Upper Burmah, which is largely peopled by wild tribes with whom even to-day it is almost impossible for aliens to have intercourse."

Kuleshov stated the crux as he saw it: "Now concerning the time interval in question, one must understand when and how maize could have been removed from America into this isolated wild land, given there a mutation and as a mutant diffused from the Philippines to Manchuria." He offered a tentative solution: ". . . as a conjecture we should suppose that likely there was an earlier cultivation of maize in Asia than the time of the first landing by the Portuguese on the shores of Asia in 1516. . . . The facts, which were established by us, return us anew to this supposition and this time with a great deal of conviction."

I shall proceed to examine in detail India, the Philippines, China, Persia, and Asia Minor for evidence of maize in Asia earlier than the first arrival of Europeans.

INDIA

The earliest European reference to maize in Asia comes from Portuguese sources. Duarte Barbosa, who controlled Portuguese interests in the Orient from 1500 to 1516, left a record of his administration. Dames's (1918: I, 155) translation of Barbosa's conquests gives Barbosa's description of the merchandise exported from Gujarat as including "abundance of wheat and of great millet [milho grosso]." Today *milho grosso* in any Portuguese dictionary means

Zea mays. Boxer (1952a: 178) wrote, "I daresay there are earlier Portuguese references to *milho grosso* than 1712 but so far I have not come across them." But the next instance I have found is much earlier and comes from the Americas, the home of maize. De Macedo (1817: 117), a Portuguese, stated in 1675 that in America *milho grosso* was the food of the Indians. The next instance of the use of the term *milho grosso* indicates a period before the discovery of America and refers to the Portuguese tradition of the arrival of maize in Portugal from Guinea. Ribeiro (1941: 657), quoting from the *Elucidario* under the heading *Maçaroca,* wrote: "In the time of King John II [1481–1495] on the discovery of Guinea, so say some authors, the Portuguese discovered the *milho grosso de maçaroca* and brought it to Portugal." There can be no two opinions over what is meant by this cereal; it is maize, as Ribeiro pointed out when he gave an alternative name, "milho americano [maize]." Bock in 1532 referred to maize as "great wheat." Maize is often described by the name of an Old World cereal prefixed by a word meaning "great." Consequently one may take Barbosa's "milho grosso" to be maize. Moore (1785: I, 280), in his translation of the raid in 1508 by Cunna and Albuquerque on Socotra in the Red Sea, mentioned that "the common food is maize or Indian wheat, tamarinds and milk.' Cortesão (1944: I, 44) in his translation of Tomé Pires' administrative work in India, which was published in Portugal in 1514, listed the following merchandise in Cambay: "wheat, barley, millet, sesame oil, rice." The Portuguese word translated as *millet* was *milho.* I (Jeffreys, 1967a: 24–40) have shown that by 1505 *milho,* as used for example, at Sofala, meant maize to the Portuguese.

"The most general vernacular name in India" for maize is, according to Watt (1908: 1132), "makhai (Mecca corn)." Inquiries in India have elicited the following variations. Maize is known as "*Makhai* in north India and as *Mecca cholam* in the Tamil parts of India. In the Andhra areas of the Madras Presidency it goes by the name of *Mokka jonna.* In the Canarese speaking areas it is known as *Mekka jola.* All the three suffixes mentioned i.e. *cholam, jonna, jola* mean sorghum. In the whole of southern India maize is known as Mekka sorghum, the word sorghum being rendered into the respective local Indian languages. The names all strongly point to the fact that maize has come from Mecca" (Sri. P. Krishna Rao, L. Ag. Assoc. I. A. R. I., personal communication). In other words, maize was introduced by Arabs. Gode (1950: 8) gave a similar list of maize names and then commented, "In particular it would be useful to study historically the terms: *Makā, Makka, Makai, Mukka,* and *Mukha.*"

Vishnu-Mittre, (1966: 155)[4] describing carbonized food grains and their impressions on potsherds from Kaundinyapar, an archaeological site in Madhya Pradesh, north India, wrote that "the evidence of maize in India is not in any case later than 1435 A.D. . . . and tends to establish its pre-Columbian age." Vishnu-Mittre and Gupta (1966: 176, 184) in their study of pollen grains wrote: "The paper describes the pollen statistics of ten primitive varieties of maize from Assam and Mexico. The pollen statistical data are used to recognize sub-fossil maize pollen from amongst the pollen of Cerealia recovered from the Post glacial deposits of Kashmir valley." These two researchers then concluded that "taking into consideration the lowest extreme size and high pore-axis ratio of subfossil pollen in stages 'e' and 'f' approaching that of maize it may be said that the maize cultivation in Kashmir began in the thirteenth-fourteenth century." Maize cultivation did not start in Kashmir, and therefore it must have been cultivated elsewhere in Asia earlier still.

THE PHILIPPINES AND BEYOND

The evidence of Magellan's voyage showed that his arrival in the Philippines had been preceded by the arrival of Arabs. The earlier arrival of the Arabs offers an explanation for Magellan's finding maize there as a cultivated crop. On April 7, 1521, Magellan's ships anchored off the island of Cebu, and, according to Robertson's translation (1906: I, 135), "the Moro merchants said to the King . . . 'These men are the same who have conquered Calicut, Malacca, and all India Majiora.'" *Moro* is a form of the word *Moor,* used to designate Arabs and Muslims.

Weatherwax (1954: 35) remarked, though on what authority he did not disclose, that "Magellan's voyage introduced Caribbean and Mexican varieties [of maize] into the East Indies and the Philippines, from which they soon spread to the mainland of eastern Asia." What, however, are the facts?

---

[4] Dr. Edna Plumstead, Department of Paleontology, Witwatersrand University, Johannesburg, South Africa, kindly drew my attention to this article.

On March 16, 1521, Magellan, out of food, his crews starving and reduced to boiling old bits of leather for sustenance, reached the eastern shores of Suma Island in the Philippines. His ships provided the first contacts that the Philippines had had with Europeans. Magellan had never visited the coasts of Mexico or the Caribbean Sea, and his starving crews would have demolished any grain that he might have been conveying. Sturtevant (1919: 616; quoting A. Adams, *Voy. Samarang* II, 424, 1824), noted that "in 1521 maize was found by Magellan at the island of Limasava." Krieger (1942: 23) likewise was satisfied that Pigafetta, an Italian chronicler who sailed with Magellan in 1519, had observed the cultivation of maize on the island of Limasava.

During his stay in the Philippines, Magellan loaded up with local food stuffs, and, according to Richardson's account (1789: 496), the islanders "invited the General into their boats, in which were their merchandise, viz. cloves, cinnamon, ginger, pepper, nutmegs, maize and gold made in divers things which they carry to and from in their boats." On consulting the original Italian text, one finds that the word translated as *maize* is the Italian word *miglio*. In this context the meaning of *miglio* may be checked by reference to Pigafetta's own Brazilian notes, in which he wrote against the Italian word *miglio* the Caribbean word *maiz*. Sauer (1960: 784) pointed out that part of Magellan's crew were Spaniards who had been in the Caribbean, where the local name for this American grain was *maiz*. It was from them that Pigafetta learned that there *miglio* was called *maiz*. "As *miglio*, the grain, was familiar, the new thing about it was that it had an Indian name."

Although the late Professor Merrill (1954: 364) was unable to find any evidence that maize was cultivated in the Philippines before the arrival of Magellan in 1521, I have found ample evidence that maize was then already a staple crop. According to Robertson's (1960; I, 128) Italian text, among other items cultivated by these islanders were "rizo . . . miglio, panizo, sorgo." *Rizo, panizo,* and *sorgo* are clearly rice, panicum, and sorghum. These cereals grow in the Philippines. From this list it is clear that there is no confusion of *miglio* with other known grains. Pigafetta (1906: 164, 182) also mentioned cakes of "rizo et miglio" and stated that on the island of Zubu [Cebu in the Philippines] were found "cani gati rizo millio [*sic*] panizo sorgo gengero." Here the Portuguese term *millio* (maize) is used for the more usual Italian *miglio*. *Millio* or *milho* was at that date a well-established Portuguese name for maize (Jeffreys, 1967a, 1967b). In his Philippine word list, Pigafetta (1906: 186) gave the Italian names for the corresponding Philippine names for a number of local cereals.

Al Rizo	bughaz baras
Al Miglio	humas
Al Sorgo	batat
Al Panizo	dana

Here one recognizes the cereals rice, maize, sorghum, and millet. The corresponding Philippine words, with the exception of *humas*, which has disappeared, still exist with the same meanings as listed by Pigafetta. Consequently there is no occasion to doubt the accuracy of Pigafetta's observations. Pigafetta (1906: 154) also remarked that "the round pepper grows . . . in ears like Indian corn and is shelled off; and is called *lada*." So it is evident that Pigafetta knew what Indian corn, or maize, looked like, and there is no reason for not treating his evidence on maize in the Philippines seriously.

It is interesting to note the late Professor Merrill's handling of Pigafetta's evidence for maize in the Philippines. He expected to find the actual word *mais* in Pigafetta's text and, not finding it, concluded that maize was nonexistent when Magellan arrived there. Merrill's (1954: 364) remarks on his inability to find *mais* in Pigafetta's text run as follows: "I have read through the Italian and English text of Robertson's account of 1906 without locating any statement about maize in the Philippines. Because *mais* does not appear in the detailed 88-page index, I scanned, as a last resort, all the explanatory notes and found the answer in note 370 of the first volume (p. 269)."[5] Why Merrill should expect to find in use in the Philippines in 1521 a Brazilian word, *maiz*, as a name for a cereal in this region is incomprehensible. The word *maiz* was new to Pigafetta, but what of Pigafetta's use of the Italian word *miglio*, a well-established word for maize?

The reference that Merrill found occurred in a footnote by the editor. Merrill unconcernedly continued: "The reference is from 'Al

[5] E. D. Merrill, *The Botany of Cook's Voyages*, Copyright 1954 The Ronald Press Company, New York. This and subsequent quotations are used by permission of the publisher.

panizo' = *dana* (correctly *daua*) = *Panicum* = *Setaria italica* (L.) Beauv. (pp. 183, 187). The note is a confused one and reads: 'The equivalent of Pigafetta's *dana* is *daoa* or *daua*, Millet. *Mais*, (our Maize), probably the equivalent of *humas*, is the word for *panicum*.'" Merrill (1954: 186) adds: "Pigafetta correctly recorded *miglio*, the classical millet (*Panicum miliaceum* L.) which was widely cultivated in Italy from Roman times on, as well as in India and China and, to a less degree, in Malaysia and the Philippines." Merrill concerned himself with an editor's guesswork in a footnote, instead of with Pigafetta's Italian text itself. Merrill wrote that Pigafetta recorded *miglio* as the classical millet (*Panicum miliaceum*), but Pigafetta never once had mentioned *Panicum miliaceum* under the name *miglio*. He does call *mais* in Brazil *al miglio*, and *humas* in the Philippines *al miglio*.

The present exposition of Pigafetta's observations has revealed what Merrill omitted to disclose. Merrill (1954: 364) also wrote: "We have no modern record of any plant name corresponding to *humas* in the Philippines: but, in 1521, this name was surely used in Negros for *Panicum miliaceum* L., an ancient, Old World cultigen." This is baseless speculation. It is safer to rely on the evidence of Pigafetta, an observer, who in 1519 recorded that *miglio* represented *maiz* in Brazil and in 1521 that *miglio* represented *humas* in the Philippines, and to accept that in each instance the grain was *Zea mays*. Both *maiz* and *humas* were for Pigafetta new words, indigenous native names for a cereal already known to him as *al miglio*.

Sauer (1960: 784) summed up the situation succinctly: "In the Vizayan part of the Philippine islands Pigafetta noted miglio/millio repeatedly. This may be entered as the first record of maize in the Philippines, antedating by half a century the introduction from New Spain. Pigafetta may be accepted as knowing what he saw. He was not only a good observer, but (1) he had been correct in Brazil in identifying miglio with maize, (2) he recognised sorghum when he saw it in the Philippines . . . , (3) when forced tribute was levied on the Vizayan natives these were required to bring equal quantities of rice and miglio, rice and maize being most desirable and familiar as ships stores to those who had sailed African shores."

The presence of the Arab and of maize in the Philippines, both reported by Pigafetta in 1521, clears up the anomalies that faced

Stonor, Anderson, and others in their researches on the antiquity of
maize in Asia.[6] The only authentic Portuguese claim to introducing
maize to any people in the Old World is that of introducing it to
Japan. In Formosa and Japan, further north, the names for maize
are respectively *fan meh* and *nan bamthbi;* both mean "foreign
grain." But another Japanese name for maize, according to Buxton
(1929: 100), is "southern barbarian millet." The Japanese referred to
the Portuguese as "southern barbarians."

CHINA

Chinese sources provide the earliest documentary indications so
far of pre-Columbian maize in Asia. Duyvendak (1949: 30) called
attention to six Chinese expeditions by sea to east Africa between
1405 and 1422. Malinde was one of the ports visited. These Chinese
navigators sent to China accounts of things they had seen. Duyvendak
(1949: 32) records that in the years previous to the arrival of a giraffe
at the Imperial Court in 1414 "several supernatural appearances had
been reported, such as vegetarian tigers, extraordinary large ears of
grain, sweet dew." At first this Chinese report raises skepticism, but
"sweet dew" was also described on the east African coast by Dos
Santos in 1597.[7] "Vegetarian tigers" is an obvious description of the
zebra by those who knew only the striped Indian tiger. The skin of
the Indian tiger and that of the African zebra are superficially alike—
each has dark stripes on a light background. One is a carnivore, the
other a vegetarian. As for "the extraordinary large ears of grain," only
maize would fit the description. The size of maize would strike the
Chinese, who, according to Candolle (1967: 355), have annually
since 2200 B.C. ceremonially sown five kinds of seeds—wheat, rice,
sorghum, *setaria italica,* and soy. None of these cereals carry "extraordinary large ears." This date of about 1414 for maize is

[6] There remains now to connect the Arab with Caribbean maize before Columbus' discovery of the Americas. I have dealt with the Arab as the probable
introducer to the Old World of the Caribbean type of maize in pre-Columbian
times in four articles (see Jeffreys, 1953, 1954, 1967a, 1967b).

[7] "In the wilderness of the Ile Cabo de Gado is a store of Manna, procreated
by the dew of Heaven falling on certain trees, on which it hardens as it were
Sugar candide, sticking to the wood like Rozin, and hanging on the leaves is
gathered and sold in jarres by the inhabitants. It tastes sweet as Sugar. . . . I
have often been in the place, and gathered it with my hand. It grows only on one
kind, although there be many other trees in the Island" (Purchas, 1905: X, 250).

not beyond the realm of possibility for pre-Columbian maize in Africa (Jeffreys, 1967a, 1967b).

Maize in China itself appears to have entered by the Great Silk Road and at an early date. Candolle scorned the idea. For him, maize entered China from the sea, brought by the Portuguese. Candolle's claim is made in the teeth of evidence available from historical sources.

One source is Li Shih-chên's *Pun Ts'ao Kang-mu,* begun, according to Bonafous, in 1552 and completed in 1578. A reproduction of the illustration of maize in this book appears in Bonafous' *Histoire Naturelle, Agricolle et Economique de Mais,* published in 1836. In the Chinese book the item on maize does not refer to it as being newly introduced. In fact, Li Shi-chên stated that maize was introduced from lower Mongolia—that is, from the west—at an early date. Candolle (1836: 392) held that "the importation through Mongolia is improbable to such a degree that it is hardly worth speaking of it." Even if maize had reached China overland, he claimed that it also reached China by sea. He held that it "may be admitted that maize was brought to China after the discovery of America. The Portuguese came to Java in 1496, that is to say four years after the discovery of America, and to China in 1516. Magellan's voyage from South America to the Philippine Islands took place in 1520. During the fifty-eight or seventy-seven years between 1516 and the dates assigned in the Chinese work, seeds of maize may have been taken to China by navigators from America or from Europe." Candolle's dates are inaccurate. He stated that the Portuguese reached Java in 1496, but Vasco da Gama crossed the Indian Ocean only in 1498. The Portuguese reached Java in 1511. Magellan reached the Philippines in 1521, without bringing any maize. However, these are minor inaccuracies. What is of greater importance is the relations between Chinese and Europeans during the "fifty-eight or seventy-seven years" that intervened between 1516 and the appearance of Li Shih-chên's work. Candolle ignored them.

The opportunities for the introduction of maize into China by the Portuguese were nonexistent. Boxer (1953: xix, xx, xxi) pointed out that in 1498, "when the Portuguese opened the maritime route round the Cape of Good Hope to India, the emperors of the Ming dynasty, reversing the expansionist policy of the third emperor, Yung-lo (1403–1424), which had carried Chinese fleets as far as the Persian

Gulf and the Somali coast, officially forbade their subjects from emigrating or trading overseas, on pain of death. . . . In 1517, a Portuguese squadron commanded by Fernão Pires de Andrade, carrying Tomé Pires as ambassador, anchored in the Pearl River off Canton."[8] This is the first recorded contact between the Portuguese and China. The isolationist policy of the emperor is disclosed in what follows. This policy minimized contacts with Europeans and reduced the possibility of introducing maize.

Boxer continued: "After some hesitation on the part of the Chinese, Tomé Pires was eventually allowed to proceed to Peking and Fernão Pires de Andrade established peaceful and profitable relations with the local officials at Canton." However, the arrogant, swashbuckling behavior of the Portuguese on their next visit so enraged the Chinese that "Tomé Pires and his suite were sent back to Canton, where they were arrested, tortured and imprisoned. Some of them were executed; others, including the ambassador himself, died of the hardships to which they were subjected. . . . The Portuguese ships which attempted to renew the trade in 1521–22 were forcibly expelled . . . and an imperial decree was promulgated, banning all dealings with the 'barbarian devils' or fan-kuei, as well as with other foreigners." It was not until 1557, according to Prestage (1933: 309), that the Portuguese were allowed to settle in Macau.

It was in such an atmosphere of hostility and exclusion, with the death penalty for trafficking with foreigners, that Candolle expected maize to have been introduced by the Portuguese.

Candolle's judgments were based on little evidence. Laufer (1919: 205) summarized Candolle's position: ". . . it must be said that since his days Oriental studies have made such rapid strides, that his notes with regard to India, China and Japan, are thoroughly out of date. As to China, he possessed no other information than the superficial remarks of Bretschneider in his *Study and Value of Chinese Botanical Works* which teem with misunderstandings and errors. De Candolle's conclusions as to things Chinese are no longer acceptable."

The *Nung Chêng Ts'üan Shu* was also published in the Ming dyn-

---

[8] C. R. Boxer, *South China in the Sixteenth Century*, Hakluyt Society, 2d series, vol. 106 (London: Cambridge University Press, 1953). This and subsequent quotations are used by permission of the publisher.

asty (1368–1644) and attracted the attention of European scholars. The date of the first introduction of maize interested Hance, who persuaded W. F. Mayers, Her Britannic Majesty's vice-consul at Canton to engage Chinese scholars to search Chinese records, including the *Nung Chêng Ts'üan Shu,* the *Kê Chih King-yüan,* or *Mirror of Classified Research,* published in 1753 by Chên Yüan-lung, and the *Pun Ts'ao Kang-mu.*

Hance and Mayers (1870: 523) wrote, on the assertion in the *Pun Ts'ao Kang-mu's* statement for the origin of maize in the countries to the west of China, as follows:

I am far from maintaining that the evidence adduced is sufficient to establish the claims of Asia to rank as a native country of this cereal. But, for my own part, I am much disposed to coincide in a remark made to me by Mr. Mayers, "that the unhesitating statement of the *Pun Ts'ao Kang-mu,* as to its [maize's] origin in the countries west of China, goes a considerable way to-wards establishing this origin, the assertion being so unqualified that I think it must be founded on antecedent evidence, although this is now untraceable." And I may add that in my judgement, the remote date assigned by Chinese records to its [maize's] introduction, and the circumstances that the introducer is unknown are irreconcilable with the supposition that it was brought into this country by the Portuguese.

Hance and Mayers (1870: 524) stated that maize "was first brought from Si-Fan; but of the period at which this took place there is no word. It is further noted that this grain was heretofore presented as tribute, but again no date is assigned. It is evident that its introduction must have taken place at a very early period, as, at the time when these works were compiled, no information could be procured." According to Hance and Mayers (1870: 525), the *Kê Chih King-yüan* stated that "Yü-me or Imperial Wheat originated in the Si-fan territory (the lands beyond the western frontier of China Proper)." The authors pointed out that the territory to the northwest of Tibet, Inner Mongolia, had "been known to the Chinese from the earliest times by the name of Si-fan" and that this "western alien territory" borders on the present territories of Sz'ch'uan and Kan-su" (Hance and Mayers, 1870: 523). An earlier name for Si-fan was Si-yü. It was in Kan-su that there was a large settlement of Arabs.

Linguistic evidence offered in the historical sources strongly supports an early importation from the west. Hance and Mayers (1870:

523, 525) noted that maize "having been formerly presented as tribute . . . is called imperial wheat, Yü-mě"; that having originated in
the Si-fan territory, an ancient Chinese name for maize "*Fan-mé,* or
wheat of the foreign lands of the west"; that "from its seed having
been brought originally from the country of Si-fan, it is likewise
called *Fan-mé* or Fan wheat" (wheat of the western barbarians).

Hance and Mayers (1870: 523) also noted that maize under the
name "*Pao-ku* is identical with *Yü shŭ-shú* or the jade-like *shü* millet."
In their second example there is a possibility that there is another
synonym for Arabs or westerners or foreigners, as *Si-fan* has also
been known as *Si yü.* Hance and Mayers (1870: 525) also noted that
"in the neighbourhood of Peking" the "common name" for maize is
"*yü-mi* or jade rice." Merrill (1954: 290) remarked that "on the sea
board of eastern China (Kiansu province) the common name for
maize is still *yu shu shu* which means 'jade millet of the west.' " Merrill added that "there was no doubt in the minds of the Chinese . . .
that it originally came . . . from the west, and not from the sea route."
Weatherwax (1954: 133) wrote that the name *yü-cho-shu,* which is
but another way of writing *yü-shŭ-shú,* breaks up into *yü,* meaning
"gem" or "precious stone," and *cho-shu,* meaning "sorghum." It depends, I presume, upon the tones actually employed whether *yü-
shŭ-shú* may mean the gemlike sorghum or the sorghum of the west.

Heine-Geldern (1958: 369), discussing early maize in China, remarked: "All these early Chinese reports on maize state consistently
that maize came to them from Tibet and the western parts of China.
They therefore call it, among other names, *Hsi fan mai,* 'Tibetan
wheat.' Of special importance is a statement by T'ien-I-heng: 'Maize
(*yu mai,* "Imperial wheat") is produced in Tibet (*Hsi fan*). Its former
name is "Tibetan wheat" (*Fan mai*). Since it was formerly brought
as tribute to the court, it received for this reason the name "Imperial
wheat" (*yu mai*).' " T'ien-I-heng apparently lived in the mid-sixteenth
century, according to Heine-Geldern.

The information from Chinese sources is corroborated by data
from European sources. A Portuguese emissary to China in 1575,
Martin de Rada, is quoted by Boxer (1953: 277) in his translation
as recording that among the taxes paid in kind as tribute to the
Chinese emperor was one of "another kind of grain, 139, 535 quin-
tals." Boxer (1952b: 179), had noted: "Juan Gonzales de Mendoza,
OSA, *Historia de las cosas maz notables ritos y costumbres del gran*

Reino de la China (Rome 1585, Pt. I. Bk. III, Cap. 4) in a list which
he gives of the tribute paid annually to the Emperor of China by his
subjects, after mentioning rice, 'trigo como el de España' and milho
(modern mijo), has an item—'De trigo clamado maize, veinte
millones doscientas circuenta [*sic*] mil fanegas'—which implies that a
great quantity of maize was grown in China as early as 1575, which
was the year in which Mendoza's informants had visited China."

Boxer (1953: 277), commenting on 20.25 million *fanegas*, or bushels
of maize paid in taxes in 1575, remarked: "This seems to be rather an
early date for the large scale cultivation of maize in China, but Gonzales de Mendoza refers elsewhere to its growth—'between these
trees they sow maize, which is the ordinary food of the Indians of
Mexico and Peru' (*Historia*, pt. I. Bk. I, Ch. iii)." From the reference
to Mexico and Peru it is clear that Mendoza knew what grain he
meant. Boxer was highly skeptical of the alleged recent introduction
of maize into China and wrote that "the spread of maize from the
New World to the Old World merits further study." For maize to be
brought by foreigners to Peking as tribute in such quantities in
1575, maize must have been a well-established crop cultivated by
these western foreigners long before 1540—say by 1510. As these
western foreigners were not in touch with either the Portuguese or
the Spaniards, they must have obtained maize from places farther
west, where maize would have been growing long before 1510—
say by 1490. Columbus returned in 1493 from his first voyage to
America. Whatever the dating be, it is evident that maize was being
cultivated in places west of China in pre-Columbian times.

There is a further interesting source in the *Chu-fan-chi* of the
Chinese historian, Chau Ju-kua, compiled, according to Hirth and
Rockhill (1911: 35), about A.D. 1250. In Hirth and Rockhill's translation (1911: 48), Chau Ju-kua mentioned that the people of Annam
"have no wheat; but have millet, hemp and beans. . . . As to fruits,
they have the lotus, sugar-cane, bananas and cocoanuts." These fruits
are tropical rainforest fruits and the rainfall in Annam is heavy, being
anything from sixty inches a year upward. This high rainfall accounts
for the absence of wheat. Indeed, there are no cereals, except rice
and maize, which could be successfully cultivated under these humid
conditions. The translators have a footnote: "*Su* which is rendered
as 'millet' in the text, is in more modern works used for maize, Indian
corn (Hirth and Rockhill, 1911: 50, n. 6). Here is an example of the

manner in which evidence of the antiquity of maize may be buried by presuming that a word in the literature of the Old World cannot refer to a New World plant before 1492. *Su* today stands for maize in Chinese. If it is claimed that *su* stood for some other cereal, then the onus is on that claimant to show how *su* ceased to apply to that other cereal or how it came to apply to maize, what that other cereal was, and what it is called today. If one accepts that *su* stands for maize in this Chinese context, then there is a written record of maize cultivation in Indo-China about A.D. 1250, the date to which Firth and Rockhill assign the work of Chau Ju-kua.

Three sixteenth-century Chinese references are noted by Ping-ti Ho. Though he is skeptical about a pre-Columbian introduction of this American cereal into China, the works he mentioned yield interesting data. Ping-ti Ho (1955: 194) wrote: "So far, the earliest reference to maize is found in the 1555 edition of the history of Kung-hsien, a district in western Honan. . . . Since this locality is far from the southeast coast and the Yunnan Burma border, the two regions where a New World crop was likely to be brought into China, and since it took considerable time for a new crop to be grown on a scale sufficiently significant to be recorded in local history, it seems reasonable to suggest that maize was introduced into China at least two or three decades prior to its first written account." This conclusion implies that, on Ping-ti Ho's reckoning, maize was being cultivated in central China by about 1525.

Ping-ti Ho (1955: 194) also noted that in the *Ta-li fuchih* edition of 1563 and in the *Yannan t'ung-chih* edition of 1574, maize "is recorded as being grown in six prefectures and two department counties, mostly in the western and northwestern parts of the province." Ping-ti Ho (1955: 195) added: "It is fairly certain that maize was first brought to Peking as tribute by . . . western tribesmen before the middle of the sixteenth century, hence the early Chinese name for maize, *yü-mai* (Imperial wheat) and its early vulgar name, the homonym, *yü mai* (jade wheat)."

Three points require consideration. First, between 1525 and 1563 the cultivation of maize had become common in six prefectures and two department counties. Second, the quantity of maize paid in 1575 as tribute, not the total quantity grown, was over twenty million bushels. On the basis of this quantity any agronomist would reject 1525 as the date for the first arrival of maize in China. Third, maize is stated to have entered China from the west. Before reaching western China, maize would have been cultivated in lands further west of China—for instance, in Asia Minor. Accepting Ping-ti Ho's estimate to about three decades, then somewhere west of China maize was introduced into Asia Minor in about 1495. Columbus had returned in 1493 from his first voyage to America. From Spain to Asia Minor is far for this American crop to have traveled in two years.

The Chinese historical evidence is clear that maize reached China overland from the west and that maize had long been cultivated before the arrival of the Europeans.

PERSIA

Is it possible to trace migration of maize into the lands to the west of China? Burtt-Davy (1914: 15) remarks that "it is instructive to note that the modern Persian names for maize are *ghendum, gandumi-makkah* (i.e. Mecca corn) and *haldah*. The word *haldah,* according to Meninski (*Lex. Arab., Pers.,* Turk. 1780), was a name for *frumentum sarracenicum,* i.e. Saracens' corn, also pointing to its western origin." The name *gandumi-makkah* likewise indicates a western origin.

The Persian historian, Mirkhond (1433–1498), is alleged to have stated that maize was planted in the delta of the Volga by Rous, an ancestor of Genghis Khan, who ruled from 1206 to 1227. De Herbelot (1783: V, 42) wrote that "Rous planted in all these islands the corn which we call Turkey, and which the Turks to this very day call in their language by the name of Rous and Bulgar."

An interesting connection with the tradition of Rous is the French name for maize, *blé d'Astrakan,* quoted by Burtt-Davy (1914: 9); Astrakan, as well as being the name of the capital of the Tartar state, destroyed by Tamerlane in 1395, is also the name of a Russian province on the delta of the Volga. Bonafous (1836: 22) was impressed by the evidence in the passage on Rous and remarked: "The celebrated orientalist, d'Herbelot, quotes a passage from Mirkhond . . . of which the version, if it is correct, leaves no doubt that maize was known in the Old World before the discovery of the new." Here Miss Lacy (1911: 969) commented:

Bonafous proceeds to say, however, that after an examination of the text of Mirkhond, at the place indicated by Herbelot, he finds nothing to justify the latter's statement in regard to *rous* and adds, as he dismisses the subject, "Either this author must have drawn from some other source than that which he indicates, or a strange confusion must have prevailed among the notes which he had collected. This judgement of Bonafous's seems for the time to have closed the question, but the investigation of the subject of the origin of maize in connection with some bibliographical work being done in the Bureau of Plant Industry, of the United States Department of Agriculture, has revealed the fact that several scholars of note agree that Herbelot and others often ascribed to Mirkhond statements which were really taken from the writings of Khondemir (1475–1534).[9]

Miss Lacy then proceeded to clarify the issue: "Khondemir wrote at almost the same time as Mirkhond, although he [Khondemir] was his grandson, and his best known work, the *Khelassé-al-âkhbar*, is very nearly identical in subject matter with Mirkhond's *History of the World*, the *Rauzet-al-Safa*."

Miss Lacy explained how confusion had arisen over these Persian authors and their texts. She said:

Having thus seen, first, that the two authors, Mirkhond and Khondemir, were often confused, and second, as a reason for the confusion, that the subject matter of the *Khelassé-al-âkhbar* of Khondemir and the *Rauzet-al-Safa* of Mirkhond, is for the most part, the same, it seems reasonable to advance the conjecture that Herbelot drew his information from Khondemir rather than from Mirkhond, and that this probable error in crediting the quotation accounts for the failure of Bonafous to verify the reference. The statement concerning maize ascribed to Mirkhond loses none of its value in the investigation of the early history of maize, if taken from the writings of Khondemir, so that an examination of his writings, especially part 9 of the *Khelassé-al-âkhbar*, becomes important. A copy of this work is in the library of the British Museum.

I wrote to the British Museum asking if a translation of the relevant passage of Khondemir could be made. The reply was that there was at that time no Persian scholar on the staff to undertake the task. I wrote to librarians in Moscow, in Tehran, and in Baghdad for information on this matter but obtained none.

Asia Minor

Asia Minor will be found to be the point from which maize spread

[9] M. G. Lacy, "Pre-Columbian References to Maize in Persian Literature," *Science*, 33: 968–970. This and subsequent quotations are used by permission of the publisher.

eastward into Persia and China and westward into Europe. In this area there is such a plethora of maize names that it is difficult to trace whence maize came.

In Turkey maize has several distinct names—*rous* or *kokoroz, boulgar, durah Shamai* or *durah de Syrie* and *boghdai Misr*. The *rous* and *kokoroz* names suggest that some maize reached Turkey from the region of the Volga delta in the northeast. The name *boulgar* indicates that some maize penetrated Turkey from Bulgaria in the west. In Bulgaria, however, maize is known as *kukuruza*, which indicates that maize reached Bulgaria from the east. The names *durha Shamai* and *durah de Syrie* mean "sorghum of Sham," a city in Syria, called Damasacus by the Turks. *Boghdai Misr* means "wheat of Misr," or Egypt. Here the name suggests that some maize entered Turkey from Egypt. Only *boulgar* is associated with Europe, but Europe as an introducer of maize to Asia Minor can be excluded.

The maize names based on K–K + R–S are puzzling. In India the Arabs, according to Sir George Watt, call maize *khandarus*. If *russ*, according to Crawfurd (1867: V, 186) derives from the Arabic *arus*, meaning "rice," then *khandarus* may mean "rice of Khanda," that is, Khandahar in Afghanistan, an ancient and important trading junction.

A glance at the distribution of the K–K + R–S names for maize, however, rules out the idea that R–S stands for rice in all areas. According to Buck (1949: 518) maize is called *kukuruza* in Bulgaria, Latvia, Lithuania, Rumania, and Russia; *kukurydza* in Poland; *kukurice* in Bohemia; *kukuruz* in Croatia and Serbia; *kukurutz* in Austria; *kukurieza* in Hungary; *kokoroz* in Turkey.[10] In these names I consider that R–S is connected with a Slavonic root for *rye*. The *Oxford English Dictionary* under *rye* gives *ryzi, ryze, ruze,* and others and remarks that "it is probable that the original home of the word was eastern Europe."

The next point is to assign a plausible meaning to K–K. There is

---

[10] Concerning the names *boghdai Misr* and *kokoroz* as maize names in Turkey, Mr. A. C. I. Samuel of the British Embassy in Ankara wrote to me on December 12, 1947: "The Turkish terms for maize should read *misir bugdayi* and *kokoroz* respectively. The former means literally *Egyptian wheat*, but the word *misir* by itself is the word currently used for maize. It is also the normal word for Egypt. The word *kokoroz* probably connotes a complete ear of maize, but it may be used locally for the plant itself."

the possibility that, because maize was regarded as animal food, K–K could refer to fowls or chickens, as in *kukus*. In the *Oxford English Dictionary* under *cock* one notes: " . . . O. Teut. *kukko-*, from the same root as *chicken (keukino)* viz. *keuk, kuk.*" On this derivation, then, the K–K + R–S names for maize would mean "chicken feed." On the other hand, as Mrs. Veller, my assistant, pointed out, the German word for cow is *kuh* and the *Oxford English Dictionary* states that *cow* is "a common Teut. and common Indo-Germanic word" with a number of forms. *Cow* is used in English to describe large coarse plants—cowpea, cowparsley, cow parsnip, cow thistle, cowwheat. Maize is a large, coarse grain, and I suggest that *kukurus* refers to a large, coarse rye, a cowrye, cattle feed, or fodder. In this case *kukurus* would be analogous to the Portuguese *milho zaburro*, cattle fodder (Jeffreys, 1963b). Maize was, on its introduction into the Old World, regarded as cattle food, and only in times of famine was it used as human food. Rendón (1953) had pointed to the Hindi and Slavic names for corn (*kukuri* and *kukurusa*) and their phonetic-semantic correspondence with the Greek *kegekrous*, or *kekkrus*, meaning "millet of the scythes." "Millet of the scythes"—that is, cattle fodder—would support my contention.

Candolle (1967: 371, 376) remarked that the Greeks did not know the cereal, rye, whereas the Greeks called *Panicum miliaceum* by the name *kegchros*. Liddle and Scott in their lexicon state that κέγχρος meant *Holcus sorghum*.

Asia Minor Introduces Maize to Europe

Italian reports hold that maize was brought to Italy early and from the east. Bertagnolli (1881: 310) maintained that maize first appeared in Italy during the Crusades, that it came from Asia, and that this claim was vouched for in the much disputed "Charter of Incisa" found by Judge Francesco Turzano in the archives of Asti and published in 1515. Bertagnolli wrote: "According to this document called *Carta donationis Verae Crucis et primi seminis meligae*, maize was introduced into the Incisa Marquisate in 1204 by Jacopo, the local marquess, and by Antoniello Molinari, both captains under Bonifacio di Monferrato, on their return from the siege of Constantinople."

Dr. Ramalhete drew my attention to Silva Marques, who in the *Descobrimentos portuguesas* (1944: 1–12) lists (in 1223–1279) *milho* among items imported from abroad through the port of Atonguio.

The opinion of Valcarcel and others mentioned by Bonafous (1836: 14, 15) is that Arabs had brought maize to the Iberian peninsula in the thirteenth century; such an introduction explains the early Spanish name for maize, *trigo de turquina*.

Negri, in his publication *La Macinazione agricola deo cereali* (1930: 79), stated that though the cultivation of maize in Italy began in earnest only after the discovery of America, it apparently had already been grown much earlier in Asia and had actually reached Italy from the east. Bon (1924–1932; XXI, 970) stated that maize was being cultivated in Italy about 1500. The late Professor Pagnucco drew my attention to a passage in Leonardo da Vinci. Between 1495 and 1497 Leonardo, while at Milan, jotted down the following note: ". . . ducati 2—fave—melica biaca—melica rossa—panica—miglio—figiuoli—fave—pisegli." Here the words red and white *melica* occur, as also does the word *miglio*. The translation as given by Richter (1939: II, 378) is: "2 ducats, beans, white maize, red maize, millet, buck wheat, kidney beans, beans, peas."

A further indication of early maize in Milan comes from Peter Martyr, who, according to MacNutt (1912: I, 64), in 1493 compared the millet with which the inhabitants of the Caribbean "easily make bread" with that which "exists plenteously among the Milanese." Peter Martyr's description of this millet might be a description of maize: "This millet is little more than a palm in length, ending in a point, and is about the thickness of the upper part of a man's arm. The grains are about the form and size of peas."

I am doubtful about Richter's translation of the word *miglio* as buckwheat, since the Italian for buckwheat is *grano saracina*. *Miglio*, as used by Ramussio in 1554, meant "maize," and Pigafetta used *miglio* for maize in 1519. Ricci in his *Compendio storico della agricoltura italiano*, published in 1920, stated (1920: 133–134) that maize was cultivated in Italy before Columbus discovered America. Maize names in Europe show that Asia Minor was a center of diffusion for this crop, and hence maize would have been present in Asia Minor prior to its arrival in Europe.

Maize was called "wheat of Asia, great wheat and great reed (tipha magna)" by Bock, who, according to Bonafous (1836: 11), was the first botanist to speak of "maize . . . in a German book printed in 1532, forty years after the discovery of America." Bock "said that this plant was brought from Arabia Felix [the Hadramaut] to Germany." Ruel and Fuchs also, according to Bonafous, about 1532 confirmed that maize came from the Orient. Bonafous quotes Fuchs as having said: "This wheat came from Asia and from Greece it passed into Germany where it is called Turkish wheat because the Turks of that day were in possession of the whole of Asia, and it is because of the country from which it was introduced that the Germans call it Turkey wheat." The name *Frumentum turcicum asiaticum* was, according to Bonafous, given to maize by Taberna-Montanus and he, with Loncier and other contemporary botanists, repeated the assertion of Fuchs.

Another early European name for maize connected with Asiatic diffusion was *Turcicum frumentum*, or Turkish corn, which, according to Miss Barber (1934: 28), was first recorded by Ruellius in 1536.[11] She then noted that this name "was more widespread in Europe than any other and though misleading, is not so meaningless as the rest." So far from being misleading or meaningless, this name reflects an early source of maize for Europe. Miss Barber continued: "Ruellius says that maize is so named because it came *in the days of our grandfathers* (*avorum nostrorum aetate*) from Greece or Asia." In Greece maize is called *arabosite* or "Arabian wheat," an indication of its arrival in Greece via Arabia. Ruellius claimed that maize reached southern Europe from Asia "in the days of our grandfathers." How many years does one deduct from 1536 to get the date when maize arrived in Europe "in the days of our grandfathers"? Would forty years be too much? Deducting forty years from 1536 gives the date 1496. It would have been cultivated in Asia Minor and in Greece prior to 1496. Columbus sailed on his first voyage to America in 1942.

According to Miss Barber, Bock (1539: XXI–XXII) wrote that maize "is new in Germany and probably came from India. . . . One wants to name it *Frumentum Asiaticum* (wheat of Asia) because in Assyria . . . such a fruit is found whose grains or kernels grow as large as olives. . . . I myself have seen four or five such grains at a country merchant. . . . When I made a thorough enquiry about such

---

[11] The interpretation of the *Turcicum frumentum* of Ruellius as maize has been challenged by Hemardinquer. In view, however, of the imposing evidence for the pre-Columbian presence of maize in India, China, and elsewhere, Hemardinquer's arguments are open to objections.

a fruit I was told it came from India." The information given by Bock would have been garnered before 1539. He had seen and handled grains as large as olives, and no cereal other than maize has grains comparable with olives. He had made enquiries about this grain and was told it came from India. There is no doubt about this information, which led him to name this grain *Frumentum asiaticum*.

Among the early botanists who were convinced of the Asiatic origin of maize were Ruellius, Fuchs, Bock, Tragus, and Dodoens. Some of these men were contemporaries of Columbus. To this list Mangelsdorf and Oliver (1951: 264) add Sismondi, Michana, Gregory, Loncier, Amoreux, Regnier, Viterbo, Doncier, Taberna-montanus, Bonafous, St. John de Turre, Daru, de Herbelot, and Klippart. Bertagnolli is another.

Until 1570 all commentators on maize were agreed that it reached Europe via Asia. On this unanimity of opinion Finan (1950: 156) remarked: "For the first thirty years in which maize is discussed in the herbals there is no mention that it had been brought in from America. . . . During this period the general opinion among the herbalists was that maize came to Europe from the Orient. It was not until 1570, with the herbal of Matthiolus (1570, p. 305) who had seen the text in Oviedo's *General and Natural History*, that an American origin for maize is suggested."[12]

In exemplification of the fact that Europe first obtained maize from Asia Minor, which about A.D. 1320 was called the empire of the Turks or Saracens, I give a short list of European names for maize: Italy has *grano Turco, grano Saraceno, frumentum Saracenium, frumentum Asiaticum*; Great Britain, *Turkish corn* and *Tartarian wheat*; Holland, *Turks tarwe*; Germany, *Turkischer körn*; Sweden, *Turkish hvede*; Russia, *Turetzki chelb*; Greece, *Arabosite*; France, *blé de Turquie* and *blé d'Astrakan*; Morocco, *Tshurkiya*.

Europe has maize names associated with Asia. Asia, with the single exception of Bulgaria, has no maize names associated with Europe. Those who claim that maize was first introduced into the

---

[12] Oviedo's *General and Natural History* was published in 1526. Even though this work established the fact that maize appeared to be an American plant, it supplied no evidence to invalidate a pre-Columbian entry of this crop into the Old World.

Old World by Columbus, an employee of Spain, will find it difficult to explain why in Spain, of all places, an early name for maize was, according to Culloch (1849: 831) *trigo de Turquia*.

In spite of this evidence for the movement of maize from Asia Minor into Europe and into Spain, evidence available to any botanist, the late Professor Merrill (1954: 290) clung to the surmise that it was only after maize had been introduced by Columbus into Spain that maize moved into the eastern Mediterranean and from there "along the old silk route."

CONCLUSION

Enough evidence has been presented for the presence of maize in Asia in pre-Columbian times to recommend a reassessment of contacts between America and the Old World. The fact that maize entered China from the west suggests early transatlantic rather than transpacific contacts.[13]

---

[13] The article by professor Hui-Lin Li (1961), "A Case for Pre-Columbian Trans-Atlantic Travel by Arab Ships," should be studied.

22. Some Problems of Interpreting Transoceanic Dispersal of the New World Cottons

S. G. STEPHENS

Background

Of more than twenty species of *Gossypium* that have been recognized, only four include cultivated forms. These are the lint-bearing species, that is, those which have nonadherent, convoluted seed fibers capable of being spun. Two of the species, *G. arboreum* L. and *G. herbaceum* L., have thirteen pairs of chromosomes and are confined to the Old World continents and neighboring islands. So far there is no convincing evidence that these species, or any nearly related wild species, have existed in the New World except in recent experimental culture. *G. arboreum* is known only as a cultivated or commensal form. *G. herbaceum* is mostly cultivated, but there is also a "wild" form, var. *africanum,* which is found established independently of human activities in southern Africa (fig. 22.1). I have written the word *wild* in quotes, because it is really a matter of interpretation whether one considers this to be an originally wild form, never cultivated, or a feral form, long reestablished in the wild from a former cultivated state.

NOTE: This paper is a contribution from the North Carolina State University Agricultural Experiment Station, Raleigh, North Carolina. The research on which it is based is supported in part by NSF Grant GB 4016.

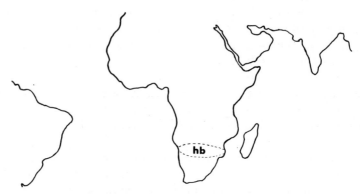

Figure 22.1. Geographical distributions of the "wild" forms of cultivated species of *Gossypium*. *hb*, Diploid species, *G. herbaceum* var. *africanum*.

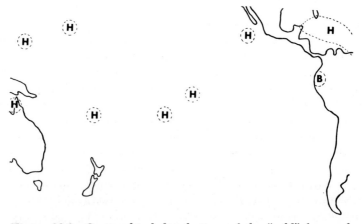

Figure 22.2. Geographical distributions of the "wild" forms of cultivated species of *Gossypium*. Amphidiploid species: *B*, *G. barbadense*; *H*, *G. hirsutum*.

The other two species, *G. hirsutum* L. and *G. barbadense* L., have twenty-six pairs of chromosomes. They are commonly known as the New World cottons, because their centers of variability and archaeological prehistory lie in Mesoamerica and northern South America, respectively. Cultivated forms of both species, however, are widely distributed in the subtropics of both Eastern and Western hemispheres and in Polynesia. "Wild" forms of both species are known (fig. 22.2). "Wild" forms of *barbadense* have been found only in coastal Ecuador and in the neighboring Galápagos Islands (*G. barbadense var. darwinii*).[1] "Wild" forms of *hirsutum* have a remarkably wide and disjunct distribution: in the Caribbean from the Guiria peninsula through the Antilles as far as the north Yucatán coast, and on many Pacific islands that lie in the triangle formed by New Guinea, Wake Island, and the Marquesas. On the whole, each island tends to have developed its own particular morphological form, which suggests either a variable ancestral population from which they were derived in common, or, more probably, that they resulted from several independent establishments separated in time. An exception to the general picture of localized forms is found in Polynesia. In experimental culture, types from the Marquesas, Samoa, and the Society Islands differ only in minor details.

As is well known, cotton has a long history of cultivation in both the Old World and New World. Cotton fabrics dated around 3000 B.C. were found in the excavations at Mohenjo-Daro in Sind, west Pakistan (Gulati and Turner, 1928). More recently "archaeological cotton" has been found in the Zambesi Valley—I do not know the age of this material. In the New World, the Huaca Prieta site in Peru yielded materials dating back to 2500 B.C. (Bird and Mahler, 1951), and the Tehuacán Valley excavations in Mexico discovered cotton dating back to 2000–3000 B.C. and possibly earlier (Smith and Mac-Neish, 1964). These dates, of course, provide only minimal estimates of the time during which cotton has been domesticated in various parts of the world. They give us no information at all concerning the time during which the species were *available* for domestication— that is, how long they existed as wild plants possessing some of the properties that would make them attractive to man. From the botani-

---

[1] Some authorities regard the Galápagos form as a distinct species, *G. darwinii*. But under either interpretation, the island and mainland forms are more closely related to each other than to any other species.

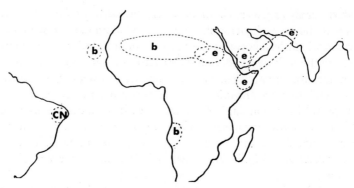

Figure 22.3. Geographical distributions of exclusively wild species of *Gossypium*. *b*, African diploid species. *e*, Afro-Arabian diploid species. *CN*, amphidiploid species, *G. caicoense.*

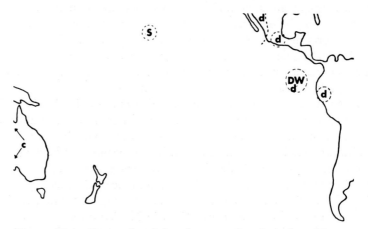

Figure 22.4. Geographical distributions of exclusively wild species of *Gossypium*. *c*, Australian diploid species. *d*, American diploid species. Amphidiploid species: *DW*, *G. darwinii*; *S*, *G. sandvicense.*

cal point of view, it is important to remember that the exclusively wild species of *Gossypium* (excluding the four species with which we are concerned here) have established themselves successfully on all the continents that provide arid, frost-free environments (Africa, Asia, North America, South America, and Australia) and also on isolated islands (Hawaii, Galápagos, Cape Verde). Their wide distribution is shown in figures 22.3 and 22.4. The climatic and oceanic barriers, which have not proved insurmountable for the natural dispersal of the wild species, cannot logically be assumed to be insurmountable for "wild" forms of the cultivated species. In short, one cannot exclude from consideration the possibility that natural means of dispersal have contributed to the wide distribution of primitive cultigens, however formidable these barriers appear to be. This is a primary difficulty when one tries to relate the geographical distribution of primitive cultigens to independent evidence of human cultural movements.

A second difficulty in using the geographical distribution of the cultivated cottons as tracers of human cultural movements is that cotton was grown for export from the sixteenth century on in the colonies established by European powers in both the Old and New Worlds. The historical record shows that remarkably short periods of time elapsed (1) between the discovery of the New World and the first exports of New World cotton to European markets (Acosta, 1590) and (2) between Cook's third voyage into the Pacific and the introduction of cotton varieties into Polynesia by the early missions (Ellis, 1831). There can be no doubt at all that during the sixteenth to eighteenth centuries, there was considerable exchange of cotton varieties among most of the cotton-growing areas of the world. Thus one does not have to consider early transoceanic cultural contacts to explain the presence of New World cottons in the Old World and in Polynesia, particularly when these cottons show virtually no correlation between degree of taxonomic differentiation and geographical distance. For example, samples of kidney cotton (a form of *barbadense*) collected in Mexico, the West Indies, Goa, and Tonga may show less morphological differentiation than samples of kidney cotton collected from different Brazilian populations. The fact that our present information on the geographical distribution of these cottons can be interpreted satisfactorily as a result of post-Columbian events does not, of course, prove that earlier contacts did not occur. The point is that it is not a simple matter to obtain critical evidence of *early* contacts when the existence of *later* contacts is well established.

These problems of cotton distribution, considered in more detail, suggest the kinds of information (now lacking) that might provide unequivocal evidence of pre-Columbian transoceanic contacts. Out of such consideration, two interesting situations arise that seem worthy of further investigations.

TRANSOCEANIC DISPERSAL OF "WILD" FORMS AND CULTIGENS

"Wild" forms

The "wild" forms, in common with their cultivated relatives, have nonadherent convoluted fibers that can be easily removed from the seeds and spun. But in other respects related to seed survival, establishment, and dispersal, they differ markedly from cultigens. The seed fibers are sparse so that the seeds do not form compact "locks" in the opened boll but are easily scattered by wind for considerable distances. The seeds are small, hard coated, and extremely long lived: they can survive prolonged soaking in salt water without appreciable loss of viability, and laboratory tests indicate that they have sufficient buoyancy to be carried by ocean currents for relatively short distances, perhaps of the order of five hundred to one thousand miles (Stephens, 1966). Since many of the "wild" forms are established coastal ecotypes, it is entirely possible that their seeds could have been carried by a process of island hopping throughout the Caribbean islands and from Ecuador throughout the Galápagos archipelago. Transoceanic dispersal by drift is a different matter and would require some form of natural rafting. Unlikely as this may appear, we must remember that the exclusively wild species, *G. sandvicense* Parl., which has no nearly related mainland relatives, has somehow become established in Hawaii.

A second possibility of natural dispersal that may have been underestimated is transport by birds. Recently Dr. Vernon Proctor in Texas has been carrying out feeding experiments of "wild" cotton seeds to captive birds (killdeer). His preliminary findings indicate that the seeds may be retained in the gut for several days between ingestion and evacuation, without apparent loss of viability.

A third possibility, not submitted seriously as a general mechanism, is the freak accident associated with unconscious human dispersal. Even today "seed cotton" (that is, the unginned seed) is sometimes used for stuffing pillows and mattresses. Apparently this was a common practice in early colonial days. Writing about the eighteenth-century European settlements in the West Indies, Raynal (1774) distinguished between the cultivated cottons grown for export and "wild" cottons with short and fine, reddish fiber, used locally for stuffing mattresses and pillows. There is a curious story (Thompson, 1845: 31) that cotton was introduced into the Marquesas accidentally "by a seaman turning out the contents of his bed, which being cotton, contained a few seeds still containing the vegetating principle." This story is interesting, not as a reliable explanation for the origin of cotton in the Marquesas, but for the implication it contains that seamen's beds of the period were stuffed with seed cotton. One wonders how many such beds may have been flung over the side and washed up on remote shorelines, how many discarded at ports of call? In this connection one thinks of the flourishing population of "wild" *hirsutum* on Wake Island and what is known of the history of that island. Discovered by Captain William Wake in 1796, it was visited and mapped by Captain Charles Wilkes during the U.S. Exploring Expedition of 1841 (Wilkes, 1845). In 1866 a German ship, *Libelle,* was wrecked on Wake, and several attempts were made to salvage her cargo. Subsequently there were other temporary landings, including some by Japanese who made camps there and collected sea birds' feathers. In 1912, attempts were made to plant coconuts without success. It was not until the Tanager Expedition of 1923 that a single clump of the "wild" cotton was found. By 1952 it was fairly common around abandoned Japanese installations (Fosberg, 1959). We will probably never know how or when the "wild" cotton arrived on Wake Island, but the possibility of an accidental introduction by one of the numerous visitors between 1786 and 1923 would seem to provide as plausible a mechanism as any alternative.

Because of the possibilities of natural and accidental dispersal, one is forced to the conclusion that the geographical distribution of the "wild" forms of cotton per se cannot be used critically as supporting evidence for early transoceanic cultural contacts. Archaeological evidence of spindle whorls, cordage, fabrics, or any artifact indicating the *use* of cotton would be far more satisfactory.

Cultivated forms

The geographical distribution of cultivated forms offers different problems of interpretation. Here the issues are confused by the existence of post-Columbian contacts. On the other hand the possibilities of natural dispersal are greatly reduced and in certain cases minimized to the point that only human dispersal can be seriously

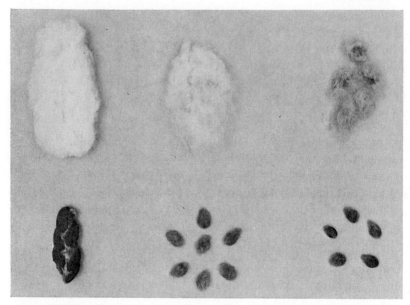

Figure 22.5. Individual locks of cotton bolls. *Left,* Kidney cotton (cultivated), *G. barbadense* var. *brasiliense. Center,* Caribbean cotton (cultivated), *G. hirsutum* var. *marie- galante. Right,* "Wild" form of *G. hirsutum* from Socorro Island, Revillagigedos.

entertained. All cultivated forms have the seed fibers aggregated into compact locks, with the result that seed dispersal is greatly restricted. One finds such forms in small field plantings, as individual dooryard plants, and as escapes from cultivation along roadsides or in open disturbed areas. But rarely do they establish themselves as a permanent component of natural vegetation.

The possibilities of dispersal by natural means are apparently considerably less in *barbadense* than in *hirsutum* cultigens. Many, though not all, cultivated types of *hirsutum* have hard seed coats, so that the seeds are resistant to weathering and can retain their viability for a long period under adverse conditions. On the contrary, cultivated forms of *barbadense* have large seeds with thin seed coats: they germinate promptly in moist conditions. It is unlikely that such seeds, aggregated in compact locks and exposed to weathering, would retain sufficient viability for natural seed dispersal. The chances of natural seed dispersal are still further reduced in the kidney-seeded forms of *barbadense*, where the seeds in each lock are fused together in a hard mass (fig. 22.5).

Now the kidney-seeded condition is peculiar to *barbadense* var. *brasiliense*; it is unknown in the other cultivated species. To any pre-Columbian visitor from outside the New World, kidney seeds would have been a curiosity and hence likely to have been noted and collected. Kidney-seeded cottons today are the types most commonly found in primitive usage in north-central Brazil and the Guianas. They were the first cottons to be described by early European travelers in Brazil (de Lery, 1594) and in the West Indies (du Tertre, 1667). Thus it is likely that any pre-Columbian visitors from the Mediterranean region or West Africa would have seen them. It follows that an archaeological discovery of authentic pre-Columbian date, beyond the limits of the New World continents and including a sample of kidney seeds, would amount to a virtual proof of early transoceanic contact. It would seem that a kidney-seeded mass, enveloped in its "cocoon" of fiber, would be as likely to be preserved as the raw cotton and boll fragments that have been identified in several excavations.

THE IDENTIFICATION OF ARCHAEOLOGICAL MATERIAL

Most excavated cotton materials that find their way into the hands of botanists consist of raw fibers, cordage, textile fragments, and, less frequently, boll fragments and seeds. Unfortunately, although such materials are readily identifiable as cotton, they are of limited value for discriminating between species of cotton. Perhaps a more tactful way of expressing this would be to say that techniques for distinguishing critically between species on the basis of such material have not yet been developed. Although quite sophisticated techniques are available to the fiber technologist, most of his experience is based on the properties of modern commercial cottons that are readily available to him. Far less is known concerning the fiber properties of primitive cultigens, these being available in only a few small botanical collections. Most cotton geneticists would be skeptical of comparisons made between archaeological material and a few selected samples of modern Old World and New World cotton varieties. One needs to know the range of variability expressed by a

Figure 22.6. Dried and open bolls of a New World cotton. *Left*, Bracteoles removed but otherwise intact. *Right*, Boll segments and peduncle (stalk) disassembled.

representative sample of primitive cultigens before meaningful comparisons can be attempted.

On the other hand, it is quite possible that in future excavations cotton materials may become available that are sufficiently well preserved and of sufficient diagnostic value for probable identification. I have already mentioned that kidney seeds alone are sufficient to identify a particular race of the New World cotton, *G. barbadense*. The remarkable preservation of the Tehuacán boll fragments and of one complete boll from the Huaca Prieta site leads one to hope that the woody stalks (peduncles) on which the bolls are borne might also be preserved and occasionally recovered. Potentially these may be of more diagnostic value than the boll itself. In living material each flower stalk bears a whorl of three leafy bracteoles surrounding the boll. At the base of each bracteole is a circular depression or pit in which a nectary is located, which I will call the "outer" nectary. Alternating with each bracteole and located inside the bracteole

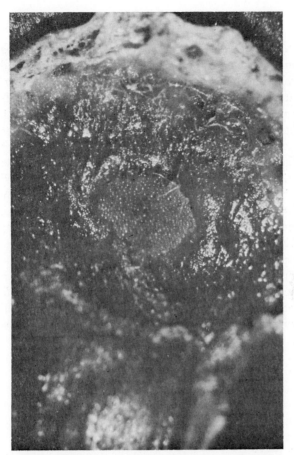

Figure 22.7. An "outer" (external extra-floral) nectary as seen in surface view on a dried peduncle. The peduncle from a herbarium specimen of *G. barbadense* was swollen in boiling water and photographed under low-power magnification (10×). The secretory hairs lining the circular nectary are clearly distinguishable from the surrounding tissues.

whorl are three triangular depressions—the "inner" nectaries. In all four cultivated species the nectaries are sometimes missing entirely or erratically developed. "Outer" nectaries, however, are not known to occur in the Old World species, *arboreum* and *herbaceum;* "inner" nectaries, when present, are well developed. In the New World species, *barbadense* and *hirsutum*, it is the "outer" nectary that is most conspicuous. The nectaries can usually be identified in dried material (as in a herbarium specimen) and certainly after swelling in water. They can also be identified when the bracteoles and other leafy parts have been damaged or lost (figs. 22. 6 and 22. 7). Optimistically, one might hope that nectaries might be sufficiently well preserved even in archaeological material to be identified by water soaking—a technique that has been applied successfully to boll fragments. An Old World site that yielded convoluted fibers, boll fragments, and peduncles bearing outer nectaries would provide good presumptive evidence for the presence of a New World cotton.

The number of locks (compartments) into which an intact boll is divided provides evidence of limited diagnostic value. Appropriate measurements of a single, isolated boll segment can sometimes be used to make an intelligent guess at the number of locks present in the intact boll, but the method is not critical. Most *barbadense* bolls are three-locked, though four-locked bolls are occasionally found. *Hirsutum* bolls may have from three to five locks, even on the same plant. *Arboreum* bolls are usually three-locked—*herbaceum* bolls may have from three to five locks. Clearly lock number is valuable only as supplementary evidence in an attempted identification. Smith and MacNeish (1964) have shown that it is possible to restore dry boll segments to something approaching their original conformity in the living state by swelling them in water. Thus one can obtain a good indication of the shape of the living boll and compare it with those of existing species. In general, *arboreum* bolls tend to be pyramidal, *barbadense* pyramidal to ellipsoidal, *hirsutum* oval to spherical, and *herbaceum* spherical. These rough categories, however, may show considerable overlapping.

It seems highly probable that as more archaeological material becomes available for study, these crude methods of identification will be greatly refined or replaced by more sophisticated techniques. The taxonomist who can classify living material on the basis of readily observable morphological differences in a number of plant parts is unlikely to search for subtle but consistent differences in isolated plant fragments unless he has a particular reason for doing so. Archaeological material clearly provides a reason and the necessary stimulus for such research.

SPECIFIC UNRESOLVED PROBLEMS

There are two puzzling cases of cotton distribution that might be related to early transoceanic contacts, though alternative interpretations cannot be excluded. They are of particular interest because one case (cotton in the Cape Verde Islands) requires some form of transatlantic distribution; the other (cotton in the Marquesas Islands) may involve a transpacific contact.

Cape Verde Islands

According to Ribeiro (1962), the Cape Verde Islands were discovered between the years 1460 and 1462, at which time there were no signs of former habitations. This was approximately thirty years before the discovery of the New World. Attempts at settlement quickly followed, and by 1466 cottons from Guinea had been introduced and had already become semiferal. During the subsequent colonial period, cotton was collected in the wild and also grown under primitive cultivation for export. Today, according to Teixeira and Barbosa (1958), it occurs in a feral (subspontaneous) state in the arid areas of most of the islands. It is a New World cotton, *G. hirsutum* var. *punctatum*. It is clear that if the feral cottons today are the descendants of the cottons introduced from Guinea between 1462 and 1466, then a New World cotton must have been established in Africa approximately thirty years before Columbus' first voyage. The difficulty here, of course, is the critical identification of the early introduction with the present-day feral type. In the sixteenth century many New World crops were brought into the Cape Verde Islands, and these probably included cotton. A later introduction from the New World may have replaced an earlier Old World species. In that case, however, one would not expect the original, well-established feral form to have disappeared completely. It would be interesting to know whether an Old World cultivated species also exists on the islands. At present the only species, other than *hirsutum*, that have been recorded are the following:

1. *G. barbadense* var. *brasiliense*. According to Teixeira and Barbosa (1958), this kidney cotton occurs much more rarely than the feral *hirsutum* type.

2. *G. barbosanum* Phillips and Clement. This species was described

by Clement and Phillips (1963). It is a wild form with undifferenti-
ated seed fibers, closely related to the wild African species, *G. ano-
malum* Wawra and Peyr., and therefore not pertinent to this problem.

3. *G. capitis viridis* Mauer. This species is apparently unknown in
culture, and information on its relationships to other species is presently lacking.

Marquesas Islands

The historical record indicates that the Marquesas Islands were
discovered by Mendaña in 1595 and rediscovered by Captain Cook
in 1774, almost two hundred years later. Between 1774 and 1792, according to Rollin (1929), there were six more recorded visits to the
islands. Only the last of these (Captain Roberts in 1792) involved
an extended stay in the islands. Roberts stayed four months and at
the end of his visit found cotton on the island of Waitahu or Christina.
He brought back a sample of the cotton and deposited it in the Boston
Museum. This interesting sample has unfortunately disappeared.
According to Roberts (1795: 245), the island of Waitahu "produced
cotton, superior in fineness to any which they had seen" and he was
told by the natives that "it grew in great plenty on all the islands."

These dates show conclusively that cotton was established in the
Marquesas before any possible introduction by European missionaries. The mission ship *Duff* did not arrive from Tahiti until 1797.
Further, cotton could not have become "established on all the islands"
in the brief period between 1774 and 1792 from an accidental introduction.

Is it possible that Roberts' cotton was the "wild" form of *hirsutum*
found in the Marquesas today? Certainly his rather glowing description does not seem particularly appropriate for a short, sparse, tawny-
colored fiber. But the "wild" *hirsutum* of the Marquesas is remarkably
similar to the "wild" form in Tahiti, and this or a close relative was
collected and preserved by Solander, the botanist on Cook's first
voyage (1768–1771). It is reasonably certain that these "wild" forms
were established in several Polynesian islands long before the eighteenth-century visitors. Their origin must remain controversial and
speculative, unless, or until, evidence of an early native usage becomes available. It should be remembered also that native usage of
the cotton plant would not necessarily be restricted to spinning and
weaving.

Subsequent attempts by the early missions to establish a cotton industry in Polynesia involved not only the introduction of foreign varieties but also the introduction of machinery to handle the product. One of the early missionaries (Ellis, 1831) states that the natives were taught how to operate this machinery. In the eighteenth-century colonial plantations in the southern United States and the West Indies, cotton fiber was removed from the seed by hand (a tedious and time-consuming process) until the adoption of a primitive, hand-operated roller gin, copied from the Indian *churka*. This machine must have been known and available to the early missionaries in Polynesia. If the use of cotton was unknown in Polynesia prior to the mission activities, it seems unlikely that new tools would be developed when more efficient machinery was available. Yet Linton (1923), discussing the material culture of the Marquesas Islands, described a hand implement, much like a modern swizzlestick, used by the Marquesans to separate the fibers from a mass of unginned cotton, and questioned whether it was an introduction or a Marquesan invention.

Nineteenth-century writers (Vincendon-Dumoulin and Desgroz, 1843; Des Vergnes, 1877) distinguished between cotton they considered indigenous in the Marquesas and superior kinds introduced later. The indigenous type was called *haavai* or *pulupulu* and was used in tinderboxes.

These scattered fragments of information do seem collectively to indicate that cotton was available in the Marquesas long before any known European influence. In all probability it was used for purposes unconnected with spinning, but whether this implies anything more than the casual use of a wild plant that happened to be available in the islands cannot be determined from the botanical and historical information that has been presented. The main problem of how a cotton with Central American affinities became established in southern Polynesia remains an open question.

23. *Phaseolus*: Diffusion and Centers of Origin

LAWRENCE KAPLAN

The genus *Phaseolus* comprises some 160 species, about 80 of which are New World natives. The remainder are Asiatic and African. Six Asian-African species, including the grams, urds, mung, and rice beans, are widely cultivated in Asia. These are annuals and have small seeds and small cylindrical pods.

THE NEW WORLD SPECIES

Four New World species have been prominent food crops: *P. vulgaris* L., *P. acutifolius* Gray var. *latifolius* Freeman, *P. lunatus* L., and *P. coccineus* L.

P. vulgaris L., common bean, frijol (derived from a name for the Old World *Vicia faba*); *etl, yetl* (Nahuatl); *buul, chenek* (Mayan); *poroto* (Quechua and Aymará). This polymorphic, poorly understood species includes hundreds of such cultivated varieties as navy, red kidney, and pinto. *P. vulgaris* and the three species discussed subsequently include strongly to weakly vining forms as well as bush or erect forms. The distinctions between green, string, or snap beans, and dry or field beans is based on use rather than on botanical characters. *P. vulgaris* is the most widely grown of all food beans. In tropical, indigenous American agriculture, common beans are grown on neutral to slightly alkaline soils from sea level to over two thousand meters. The relatives of the common beans have been said by Burkart

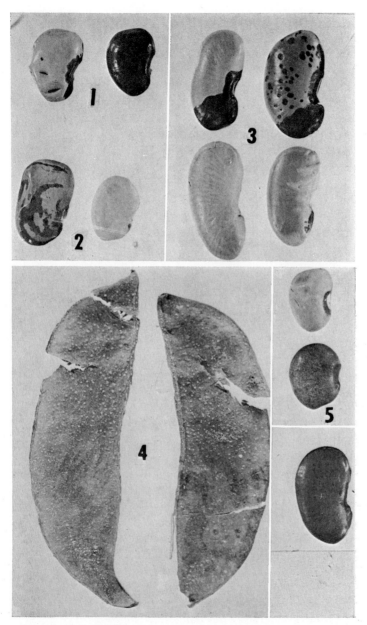

Figure 23.1. *P. lunatus*—Peru. *1,* San Nicolas, near Supe (407382). *2,* Galegarza, site Z, Ica (4–4831). *3,* San Nicolas, near Supe (407242). *4,* Nazca Valley 8/293. *5,* Galegarza, site Z, Ica (4–4831). (*1–3, 5,* Museum of Anthropology, University of California, Berkeley. *4,* Botanical Museum, Harvard).

and Brücher (1953) and Gentry (1969) to occur widely from Durango, Mexico, to Argentina.

P. acutifolius Gray var. *latifolius* Freeman, tepary, *escomite*. At the present time this bean is not cultivated on a commercial scale, although some field stations have been investigating its potential as a dry-land seed or forage crop. The seeds are smaller than those of other cultivated American beans, but they overlap in size the smaller-seeded common bean varieties. Collections made a few decades ago show the tepary to have been common then in markets along the Pacific coast of northern Mexico. In 1954 it was infrequent in that region. The disjunct range of this bean—the Sonoran desert region south through Jalisco and then a gap until the Tapachula-Guatemala border region—suggests that the present distribution is a relic one. The tepary appears to be derived from a Sonoran species (Freeman, 1912), but the relationship has been questioned (Kaplan, 1965, 1967).

P. lunatus L., Sieva, small Lima, *frijol de haba* (this also applies to the introduced *Vicia faba,* the broad bean), *comba* (Guerrero), *patashete,* (Chiapas), *guaracara* (Venezuela), *cubace* (Costa Rica). The curved pod and smaller, often flat seed distinguishes the Sieva from the Lima. *P. lunatus* var. *macrocarpus* Bentham (synonym *P. limensis* Macf.), big Lima, *pallar,* in Peru. Any Lima bean encountered in Mexico, Central America, or in indigenous areas of the southwestern United States is likely to be a Sieva bean. Peruvian Limas, the big Limas, are grown commercially in humid coastal valleys of California. The morphologically similar Sievas and Limas are fully interfertile and produce viable, fertile offspring (Mackie, 1943). This, in the genus *Phaseolus,* where interspecific crosses do not really occur (*P. coccineus* × *P. vulgaris* is a noteworthy exception), leaves little question but that the two groups should be regarded as conspecific. On the basis of the distribution of the wild species and the archaeological evidence, it is now clear that these groups are independent domesticates deriving from geographically separate races or subspecies (figs. 23.1, 23.2).

Wild *P. lunatus* (R. W. Allard, personal communication), ranging from Mexico to northern South America, evidently has developed South American and Central American subspecies that correspond to the differences separating the domesticated groups. The geographic separation of Sievas and Limas in pre-Columbian times attests to independent domestication. The Lima was present in preceramic,

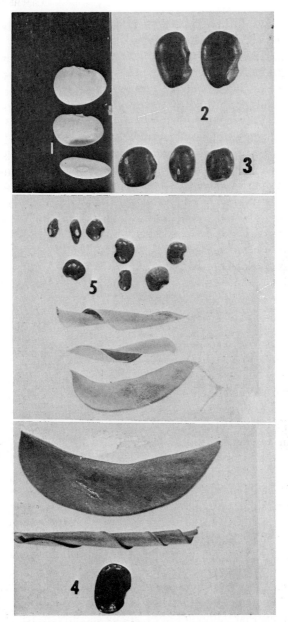

Figure 23.2. *P. lunatus*—Mesoamerica. *1*, Hopi contemporary. *2*, Hopi contemporary. *3*, Río Zape, Chihuahua, 1300 B.P. *4*, Wild *P. lunatus,* Oaxaca coast. *5*, Tehuacán, 1000 B.P.

pre-agricultural times (5,200 years ago; collections from Chilca by Dr. Frederic Engel) and continued into later times on the north coast of Peru. The evidence now available suggests that no movement of *P. lunatus* cultivars between South America and Mesoamerica took place in pre-Columbian times. Restudy of materials from Huaca Prieta, Cupisnique times (Towle, 1961: 53), has removed doubt as to their identity as *macrocarpus* limas.

P. coccineus L., runner beans, *ayecote* (Nahuatl derivation), *botil* in Chiapas, *patol* in Northern Mexico. Perennial semidomesticates are abundant in the southern Mexican-Guatemalan highlands. The most common variety in the United States is the large-seeded scarlet runner, often listed in seed catalogues as an ornamental with edible seeds. Seeds of most varieties are larger than those of Sieva beans and common beans and are usually purple or variegated purple, although there are white-seeded varieties. The flowers of the purple-seeded varieties are a striking red; those of the white-seeded kinds are white.

OLD WORLD–NEW WORLD *Phaseolus*

Botanical Distinctions

Although a critical taxonomic survey of the entire genus has not been made, studies of the cultivated species provide good cause for viewing Old World and New World *Phaseolus* as distinct sections of the genus (Piper, 1926) or even as different genera (Ohwi, 1965). The differences between these groups of *Phaseolus* include differences in susceptibility and resistance to pathogenic fungi; flower color, seed size, and color pattern; pod form; flower morphology, and growth habit. These have been reviewed (Kaplan, 1956). By electrophoresis and immunity reactions, Klotz (1962) has demonstrated significant differences between certain Old World and New World cultivars with respect to the structure of their protein molecules. Whether or not these distinctions among cultivars can be extended to the entire genus remains to be determined. It does, however, seem clear that the botanical origins of these two groups of cultivars are separate. Without a discussion of the fundamental differences in the economic botany and utilization of the Old World beans, it may be pointed out that, although both supply the protein fractions in predominantly vegetable native diets, they are not likely to be substituted for one another. Thus, for example, no American bean is used for sprouting or fermenting, and no Asiatic bean is used in combination with corn in Indian North America.

In growth requirements and general ecological behavior, the two groups of cultivars differ strikingly in the range of variation in adaptation to growing conditions. The most notable difference has been the ability of the New World *P. vulgaris* and *P. coccineus* to form cool temperature ecotypes and to extend their ranges under cultivation into regions of Asia and Europe, whereas the Asiatic *Phaseolus* cultivars could not. The ability of *P. vulgaris* and *P. coccineus* to so adapt is likely the result of genetic material selected for in the cool highlands of Mesoamerica and Andean South America. The thermophilic Asiatic-African species that might have been acceptable for food in northern Asia and Europe evidently are without an equivalent preadaptive source.

For a variety of reasons, then, it may be concluded that the cultivated *Phaseolus* beans of the New World and the Old World evolved independently, and that their botanical traits are so distinct that it is not possible for an experienced botanist familiar with the genus to mistake a representative of one group for a member of the other.

Pre-Columbian Transoceanic Contact

From our present knowledge of the botanical-archaeological record in the New World and the absence of Asiatic beans in these records, it seems clear that no Asiatic beans were brought to the Americas in pre-Columbian times, or that if they were brought, they had no perceptible influence on the native agriculture.

What about pre-Columbian evidence of American beans in the Old World? In his classic 1855 and 1886 treatments of the origins of cultivated plants, Candolle (1964) reviewed the etymology of common names and the evidence on origins provided by the ancient literature and the pre-Linnaean herbals. Such studies have been repeated many times since Candolle, but the methodology remains the same. For the common bean, *P. vulgaris*, Candolle pointed out that no Sanskrit name was known. No archaeological remains of any American *Phaseolus* species has ever been reported from any Asiatic or other Old World site. Candolle was satisfied that in any event the common bean was not of great antiquity in India. However, confusion persisted for some time with respect to the significance of the name *faseolos* in Greek and the genus name *Phaseolus*. The derivation of the genus name from an ancient Greek name led Candolle to accept a thirteenth-century European description by Albertus Magnus of cultivated "faseolus" as indicative of pre-Columbian common beans in Europe. The extensive researches of Sturtevant (Hedrick, 1919) show that the varieties described by Magnus had to be either the cow pea, *Vigna sinensis,* or the hyacinth bean, *Dolichos lablab*. Both of these are Asiatic-African in origin. The name "faseolus" or "faseolos" in the classical Mediterranean world, according to Sturtevant's interpretation, refers to the dwarf field-grown *dolichos* beans. There is no reference to garden-grown, vining beans in Europe until the sixteenth-century herbals, when every author mentions them in great detail. These sixteenth-century and later depictions of garden beans are *P. vulgaris, P. coccineus,* and *P. lunatus.*

It is certainly possible to derive from some of the literature misconceptions that bear upon the question of transoceanic diffusion. Fairservis (1959: 150) mentions "kidney beans" as one of the crops of the agricultural Jomon period in Japan over two thousand years ago. To any English-speaking reader a "kidney bean" is any one of several varieties of the common bean *P. vulgaris.* But when we read in Kidder (1966) that after middle Jomon, presumably later than 2000–3000 B.C., the "hairy-podded kidney bean" was cultivated, the misunderstanding clears up. No American *Phaseolus* bean is anything approaching hairy-podded. The Asiatic *P. aureus* Roxb., the mung, or green gram, and *P. mungo* L., the urd or black gram, are markedly hairy, as is the soy bean, *Glycine Soja* Sieb. and Zucc. The soy, however, is probably a later introduction to Japan.

NEW WORLD DIFFUSION

Historical records point to the extensive diffusion of beans in recent times. Peruvian Lima beans were brought into California extensively in the 1840's to supply food for the gold miners (Hedrick, 1931) and are now grown in the humid coastal valleys of that state. The pinto bean was rare in the pre-Columbian Southwest (Kaplan, 1956) but in historic times has adapted widely to growing and market conditions in the Southwest. In the valley of Oaxaca, runner and common bean varieties that now predominate were not present in the archaeological record. The extent to which common beans of North

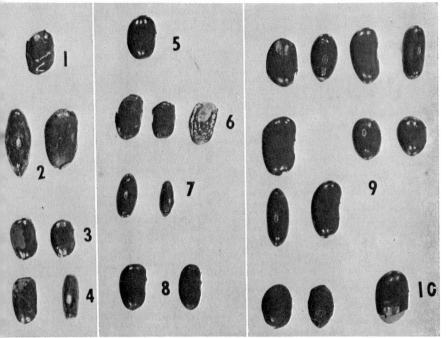

Figure 23.3. *P. vulgaris*—Peru. *1*, Pachacamac 5/221. *2*, Pachacamac 5/222. *3*, Estaqueria, Nazca Valley 8/38. *4*, Estaqueria, Nazca Valley 8/52. *5*, Estaqueria, Nazca Valley 8/45. *6*, Cahuachi, Nazca Valley 8/451. *7*, Cahuachi, Nazca Valley 8/451. *8*, Cahuachi, Nazca Valley 8/410. *9*, Middle Supe, San Nicholas, near Supe (4–7255). *10*, Chincha, 16th century (4–9412). (*1–8*, seeds in Ethnobotanical Collection, Botanical Museum, Harvard. Courtesy of Margaret A. Towle. *9, 10*, Museum of Anthropology, University of California, Berkeley.)

and South America have been interchanged since the conquest has not been extensively documented. However, insofar as North and South American archaeological beans have been investigated, there appears to be no overlap in varieties (figs. 23.1, 23.2, 23.3, 23.4, 23.5).

The confidence that may accompany these conclusions on diffusion within the New World must be tempered by the realization that the sample of archaeological material is small. Furthermore, areas critical for comparisons of ancient North and South American varieties have not yet been excavated by methods that might produce sig-

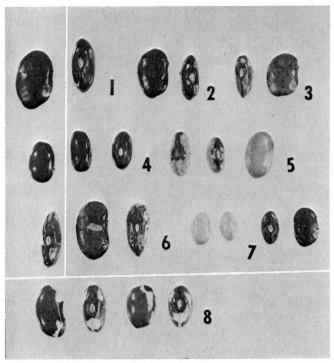

Figure 23.4. *P. vulgaris*—Mesoamerica. *1*, Río Zape Chihuahua, 1300 B.P. *2*, Río Zape, Chihuahua, 1300 B.P. *3*, Río Zape, Chihuahua, 1300 B.P. *4*, Tehuacán, 1000 B.P. *5*, Tularosa Cave. *6*, Verde Valley, PIII. *7*, Tehuacán, 1000 B.P. *8*, Verde Valley, PIII.

nificant remains. The humid eastern slopes of the Andes and the wet coastlands of Mesoamerica must be excavated by methods that will recover carbonized plant material. None of this has yet come to the attention of this writer.

The possible significance of bias in archaeological sample is perhaps best illustrated by the *P. lunatus* beans. The Sievas are dry-land adapted, whereas the Peruvian Limas are humid-land adapted. Archaeological records in areas that would be expected to produce remains of the Peruvian varieties in Mesoamerica are not now available. Almost all Mesoamerican archaeological plant materials are derived from too high elevations, from environments of too little rainfall, or from geographic locations remote from possible routes of introduction or areas of cultivation of Peruvian plants.

As Carl Sauer has suggested, the widespread, predominant beans of historic Mexican agriculture are likely to have achieved their present distribution as a result of having been carried by the sixteenth-century Spanish explorers. This view should be contrasted with that of Gentry (1969), who finds the wild races of *P. vulgaris* most closely related to certain regional cultivars extant in those regions. Thus, for example, bay-seeded (*vayo*) wild *vulgaris* can still be collected in northern Mexico where bay-seeded cultivars predominate. This, of course, assumes that the bay-seeded cultivars are indeed derived from these proposed wild *vulgaris* ancestors. The problem of ancestry of the major bean cultivars is far from approaching a botanical solution. We must be cognizant of the fact that when cultivar populations are established in a region where related wild populations exist, gene flow may proceed in both directions. Genetic influence of the cultivars may be expected to alter the characteristics of the wild populations quite as readily as the reverse influence.

P. vulgaris wild collections have been made widely in Mexico (Gentry, 1969) and include the regions from which archaeological records are available. Given the varietal distinctions between these regions, the over-all evidence suggests multiple domestication and, with some notable exceptions, only limited diffusion in prehistoric times.

NORTH AMERICAN DIFFUSION

The northeastern United States is the region most remote from any center of bean domestication for which archaeological-botanical data are available. Here (Kaplan, in Prufer, 1970) *P. vulgaris* appeared in Ohio nine hundred years ago along with the earliest remains of eight-rowed corn (Galinat, unpublished manuscript). Galinat has suggested (in conversation) that this date was very likely the starting point in the northeast for this corn of remote South American ancestry, which was acclimatized in the Mexican highlands before diffusing into the southwest Pueblos, then to Colorado, and ultimately to the northeast. I can say nothing about the origin of the corn in this Ohio site, but the charred beans resemble a frequently encountered, southwestern vining *P. vulgaris* (fig. 23.4, 6) that is not found among South American collections.

ARCHAEOLOGICAL PHASEOLUS
VARIETAL–GEOGRAPHIC CORRELATIONS

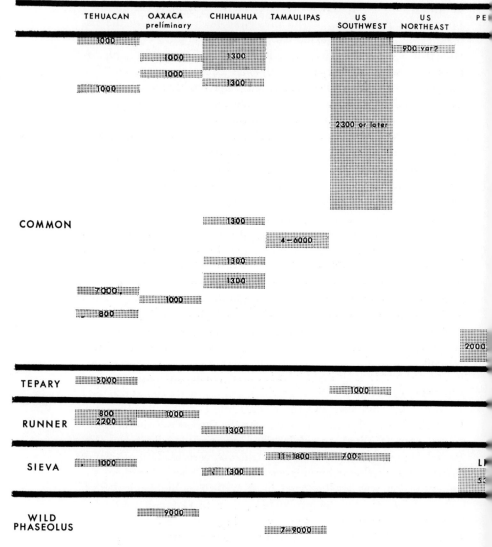

Figure 23.5.

By 2,300 years ago, common beans were well established in the Southwest (Kaplan, 1956). Twenty-one varieties of the common bean are present in the entire available archaeological record in the southwestern United States; six of these are in Chihuahua and two each are in Tehuacán and Oaxaca. The degree of identity among these areas can be determined from figure 23.5. The southwestern United States gives the appearance of being a reception and collecting center for varieties domesticated elsewhere. Most of these varieties entered the Southwest at least 1,000 years after the early date of 2,300 years ago, indicated in figure 23.5. Pueblo III times in the Verde Valley account for most of the varieties recorded.

The *P. vulgaris* beans of Chihuahua, Río Zape (Brooks *et al.*, 1962), nine in all, appear to be one of the varietal arrays from which the southwestern United States beans were selected. That diffusion was a selective process is indicated by the appearance in the Southwest of only five of the nine available Río Zape varieties.

Elsewhere—Tehuacán, Oaxaca, Tamaulipas, Peru—the number of varieties of *P. vulgaris* recovered is small, but each area is sufficiently distinctive to argue for independent regional domestication and little diffusion. The most critical question of pre-Columbian diffusion in the New World remains the relationship between North and South America. The evidence cited here supports the idea that there was no exchange or intercontinental movement of bean cultivars in pre-Columbian times. Further archaeological and botanical collections are necessary to substantiate this argument. South American botanical collections and archaeological materials from the Andean highlands and the eastern Andean slopes are particularly needed.

24. Commentary: Section III

In biology, evolutionists and ecologists are commonly criticized by their more narrowminded colleagues for their willingness to undertake the synthesis of what they hope will be a picture of the natural world, taking their information from a wide variety of disciplines. Of necessity, their panorama lacks the clarity of focus that the specialist can give to his photomicrograph; it may even include a number of optical illusions. But, heaven help them, they try.

Comparable in many ways is the position of the archaeologist who attempts to trace the pattern of intercontinental and intracontinental human contacts and influences; he must be a Jack-of-all-trades, yet he cannot afford not to be a master of each one. Or else he must be a member of a team.

Strangely, however, whether it be the nature of the subject, the natures of the investigators, or the natural disinclination of the fund-granting agencies to support the study of human history rather than forward-looking science, it is notable that the study of pre-Columbian contacts (or at least the botanical side of things) has not attracted many teams. The work that has been reported in this symposium, like work that would have been reported a decade or two ago (before the large-scale funding of science), is generally the product of individual ingenuity, opportunism, and industry. As such, it is not to be criticized lightly, particularly by a botanist who is not even an ethnobotanist. Nevertheless, in addition to the methodological suggestions made by a number of the speakers themselves, it may be possible for an interested outsider, looking at developments in the last couple of decades, to produce some useful ideas for future work based on his experience in other areas of environmental biology.

And, straightaway, I will run the risk of being offensive. Compared with the informational situation that prevailed when Carleton Coon wrote the book that stimulated my interest in the subject of pre-Columbian contacts (*The History of Man,* published in 1954), there has not been a very great change in the botanical picture. At least nothing obviously revolutionary has come to light. Those who used to believe that there is botanical evidence of significant pre-Columbian contacts between the Americas and the rest of the world can carry on in their belief; those who doubted it may remain disbelieving. Agnosticism has not yet been put to flight by revelation.

Perhaps we can never hope for incontrovertible proof of the existence or the absence of influential pre-Columbian contacts, but we might expect to be able to achieve the resolution of such a direct conflict of views as prevails in relation to the introduction of the sweet potato into Polynesia. Was it carried there in prehistoric times, or does its presence there depend entirely upon the Spaniards and Portuguese who sailed into the Pacific Ocean in the sixteenth century and later? Even though the speakers on this subject in this symposium have each utilized new sources of information that were not available when Dr. E. D. Merrill and his opponents were hammering at each other nearly twenty years ago, it is my optimistic belief that the limit has not yet been reached. We should plan for the acquisition of new kinds of data—and, in so doing, realize one of the objects of the organizers in setting up the symposium.

PRE-COLUMBIAN TRANSOCEANIC CONTACTS

In 1954, six taxa were generally considered most worthy of discussion for the evidence they could provide in favor of or against pre-Columbian culture contacts between the Americas and the Old World. These were the coconut (*Cocos nucifera*), the calabash or gourd (*Lagenaria siceraria*), the sweet potato (*Ipomoea batatas*), the peanut (*Arachis hypogaea*), maize (*Zea mays*), and the cotton genus (*Gossypium*). Only the peanut appears to have lost status and has been deemed unworthy of discussion at this symposium in 1968. The dropping of the peanut will raise no protests—the evidence of its pre-Columbian occurrence in the Old World was never better than tenuous and has been adequately discredited (Merrill, 1954). But how much new evidence of significant import has come to light for the other plants?

The Coconut Palm

Jonathan D. Sauer presented in this symposium a convincing account of human *and* natural dispersal of the coconut palm from an Indo-Pacific center. It is very important that he is able to demonstrate that *Cocos nucifera* need not be thought of as a strictly cultigen species (as had been proposed as recently as 1962 by a well-known botanist). Apart from the fossil and historical evidence, the adaptations that the species shows to strand habitats and dispersal by ocean currents are too obvious to be missed, and their evolution must have required hundreds of thousands, if not millions of years. It is not to be expected that botanical guides will always be as obvious as these, but, for their positive or negative influences on the likelihood of natural dispersal, they should be looked for in all the taxa that come under discussion. They may be derived from the reproductive biology of the plants, the ecology of their seedling establishment, vegetative growth, and competitive abilities, as well as their susceptibility to parasites and predators.

The combination of natural and human seaborne dispersal of the coconut is reminiscent of the probable history of another more or less cultivated tropical tree, the kapok tree (*Ceiba pentandra*) of the Bombacaceae (although the direction of dispersal is very different). Here there is evidence (Baker, 1965a) that the species is native in tropical America and in West Africa (and dispersal from the former to the latter may have involved the flotation of the fruits). The cultivated form, however, arose in West Africa and was carried by man across the continent to the east coast and thence around or across the Indian Ocean to Southeast Asia before European explorers reached there. It is primarily botanical evidence that invites these conclusions and it includes a measure of experimentally acquired data. Even though, as Sauer makes clear, *Cocos nucifera* is not ideal material for a breeding program, this does not mean that all experiments are impossible with it.

In both *Cocos nucifera* and *Ceiba pentandra* we have trees that are self-compatible despite a significant rate of outcrossing. A theoretical consequence of this ability to set seed from self-pollination is that seed-reproducing colonies can be started in a new locality even if only a single propagule arrives. Why, therefore, do the occasional volunteer coconut palms that Sauer reports seeing on Caribbean shores not produce groves, as their Pacific Ocean counterparts seem to have done? It would be useful to know whether this is due to biotic factors in one region that are not operative in the other or whether it indicates the baleful effects of inbreeding depression following self-pollination. If the latter is true (and this could be determined by experiment), it implies that multiple natural introductions must have occurred during the dispersal history of the coconut palm in the Pacific area (avoiding inbreeding depression there), again suggesting that a longer time period than that of human occupation of the Pacific Ocean is involved. This conclusion is in accord with all Sauer's evidence. Fortunately for the coconut palm, the longevity of the individual trees improves the likelihood of a second establishment from a wayward seed before the original immigrant dies (and, unlike human beings, all trees are potentially reproductive until their death).

The Calabash or Gourd

The calabash or gourd, *Lagenaria siceraria,* is the other obvious candidate for natural rather than human transportation through ocean waters. Here, Thomas W. Whitaker was able to report experimental work. For some years we have been familiar with the outcome of the studies that he made with George Carter on the capacity of *Lagenaria* seed to survive while the gourds floated in seawater. I have always been surprised that these gentlemen have been so reluctant to accept natural floating of the fruit from Africa to the Americas, in view of their positive demonstrations of the retention of seed viability in floating fruits. Their doubts have been raised, of course, by the fact that *Lagenaria* does not grow as a strand plant. However, I imagine that men were beachcombers even more in the past than they are now; and strange fruit that was washed up from the sea might be expected to be carried to the finder's village to be opened out of curiosity, with the contents finally being thrown onto a trash pile.[1] *Lagenaria* grows very well in such a fertile place. Once in the Americas, *Lagenaria* might move around rather freely by human carriage on land, or further intracontinental sea voyages are possible.

As in the coconut palm, the stigmas of *Lagenaria siceraria* can be successfully pollinated with pollen from the same plant. Thus, the establishment of a seed-reproducing population from even a single seed is possible. Actually, however, seeds are not dispersed singly—the whole fruit, containing many seeds, is the unit of dispersal—so that even inbreeding depression may be alleviated by some cross-pollination between several plants derived from a single fruit.

Experiment has also served *Lagenaria* well through the work carried out by Whitaker and C. B. Heiser, Jr., on the genetic differentiation and fertility barriers between *L. siceraria* and *L. sphaerica*. Work like this increases our confidence in the judgment by Charles Jeffrey (1961, 1967) that there are at least four species of *Lagenaria* in Africa—and, as a consequence, that *L. siceraria* probably originated there rather than in the Americas.

The enormous differences in seed size and morphology that Dr. Whitaker has been able to demonstrate in *L. siceraria* are interesting as indicators of a sizable gene pool in this species. In addition, they may reflect differences in germination requirements between races, for there is a growing body of evidence that the balance between seed output and the size of individual seeds may be of real adaptational significance. Large seeds may be of special value to plants that germinate in conditions of shade or heavy competition (Salisbury, 1942) or in potential drought (Baker, unpublished data); another positive correlation, worked out by Janzen (1969), is between seed size and the presence of substances toxic to insect seed-eaters in some wild members of the Leguminosae (where the larger seeds are rendered possible by release from the necessity of producing a larger number than pests can destroy). It remains to be seen if any of these considerations apply to *Lagenaria*. Whatever is learned in the future about its ecology and evolution is likely to be of greater assistance

---

[1] In the printed version of his paper, Dr. Whitaker inclines more toward this view.

to the explanation of its history in the Americas than of the circumstances of its arrival in this continent, but this is particularly desirable now that the chronology of its travels on this continent is becoming rather well known through the efforts of Dr. Whitaker and others.

The Sweet Potato

In the case of *Lagenaria siceraria*, it seems to be satisfactorily established now that Africa is its home. It seems equally certain that the sweet potato, *Ipomoea batatas*, began its travels in tropical America. Even though Donald D. Brand and Douglas E. Yen do not agree on Nishiyama's claim that *I. trifida* is the tuberless ancestor of the sweet potato, both have their good reasons for believing that the latter was domesticated in this hemisphere. If anything, however, we are now farther from any agreement as to how it reached Oceania.

Even Merrill (1954) was willing to accept human carriage in pre-Columbian time. Yet now we have Yen following Barrau (1957) in suggesting a prehistoric carriage from South America to Polynesia (where, however, its arrival was recent enough for it to be rather clearly superimposed on an agricultural pattern of Asian origin) while allowing the Spanish credit for its introduction to Asia (via Acapulco and Manila) and the Portuguese the responsibility for getting it to western Melanesia from Brazil. Brand considers that there was no prehistoric transportation at all and credits the Portuguese with introducing the sweet potato to strategic places in Asia whence others could pick it up and spread it. Finally, in a book recently published, Purseglove (1968) reiterates his belief (Purseglove, 1963, 1965) that *Ipomoea batatas* spread by natural means across the Pacific Ocean and that tuber-bearing forms arose and were domesticated separately in various places.

Purseglove (1968: 80) asks, rhetorically, why sweet potatoes alone should have been carried by man from the New World to the Old World before 1492. "Sweet potatoes are invariably propagated by stem cuttings in the tropics and these would not survive the voyage unless planted and watered. They can also be grown from tubers, but these keep badly unless cured, and curing is not done in the tropics. . . . As there is no tradition of growing *I. batatas* from seed, it is unlikely that seed would have been taken." Sweet potato seed capsules float in water, and the hard-coated seeds can survive immersion in the sea. Consequently, Purseglove (1965, 1968) suggests that either fruits or a fruiting vine attached to a branch or log drifted from the New World to Polynesia.

It is with a twinge of regret that I observe all three authors to be agreed that the similarity of the Maori name *kumara* to others in use in Polynesia and to the name *cumar* from Peru is *not* good evidence of human carriage of the plant over the Pacific Ocean. Students have been very fond of this piece of "evidence." We shall miss it.

All three of these authors, however, make suggestions upon which botanical comment is in order. Purseglove makes a very good point in stressing the difficulties of transporting viable tubers and sprouting them successfully at the end of their long voyage, but he should also consider the disadvantage, for establishment of the plant from naturally dispersed seed, of the very irregular germination of that seed. In addition, any plant derived from a seed will be self-incompatible, so that further reproduction will have to be by vegetative means until, or unless, another plant also gets started from more immigrant seed. Generally speaking, self-compatibility rather than self-incompatibility is found in plants that there is reason to suppose have established themselves naturally after long-distance dispersal (Baker, 1955). I do not think that natural transportation provides the most likely answer to the sweet potato problem.

Brand's apparently very complete critical review of the sweet potato literature also contains suggestions for future investigations. Included among these is a recommendation that a study of the pollen of *Ipomoea* species be made, followed by attempts to find such pollen in remains datable by the C-14 technique. By such means it might be possible to determine the minimum length of time during which *Ipomoea batatas* has been growing in different areas. Ikuse (1956), for example, described the pollen of this species in detail, but the scanty evidence available when Erdtman (1952) wrote his book on comparative pollen morphology suggested to him that the pollen is rather uniform throughout the genus. If this is true, the pollen contribution of all the naturally occurring species of *Ipomoea* in the tropics of the world will have to be taken into account. In addition, even where the sweet potato is grown, its pollen production is very limited; not only is its flowering far from prolific but each flower produces relatively few grains (as befits its insect-pollination mechanism.) Finally, most pollen preservation occurs in soil subject to waterlogging; this is not a usual habitat for sweet potatoes. Consequently, the chances of pollen from this species turning up in any soil sample that is examined do not seem to be very good.

Drs. Brand and Yen do not disagree on most sweet potato topics, except the big one of how the sweet potato reached Polynesia after an American origin. Yen is commendably modern in taking account of the ranges of variation in *a large number of characters* that characterize *populations* of sweet potatoes he has sampled in different regions of the Pacific basin. He has also taken good account of the influence of vegetative reproduction in producing this picture of variation—one that might have been very different if there should have been much seed reproduction (by outcrossing, no less, because the plants are self-incompatible). By vegetative reproduction the characteristics of clones tend to be passed on unchanged from generation to generation instead of being continuously recombined.

Yen's evidence points to a conclusion that Polynesia, Melanesia, and the Asiatic mainland have received separate introductions of sweet potatoes from a common provenance rather than there having been a linear transmission from South America through the islands to the opposite side of the ocean. But how much of this picture may have been produced by *post*-Columbian, separate introduction?

It seems to me that the truth about the travels of the sweet potato to and through Oceania may quite possibly never be revealed to us. But this is hardly likely to prevent future arguments over this species.

Maize

It is with reluctance that I comment at all upon maize. A vast amount of attention has been given to this cultigen, with most of the conclusions from recent studies labeling it a New World domesticate that remained just that until it was carried to Europe by returning Spanish explorers. Goodman (1965) has reviewed recent literature on the biology of *Zea mays*, but he reaches no conclusion regarding pre-Columbian export of maize.

Hugh C. Cutler and Leonard W. Blake in the present symposium come to the conclusion that there is no satisfactory evidence favoring a belief in pre-Columbian transportation of maize away from the New World. M. D. W. Jeffreys, however, disagrees, although most of the arguments advanced by him in favor of its introduction into the Old World in pre-Columbian time depend upon the interpretation of vernacular names and ambiguous statements by classical authors. Nevertheless, he does make passing reference to some botanical evidence that must be looked into: the claimed finding in India of carbonized maize grains and their impressions upon potsherds (Vishnu-Mittre, 1966) and pollen grains (Vishnu-Mittre and Gupta, 1966) that are slightly pre-Columbian. In addition to the obvious necessity of checking the age of these botanical remains, it must also be made certain that there is no error in identification. For the pollen, at least, this is not easy, as Barghoorn, Wolfe, and Clisby (1954) found in defending their identification of sixty-thousand-year-old remains from Mexico. Nevertheless, by the application of a variety of scientific tests Barghoorn has been, to all appearances, successful. Corresponding tests should be applied to the Indian pollen. The most obvious characteristic of maize pollen is that it is larger than that of any other grass (Erdtman, 1943, 1952), but some other cereals have large grains (for example, *Coix, Sorghum, Eriochloa,* and *Triticum*), and it must be demonstrated beyond doubt that the Indian remains do not represent one of these indigenous genera.

Cotton

An interesting feature of the extremely relevant presentation on cotton by S. G. Stephens is that he concerns himself with problems not envisaged in 1954. The major problem at that time seemed to be one of explaining how the A genome from the Old World could have been combined with the D genome of diploid New World cottons to produce the AD genome (or genomes) of the cultivated tetraploid New World cottons (*Gossypium hirsutum* and *G. barbadense*). It was the prevailing view then that these tetraploids did not occur as genuinely wild plants, being feral at best. The Old World diploids are linted and are used for textile production; New World diploids are lintless. Consequently, it seemed very likely that men brought Old World linted diploid cotton to the New World, where it hybridized with indigenous lintless species. With a doubling of the chromosome number in the hybrids, the luxuriantly linted tetraploids would have been born, and it was supposed that with selection in favor of these tetraploids by the growers, the diploid (Old World) cultivated cotton became extinct in the New World.

There is no need to review the various theories of transatlantic and transpacific transportation of such an Old World cotton; these have been reviewed most recently by Purseglove (1968), who also includes in his consideration the theories of *natural* immigration of Old World cotton into the New World. In any case, the switch away from preoccupation with the origin of the tetraploids appears to stem simply from the acceptance of the natural occurrence of both *Gossypium hirsutum* and *G. barbadense* variously in Antillean, Central American, and South American locations. Certainly, the problem of how and where the tetraploids evolved has not been solved, but the necessity of human involvement in their origin appears to have been removed. The natural meeting of the diploids and the origin of the tetraploids may have occurred a very long time ago, when climates and continental outlines could have been very different from what they are now.

Nevertheless, *Gossypium* does not disappear from our concern with possible pre-Columbian transoceanic transportation, although now it is the tetraploids that are under scrutiny. Stephens' consideration of the capacity for natural transoceanic dispersal of the "wild" tetraploid cottons, including the ancestor of *G. sandvicense* (otherwise known as *G. tomentosum*) to Hawaii from Central America and *G. barbadense* var. *darwinii* to the Galápagos Islands from Ecuador, leads him to the conclusion that their geographical distribution in itself cannot be used critically as supporting evidence for early transoceanic contacts. At the same time, however, he is able to point to features of cultivated cotton that leave them virtually dependent upon human dispersal. As a consequence, the possible early occurrences of the linted *G. hirsutum* in the Cape Verde Islands and the Marquesas Islands become much more significant and worthier of further investigation.

An extremely important part of Stephens' contribution is the plea, with examples, that he makes for an appreciation by the archaeologist of what a botanist needs in plant remains before he can make an accurate identification.[2] This matter deserves careful consideration, not merely in relation to cotton problems, but for all plant materials unearthed in any archaeological investigation. Another important contribution Stephens has made (1967) is the demonstration that areas with greatest variability (Vavilov notwithstanding) are not

---

[2] In their paper, Cutler and Blake reverse the signals and call for more botanists to be trained as specialists in the identification of economic plants.

necessarily centers of distribution. In the case of *Gossypium hirsutum* they probably have been produced by introgressive hybridization with *G. barbadense* in Central America and northwestern South America.

The relevance of Stephens' methodological suggestions to the theme of this symposium must be emphasized; it is by the acquisition of new *kinds* of data that progress in understanding plants in relation to man will come, instead of by mere prolongation of what is often futile argument.

Conclusions on Transoceanic Contacts

These are the papers primarily concerned with potential transoceanic contacts in pre-Columbian times. How much clearer is the picture they present compared with that prevailing in 1954? Surely there cannot now be any question but that there *were* visitors to the New World from the Old World (or vice-versa) in historic and even prehistoric time before 1492. The big problem is whether these visits were at all significant culturally.

One of the dangers of considering crop plants one at a time, as they are in this symposium, is that they are not viewed in perspective. Every small suggestion of an influence from one continent on another looms largely in the account of a single species of crop plant, even though it may be trivial in the total agricultural context. Evidence from sweet potatoes, from maize, and from cotton may suggest minor transfers from the New World to the Old World, but these must always be viewed against a background of enormous differences between the agricultural materials and methods in the two hemispheres.

The presentation of evidence in this symposium leaves me with the impression that such contacts as may have occurred—whether by Polynesian argonauts, Peruvian rafters, Japanese fishermen, Vikings, or Irish priests—were remarkably unproductive of botanical or agricultural effects. From the speed with which many New World crop plants were spread to and through the Old World and vice-versa *after* the Columbian discovery, it would seem that they would have been highly appreciated before that time. Furthermore, an inevitable implication is that if pre-Columbian contacts were not very effective in modifying the food-producing aspects of cultures, they probably were not much more effective in any other way.

Pre-Columbian Contacts within the Americas

So little controversy attends the movements of plant materials useful to man within the Americas in pre-Columbian times that this
commentator feels little stimulus to intervention in the discussion.
Cutler and Blake point out in their paper that maize appears late in
South America (no earlier than 1400 B.C., according to remains available so far) and seems to have been added to an existing agriculture
that included beans, gourds, and squashes. These authors believe that
that the beans, gourds, and squashes may have been domesticated
locally from wild-growing plants. Fortunately, we have the contributions of specialists on each of these kinds of plant; they do not agree
in all cases with this theory, which implies domestication in South
America independent from that in Mesoamerica. Consequently, some
extra consideration is in order.

Beans

Lawrence Kaplan, in an exhaustive discussion of beans in the genus
Phaseolus, presents evidence that the common bean (*P. vulgaris*)
was domesticated (probably several times) in Mesoamerica by 5000
B.C., that the tepary (*P. acutifolius* var. *latifolius*) was domesticated
by 3000 B.C., and that the runner bean (*P. coccineus*) entered a
domestic state a few hundred years before the birth of Christ. Of
these species, only common beans appear to have spread to South
America before 1492, and their datings there are considerably later
than those from Mesoamerica. Kaplan does not discuss the suggestion
by Heiser (1965) that common beans in coastal Peru were domesticated separately from the wild *P. arborigeus* Burkhart. *Phaseolus
lunatus* provides an interesting contrast (and one that does agree
with the Cutler and Blake postulate). In this case, Kaplan and also
Heiser (1965) point out that the species appears to have differentiated subspecifically while still a wild plant and that the two forms
were domesticated separately (to give big Limas in Peru and small
Limas or Sievas in Mesoamerica). All this seems very reasonable
botanically.

The Calabash or Gourd

Whitaker adds to this generally harmonious picture by the presentation of a chronology for *Lagenaria siceraria*, the calabash or gourd.

Here the archaeological record indicates that the plant was on the northern boundary of Mesoamerica in preagricultural times, prior to 7000 B.C. Whitaker demonstrates clearly the progressive spread of the gourd into the Southwest, the Eastern Woodlands, and the Plains area of the present-day United States.

For South America, the situation is less clear; Whitaker claims that the gourd was *cultivated* at Huaca Prieta on the northern coast of Peru as early as 3000 B.C. but does not make a final decision as to whether it was deliberately grown or merely collected on the central coast of Peru where Lanning (1963) examined remains. Lanning's materials could be very important, because he speculates that the deposits containing them may have ages of up to ten thousand years or more (in an area where the preagricultural stage is believed to have persisted until 2500–2000 B.C.). Cutler and Blake, referring to a gourd rind estimated to date from 5500 to 4500 B.C. and found at a site near Talcara, Peru, also do not indicate whether they believe the plant to have been cultivated or not. Presumably it was not.

Consequently, it cannot yet be decided whether the gourd traveled from Mesoamerica to South America as a cultivated plant, as a wild one, or as a weed (or even whether it was separately introduced there from the Old World). Of the various possibilities, travel as a weed—or, at any rate, as a camp-follower—seems the most likely. Incidentally, more attention could be given with advantage to the study of weeds, not only as potential crop plants, but also for what they, like the deliberately cultivated plants, can tell about human migration (see Baker, 1962, 1965b).

Squashes

For *Cucurbita,* Cutler and Blake offer the alternative suggestions that the ancestors of *C. maxima* and *C. andreana* were either distributed more or less continuously through Central America to Andean South America (and subsequently became extinct in the former) or that fruits of an ancestral species drifted there and that evolution on the Peruvian coast produced the weedy plants whose fruits were gathered by men. Evidence has come to light that makes the former hypothesis the more likely one.

In a series of studies, Hurd and Linsley (1964, 1966, 1967a, 1967b) have traced the origin and distribution of squashes, gourds, and pumpkins throughout the Americas by investigating the pollen-collecting relationships of two genera of solitary bees (*Peponapis* and *Xenoglossa*) with the genus *Cucurbita*. *Xenoglossa* is restricted to North America, whereas *Peponapis* occurs in North and South America. The females of these two bee genera are known to obtain pollen solely from wild and domesticated *Cucurbita* plants. Seventeen wild species of *Cucurbita* are restricted to North America and the group is centered south of Mexico City, but none occurs in Central America south of San Salvador (Hurd and Linsley, 1967a). Nevertheless, cultivated *Curcurbita* and the genus *Peponapis* occur in South America, where there are three quite distinct endemic species of the bees. "Even if domesticated *Cucurbita* were introduced as early as 25,000 years ago, this period of time is insufficient to account for the evolution of three such distinctive species of bees" (Hurd and Linsley, 1967a: 649). From the distribution of these bees (two in northwestern South America and one in the southeast of the sub-continent) it would seem that two, possibly three, species of wild *Cucurbita* must have been present in South America. Before they became extinct, domestication of the cucurbits occurred and the bees were saved.

Interestingly, on a collecting trip for *Peponapis* made to Ecuador in 1965 by Dr. and Mrs. A. E. Michelbacher, a large wild gourd was discovered and three collections of seeds were made. It appears to be a new species related to *C. maxima* and *C. andreana* and will be described as such by Dr. Cutler and Dr. Whitaker. Thus a conclusion drawn from the bee biology appears to be borne out by the revelation of the continued, rare existence of a wild cucurbit.

Cultivated *Cucurbita* alone occurs in Central America south of San Salvador, but it is accompanied by five species of *Peponapis*—all recruited from the North American fauna. Presumably man has reestablished *Cucurbita* in this area where it had long been extinct (possibly since the submergence of the land in the early Tertiary) and the bees have followed it southward.

In the case of the South American cucurbits, it looks as if we are up against a familiar problem. Why is it that the ancestors of domesticated plants are now so rare (or even extinct)? It is hard to see how domestication of *Cucurbita* would make life any more difficult for the wild species.

TABLE 24.1
Botanical Tests Distinguishing Gradual Range Expansions from Long-Distance Dispersal and Establishment, with or without Human Aid

Gradual Range Expansion	Long-distance Dispersal	Possible Evidence of Dispersal by Human Agency
1. Weeds, pests, and specialized pollinators may be accompanists	1. Usually unaccompanied	
2. Dispersal mechanisms only of short-range type	2. Fruits or seeds suitable for floating or attachment to migrating birds	2. May show loss of dispersal mechanism
3. Seed may have limited length of viability	3. Seed with extended viability	3. May show loss of seed formation
4. Flowers may be self-incompatible or dioecious	4. Usually self-compatible, apomictic, or plants have vegetative reproduction	
5. Cross-pollination may be by specialized pollinators	5. Such crossing as occurs involves generally available pollen vectors (including wind)	
6. May be close environmental control of growth and reproduction	6. Individual plants may possess rather wide environmental tolerance	6. May be unable to grow outside of cultivated land
7. May have requirement for specialized symbiont (e.g., legumes and nitrogen-fixing bacteria)	7. Probably no relationship with any *specialized* symbiont	
8. May be able to grow only in climax vegetation or in cultivated land derived therefrom	8. Often able to grow in pioneer habitats	
9. Evidence of virtually continuous array of habitats	9. Required habitats may be obviously disjunct	9. Distribution may be discordant with patterns to be seen in unquestionably wild plants

Botanical Tests of Dispersal Types

Where there were early human contacts between Mesoamerica and South America, revelation of the manner in which they were made in each case would be of great importance to students of human history in the Americas. Always there are the two alternatives —a sea passage or a land journey—and for cotton, as well as the *Lagenaria* gourd and the coconut, natural passage by sea cannot be ruled out. Even for maize, suggestions have been made that its introduction to South America may have been by sea (but, in this case, of course, carried by man); the common bean may have arrived by the same means.

There are a number of botanical tests (table 24.1) that can be applied in the hope of distinguishing between a gradual expansion of range and long-distance dispersal, even if the two pictures ultimately come to look alike. In the latter case, a disjunct distribution is set up directly; in the former it may be produced by subsequent extermination in an interior part of the range. A result from the tests can be announced only on the basis of a clear preponderance of characteristics pointing to the same means of dispersal, and it is not to be expected that this will be distinguishable in every case. A decision as to whether either kind of dispersal has been achieved naturally or with human aid can only be approached by a further series of tests.

This is one way in which the application of botanical tests may be helpful to the archaeologist. It would also be helpful if the latter would accept (as the botanical taxonomist has been forced to do) that an individual can only rarely be taken as typical of a population and that an analysis of variance wherever it can be performed is an essential act in the description of a find.

Wherever it is possible to discover the breeding system of a plant under investigation, this should also be done. Although there can be complicating factors, obligate cross-pollinators will tend to be the most highly variable, self-pollinators less variable, and those plants that do not reproduce sexually will tend to be rather highly invariable within populations. Many intermediate breeding systems exist, of course, and these, like variations in the intensity of selection pressure, will complicate the picture. Out-crossers tend to hold their variability as they migrate, while selfers and those plants which reproduce asexually tend to lose it. In all cases, however, long-distance dispersal is liable to produce a significant reduction in variability when the new colony is derived from only one or a few propagules. Such analyses of variability may be much more difficult to make with archaeological material than with living populations, but the goal is there to be aimed at.

Finally, an admonition to botanists may be in order. If archaeologists seem to be liable to draw conclusions that a botanist would not think justified by the evidence, it may be because the archaeologist is being forced to attempt a task botanists have spurned. There are still too many of our fraternity who feel that any kind of study not made upon unquestionably wild plants is somehow not respectable. Let us come down from our ivory tower and try to be rather more useful than we have been in the past.

Conclusions

Discussions of New World–Old World pre-Columbian contacts have, all too often, generated more heat than light. For example, the general ground rules and presuppositions of any two examiners are apt to differ, and the perimeters of the problem are seen differently by different people. To men like Elliot Smith and Lord Raglan it was transparently clear that a single region, blessed with circumstances that led or forced man to invent, produced much of the high culture (from Smith's writings one might think much of the *culture*) of diverse peoples around the world. Smith and Raglan, in fact, chose two different natal areas, but their underlying assumptions about the uninventiveness of man were much the same, as were the ideas of other hyperdiffusionists who chose still other (and in some cases clearly mythical) regions for this *Ursprung* of culture.

The situation was also simple enough to the unilinear evolutionists. To them, man was on a one-way track—in fact, in its more extreme form, their concept of culture progress could be thought of as a series of parallel cultural "railroad tracks" that really need *never* have interconnecting branches to arrive at the same station. The tracks did occasionally interconnect, but this, although interesting, was not of any real processual importance.

We mention these two extreme positions merely to record them; no one in the present symposium holds to either of them. They simply mark the end points of a continuum, and the positions of the various members of the symposium can be more or less spotted along this continuum.[1]

Such a view, of course, oversimplifies the problem. For example, the question of interhemispherical diffusion may be looked on as part of the larger question of culture dynamics or process. The tendency to treat diffusion versus independent invention of culture traits or complexes may in fact obscure some of the problems of the interpretation of cultural interaction. In addition, some scholars feel that the very investigation of this sort of problem is at best worthless and at worst dangerously misleading. As John H. Rowe (1966: 337) recently said:

> In altogether too many courses and symposia on New World archaeology, diffusionist fantasies are being presented as a substitute for archaeological theory, the presentation conveying to the audience that some standard diffusionist idea is the goal toward which all detailed archaeological research in the area in question is being or should be directed. But any innocent archaeologist who comes away from one of these sessions convinced that transpacific contacts are the wave of the future is sadly deluded. Diffusionism is the wave of the past. It was the favorite theory used by 16th-century travelers to explain odd similarities which struck their notice, and it has remained ever since the favorite recourse of Western folk-belief in dealing with such problems.

Such a view, obviously, is not shared by most members of this symposium. A statement of A. V. Kidder (1946: 2) more nearly sums up the spirit of the present volume: "This matter of beginnings of native American civilizations is of fundamental importance not only for the understanding of American prehistory, but also because of its bearing upon problems of culture diffusion versus the repeated invention of basic processes." The question of contacts and, more importantly, the *nature* of such contacts we believe to be basic to an understanding of a great segment of culture history and broad areas of cultural dynamics.

In examining the presence and nature of interhemispheric pre-

---

[1] By now it is obvious to the reader that the nonbotanical sections of the symposium are heavily weighted in favor of interhemispheric diffusion. Having attempted in the organization of the symposium to cover all points of view, we are led to speculate as to why many antidiffusionists seem reluctant to enter into such dialogues.

Columbian contacts, we should first consider if there is, in fact, any contact situation that specialists generally accept as valid. There does seem to be one period and one area for which pre-Columbian contact is admitted, though even here the *implications* are not wholly agreed upon. Beginning in the last years of the tenth century A.D. and continuing on into at least the early years of the eleventh century, Norse vessels did, in all probability, make landfalls on the coasts of Labrador and Newfoundland. In the present volume these have been briefly but satisfactorily sketched out by Taylor. Until recently the evidence for Norse contact has been mainly documentary, but within recent years archaeological work at the site of L'Anse aux Meadows in northern Newfoundland suggests that this site does represent a transient Norse settlement—perhaps that of Thorfinn Karlsefni. In addition, there are a few artifacts in Greenland from Viking or early post-Viking period excavations that suggest contact with the mainland of North America (Ingstad, 1969: 92–93). Taylor points out that analysis of wood found in Greenland might indicate such contacts, and surely the whole archaeological picture in Greenland will someday have to be reconsidered in terms of possible mainland influences. As far as the L'Anse aux Meadows site is concerned, however, we still await a detailed archaeological report.

There is no reliable evidence whatsoever that these Norse contacts had significant influence on indigenous populations. For one thing, the Norse seem to be restricted to the coastal area. The "finds" that place Scandinavians far inland—for example, the Kensington Stone —are almost certainly valueless. Such fanciful and farfetched ideas as derivation of Quetzalcoatl from Norse culture heroes violate the priority rule stated in our introduction (and the Quetzalcoatl flight of fancy, in particular, has been dealt with by Hedrick in this volume). The saga evidence makes it clear that Viking and Indian, or Eskimo, in continental North America had little contact, and that mostly of a violent nature. We can safely say that the Norse came, they saw, but they did not conquer or even change things very much.

We have no other convincing evidence of North Atlantic contact, although, as Kehoe so clearly points out, contact may well have been feasible. More work needs to be done, especially study of the larger European boats. In this regard, it should be noted that the physical evidence we have for pre-Viking ships (as against dugouts or smaller craft) throws some doubt on the seaworthiness of, at least, the crafts of the Migration period (see Green, 1963, for a discussion of the Sutton Hoo ship and of other Migration period ships).

In the introduction to this volume the editors suggested five major considerations—hard evidence for contacts, similar traits in the two hemispheres, linguistic resemblances, plant evidence, and theoretical implications—in investigating the whole problem of contacts. We can consider these here in the light of evidence presented in this volume and elsewhere.

It seems to be the concensus in the symposium and in the archaeological literature in general that there are, to date—excluding the Viking contacts discussed above—no verified archaeological finds of artifacts from one hemisphere in pre-Colombian context in the other. We must consider the implications of this point in detail. There are obviously many finds of similar materials that have led archaeologists and others to postulate contacts; that is, after all, a major part of the evidence. Some recent and well-publicized examples include the many examples of artistic similarities seen by Robert Heine-Geldern and Gordon Ekholm—scroll patterns from the Ulua Valley compared to Chou China; friezes from Tajín compared to Chou; pyrite mirrors, Tajín compared to China; tripod vessels, Teotihuacán style and Han China; features of temples, Yucatán Maya compared to Cambodia (Heine-Geldern, 1966: 279–282, 290), and of course many others. More recently Meggers, Evans, and Estrada (1965) have compared Valdivia and Jomon (Japanese) ceramics.

It must be stressed that these similarities represent, not actual spread of artifacts, but possible copying of one technique or design element of one culture by the other. If actually copied, these examples obviously are proof of contact from one area to the other, but, of course, the question here centers on the meaning of the resemblances. All such similarities have been challenged, Ekholm and Heine-Geldern by Phillips (1966: 296–314), among others; Meggers, Evans, and Estrada by Muller (this volume), by Pearson (1968: 85–86), and by Lathrop (1967: 96–97), among others.

These, of course, represent only a tiny sample of the many alleged examples of contact between the Old World and the New World. In the present symposium Doran suggests a link up in boat types, Beirne in axes and adzes; Sorenson tabulates a large number of interhemispherical correspondences (without, of course, claiming that they were necessarily the result of diffusion); Kelley deals with calendrical systems, Kehoe with pottery. These cover a vast range of time and contact across both major bodies of water, Atlantic and Pacific.

The symposium members have generally been sensitive to the problems of time and space correspondences. Several writers point out the desirability of comparing complexes that are *in fact* comparable in the sense that they appear either at the same time, or with some reasonable time lag between the donor and recipient culture. Naturally, it is important that the time differential between the hemispheres not be overwhelmingly great. As one of the present editors pointed out in another context, Inca *aryballi* "are covered with geometric decorations and have a freakish resemblance to Greek Geometric period pots" (Riley, 1969: 205). No one (certainly not the author of the statement) seriously claims that there was direct contact over a chasm of two thousand years between the early Greeks and the Inca.

Actually, the lack of direct evidence for contact has led several members of the symposium to turn to a consideration of large-scale patterned similarities. Both Sorenson and Borhegyi are interested in the Kroeberian concept of oikoumene as a heuristic device for examining extensive parallels between Old World and New World cultures. Ekholm, who suggests that concrete evidence may *never* be found for transpacific (or, by implication, transatlantic) diffusion, is also mainly concerned, not with possible incidental diffusions, but with diffusion as a major factor in the evolution of culture.

The lack of absolute evidence for transhemispherical contact is, of course, significant. After all, the two worlds, inhabited by rather advanced cultures, were in juxtaposition for many, many centuries, and zero evidence of an artifactual type must be explained. We should be careful, however, not to overemphasize negative evidence. For one thing, as Ekholm points out in this volume, archaeological evidence, by its very nature, is incomplete, not only because of the natural attrition of time but also because many important contacts may be nonmaterial in nature. In addition, archaeological exploration, to date, is far from complete—in fact, certain crucial regions in both the New World and the Old World (western Mexico and much of Southeast Asia, for example) are hardly known at all. The possibility must also be considered that actual artifacts *may* have been discovered but discarded, misunderstood, or incompletely reported. In fact, there have been claims for a considerable number of Old World artifacts in pre-Columbian contexts. Sorenson mentions "patently Egyptian" statuettes supposedly found in strata three meters deep in El Salvador. A recent Greco-Roman head has been discovered in an alleged pre-Columbian context in Veracruz, and there are many more. Obviously, one or the other of these finds might, indeed, be valid.

The stress on large-scale contacts as against incidents that deposited isolated artifacts on one shore or the other brings us to the major question of the nature of contacts. The editors feel that the important question is, ultimately, whether one hemisphere was significantly modified in major cultural trends by the other. Does the evidence reinforce or weaken the case for broad similarity in the human response to comparable conditions? This similarity, which is basic to all evolutionary approaches to man and is inherent in Bastian's concept of the psychic unity of mankind, cannot, of course, actually be disproved by a demonstration of wide-scale contact around the world. The case for multilinear evolution would, however, be significantly weakened, for the "laboratory" situation would be lost.

One of the most pervasive types of evidence for interhemispheric diffusion is that of language. It is a key factor in the attempts by men like García and Grotius to demonstrate contact across the Atlantic and Pacific. In the nineteenth and twentieth centuries, especially, it has been drawn on by amateurs to bolster pet ideas. Theories of contacts between widespread areas, some plausible, others wildly improbable, have been suggested in the last century. Enthusiastic workers have "demonstrated" historical linguistic relationships between Algonkian and Norse, Polynesian and Inca, Aboriginal Australian and one or the other American Indian languages, Chinese and Yuman, and so on *ad nauseam.*

This is not to say that linguistic relationships cannot be traced over a large distance; indeed there are language stocks that extend over thousands of miles and thousands of years—Indo-European, for example, or Uto-Aztecan. As yet, however, no linguist has established (perhaps with the minor exception of Eskimo-Aleut) a continuity of a language family from one hemisphere to the other on a pre-Columbian level.

The standard position of the historical linguistic relationship is stated by Leonard Bloomfield (1933: 297):

Such features as phonemes, morphemes, words, sentences, constructions, and substitution-types, appear in every language; they are inherent in the nature of human speech. Other features, such as noun-like and verb-like form-classes, categories of number, person, case, and tense, or grammatical positions of actor, verbal goal, and possessor, are not universal, but still so widespread that better knowledge will doubtless some day connect them with universal characteristics of mankind. Many features that are not wide-spread—among them some very specific and even minute ones—are found in distant and wholly unrelated languages; these features, too, may be expected some day to throw light on human psychology.

Bloomfield goes on to warn specifically against incidental resem-blances of isolated, similar words that have similar meanings in two disconnected languages; resemblances that "bear no significance whatever" (1933: 297).

In the present symposium we are not, in fact, concerned with schemes of relationships of whole languages. Two limited and rather different uses of language to support contact are drawn on by certain of the participants. The first of these is the identification of individual words that may be related in Old World and New World languages. Carter uses this technique to trace names of chickens, and Jett to compare series of words representing possible contact across the Pacific. Both Carter and Jett emphasize that they regard these words as leads to be followed up rather than as definite proof of contact. For this kind of evidence we have very little to say, except perhaps to stress again the suspicion with which professional linguists view com-parison of isolated words with the idea of demonstrating either his-torical relationships of the languages or (more germane in this case) vocabulary borrowing. A few specific comments on name diffusion as discussed by symposium members may be made here. Carter is perhaps a bit too cavalier in dismissing onomatopoeia as an explana-tion for similarity in chicken names (especially the *kuk* words). In addition, his suggestion that the Tarahumar word for chicken, *totori*, is derived from, or related to, Japanese is likely without merit. These are very minor things; perhaps more to the point, because it figures importantly in hypotheses about contact across the Pacific, is the alleged relationship between the Quechua name for sweet potato, *kumar*, with the Polynesian *kumara*. This point is mentioned by Carter (quoting Rivet, 1957) and Jett. Yen, however, is hesitant to assign much importance to it, and Brand has telling arguments against the diffusion of this word from a Polynesian language to

Quechua. The present editors feel with H. G. Baker "a tinge of regret" that the *kumar-kumara* link is now very suspect. We too shall miss it.

The other use of word analysis in the symposium is that of Jeffreys, who in this paper, as in a number of previous ones, attempts to place pre-Columbian maize in Africa and Asia by establishing that certain Portuguese, Italian, and Spanish words for some cereal grain (or grains) in pre-Columbian or early post-Columbian times actually referred to maize. If Jeffreys' inferences are correct, it is certainly true that maize is old in the Eastern Hemisphere. As Reed in this volume points out, however, there is considerable uncertainty in Jeffreys' approach and, though it points up interesting possibilities, it can hardly stand as proof.

In the present volume there has been relatively little use of linguistic evidence. Generally, linguistic comparisons have played a small part in scholarly consideration of the problem of interhemispheric contacts (Heyerdahl's work is a notable exception). We editors feel that linguistic evidence will always have a place in future consideration of diffusion problems but disagree somewhat among ourselves as to how important a place.

At one time in the past a great deal of emphasis was placed on comparisons of physical type for a contribution to the problem of contacts. In this volume Jett summarizes some of the physical anthropological evidence and is cautiously optimistic that this approach may help solve the problem of transoceanic contacts. The editors do not share this optimism. The limitations of osteological comparisons are generally recognized, and studies of modern groups after four centuries of massive contact can hardly produce anything but suspect data.

The question of plant and animal transferences is of crucial importance to this symposium. The point has been made over and over that here we have the possibility of firm evidence; that identity in plants, especially the man-modified cultigens, must mean some sort of contact between the hemispheres. The problem turns out to be more complicated than is generally recognized. The possibility of parallel development of cultivated plants from related wild forms cannot be ignored. Alternate methods of transport can be suggested— flotation and birds as carriers, for example. The concensus of botanical evidence given in this symposium seems to be that *there is no hard and fast evidence for any pre-Columbian human introduction of any single plant or animal* across the ocean from the Old World to the New World, or vice-versa. This is emphatically *not* to say that it could not have occurred. H. G. Baker, whose excellent commentary on the botanical section of this volume obviates any necessity for detailed comments by the editors, thinks (without committing himself very strongly) that a case can be made for the sweet potato, perhaps for cotton, possibly for maize.

The arguments of Carter for pre-Columbian chickens in America, based on such diverse considerations as rate of diffusion in the Old World, comparison of names for separate areas, and physical descriptions, is ingenious and we certainly agree with Carter that further study is desirable.

One facet touched on in the introduction to this volume and discussed briefly by Jett, but not considered in detail by any symposium member, is the question of macro- or micro-organism parasites. The lack of evidence of malaria in early contact times strongly suggests that the parasite *Plasmodium sp.* was originally absent in America, although it was widespread and probably ancient in Africa and Europe. The rapid spread of the Old World "children's diseases," with terrifying results, throughout the Americas and the deadly spread of syphilis in Europe in immediate post-conquest times suggest that the various viruses of measles, chicken pox, and smallpox were unknown in native America and that the organism *Treponema pallidum*, causing syphilis, was unknown in Europe. If such is true, it must be taken into account when we consider the feasibility of large-scale pre-Columbian contacts.

The most serious problem in a symposium such as this is not a tabulation of the pros and cons in box-score fashion, but an attempt to lay the groundwork for further exploration of the field and a delineation of further problems. A very central question is that of our goal. If we are looking simply for pre-Columbian contacts from one hemisphere to the other, the chances are that some did, indeed, occur and that we may reasonably expect to find them. Certain data already point the way to such contacts—the distribution of sweet potatoes, similarities of stonework between Easter Island and the central Andes, a series of tantalizing (albeit indefinite) similarities in art forms, tool types, architectural features, boats, rafts, and the like. In addition, there is the often demonstrated ability of man to cross, at least, the Atlantic in small or makeshift crafts. Finally, one or more of the numerous unverified finds of actual trade objects in pre-Columbian contexts may indeed be valid, or a verifiable one may appear tomorrow or next year. In this kind of contact, Atlantic journeys may actually have been more common than Pacific ones. Atlantic crossings have received little attention in the past, primarily because they involved Africa. Until recently, most specialists believed—incorrectly, it would now seem—that African cultures vigorous or complex enough to contribute to the New World were too late to have any important effect. Schwerin (1970) and Reed in this volume point up the possible importance of early African contacts with America.

The question of sporadic pre-Columbian contacts is interesting but ultimately not very important. Those members of the symposium who feel most strongly about the validity of transoceanic diffusion normally consider that contact was massive and prolonged, that it may have come in several waves, and that it profoundly influenced the art, architecture, political and social systems, crafts, religion, and other uses of culture. In other words, they feel that the obvious similarities of great complexes between the Old World and the New can only mean that at one or the other time the Old World oikoumene reached out to encompass the New. Those members less convinced of massive diffusion are particularly puzzled at the lack of hard (artifactual) evidence for contact, the curious dissimilarity of agricultural systems between the hemispheres, the increasing evidence of formative cultural sequences in the New World that match those already delineated in the Old World, and, of course, the real space and time problems of massive contact. Outside the symposium the same sharp division of view appears. For example, consider a recent comment by Sanders and Price (1968: 60):

Assumption of diffusion between widely spaced culture areas in the New World and particularly between the New World and the Old should be very critically examined. Similarity in culture traits between two groups can be the product of convergence as well as diffusion. The reasons for convergence, or the independent invention of custom in different cultures, are numerous. Some traits are directly linked to the use of particular types of environment; thus groups living in the tropical forests of the Congo and Amazon basin will share some customs simply because they have similar geographical resources which they exploit in similar fashion. Examples of convergence on this level would be slash-and-burn agriculture, dispersed settlement pattern, and pole-and-thatch dwellings. Such inventions as ceramics, weaving, and metallurgy are so useful and generalized that the probability of their multiple reinvention would be high. Arguments that pottery making and metallurgy are such complex crafts that they could not have been reinvented independently seem highly illogical: If they are so complex that duplicate invention is improbable how were they ever invented in the first place?

On the other hand, Heine-Geldern (1966: 293) stresses what he feels to be the strong Asiatic flavor of Mesoamerican civilization in these words:

> There is no evidence of large-scale Asiatic sea-borne migrations to Mesoamerica. However, the native cultures could not have been so deeply affected as they actually were, if considerable numbers of single persons and small groups had not settled among them more or less permanently. The whole process may be compared to that which led to the formation of Indian colonial cultures in southeast Asia: the implantation of a foreign civilization on more primitive indigenous cultures by small groups of immigrants, soon absorbed by the local population, and, in consequence, the emerging of new civilizations which, despite all their own new creations, despite their original and unique characters, still allow us to recognize many of the features of both the foreign and native parent cultures from which they were derived.

James A. Ford (1967: 259), in an enthusiastic review of Meggers, Evans, and Estrada (*Early Formative Period of Coastal Ecuador*), feels that they have produced the key to the understanding of interhemispherical contact and of human history in general:

> There are also important implications for Cultural Anthropology in general. Old World archaeologists have clearly demonstrated that Neolithic culture diffused—it was not reinvented in the Near East, China, and Africa. The last stronghold for those who argued that culture was produced by some innate capability in man and had not evolved from preceding culture was the American example. Here man crossed Bering Straits with upper Paleolithic baggage and, without help, created the Inca, Maya, and Aztec civilizations. Now the Meggers, Evans, Estrada evidence for early trans-Pacific contacts opens wide the door for the theories of Heine-Geldern and Ekholm for the coming of later traits.
>
> I think that Meggers, Evans, and Estrada have demonstrated that human culture history is a single connected story.

Compare, however, the comments of John H. Rowe (1966: 339):

The most serious reason for concern about the current activities of the doctrinaire diffusionists is that they are not only avoiding general theoretical problems themselves but are also discouraging the development of general and comparative studies in archaeology. It is partly a matter of distraction; in so far as the diffusionists succeed in persuading archaeologists to discuss cultural similarities on their terms, they are distracting them from working on comparative problems. More important, however, is the fact that the assumptions of the diffusionists undermine the very foundations of comparative study. If all the world can be linked in a single oneway chain of diffusion, comparison is unnecessary. Why compare the rise of civilization in Mesopotamia, China, Mexico, and Peru if China received all its significant ideas from Mesopotamia, Mexico from China, and Peru from Mexico (or Peru from Ecuador from Japan)?

If we admit that it is important to know the nature and extent of diffusion, it then becomes necessary to discover wherein lies acceptable evidence. This is the major problem facing scholars today in any discussion of diffusion. As we pointed out in the introduction, two people can interpret the same evidence in very different ways. Even such a phenomenon as geographically patterned change in culture elements means quite diverse things to different culture historians. Until some procedures for verification of evidence are developed and agreed upon, the problem of pre-Columbian contacts will never rise above the level of dogmatic assertion and more or less polite name-calling. Since incontrovertible hard evidence is signally lacking and all other evidence is disputed, any common agreement must be on the broader grounds of universal human activities. We will suggest some here, realizing that they are not all of equal value and recognizing that our list is not complete. Some will take the nature of truisms, perhaps, but this seems unavoidable.

1. Man is a closely knit species in which any fully functioning adult can participate at about the same level of culture as any other adult.
2. Human beings, universally, have certain kinds of reactions to certain situations, these reactions dictated both by man's physical make-up and by his long cultural heritage.
3. Man is inventive but, because of the conservative and conformistic nature of culture, is not obsessively so.
4. Invention of new items or new systems is not psychologically very different from accepting the same item from a foreign

source. The same cultural integrative mechanisms are brought into play whether a trait is invented or diffused. To that extent, the idea of independent invention versus diffusion is misleading. Periods of rapid culture change are normally brought about by diffusion, but the social acceptance of rapid, introduced change is accompanied by an unusual acceptance of internal change (invention). For the culture historian this creates something of a paradox: How does one sort out what is diffused from what is invented, especially as the "inventions" may draw on and incorporate diffused traits?

5. Additions to man's cultural inventory, whether invented or diffused, tend to be elaborated according to patterns channeled by the environment, the particular cultural uses of the group, and, perhaps, by psychological factors still not completely understood.

Accepting these points, we stress again that random contact between the hemispheres has no processual importance. An introduced plant or a ceramic technique would probably be treated in much the same way by the recipient culture if it had been invented locally. The basic question, as we have stressed over and over, is whether the channeled nature of man's responses to cultural situations will, in fact, lead him to develop complex cultures, and particularly civilization, along parallel lines. Is the New World a laboratory situation for testing this kind of evolutionism or is it not? We feel that it is essential to find out, and so we must reject the position of Rowe that the unimportance of wide-scale diffusion can be simply assumed.

The underlying problem that must be solved is that of the origins of New World civilization. Clearly, the present status of our knowledge of American archaeology does not allow us to attribute the origins of New World civilization to diffusion from the Old World with assurance. Equally, however, it does not demonstrate the independent origin of New World high culture. Just as the zero occurrence of artifacts originating in the Old World and found in America may be taken as a strong argument against the diffusionist explanation, so the early occurrence of a complex of Old World–like traits—often very sophisticated—in early levels of Nuclear American civilization casts a strong reflection against the independent origins hypothesis. Of course, it is also possible that the New World was a "laboratory" situation as regards *origins* of civilization but received significant influence from the Old World at one or more later but still pre-Columbian dates. This presents us with a different problem, but still an important one in terms of an understanding of cultural dynamics.

The present symposium, though it has not answered our questions, has by itself set up certain guidelines. It is clear that we must involve several disciplines—anthropology, botany, geography, history, and certainly paleontology and zoology. The experts in each field must acquaint themselves with both the data and the most current thinking from the other disciplines. Cross-disciplinary evidence must be closely scrutinized and weighed with great caution. Particularly, we must guard against ideas becoming so imbedded that they are accepted as gospel without check or challenge.

In comparing complexes, particularly where style, type, or other variation in form is involved, we are probably going to need much more exact tools than the subjective ones now generally used (see, for example, the discussion by Tolstoy, 1969). It is possible that generative models of the type Muller suggests (this volume) will provide us with a major break-through, particularly in the field of stylistic comparisons.

With such guidelines we should eventually be able to reach the point where given pieces of evidence can be generally accepted, rejected, or at least assigned a level of high or low probability. Eventually many such pieces of evidence may allow us, no doubt slowly and painfully, to fill in the puzzle, the outlines of which are only now beginning to form.

BIBLIOGRAPHY

ABADIANO, F.
1910   Quetzalcóatl, el gran constructor de Palenque. Xochicalco-Chicomostoc-Culhuacán. Mexico City.

ABERG, N.
1918   Die Typologie der nordischen Streitäxte. Edited by G. Kossinna. *Mannus-Bibliothek,* no. 17.

ABREU GÓMEZ, E.
1944   El Popol Vuh: advertencia y selección. Mexico City.
1947   Quetzalcóatl: sueño y vigilia. Mexico City.

———— AND J. S. FLORES
1951   Leyendas Mexicanas. New York.

ACKERMAN, P.
1950   The dawn of religions. *In* Ancient religions: a symposium, edited by V. Ferm, pp. 3–24. New York.

ACOSTA, J. DE
1590   Historia natural y moral de las Indias. Seville. Also Hakluyt Soc., 1880; Mexico City, 1940.

ACOSTA SAIGNES, M.
1945   Los pochteca. *Acta Antropológica,* vol. 1. Mexico City.

ADAMS, R. M.
1966   The evolution of urban society: early Mesopotamia and pre-hispanic Mexico. Chicago.

ALBRIGHT, W. F.
1938   What were the cherubim? *Bibl. Archaeologist,* 1: 1–2.
1942–43   The excavation of Tell Beit Mirsim. *Amer. Schools of Oriental Res. Annual,* vols. 20–22.
1949   The archaeology of Palestine. Baltimore.

ALCINA FRANCH, J.
1955   El neolítico Americana y su problemática. *Acts 31st Int. Cong. Amer.* (São Paulo), pp. 871–882.

ALDROVANDI, U.
  1963   Aldrovandi on chickens: the ornithology of Ulisse Aldrovandi
         (1600), vol. 2, bk. 4. Translated by L. R. Lind. Norman, Okla.
ALEXANDER, H. B.
  1916   The mythology of all races. Vol. 10, North American. New York.
  1920   The mythology of all races. Vol. 11, Latin American. Boston.
ALLCARD, E. C.
  1964   Voyage alone. New York.
ALLEN, P. H.
  1956   The rain forests of Golfo Dulce. Gainesville, Fla.
ALMAGRO-BASCH, M.
  1946   Prehistoria del norte del Africa y del Sahara español. Barcelona.
ALPHONSE, E. S.
  1956   Guaymi grammar and dictionary. *Smithsonian Inst., Bur. Amer.*
         Ethnol., bull. 162.
ANALES DE CUAUHTITLÁN
  1906   Paris.
ANDERSON, E.
  1954   Plants, man, and life. Tiptree, Essex.
ANDERSON, J.
  1967   Vinland voyage. New York.
ANDERSON, R., AND R. C. ANDERSON
  1963   The sailing-ship. New York.
ANDERSSON, O.
  1967   Seal-folk in East and West. *In* Folklore international, edited by
         D. K. Wilgus, pp. 1–6. Hatboro, Penn.
ARMILLAS, P.
  1947   La serpiente emplumada, Quetzacoatl y Tlaloc. *Cuad. Amer.*,
         31: 161–179.
  1964   Northern Mesoamerica. *In* Pre-historic man in the New World,
         edited by J. D. Jennings and E. Norbeck, pp. 291–329. Chicago.
———, A. PALERM, AND E. R. WOLF
  1956   A small irrigation system in the valley of Teotihuacán. *Amer.*
         Antiquity, 21: 396–399.
ARTE, Y VOCABULARIO EN LA LENGUA GENERAL DEL PERU LLAMADA
    QUICHUA, Y EN LA LENGUA ESPAÑOLA LOS REYES
  1586   Attributed to J. Martínez. Lima.
ARUTIUNOV, S. A.
  1966   Problems of the historical-cultural connections of the Pacific
         Basin. *Soviet Anthr. & Archeol.*, 5(1): 26–31.

ASCHER, R.
  1961   Analogy in archaeological interpretation. *SW. Jour. Anthr.*, 17: 317–325.
BABCOCK, W. H.
  1922   Legendary islands of the Atlantic. New York.
BADIAN, E.
  1958   Alexander the Great and the unity of mankind. *Historia*, 7(4): 425–444.
BAESSLER, A.
  1906   Altperuanische Metallgerate. Berlin.
BAILEY, A. E.
  1943   Daily life in Bible times. New York.
BAKER, H. G.
  1955   Self-compatibility and establishment after "long-distance" dispersal. *Evolution*, 9: 347–348.
  1962   Comments on the thesis that there was a major center of plant domestication near the headwaters of the River Niger. *Jour. African Hist.*, 3: 229–233.
  1965a The evolution of the cultivated kapok tree: a probable West African product. *In* Ecology and economic development in tropical Africa, edited by D. Brokensha, pp. 185–216. Univ. of Calif. (Berkeley), Inst. of International Studies, Res. Ser., no. 9.
  1965b Characteristics and modes of origin of weeds. *In* The genetics of colonizing species, edited by H. G. Baker and G. L. Stebbins, pp. 147–172. New York.
  1965c Plants and civilization. Belmont, Calif.
BALDWIN, J. D.
  1869   Pre-historic nations. New York.
  1871   Ancient America. New York.
BALL, S. C.
  1933   Jungle fowl from Pacific islands. *Bishop Mus. Bull.*, no. 108.
BANCROFT, H. H.
  1883   The native races of the Pacific states. 5 vols. San Francisco.
BAQUEIRO ANDUZE, O.
  1941   Los mayas: fin de una cultura. Mexico City.
BARBER, A.
  1934   The Graminae: a study of cereal, bamboo, and grass. Cambridge, Eng.
BARDARSON, I.
  1873   Description of Greenland in the fourteenth century. *In* The voyages of the Venetian brothers to the northern seas, in the XIVth century, by R. H. Major. Hakluyt Soc., 1st ser., no. 50.

1906   A treatise of Iver Boty, a Gronlander. *In* Purchas his pilgrimes, by S. Purchas, vol. 13. Glasgow.

BARGHOORN, E. S., M. K. WOLFE, AND K. H. CLISBY
1954   Fossil maize from the Valley of Mexico. *Bot. Mus. Leafl., Harvard Univ.*, 16: 229–240.

BARLOW, R.
1954   Las joyas de Martín Ocelotl. *Yan,* vol. 3.

BARNETT, H. G.
1942   Invention and culture change. *Amer. Anthr.*, 44: 14–30.
1953   Innovation: the basis of cultural change. New York.

BAROCIO, A., AND OTHERS
1946   México y la cultura. Mexico City.

BARRAU, J.
1957   L'énigme de la patate douce en Océanie. *Études d'Outre Mer,* 40: 83–87.
1958   Subsistence agriculture in Melanesia. *Bishop Mus. Bull.,* no. 219, pp. 47–48.
1961   Subsistence agriculture in Polynesia and Micronesia. *Bishop Mus. Bull.,* no. 223, pp. 47–48.
1963   [ed.] Plants and the migrations of Pacific peoples. Honolulu.

BASS, G. F.
1961   The Cape Gelidonya wreck. *Amer. Jour. Archaeol.*, 65(3): 267–276.
1963a Promise of underwater archaeology. *Amer. Scholar,* 32: 241–255.
1963b Underwater archaeology: key to history's warehouse. *Nat. Geog. Mag.,* 124: 138–156.

BATRES, J. A.
1892   Los indios, su historia y su civilización. Guatemala.
1915–17   La América Central ante la historia. Guatemala.

BEAGLEHOLE, J. C.
1967   The journals of Captain James Cook on his voyages of discovery. Vol. 3, The voyage of the Resolution and Discovery, 1776–1780. Hakluyt Soc., extra series, no. 34.

BEALS, R. L.
1932   The comparative ethnology of northern Mexico before 1750. *Ibero-Amer.,* no. 2.

BEEBE, W.
1931   Pheasants, their lives and homes. New York.

BEEL, F. L. S.
1949   The industrial arts in Tanga. *Oceania,* 19: 208–233.

BENITEZ, F.
1952   In the footsteps of Cortes. New York.

BENNETT, W. C., AND J. B. BIRD
  1964   Andean culture history. New York.
BENNINGTON, F. C. M., AND P. J. WATSON
  1962   Carbon dating prehistoric soot from Salts Cave, Kentucky. *Amer. Antiquity*, 28(2): 238–241.
BENZONI, G.
  1857   History of the New World. London.
BERLIN, H., AND S. RENDÓN, eds.
  1947   Historia Tolteca-Chichimeca: anales de Quauhtinchan. Preface by P. Kirchhoff. Mexico City.
BERNAL, I.
  1955   Remarks on the origin of Mesoamerican civilization. *Acts 4th Int. Cong. Anthr. Ethnol. Sci.* (Vienna), 2: 347–350.
  1963   Teotihuacán. Mexico City.
BERNERS, J.
  1486   The boke of Saint Albens. Facsimile reproduction, London, 1901.
BERTAGNOLLI, C.
  1881   Delle vicende dell' agricultura in Italia. *In* L'agricultura Italiana nell' eta moderna. Florence.
BEST, E.
  1923   Polynesian voyagers: the Maori as a deep-sea navigator, explorer, and colonizer. *N. Z. Dom. Mus. Monogr.*, no. 5.
  1925   Maori agriculture. *N. Z. Dom. Mus. Bull.*, no. 9.
BESTERMAN, T.
  1965   Crystal-gazing. New Hyde Park, N. Y.
BEYER, H. O.
  1948   Philippine and East Asian archaeology and its relation to the origin of the Pacific Islands population. *Nat. Res. Council of the Philippines Bull.*, no. 29. Quezon City.
BIART, L.
  1885   Les Azteques: histoire, moeurs, coutumes. Paris.
BINFORD, R.
  1967   Smudge pots and hide smoking: the use of analogy in archaeological reasoning. *Amer. Antiquity*, 32: 1–12.
BIRD, J.
  1951   South American radiocarbon dates. Suppl. to *Amer. Antiquity* 17: 37–49.
  ——— AND J. MAHLER
  1951   America's oldest cotton fabrics. *American Fabrics*, 20: 73–78.
BIRKET-SMITH, K.
  1943   The origin of maize cultivation. *Det Kgl. Danske Videnskabernes Selskab, Historisk-Filologiske Meddelelser*, vol. 29, no. 3.

BIRRELL, V.
   1964   Transpacific contacts and Peru. *Acts 35th Int. Cong. Amer.*
           (Mexico City), 1: 31–38.
BISSCHOP, E. DE
   1959   Tahiti Nui. New York.
BLANCE, B.
   1961   Early Bronze Age colonists in Iberia. *Antiquity,* 35: 192–202.
BLOOMFIELD, L.
   1933   Language. New York.
BOBÉ, L.
   1928   Early explorations of Greenland. *In* Greenland, vol. 1. London.
BOCK, H.
   1539   Neu Kreuterbuch von Underscheid. Strassburg.
BOGGS, R. S.
   1939   Bibliografía del folklore mexicano. *Actos Instituto panamericano
           de geografía e historia,* pp. 1323–1223 [*sic*].
BOIS, D.
   1927–28 Les plantes alimentaires chez tous les peuples et à travers
           les ages. 2 vols. Paris.
BÖKÖNYI, S., AND D. JANOSSY
   1958   Data about the occurrence of the turkey in Europe before the
           time of Columbus. *Aguila,* 65: 265–269.
BOMBARD, A.
   1954   The voyage of the Hérétique. New York.
BON, M.
   1924–32 Mais. *In* Enciclopedia Italiana, 21: 970. Rome.
BONAFOUS, M.
   1836   Histoire naturelle, agricole et économique du mais. Paris.
BORDEN, C. A.
   1967   Sea quest. Philadelphia.
BORDEN, E., ed.
   1963   Current research. *Amer. Antiquity,* vol. 28, no. 4.
   1964   Current research. *Amer. Antiquity,* vol. 29, no. 4.
   1965   Current research. *Amer. Antiquity,* vol. 31, no. 2.
BORHEGYI, S. F. DE
   1948   Statuette Égyptienne en terre-cuite au Musée Hongrois des
           Beaux-Arts. *Bull. du Musée Hongrois des Beaux-Arts,* 1 (2):
           5–10, 46–49.
   1950a   Tlaloc effigy jar from the Guatemalan National Museum. *Car-
           negie Inst. Wash., Notes Middle Amer. Archaeol. Ethnol.,* no. 96.
   1950b   Rim-head vessels and cone-shaped effigy prongs of the Pre-

classic period at Kaminaljuyu, Guatemala. *Carnegie Inst. Wash., Notes Middle Amer. Archaeol. Ethnol.*, no. 97.

1950c Notas sobre sellos de barro, existentes en el Museo Nacional de Arqueología y Etnología de Guatemala. *Rev. Inst. Antr. Hist. Guatemala*, 2 (2): 16–26.

1951a A study of three-pronged incense burners from Guatemala and adjacent areas. *Carnegie Inst. Wash., Notes Middle Amer. Archaeol. Ethnol.*, no. 101.

1951b Further notes on three-pronged incense burners and rim-head vessels in Guatemala. *Carnegie Inst. Wash., Notes Middle Amer. Archaeol. Ethnol.*, no. 105.

1953 The miraculous shrines of Our Lord of Esquipulas in Guatemala and Chimayo, New Mexico. *El Palacio*, 60: 83–111.

1954a The cult of Our Lord of Esquipulas in Middle America and New Mexico. *El Palacio*, 61: 387–401.

1954b Jointed figurines in Mesoamerica and their cultural implication. *SW. Jour. Anthr.*, 10: 268–277.

1956a The development of folk and complex cultures in the southern Maya area. *Amer. Antiquity*, 21: 343–356.

1956b Settlement patterns in the Guatemalan highlands: past and present. *In* Prehistoric settlement patterns in the New World, edited by G. R. Willey. *Viking Fund Pub. Anthr.*, no. 23, pp. 101–106.

1958a Aqualung archaeology. *Natural Hist.*, 67: 120–125.

1958b Hallazgos arqueológicos in aguas del Lago de Amatitlán. *Rev. Inst. Antr. Hist. Guatemala*, 10 (1): 3–12.

1959a Pre-Columbian cultural connections between Mesoamerica and Ecuador. *Tulane Univ., Middle Amer. Research Records*, 2 (6): 141–156.

1959b Underwater archaeology in the Maya highlands. *Sci. Amer.*, 200: 100–113.

1959c Culto a la imagen del Señor de Esquipulas en Centro América y Nuevo México. *Rev. Inst. Antr. Hist. Guatemala*, 2 (1): 44–49.

1960a America's ball game. *Natural Hist.*, 69: 48–59.

1960b Pre-Columbian cultural connections between Mesoamerica and Ecuador: addenda. *Tulane Univ., Middle Amer. Research Records*, 2 (7): 159–160.

1960c Underwater archaeological studies in Lake Amatitlán, highland Guatemala. *Year Book Amer. Phil. Soc.*, pp. 56–57.

1961a Miniature mushroom stones from Guatemala. *Amer. Antiquity*, 26: 498–504.

1961b Shark teeth, stingray spines, and shark fishing in ancient Mexico and Central America. *SW. Jour. Anthr.*, 17: 273–296.

1961c Ball game handstones and ball game gloves. *In* Essays in pre-Columbian art and archaeology, by S. K. Lothrop, D. Z. Stone, J. B. Bird, G. F. Ekholm, and G. R. Willey, pp. 126–151. Cambridge, Mass.

1963a Pre-Columbian pottery mushrooms from Mesoamerica. *Amer. Antiquity*, 28: 328–338.

1963b The rubber ball game in ancient America. *Lore*, 13: 44–53.

1964a Pre-Columbian cultural similarities and differences between the highland Guatemalan and tropical rainforest Mayas. *Acts 35th Int. Cong. Amer.* (Mexico City), pp. 215–224.

1964b The art of the ancient Maya. *Lore*, 15: 18–28.

1965a Archaeological synthesis of the Guatemalan highlands. *In* Handbook of Middle American Indians, edited by R. Wauchope. Vol. 2, Archaeology of southern Mesoamerica, edited by G. R. Willey, pp. 3–58. Austin.

1965b Settlement patterns of the Guatemalan highlands. *In* Handbook of Middle American Indians, edited by R. Wauchope. Vol. 2, Archaeology of southern Mesoamerica, edited by G. R. Willey, pp. 59–75. Austin.

1965c Some unusual Mesoamerican portable stone sculpture in the Museum für Völkerkunde, Berlin. *Baessler-Archiv, N.F.*, 13: 171–206.

1965d The first printers of the New World. *Lore*, 16: 5–9.

1966a The wind god's breastplate. *Expedition*, 8 (4): 13–15.

1966b Shell offerings and the use of shell motifs at Lake Amatitlán, Guatemala, and Teotihuacán, Mexico. *Acts 36th Int. Cong. Amer.*, pp. 355–371.

1968a Piedras semiesféricas con asas para el juego de pelota y "manoplas" en Mesoamérica: una posible alternativa para su función. *Estud. Cultura Maya*, 6: 215–219.

1968b Una fecha de C-14 para la influencia Teotihuacán en Guatemala. *Estud. Cultura Maya*, 6: 221–224.

1968c Hoops, yokes, and rubber balls. *Pacific Discovery*, 21 (3): 10–15.

BORN, W.

1937 The use of purple among the Indians of Central America. *Ciba Rev.*, 4: 124–127.

1938 Scarlet. *Ciba Rev.*, 7: 206–217.

BORSSUM WAALKES, J. VAN

1960 Botanical observations on the Krakatau Island in 1951–52. *Ann. Bogoriensis*, 4: 5–64.

BOSSERT, A. T.
  1951 Altsyrien. Tübingen.
BOSWELL, C.
  1959 The last long voyage. *Argosy*, 348(2): 36–38, 87–90.
BOUMAN, C.
  1911 Het Journaal van Cornelis Bouman, 1721–1722. *In* De Reis van
        Mr. Jacob Roggeveen (1721–1722), pp. 178–205. Linschoten-
        Vereeniging, Werken No. 4. The Hague.
BOWEN, R. L., JR.
  1953a Eastern sail affinities, pt. 1. *Amer. Neptune*, 13: 81–117.
  1953b Eastern sail affinities, pt. 2. *Amer. Neptune*, 13: 185–211.
  1956 Boats of the Indus civilization. *Mariner's Mirror*, 42: 279–290.
  1959a The origins of fore-and-aft rigs, pt. 1. *Amer. Neptune*, 19: 155–
        199.
  1959b The origins of fore-and-aft rigs, pt. 2. *Amer. Neptune*, 19: 274–
        306.
BOXER, C. R.
  1952a Maize names. *Uganda Jour.*, vol. 16, pt. 2.
  1952b Maize names. *Uganda Jour.*, vol. 17, pt. 1.
  1953 South China in the sixteenth century. Hakluyt Soc., 2d ser.,
        vol. 106.
BRASSEUR DE BOURBOURG, C. E.
  1851 Cartas para servir de introducción a la historia primitiva de las
        naciones civiliçadas de la América septentrional. Mexico City.
  1866 Recherches sur les ruines de Palenque. Paris.
BRAVO, J. U.
  1952 Compendio de historia de México. Mexico City.
BREA, L. B.
  1957 Sicily before the Greeks. New York.
BRETSCHNEIDER, E.
  1888 Mediaeval researches from eastern Asiatic sources. London.
BRIGGS, C. W.
  1955 Eastern sage to western man. *Rev. Religion*, 19: 115–130.
BRIGGS, I.
  1950 The tree of life symbol: its significance in ancient American
        religion. Master's thesis, Brigham Young University.
BRINDLEY, H. H.
  1926 A Solomon Islands catamaran. *Mariner's Mirror*, 12: 444–445.
BRINTON, D.
  1885 The annals of the Cakchiquels. Philadelphia.
BRITISH MUSEUM
  1904 A guide to the antiquities of the Bronze Age. London.

BRONSON, B.
  1966   Roots and the subsistence of the ancient Maya. *SW. Jour. Anthr.*,
          22: 251–279.
BROOKS, C. W.
  1875   Reports of Japanese vessels wrecked in the North Pacific: from
          the earliest records to the present time. *Proc. California Acad.
          Sci.*, 6: 50–66.
BROOKS, R. H., L. KAPLAN, H. C. CUTLER, AND T. W. WHITAKER
  1962   Plant material from a cave in the Rio Zape, Durango, Mexico.
          Amer. Antiquity, 27: 356–369.
BROWN, E.
  1929   Poultry breeding and production, vol. 1. New York.
BROWN, F. B. H.
  1935   Flora of southeastern Polynesia. Vol. 3, Dicotyledons. *Bishop
          Mus. Bull.*, no. 130.
BRUMAN, H. J.
  1947   A further note on coconuts in Colima. *Hisp. Amer. Hist. Rev.*,
          27: 572–573.
BRUUN, D.
  1905   De gamle Nordbokolonier i Grønland, Tidsakrift for Lando-
          kønomi. Copenhagen.
  1917   The Icelandic colonization of Greenland and the finding of Vine-
          land. *Meddelelser om Grønland*, 57: 1–228.
BUCK, C. D.
  1949   Dictionary of selected synonyms in the principal Indo-European
          languages. Chicago.
BUCK, P. H.
  1938   Vikings of the sunrise. New York.
  1944   Arts and crafts of the Cook Islands. *Bishop Mus. Bull.*, no. 179.
  1959   Vikings of the Pacific. Chicago.
BUDGE, E. A. T.
  1926   Babylonian life and history. Revised edition. New York.
BULLEN, R. P.
  1961   Radiocarbon dates for southeastern fiber-tempered pottery.
          Amer. Antiquity, 27 (1): 104–106.
BULMER, R.
  1964   The prehistory of the Australian New Guiana highlands. *Amer.
          Anthr.*, 66 (4): 39–76.
  1965   Beliefs concerning the propagation of new varieties of sweet
          potatoes in two New Guinea highland societies. *Jour. Polynesian
          Soc.*, 74: 237–309.

BURKART, A., AND H. BRÜCHER.
1953 *Phaseolus aborigineus* Burkart, die mutmassliche audine Staimform der Kulturbohne. *Der Zuchter*, 23: 65–72.

BURKILL, I. H.
1935 A dictionary of the economic products of the Malay peninsula. London.
1954 Aji and batata as group-names within the species *Ipomoea batatas. Ceiba*, 4: 227–240.

BURLAND, C. A.
1948 Art and life in ancient Mexico. Oxford.

BURN, A. R.
1962 Alexander the Great and the Hellenistic world. New York.

BURROWS, M.
1941 What mean these stones. New Haven.

BURTON, R. F.
1875 Ultima Thule, vols. 1–2. London.

BURTT-DAVY, J.
1914 Maize: its history, cultivation, handling, and uses. London.

BUSHNELL, G. H. S.
1951 The archaeology of the Santa Elena Peninsula in southwest Ecuador. Cambridge, Eng.
1956 Peru. London.

BUXTON, L. H. D.
1929 China. London.

CABELLO DE BALBOA, M.
1586 Miscelanea antartica. Lima, 1951.
1945 Obras, vol. 1. Quito.

CALLEN, E. O.
1967 Analysis of Tehuacan coprolites. *In* The prehistory of the Tehuacan Valley, edited by D. S. Byers. Vol. 1, Environment and subsistence, pp. 261–289. Austin.

CAMPBELL, D. H.
1926 An outline of plant geography. New York.

CAMPS, G.
1961 Monuments et rites funéraires protohistoriques. Paris.

CANALS FRAU, S.
1956–57 Las Dioscoreas cultivadas (ñames) y su introducción en el Nuevo Mundo. *Runa*, 8: 28–52.

CANBY, C.
1963 A history of ships and seafaring. New York.

CANDOLLE, A. DE
1886   Origin of cultivated plants. New York. Also Paris, 1836; London, 1967.

CAPA, P. R.
1915   Estudios críticos acerca de la dominación española en América. Pt. 3, Industria agricola-pecuaria llevada a América por los Españoles. 4th edition. Madrid.

CÁRCER Y DISDIER, M. DE
1953   Apuntes para la historia de la transculturación Indoespañola, pp. 247–264. Mexico City.
1955   Disertaciones sobre la papa (patata) y la batata (patata). *Cuad. Inst. Hist.*, no. 1.

CARRERA, F. DE LA
1644   Arte de la lengua Yunga. Edited by R. A. Alfieri. Tucumán, 1939.

CARTER, G. F.
1950   Plant evidence for early contacts with America. *SW. Jour. Anthr.*, 6: 161–182.
1953   Plants across the Pacific. *Amer. Antiquity*, vol. 18, no. 3, pt. 2: *Mem. Soc. Amer. Archaeol.*, no. 9, pp. 62–71.
1963   Movement of people and ideas across the Pacific. *In* Plants and the migrations of Pacific peoples, edited by J. Barrau, pp. 7–22. Honolulu.
1964   Man and the land: a cultural geography. New York.

CASANOVA, E.
1946   The cultures of the Puna and the Quebrada de Huma Huaca. *In* Handbook of South American Indians, edited by J. H. Steward. Vol. 2, The Andean civilizations, pp. 619–632. *Smithsonian Inst., Bur. Amer. Ethnol.*, bull. 143.

CASELLA, D.
1950   La frutta nelle pinture Pompeiane. *In* Pompeiane: racolta di scavii di Pompei, pp. 355–386. Naples.

CASO, A.
1937   Tenían los Teotihuacanos conocimiento del Tonalpohualli? *El México antiguo*, 4: 131–143.
1942   El Paraíso terrenal en Teotihuacán. *Cuad. Amer.*, 6(6): 127–136.
1945a   El complejo arqueológico de Tula y las grandes culturas de México. *Rev. Mex. Estud. Arqueol.*, 5: 11–45.
1945a   El complejo arqueológico de Tula y las grandes culturas de México. *Rev. Mex. Estud. Arqueol.*, 5: 11–45.
1945b   La religión de los aztecas. Mexico City.

1947   Calendario y escritura de antiguas culturas de Monte Albán.
        Mexico City.
1958   The Aztecs, people of the sun. Norman, Okla.
1964   Relations between the Old and New Worlds: a note on method-
        ology. *Acts 35th Int. Cong. Amer.* (Mexico City), 1: 55–71.
CASSON, L.
1956   Fore-and-aft sails in the ancient world. *Mariner's Mirror*, 42: 3–5.
1963   Sewn boats. *Classical Rev.*, n.s., 13: 257–259.
1964   Illustrated history of ships and boats. Garden City, N. Y.
1966   The lateen sail in the ancient world. *Mariner's Mirror*, 52: 199–
        200.
CASTELLO, S.
1924   The *Gallus inauris* and the hen which lays blue eggs. *In* 2d World
        Poultry Cong. (Barcelona), pp. 113–118.
CEBALLOS NOVELO, J.
1934   Quetzalcóatl, los dos templos que sucesivamente tuvo en Cholula,
        estado de Puebla. Mexico City.
CHANCA, D. A.
1945   A letter of 1494 written in Hispaniola. *In* Colección de los viajes
        y descubrimientos, edited by M. F. de Navarrete, vol. 1.
CHANDLER, T.
1960   Duplicate inventions? *Amer. Anthr.*, 62: 495–498.
CHANG, K. C.
1959   A working hypothesis for the early cultural history of South
        China. *Bull. Inst. Ethnol., Acad. Sinica*, no. 7, pp. 43–103.
1967   Rethinking archaeology. New York.
1968   The archaeology of ancient China. Revised edition. New Haven.
CHAPELLE, H. I.
1935   American sailing ships. New York.
CHARD, C. S.
1950   Pre-Columbian trade between North and South America. *Kroeber
        Anthr. Soc. Papers*, no. 1, pp. 1–27.
CHARLES, A. E.
1961   Selection and breeding of the coconut palm. *In* Symposium on
        tropical crops improvement, edited by J. Barrau, pp. 51–54.
        Honolulu.
CHAVERO, A.
1895   México á traves de los siglos, vol. 1. Barcelona.
1930   Libro de Chilam Balam de Chumayel. Translated by A. Mediz
        Bolio. San José de Costa Rica.
CHENG, T. K.
1960   Archaeology in China, vols. 1–2. Cambridge, Eng.

CHIERA, E.
1938   They wrote on clay. Chicago.
CHILDE, V. G.
1926   The Aryans: a study of Indo-European origins. New York.
1930   The Bronze Age. London.
1937   A prehistorian's interpretation of diffusion. *In* Independence, convergence, and borrowing in institutions, thought, and art, pp. 3–21. Cambridge, Mass. Also *in* Readings in cultural geography, edited by P. L. Wagner and M. W. Mikesell, pp. 209–217. Chicago, 1962.
1940   Prehistoric communities of the British Isles. London.
1944   The story of tools. London.
1957   The dawn of European civilization. London.
CHIOVENDA, E.
1921–23   La culla del cocco. *Webbia*, 5: 199–294, 349–449.
CHUNG, H. L.
1923   The sweet potato in Hawaii. *Hawaii Agr. Exp. Sta. Bull.*, no. 50.
CIEZA DE LEÓN, P. DE
1553   Parte primera de la crónica del Perú. Madrid. Also published as The travels of Pedro de Cieza de León, translated and edited by C. Markham. London, 1864. Hakluyt Soc., 1st ser., no. 68.
1553   Del señorio de los Incas. Buenos Aires, 1943. This is the second part of the Crónica del Perú.
CLARK, J. D.
1959   The prehistory of southern Africa. Baltimore.
CLARK, J. G. D.
1952   Prehistoric Europe: the economic basis. London.
1954   Excavations at Star Carr. Cambridge, Eng.
1961   The first half-million years. *In* The dawn of civilization, edited by S. Piggott. New York.
1966   The invasion hypothesis in British archaeology. *Antiquity*, 40: 172–189.
CLAVIJERO, F. J.
1948   Historia antigua de México. Mexico City.
CLEMENT, D., AND L. L. PHILLIPS
1963   A new species of *Gossypium* from the Cape Verde Islands. *Bot. Mus. Leafl., Harvard Univ.*, 20: 213–218.
COBO, B.
1890–95   Historia del Nuevo Mundo, vol. 1. Seville.
COE, M. D.
1956   The Khmer settlement pattern: a possible analogy with that of the Maya. *Amer. Antiquity*, 22: 409–410.

1960 Archaeological linkages with North and South America at La Victoria, Guatemala. *Amer. Anthr.*, 62: 363–393.

1962 Mexico. New York.

COE, W. R.

1962 A summary of excavation and research at Tikal, Guatemala. *Amer. Antiquity*, 27: 479–507.

COLE, S.

1963 The prehistory of East Africa. New York.

COLECCIÓN DE DOCUMENTOS INÉDITOS . . . DE INDIAS

1866 Vol. 5. Madrid.

COLECCIÓN DE DOCUMENTOS INÉDITOS . . . DE LAS ANTIGUAS POSESIONES ESPAÑOLAS DE ULTRAMAR

1886–87 Series 2, Madrid. Vol. 2, 1886, pp. 217–351: Relación . . . de Legazpi; pp. 373–427: Relación . . . del piloto mayor Estevan Rodríguez 1565. Vol. 3, 1887, pp. 226–243: Relación de Juan de las Islas; pp. 371–475: Relación de Juan Martínez.

COLLIER, C.

1967 Who discovered America? S. *Atlantic Quart.*, 66: 31–41.

COLLIER, D.

1946 The archaeology of Ecuador. *In* The handbook of South American Indians, edited by J. H. Steward. Vol. 2, The Andean civilizations, pp. 767–784. *Smithsonian Inst., Bur. Amer. Ethnol.*, bull. 143.

1961 Agriculture and civilization on the coast of Peru. *In* Symposium on the evolution of horticultural systems in native South America, *Antropológica Suppl.*, 2: 101–109.

COMAS, J.

1965 Significado de la presencia del Antigeno Diego entre los amerindios. *An. Antropol.* (Mexico), 2: 89–112.

COMENTARIOS DE ALVAR NÚÑEZ CABEZA DE VACA

1877 *In* Biblioteca de autores Españoles, 22: 548–599. Madrid.

COMMONWEALTH BUREAU OF PASTURES AND FIELD CROPS

1963 *Field Crop Abstracts*, vol. 16. Hurley, Eng.

CONKLIN, H. C.

1963 The Oceanian-African hypothesis and the sweet potato. *In* Plants and the migrations of Pacific peoples, edited by J. Barrau. Honolulu.

COOK, O. F.

1901 The origin and dispersal of the cocoa palm. *Contr. U.S. Nat. Herb.*, 7: 247–93.

1910 History of the coconut palm in America. *Contr. U.S. Nat. Herb.*, 14: 271–342.

1916   Quichua names of sweet potatoes. *Jour. Wash. Acad. Sci.,* 6: 86–90.

1925   Peru as a center of domestication. *Jour. Heredity,* 16: 33–46, 95–110.

1940   An endemic palm on Cocos Island near Panama mistaken for the coconut palm. *Science,* 91 (2354): 140–142.

———— AND R. C. COOK

1916   Polynesian names of sweet potatoes. *Jour. Wash. Acad. Sci.,* 6: 339–347.

COOK, S. A.

1930   The religion of ancient Palestine in the light of archaeology. London.

COOLEY, J. S.

1951   The sweet potato—its origin and primitive storage practices. *Econ. Botany,* 5: 378–386. Reprinted from *Scientific Monthly* (May, 1951).

COON, C. S.

1954   The story of man: from the first human to primitive culture and beyond. 1st edition. New York.

1962   The story of man. 2d edition. New York.

1965   The living races of man. New York.

COPELAND, E. B.

1906   On the water relations of the coconut palm. *Philippine Jour. Sci.,* 1: 6–57.

COPLESTON, F. C.

1962   A history of philosophy. Vol. 1, pt. 2, Greece and Rome. New York.

CORDERO, L.

1955   Diccionario Quichua-Español Español-Quichua. Quito. Written in 1892.

CORDERO PALACIOS, O.

1924   El Quechua y el Cañari. Cuenca.

CORNER, E. J. H.

1966   The natural history of palms. Berkeley.

CORNEY, B. G.

1908   The voyage of Captain Don Felipe Gonzalez to Easter Island in 1770–1. Hakluyt Soc., 2d ser., no. 13.

CORTESÃO, A.

1944   The Suma Oriental of Tomé Pires. Hakluyt Soc., 2d ser., nos. 89–90.

CORYN, J. H.
  1930   Epic of the Aztecs: review of Son of Quetzalcoatl. *Pan Amer. Mag.*, 43: 127–131.
COTTER, J. L.
  1966   Current research, Northeast. *Amer. Antiquity*, 31: 295–297.
COUNT, E. W.
  1952   The earth-diver and the rival twins: a clue to time correlation in North-Eurasiatic and North American mythology. *In* Indian tribes of aboriginal America, edited by S. Tax, pp. 55–62. Chicago.
COVARRUBIAS, M.
  1946   Mexico south, the isthmus of Tehuantepec. New York.
  1955   The eagle, the jaguar, and the serpent. New York.
  1957   Indian art of Mexico and Central America. New York.
CRAIGIE, W. A.
  1913   The Icelandic sagas. London.
CRAWFURD, J.
  1820   History of the Indian Archipelago. Edinburgh.
  1867   On the migration of cultivated plants in reference to ethnology. *Trans. Ethnol. Soc. London*, vol. 5.
CRITCHLEY, M.
  1943   Shipwreck survivors: a medical study. London.
CRONE, G. R.
  1966a How authentic is the "Vinland Map"? *Encounter*, 26: 75–78.
  1966b The Vinland map cartographically considered. *Geog. Jour.*, 132 (1): 75–80.
CULIN, S.
  1898   Chess and playing cards. *U.S. Nat. Mus. Rept.* (1896), pp. 665–942.
CULLOCH, C.
  1849   Maize. *In* Dictionary of commerce. London.
CULVER, H. B., AND G. GRANT
  1935   The book of old ships and something of their evolution and romance. Garden City, N.Y.
CUMONT, F.
  1956a The oriental religions in Roman paganism. New York.
  1956b The mysteries of Mithra. New York.
  1959   After life in Roman paganism. New York.
CURRAY, J. R.
  1965   Late Quaternary history: continental shelves of the United States. *In* The Quaternary of the United States, edited by H. E. Wright, Jr. and D. G. Frey. Princeton, N.J.

CUTLER, H. C.
1946   Races of maize in South America. *Bot. Mus. Leafl., Harvard Univ.*, 12: 257–291.
1957   The current status of the identification problem—the non-archaeological specialist viewpoint—botany. *In* The identification of non-artifactual archaeological materials, edited by W. W. Taylor. *Nat. Acad. Sci., Nat. Res. Council Pub.*, no. 565.
1960   Cultivated plant remains from Waterfall Cave, Chihuahua. *Amer. Antiquity*, 26: 277–279.
——— AND T. W. WHITAKER
1961   History and distribution of the cultivated cucurbits in the Americas. *Amer. Antiquity*, 26: 469–485.
1969   A new species of *Cucurbita* from Ecuador. *Ann. Missouri Botanical Garden*, 55: 392–396.

D'ALVIELLA, E. G.
1894   The migration of symbols. London.

DALY, D.
1891   Mexican Messiah [an attempt to identify Quetzalcoatl with St. Brendan]. *Pop. Sci.*, 39: 95–105.

DAMES, M. L.
1918   The book of Duarte Barbosa, vol. 1. Hakluyt Soc., 2d ser., vol. 44.

DANIEL, G.
1963   The idea of prehistory. Cleveland.

DANIELSSON, B.
1960   From raft to raft. Garden City, N.Y.

DARLING, S. T.
1920   Observations on the geographical and ethnological distribution of hookworms. *Parasitology*, 12: 217–233.

DAWSON, E. Y.
1959   Changes in Palmyra Atoll and its vegetation through the activities of man, 1913–1958. *Pacific Naturalist*, 1: 2–51.

DE BOOY, T.
1915–16   Notes on the archaeology of Margarita Island, Venezuela. *Contrib. Mus. Amer. Indian, Heye Found.*, vol. 2, no. 5.

DEGENER, O.
1930   Ferns and flowering plants of Hawaii National Park. Honolulu.

DE HERBELOT, B.
1781–83   Bibliothèque orientale. Paris.

DE MACEDO, D. R.
1817   Obras inéditas. Lisbon.

DE TENA, T. L.
1966   The influence of literature on cartography and the Vinland Map. *Geog. Jour.*, 132: 515–518.

DISSELHOFF, H. D.
1967 Daily life in ancient Peru. New York.

DIXON, R. B.
1932 The problem of the sweet potato in Polynesia. *Amer. Anthr.*, 34: 40–66.
1934 The long voyages of the Polynesians. *Proc. Amer. Philos. Soc.*, 74: 167–175.

DOCTERS VAN LEEUWEN, W. M.
1936 Krakatau, 1883–1933. *Ann. Jard. Bot. Buitenzorg*, 16: 1–506.

DÖLLINGER, J. J.
1862 The Gentile and the Jew in the courts of the temple of Christ. Translated by N. Darnell. 2 vols. London.

DORAN, E., JR.
1967 The origin of leeboards. *Mariner's Mirror*, 53: 39 53.

DOSAL, P. J.
1925 Descubrimientos arqueológicos en el templo de Quetzalcóatl (Teotihuacán). Mexico City.

DOW, J. W.
1967 Astronomical orientations at Teotihuacán: a case study in astro-archaeology. *Amer. Antiquity*, 32: 326–334.

DOWNIE, N. M., AND R. W. HEATH
1959 Basic statistical methods. New York.

DRUCKER, P., R. HEIZER, AND R. SQUIER
1959 Excavations at La Venta, Tabasco, 1955. *Smithsonian Inst., Bur. Amer. Ethnol.*, bull. 170.

DRURY, H.
1858 The useful plants of India. Madras.

DUFF, R.
1959 Neolithic adzes of eastern Polynesia. *In* Anthropology in the south seas, edited by J. D. Freeman and W. R. Geddes, pp. 121–148. New Plymouth, N.Z.

DURÁN, D.
1951 Historia de las Indias de Nueva España e islas de Tierra Firma, vol. 2. Mexico City.

DU SOLIER, W.
1939 Una representación pictórica de Quetzalcóatl en una cueva. *Rev. Mex. Estud. Antropol.*, 3: 129–641.

DUYVENDAK, J. J. L.
1949 China's discovery of Africa. London.

EASBY, D. T., JR.
1966 Early metallurgy in the New World. *Sci. Amer.*, 214: 73–81.

EDGERTON, W.
1880   An illustrated handbook of Indian arms. London.

EDMONSON, C. H.
1941   Viability of coconut seeds after floating in the sea. *Bishop Mus. Occas. Papers*, 16: 293–304.

EDMUNDSON, M.
1961   Neolithic diffusion rates. *Cur. Anthr.*, 2: 71–102.

EDWARDS, C. R.
1956   Formosan sea-going raft and its origin in ancient China. *Bull. Inst. Ethnol., Acad. Sinica,* no. 1, pp. 1–54.

1960   Sailing rafts of Sechura: history and problems of origin. *SW. Jour. Anthr.*, 16: 368–391.

1965   Aboriginal watercraft on the Pacific coast of South America. *Ibero-Amer.*, no. 47.

1969a   New World perspectives on pre-European voyaging in the Pacific. *In* The proceedings of a symposium: early Chinese art and its possible influences in the Pacific Basin, edited by N. Bernard. New York.

1969b   Possibilities of pre-Columbian maritime contacts among New World civilizations. *In* Precolumbian contact within Nuclear America, edited by J. C. Kelley and C. L. Riley. *Res. Rec. Univ. Mus.*, Southern Illinois University, Mesoamerican Studies, no. 4, pp. 3–10.

EDWARDS, I. E. S.
1961   The pyramids of Egypt. London.

EKHOLM, G. F.
1946   Wheeled toys in Mexico. *Amer. Antiquity*, 11: 222–228.

1950   Is American Indian culture Asiatic? *Natural Hist.*, 59: 344–351, 382.

1953   A possible focus of Asiatic influence in the Late Classic cultures of Mesoamerica. *Mem. Soc. Amer. Archaeol.*, no. 9: *Amer. Antiquity*, 18: 72–89.

1955   The new orientation toward problems of Asiatic-American relationships. *In* New interpretations of aboriginal American culture history, pp. 95–109. Washington.

1964a   The possible Chinese origin of Teotihuacán cylindrical tripod pottery and certain related traits. *Acts 35th Int. Cong. Amer.* (Mexico City), pp. 39–45.

1964b   Transpacific contacts. *In* Prehistoric man in the New World, edited by J. D. Jennings and E. Norbeck, pp. 489–510. Chicago.

ELDERKIN, K. M.
  1930   Jointed dolls in antiquity. *Amer. Jour. Archaeol.*, 2d ser., 34: 455–479.

ELLAM, P., AND C. MUDIE
  1953   Sopranino. New York.

ELLIS, W.
  1831   Polynesian researches. 4 vols. London.

EMERY, K. O., AND R. L. EDWARDS
  1966   Archaeological potential of the Atlantic continental shelf. *Amer. Antiquity*, 31: 733–737.

EMERY, W. B.
  1961   Archaic Egypt. Baltimore.

ENCISO, M. F. DE
  1519   Suma de geographia, etc. Seville.

ENGEL, F.
  1963   A preceramic settlement on the central coast of Peru: Asia, unit 1. *Trans. Amer. Phil. Soc.*, 53: 1–139.

ERASMUS, J.
  1950   Patolli, pachisi, and the limitation of possibilities. *SW. Jour. Anthr.*, 6: 369–387.

ERDTMAN, G.
  1943   An introduction to pollen analysis. Waltham, Mass.
  1952   Pollen morphology and plant taxonomy: angiosperms. Stockholm.

ESPINOSA, A. DE
  1907   The Guanches of Tenerife. Hakluyt Soc., 2d ser., vol. 21.

ESTRADA, E., AND B. J. MEGGERS
  1961   A complex of traits of probable transpacific origin on the coast of Ecuador. *Amer. Anthr.*, 63: 913–939.

EVANS, J. D.
  1958   Two phases of prehistoric settlement in the western Mediterranean. *London Univ., Inst. Archaeol. Ann. Rept.*, no. 13, pp. 49–70.

EYRIAUD DES VERGNES, P. E.
  1877   L'archipel des Iles Marquises. Paris.

FAIRSERVIS, W. A., JR.
  1959   The origins of Oriental civilizations. New York.

FARADAY, W.
  1902   The Edda: the divine mythology of the North. *In* Popular studies in mythology, romance, and folklore, edited by A. Nutt, nos. 12, 13. London.

FARMER, W. R.
1956   The geography of Ezekiel's river of life. *Bibl. Archaeologist,* 19: 17–22.

FERDON, E. N., JR.
1963   Polynesian origins. *Science,* 141 (3580): 499–505.

FERGUSON, T. S.
1958   One fold and one shepherd. San Francisco.

FERGUSON, W.
1939   Humanist views of the Renaissance. *Amer. Hist. Rev.,* 45: 1–28.

FEWKES, J. W.
1909   Antiquities of Mesa Verde National Park: Spruce-Tree House. *Smithsonian Inst., Bur. Amer. Ethnol.,* bull. 41, pl. 21.

1911   Antiquities of Mesa Verde National Park: Cliff Palace. *Smithsonian Inst., Bur. Amer. Ethnol.,* bull. 51, pl. 20.

1914a Prehistoric objects from a shell-heap at Erin Bay, Trinidad. *Amer. Anthr.,* 16: 200–220.

1914b Relations of aboriginal culture and environment in the Lesser Antilles. *Bull. Amer. Geog. Soc.,* 46 (9): 662–678.

1922   A prehistoric island culture area of America. *Smithsonian Inst., Bur. Amer. Ethnol.,* ann. rept. 34 (1912–13), pp. 35–281.

FINAN, J. J.
1950   Maize in the great herbals. Waltham, Mass.

FINEGAN, J.
1964   Handbook of biblical chronology, principles of time reckoning in the ancient world and problems of chronology in the Bible. Princeton, N.J.

FINSTERBUSCH, C. A.
1929   Cock fighting all over the world. Gaffney, S. C.

1931   The Araucano, the blue egged fowl of Chile. *The Feathered World,* 85 (2201): 465–470.

FISCHER-MØLLER, K.
1942   The mediaeval Norse settlements in Greenland. *Meddelelser om Grønland,* 89 (2): 1–82.

FISKE, J.
1902   The discovery of America, vols. 1–2. New York.

FOLLETT, P. H. F.
1932   War and weapons of the Maya. *Tulane Univ., Middle Amer. Res. Inst., Res. Ser.,* no. 4.

FORD, C. S., AND F. A. BEACH
1951   Patterns of sexual behavior. New York.

FORD, J. A.
1966 Early Formative cultures in Georgia and Florida. *Amer. Antiquity*, 31: 781–799.
1967 *Review of* B. J. Meggers, C. Evans, and E. Estrada, Early Formative period of coastal Ecuador. *Amer. Antiquity*, 32: 258–259.
1969 A comparison of the Formative cultures in the Americas. *Smithsonian Contrib. Anthr.*, vol. 11.

FORDE, D.
1954 Foraging, hunting, and fishing. *In* The history of technology. Vol. 1. From early times to the fall of the ancient empires, edited by C. Singer, E. J. Holmyard, and A. R. Hall, pp. 154–168. Oxford.

FORDE-JOHNSTON, J.
1959 Neolithic cultures of North Africa. Liverpool.

FOROUGHI COLLECTION
Iranian art through 7,000 years.

FORSTER, E. M.
1961 Alexandria: a history and a guide. New York.

FOSBERG, F. R.
1959 Vegetation and flora of Wake Island. *Atoll Res. Bull.*, no. 67.
1962 A theory on the origin of the coconut. *In* Symposium on the impact of man on humid tropics vegetation: Goroka, Territory of Papua and New Guinea, pp. 73–75. Canberra.
———— AND G. CORWIN
1958 A fossil flora from Pagan, Mariana Islands. *Pacific Science*, 12: 2–16.

FOWLER, E. W.
1965 English sea power in the early Tudor period (1485–1558). Ithaca, N.Y.

FRANKEN, H. J., AND C. A. FRANKEN-BATTERSHILL
1963 A primer of Old Testament archaeology. Leiden.

FRANKFORT, H.
1939 Cylinder seals. London.
1948 Kingship and the gods. Chicago.
1954 The birth of civilization in the Near East. Bloomington, Ind.
1955 The art and architecture of the ancient Orient. Baltimore.
————, H. A. FRANKFORT, J. A. WILSON, AND T. JACOBSEN
1949 Before philosophy.

FRASER, D.
1962 Primitive art. Garden City, N.Y.

1965   Theoretical issues in the transpacific diffusion controversy. *Social Research*, 32: 452–477.

1966a   The heraldic woman: a study in diffusion. *In* The many faces of primitive art, edited by D. Fraser, pp. 36–99.

1966b   [ed.] The many faces of primitive art: a critical anthology. Englewood Cliffs, N.J.

1967   [ed.] Early Chinese art and the Pacific Basin: a photographic exhibition. Columbia University. New York.

FREE, J. P.
1956   The excavation of Dothan. *Bibl. Archaeologist*, 19: 43–48.

FREEMAN, G. F.
1912   Southwestern beans and teparies. *Ariz. Agr. Exp. Sta. Bull.*, no. 68.

FREER GALLERY OF ART, WASHINGTON, D.C.
Chinese Bronzes: collection.

FRIEDERICI, G.
1929   Zu den vorkolumbischen Verbindungen der Südseevölker mit Amerika. *Anthropos*, 24: 441–487.

1936   Die Süsskartoffel in der Südsee. *Mitt. der Gesellschaft für Völkerkunde*, no. 7, pp. 2–7.

1947   Amerikanistisches Worterbuch. Hamburg.

FRIIS, H. R., ed.
1967   The Pacific Basin: a history of its geographical exploration. *Amer. Geog. Soc.*, spec. pub. 38.

FUNK AND WAGNALLS NEW STANDARD BIBLE DICTIONARY
1936   New York.

FUNK AND WAGNALLS STANDARD DICTIONARY OF FOLKLORE, MYTHOLOGY, AND LEGEND
1950   2 vols. New York.

GANN, T.
1926   Ancient cities and modern tribes. London.

1936   Mexico: from the earliest times to the conquest. London.

———— AND J. E. THOMPSON
1931   The history of the Maya from the earliest times to the present day. New York.

GARCÍA PAYON, J.
1942–59   Prehistoria de Mesoamérica. Excavaciones en Trapiche y Chalahuite, Veracruz, México, 1942, 1951 y 1959. Cuadernos de la Facultad de Filosofía, Letras, y Ciencias, Universidad Veracruzana, Xalapa, V.C., Mexico.

1948–49   Una "palma" in situ. *Rev. Mex. Estud. Antropol.*, 10: 121–124.

GARCILASO DE LA VEGA (EL INCA)
  1943 Comentarios reales de los Incas. 2 vols. Buenos Aires. Written before 1604.
GARDINER, A.
  1950 The baptism of Pharoah. *Jour. Egyptian Archaeol.*, 36: 3–12.
GARLAND, J. E.
  1963 Lone voyager. Boston.
GARN, S. M.
  1957 Race and evolution. *Amer. Anthr.*, 59: 218–224.
GATTY, H.
  1958 Nature is your guide: how to find your way on land and sea by observing nature. New York.
GEIST, O., AND F. RAINEY
  1936 Archaeological excavations at Kukulik, St. Lawrence Island, Alaska. *Misc. Pub. Univ. Alaska*, vol. 2.
GENTLEMAN OF ELVAS
  1905 Discovery of Florida: the true relation by a Fidalgo of Elvas. *In* Narratives of the career of Hernando de Soto, edited by E. G. Bourne. London.
GENTRY, H. S.
  1969 Origin of the common bean, *Phaseolus vulgaris. Econ. Botany,* 23 (1): 55–64.
GHIRSHMAN, R.
  1961 Iran. Baltimore.
GILMORE, R. M.
  1950 Fauna and ethnozoology of South America. *In* Handbook of South American Indians, edited by J. H. Steward. Vol. 6, Physical anthropology, linguistic and cultural geography of South American Indians, pp. 345–464. *Smithsonian Inst., Bur. Amer. Ethnol.*, bull. 143.
GINSBERG, H. L.
  1945 Ugaritic studies and the Bible. *Bibl. Archaeologist,* 8: 41–58.
GODE, P. K., ed.
  1950 The history of maize (maka) in India. *Reprinted from* Commemorative Volume, pp. 14–25. Poona.
GODFREY, W. S., JR.
  1951 The archaeology of the old stone mill in Newport, Rhode Island. *Amer. Antiquity,* 17: 120–129.
  1954 Answer to Plaster under the tower. *Amer. Antiquity,* 19: 277–279.
  1955 Vikings in America: theories and evidence. *Amer. Anthr.*, 57: 35–43.

GOETZ, D., and S. G. MORLEY
   1950   Popul Vuh: the sacred book of the ancient Quiche Maya. From
          a translation by A. Recinos. Norman, Okla.
GOLSON, J.
   1959   Culture change in prehistoric New Zealand. *In* Anthropology in
          the South Seas, edited by J. D. Freeman and W. R. Geddes, pp.
          29–74. New Plymouth, Avery.
   1963   [ed.] Polynesian navigation: a symposium on Andrew Sharp's
          theory of accidental voyages. *Supl. Jour. Polynesian Soc. Mem.*,
          no. 34. Wellington.
   1965   Some considerations of the role of theory in New Zealand ar-
          chaeology. *N. Z. Archaeol. Assn. Newsletter*, 8: 79–92.
GÓMARA, F. L. DE. *See* LÓPEZ DE GÓMARA
GONZALEZ, A. R.
   1961   The La Aguada culture of northwestern Argentina. *In* Essays in
          pre-Columbian art and archaeology, by S. K. Lothrop, D. Z.
          Stone, J. B. Bird, G. F. Ekholm, and G. R. Willey, pp. 389–420.
          Cambridge, Mass.
GONZÁLEZ HOLGUÍN, D.
   1608   Vocabulario de la lengua general de todo el Perú llamada lengua
          Quichua, o del Inca. Lima. We used the reissue of 1952.
GOODMAN, M. M.
   1965   The history and origin of maize: current theories on the relation-
          ships between maize and some of its relatives. *N. Carolina Agr.
          Exp. Sta. Tech. Bull.*, no. 170, pp. 1–25.
GORDON, C. H.
   1968   The authenticity of the Phoenician text from Parahyba. *Orien-
          talia*, 37: 75–80.
GORDON, D. H.
   1958   The prehistoric background of Indian culture. Bombay.
GORODZOV, V. A.
   1933   The typological method in archaeology, *Amer. Anthr.*, 35: 95–
          102.
GOSCH, C. C. A.
   1897   Danish Arctic expeditions, 1605–1620. Vols. 1–2. Hakluyt Soc.
GRACE, G. W.
   1964   Movement of the Malayo-Polynesians. *Current Anthr.*, 5: 361–
          368.
GRAHAM, R. L.
   1968   A teen-ager sails the world alone. *Nat. Geog. Mag.*, 134: 445–
          491.
GRAY, A., AND J. H. TRUMBULL
   1883   *Review of* De Candolle's Origin of cultivated plants; with an-

notations upon certain American species. *Amer. Jour. Sci*, 25: 241–255.

GREEN, R. C.
  1963 A review of the prehistoric sequence in the Auckland Province. *Auckland Archaeol. Soc. Pub.*, no. 1: *N. Z. Archaeol. Assn. Pub.*, no. 2.
  1967 The immediate origins of the Polynesians. *In* Polynesian culture history, edited by G. Highland, R. W. Force, A. Howard, M. Kelly, and Y. H. Sinoto. Honolulu.

GREENE, V., AND H. MOHOLY-NAGY
  1966 A Teotihuacán-style vessel from Tikal: a correction. *Amer. Antiquity*, 31: 432–434.

GREENHILL, B.
  1956 The Karachi fishing boats. *Mariner's Mirror*, 42: 54–66.

GRESSMAN, H.
  1928 The tower of Babel. New York.

GRIFFIN, J. B.
  1952 [ed.] Archaeology of eastern United States. Chicago.
  1964 The Northeast Woodlands area. *In* Pre-historic man in the New World, edited by J. D. Jennings and E. Norbeck, pp. 223–258. Chicago.

GROOT, G.
  1951 The prehistory of Japan. New York.

GROTH, B. H. A.
  1911 The sweet potato. *Contrib. Bot. Lab. Pennsylvania Univ.*, vol. 4, no. 1.

GROTH-KIMBALL, J., AND F. FEUCHTWANGER.
  1954 The art of ancient Mexico. London and New York.

GROUBE, L. M.
  1967 Models in prehistory: a consideration of the New Zealand evidence. *Archaeol. Phys. Anthr. Oceania*, 2: 1–27.

GULATI, A. M., AND A. J. TURNER
  1928 A note on the early history of cotton. *Indian Central Cotton Committee, Bombay. Technological Lab. Bull.*, no. 17.

GUPPY, H. B.
  1906 Observations of a naturalist in the Pacific between 1896 and 1899. Vol. 2, Plant-dispersal. London.

GURNEY, O. R.
  1961 The Hittites. Baltimore.

GUZMÁN, M.
  1920 Vocabulario de la lengua quichua cual se habla hoy en la República del Ecuador. Quito.

HABERLAND, W.
  1960   Ceramic sequences in El Salvador. *Amer. Antiquity*, 26: 21–29.
HADDON, A. C.
  1934   Introductory address. *1st Int. Cong. Sci. Anthr. Ethnol.* (London), 1: 179–182.
  1937   The canoes of Melanesia, Queensland, and New Guinea. *Bishop Mus. Spec. Pub.*, no. 28.
HAGEN, A.
  1967   Norway. New York.
HAGEN, S. N.
  1950   The Kensington runic inscriptions. *Speculum*, 25: 321–356.
HANCE, H. F., AND W. F. MAYERS
  1870   Introduction of maize into China. *Pharmaceutical Jour. Trans.*, Dec. 31, 1870.
HANDY, E. S. C.
  1936   Dreaming in relation to spirit kindred and sickness in Hawaii. *In* Essays in anthropology, presented to A. L. Kroeber, pp. 119–128. Berkeley.
  1943   Two unique petroglyphs in the Marquesas which point to Easter Island and Malaysia. *In* Studies in anthropology of Oceania and Asia, *Papers Peabody Mus., Harvard Univ.*, 20: 22–31.
HANSEN, C. C.
  1915   Outlines of the geography and history of Greenland. Copenhagen.
  1924   Anthropologia medico-historica groenlandiae antiquae. Vol. 1, Herjolfsnes. *Meddelelser om Grønland*, 67: 291–547.
HANSON, P. M.
  1949a   In the land of the feathered serpent. Independence, Mo.
  1949b   Jesus Christ among the ancient Americans. Independence, Mo.
HARMS, H.
  1922   Übersicht der bisher in altperuanischen Grabern gefundenen Pflanzenreste. Festschrift Eduard Seler, pp. 157–186. Stuttgart.
HARRIS, D. R.
  1967   New light on plant domestication and the origins of agriculture: a review. *Geog. Rev.*, 57: 90–107.
HASSLÖF, O.
  1963   Wrecks, archives, and living tradition. *Mariner's Mirror*, 49: 162–177.
  1966   Sources of maritime history and methods of research. *Mariner's Mirror*, 52: 127–144.
HASTINGS, J., ed.
  1951   Encyclopedia of religion and ethics. 12 vols. New York.

HATT, G.
1949 Asiatic influences in American folklore. Copenhagen.
1951 The Corn Mother myth in America and in Indonesia. *Anthropos*, 46: 853–914.

HAUDRICOURT, A. G., AND L. HEDIN
1943 L'Homme et les plantes cultivées. Paris.

HAWKES, J.
1962 Man and the sun. New York.

HAWKES, J. G.
1947 On the origin and meaning of South American Indian potato names. *Jour. Linnean Soc., London (Botany)*, 53: 205–250.

HAWKINS, G. S.
1965 Stonehenge decoded. Garden City, N. Y.

HAZARD, H. W.
1954 Atlas of Islamic history. Princeton.

HEDRICK, B. C.
1957 Quetzalcoatl: man, god, and myth. University of Florida, Gainesville. Manuscript.

HEDRICK, V. P.
1931 The beans of New York. *In* The vegetables of New York, 1: 1–110. *N. Y. Agr. Exp. Sta. Rept.*

HEHN, V., AND S. STALLYBRASS
1885 Wanderings of plants and animals. London.

HEINE-GELDERN, R.
1937 L'Art prébouddhique de la Chine et de l'Asie du Sud-Est et son influence en Océanie. *Rev. Arts Asiatiques*, 11: 177–206.
1945 Prehistoric research in the Netherlands Indies. *In* Science and scientists in the Netherlands Indies, pp. 129–167. New York.
1952 Some problems of migration in the Pacific. *In* Kultur und Sprache, edited by W. Koppers. Wiener Beiträge zur Kulturgeschichte und Linguistik, Annual, 9: 313–362.
1954 Die asiatische Herkunft der südamerkanishen Metalltechnik. *Paideuma*, 5: 347–423.
1956 The origin of ancient civilizations and Toynbee's theories. *Diogenes*, no. 13, pp. 81–99.
1958 Kulturpflanzengeographie und das Problem vorkolumbischer Kulturbeziehungen zwischen Alter und Neuer Welt. *Anthropos*, 53: 361–402.
1959a Chinese influences in Mexico and Central America: The Tajín style of Mexico and the marble vases from Honduras. *Acts 33rd Int. Cong. Amer.* (San José), 1: 195–205.
1959b Chinese influence in the pottery of Mexico, Central America, and

Colombia. *Acts 33rd Int. Cong. Amer.* (San José), 1: 207–210.

1960   Theoretical considerations concerning the problem of pre-Columbian contacts between the Old World and the New. *In Selected papers 5th Int. Cong. Anthr. Ethnol. Sci.* (Philadelphia), edited by A. Wallace, pp. 277–281.

1964   Traces of Indian and Southeast Asiatic Hindu-Buddhist influences in Mesoamerica. *Acts 35th Int. Cong. Amer.* (Mexico City), 1: 47–54.

1966   The problem of transpacific influences in Mesoamerica. *In* Handbook of Middle American Indians, edited by R. Wauchope. Vol. 4, Archaeological frontiers and external connections, edited by G. F. Ekholm and G. R. Willey, pp. 277–295. Austin.

1967   A Roman find from pre-Columbian Mexico. *Anthr. Jour. Canada,* 5: 20–22. Translated from *Anzeiger der philosophischehistorische Klasse der Oesterreichischen Akademie der Wissenschaften,* 98: 117–119. 1961.

1968   Tranzozeanisch Kultureinflüsse im Alten Amerika: der Gegenwärtige Stand der Forschung. *Zeitschrift für Ethnologie,* 93 (1–2): 2–22. Brunswick.

——— AND G. F. EKHOLM

1951   Significant parallels in the symbolic arts of southern Asia and Middle America. *In* The civilizations of ancient America, edited by S. Tax, 1: 299–309. Chicago. This collection comprises selected papers of the 29th Int. Cong. Amer.

HEISER, C. B.

1965   Cultivated plants and cultural diffusion in Nuclear America. *Amer. Anthr.,* 67: 930–949.

HELBAEK, H.

1963   Palaeo-ethnobotany. *In* Science in archaeology, edited by D. Brothwell and E. Higgs. New York.

HENNING, P.

1911   Apuntes sobre la historia del Chalchiuitl en América. *Mem. Soc. "Alzate,"* no. 31: 29–46.

HENRÍQUEZ UREÑA, P.

1938   Para la historia de los indigenismos papa y batata, etc. Univ. Buenos Aires, Inst. de Filología. Biblioteca de dialectología hispanoamericana, suppl. 3.

HERMANNSSON, H.

1944   The Vinland sagas. *Islandica,* vol. 30.

HERNÁNDEZ, F.

1959–60   Various materials composed about 1570, from his Obras completas, 3 vols. Mexico City.

HERRERA, F. L.
1941 Sinopsis de la flora del Cuzco. Lima.
1942 Plantas tropicales cultivados por los antiguos Peruanos. *Rev. Mus. Nac.* (Lima), 11: 179–195.

HERRERA FRITOT, R.
1938 Revisión de las hachas de ceremonia de la cultura Taina. Havana.

HERRERA Y TORDESILLAS, A. DE
1601–15 Historia general de los hechos de los castellanos en las islas y tierra firma del mar Océano, vol. 1. Madrid.

HEWES, G. W.
1961 The ecumene as a civilizational multiplier system. *Kroeber Anthropol. Soc. Papers*, no. 25, pp. 73–109.

HEWETT, E. L.
1943 Ancient life in Mexico and Central America. New York.

HEYERDAHL, T.
1950a The voyage of the raft Kon-Tiki. *Geog. Jour.*, 115: 20–41.
1950b The Kon-Tiki expedition. London. Also published as Kon-Tiki. Chicago.
1952 American Indians in the Pacific: the theory behind the Kon-Tiki expedition. London, Oslo, and Stockholm.
1959 Guara sailing technique indigenous to South America. *Acts 33rd Int. Cong. Amer.* (San José), 1: 333–340.
1963 Prehistoric voyages as agencies for Melanesian and South American plant and animal dispersals to Polynesia. *In* Plants and the migrations of Pacific peoples, edited by J. Barrau. Honolulu.
1964 Feasible ocean routes to and from the Americas in pre-Columbian times. *Acts 35th Int. Cong. Amer.* (Mexico City), 1: 133–142. Same title in *Amer. Antiquity*, 28 (1963): 482–488.
1966a Discussions of transoceanic contact: isolationism, diffusionism, or a middle course? *Anthropos*, 61: 689–707.
1966b The Inca inspiration behind the Spanish discoveries of Polynesia and Melanesia. *Acts 36th Int. Cong. Amer.* (Seville-Barcelona), 1: 93–104.
———— AND E. N. FERDON, JR., eds.
1961–65 Reports of the Norwegian archaeological expedition to Easter Island and the East Pacific. Vol. 1, 1961; vol. 2, 1965. Santa Fe, N. M., and London.

HINDERLING, P.
1949 Über steinzeitliche Beile der Südsee. Aarau, Switzerland.

HINKE, J.
1907 A new boundary stone of Nebuchadnezzar I from Nippur. The

Babylonian expedition of Pennsylvania Univ., ser. D, vol. 4. Philadelphia.

HIRTH, F., AND W. W. ROCKHILL
1911   Chau Ju-Kua. St. Petersburg.

HISTORIA DE LOS MEXICANOS POR SUS PINTURAS (CÓDICE RAMÍREZ)
1886   An. Mus. Nac. (Mexico), ser. 1, 3: 83–106.

HO, P.-T.
1955   The introduction of American food plants into China. Amer. Anthr., 57: 191–201.

HOBBS, W. H.
1951   The fourteenth-century discovery of America by Antonio Zeno. Scientific Monthly, 72: 24–31.

HODGE, F. W.
1905   Handbook of American Indians north of Mexico. Smithsonian Inst., Bur. Amer. Ethnol., bull. 30.

HODGEN, M. T.
1952   Change and history. Viking Fund Pub. Anthr., no. 18.

HOEBEL, E. A.
1949   Man in the primitive world. New York.
1966   Anthropology: the study of man. New York.

HOEHNE, F. C.
1937   Botanica e agricultura no Brasil (Século XVI). São Paulo.

HOLAND, H. R.
1940   Westward from Vinland. New York.
1946   America: 1355–1364. New York.

HOLLAND, W. R.
1964   Contemporary Tzotzil cosmological concepts as a basis for interpreting prehistoric Maya civilization. Amer. Antiquity, 29: 301–306.

HOLLIS, F. J.
1933   The sun-cult and the temple at Jerusalem, myth and ritual. London.

HOLM, B.
1965   Northwest coast Indian art: an analysis of form. Seattle.

HONORÉ, P.
1964   In quest of the White God. New York.

HOOKER, J. D.
1867   Cucurbitaceae. In Genera plantarum, by G. Bentham and J. D. Hooker, 1: 816–841. London.

HOOTON, E. A.
1925   The ancient inhabitants of the Canary Islands. Harvard African Studies, vol. 7.

HORNELL, J.
1923   The origins and ethnological significance of Indian boat designs. *Mem. Asiatic Soc. Bengal*, 7: 139–256.
1931   South American balsas: the problem of their origin. *Mariner's Mirror*, 17: 347–355.
1936a   British coracles. *Mariner's Mirror*, vol. 22, no. 1.
1936b   British coracles. *Mariner's Mirror*, vol. 22, no. 3.
1936c   The canoes of Polynesia, Fiji, and Micronesia. *Bishop Mus. Spec. Publ.*, no. 27.
1937   The curraghs of Ireland. *Mariner's Mirror*, vol. 23, nos. 1–2; vol. 24, no. 1.
1946a   How did the sweet potato reach Oceania? *Jour. Linnean Soc., London (Botany)*, 53: 41–62. This is a revised version of an article in *Jour. Polynesian Soc.*, 54 (1945): 167–191.
1946b   Water transport: origins and early evolution. Cambridge, Eng.

HOUSE, H. D.
1908   The North American species of the genus *Ipomoea. Ann. New York Acad. Sci.*, 18: 181–263.

HRDLIČKA, A.
1912   Early man in South America. *Smithsonian Inst., Bur. Amer. Ethnol.*, bull. 52.

HSIEH, C.
1967   Geographical exploration by the Chinese. *In* The Pacific Basin, edited by H. R. Friis, pp. 87–95. New York.

HUDDLESTON, L. E.
1967   Origins of the American Indians: European concepts, 1492–1729. Austin.

HUMBOLDT, A. DE
1811   Essai politique sur le royaume de la Nouvelle-Espagne. Paris.

HURD, P. D., JR., AND E. G. LINSLEY
1964   The squash and gourd bees—genera *Peponapis* Robertson and *Xenoglossa* Smith—inhabiting America north of Mexico. (Hymenoptera: Apoidea). *Hilgardia*, 35 (15): 375–477.
1966   The Mexican squash and gourd bees of the genus *Peponapis* (Hymenoptera: Apoidea). *Ann. Entom. Soc. Amer.*, 59: 835–851.
1967a   South American squash and gourd bees of the genus *Peponapis* (Hymenoptera: Apoidea). *Ann. Entom. Soc. Amer.*, 60: 647–661.
1967b   Squash and gourd bees of the genus *Xenoglossa* (Hymenoptera: Apoidea). *Ann. Entom. Soc. Amer.*, 60: 988–1007.

HUTCHINSON, J. B.
  1959   The application of genetics to cotton improvement. Cambridge,
         Eng.
  1962   The history and relationships of the world's cottons. *Endeavour*,
         21(5): 5–15.
  ———, R. A. SILOW, AND S. G. STEPHENS
  1947   The evolution of *Gossypium* and the differentiation of the culti-
         vated cottons. Oxford.
HUTCHINSON, R. W.
  1962   Prehistoric Crete. Baltimore.
HUTT, F. B.
  1949   Genetics of the fowl. New York.
IKUSE, M.
  1956   Pollen grains of Japan. Tokyo.
IMBELLIONI, J.
  1940   Kumara, Amu et Hapay. *An. Inst. Etnogr. Amer., Univ. Nacional
         de Cuyo, Mendoza,* 1: 201–216.
  1956   La Segunda esfinge indiana. Buenos Aires.
INGSTAD, H.
  1964   Vinland ruins prove Vikings found the New World. *Nat Geog.
         Mag.,* 126: 708–734.
  1969   Westward to Vinland. Translated by E. J. Friis. London.
IRWIN, C.
  1963   Fair gods and stone faces. New York.
ITURRIBARRÍA, J. F.
  1951   Historia de México. Mexico City.
IXTLILXÓCHITL, F. DE ALVA
  1891   Relaciones . . . Mexico City.
  1952   Obras históricas. 2 vols. Mexico City.
JACKSON, J. W.
  1916   The geographical distribution of the shell purple industry. Man-
         chester Literary and Philosophical Soc., *Mem. and Proc.,* vol. 60.
JACOBS, J.
  1969   The economy of cities. New York.
JACOBSEN, T.
  1949   Mesopotamia. *In* Before philosophy, by H. Frankfort, H. A.
         Frankfort, J. A. Wilson, and T. Jacobsen, pp. 137–234. Balti-
         more.
JACOBUS, M. W.
  1936   A new standard Bible dictionary. London.
JAMES, E. O.
  1966   The tree of life. Leiden.

JANE, C., ed. and trans.
  1960   The journal of Christopher Columbus. Revised by L. A. Vigneras. London.
JANSE, O.
  1947–58   Archaeological research in Indo-China, vols. 1–3. Cambridge, Mass.
JANZEN, D. H.
  in press   Seed eaters, and seed size, number, toxicity and dispersal. *Evolution*.
JEFFREY, C.
  1961   Notes on Cucurbitaceae, including a proposed new classification of the family. *Kew Bull.*, 15 (3): 337–371.
  1967   Flora of tropical East Africa: Cucurbitaceae. London.
JEFFREYS, M. D. W.
  1953a   Arabs discover America before Columbus. *Ramadan Annual of the Muslim's Digest*, 3 (11): 67–74. Durban.
  1953b   Pre-Columbian Negroes in America. *Scientia* (July–August), pp. 1–16.
  1954   Pre-Columbian Arabs in the Caribbean. *The Muslim Digest*, 5(1): 25–29.
  1963a   How ancient is West African maize? *Africa* (January, 1963), pp. 115–131.
  1963b   Milho zaburro=milho de Guynee=maize. *Garcia de Orta*, 2 (2): 213–226.
  1967a   Who introduced maize into southern Africa? *South African Jour. Science*, 63: 23–40. Johannesburg.
  1967b   Pre-Columbian maize in Southern Africa. *Nature*, 215 (5102): 695–697.
JENNINGS, J. D., AND E. NORBECK, eds.
  1964   Prehistoric man in the New World. Chicago.
JENSEN, S.
  1939   Concerning a change of climate during recent decades in the Arctic and subarctic regions, from Greenland in the west to Eurasia in the east, and contemporary biological and geo-physical changes. *Danske Videnskabernes Selskab. Biologiske Medd.*, vol. 14, no. 8.
JETT, S. C.
  1968   Malaysia and tropical America: some racial, cultural, and ethno-botanical comparisons. *Acts 37th Int. Cong. Amer.* (Buenos Aires), 4: 133–177.
  1971   The development and distribution of the blowgun. *Ann. Assoc. Amer. Geog.*, vol. 60, no. 4.

494   BIBLIOGRAPHY

———— AND G. F. CARTER
  1966 A comment on Rowe's "Diffusionism and archaeology." *Amer.*
         Antiquity, 31: 867–870.
JIMÉNEZ MORENO, W.
  1966 Mesoamerica before the Toltecs. *In* Ancient Oaxaca, edited by
         J. Paddock, pp. 1–82. Stanford.
JOHNSON, W. G. AND G. O. BROWN, eds.
  1913 The poultry book. Garden City, N. Y.
JONES, A.
  1965 Cytological observations and fertility measurements of sweet
         potato (*Ipomoea batatas* [L.] Lam.). *Proc. Amer. Soc. Hort.*
         Sci., 86: 527–537.
  1967 Should Nishiyama's K123 (*Ipomoea trifida*) be designated *I. ba-*
         tatas? Econ. Botany, 21: 163–166.
JONES, G.
  1964 The Norse Atlantic saga. London.
JÓNSSON, A.
  1643 Specimen Islandiae historicum. Amsterdam.
JÓNSSON, F. (1704–1789)
  1772–78 Historia ecclesiastica Islandiae, vols. 1–4. Copenhagen.
JÓNSSON, F. (1858–1934)
  1924 Interpretation of the runic inscriptions from Herjolfsnes. *Med-*
         delelser om Grønland, 67: 271–290.
  1928 On the Icelandic colonization of Greenland. Greenland, vol. 2.
         London.
JOYCE, T. A.
  1916 Central America and West Indian archaeology. London.
  1920 Mexican archaeology. London.
KANTOR, H. J.
  1947 The shoulder ornament of Near Eastern lions. *Jour. Near Eastern*
         Studies, 6: 250–274.
KAPLAN, L.
  1956 Cultivated beans of prehistoric Southwest. *Ann. Missouri Bo-*
         tanical Garden, 43: 189–251.
  1965 Archaeology and domestication in American *Phaseolus* (beans).
         Econ. Botany, 19: 358–368.
  1967 Archaeological Phaseolus from Tehuacan. *In* The prehistory of
         the Tehuacan Valley, edited by D. S. Byers. Vol. 1, Environ-
         ment and subsistence, pp. 201–212. Austin.
KEHOE, A. B.
  1962 A hypothesis on the origin of northeastern American pottery.
         SW. Jour. Anthr., 18: 20–29.

KELLETT, E. E.
1929   The northern saga. London.
KELLEY, J. C., AND C. L. RILEY
1969   Pre-Columbian contact within Nuclear America. *Res. Rec. Univ. Mus.*, Southern Illinois University, Mesoamerican Studies, no. 4.
KELLY, C., ed.
1966   La Austrialia del Espiritu Santo. 2 vols. Hakluyt Soc., 2d ser., nos. 126–127.
KELLY, D.
1960   Calendar animals and deities. *SW Jour. Anthr.*, 16: 317–337.
1964   Linguistics and problems of trans-Pacific contacts. *Acts 35th Int. Congr. Amer.* (Mexico City), 1: 17–19.
KELSO, J. L., AND J. P. THORLEY
1945   Palestinian pottery in Bible times. *Bibl. Archaeologist*, 8: 82–93.
KENNARD, G. B.
1944   Sweet potato variety experiments at the Imperial College of Tropical Agriculture, 1927–43. *Tropical Agriculture*, 21:69–77.
KENNEDY, R. A.
1960   Necked and lugged axes in Nigeria. *Antiquity*, 34: 54–58.
1965   The spread of Neolithic modes of life in Africa. Thesis. Oxford.
———— AND VITA-FINZI, C.,
1965   Seven Saharan sites. *Jour. Royal Anthr. Inst.*, 95: 195–207.
KENYON, K. M.
1931   Settlement of the east coast of Africa, being appendix V *in* Zimbabwe culture, by G. Canton-Thompson. Oxford.
KIDD, H. J., AND H. C. REYNOLDS, trans.
1954   Kuleshov's 'Some peculiarities of maize in Asia.' *Ann. Missouri Botanical Garden*, vol. 41, no. 3.
KIDDER, A. V.
1946   Introduction. *In* Excavations at Kaminaljuyu, Guatemala, by A. V. Kidder, J. D. Jennings, and E. M. Shook. *Carnegie Inst. Wash. Pub.* no. 561.
1953   Transpacific influences. *In* An appraisal of anthropology today, by S. Tax, L. C. Eiseley, I. Rooser, and C. Voegelin, p. 47. Chicago.
1964   South American high cultures. *In* Prehistoric man in the New World, edited by J. D. Jennings and E. Norbeck, pp. 451–486. Chicago.
————, J. D. JENNINGS, AND E. M. SHOOK
1946   Excavations at Kaminaljuyu, Guatemala. *Carnegie Inst. Wash. Pub.*, no. 561.

KIDDER, J. E., JR.
  1957   The Jomon pottery of Japan. Ascona, Switzerland.
  1959   Japan before Buddhism. London. Also New York, 1966.
KING, J. R., AND R. BANFORD
  1937   The chromosome number in *Ipomoea* and related genera. *Jour.
         Heredity*, 28: 278–282.
KIRCHOFF, P.
  1943   Mesoamerica. *Acta Amer.*, 1: 92–107.
  1944   The problem of the origin of Mexican civilization. *Esta Semana*
         (Mexico), July 22–28.
  1964   The diffusion of a great religious system from India to Mexico.
         Acts 35th Int. Cong. Amer. (Mexico City), 1: 73–100.
KIVIKOSKI, E.
  1967   Finland. New York.
KLOZ, J.
  1962   An investigation of the protein characters of four *Phaseolus*
         species with special reference to the question of their phylogene-
         sis. *Biologia Plantarum*, 4 (2): 85–90.
KRAMER, S. N.
  1952   Enmerkar and the Lord of Aratta. Philadelphia.
KRIEGER, H. W.
  1942   Peoples of the Philippines. Smithsonian Institution War Back-
         ground Studies, no. 4. Washington.
KROEBER, A. L.
  1925   Handbook of the Indians of California. *Smithsonian Inst., Bur.
         Amer. Ethnol.*, bull. 78.
  1948   Anthropology. New York.
  1952   The ancient oikoumene as a historical culture aggregate. *In* The
         nature of culture, pp. 379–395. Chicago.
———— AND C. KLUCKHOHN
  1952   Culture, a critical review of concepts and definitions. *Papers
         Peabody Mus., Harvard Univ.*, vol. 47, no. 1.
KROM, N. J.
  1920–22   Beschrijving van Bara Budur. The Hague.
KUBLER, G.
  1961   On the colonial extinction of the motifs of pre-Columbian art. *In*
         Essays in pre-Columbian art and archaeology, by S. K. Lothrop,
         D. Z. Stone, J. B. Bird, G. F. Ekholm, and G. R. Willey, pp.
         14–34. Cambridge, Mass.
  1962   The art and architecture of ancient America. Baltimore.
  1967a Pintura mural precolombina. *Estud. de Cultura Maya*, no. 6.
  1967b The iconography of the art of Teotihuacán. *Studies in Pre-
         Columbian Art and Archaeology*, no. 4. Washington.

KUNZ, G.
1938   The curious lore of precious stones. New York.
KURTZ, E. B., JR., J. L. LOVERMAN, AND H. TUCKER
1960   Some problems concerning fossil and modern corn pollen. *Torrey Bot. Club Bull.*, 87: 85–94.
LACY, M. G.
1911   Pre-Columbian references to maize in Persian literature. *Science*, 33: 968–970.
LANE-POOLE, R. H.
1940   Primitive craft and mediaeval rigs in South America. *Mariner's Mirror*, 26: 333–338.
LANGDON, S. H.
1931   The mythology of all races. Vol. 5, Semitic. Boston.
LANNING, E. P.
1963   A pre-agricultural occupation on the central coast of Peru. *Amer. Antiquity*, 28: 360–371.
1965   Early man in Peru. *Sci. Amer.*, 213: 68–76.
1967   Peru before the Incas. Englewood Cliffs, N. J.
LARCO HERRERA, V.
1934   Cobrizos, blancos y negros: aborígenes de América. Santiago de Chile.
LARCO HOYLE, R.
1938–39   Los mochicas. 2 vols. Lima. Our material is in 2: 44–82.
LARSON, R.
1966   Was America the wonderful land of Fusang? *Amer. Heritage*, 17 (3): 42–45, 106–109.
LAS CASAS, B. DE
1957–61   Historia de las Indias. Biblioteca de Autores Españoles, vols. 95–96. Madrid.
LATCHAM, R.
1922   Los animales domésticos de la America pre-Columbiana. *Mus. Etnol. Antr.* (Santiago), pub. 3, 1: 1–199.
1936   La agricultura precolombiana en Chile y los países vecinos. Santiago.
LATHRAP, D.
1967   *Review of* B. J. Meggers, C. Evans, and E. Estrada, Early formative period of coastal Ecuador. *Amer. Anthr.* 69: 96–98.
———— AND L. ROYS
1963   Archaeology of the cave of the owls in upper Montana of Peru. *Amer. Antiquity*, 29: 27–38.
LAUFER, B.
1919   Sino-Iranica: Chinese contributions to the history of civilization

in ancient Iran. Field Mus. *Natural Hist., Anthr. Series*, vol. 15, no. 3.

1938   The American plant migration, pt. 1: the potato. *Field Mus. Natural Hist., Anthr. Ser.*, vol. 28, no. 1.

L'ECLUSE, J. C. DE

1576   Rariorum aliquot stirpium per Hispanias observatorum Historia. Antwerp.

LEEDS, A.

1961   Yarura incipient tropical forest horticulture—possibilities and limits. *In* The evolution of horticultural systems in native South America, causes and consequences, edited by J. Wilbert. Caracas.

LEÓN-PORTILLA, M.

1959   La filosofía náhuatl estudiada en sus fuentes. Mexico City.

1963   Aztec thought and culture. Norman, Okla.

LE PLONGEON, A.

1886   Sacred mysteries among the Mayas and the Quiches, etc. New York.

LERY, J. DE

1594   Histoire d'un voyage fait en la terre du Brasil, dite Amerique. 4th edition. Geneva.

LETHBRIDGE, T. C.

1950   Herdsmen and hermits. Cambridge, Eng.

1952   Boats and boatmen. London.

1956   Shipbuilding. *In* A history of technology. Vol. 2, The Mediterranean civilizations and the Middle Ages, edited by C. Singer, E. J. Holmyard, A. R. Hall, and T. I. Williams, pp. 563–588. London.

LE TOUMELIN, J. Y.

1955   Kurun around the world. New York.

LEUZINGER, E.

1960   Africa, the art of the Negro peoples. New York.

LÉVI-STRAUSS, C.

1960   On manipulated sociological models. *Bijdragen tot deTaal, Land-en-Volkenkunde*, 116: 45–54.

LEVY, G. R.

1953   The gate of horn. New York.

LEWER, S. H., ed.

n.d.   Wright's book of poultry. Revised edition. London.

LEWIS, A. R.

1958   The northern seas. Princeton, N. J.

LEWIS, D.
   1964   Polynesian navigational methods. *Jour. Polynesian Soc.*, 73: 364–374.
LEWTHWAITE, R.
   1966   Tupaia's map: the horizons of a Polynesian geographer. *Yearbook Assn. Pacific Coast Geog.*, 28: 41–53.
LI, H.-L.
   1961   Pu-Lan-Pi: a case for pre-Columbian transatlantic travel by Arab ships. *Harvard Jour. Asiatic Studies*, 23: 114–126.
LINDEMANN, H.
   1957   Alone at sea for 72 days. *Life*, 43 (4): 92–108. Also published as book, edited by J. Stuart. New York, 1958.
LINDQUIST, S.
   1913   De Svenska Holkyxorna Fran Bronsaldern. Stockholm.
LING, S.-S.
   1956   Formosan sea-going raft and its origin in ancient China. *Bull. Inst. Ethnol., Acad. Sinica*, no. 1, pp. 1–54.
LINNÉ, S.
   1934   Archaeological researches at Teotihuacán, Mexico. *Ethnog. Mus. Sweden, Pub.*, n.s., no. 1.
   1938   Zapotecan antiquities. *Ethnog. Mus. Sweden Pub.*, n.s., no. 4.
   1941   Teotihuacán symbols. *Ethnos*, 3: 164–186.
   1942   Mexican highland cultures. *Ethnog. Mus. Sweden Pub.*, n.s., no. 7.
LINTON, R.
   1923   The material culture of the Marquesas Islands. *Mem. Bernice P. Bishop Mus.*, vol. 8, no. 5.
LIYENAGE, D. V.
   1961   Genetic improvement of the coconut palm. *In* Symposium on tropical crops improvement, edited by J. Barrau, pp. 39–50. Honolulu.
LOEB, E.
   1923   The blood sacrifice complex. *Mem. Amer. Anthr. Assn.*, no. 30.
LOEHR, M.
   1956   Chinese Bronze Age weapons. Ann Arbor, Mich.
LOPATIN, I. A.
   1960   Origin of the native American steam bath. *Amer. Anthr.*, 62: 977–993.
LÓPEZ DE GÓMARA, F.
   1877   La historia de las Indias y conquista de México. First published 1552–53. Biblioteca de Autores Españoles, 22: 155–455. Madrid.
   1943   Historia de la conquista de México, vol. 2. Mexico City.

LOTHROP, S. K.
  1926   Pottery of Costa Rica and Nicaragua. *Contrib. Mus. Amer. Indian, Heye Found.*, no. 8.
  1964   Treasures of ancient America. Geneva.
  ———, D. Z. STONE, J. B. BIRD, G. F. EKHOLM, AND G. R. WILLEY
  1961   Essays in pre-Columbian art and archaeology. Cambridge, Mass.
LOU, D. W.
  1957   Rain worship among the Chinese and the Nahua-Maya Indians: a comparative study of cultural similarities. *Bull. Inst. Ethnol., Acad. Sinica*, no. 4, pp. 31–108.
  in press   Early Chinese sea-faring activities and the trans-Pacific cultural contact. *Acts 38th Int. Cong. Amer.* (Stuttgart).
LOUD, G.
  1949   Megiddo, vol. 2. Chicago.
LOWE, P. R.
  1929   A note on the earliest appearance of the cock in Egypt. *Ibis*, 5: 40–41.
  1943   A further note on the appearance of the cock in Egypt. *Ibis*, 9: 378–382.
LOWIE, R. H.
  1937   The history of ethnological theory. New York.
  1956   The Crow Indians. New York.
LUOUMALA, K.
  1940   Oceanic, American Indian, and African myths of snaring the sun. *Bishop Mus. Bull.*, no. 168.
  1953   Ethnobotany of the Gilbert Islands. *Bishop Mus. Bull.*, no. 213, pp. 1–129.
MACALISTER, R.
  1912   The excavations of Gezer. 2 vols. London.
MACBRIDE, J. F.
  1959   Flora of Peru, pt. 5, no. 1, pp. 455–536, *Field Mus. Natural Hist., Bot. Ser.*, no. 13.
McBRYDE, F. W.
  1945   Cultural and historical geography of southwestern Guatemala. *Smithsonian Inst. Social Anthr. Pub.* no. 4.
McBURNEY, C. B. M.
  1960   The stone age of northern Africa. Baltimore.
McCOWN, C. C.
  1947   Tell en-Nasbeh. Palestine Inst. and Amer. Schools of Oriental Research. Berkeley.
  1950   Hebrew high places and cult remains. *Jour. Bibl. Lit.*, 69: 205–219.

MacDonald, A. S.
  1963 Sweet potatoes, with particular reference to the tropics. *Field Crop Abstracts*, 16: 219–225.
  1969 Some aspects of sweet potato breeding at the Kabahyolo University Farm. Proc. Int. Symposium on Tropical Root Crops, 1967, I: 131–143. St. Augustine, Trinidad.
McGrew, T. F.
  1926 The book of poultry. New York.
MacKendrick, P.
  1966 The Hellenistic age. *In* The Greek stones speak. New York.
McKern, W. C.
  1937 An hypothesis for the Asiatic origin of the Woodland pattern. *Amer. Antiquity*, 3: 138–143.
Mackie, W. W.
  1943 Origin dispersal and variability of the lima bean, Phaseolus lunatus. *Hilgardia*, 15: 1–24.
Mackiner, H. I.
  1929 Trade routes. *In* Encyclopedia Britannica. 14th edition. London.
McKnight, R. K.
  1968 Palauan culture heroes as agents of change. *In* Abstracts of SW. Anthr. Assn. and Soc. for Calif. Archaeol. 1968 meetings, edited by J. A. Price, p. 30.
McKusick, M. B.
  1960 Aboriginal canoes in the West Indies. *Yale Univ. Pub. Anthr.*, no. 63. New Haven.
Macleod, D.
  1967 Paper given before the Society for American Archaeology, May 5, 1967, at the University of Michigan, Ann Arbor.
MacLeod, W. C.
  1929 On the diffusion of Central American culture to coastal British Columbia and Alaska. *Anthropos*, 24: 417–439.
MacNab, J. W.
  1967 Sweet potatoes and settlement in the Pacific. *Jour. Polynesian Soc.*, 76: 219–221.
McNeill, W. H.
  1965 The rise of the West. *In* Hellenism, pp. 298–346. New York.
MacRitchie, D.
  1912 The kayak in north-western Europe. *Jour. Royal Anthr. Inst.*, 42: 493–510.
Major, R. H.
  1873 The voyages of the Venetian brothers, to the northern seas, in the XIVth century. Hakluyt Soc., 1st ser., no. 50.

MALLERY, A. H.
  1958   The pre-Columbian discovery of America: a reply to W. S. God-
         frey. *Amer. Anthr.*, 60: 141–152.
MANGELSDORF, P. C., R. S. MACNEISH, AND W. C. GALINAT
  1964   Domestication of corn. *Science*, 143 (3606): 538–545.
  1967   Prehistoric wild and cultivated maize. *In* The prehistory of the
         Tehuacan Valley, edited by D. S. Byers. Vol. 1, Environment
         and subsistence, pp. 178–200. Austin.
  ————, ————, AND G. R. WILLEY
  1964   Origins of agriculture in Middle America. *In* Handbook of Mid-
         dle American Indians, edited by R. Wauchope. Vol. 1, Natural
         environment and early cultures, edited by R. C. West, pp. 427–
         445. Austin.
  ———— AND D. L. OLIVER
  1951   Whence came maize to Asia? *Bot. Mus. Leafl., Harvard Univ.*,
         14 (10): 263–291.
  ———— AND R. G. REEVES
  1959   The origin of corn. Cambridge, Mass.
MANRY, R.
  1966   Tinkerbelle. New York.
MARCGRAVE, G.
  1648   Historiae rerum naturalium Brasiliae, bk. 8. Lugdun. Held in
         Beinecke Rare Book Library, Yale University.
MARKHAM, C. R.
  1862   Travels in Peru and India while superintending the collection
         of Chinchona plants and seeds in South America, and their in-
         troduction into India. London.
  1904   [Trans. and ed.] The voyages of Pedro Fernández de Quiros,
         1595–1606. 2 vols. Hakluyt Soc., 2d ser., nos. 14–15.
MARQUES, S.
  1944   Descobrimentos Portugueses. 12 vols. Lisbon.
MARSDEN, P. R. V.
  1965   The Blackfriars ship. *Mariner's Mirror*, 51: 59–62.
MARSHALL, DONALD
         Polynesian adzes, Austral Islands: collection.
MARTIN, F. W.
  1965   Incompatibility in the sweet potato: a review. *Econ. Botany*,
         19: 406–15.
MARTIN, P. S., G. QUIMBY, AND D. COLLIER
  1947   Indians before Columbus. Chicago.
  ————, J. B. RINALDO, E. BLUHM, H. C. CUTLER, AND R. GRANGE, JR.

1952 Mogollon cultural continuity and change. *Fieldiana: Anthropology*, 40: 461–479.

MARTÍNEZ, P.
1868 Descripciones . . . Pánuco, Tampico. *In* Colección de documentos inéditos . . . de Indias, vol. 9. Madrid.

MARTÍNEZ DEL RIO, P.
1952 Los orígenes americanos. 3d edition. Mexico City.

MARTÍNEZ-HIDALGO, J.
1966 Columbus' ships. Barre, Mass.

MARTYR, P. (P. MARTIRE D'ANGHIERA)
1912 De orbe novo: the eight decades of Peter Martyr d'Anghiera. Translated by F. A. MacNutt. 2 vols. New York. First decade published Acalá, 1511. Spanish edition, Buenos Aires, 1944.

MARX, E.
1947 Egyptian shipping. *Mariner's Mirror*, 33: 139–169.

MASCAL E., AND J. BARRAU
1956 Food plants of the South Sea islands. *South Pacific Commission* (*Noumea*), *Technical paper* no. 94, pp. 1–51.

MATHIOLUS, P. A.
1570 Commentarij in sex libros Pedacij Dioscordis Anazarhei de Medica Materia. Venice.

MATSON, G., H. SUTTON, R. ETCHEVERRY, B. SWANSON, AND A. ROBINSON
1967 Distribution of hereditary blood groups among Indians in South America, pt. 4: in Chile, with inferences concerning genetic connections between Polynesia and America. *Amer. Jour. Phys. Anthr.*, 27: 157–193.

MATUDA, E.
1964–66 El género *Ipomoea* en México. *An. Inst. Biología* (Universidad Nacional Autónoma de México), 34: 85–145, 35: 45–76, 36: 83–106. Our material is in 34: 140–142, dated 1963, but published in May, 1964.

MAY, H. G.
1931–32 The fertility cult in Hosea. *Amer. Jour. Semitic Languages*, 48: 73–98.
1935 Material remains of the Megiddo cult. *Univ. Chicago. Oriental Inst. Pub.*, vol. 26.

MEAD, C.
1924 Old civilizations of Inca land. New York.

MEADE, J.
1948 Izis Centli (El maíz). Mexico City.

MEEUSE, A. D. J.
1962 The Cucurbitaceae of southern Africa. *Bothalia*, 8: 1–111.

504   BIBLIOGRAPHY

MEGGERS, B. J.
    1954   Environmental limitation on the development of culture. *Amer.
            Anthr.*, 56: 801–824.
    1963a   Cultural development in Latin America: an interpretative over-
            view. *In* Aboriginal cultural development in Latin America: an
            interpretative review, edited by B. J. Meggers and C. Evans.
            Smithsonian Inst., Misc. Coll., 146 (1): 131–148.
    1963b   Aboriginal cultural development in Latin America: an interpre-
            tative review. *Smithsonian Inst., Misc. Coll.*, vol. 146, no. 1.
    1964   North and South American cultural connections and conver-
            gences. *In* Prehistoric man in the New World, edited by J. D.
            Jennings and E. Norbeck, pp. 511–526. Chicago.
    1966   Ecuador. New York.
    —————— AND C. EVANS
    1960   Archaeological investigations in British Guiana. *Smithsonian
            Inst., Bur. Amer. Ethnol.*, bull. 177.
    1962   The Machalilla culture: an early Formative complex on the Ecua-
            dorian coast. *Amer. Antiquity*, 28: 186–192.
    ——————, ——————, AND E. ESTRADA
    1965   Early Formative period of coastal Ecuador: the Valdivia and
            Machalilla phases. *Smithsonian Contrib. Anthr.*, vol. 1.
MEINETZHAGEN, R., ed.
    1930   Nicoll's birds of Egypt. London.
MELVILLE, H.
    1847   Omoo. New York.
MENDIETA, G. DE
    1870   Historia eclesiástica indiana. Mexico City.
MENDIZABAL, M. O. DE
    1946   Obras completas, vol. 2. Mexico City.
MERRIEN, J.
    1954   Lonely voyagers. Translated by J. H. Watkins. New York.
MERRILL, E. D.
    1950   Observations on cultivated plants with reference to certain Amer-
            ican problems. *Ceiba*, 1: 161–384.
    1954   The botany of Cook's voyages. *Chronica Botanica*, 14 (5–6):
            164–384.
METRAUX, A.
    1940   Ethnology of Easter Island. *Bishop Mus. Bull.*, no. 160.
METROPOLITAN MUSEUM OF ART
            Ancient Near East, China: collections.
MICHELS, J. W.
    1967   Paper given before the Society for American Archaeology, May
            5, 1967, at the University of Michigan, Ann Arbor.

MILES, S.
  1966   Sculpture of the Guatemala-Chiapas highlands and Pacific slopes. *In* Handbook of Middle American Indians, edited by R. Wauchope. Vol. 3, The archaeology of Southern Mesoamerica, edited by G. R. Willey, pp. 237–275. Austin.

MILLER, J. C.
  1939   Further studies and technic used in sweet potato breeding in Louisiana. *Jour. Heredity*, 30: 485–492.

MILLER, M. S., AND J. L. MILLER
  1944   Encyclopedia of Bible life. New York.

MILLON, R.
  1960   The beginnings of Teotihuacán. *Amer. Antiquity*, 26: 1–10.
  1964   The Teotihuacán mapping project. *Amer. Antiquity*, 29: 345–352.

MIRANDA, F. M.
  1946   The Diaguita of Argentina. *In* Handbook of South American Indians, edited by J. H. Steward. Vol. 2, The Andean civilizations, pp. 637–660. *Smithsonian Inst., Bur. Amer. Ethnol.*, bull. 143.

MITMAN, C. W.
  1923   Catalogue of the Watercraft Collection in the United States National Museum. *U. S. Nat. Museum Bull.*, no. 127.

MONARDES, N.
  1925   Joyfull newes out of the Newe Founde Worlde. 2 vols. London.

MOORE, J. H.
  1785   A new and complete collection of voyages and travels. 2 vols. London.

MORALES Y SÁNCHEZ, A.
  1947   Copantl: Jardín Maya, "La Concordia." Tegucigalpa.

MORENO, J.
  1942   El enigma de los Olmecas. *Cuad. Amer.*, 5: 113–646.

MORISON, S. E.
  1965   *New York Times* (Nov. 7), p. 92.

MORLEY, S. G.
  1946   The ancient Maya. 2d edition. Palo Alto, Calif. Also 3d edition, revised by G. W. Brainerd, 1956.

MOURA PESSOA, M.
  1950   O mito do diluvia nas Americas. *Rev. Mus. Paulista* (São Paulo), n.s., 4: 7–48.

MULERT, F. E. B., ed.
  1911   De reis van Mr. Jacob Roggeveen (1721–1722). Linschoten-Vereeniging, Weerken no. 4. The Hague.

MULLER, H. J.
  1958   The loom of history. New York.
MULLER, J.
  1966   Archaeological analysis of art styles. *Tenn. Archaeol.*, 22 (1): 25–39.
  1967   Style: a generative theory. Manuscript.
  1968   A comment on Ford's review of Early Formative period of coastal Ecuador. *Amer. Antiquity*, 33: 254–255.
MURDOCK, G. P.
  1945   The common denominator of cultures. *In* The science of man in the world crisis, edited by R. Linton, pp. 123–142. New York.
  1959   Africa: its peoples and their culture history. New York.
MUSEUM OF PRIMITIVE ART (NEW YORK)
  1965   The jaguar's children, edited by M. Coe. New York.
NANSEN, F.
  1911   In northern mists. Translated by A. G. Chater. 2 vols. London.
NAROLL, R.
  1961   Two solutions to Galton's problem. *Phil. Science*, 28: 16–39.
NATIONAL GEOGRAPHIC SOCIETY
  1967   Everyday life in Bible times. Washington.
NAUDOU, J.
  1962   À propos d'un eventuel emprunt de l'art Maya aux arts de l'Inde Extérieure. *Acts 34th Int. Cong. Amer.* (Vienna), pp. 340–347.
NAVAGIERO, A.
  1879   Viajes por España. Madrid.
NAVARRETE, M. F. DE
  1825–37   Colección de los viajes y descubrimientos que hicieron por mar los Españoles desde fines del siglo XV. 5 vols. Madrid, 1825–37, and later editions. We have used the Buenos Aires edition of 1945–46.
NAVARRO, M.
  1903   Vocabulario Castellano-Quechua-Pano. Lima.
NEEDHAM, J.
  1959   Science and civilization in China, vol. 3. Cambridge, Eng.
  1962   Science and civilization in China, vol. 4, pt. 1. Cambridge, Eng.
  1971   Science and civilization in China, vol. 4, pt. 3. Cambridge, Eng.
NEGRI, G.
  1930   La macinazione agricola des cereali. Milan.
NELSON, J. G.
  1961   The geography of the balsa. *Amer. Neptune*, 21: 157–195.
  1962   Drift voyages between Asia and the Americas. *Canad. Geographer*, 6: 54–59.

1963   Drift voyages in the Pacific. *Amer. Neptune,* 23: 113–130.

NEUGEBAUER, O.

1951   The exact sciences in antiquity. Copenhagen.

NIBLEY, H.

1951   The hierocentric state. *West. Political Quar.,* 3: 226–253.

NICHIMURA, S.

1925   Ancient rafts of Japan. Tokyo.

NICHOLSON, H. B.

1967   The efflorescence of Mesoamerican civilization: a résumé. *In* Indian Mexico: past and present; symposium papers (1965), edited by B. Bell. *Univ. Calif. (Los Angeles) Latin Amer. Studies,* 7: 46–71.

NICOL, J.

1840   An historical study of Iceland, Greenland, and the Faroe Islands. Edinburgh.

NISHIYAMA, I.

1959   Collecting the sweet potato and its allied species in U.S.A. and Mexico. *Japanese Jour. Breeding,* 9: 73–78.

1963   The origin of the sweet potato plant. *In* Plants and the migrations of Pacific peoples, edited by J. Barrau, pp. 119–128. Honolulu.

────── AND T. TERAMURA

1962   Mexican wild forms of sweet potato. *Econ. Botany,* 16: 304–314.

NORDENSKIÖLD, E.

1921   The Copper and Bronze Ages in South America. *Comp. Ethnog. Studies,* no. 4. Gothenburg.

1922   Deductions suggested by the geographical distribution of some post-Columbian words used by the Indians of South America. *Comp. Ethnog. Studies,* no. 5. Gothenburg.

1924   The ethnography of South America seen from Mojos in Bolivia. *Comp. Ethnog. Studies,* no. 3. Gothenburg.

1929   The American Indian as an inventor. *Jour. Royal Anthr. Inst.,* 59: 273–309.

1930   Modifications in Indian culture through inventions and loans. *Comp. Ethnog. Studies,* no. 8. Gothenburg.

1931   The origin of the Indian civilization in South America. *Comp. Ethnog. Studies,* no. 9. Gothenburg.

NØRLUND, P.

1924   Buried Norsemen at Herjolfsnes: an archaeological and historical study. *Meddelelser om Grønland,* 67: 1–270.

1930   Norse ruins at Gardar: the episcopal seat of mediaeval Greenland. *Meddelelser om Grønland,* 76: 1–170.

1936   Viking settlers in Greenland. London.

NOTT, C.

1947   Voices from the flowery kingdom. New York.

NUTTALL, Z.

1901   The fundamental principles of Old and New World civilization. *Papers Peabody Mus., Harvard Univ.,* vol. 2.

1909   A curious survival in Mexico of the use of the Purpura shellfish for dyeing. *In* Putnam anniversary volume, edited by F. Boas, pp. 368–384. Cedar Rapids, Iowa.

OAKLEY, K. P.

1957   Man the tool-maker. London.

OBAYASHI, T.

1959   Divination from entrails among the ancient Inca and its relation to practices in Southeast Asia. *Acts 33rd Int. Cong. Amer.* (San José), 1: 327–332.

OGBURN, W. F.

1938   Social Change. New York.

OHWI, JISABURO

1965   Flora of Japan. *Contrib. U.S. Nat. Herb.,* 22: 663–701.

OOSTSTROOM, S. J. VAN

1954   *Convolvulaceae.* Flora Malesiana, ser. 1, 4: 388–512. Djakarta.

OPPENHEIM, A. L.

1944   The Mesopotamian temple. *Bibl. Archaeologist,* 7: 54–63.

1950   Assyro-Babylonian religion. *In* Ancient religions: a symposium, edited by V. Ferm, pp. 63–79. New York.

OROZCO Y BERRA, M.

1880   Historia antigua y de la conquista de México. 5 vols. Mexico City.

ORTIZ DE ZÚÑIGA, I.

1920   Vista . . . 1562. *Rev. Arch. Nac. Perú,* 1 (1): 1–48.

OTERO, J. I., R. A. TORO, AND L. PAGAN DE OTERO

1945   Catálogo de los nombres vulgares y científicos de algunas plantas puertorriqueñas. *Univ. Puerto Rico, Estación Experimental Agrícola Boletín,* no. 37.

OTTEN, C.

1967   On pestilence, diet, natural selection, and the distribution of microbial and human blood group antibodies. *Cur. Anthr.,* 8: 209–216.

OVIEDO Y VALDES, G. F. DE

1526   Sumario de la natural historia de las Indias. Toledo. We have used the Mexico City edition of 1950.

1535   Historia general y natural de las Indias, islas y tierra firme del mar oceano. The first part appeared in Seville in 1535. We have used the 1959 edition in Biblioteca de Autores Españoles, vol. 117, bk. 7.

PADDOCK, J.
1955   The first three seasons at Yagul. *Mesoamerican Notes,* no. 4, pp. 25–47.

PALACIOS, E. J., AND M. O. DE MENDIZABAL
1921   Quetzalcoatl y la irradiación de su cultura en el antiguo pueblo mexicano. Mexico City.

PARIS, P.
1952   Quelques dates pour une histoire de la jonque chinoise. *Bulletin de l'Ecole Française de l'Extrême-Orient,* 46: 267–278.
1955   Esquisse d'une ethnographie navale des peuples annamites. 2d edition. Rotterdam.

PARKES, H. B.
1950   A history of Mexico. Boston.

PARROT, A.
1949   Ziggurats et tour de Babel. Paris.

PATIÑO, V. M.
1963   Plantas cultivadas y animales domésticos en América equinoccial. Cali, Colombia.

PEAKE, H., AND H. J. FLEURE
1931   Merchant venturers in bronze. London.
1933   The horse and the sword. London.

PEARSON, R.
1968   Migration from Japan to Ecuador: the Japanese evidence. *Amer. Anthr.,* 70: 85–86.

PEDERSON, J.
1945   Israel, its life and culture. 4 vols. Copenhagen.

PENNSYLVANIA UNIVERSITY, UNIVERSITY MUSEUM
  Collections: Near and Middle East, Africa, South and Central America.

PÉREZ ARBELAEZ, E.
1956   Plantas útiles de Colombia. 3d edition. Bogotá.

PERROT, G., AND C. CHIPIEZ
1884   History of art in Chaldea and Assyria. London.

PERRY, W. J.
1923   The children of the sun. London.

PETRIE, W. M. F.
1917   Tools and weapons. London.
1920   Prehistoric Egypt. London.

Petróleos Mexicanos, eds.
1948   México arqueológico. Mexico City.
Phillips, P.
1966   The role of transpacific contacts in the development of New World pre-Columbian civilizations. *In* Handbook of Middle American Indians, edited by R. Wauchope. Vol. 4, Archaeological frontiers and external connections, edited by G. F. Ekholm and G. R. Willey, pp. 296–315. Austin.
Phillpotts, S.
1931   Edda and saga. New York.
Pickering, C.
1879   Chronological history of plants. Boston.
Pierce, W. D.
1940   A few remarks on the possible origin of the sweet potato. *Bull. S. Calif. Acad. Sci.*, 39: 229–230.
Pigafetta, A.
1906   Primo viaggio intorno al mondo. Manuscript version of about 1524, translated into English by J. A. Robertson. *In* The Philipine Islands, 1493–1898, by E. H. Blair and J. A. Robertson, vols. 33, 34.
Piggott, S.
1950   Prehistoric India to 1000 B.C. Baltimore.
1965   Ancient Europe. Chicago.
Piper, C. V.
1926   Studies of American Phaseolinae. *Contr. U. S. Nat. Herb.*, 22: 663–701.
Pittier, H.
1926   Plantas usuales de Venezuela. Caracas.
Polunin, N.
1960   Introduction to plant geography and some related sciences. New York.
Poma de Ayala, P. G.
1944   Primer nueva coronica y buen gobierno. La Paz. Written between 1584 and 1614.
Poole, C. F.
1952   Seedling improvement in sweet potato. *Hawaii Univ. Agr. Exp. Sta. Tech. Bull.*, no. 17.
1955   Sweet potato genetic studies. *Hawaii Univ. Agr. Exp. Sta. Tech. Bull.*, no. 27.
Pounds, J. G.
1966   *Review of* The Vinland map and The Tartar relation. *Jour. Amer. Hist.*, 53: 107–108.

POWELL, B. W.
1965   Spruce swamp: a partially drowned coastal midden in Connecti-
        cut. *Amer. Antiquity,* 30: 460–469.

POWELL, T. G. E.
1961   Barbarian Europe—from the first farmers to the Celts. *In* The
        dawn of civilization, edited by S. Piggott, pp. 329–358. New
        York.

PREISSIG, E. R. VON
1918   Dictionary and grammar of the Chamorro language of the island
        of Guam. Washington.

PRESCOTT, W. H.
1877   History of the conquest of Mexico. 3 vols. Philadelphia.
1900   Mexico and the life of the conqueror, Fernando Cortez, vol. 1.
        New York.

PRESTAGE, E.
1933   The Portuguese pioneers. London.

PRICE, R. H.
1896   Sweet potato culture for profit. Dallas.

PRIDGEN, T.
1938   Courage: the story of the modern fighting cock. Boston.

PRITCHARD, J. B.
1943   Palestinian figurines in relation to certain goddesses known
        through literature. Amer. Oriental Series, no. 24. New Haven.

PROCTOR, V.
1968   Long-distance dispersal of seeds by retention in digestive tract
        of birds. *Science,* 160 (3825): 321–322.

PROSKOURIAKOFF, T.
1960   Historical implications of a pattern of dates at Piedras Negras,
        Guatemala. *Amer. Antiquity,* 25: 454–475.

PRUFER, O.
1970   Studies in Ohio archeology. Cleveland.

PUNNETT, R. C.
1933   Genetic studies in poultry, pt. 9: the blue egg. *Jour. Genetics,*
        27: 465–470.

PURCHAS, S.
1906   Purchas his pilgrimes, vols. 10, 13–14. Glasgow.

PURSEGLOVE, J. W.
1963   Some problems of the origin and distribution of tropical crops.
        Genetica Agraria, 17: 105–122.
1965   The spread of tropical crops. *In* The genetics of colonizing spe-
        cies (Proceedings of the First International Union of Biological

Sciences Symposia on General Biology), edited by H. G. Baker and G. L. Stebbins. New York and London.

1968   Tropical crops: Dicotyledons. 2 vols. New York.

QUENNEL, C. H. B., AND M. QUENNEL

1959   Everyday life in prehistoric times. London.

QUIMBY, G. I.

1961   Cord marking versus fabric impressing of Woodland pottery. *Amer. Antiquity*, 26: 426–428.

QUINN, D. B.

1961   The argument for the English discovery of America between 1480 and 1494. *Geog. Jour.*, 127: 277–285.

RAGLAN, LORD (FITZROY RICHARD SOMERSET)

1939   How came civilization? London.

1945   Death and rebirth: a study in comparative religion. London.

RAINEY, F.

1953   The significance of recent archaeological discoveries in inland Alaska. *Mem. Soc. Amer. Archaeol.*, no. 9: *Amer. Antiquity*, 18: 43–46.

RANDS, R. L.

1953   The water lily in Maya art: a complex of alleged Asiatic origin. *Smithsonian Inst., Bur. Amer. Ethnol.*, bull. 151: 75–153.

———— AND C. L. RILEY

1958   Diffusion and discontinuous distribution. *Amer. Anthr.*, 60: 274–279.

———— AND R. E. SMITH

1965   Pottery of the Guatemalan highlands. *In* Handbook of Middle American Indians, edited by R. Wauchope. Vol. 2, Archaeology of southern Mesoamerica, edited by G. R. Willey, pp. 95–145. Austin.

RAYNAL, G. T. F.

1774   Histoire philosophique et politique des établissements et du commerce des Européens dans les deux Indes. La Haye.

REISS, W., AND A. STÜBEL

1880–87   The necropolis of Ancon in Peru. 3 vols. Berlin.

LA RELACIÓN DE GENEALOGÍA Y LINAGE DE LOS SEÑORES QUE HAN SEÑORADO ESTA TIERRA DE NUEVA ESPAÑA

1886–92   Vol. 3. Mexico City.

RELACIONES GEOGRÁFICAS DE INDIAS

1881–87   Edited by Marcos Jiménez de la Espada. 4 vols. Madrid.

RENDÓN, S.

1953   Fué el maíz originario de América? *América Indígena*, 13(3): 223–230.

RENFREW, C.
1969 Trade and culture process in European prehistory. *Current Anthr.*, 10 (2–3): 151–169.

REYES, C. V.
1968 La pila bautismal de Zinacantepec, estado de México. *Boletín Mex. Inst. Nac. Antr. Hist.*, 31 (March, 1968): 24–27.

RIBEIRO, O.
1941 Cultura do milho economia agraria e povomento. *Biblos*, vol. 17, bk. 2. Lisbon.
1962 Aspectos e problemas da expansão Portuguesa. *Estudos de Ciências Politicas e Sociais*, no. 59. Lisbon.

RICCI, R.
1920 Compendio storico della agricultura italiana. Catania.

RICHARDSON, W., ET AL.
1789 General collection of voyages and discoveries made by the Portuguese and Spaniards during the 15th and 16th centuries. London.

RICHTER, J. P.
1939 The literary works of Leonardo da Vinci. Oxford.

RIDGEWAY, J., AND C. BLYTH
1967 A fighting chance. Philadelphia.

RIEFSTAHL, E.
1943 Doll, queen, or goddess. *Brooklyn Mus. Jour.*, 44: 7–23.

RILEY, C. L.
1967 American historical anthropology—an appraisal. *In* Essays in honor of Leslie Spier, edited by C. L. Riley and W. W. Taylor, pp. 3–21. Carbondale and Edwardsville, Ill.
1969 The origins of civilization. Carbondale, Ill.

RITCHIE, W. A.
1955 Recent discoveries suggesting an early Woodland burial cult in the Northeast. *New York State Mus. and Science Service*, circ. 40.
1965 The archaeology of New York State. Garden City, N.Y.

RIVET, P.
1928 Relations commerciales precolombiennes entre l'Océanie et l'-Amérique. *In* Festschrift publication d'hommage offerte au P. W. Schmidt, pp. 583–609. Vienna.
1949 Les Langues de l'ancien diocèse de Trujillo. *Jour. Soc. Amér.* (Paris), n.s., 38: 1–52.
1957 Les Origines de l'homme Américain. 6th edition. Paris.
———— AND G. DE CREQUI-MONTFORT
1951 Bibliographie des langues Aymará et Kicua, vol. 1 (1540–1875). *Univ. Paris, Travaux et Mém. Inst. Ethnol.*, no. 51.

———— AND R. VERNEAU
1912 Mission du service géographie de l'armée pour la mesure d'un arc de méridien équatorial en Amérique du Sud 1899–1906. *In* Ethnographie ancienne de l'équateur, vol. 6. Paris.

ROARK, R. P.
1965 From monumental to proliferous in Nasca pottery. *Ñawpa Pacha,* 3: 1–92.

ROBERTS, J.
1795 The discovery and description of the islands called the Marquesas in the South Pacific Ocean. *Mass. Hist. Soc.,* ser. 1, 4: 238–246.

ROBINSON, J. H.
1913 Our domestic birds. Dayton, Ohio.

ROCK, J. F.
1916 Palmyra Island, with a description of its flora. *Coll. Hawaii Bull.,* 4: 1–48.

ROGERS, E. S.
1965 The dugout canoe in Ontario. *Amer. Antiquity,* 30: 454–459.

ROLLIN, L.
1929 Les îles Marquises. Paris.

ROMERO, J.
1951 Monte Negro, centro de interés antropológico. *In* Homenaje al Doctor Alfonso Caso, pp. 318–320. Mexico City.

ROUSE, I.
1939 Prehistory in Haiti. *Yale Pub. Anthr.,* no. 21.
1948 The Cíbony. *In* Handbook of South American Indians, edited by J. H. Steward. Vol. 4, The circum-Caribbean tribes, pp. 497–503. *Smithsonian Inst., Bur. Amer. Ethnol.,* bull. 143.
1964 Prehistory of the West Indies. *Science,* 144: 499–513.

ROUSSELL, A.
1934–36 Sandnes and the neighboring farms. *Meddelelser om Grønland,* 88: 1–219.
1941 Farms and churches in the mediaeval Norse settlements of Greenland. *Meddelelser om Grønland,* vol. 89, no. 1.

ROWE, J. H.
1946 Inca culture at the time of the Spanish conquest. *In* Handbook of South American Indians, edited by J. H. Steward. Vol. 2, The Andean civilizations, pp. 183–330. *Smithsonian Inst., Bur. Amer. Ethnol,* bull. 143.
1953 Ethnobotany. *In* An appraisal of anthropology today, by S. Tax, L. C. Eiseley, I. Rouse, and C. F. Voegelin, pp. 53–54. Chicago.
1966 Diffusionism and archaeology. *Amer. Antiquity,* 31: 334–337.

Roys, R. L.
1933   The book of Chilam Balam of Chamayel. Washington, D.C.
Ruddock, A. A.
1966   John Day of Bristol and the English voyages across the Atlantic before 1497. *Geog. Jour.*, 132: 225–233.
Ruiz Lopez, H.
1952   Relación histórica del viage a los reynos del Perú y Chile. Madrid.
Russell, R. J.
1967   Aspects of coastal morphology. *Geografiska Annaler*, 49A (2–4): 299–309.
Sáenz, C. A.
1945   Tula y los Toltecas. Mexico City.
1946   Quetzalcoatl en México y Centro América. Mexico City.
1962   Quetzalcoatl. Mexico City.
Safford, W. E.
1905   The useful plants of the island of Guam. *Contrib. U. S. Nat. Herb.*, 9: 1–416.
1925   The potato of romance and reality. *Jour. Heredity*, 16: 113–126.
Sahagún, B. de
1932   A history of ancient Mexico. Translated by F. R. Bandelier. Nashville.
1938   Historia general de las cosas de Nueva España. 5 vols. Also 3 vol. edition, edited by M. Acosta Saignes. Mexico City, 1946.
1943   Suma indiana. Mexico City.
1950   General history of the things of New Spain; Florentine codex. Translated by A. J. O. Anderson and C. E. Dibble. *School of Amer. Research* (Santa Fe) *Monogr.* no. 14.
St. John, H.
1953   Origin of the sustenance plants of the Polynesians. *Proc. 7th Internat. Bot. Congr.*, pp. 152–154.
St. Pierre, G. de
1866   Note sur le *Lagenaria sphaerico-vulgaris*, hybride obtenue à Hyenes et description des espèces du genre *Lagenaria*. *Bull. Soc. Bot. France*, 13: 301–304.
Salisbury, E. J.
1942   The reproductive capacity of plants. London.
Salwen, B.
1967   A comment on Emery and Edwards' Archaeological potential of the Atlantic continental shelf. *Amer. Antiquity*, 32: 546–547.
San Juan, A. de
1872   Relación breve y verdadera de algunas cosas de las muchas que sucedieron al Padre Fray Alonso Ponce en las provincias de la

Nueva España. *In* Colección de documentos inéditos para la historia de España, vols. 57–58. Madrid.

SAPIR, E.
1916 Time perspective in aboriginal American culture: a study in method. *Canad. Dept. Mines, Geol. Sur., Mem. 90, Anthr. Ser.,* no. 13.

SAPPER, K.
1936 Geographie und Geschichte der indianischen Landwirtschaft. Hamburg.

SATTERTHWAITE, L.
1944 Archaeological reconnaissance in Campeche, Quintana Roo, and Peten: a review. *Amer. Antiquity,* 10: 216–218.
1946 Incense burning at Piedras Negras. *Pennsylvania Univ., Univ. Mus. Bull.,* no. 11.

SAUER, C. O.
1950 Cultivated plants of South and Central America. *In* Handbook of South American Indians, edited by J. H. Steward. Vol. 6, Physical anthropology, linguistics, and cultural geography of South American Indians, pp. 487–543. *Smithsonian Inst., Bur. Amer. Ethnol.,* bull. 143.
1952 Agricultural origins and dispersals. New York.
1959 Middle America as a culture historical location. *Acts 33rd Int. Cong. Amer.* (San José) 1: 115–122.
1960 Maize into Europe. *Acts 34th Int. Cong. Amer.* (Vienna), pp. 777–788.
1968 Northern mists. Berkeley and Los Angeles.

SAUER, J. D.
1962 Effects of recent tropical cyclones on the coastal vegetation of Mauritius. *Jour. Ecology,* 50: 275–290.
1967 Plants and man on the Seychelles coast: a study in historical biogeography. Madison, Wisc., and London.

SAVILLE, M. H.
1915–16 Monolithic axes and their distribution in ancient America. *Contrib. Mus. Amer. Indian, Heye Found.,* 2 (6): 1–13.
1925 The wood carver's art in ancient Mexico. *Contrib. Mus. Amer. Indian, Heye Found.,* vol. 9.

SCHAEFFER, C. F. A.
1936 La septième campagne de fouilles à Ras-Shamra (Ugarit). Paris.
1948 Stratigraphie comparée et chronologie de l'Asie occidentale (III et II millénaires). London.

SCHAFER, J. P., AND J. H. HARTSHORN
1965 The Quaternary of New England. *In* The Quaternary of the

United States, edited by H. E. Wright, Jr., and D. G. Frey. Princeton, N. J.

SCHAPIRO, M.
1953   Style. *In* Anthropology today, edited by A. L. Kroeber, pp. 287–312. Chicago.

SCHELTEMA, J. F.
1912   Monumental Java. London.

SCHMIDEL, U.
1938   Derrotero y viaje a España y las Indias por Ulrico Schmidl. Santa Fe.

SCHORGER, A. W.
1966   The wild turkey: its history and domestication. Norman, Okla.

SCHULTZ, J.
1962   Sea fever. *In* Men, ships, and the sea, edited by A. Villiers, pp. 398–403. Washington.

SCHUYLER, R. L.
1968   The use of historic analogs in archaeology. *Amer. Antiquity,* 33: 390–392.

SCHWERIN, K. H.
1970   Winds across the Atlantic—possible African origins for some pre-Columbian New World cultures. *Res. Rec. Univ. Mus.,* Southern Illinois University, Mesoamerican Studies, no. 6.

SCULLY, V.
1962   The earth, the temple, and the gods: Greek sacred architecture. New Haven.

SEEMANN, B. C.
1852–57   The botany of the voyage of the H.M.S. *Herald.* London.
1853   Narrative of the voyage of the H.M.S. *Herald* 1845–51. 2 vols. London.

SÉJOURNÉ, L.
1954   El mensaje de Quetzalcoatl. *Cuad. Amer.,* 77: 159–172.
1966   El lenguaje de las formas en Teotihuacán. Mexico City.

SELER, C.
1900   Auf alten Wegen in Mexiko und Guatemala, vol. 2. Berlin.
1904a   Borgia Codex. (A facsimile). Mexico City.
1904b   Quetzalcoatl-Kukulcan en Yucatán, vol. 2.

SELER, E.
1902–03   Codex Vaticanus, no. 2773. London and Berlin.
1904   Mexican and Central American antiquities calendar, systems and history. *Smithsonian Inst., Bur. Amer. Ethnol.,* bull. 28.
1906   Codex Borgia. 2 vols. Berlin.

1961   Die Teotiuakan-Kultur des Hochlands von Mexiko. *In* Gesammelte Abhandlungen zur Amerikanischen Sprachund Altertumskunde, vol. 5, pt. 2, no. 5, pp. 405–585.

SELLARS, O. R.
1945   Israelite belief in immortality. *Bibl. Archaeologist,* 8: 1–16.

SELLING, O. H.
1947   Studies in Hawaiian pollen statistics. *Bishop Mus. Spec. Pub.,* nos. 37–39.

SHARP, A.
1960   The discovery of the Pacific Islands. Oxford.
1964   Ancient voyagers in Polynesia. Berkeley and Los Angeles.

SHEPARD, A.
1963   Ceramics for the archaeologist. *Carnegie Inst. Wash. Pub.,* no. 609.

SHEPARD, F. P.
1964   Sea level changes in the past 6000 years: possible archeological significance. *Science,* 143: 574–576.

SHOOK, E. M.
1952   Lugares arqueológicos del altiplano meridional central de Guatemala. *Antropol. e Hist.* 4: 3–40.

SHUTLER, R., JR.
1961   Applications of palynology to archaeological and environmental problems in the Pacific. 10th Pacific Sci. Cong., 1961. Abstracts of papers, p. 79.

SIERRA, J.
1948   Evolución política del pueblo mexicano, vol. 1. Mexico City.

SIMMONDS, N. W.
1962   The evolution of the bananas. London.

SIMMONS, R. T.
1966   The blood group genetics of Easter Islanders (Pascuense), and other Polynesians. *In* Reports of the Norwegian archaeological expedition to Easter Island and the East Pacific. Vol. 2, Miscellaneous papers, edited by T. Heyerdahl and E. N. Ferdon, Jr. Stockholm.

SIMOONS, F. J.
1970   The traditional limits of milking and milk use in southern Asia. *Anthropos,* vol. 65 (in press).

SITTIG, O.
1896   Compulsory migrations in the Pacific Ocean. *Smithsonian Inst. Ann. Rept. of Board of Regents . . . to Jly. 1895,* pp. 519–535.

SKELTON, R. A., T. E. MARSTON, AND G. D. PAINTER
1965   The Vinland map and The Tartar relation. New Haven and London.

SKJÖLSVOLD, A.
  1961 Site E-2, a circular stone dwelling, Anakena. *In* Reports of the Norwegian archaeological expedition to Easter Island and the East Pacific. Vol. 1, Archaeology of Easter Island. London.
SMITH, C. E., JR., AND R. S. MACNEISH
  1964 Antiquity of American polyploid cottons. *Science*, 143 (3607): 675–676.
SMITH, C. H.
  1905 Arms, armor. *In* The popular and critical Bible encyclopedia and scriptural dictionary, edited by S. Fallows, 1: 155–159.
SMITH, G. E.
  1919 Dragons and rain-gods. *John Rylands Library* (Manchester), *Bull.*, 5: 317–380.
  1928 In the beginning: the origin of civilization. London.
SMITH, R. H.
  1966 The household lamps of Palestine in Old Testament times. *Bibl. Archaeologist*, 27: 2–31.
SMITHSONIAN INSTITUTION
        Collections: Indians of North and South America.
  1883 U.S. Bureau of Amer. Ethnol., ann. rept. for 1882–1883.
SOCIEDAD DE ANTROPOLOGÍA Y ETNOGRAFÍA DE MÉXICO
  1911 Quetzalcoatl. Mexico City.
SOPER, F. L.
  1927 The report of a nearly pure *Ancylostoma Duodenalo* infestation in native South American Indians and a discussion of its ethnological significance. *Amer. Jour. Hygiene*, 7: 174–184.
SPEISER, E.
  1935 Excavations at Tepe Gawra, vol. 1. Philadelphia.
SPENCE, L.
  1912 The civilization of ancient Mexico. Cambridge, Eng.
SPENCE, M. W.
  1967 The obsidian industry of Teotihuacán. *Amer. Antiquity*, 32: 507–514.
SQUIER, E.
  1860 Collection of rare and original documents and relations. No. 1, Carta por . . . el Lic. Garcia de Palacio, 1576. New York.
STADEN, H.
  1964 Hans Staden's Wahrhaftige Historia. Edited by R. Maack and K. Fouquet. Marburg.
STAMP, G.
  1968 Jeffreys, M.D.W. milho zaburro = milho de Guynee = maize in *Garcia de Orta*, 11: 213 226. *African Abstracts*, 19: 99.

STARR, R. S.
  1937   Nuzi, vol. 2. Cambridge, Mass.
STEENSBY, H. D.
  1924   The Norsemen's route from Greenland to Wineland. *An. 20th Int. Cong. Amer.* (Rio de Janeiro), vol. 1.
STEFANSSON, V.
  1938   The three voyages of Martin Frobisher, vols. 1–2. London.
  1940   Ultima Thule. New York.
STENBERGER, M.
  1962   Sweden. New York.
STEPHENS, S. G.
  1966   The potentiality for long range oceanic dispersal of cotton seeds. *Amer. Naturalist,* 100: 199–210.
  1967   Evolution under domestication of the New World cottons (*Gossypium spp.*). *Ciencia e Cultura,* 19 (1): 118–134.
STEVENS, H. N., ed.
  1930   New light on the discovery of Australia as revealed by the journal of Captain Don Diego de Prado y Tovar. Hakluyt Soc., 2d ser., no. 64. London.
STIRLING, M. W.
  1940   Great stone faces in the Mexican jungle. *Nat. Geog. Mag.,* 77: 309–334.
  1943   Stone monuments of southern Mexico. *Smithsonian Inst., Bur. Amer. Ethnol.,* bull. 138.
STONE, D.
  1958   Introduction to the archaeology of Costa Rica. *Museo Nacional.* San José, C. R.
STONOR, C. R., AND E. ANDERSON
  1949   Maize among the hill peoples of Assam. *Ann. Missouri Botanical Garden,* no. 36.
STRANWOLD, O.
  1948   Norse inscriptions on American stones. Wehauken, N.J.
STRONG, W.D.
  1935   An introduction to Nebraska archeology. *Smithsonian Inst. Misc. Coll.,* 93 (10): 1–315.
  1948   The archaeology of Honduras. *In* Handbook of the South American Indians, edited by J. H. Steward. Vol. 4, The circum-Caribbean tribes, pp. 69–140. *Smithsonian Inst., Bur. Amer. Ethnol.,* bull. 143.
STURTEVANT, E. L.
  1919   Notes on edible plants. New York State Dept. Agr. 27th Ann. Rept.

STURTEVANT, W. C.
1960 The significance of ethnological similarities between southeastern North America and the Antilles. *Yale Univ. Pub. Anthr.*, no. 64.

SUDER, H.
1930 Vom Einbaum und Floss zum Schiff. *Univ. Berlin, Inst. für Meereskunde Veröff.*, N.F.B., bk. 7.

SUGGS, R. C.
1960 The island civilization of Polynesia. New York.

SWADESH, M.
1964 Linguistic overview. *In* Prehistoric man in the New World, edited by J. D. Jennings and E. Norbeck, pp. 527–556. Chicago.

TAPSELL, E.
1947 Original Kumara. *Jour. Polynesian Soc.*, 56: 325–332.

TARN, W. W.
1961 Hellenistic civilization. Cleveland.

TAX, S., ed.
1951 The civilization of ancient America. Chicago.

TAYLOR, D.
1957 Aji and batata. *Amer. Anthr.*, 59: 704–705.

TAYLOR, E. G. R.
1964 Imaginary islands: a problem solved. *Geog. Jour.*, 130: 105–109.

TAYLOR, H. C., JR.
1951 Social change and cultural death: a diachronic study. *Microfilm Publ. Univ. Chicago Library*, ref. no. 1139.

TAYLOR, W. W., ed.
1957 The identification of non-artifactual archaeological materials. *Nat. Acad. Sci., Nat. Res. Council Pub.*, no. 565.

TEEPLE, J. E.
1931 Maya astronomy. *Carnegie Inst. Wash., Contr. Amer. Arch.*, 1: 29–116.

TEIXEIRA, A. J. DA SILVA, AND L. A. G. BARBOSA
1958 A agricultura do arquipelago de Cabo Verde. Portugual, *Junta das Missoes Geograficas e de Investigacoes do Ultramar Memorias*, 2d ser., no. 2.

TEJA ZABRE, A.
1935 Guide to the history of Mexico: a modern interpretation. Mexico City.
1944 Guía de la historia de México. Mexico City.

TELLO, A.
1891 Libro segundo de la crónica miscelánea en que se trata de . . . la Santa Provincia de Xalisco. Guadalajara.

Tello, J. C.
1929 Antiguo Perú primera epoca. Lima.
1938 Arte antiguo peruano. *Inca, Rev. Estud. Antropol.,* vol. 2.

Tertre, J. B. du
1667 Histoire génerale des Antilles, vol. 2. Paris.

Thompson, H. C., and H. Beattie
1922 Group classification and varietal descriptions of American varieties of sweet potatoes. *U.S. Agr. Dept. Bull.,* no. 1021.

Thompson, H. O.
1967 Tell el-Husn–biblical Bethshan. *Bibl. Archaeologist,* 30: 110–135.

Thompson, J. E. S.
1942 Civilization of the Mayas. Chicago.
1950a Canoes and navigation of the Maya and their neighbors. *Jour. Royal Anthropol. Inst.,* 79: 69–78.
1950b Maya hieroglyphic writing: introduction. *Carnegie Inst. Wash. Pub.,* no. 589.
1954 The rise and fall of Maya civilization. Norman, Okla.
1958 Symbols, glyphs, and divinatory almanacs for diseases in the Maya Dresden and Madrid codices. *Amer. Antiquity,* 23: 297–308.
1960 Maya hieroglyphic writing: an introduction. Revised edition. Norman, Okla.
1966 Maya hieroglyphic writing. *In* Handbook of Middle American Indians, edited by R. Wauchope. Vol. 3, The archaeology of southern Mesoamerica, edited by G. R. Willey, pp. 632–658. Austin.

Thompson, R.
1845 Marquesan Islands, pt. 3. *The Friend,* 3: 30–31.

Throckmorton, P.
1964 Roman shipwrecks and modern Aegean ships. *Mariner's Mirror,* 50: 205.

Time, The Weekly News-Magazine
1968a People. 91 (26): 31.
1968b Before Columbus or the Vikings. 91 (26): 62.

Ting, Y. C., and A. E. Kehr
1953 Meiotic studies in the sweet potato (*Ipomoea batatas* Lam.). *Jour. Heredity,* 44: 207–211.

———, A. E. Kehr, and J. C. Miller
1957 A cytological study of the sweet potato plant *Ipomoea batatas* (L.) Lam. and its related species. *Amer. Naturalist,* 91: 197–203.

Tioutine, M. G.
1935 Breeding and selection of sweet potatoes. *Jour. Heredity*, 26: 3–10.

Tolstoy, P.
1963 Cultural parallels between Southeast Asia and Mesoamerica in the manufacture of bark cloth. *Trans. New York Acad. of Sci.*, ser. 2, 25: 646–662.
1966 Method in long range comparison. *Acts 36th Int. Cong. Amer.* (Seville), 1: 69–89.
1969a *Review of* W. T. Sanders and B. J. Price, Mesoamerica: the evolution of a civilization. *Amer. Anthr.*, 71: 554–558.
1969b Diffusion: as explanation and as event. *In* Early Chinese art and its possible influence in the Pacific Basin, edited by N. Bernard. New York.

Torquemada, J. de
1943 Monarquía indiana, vols. 1–2. 3d edition. Mexico City.

Torres Rubio, D. de
1603 Arte y vocabulario de la lengua quichua general de los indios del Peru. First published in 1603; Chinchasuyo vocabulary added by Padre Juan de Figueredo in 1700 Lima edition; and anonymously revised in 1754 Lima edition, which we used.

Towle, M. A.
1961 The ethnobotany of pre-Columbian Peru. *Viking Fund Pub. Anthropol.*, no. 30.

Tozer, H. F.
1964 A history of ancient geography. New York.

Tozzer, A. M., ed.
1941 Landa's Relación de las cosas de Yucatán. Papers *Peabody Mus., Harvard Univ.*, vol. 18.

Tschopik, H., Jr.
1946 The Aymara. *In* Handbook of the South American Indians, edited by J. H. Steward. Vol. 2, The Andean civilizations, pp. 501–573. *Smithsonian Inst., Bur. Amer. Ethnol.*, bull. 143.

Tweedy, M. W. F.
1953 The Stone Age in Malaya. *Royal Asiatic Soc., Malayan Branch, Jour.*, 26 (pt. 2): 1–90.

Tylor, E. B.
1879 On the game of patolli in ancient Mexico, and its probable Asiatic origin. *Jour. Royal Anthropol. Inst.*, 8: 116–129.
1896 On American lot-games, as evidence of Asiatic intercourse before the time of Columbus. *Int. Archiv für Ethnog.*, suppl. to vol. 9, pp. 55–67.

UNITED STATES DEPARTMENT OF AGRICULTURE
1950　Commercial growing and harvesting of sweet potatoes. *Farmers'
Bull.*, no. 2020.

VAILLANT, G. C.
1935　Excavations at El Arbolillo. *Amer. Mus. Natural Hist. Papers*,
35: 137–279.
1951　The Aztecs of Mexico. Bungay, Suffolk. Also 1941, Garden City,
N.Y.

VALVERDE, V. DE
1865　Carta del obispo de Cuzco al emperador Marzo 20, 1539. Colección de documentos inéditos . . . de Indias, 3: 92–137. Madrid.

VAN BUREN, E. D.
1933　The flowing vase and the god with streams. Berlin.

VAN HEEKEREN, H. R.
1958　The Bronze-Iron Age of Indonesia. The Hague.

VARGAS, C.
1962　Phytomorphic representations of the ancient Peruvians. *Econ.
Botany*, 16: 106–115.

VARRON, A.
1942　The umbrella as an emblem of dignity and power. *Ciba Rev.*,
9: 42.

VAVILOV, N. I.
1931　Mexico and Central America as the principal center of origin
of the cultivated plants of the New World. *Bull. Applied Bot.,
Genetics and Plant Breeding*, 26 (3): 135–199.
1933　The problem of the origin of the world's agriculture in the light
of latest investigations. *In* Science at the cross roads. London.
1951　The origin, variation, immunity and breeding of cultivated
plants. Translated by K. S. Chester. *Chronica Botanica*, 13:
1–366.

VEBAEK, C. L.
1943　Inland farms in the Norse east settlement. *Meddelelser om Grønland*, 90: 1–119.

VEEDAM, V., AND C. B. WALL
1952　Sailing to freedom. New York.

VERGNES, P. E. E. DES
1877　L'archipel des Îles Marquises. Paris.

VERRILL, A. H.
1937　Foods America gave the world. Boston.
1945　Antiguas civilizaciones de América. Mexico City.

VIGFUSSON, B. G., AND F. Y. POWELL, eds.
1905　Origines Islandicae, vols. 1–2. Oxford.

VILLAREAL, F.
　1921　La lengua Yunga o Mochica. Lima.
VILLIERS, A.
　1957　Wild ocean. New York.
　1962　Men, ships, and the sea. Washington.
VINCENDON-DUMOULIN, C. A., AND C. L. F. DESGROZ
　1843　Îles Marquises ou Nouka Hiva. Paris.
VISHNU-MITTRE
　1966　Kaundinyapur plant economy in protohistoric and historic times. *Paleobotanist*, 15: 152–156.
———— AND H. P. GUPTA
　1966　Pollen morphological studies of some primitive varieties of maize (*Zea Mays* L.) with remarks on the history of maize in India. *Paleobotanist*, 15: 176–185.
VOSBURGH, F. G.
　1948　Easter egg chickens. *Nat. Geog. Mag.*, 94: 377–387. Vosburgh cites Alexander Wetmore on 1880 date for blue eggs.
WAFER, L.
　1903　A new voyage and description of the isthmus of America. Edited by George Winship. Cleveland. Reprinted from the original edition of 1699.
WAGNER, F. A.
　1959　Indonesia, the art of an island group. London.
WALKER, D.
　1966　Vegetation of the Lake Ipea region, New Guinea highlands. *Jour. Ecol.*, 54: 503–533.
WALLACE, L.
　1873　The fair god. Boston.
WALLACKER, B. E.
　n.d.　The sweet-tuber re-examined. Manuscript.
WARD, W. H.
　1910　Seal cylinders of western Asia. Washington.
WARNER, J. N.
　1962　Sugar cane: an indigenous Papuan cultigen. *Ethnology*, 1: 405–411.
WARREN, D. C.
　1949　The origin of breeds of chickens. *Jour. Agr. Research*, 78: 397–403.
WASHBURN, W. E.
　1966　The Vinland map and The Tartar relation. *Amer. Hist. Rev.*, 71: 927–928.

WATERMAN, T. T.
1925   Feathered snake of the winds. *Art and Archaeol.*, 20: 61–64.
WATSON, J. B.
1965   The significance of a recent ecological change in the central highlands of New Guinea. *Jour. Polynesian Soc.*, 74: 438–450.
1967   Horticultural traditions of the eastern New Guinea highlands. *Oceania*, 38: 81–98.
WATSON, W.
1962   China before the Han dynasty. New York.
1966   Early civilization in China. New York.
WATT, G.
1908   The commercial products of India. London.
WATT, W. C.
1966   Morphology of the Nevada cattlebrands and their blazons, pt. 1. Washington.
1967   Morphology of the Nevada cattlebrands and their blazons, pt. 2. Pittsburgh, Penn.
WAUCHOPE, R.
1962   Lost tribes and sunken continents. Chicago.
1964   Southern Mesoamerica. *In* Prehistoric man in the New World, edited by J. D. Jennings and E. Norbeck, pp. 331–386. Chicago.
1966   Archaeological survey of northern Georgia. *Soc. Amer. Archaeol. Mem.*, no. 21: *Amer. Antiquity*, vol. 31, no. 5, pt. 2.
WEATHERWAX, P.
1954   Indian corn in old America. New York.
WEAVER, J. C.
1965   Beyond the "Western sea." *Riecker Mem. Lecture* no. 10, *Univ. Arizona Bull. Ser.*
WEBERBAUER, A.
1945   El mundo vegetal de los Andes peruanos. Translated and revised from Leipzig edition of 1911. Lima.
WELLHAUSEN, E. J., L. M. ROBERTS, AND E. HERNANDEZ
1952   Races of maize in Mexico. Jamaica Plain, N.Y.
WENSINCK, A. J.
1916   The ideas of the western Semites concerning the navel of the earth. *Koninklijke Akademie van Wetenschappen. Verhandelingen*, Nieuwe reeks, vol. 17, no. 1.
WERTH, E.
1954   Grabstock, Hacke und Pflug. Ludwigsburg, Germany.
WHEELER, J. M., AND D. E. YEN
1964   Unpublished data on cytology of Pacific sweet potato collection.

WHEELER, M.
1954 Rome beyond the imperial frontiers. Baltimore.
1959 Early India and Pakistan. New York.
WHITAKER, I.
1954 The Scottish kayaks and the "Finn-men." *Antiquity*, 28: 110.
WHITAKER, T. W., AND J. B. BIRD
1949 Identification and significance of the cucurbit materials from Huaca Prieta, Peru. *Amer. Mus. Natural Hist., Amer. Mus. Novitates*, no. 1426, pp. 1–15.
———— AND G. F. CARTER
1954 Oceanic drift of gourds: experimental observations. *Amer. Jour. Bot.*, 41 (9): 697–700.
1961 Note on the longevity of seed of *Lagenaria siceraria* (Mol.) Standl. after floating in water. *Torrey Bot. Club Bull.*, 88: 104–106.
————, H. C. CUTLER, AND R. S. MACNEISH
1957 Cucurbit materials from three caves near Ocampo, Tamaulipas. *Amer. Antiquity*, 22: 352–358.
———— AND G. N. DAVIS
1962 Cucurbits: botany, cultivation, and uses. London.
WHITEHEAD, R. A.
1966 Sample survey and collection of coconut germ plasm in the Pacific Islands. London.
WICKE, C. R.
1965 Pyramids and temple mounds: Mesoamerican ceremonial architecture in eastern North America. *Amer. Antiquity*, 30: 409–420.
WILKES, C.
1845 Narrative of the U.S. Exploring Expedition during the years 1838–42. 5 vols. Philadelphia.
WILKES, H. G.
1967 Teosinte: the closest relative of maize. Jamaica Plains, N.Y.
WILL, G. F., AND G. E. HYDE
1917 Corn among the Indians of the upper Missouri. St. Louis.
WILLARD, T. A.
1941 Kukulcan: the bearded conqueror. Hollywood, Calif.
WILLEY, G. R.
1946 La candelaria. *In* Handbook of South American Indians, edited by J. H. Steward. Vol. 2, The Andean civilizations, pp. 661–662. *Smithsonian Inst., Bur. Amer. Ethnol.*, bull. 143.
1955 The prehistoric civilizations of Nuclear America. *Amer. Anthr.*, 57: 571–593.

528 BIBLIOGRAPHY

1966   An introduction to American archaeology. Vol. 1, North and
        Middle America. Englewood Cliffs, N. J.
——— AND P. PHILLIPS
1958   Method and theory in American archaeology. Chicago.
WILLIAMS, O.
1953   Plant evidence for early contacts with America: a review. *Ceiba*,
        3: 220–221.
WILLIAMSON, G.
1879   Antiquities in Guatemala. *Smithsonian Inst. Ann. Rept. for 1877*,
        pp. 418–421.
WILLIAMSON, J. A.
1962   The Cabot voyages and Bristol discovery under Henry VII.
        Hakluyt Soc., 2d ser., vol. 120.
WILLIS, W.
1965   Alone against the sea. *Sat. Eve. Post* (September 25, 1965),
        pp. 38–42, 45–46, 51–52.
WILSON, K. A.
1960   The genera of *Convolvulaceae* in the southeastern United States.
        Jour. Arnold Arboretum, 41: 298–317.
WINNING, H. VON
1947   A symbol for dripping water in the Teotihuacán culture. *El
        México Antiguo*, 6: 333–341.
1948   The Teotihuacán owl-and-weapon symbol and its association
        with "serpent head X" at Kaminaljuyu. *Amer. Antiquity*, 14:
        129–132.
1949   Shell designs on Teotihuacán pottery. *El México Antiguo*, 7:
        126–153.
1961   Teotihuacán symbols: the reptile's eye glyph. *Ethnos*, 26: 121–
        166.
WINSOR, J., ed.
1886–89 Narrative and critical history of America, vol. 1 (1889) and
         vol. 2 (1886). New York.
WITTHOFT, J.
1966   A history of gunflints. *Penn. Archaeologist*, 36: 1–49.
WOLF, A. V.
1956   Thirst. *Sci. Amer.*, 194: 70–76.
WOODBURY, R. B.
1965   Artifacts of the Guatemalan highlands. *In* Handbook of Middle
        American Indians, edited by R. Wauchope. Vol. 2, Archaeology
        of southern Mesoamerica, edited by G. R. Willey, pp. 163–179.
        Austin.

WOOD-GUSH, D. G. M.
1959   A history of the domestic chicken from antiquity to the 19th century. *Poultry Science*, 38: 321–325.

WOOLLEY, L.
1934   Ur excavations. Vol. 2, The royal cemetery. London.
1937   Digging up the past. Baltimore.

WORCESTER, G. R. C.
1966   Sail and sweep in China. London.

WRIGHT, E. V.
1964   The North Ferriby boats—a reappraisal. *Mariner's Mirror*, 50: 83–91.

WRIGHT, G. E.
1938   Lachish—frontier fortress of Judah. *Bibl. Archaeologist*, 1: 28–29.
1943   How did early Israel differ from her neighbors? *Bibl. Archaeologist*, 6: 1–20.

WRIGHT, J. V.
1967   The laurel tradition and the Middle Woodland period. *Nat. Mus. of Canada Bull.* no. 217.

XIMÉNEZ, F.
1857   Las historias del orígen de los indios de esta provincia de Guatemala. Vienna.

YACOVLEFF, E., AND F. L. HERRERA
1934–35   El mundo vegetal de los antiguos peruanos. *Rev. Mus. Nac.* (Lima), 3: 243–322, 4: 31–102.

YADIN, Y.
1963   The art of warfare in biblical lands in light of archaeological study, vols. 1–2. New York.

YÁÑEZ, A., ed.
1942   Mitos indígenas. Mexico City.

YANG, M. C.
1945   A Chinese village. New York.

YARNELL, R. A.
1964   Aboriginal relationships between culture and plant life in the upper Great Lakes region. *Univ. Mich. Mus. Anthr. Pub.*, no. 23.

YEN, D. E.
1960   The sweet potato in the Pacific. The propagation of the plant in relation to its distribution. *Jour. Polynesian Soc.*, 69: 368–375.
1961   The adaptation of Kumara by the New Zealand Maori. *Jour. Polynesian Soc.*, 70: 338–348.
1963   Sweet-potato variation and its relation to human migration in the

Pacific. *In* Plants and the migrations of Pacific peoples, edited by J. Barrau, pp. 93–117. Honolulu.

1968   Natural and human selection in the Pacific sweet potato. *In* Evolution and environment, edited by E. T. Drake, pp. 387–412.

ZARAGOZA, J., ed.

1876–82   Historia del descubrimiento de las regiones austriales hecho por el general Pedro Fernández de Quiros. 3 vols. Madrid.

ZARATE, A. DE

1555   Historia del descubrimiento y conquista del Perú. Anvers. Also Lima, 1944.

ZAYAS Y ALFONSO, A.

1914   Lexicografía Antillana. Havana.

ZEUNER, F. E.

1956   The domestication of animals. *Scientia,* 91: 23–28.

ZEVALLOS QUIÑONES, J.

1946   Un diccionario Yunga. *Rev. Mus. Nac.* (Lima), 15: 163–188.

ZURITA, A. DE

1964   Life and labour in ancient Mexico: the brief and summary relation of the Lords of New Spain. Translated with an introduction by B. Keen. New Brunswick, N. J.

LIST OF CONTRIBUTORS

Dr. Herbert G. Baker
Director of the Botanical Garden
Department of Botany
University of California
Berkeley, California 94720

Mr. Daniel R. Beirne
Assistant Professor, Department of Science
University of Baltimore
1420 North Charles Street
Baltimore, Maryland 21201

Mr. Leonard W. Blake
Missouri Botanical Garden
2315 Tower Grove Avenue
St. Louis, Missouri 63110

Dr. Stephan F. Borhegyi, Director (late)
Milwaukee Public Museum
Milwaukee, Wisconsin 53233

Dr. Donald D. Brand
Professor of Geography
University of Texas
Austin, Texas 78712

Dr. George F. Carter
Distinguished Professor of Geography
Department of Geosciences
Texas A&M University
College Station, Texas 77843

Dr. Hugh C. Cutler
Curator of Useful Plants
Missouri Botanical Garden

2315 Tower Grove Avenue
St. Louis, Missouri 63110

Dr. Edwin Doran, Jr.
Assistant Dean and Professor, College of Geosciences
Texas A&M University
College Station, Texas 77843

Dr. Clinton R. Edwards
Professor of Geography
University of Wisconsin, Milwaukee
Milwaukee, Wisconsin 52301

Dr. Gordon F. Ekholm
Curator of Mexican Archaeology
American Museum of Natural History
Central Park West at 79th Street
New York, New York 10024

Dr. Basil C. Hedrick
Director, University Museum
Southern Illinois University
Carbondale, Illinois 62901

Dr. M. D. W. Jeffreys
Department of Anthropology
Witwatersrand University
Johannesburg, South Africa

Dr. Stephen C. Jett
Assistant Professor of Geography
University of California, Davis
Davis, California 95616

Dr. Lawrence Kaplan
Professor of Biology
University of Massachusetts, Boston
100 Arlington Street
Boston, Massachusetts 02116

Dr. Alice B. Kehoe
Associate Professor
Department of Sociology and Anthropology

Marquette University
627 North 13th Street
Milwaukee, Wisconsin 53222

Dr. David H. Kelley
Associate Professor of Archaeology
University of Calgary
Calgary, Alberta, Canada

Dr. J. Charles Kelley
Professor and Coordinator of Museum Research
Southern Illinois University
Carbondale, Illinois 62901

Mr. Robert A. Kennedy
Curator/Director
County Museum, The Castle
Haverfordwest
Pembrokeshire, Wales

Dr. Jon M. Muller
Assistant Professor of Anthropology
Southern Illinois University
Carbondale, Illinois 62901

Dr. Campbell W. Pennington
Professor of Geography
Southern Illinois University
Carbondale, Illinois 62901

Dr. Robert L. Rands
University Museum
Southern Illinois University
Carbondale, Illinois 62901

Dr. Erik K. Reed
Research Anthropologist, U.S. Department of the Interior
National Park Service, Southwest Region
P.O. Box 728
Santa Fe, New Mexico 87501

Dr. Carroll L. Riley
Professor of Anthropology
Southern Illinois University
Carbondale, Illinois 62901

Dr. Jonathan Sauer
Professor of Geography
University of California, Los Angeles
Los Angeles, California 90024

Dr. John L. Sorenson
Professor in Anthropology and Political Science
Department of Political Science
Maeser Building
Brigham Young University
Provo, Utah 84601

Dr. S. G. Stephens
Department of Genetics
North Carolina State University, Raleigh
Box 5487
Raleigh, North Carolina 27607

Dean Herbert C. Taylor, Jr.
Professor of Anthropology
Dean for Research and Grants
Western Washington College
Bellingham, Washington 98225

Dr. Thomas W. Whitaker
Research Geneticist
U.S. Department of Agriculture
P.O. Box 150
La Jolla, California 92037

Dr. Douglas E. Yen, Ethnobotanist
Bernice P. Bishop Museum
Honolulu, Hawaii 96819

INDEX

In this index, NW indicates the New World, OW the Old World.